Glencoe

Childcare Today

Mc
Graw
Hill
Education

About the Author

Karen Stephens, M.S. in Education, has been in the early childhood field since 1975. She is Director of the Illinois State University Child Care Center, as well as a child development and early childhood program administration instructor for Illinois State University's Family and Consumer Sciences Department. She has published books and articles and is a regular contributor to early childhood education magazines. She is best known for her contributions to family-friendly early childhood programming and implementing nature-based preschool curriculum. Ms. Stephens is a past president of the Midwest Association for the Education of Young Children and has received the Distinguished Service Award for her contributions to Illinois State University.

COVER: Mike Watson Images Limited/Glow Images

MHEonline.com

Send inquiries to:
McGraw-Hill Eduction
8787 Orion Place
Columbus, OH 43240

ISBN: 978-0-02-1405169
MHID: 0-02-140516-6

Printed in the United States of America.

1 2 3 4 5 6 7 8 9 DOW 22 21 20 19 18 17 16 15

REVIEWERS

TEACHER REVIEWERS

Ruth R. Baker
Family and Consumer Sciences Teacher
Ardrey Kell High School
Charlotte, North Carolina

Suzi Beck
Family and Consumer Sciences Teacher
Trenton R-9 School
Trenton, Missouri

Diane Bollinger
Family and Consumer Sciences Teacher
Wichita High School West
Wichita, Kansas

Christine Bunte Halweg
Family and Consumer Sciences Teacher
Peotone High School
Peotone, Illinois

Pat M. Carpenter
Family and Consumer Sciences Teacher
Greeneville-Greene County Center for
Technology
Greeneville, Tennessee

Kathryn A. Cox
Family and Consumer Sciences Teacher
William G. Enloe Magnet High School
Raleigh, North Carolina

Brenda Dishman Eggers
Family and Consumer Sciences Teacher
Johnson County High School
Mountain City, Tennessee

Libby Helle
Family and Consumer Sciences Teacher
West High School
Knoxville, Tennessee

Cathy Kloch
Family and Consumer Sciences Teacher
Alliance High School
Alliance, Nebraska

Barbara A. Mikler-Crandon
Family and Consumer Sciences Teacher
Newark High School
Newark, New York

Julie Pagnotta
Early Childhood Education Instructor
Mahoning County Career and
Technical Center
Canfield, Ohio

Shirley Rauh
Family and Consumer Sciences Teacher
Mehlville High School
St. Louis, Missouri

Nancy Rebar
Early Childhood Education Instructor
North Technical High School
Florissant, Missouri

Carla Robinson
Child Development Teacher
Millard South High School
Omaha, Nebraska

Marilyn Spencer
Family and Consumer Sciences Teacher
Oakland High School
Murfreesboro, Tennessee

Cynthia Theiss
Family and Consumer Sciences Teacher
Babylon High School
Babylon, New York

Elissa Greg Twachtman
Child Guidance/Practicum in
Human Services Instructor
Cy-Fair High School
Cypress, Texas

TECHNICAL REVIEWERS

Alia Antoon, MD
Chief of Pediatrics
Shriners Hospital for Children
Assistant Clinical Professor of Pediatrics
Harvard Medical School
Boston, Massachusetts

Keith-Thomas Ayoob, EdD, RD, FADA
Associate Clinical Professor of Pediatrics
Albert Einstein College of Medicine
Bronx, New York

Roberta L. Duyff, MS, RD, FADA, CFCS
Food and Nutrition Consultant
Duyff Associates
St. Louis, Missouri

Mary Jane Grayson
Family and Consumer Sciences Education
Program Specialist
Oklahoma Department of Career and
Technology Education
Stillwater, Oklahoma

Jean A. Kelleher
Family and Consumer Sciences Program
Specialist
Pennsylvania Department of Education
Harrisburg, Pennsylvania

Stacey Payton
Elementary Technology Specialist
Beaver and Watson Technology Centers for
Math & Science
Garland, Texas

Pamela S. Raffurty
Director, Workshop on Wheels Child Care
Resource and Referral
University of Central Missouri
Warrensburg, Missouri

Marcia A. Rossi, MEd
Adjunct Assistant Professor, Department
of Educational Administrative Foundations
Illinois State University
Normal, Illinois

Dr. Robert Wandberg
Language Diverse Literacy Coach
Columbia Heights Public School
Columbia Heights, Minnesota

SCAVENGER HUNT

Child Care Today: Becoming an Early Childhood Professional contains a wealth of information. The trick is to know where to look to find the information. Use this Scavenger Hunt to preview the text and help you get the most out of this book.

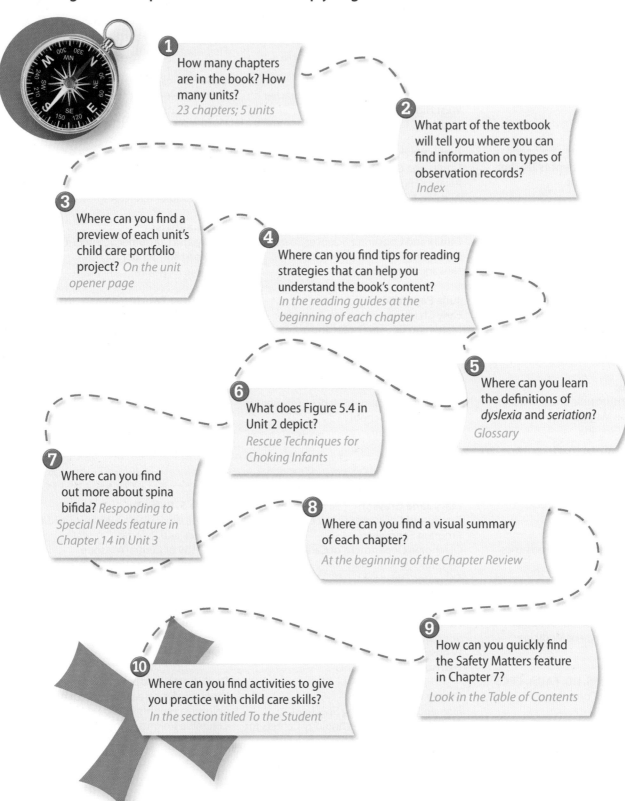

1 How many chapters are in the book? How many units? *23 chapters; 5 units*

2 What part of the textbook will tell you where you can find information on types of observation records? *Index*

3 Where can you find a preview of each unit's child care portfolio project? *On the unit opener page*

4 Where can you find tips for reading strategies that can help you understand the book's content? *In the reading guides at the beginning of each chapter*

5 Where can you learn the definitions of *dyslexia* and *seriation*? *Glossary*

6 What does Figure 5.4 in Unit 2 depict? *Rescue Techniques for Choking Infants*

7 Where can you find out more about spina bifida? *Responding to Special Needs feature in Chapter 14 in Unit 3*

8 Where can you find a visual summary of each chapter? *At the beginning of the Chapter Review*

9 How can you quickly find the Safety Matters feature in Chapter 7? *Look in the Table of Contents*

10 Where can you find activities to give you practice with child care skills? *In the section titled To the Student*

Table of Contents

focus ON

Reading Strategies

In each chapter, look for these reading strategies:

- **Before You Read**
- **Graphic Organizer**
- **As You Read**
- **Reading Checks**
- **After You Read**

TABLE OF CONTENTS

focus ON

Academic Success

To help you succeed in your classes and on tests, look for these academic skills:

- **Reading Guides**
- **Math Concepts**
- **Financial Literacy**
- **Science for Success**

© Paul Bradbury / age fotostock

focus ON

Visuals

Images help you learn key ideas. Answer all the questions for:
- **Unit and Chapter Openers**
- **Photos**
- **Figures**

TABLE OF CONTENTS

focus ON

Assessment

Look for review questions and activities to help you remember important topics:

- **Reading Checks**
- **Chapter Reviews**
- **Child Care Labs**
- **Child Care Portfolio Projects**

SolStock/Getty Images

Features Table of
Contents

Build Academic and Financial Literacy Skills

Do you understand the connection between nutrition and brain development? Do you know how to calculate paycheck deductions? These standards-based academic features will help you succeed in school and at work.

(l) McGraw-Hill Education; (r) ©Comstock/Alamy

Strengthen Your Safety Knowledge

How do you know if a toy is safe? What should you do to handle children's allergies? Learn about safety issues that affect early childhood professionals on the job.

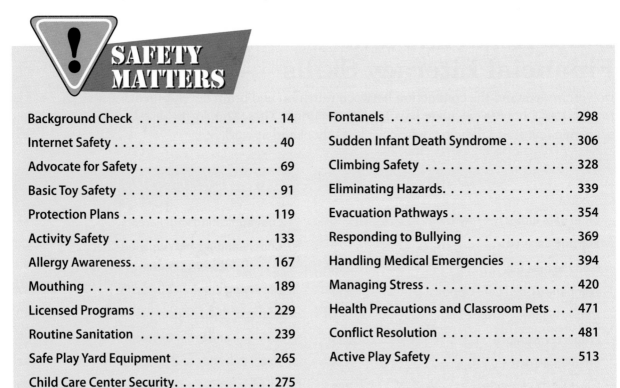

SAFETY MATTERS

© Keith Eng 2007

Develop Real-World Skills

Learn basic skills that you can use as an early childhood professional. Also learn how special needs can affect child development and child care.

A Matter of ETHICS

Respond to SPECIAL NEEDS

Child Care LAB

Apply Essential Child Care Skills

What is the proper hand-washing procedure? How can you effectively manage an meeting? These features should show you how to apply your skills to the work environment.

How to . . .

PhotoAlto/Alamy

College and Career Readiness

Are you prepared for life after you graduate from school? As you get ready to continue your education or enter the workplace, these features will teach you the skills you need to succeed.

PATHWAY TO COLLEGE

PATHWAY TO YOUR CAREER

UNIT CAREER SPOTLIGHT

Becoming a Child Development Associate (CDA)

As a student in an occupational early childhood program, you might be wondering, "Why should I work toward acquiring the Child Development Associate (CDA) credential?" The personal and professional rewards are numerous and include

- growing as a professional in knowledge and skill.
- improving yourself in ways that benefit children.
- developing a support network of professionals experienced with early childhood development and care.
- evaluating your knowledge and skills against national standards.
- acquiring a credential that is nationally recognized by early childhood professionals.

The information in this section offers you an overview of the CDA requirements and assessment process. The training and education required, along with the credential itself, can be a real asset in obtaining gainful employment.

CDA Eligibility Requirements

Personal

At least eighteen years of age with a high school diploma or equivalent.

Ability to speak, read, and write well enough to fulfill all CDA requirements.

Distribute and collect Family Questionnaires.

Setting

Must be in a state-approved center.

Candidate must work as a lead caregiver for a group of at least eight children ages three to five.

At least ten children must be enrolled in the program with at least two caregivers present.

Experience

At least 480 hours work experience with three- to five-year-olds in a group setting within "three years prior to CDA application.

Prepare a Professional Portfolio.

Education

120 clock hours with at least ten hours in each of the eight prescribed areas ranging from planning a safe, healthy learning environment to principles of child development and learning.

CDA Competency Goals

The Council for Professional Recognition in Washington, D.C., is the sponsoring agency for the CDA credential. The Council created the CDA credentialing program as a way to assure families of quality child care.

The CDA Competency Goals identify the necessary skills for qualified early childhood professionals in a variety of early childhood settings that include center-based programs for infants, toddlers, and preschoolers; family day care; and home visitor programs. The six CDA Competency Goals are:

- **Goal I** To establish and maintain a safe, healthy learning environment
- **Goal II** To advance physical and intellectual competence
- **Goal III** To support social and emotional development and to provide positive guidance
- **Goal IV** To establish positive and productive relationships with families
- **Goal V** To ensure a well-run, purposeful program responsive to participant needs
- **Goal VI** To maintain a commitment to professionalism

Ariel Skelley/Blend Images LLC

The Assessment Process

The process for becoming a CDA is designed to thoroughly assess each candidate in terms of his or her professional skills. The process involves six steps.

Step 1 Explore After eligibility requirements are met, candidates will be asked to demonstrate competency based on the CDA Competency Goals.

Step 2 Prepare Next, the candidate must complete formal training and work experience, and put together the required documentation showing his or her skills.

- **Professional Portfolio.** This portfolio includes a collection of resource materials related to his or her work. Instructions are provided in the Competency Standards book.

- **Family Questionnaires.** The parent or guardian of each child in the candidate's care completes a questionnaire giving his or her perceptions about the candidate's skill and knowledge.

The candidate also needs to identify a CDA Professional Development Specialist to coach skills and conduct a Verification Visit. This visit will not occur until after the application is approved.

Step 3 Apply After the candidate and his or her advisor collect the necessary documentation, the application for final assessment and required fee is sent to the Council via paper or online.

Step 4 Demonstrate Candidate will complete the Verification Visit and CDA exam. The Professional Development Specialist will submit the results of the candidate's Visit to the Council.

Step 5 Earn A committee from the Council for Professional Recognition reviews the results of the candidate's assessment. If all the documentation is favorable, the Council awards the CDA credential to the candidate. If for some reason the candidate needs further education and training, he or she will be notified concerning the specifics of that education and training.

Step 6 Renew After an individual receives the CDA credential, the initial credential is valid for three years. The credential must be renewed every three years.

Correlation to the Child Development Associate (CDA) Competency Goals and Functional Areas

The following charts show how *Child Care Today* addresses the competency goals and functional areas outlined by the Council for Professional Recognition.

Competency Goal I	
To establish and maintain a safe, healthy learning environment	
Functional Area 1: Safe Candidate provides a safe environment to prevent and reduce injuries.	**Chapters 2, 3, 5, 10, 12, 14–16, 23**
Functional Area 2: Healthy Candidate promotes good health and nutrition and provides an environment that contributes to the prevention of illness.	**Chapters 1, 4, 5, 7, 8, 11–14, 17, 18**
Functional Area 3: Learning Environment Candidate uses space, relationships, materials, and routines as resources for constructing an interesting, secure, and enjoyable environment that encourages play, exploration, and learning.	**Chapters 1, 9, 11, 12, 14–23**

Corbis/SuperStock

CHILD DEVELOPMENT ASSOCIATE CREDENTIAL

Competency Goal II
To advance physical and intellectual competence

Functional Area 4: Physical Candidate provides a variety of equipment, activities, and opportunities to promote the physical development of children.	**Chapters 4, 8, 11, 12, 14–19, 23**
Functional Area 5: Cognitive Candidate provides activities and opportunities that encourage curiosity, exploration, and problem-solving appropriate to the developmental levels and learning styles of children.	**Chapters 4, 11–23**
Functional Area 6: Communicative Candidate actively communicates with children and provides opportunities and support for children to understand, acquire, and use verbal and nonverbal means of communicating thoughts and feelings.	**Chapters 3, 9, 13,–20, 22, 23**
Functional Area 7: Creative Candidate provides opportunities that stimulate children to play with sound, rhythm, language, materials, space, and ideas in individual ways and to express their creative abilities.	**Chapters 12, 19, 20, 22, 23**

Competency Goal III
To support social and emotional development and to provide positive guidance

Functional Area 8: Self Candidate provides physical and emotional security for each child and helps each child to know, accept, and take pride in himself or herself and to develop a sense of independence.	**Chapters 4, 7–9, 11, 14–19, 22**
Functional Area 9: Social Candidate helps each child feel accepted in the group, helps children learn to communicate and get along with others, and encourages feelings of empathy and mutual respect among children and adults.	**Chapters 4, 9, 14–18, 20, 22**
Functional Area 10: Guidance Candidate provides a supportive environment in which children can begin to learn and practice appropriate and acceptable behaviors as individuals and as a group.	**Chapters 9, 11, 15–18, 22**

Competency Goal IV
To establish positive and productive relationships with families

Functional Area 11: Families
Candidate maintains an open, friendly, and cooperative relationship with each child's family, encourages their involvement in the program, and supports the child's relationship with his or her family.

Chapters 1, 3–6, 8–10, 12, 13, 18, 22

Competency Goal V
To ensure a well-run, purposeful program responsive to participant needs

Functional Area 12: Program Management
Candidate is a manager who uses all available resources to ensure an effective program operation. Candidate is a competent organizer, planner, recordkeeper, communicator, and a cooperative co-worker.

Chapters 2–8, 10, 12, 13

Competency Goal VI
To maintain a commitment to professionalism

Functional Area 13: Professionalism
Candidate makes decisions based on knowledge of early childhood theories and practices, promotes quality in child care services, and takes advantage of opportunities to improve competence, both for personal and professional growth and for the benefit of children and families.

Chapters 1–4, 7, 10, 13

*Reprinted with permission from the Council for Professional Recognition, www.cdacouncil.org

Exploring Career Opportunities

Chapters

1 **Early Childhood Careers**
2 **Employability Skills**
3 **Professional Skills**

©Nova Development

Project Preview

Job Search Skills

After completing this unit, you will know more about child care careers and the skills you will need to find work with children as an early childhood professional. In your Unit 1 child care portfolio project, you will prepare to apply for a job. You will complete application materials, develop a list of professional references, write a cover letter, and create a portfolio before conducting a mock job interview.

My Journal

Write a journal entry about your experiences with child care and how that experience can help you become a child care professional.

- What experience do you have taking care of children?
- Did you have a child care provider when you were young? If yes, how might this experience influence your role as a child care professional?
- How do you think quality child care affects both children and families?

Explore the Photo
There are many career opportunities for people who want to work with children. *What skills might this early childhood professional need when working with children?*

CHAPTER 1

Early Childhood Careers

Writing Activity

21st Century Skills

Self-Direction Think about the various jobs within a child care center. Then freewrite for five minutes about the traits, skills, and abilities you would need for each of these jobs. Identify other jobs or areas within the early childhood industry about which you would like to learn more.

Writing Tips

1. Write the topic at the top of the paper to keep you focused.
2. Continue writing for the entire time period.
3. Write anything that comes to mind. If you cannot think of the correct word, just draw a blank line in that spot and keep going.
4. Do not worry about form or structure. You can edit your writing or fix mistakes later.

Explore the Photo
This child care professional is working with Kindergarteners. *What skills might you need for this job?*

Blend Images/Ariel Skelley/Getty Images

Reading Guide

Preview Read the Key Concepts. Write one or two sentences predicting what the chapter will be about.

Read to Learn

Key Concepts

- **Identify** three factors that contribute to an increasing demand for early childhood professionals.
- **Describe** ten characteristics of successful child care professionals.
- **Identify** places to work in the early childhood industry.
- **Summarize** three major legal responsibilities of early childhood professionals.

Content Vocabulary

- ◇ child care
- ◇ trend
- ◇ nanny
- ◇ au pair
- ◇ entrepreneur
- ◇ Child Development Associate (CDA)
- ◇ mandated

Academic Vocabulary

- ■ comply
- ■ initiative

Main Idea

There is a demand for qualified professionals to work in early childhood careers. These jobs require specific characteristics, skills, education, training, and responsibilities.

Graphic Organizer

As you read, you will discover the traits, attitudes, skills, and abilities that are helpful when working with young children. Use a ladder organizer like the one shown to list ten characteristics that describe a successful child care professional.

Characteristics of Successful Child Care Professionals
1.
2.
3.
4.
5.
6.
7.
8.
9.
10.

Graphic Organizer *Go to* **connected.mcgraw-hill.com** *to print this Graphic Organizer.*

◇**Vocabulary**

You can find definitions in the glossary at the back of this book.

Demand for Early Childhood Professionals

Good child care makes a difference. **Child care** is the broad term that describes any situation in which children are provided with supervision, support, and education by individuals outside the child's immediate family. For a parent who entrusts the care of a child to others, the quality of that care is critical. Can you imagine what it would be like as a parent to leave your child with people you do not know? What would you want to know about the people and location where your child receives care? How would you find quality care? These are very real questions that families face. The demand for more and better child care has grown significantly over the last few decades, and it will continue to do so. Identifying and insuring quality child care is a common goal.

More Americans than ever rely on early childhood professionals to care for their young children outside their homes. Recent studies show almost two-thirds of all children under age five spend at least some time in someone's care other than their parents. This development is called a **trend**, or the overall direction in which a society moves within a given time frame. Several factors contribute to this trend:

▶ The United States is a society with many families moving to find employment.

▶ Grandparents and other family often live far away or are stil in the workforce.

▶ Single parents rely on quality child care to work outside the home.

▶ In many dual-career families, both parents work outside the home.

The availability of quality child care has given both men and women the opportunity to successfully balance career and family.

Quality programs help prepare children for school both intellectually and socially. Numerous studies show that students who receive quality early childhood education before the age of five have better academic achievement and are less likely to act out. Research such as this has made parents more willing to enroll their children in child care programs or preschools, especially if the programs and schools have a reputation for providing quality care and education. Many states have responded to this research by offering a variety of school-based programs for three- and four-year-olds.

Financial *Literacy*

Child Care Industry Growth

The Bureau of Labor Statistics projects that jobs in the child care industry will grow 11 percent in the next 10 years. Alana's community currently has 278 child care positions. If her community gains 2 child care jobs a year for the next 10 years, what percentage of growth will her local economy experience in the child care industry? Is this above or below the national average? What local economic factors might have contributed to this growth?

Math Concept **Percent** A percent is a ratio of a number to 100. For example, 27 percent is the same as 27/100, or 27 divided by 100. To find the percent of a number, multiply the number by the percent. Convert a percent to a decimal by moving the decimal point two places to the left.

Starting Hint To determine the percentage of growth, first determine the total number of new jobs (2×10). Then divide the total number of new jobs by the original number of jobs.

 For more math practice, go to the Math Appendix at the back of the book.

McGraw-Hill Education

Early Care and Education Programs

No two children or two families are exactly alike; therefore, no one type of care is right for all families. Parents look for early childhood programs and providers that suit their needs.

In the past, many providers offered simple child care. They offered parents a safe place for their children. They served children snacks or meals and watched over them as the children played and napped. The provider offered few, if any, educational activities.

Today, quality child care goes far beyond basic care. Early childhood programs focus on meeting children's overall developmental needs, such as secure attachments and positive self-esteem, while nurturing their emerging skills and abilities.

Child Care Centers

Many early childhood programs aim to create a family-friendly environment. They know that children develop within a family unit, so providers often encourage parents to participate. They may ask parents, whenever possible, to serve as a field trip chaperone or a monitor for outdoor play periods.

Early childhood professionals also help parents better manage their child-rearing responsibilities by offering parent education classes. Referring families to services they need, such as family counseling, is another important role for trained early childhood professionals.

Family Child Care Homes and In-Home Care

There are many options for child care beyond the child care center. The most common is a family child care home. In a family child care home, a provider cares for children in his or her own home. Most states require a license or certification for family child care homes. Family child care homes are often less expensive than child care centers, and there are usually fewer children in this setting.

Some parents choose to find a caregiver who will come to their home to care for their children. A **nanny** is an in-home care provider who may or may not live with the family. Most nannies work with only one family at a time. Another option for in-home care is an **au pair** ('ō-'per), a person from another country who lives with

▲ **Program Options**

Many program options are available for children and early childhood professionals ranging from early childhood centers to family child care homes. *What factors influence the willingness of parents to enroll their children in child care programs or centers?*

Glow Images

a family and cares for its children to receive exposure to American culture as part of his or her employment. Nannies and au pairs give parents an option for greater interaction between child and caregiver and allow children the comfort of staying at home. They are also a good option for people who work hours that are not part of the typical workday.

▲ Opportunities for All

The Americans with Disabilities Act requires child care centers to accept children with disabilities when a center can meet the child's needs. *What might a child care center need to be equipped with to help meet the needs of a Child in a wheelchair or with developmental delays?*

Increasingly, families require flexible care to serve as a "backup" when their regular care arrangements cannot meet temporary changes in their child care needs. This has created jobs for early childhood professionals willing to provide care in a family's home when a child is mildly ill, recovering from illness, or needs overnight care due to parents' business travel. Such individuals also frequently serve as "on call" substitute teaching staff in local early childhood programs.

Inclusive and Diverse Environments

Early childhood programs and centers must comply with, or follow the rules of, Title III of the Americans with Disabilities Act (ADA). These programs and centers cannot discriminate against people with disabilities, including children and their parents or guardians. They must provide equal participation opportunities for all people. Exceptions to Title III include:

▶ An individualized assessment shows the presence of children with disabilities would pose a direct threat to the health or safety of others or require a fundamental alteration of the program or facility.

▶ Centers operated by religious organizations.

If a center can meet a child's needs, it is required by law to include the child. The ADA Web site contains more information and a complete listing of the requirements.

Early childhood professionals ensure that the children's classroom environment and routines—such as discipline, meal service, and toilet training—respect individual family traditions and beliefs. They encourage children of varying abilities and diverse backgrounds to enroll in their programs. Professional staff members become acquainted with the varying needs of these children and their families and try to accommodate them. Today's professionals show their respect of children and families of all racial, ethnic,

Realistic Reflections

and cultural backgrounds. This includes providing information to children and their parents in their native languages, if possible. In addition, some early childhood providers provide opportunities for children to acquire a second language. They strive to communicate effectively with everyone and to work in a professional manner.

READING CHECK ✔ Describe What are two benefits of home-based care?

Your Role in Child Care

Many opportunities exist for a career in early care and education or in other child-related careers. However, not everyone is suited for the responsibilities of an early care educator or to the child care center environment. Your success as an early childhood professional depends on a combination of your personal traits, attitudes, skills, and abilities. **Figure 1.1** lists characteristics of a successful child care professional. Additional education and training can also help prepare you for a career working with young children. Understanding what characteristics help a child care provider become successful can help you determine if this career is right for you.

Figure 1.1 **Characteristics of Early Childhood Professionals**

Keys to Success Caring for children requires many talents. *How do you think the characteristics listed help a child care professional do his or her job?*

Successful Early Childhood Professionals

- enjoy working with children.
- have good physical health.
- are kind and compassionate
- have a positive, "can-do" attitude.
- show a sense of humor.
- are dedicated to serving children and families.
- respect diverse family backgrounds.
- understand how children grow and develop.
- can see the world from both a child's and a parent's point of view.
- communicate effectively.
- show consistency in ways of responding to children.
- adapt easily to changes in schedule and plans, as needed.
- show creativity and resourcefulness in solving problems.
- make decisions as a team player.
- are reliable and dependable.
- display self-starting **initiative**, the ability to take first steps.

Christopher Futcher/Getty Images

Traits, Skills, and Abilities

In early childhood programs, providers work with people of all ages. It is important to maintain good working relations with parents, children, and coworkers. This also involves keeping private information confidential and communicating professionally.

The ability to "think on your feet" in a child care setting is a necessity. Settings with children are very busy places because they typically involve games, activities, meals, naps, and other daily routines. A child care professional must show patience and understanding to help children learn and grow in a nurturing environment. Review Figure 1.1 on page 9, and think about which of these characteristics describe you.

Managing Stress

Working with children can be rewarding and challenging. Anticipating and meeting the needs of children and families can be stressful at times. It is important for child care providers to learn to manage stress in healthful ways. When you manage stress well, you feel better and your job remains fulfilling and enjoyable. Here are some ways to help you manage stress:

▶ Eat nutritious meals and snacks.

▶ Get plenty of rest.

▶ Set realistic expectations for yourself.

▶ Practice good time management.

▶ Learn to say "no" to avoid taking on too many commitments.

▶ Set and prioritize goals.

▶ Break each goal into tasks, and work on one task at a time.

▶ Share home and work responsibilities with others, whenever possible.

▶ Learn what balance between work and personal life works for you.

▶ Look for ways to reduce unnecessary stress.

▶ Use problem solving skills to meet challenges.

▶ Maintain friendships by spending time regularly with friends.

▶ Take up a hobby, and participate in it regularly.

▶ Seek help from a trusted counselor if needed.

▼ **Stress Relief**
....

Taking time for personal interests is part of maintaining balance between work and personal life. *How will your career choice affect your family life? How can you balance your work and home life?*

READING CHECK ✔ **Reflect** In what ways can your personal traits and skills influence the career you select?

Purestock/SuperStock

Careers in Early Childhood

Working in an early childhood program helps you see and hear about the world from a child's perspective. Children's natural curiosity and high activity levels create an active environment. Teaching and guiding children allow you to develop many talents and skills. Each early childhood professional chooses the field for his or her own reasons. Most agree that a love of children is at the top of the list. Your training in the field of early childhood care opens other career opportunities as well, including owning or managing a child care center, working with children and parents as a social worker or other human services professional, and teaching other adults about children. See **Figure 1.2** for additional ideas.

Figure 1.2 **Places You Can Work With Children**

Early Childhood Settings Not everyone who works in early childhood works at a child care center or preschool. Choose five settings below and research the type of early childhood professionals they employ. *How can you benefit from comparing the rewards and responsibilities of various early childhood careers?*

- Organizations such as the Boys and Girls Clubs
- Child care resource and referral agencies
- Children's hospital or hospice
- Children's section of a library
- Children's zoos, gardens, and nature centers
- Cruise ships, shopping malls, or fitness centers
- Domestic violence or homeless shelters
- Early childhood professional organizations
- Elementary before- and after-school programs
- Family education agencies
- High school or university child care centers
- Human services departments in government agencies
- Intergenerational care centers
- Kindergartens
- Mental health agencies
- Children's museums
- Parks and recreation programs
- Prisons with in-house child visitation
- Public or private preschool programs
- School health center or office
- State education boards
- Summer camps and sports clinics
- U.S. military bases

Bananastock/AGE Fotostock

You can learn more about these and other careers in the Pathway to Your Career and Career Spotlight features.

Expert *Advice* . . .

"It may be that the benefits of investing in child care and preschool learning could be greater than investment in education at later ages, given that a significant part of cognitive and non-cognitive skills development occurs before children start school."

— David Armstrong,
author and researcher

Working with Children

Children usually view anyone who spends time with them in a classroom setting as a teacher. However, the people who work at a child care center or in home-based care have various titles, such as director, teacher, care giver, care provider, child care worker, teacher's assistant, and teacher's aide. Each title generally refers to the level of training the position requires. Note that job titles and training requirements may vary from program to program and from state to state.

Early childhood programs are now available at a variety of settings. Figure 1.2 includes an array of settings that involve working with or providing support to young children and their parents. Which ones appeal to you for your professional career?

Choosing a Career Path

Setting educational and career goals is the first step in planning your career. Gaining the education and training that qualifies you for early childhood positions will help you achieve your career goals. The education, training, and experience you need, however, will depend upon the specific job you seek and where you live.

Many states require only a high school diploma to work in an entry-level position, such as a teacher's aide, although additional classes and training is often recommended. Many states and most employers require that the mid-level teacher complete additional child development coursework or an associate's degree. Center directors, and those in high-level positions, usually have a bachelor's or master's degree in education, child development, or business.

The United States has no uniform national licensing or registration standards for education, training, and experience in the early childhood care profession. Each state sets its own standards, and many states have created a career lattice, or framework of information, to help determine what skills, knowledge, or credentials you need to pursue various positions or career pathways within that state. Different job titles and settings have different standards and requirements. Programs in public schools usually have higher requirements than those of privately owned early childhood centers or home-based care. You may obtain a school district's standards directly from the school board office or from the state board of education. Contact the local agency that licenses or regulates early childhood centers and home-based care in your area to find out about your state's requirements.

To help you determine the right career path for you, look for practical intern or volunteer experiences in early childhood careers before you graduate. During high school, you can gain firsthand experience in working with young children. Exposure to and comparing various early childhood careers will help you confirm whether you have the traits, attitudes, skills, and abilities to be a successful early childhood professional. It is also an excellent way to watch how professionals teach and care for young children.

Entrepreneurship Opportunities

As you examine your interests and abilities, you may discover things about yourself that guide you toward other career directions. Perhaps you could be a successful **entrepreneur** (äⁿn-trə-p(r)ə-ˈnər), or a person who owns and operates a business.

Your business may be owning and managing a child care center or family child care home, but there are other possibilities for entrepreneurs trained to work with children. You could use your knowledge of child development to design toys or educational materials. You could work as an independent curriculum specialist or parent educator. As a business owner, you are your own boss. You get to choose the type of work you do and make all the decisions. You also take on the risks and challenges involved in building a quality, profitable business.

If owning a child-centered business appeals to you, think about the education, experience, and financing you will need to open a business.

Provider Certification

In order to identify individuals who can successfully perform the duties of an early childhood professional, federal, state, and county or city government agencies have created certification and credentialing programs. These requirements may not be required if you obtain a four-year college degree.

▲ **Owning a Business**

Owning a child care center comes with many additional responsibilities and rewards. *What are some of the rewards of being an entrepreneur?*

SAFETY MATTERS

Background Check

Most jobs require some kind of background check. Federal and state laws require that background checks be conducted for certain jobs. Most states require criminal background checks for anyone who works with children, the elderly, or people who are disabled. A child care center or family child care home may choose to do more research than the state or city requires but cannot legally do less.

Depending on your location, employers may use a variety of sources to conduct a background check. They may check the child abuse and neglect registry, conduct a fingerprint check at the state and/or federal level, research your criminal record, and check the sex offender registry.

What Would You Do? You find out that one of your coworkers has an arrest record. She seems like a nice person, but she has not told the child care center director about her past arrest. What would you do?

To earn a certificate or a credential, you must satisfactorily complete on-the-job training and formal education. Public schools typically require certification for early childhood educators. The board of education in each state determines certification requirements for a variety of early childhood careers. A nationally recognized credential program for early childhood professionals is the **Child Development Associate (CDA)** credential. Many states require the CDA or similar training and education for child care professionals. To receive a CDA credential, you must complete the following steps:

▶ Show your knowledge of six specific areas of child care by completing classes in child development and child care.

▶ Demonstrate your experience working with children in a formal child care setting.

▶ Have your teaching skills evaluated by an experienced professional.

▶ Complete a multiple-choice test, the CDA Exam, to demonstrate your knowledge of child care.

The Child Development Associate credential is offered in four areas: infant/toddler caregivers in center-based programs, preschool caregivers in center-based programs, family child care providers, and home-based programs. Meeting this credential's standards prepares people for a variety of positions in early childhood programs. More and more states also offer the director credential to prepare administrators for managing children's programs. Some states also offer child care professionals' credentials for specific age ranges, such as infant care, preschool age, and school-age children. These credentials allow professionals to improve their skills and to increase their knowledge in a specialized area.

READING CHECK ✔ **Plan** What education is required for mid-level and high-level careers in early childhood education?

Legal Responsibilities

Early childhood professionals must abide by the laws that apply to their job responsibilities. Laws help protect the rights and welfare of children, families, and staff. Three major legal responsibilities in the early childhood profession are criminal background checks, maintaining privacy and confidentiality, and mandated reporting of abuse and neglect.

Criminal Background Checks

Many states now require confidential criminal background checks before a person can be employed in early childhood care and education. If a background check reveals a person has been convicted of a crime against children, state law requires that the employer reject the prospective candidate or dismiss him or her if already hired.

Privacy and Confidentiality

The Family Educational Rights and Privacy Act (FERPA) is a federal law that protects the privacy of personal and educational records. It says that only parents or legal guardians may have access to their children's records. To share the information with another person, such as a counselor, physician, or other child care setting, the parents or guardians must give written permission.

Although it is tempting to discuss children's development issues with fellow staff members, it is your professional responsibility to maintain confidentiality. FERPA specifies that personal, developmental, or educational information about a child should be shared only with staff members who have necessary involvement in a child's care and education.

Mandated Reporting

All states have child abuse and neglect laws, which protect children from harm inside or outside their homes. Anyone can report a case of child abuse or neglect. Early childhood professionals, however, along with health-care workers and teachers, are **mandated**, or required by law, to report each suspected abuse or neglect case. People in these professions are called mandated reporters.

Most states have hotlines that make it easy to make mandated-reporter calls to the appropriate office. Licensing laws often require that staff members receive training in identifying symptoms of child abuse and neglect and in reporting these incidents.

READING CHECK ✔ **Review** What sources can be used to conduct a background check?

▼ **Reporting Abuse and Neglect**
....
Mandated reporting is just one of the legal responsibilities of those who work with children. *How can this practice benefit the children and the profession?*

Purestock/SuperStock

Teacher's Aide

What Does a Teacher's Aide Do?

A teacher's aide works to support classroom teachers and students. Aides work with teachers, supervise cafeterias and playgrounds, and help with administrative tasks. They often work with special education students to help them succeed in their classes. In child care centers, they work with children who have developmental delays and assist lead teachers to make sure that all the children in the room get individual attention.

Career Readiness Skills

As with all careers related to children, teacher's aides should enjoy working with children. They are usually required to pass a background check. Teacher's aides should have a lot of patience and a willingness to follow directions. They need to be able to communicate with students, teachers, and parents. Because teacher's aides are called on to complete a variety of tasks, flexibility and creativity are essential skills.

Education and Training

In many states, the basic education requirement for a teacher's aide is a high school diploma. Coursework in child development and early childhood education is helpful when considering working as a teacher's aide. An associate's degree or passing state testing is required to work in schools that get federal funding. Previous experience working with children is often required.

Job Outlook

Employment of teacher's aides is expected to continue growing as the number of children in school increases. Teacher's aides also allow schools to place more students in a single classroom. Teacher's aides who have attended at least two years of college, have experience working with special needs students, or who speak a second language are particularly in demand.

Critical Thinking Because teacher's aides are not always required to have a college degree, this is often a career pursued at the beginning of a career. Propose the possible short-term and long-term goals that will help you prepare for this career.

Career Cluster

Human Services Teacher's aides work in the Human Services career cluster. Here are some other child-related jobs in this career cluster:

- Nanny
- Preschool teacher
- Psychologist and children's play therapist
- Staff development trainer
- Child care resource and referral specialist
- Early intervention specialist
- Parent educator
- Child care center director
- Social worker
- Camp counselor

Explore Further The Human Services career cluster contains five pathways: Counseling and Mental Health Services, Personal Care Services, Consumer Services, Family and Community Services, and Early Childhood Development and Services. Choose one of these pathways to explore further. Write a paragraph that summarizes your findings.

Early Childhood Careers
Visual Summary

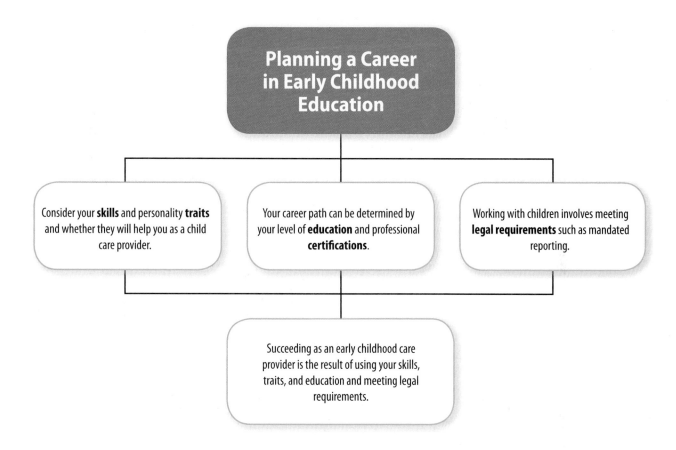

Planning a Career in Early Childhood Education

Consider your **skills** and personality **traits** and whether they will help you as a child care provider.

Your career path can be determined by your level of **education** and professional **certifications**.

Working with children involves meeting **legal requirements** such as mandated reporting.

Succeeding as an early childhood care provider is the result of using your skills, traits, and education and meeting legal requirements.

Vocabulary Review

1. Write each of the vocabulary terms below on an index card and the definitions on separate index cards. Work in pairs or small groups to match each term to its definition.

Content Vocabulary

◇ child care (p. 6)
◇ trend (p. 6)
◇ nanny (p. 7)
◇ au pair (p. 7)
◇ entrepreneur (p. 13)
◇ Child Development Associate (CDA) (p. 14)
◇ mandated (p. 15)

Academic Vocabulary

▪ comply (p. 8)
▪ initiative (p. 9)

Review Key Concepts

2. Cite three factors that contribute to the demand for early childhood professionals.
3. Identify ten characteristics of a successful child care professional.
4. Name five places where you can work with children.
5. Describe the responsibilities of a mandated reporter.

Critical Thinking

6. **Give examples** of what child care professionals can do to create a quality child care environment.
7. **Explain** the purpose of the Family Educational Rights and Privacy Act.
8. **Reflect** on why it is important to relieve stress.
9. **Examine** what questions you might have when opening a child care business. How would you find answers to those questions?
10. **Explain** why background checks are usually required before a person can be employed in early childhood care and education.

21st Century Skills

Planning Skills

11. **Career Opportunity** Investigate the rewards and challenges of a variety of levels of early childhood careers. What education and training is required for those careers? What personal traits and characteristics would you recommend for a person seeking any early childhood career? Which jobs might you apply for now? What could you do in the future? Create a chart to show your findings.

Accountability Skills

12. **Observation and Evaluation** Obtain a copy of your state's licensing laws for child care centers. Read the laws thoroughly and take notes on the requirements they give. Then visit an accredited early childhood program in your area. Record the indicators of high quality that you observe. How do these indicators compare to standards set by the state licensing laws? Write a summary of your observation.

Child Care LAB

Use the skills you have learned in this chapter.

Personal Mission Statement

13. **CDA Preparation** This activity will help you create an autobiography and personal statement such as the one required to obtain a CDA credential. This statement will be included in your Professional Resource File, and should be revised as your goals and experiences change.

    A. Create a time line. Draft a time line of the major events and accomplishments in your life so far. Include job experience, community service projects, and education experiences.

    B. Evaluate your time line. Look for events and experiences that explain why you would be a good child care provider. Remove items that are too personal or inappropriate for a professional setting.

    C. Give your reasons. List your reasons for working with young children and any role models or influences you have had. Use the characteristics covered in this chapter to help you.

    D. Personal goals. Outline your goals for the future. What education do you plan on completing? What jobs would you like to hold? Where do you think you will begin and end your career?

    E. Write your autobiography. Combine your information to create a 300-word personal mission statement that explains who you are and what about your life influenced your decision to work with young children.

Create Your Evaluation

Create a sheet with the following categories:

- Life Overview
- Influences
- Personal Goals
- Appropriateness

Ask your classmates to use the sheet to evaluate your autobiography, rating each category from 1 to 10.

Academic Skills

English Language Arts

14. Earn Your Rewards Owning your own business is a path that offers many challenges and many rewards. Think of a situation in which you worked hard to meet a goal. Create a list of the steps you had to take to accomplish the task. Write a paragraph describing some of the challenges you faced and some of the rewards you received.

Social Studies

15. Compare Child Care Choose a country other than the United States. Conduct research to learn how child care is usually handled in that country. How is it similar to or different from child care in the U.S.? Write a report with your findings, including a summary of what you feel the pros and cons are for that country's approach.

Science

16. Job Opportunities Because of changing family needs such as the number of dual-income parents and single parents, the demand for early care and education professionals is expected to continue growing.

Procedure Use the Internet and library reference resources to research the number of people employed in child care in 1960, 1970, 1980, 1990, and 2000. Then research potential job opportunities in child care from 2010 to 2040.

Analysis Draw a graph showing the past levels of employment in child care and the predictions of the number of job opportunities over the coming years. Write a brief summary of your findings. Include an explanation of how things have changed and the reasons the field has grown. List factors that could change the future outlook for jobs in the early care and education career field.

Certification Prep

Sharpen your test-taking skills to improve your certification program score.

Directions Choose the phrase that best completes the statement.

17. Child care providers demonstrate characteristics such as _____.

    A. great mood swings

    B. an inability to adapt to change

    C. an understanding of child development

    D. entrepreneurship

18. CDA stands for _____.

    A. Child-care Discipline Agency

    B. Childhood Development Application

    C. Certification for Developing Ages

    D. Child Development Associate

Test-Taking Tip

When answering a fill-in-the-blank question, silently read the sentence with each of the sample answers in the blank space. This will help you eliminate wrong answers. The best answer results in a sentence that is both factual and grammatically correct.

CHAPTER 2

Employability Skills

Writing Activity

★ 21st Century Skills

Initiative A successful interview is an important part of getting a job. Choose three early childhood jobs that interest you. For each job, make a list of questions that you would need to ask to learn more about the position. Then review all the lists and underline related question topics. How could these related topics help you plan for an interview?

Writing Tips

1. Start with a key word or phrase as you write each question.
2. Add ideas and phrases as they occur to you.
3. Do not worry about keeping your ideas in order.
4. Review your lists to look for related ideas.

Explore the Photo
Finding a job takes preparation. *What steps do you need to take in order to get a job?*

©Todd Wright/Blend Images/Corbis

Reading Guide

Predict Before starting the chapter, browse the content by reading headings, bold terms, and photo captions. Do they help you predict the information in the chapter?

Read to Learn

Key Concepts

- **Describe** the basic employability skills that applicants need for positions in early childhood care.
- **List** the qualities of effective leaders.
- **Outline** the steps of the job application and hiring process and the required actions at each step.
- **Summarize** the rights and responsibilities of employees and employers.

Main Idea

Employers look for specific skills and characteristics in employees. Finding a job requires careful preparation of application materials and making a good impression at an interview. Both employees and employers have rights and responsibilities.

Content Vocabulary

- ◇ active listening
- ◇ body language
- ◇ work ethic
- ◇ flexibility
- ◇ networking
- ◇ trade publications
- ◇ service learning
- ◇ résumé
- ◇ prioritize
- ◇ empathy
- ◇ ethics
- ◇ workers' compensation
- ◇ minimum wage
- ◇ compensatory time
- ◇ labor union
- ◇ collective bargaining
- ◇ discrimination
- ◇ sexual harassment
- ◇ probation

Academic Vocabulary

- ■ foundation
- ■ responsibility

Graphic Organizer

As you read, you will identify skills and characteristics that can help you succeed as an employee. Use a two-column chart like the one shown to help you organize the information.

Successful Employee Traits	
Skills	**Characteristics**

Graphic Organizer *Go to* **connected.mcgraw-hill.com** *to print this Graphic Organizer.*

AS YOU READ

Connect Think about how you can apply skills you have learned in school on the job.

◇ Vocabulary

You can find definitions in the glossary at the back of this book.

▼ A Smile Can Be Heard

The telephone is an important communication tool for child care professionals. *What speaking skills should you use when talking on the phone?*

Sharpening Your Basic Skills

Whether your career goal is to be a child care center owner, a preschool teacher, or a camp counselor, your next step is to sharpen the skills you need to start your professional career. Every employer expects you to have certain basic skills. These are general skills that provide you with a strong foundation, or base that you build upon, for finding and keeping a job and advancing in your career. Basic skills can also transfer from job to job. Communication, math, thinking, technology, and information skills are critical to helping you succeed in furthering your education and career.

Communication Skills

Effective communication skills are essential to any career. As a child care professional, your skills in speaking, writing, reading, and listening will play an important role in how well you exchange information and build relationships with children and their families. Choose a communication strategy appropriate for the task or situation to ensure effective communication.

Speaking Skills

Speaking skills are needed to organize ideas and communicate to individuals, to small and large groups, and to both children and adults. Verbal communication is most effective when you present information in a clear and organized way. How well other people understand you depends upon how clearly you speak. Pronounce words clearly and correctly, and speak at a pace appropriate for your audience.

Listening Skills

You will be listening constantly at work. Listening is not just appearing to hear what a person has said to you. You must listen to understand the meaning of the speaker's words, a skill called **active listening**. To be an active listener, avoid distractions and focus on what the speaker says. Paraphrase the speaker to show that you understand. Ask questions if you do not understand or need clarification.

Figure 2.1 Reading Strategies

Read to Understand
Whether reading care instructions or reading a story to children, effective reading skills are important for child care professionals. *Why is it important for child care professionals to read for understanding?*

- **Preview.** Read headlines and subtitles to get an overview.
- **Skim.** Look over the reading material for key points.
- **Focus.** Give what you are reading your full attention. As you read, think about what you are reading.
- **Use context clues.** Use clues within the text to help you determine the meaning of unfamiliar words or phrases.
- **Visualize.** Form mental pictures or charts of the events, characters, and details of what you are reading.
- **Check comprehension.** Ask yourself how well you understand what you just read.

Body Language

You might not be aware of it, but you also speak without saying a word through your body language. **Body language** is the way you move your hands and arms, hold your body, and use facial expressions. It reveals your feelings and reactions to what you say or hear. You can also observe and interpret another speaker's body language to pick up on emotions that the person does not say aloud. Pay attention to body language to practice effective nonverbal communication skills.

Writing Skills

Your ability to communicate in writing will help you find a job and perform well on the job. Job applications, business forms, and everyday work correspondence such as memos and e-mails require strong writing skills and good grammar. In providing child care services, you will document care in children's records and write letters to parents and memos to staff. Consider your audience and style when writing:

▶ **Audience.** Picture who will be reading your writing. Adjust what and how you write to what the reader needs to understand your message.

▶ **Writing style.** Your writing style comes from your choice of words and the tone, or attitude, that your words convey to the reader. Be direct and use a professional tone. Always follow basic grammar and punctuation rules. Use proper tense and syntax, and carefully proofread your writing before hitting the send button on an e-mail or mailing a letter.

Reading Skills

Reading is a very important skill. Much of the information you receive on the job is gained from reading. Child care professionals use their reading skills in many ways. They read work policies and communications and care instructions from family members. They also use reading skills to keep updated on research findings for ongoing professional development. **Figure 2.1** above describes reading techniques that can help you improve your reading skills.

Math Skills

The ability to work with numbers is a fundamental part of almost every job. You will add, subtract, multiply, and divide, and use fractions, percentages, and decimals frequently in the workplace. For example, you will use basic math skills to keep track of your work hours, wages, and vacation days. Child care directors use math skills to order supplies, complete payroll and tax forms, and maintain budgets. Sharpening your basic math skills will improve your success as a child care professional.

Thinking Skills

Employers desire employees who can think creatively and make good decisions based on reasons and facts. An employee who can think critically can respond quickly and properly to a variety of situations. For example, if a fire alarm sounds during nap or rest time, you must react immediately to evacuate children as safely as possible.

Making good decisions shows employee responsibility. Employers also value employees that can resolve small problems before they become big issues. An employee who finds quick, practical solutions to problems will help a care team provide quality child care.

Technology Skills

Knowing how to use a computer and other current technologies is essential for today's workplace. You will use technology to access, manage, and create information. Depending on your child care facility, you may need to learn how to operate a security system or update information on a Web site. During your career, you will need to keep up with the many changes and advances in technology.

Information Skills

Information comes from countless sources during your workday. To be a successful employee, you must learn and practice how to acquire and use information appropriately. Learn the difference between reliable and useful information and opinions, which can contain false or misleading information. An effective employee must be able to make sense of his or her own research and successfully communicate it to employers, coworkers, and parents. This requires knowing how to understand and interpret information in a variety of formats such as graphs, reports, manuals, and schedules.

McGraw-Hill Education

Work Ethic

In addition to skills, employers look for certain key qualities in employees. Employers want employees who have productive work habits and attitudes. Demonstrating these traits shows a strong **work ethic**—a personal commitment to work hard and do one's very best. The qualities that mark a strong work ethic include responsibility, commitment, reliability, flexibility, and honesty.

Responsibility and Commitment

Showing responsibility is one of the most important qualifications for success in any job. Responsibility means showing up for work on time. It means carrying out your job duties, even when your boss is not around. When you are responsible, you accept the consequences of your actions.

Commitment is a quality that supports your other abilities and skills. You show that you are committed to your job by following all procedures, supporting your coworkers, and doing your duties very well. Committed employees show enthusiasm for their job. They make the most of opportunities to improve their abilities and to learn new skills. Demonstrating commitment to quality and excellence on the job will set you apart as a valuable employee.

Reliability and Flexibility

Reliability means that you perform as your employer expects time after time. Reliable employees carry out assigned tasks without being reminded and with minimal supervision. **Flexibility**, the ability to adapt willingly to change, is very important in the workplace. Flexibility on the job means dealing with change without complaining. The more confident that you are in your skills, the easier you will find it to be flexible.

Honesty

Honesty is an important part of a strong work ethic. You show honesty on the job when you are truthful in what you say and do. For example, if you make a mistake, it is honest behavior to admit your error and to find out ways to prevent making the mistake again. You do not cover up the mistake or blame someone else. Employers insist on honesty, and some consider dishonesty reason for firing.

▼ **Valuable Employee**
....
Doing repetitive tasks such as preparing art supplies without complaining shows a good work ethic. *How else can an employee show a good work ethic?*

READING CHECK ✔ **Summarize** What skills and qualities do you need to be a successful employee?

Purestock/SuperStock

Leadership Skills

Employers look for employees with leadership qualities. Leadership is the ability to motivate others to accomplish goals. Every person has an individual leadership style. Some people lead quietly, preferring to lead by example. Other leaders are more vocal, frequently giving encouragement. Some leaders become involved in every part of a job. Others prefer to stay in the background until they are needed. All effective leaders share key qualities that get the job done and keep the group together.

Qualities of Effective Leaders

Effective leaders have certain qualities that are helpful in creating a productive work environment. These qualities include:

- **Integrity.** Good leaders are honest and trustworthy. They are dependable and straightforward in communicating with others. They use good judgment based on solid values and principles in working with others.

- **Vision.** Good leaders are open minded and future oriented. They look to the future for opportunities and challenges. They use their vision and creativity to motivate others.

- **Perseverance.** Good leaders are persistent even when faced with difficult challenges. They keep focused and find and use resources to achieve desired goals.

- **Consideration.** Effective leaders are aware and considerate of the feelings of others. They take time to listen to others' ideas.

- **Team oriented.** Good leaders are committed to the team effort. They collaborate, or work well with others, to achieve a common goal. They identify and value the differing backgrounds, viewpoints, skills, and talents of others on the team.

▼**Be a Leader**

Good leaders support their team by providing encouragement and feedback. *Why is a strong work ethic important for leaders?*

Effective leaders maintain a high level of commitment to their goals and the workers who help them achieve these goals. Effective leaders also desire to reach the highest standards of quality in any task. To achieve these high standards, good leaders regularly monitor team members' work. All members of a team can display leadership skills by supporting the common team goal, taking initiative to accomplish team tasks, and sharing constructive opinions and concerns about the team's plan and direction.

Developing your leadership skills will help you as you move along your career path. Employers look among their employees for those whom others respect and who can also handle more responsibility. They consider these employees first for higher-level positions. One way to improve leadership skills is through participation in educational and professional organizations.

Leadership Programs

Many organizations and programs have been designed to help students develop leadership skills. Family, Career and Community Leaders of America (FCCLA) is a national organization of middle and high school students who are either currently taking or have taken Family and Consumer Sciences courses. FCCLA activities provide opportunities for personal, career, and leadership development through activities and competitive events. Student members participate in challenging competitions such as the Students Taking Action with Recognition (STAR) Events. For example, the Early Childhood event challenges students to submit a portfolio, develop a lesson plan, and present the lesson to demonstrate their abilities in this career area.

SkillsUSA is another organization that helps students develop leadership skills. SkillsUSA is a national organization of high school and college students enrolled in training programs for technical, skilled, and service occupations. SkillsUSA programs partner students with industry professionals to provide SkillsUSA Championships. Students enrolled in occupational child care and early childhood programs can participate in the Preschool Teaching Assistant contest. Students are judged on their abilities to plan and present appropriate activities for preschool children and their general knowledge of quality child care.

▲**Leadership in Action**
....
Leadership organizations help students learn and practice leadership skills. *What are other ways you could develop your leadership skills?*

READING CHECK ✔ **Connect** How can all team members show leadership skills?

Seeking Employment

Your career as a child care professional begins with your first job. Finding a job can be a challenging process, but the key to a successful job search is to be patient. Your job search will become at least a part-time job in itself. It is also important to stay organized and to take initiative on job leads, or opportunities.

Employment Resources

Job opportunities come from many sources, such as newspaper classified ads, online job boards, and word-of-mouth. Your job search will demand that you tap many kinds of resources. Because you will learn of many job possibilities and meet many people, you will need to keep records for successful follow-up. Develop an organization system to keep track of job leads and what you have done to pursue each lead.

Networking

Networking is the most direct and successful way of finding a job. **Networking** means making use of all your personal and professional contacts to further your career goals. If you have ever asked a family member or friend about a job possibility, you have practiced networking. You can also network with:

▶ **Teachers and Mentors.** These adults know your strengths and how you could apply them in a child care setting. These are also individuals who you may ask for reference letters.

▶ **Friends and Classmates.** Other people who are interested in careers similar to yours will also be researching jobs. They may be willing to share information with you.

▶ **Employers and Coworkers.** If you already have a job, most employers post job opportunities internally before advertising them to the general public. Your coworkers also may also know about job openings outside of your workplace.

▶ **Organizations.** School organizations and community groups can often provide job information.

Building a strong network takes time. Every referral, or job lead, you receive through networking should be treated with respect. If someone gives you a job lead, follow up with the employer responsibly. Your dress and behavior not only reflect on you, but also the person who recommended you. Remember to return the favor—share job information with people in your network.

▲ Build a Network

Maintaining connections with teachers and mentors, the people who know your strengths well, is one form of networking. *What are the advantages of using networking to find job leads?*

Stewart Cohen/Getty Images

The Internet

The Internet is an important job-search tool. Thousands of employment resources are available on the Internet. There are many Web sites that provide quality job-search and career-building information. You can review job postings online and apply for jobs electronically. You can network with people around the world by participating in social network communities.

Professional Organizations

Another source of job resources is professional organizations that have members who are involved in various aspects of caring for children. Many have Web sites that list jobs on their staffs, as well as positions at member companies or member programs. **Figure 2.2** lists professional organizations you may want to explore.

You may have to pay a membership fee to join a professional organization. Many organizations have student chapters in high schools and colleges. The services they offer their members may include job listings, job placement services, scholarships, workshops, and conferences, which provide networking opportunities. Early childhood positions listed with professional organizations usually require more education and skills than those listed in local resources and, consequently, offer higher salaries.

Most early childhood professional organizations publish professional magazines and newsletters for their members. They are called **trade publications** because they are written for people in an industry by organizations that support the industry. These publications contain helpful articles on all aspects of the industry and often list job opportunities.

Figure 2.2 Early Childhood Professional Organizations

Professional Resources Membership fees may include a subscription to a professional organization's publications. *How might you use trade publications throughout your career?*

Professional Organization	Publications
National Association for the Education of Young Children (NAEYC)	*Young Children* *Teaching Young Children*
National Association of Child Care Resource and Referral Agencies (NACCRRA)	Annual reports and research reports on specific topics
National Coalition for Campus Children's Centers (NCCCC)	Fact sheets and newsletter
Association for Childhood Education International (ACEI)	*Childhood Education, Childhood Explorer* *Journal of Research in Childhood Education*
Council for Professional Recognition (CDA)	Child Development Associate credential assessment and training materials
National Association of Social Workers (NASW)	*Journals and brochures*
American Association of Family and Consumer Sciences (AAFCS)	*Journal of Family & Consumer Sciences*

Ingram Publishing

▲ Hands-On Experience

Volunteering lets you try out a job. *What are other benefits of volunteering?*

Employment Agencies

An employment agency may assist in your job search. Employment agencies are businesses that work for employers and seek potential employees for them. They keep lists of their clients' job openings and potential applicants. They will submit an applicant's credentials to the employer for consideration for a fee.

Temporary agencies offer fast placement for people looking for an entry-level position. Employers who have an ongoing need for child care professionals may rely on temporary agencies to fill their demand. This hiring arrangement gives the employer a chance to assess each agency employee as a potential team member without going through the company's hiring process. Working through a temporary agency gives you a chance to see what the child care field is like without committing to a certain employer.

Volunteering and Internships

Although volunteers do not usually get paid, they do gain valuable career experience. The information you learn can help you make valuable career decisions in the future. To gain experience working with children, consider volunteering at a preschool, library, hospital, recreation center, or child care center.

Internships are another way to gain valuable career experience. An internship is a more formal position and requires a longer time commitment than a volunteer position. Internships may be unpaid or paid depending upon the situation. Through hands-on experience at the work site, interns gain vital job skills. Internships can sometimes lead to full time, paid employment.

In addition to volunteering and internships, many schools offer service learning opportunities. **Service learning** is community service that is part of your schoolwork. For example, you might work at your community early childhood center while taking early childhood education classes.

Applying for a Job

When you have identified several job leads, you can begin applying for jobs. Most employers will first ask you to fill out an application form, either on paper or electronically. Many employers also ask you to submit a cover letter and a résumé. It is important to follow the directions for each job lead and submit only what the employer requests. Employers will be interested in the skills you have to offer. They also observe how you write, dress, speak, and behave during the job application and interview process. It is important to perform each step of the process in a professional manner.

Job Applications

Remember to make a good impression from the beginning. Do not walk into a potential workplace, even to ask for an application, unless your clothing is neat and appropriate and you are clean and well groomed. It is absolutely essential that you demonstrate appropriate appearance for the workplace when applying for a job.

Even if an application form is not your first step, you will be asked to complete one at some point during the process. You must fill out the form correctly and completely. Job application forms vary, but they all ask for the same kinds of information. Keep these tips in mind when completing an application:

▶ Read the instructions for completing each section before responding.

▶ Print neatly, using blue or black ink.

▶ Assemble key application information in one place. This includes your Social Security number; driver's license number; and the names, addresses, and phone numbers of previous employers along with the dates of your employment.

▶ You will also need the complete names, addresses, and telephone numbers of your personal references. Be sure to get permission from the people on your reference list before using their names.

▶ Do not leave any part of the application form blank unless you are asked to do so. If a question does not apply, write *N/A*, which means "not applicable," in the space provided.

▶ Always tell the truth. Submitting false information is illegal.

▼ **Application Forms**

When you fill out a job application, print neatly and use blue or black ink. *What are the ways you might apply for a job?*

Prepare Your Résumé

Your résumé will likely be the first contact an employer has with you. As with all first impressions, you want to leave a good one. A résumé should include your contact information, job objective, and relevant education, work experience, skills and abilities, awards and honors, and professional and community activities.

Simon Smith
105 Elm Street
Culver, IN 46511
(555) 555-5555
simon.smith@email.com

OBJECTIVE
An entry level teaching assistant position as a step toward a career in an early childhood education

EXPERIENCE
Family, Career and Community Leaders of America (FCCLA), Franklin High School Chapter, Culver, Indiana
Chapter President. September 2011-present.
- Developed agenda for and lead class meetings.
- Represented chapter at national leadership meetings.
- Won silver medal in Early Childhood Star Event.

Little League Baseball, Culver Department of Parks and Recreation, Culver, Indiana
Assistant Coach. May 2011–present.
- Organized and led practice sessions for 15 second-graders.
- Managed parent communications, including team blog and email newsletters.

National Honor Society, Franklin High School, Culver, Indiana
Secretary. September 2011–present.
- Coordinated fundraiser that raised $3,000 for local food pantry.

EDUCATION & TRAINING
Franklin High School, Culver, Indiana
Diploma expected June 2014. GPA: 3.8/4.0
National Honor Society member.
- Completed Early Childhood Education and Child Development classes.

Red Cross First Aid with CPR Training Program
Certificate of Completion, April 2011.

SKILLS
- Proficient in Microsoft Office and Adobe Creative Suite.
- Experienced babysitter.
- Proven ability to teach young children.
- Ability to speak and write basic Spanish.

Apply It!
Create your résumé for a specific career in early childhood care and education.

▶ **Have a Clear Objective** *Your job objective should be short and to the point. State specifically what type of position you are looking for.*

▶ **Use Key Words** *Key words are significant words that employers use to search for relevant information about your skills and work experience. Employers use key words to search for resumes on the Internet.*

▶ **Look Professional** *A well-designed, error-free résumé will stand out from other applicants'. Avoid decorative graphics. Use correct spelling and grammar.*

▶ **Highlight Skills and Experience** *Stress relevant work experience, key skills, education, and training. If your work experience is limited, organize your résumé by the kinds of skills you have, such as communication and technical skills. Use action words to describe your skills and experience.*

▶ **Be Accurate and Concise** *Include accurate contact information and honest descriptions of your experience. Do not include information unless it is related to the job you are applying to.*

Preparing Your Résumé

A **résumé** (ˈre-zə-ˌmā) is a summary of your career objectives, work experience, qualifications, education, and training. Your résumé is a very important job-seeking tool. It gives a prospective employer the information he or she needs to help determine if you are right for the position. When preparing your résumé, always be truthful and accurate. List your work experience, skills, and education or training that will convince an employer that you are the best candidate for the job.

Writing Your Cover Letter

Responding to a job lead often requires you to submit a cover letter to accompany your résumé. A cover letter introduces yourself to your prospective employer. It is an opportunity to "sell yourself" by highlighting your best qualities. **Figure 2.3** on page 34 shows a sample cover letter. Here are some tips for creating a professional, attention-getting cover letter:

▶ **Keep it short.** Your cover letter should not be longer than one page.

▶ **Explain why you are writing.** The first sentence of your letter should describe what position you are applying for and where you heard of the opening.

▶ **Introduce yourself.** Give a short description of your background and professional abilities. Refer to your attached résumé and highlight one or two specific accomplishments.

▶ **Sell yourself.** Your cover letter should leave the reader thinking, "This person is exactly what we are looking for." Relate your skills and experience to the responsibilities described in the job listing. For example, if the job ad lists specific skills or knowledge required, mention your mastery of these in your letter.

Creating Your Portfolio

A portfolio is a collection of work samples that demonstrate your skills. The work samples are assembled in a binder, folder, or in a digital format. Portfolios are presented to potential employers to show how well prepared you are for a particular job. An early childhood portfolio may include items such as sample lesson plans, sample menus, teacher evaluations of work, and observations of child development.

▼ **Do Your Research**

As you prepare your cover letter and résumé, research the position and relate your skills and experience to the position. *Why is it important to use key words in your application materials?*

© Robert Daly/age fotostock

Figure 2.3 Cover Letter

A Good Introduction A cover letter is an opportunity to highlight your strengths as a potential employee. *What are the key qualifications pointed out in this cover letter?*

3008 Oak Street
Springdale, GA 33333
(555) 555-5555

May 31, 20—

Ms. Janelle Kirchner, Director
Willow Grove Preschool
6245 Groveland Avenue
Springdale, GA 33333

Dear Ms. Kirchner:

I am responding to your ad in last Sunday's *Journal* seeking a teacher's aide for the morning pre-kindergarten class. I would like to apply for this position.

On June 3, I will graduate from Jefferson High School. In addition to the required classes I have taken child development and child care classes to prepare for a career in early childhood education. I am an active member of the local Family, Career and Community Leaders (FCCLA) chapter.

During my last year in high school, I was enrolled in a work-experience program as a teacher's aide at Sunnydale Preschool. I enjoy working with children and they respond very positively to me.

I would like the opportunity to schedule an interview to discuss the position and my qualifications. You can reach me at (555) 555-5555. Thank you for considering me as a future employee.

Sincerely,

Carla Fuentes

Carla Fuentes

State where you learned about the job.

State that you want to apply for the job.

State your education and experience.

Ask for an interview.

Sign your name.

The Interview Process

When you have completed the application process, you must prepare for your interview. During this important face-to-face meeting, you will have a chance to convince an employer that you are the right person for the job. The employer will evaluate your appearance, attitude, personality, and answers to his or her questions.

Before the Interview

The interview process starts when an employer schedules an appointment. Write down the date, time, place of the interview, and the name of the contact person. These tips will help you prepare for a successful interview:

▶ **Do your homework.** The more you know about your prospective employer and the job you are seeking, the better you will do in the interview. Learn about market trends in the industry. Check such resources as community business publications, local newspapers, Internet directories, and professional organizations.

▶ **Choose appropriate clothing.** An employer's first impression of you will be based on your appearance. Choose business clothing that fits properly, is clean, pressed, and in good condition and is appropriate for the job you are applying for. Do not wear jeans or sandals. Your hair and nails should be clean, trimmed, and neat.

▶ **Be prompt and courteous.** On the day of the interview, allow plenty of time to locate your destination. Arrive early and practice appropriate business and personal etiquette. As you introduce yourself to a receptionist, guard, or other person before meeting with the interviewer, be polite and respectful. The interviewer may check with these people later.

▼ **Look Your Best**

The first impression you make at an interview will be through your appearance. *What can you do to make sure you look your best when meeting potential employers?*

During the Interview

Because the interview is so important in the hiring process, you will do well if you are prepared, positive, and relaxed. Keep the following points in mind:

▶ **Shake hands.** The interviewer will introduce him- or herself to you. Introduce yourself in return, and give for a firm, confident handshake. The interviewer will welcome you to the interview location and initiate the discussion. He or she will probably begin with a few simple questions to help you feel more at ease.

▶ **Make eye contact.** Throughout the interview, maintain eye contact with the interviewer. Eye contact helps show that you are listening and are interested in what the interviewer is saying.

▶ **Be poised and relaxed.** Sit up straight, with both feet on the floor. Avoid nervous gestures such as fidgeting or tapping a pencil. Never chew gum during an interview.

▶ **Answer thoughtfully and completely.** The interviewer will ask questions designed to determine if you are the person the company needs. Use correct grammar and speak clearly in your answers. Do not interrupt the interviewer. If you do not understand a question or do not know the answer, say so politely. **Figure 2.4** lists common interview questions.

▶ **Ask questions.** The interview process is meant to help you gain information, too. Do not hesitate to ask the interviewer about the nature of the job, the job responsibilities, and the working environment. You should not raise questions about the rate of pay and employee benefits, such as insurance, during the first interview unless the interviewer addresses them. Most employers use the first interview to narrow the applicants to one or two. In the second interview, employers will get more specific about pay and benefits.

Figure 2.4) Common Interview Questions

Be Prepared
Interviewers often ask similar questions in order to get a sense of a job candidate's skills, abilities, and interests. *How should you prepare for an interview?*

- Tell me about yourself.
- Why would you like to work for this company?
- What are your qualifications for this job?
- Where do you see yourself in five years?
- What is your greatest strength? Your greatest weakness?
- Tell me about a challenge you met or a problem you solved in school or on a job.
- What do you like best and least about teamwork?
- What questions do you have about the position or this company?
- Why should we hire you?
- Why do you want to work with children?

▶ **Close the interview on a positive note.** If the interviewer does not explain to you the next steps, such as the time period for second interviews or hiring decisions, ask. Thank the interviewer for his or her time. A professional attitude will always be remembered. Shake hands as you leave.

After the Interview

The interview process does not end when the interview is over. After each interview, you have the following responsibilities:

▶ **Send a thank-you letter.** The day after the interview, send the interviewer a handwritten or typed thank-you letter for the interview. Do this even if you are no longer interested in the position or have been turned down for the job. You may apply for another position with this employer at some point in the future and want to leave a good impression.

▶ **Follow up.** If you have been asked to contact the employer, do so as requested. Send any materials or information requested, such as reference letters. If the employer has promised to contact you, wait the specified amount of time. If this time passes, call the employer and politely request information about the status of your application. You may be asked to go through a second interview.

▲ **A Successful Interview**

A smile and a firm handshake help make a good first impression at a job interview. *How can you show confidence to a potential employer?*

▶ **Review the session.** As soon as possible after the interview, go over the session in your mind. Think about the impression you made. Make notes on what questions you were asked and anything you could do to improve during the next interview. Note any key information, such as employer expectations and job responsibilities. List any unanswered questions you have about the job.

Responding to a Job Offer

Before you accept a job offer, it is important to determine if the job is the right one for you. Ask yourself: Is the offered wage fair? Will I be able to get along with my manager? How much time will I spend traveling to and from the job? Will the job require working extra hours? Is there opportunity for professional growth in the position? When you have considered these questions, you are ready to respond to a job offer in one of three ways:

▶ **Accept the offer.** The employer will give you specific details on pay, benefits, schedules, job expectations, and start date. You may be asked to participate in employee orientation or a training session before starting the job.

▶ **Ask for time to consider the offer.** This is the time to bring up any unanswered questions that might affect your decision. Let the employer know when you will notify him or her of your decision. Do not put off responding to the employer.

▶ **Turn down the job offer.** You may decide that the job is not right for you, or you may have been offered a better job in the meantime. Whatever the case, if you do not plan to take the position, say so. You do not need to give reasons for turning down a job offer. Simply say, "Thank you for considering me, but I am not interested in taking the position."

If you are not offered a job, do not be discouraged. You many not have the necessary qualifications or the employer may have found an applicant more suited to the position. The interviewer is under no obligation to tell you why you are not being offered the job. Accept the decision gracefully, and keep looking for a job.

READING CHECK ✔ **Describe** What are the steps in applying and interviewing for a job?

▼ **First Day**

When you start a new job, you want to do well. *What should you do to prepare for your first day in a new position?*

(c) IT Stock Free

On the Job

Whether you work for a large company or a small business, what really matters to your professional success is the relationship between you and your employer. In this relationship, both parties have rights and responsibilities. When you begin your job, your employer will explain to you specific expectations and regulations. In accepting the job, you agree to these responsibilities.

Employee Responsibilities

As an employee, your main **responsibility**, or required task or duty, is to do the very best job possible for your employer and for the children in your care. In most cases, your responsibilities to your employer are the employer's rights in the relationship. Successful employees do more than just show up for the job. They are proactive and involved in their work. In addition, they have the exact skills needed to do their jobs well. Here are some general ways to carry out your responsibilities:

▶ **Earn your pay.** Complete each task you are assigned on time. Keep your work area neat and well organized. Sometimes going the "extra mile" with your work leads to greater success.

▶ **Use time responsibly.** Be on time for work. Return promptly from breaks and meals. Use time effectively by planning how to complete tasks efficiently. You must also learn to **prioritize**, or put tasks in the order of importance, not in the order of your preference. You may need to ask your supervisor to help you prioritize your assigned tasks, especially if you have been told to do more in your workday than is humanly possible.

▲ Show You Care

Employers expect employees to do their job well and demonstrate responsibility, professionalism, and honesty. *Why are these qualities important in a child care occupation?*

Internet Safety

The Internet is a great resource for information, education, networking, shopping, and entertainment. However, you must be careful. Never save private information such as passwords or credit card information on a public computer. Think before you post personal information to a social networking site. Future and current employers may review this information and use it to make decisions about hiring you. Make sure your Internet connection is secured behind a firewall to prevent hackers from accessing your system.

What Would You Do? You log onto a shared computer in your break room and find that one of your coworkers was using the computer for online shopping. The computer saved her password and credit card information. What would you do?

▶ **Respect the rules.** Learn and follow your employer's rules and policies, typically spelled out in an employee handbook. If you are unsure about a policy, ask your employer, and if necessary, ask if it is available in writing.

▶ **Work safely.** Familiarize yourself with your job's safety requirements. Learn how to operate and maintain equipment safely. Ask your supervisor to observe you to ensure that you have learned properly. Report any damaged equipment or unsafe conditions or practices to your supervisor immediately.

▶ **Maintain confidentiality.** When you work with children, much of the information you gain about individuals may be private and personal. It is up to you to respect the rights of the children you care for and to maintain confidentiality about their personal information.

A responsible employee also uses job resources wisely. In addition to time, your resources include people, information, technology, and money.

▶ **People.** Child care professionals have constant interaction with people. You must take care to respect and communicate with children, parents, and coworkers effectively. Building positive relationships with parents and coworkers benefits the children in your care.

▶ **Information.** Effective care professionals share important information they acquire. The whole team benefits from shared knowledge. They also recognize the difference between sharing useful job information and negative information, such as gossip.

▶ **Technology.** Respect technology resources on the job and remember to use it for business purposes only. Personal e-mail, online shopping, and computer games are inappropriate uses of employer-owned computers and a waste of your employer's time.

▶ **Money.** Whenever you perform a job transaction that involves money, double-check yourself and be honest. If you are responsible for making purchases, look for good values when you spend the program's budget.

In addition to the above responsibilities, success as an employee depends upon willingness to work as a team, show a positive attitude and respect, and resolve conflicts effectively.

Teamwork

As a child care teacher, you will often find yourself part of a large care team. Every worker is an individual with his or her own personality traits, strenths, and weaknesses. A team, however, is more than a set of individuals. In order to bring individuals together into an effective team, each employee must practice good teamwork.

If you have ever played a team sport or served on a committee, you know how important it is that every member participates and completes his or her assignment. You will practice teamwork on the job by completing your duties, and in doing so, you are supporting the efforts of your coworkers. As you build and maintain relationships at work, you are investing in your career and the people with whom you work, as well as those in your care. You must get along to work well together.

Positive Attitude

An upbeat, positive outlook contributes to team spirit. Complaining can bring down the whole team and affect your job performance. A positive attitude, along with carefully thought-out responses, leads to effectiveness in the workplace and your personal life. Look beyond your personal views and understand the reality of a situation before you respond.

Respect

When you respect and appreciate the differences in people, you will be more likely to have good work relationships. You demonstrate self-respect when you accept responsibility for your actions and learn from your mistakes. Learn to practice **empathy** ('em-pə-thē), the ability to put yourself in another's place. Empathy will help you understand the feelings of your coworkers and children in your care.

Resolving Conflicts

No matter how well you and your coworkers get along, you will not always agree. Disputes and conflicts are a common part of team interaction. Use your negotiation and compromise skills to lead the way to effective problem solving. While conflict can be unpleasant, remember to focus on the problem, not the personalities involved.

▼ **Working Together**

Teamwork requires respecting others on your team. A teacher's team might include other teachers, coaches, librarians, and administrators.
Why do you think it is important to use empathy with your coworkers?

Blend Images - Hill Street Studios/Getty Images

Taking Initiative

An employee who shows initiative does not wait to be told what to do next. Initiative is part of a strong work ethic and is a key characteristic of a reliable and flexible employee.

Teamwork

Showing initiative on a team means willingly taking on a task that helps accomplish the team's goals. Taking initiative benefits the whole team. It builds team confidence in your abilities, shows leadership, and demonstrates responsibility to your employer.

Thinking Ethically

It is the end of the day and few children remain at the center. There are still many tasks to be done to get the center ready for the next day. Your coworkers do not appear to be taking the initiative to do these tasks without prompting from your supervisor, who is in her office. What can you do about your coworkers' lack of initiative?

Ethics

Ethics ('e-thiks) are your internal guidelines for distinguishing right from wrong. Ethical behavior consists of doing what is right. Some choices, however, are more difficult. When two choices appear equally right or equally wrong, ask yourself the following questions:

▶ Does the choice comply with the law?

▶ Is the choice fair to those involved?

▶ Does the choice harm anyone?

▶ Has the choice been communicated honestly?

▶ Can I live with the choice without guilt?

Behaving ethically also means taking responsibility. If you make a mistake, admit it. Responsible employees learn from their mistakes and adapt their behavior to make better choices in the future.

Wages and Benefits

When you agree to take a job, you trade your skills and services for money. Your employer sets your pay based on your level of skills and experience, the difficulty of the work, and the number of people competing for the same job. Search on the Internet to find examples of pay for the same job in your region. This will give you a market value of the position so you know whether the pay rate you are offered is fair. More information is also available from organizations that advocate for improved child care worker compensation.

Pay periods differ. Some employers pay weekly, every two weeks, or once a month. Your employer will pay you in one of two ways. If you are paid an hourly wage, your employer will pay you a certain amount for each hour you work. Your pay will vary depending on how many hours you work each pay period. If you receive a salary, you will be paid a set amount of money each pay period, regardless of the number of hours you work.

In addition to your salary, your employer may offer benefits. Benefits are considered part of the total compensation package. A generous benefits package can make up for a lower wage. Likewise, a higher wage may make up for few benefits. Benefits an employer may offer include:

▶ Paid vacation and sick days

▶ Health, life, dental, and accident insurance

▶ Disability insurance that helps pay your expenses if you become disabled and cannot work

▶ Savings and investment plans, such as a 401K plan, to help you earn money for retirement

▶ Tuition reimbursement for education courses that are related to your career

▶ Onsite child care

The total amount of money you earn is your gross pay. If you are paid an hourly wage, calculate your gross pay by multiplying the number of hours worked by your hourly wage. The amount of money you receive after deductions are taken out is called your net pay, or take-home pay. Deductions are amounts of money withheld from your gross pay for taxes, insurance, and other fees. **Figure 2.5** describes some common deductions. You can ask your employer to explain the specific deductions that will be taken out of your pay.

Figure 2.5 Paycheck Deductions

Net Pay Your pay stub provides important information about your earnings and deductions. *How much were this employee's total deductions?*

State Income Tax
A personal income tax you pay on the amount of income you receive. The amount of state income tax varies by state. Some states do not have an income tax.

FICA
Federal Insurance Contribution Act (FICA) deductions are social security taxes on the money you earn. Social security taxes are withheld in two parts. The first part goes toward pension benefits. The second part covers Medicare benefits.

Federal Income Tax
A personal income tax you pay on the amount of income you receive. This is the main source of revenue for the federal government.

SMITH, EMILY
0997423035

DESCRIPTION	HOURS	GROSS PAY	YEAR TO DATE	DEDUCTIONS	DEDUCTION	YEAR TO DATE
REGULAR PAY	54.00	380.50	2,280.05	FEDERAL	23.03	138.18
				STATE	4.29	25.74
				FICA (SOCSEC)	7.20	43.20
				FICA-HI (MEDICARE)	5.45	32.70
				MEDICAL INS	16.50	99.00

	GROSS PAY	TAXES	DEDUCTIONS	NET PAY		PAY PERIOD	CHECK NUMBER	AMOUNT OF CHECK
CURRENT	380.50 -	39.97 -	16.50 -	324.03	END	04-13	23076186	324.03
YTD	2280.05 -	239.82 -	99.00 -	1941.23				

Gross Pay
The total amount of your earnings before taxes and other deductions.

Other Deductions
Other withholdings that are taken out of your paycheck might include employee contributions to medical, dental, or life insurance or retirement savings.

Net Pay
Your take-home pay, or the amount of your earnings after all deductions are taken out.

▲ Coffee Break

Some employers provide small benefits such as free coffee in the break room. *What are other benefits an employer might provide?*

Employer Responsibilities

The employer-employee relationship works both ways. Your employer has responsibilities to you, too. Your employer's main responsibilities include supplying you with what you need to do your job, providing safe working conditions, and making sure you are treated fairly. In most cases, your employer's responsibilities to you are your rights in the relationship.

Employee Support

Your employer will outline your responsibilities and expectations clearly. Your employer is responsible for providing you with all the equipment or training you need to do your job well. You and your employer may not agree on what are necessities. If you find that you lack what you need, ask your supervisor to show you how to do an assigned task with the available resources.

Safe Working Conditions

Federal, state, and local regulations require your employer to provide you with safe working conditions. This responsibility includes the following:

▶ Providing equipment and materials necessary to do the job safely

▶ Eliminating any recognized health and safety hazards

▶ Informing employees when conditions or materials pose dangers to health and safety

▶ Maintaining records of job-related illnesses and injuries

- ▶ Complying with environmental-protection policies for safely disposing of waste materials
- ▶ Providing conditions or equipment known to prevent injury

If you are injured on the job and cannot work, state laws require your employer to provide financial help called **workers' compensation** to cover medical expenses and lost wages. Employers with fewer than four employees do not have to carry this type of insurance. If your employer does not, you might consider buying your own personal disability insurance.

Fair Labor Practices

Your employer has a legal responsibility to protect you from unfair treatment on the job. U.S. labor laws are meant to protect the following rights of employees:

- ▶ To have an equal opportunity to obtain and keep employment
- ▶ To be paid a fair wage
- ▶ To be considered fairly for promotion

Among other legally required responsibilities, employers must pay their employees at least the federal **minimum wage**, the lowest hourly amount a worker can earn. Some locations pay entry-level employees a wage higher than the federal government requires. Employers must compensate hourly employees who work overtime (more than 40 hours per week) with extra pay or time off, called **compensatory time**.

U.S. workers are guaranteed the right to join a **labor union**, an organization of workers in a similar field. Leaders of labor unions act as the voice of their members in **collective bargaining**, the process of workers and employers agreeing to working conditions, contracts, and benefits. Labor unions represent about 15 percent of U.S. workers. Some labor unions include child care teachers and aides.

Employers must protect their employees from **discrimination**—unfair treatment based on age, gender, race, ethnicity, religion, physical appearance, disability, or other factors. For example, **sexual harassment** is an act of discrimination. It is any unwelcome verbal or physical behavior of a sexual nature. It is illegal behavior in the workplace. If you think someone has sexually harassed you, report the incident to your supervisor immediately so the employer can investigate the matter and take action.

Performance Evaluations

Your employer is also responsible for giving you feedback on your job performance. Some employers consider an employee's first few months on a new job as a probation period. **Probation** is a period in which an employer observes the employee's work and behavior in order to assess whether the employee is fit to remain with the company.

Expert *Advice . . .*

"Besides formal training you must have energy and enthusiasm to work successfully with children."

— Marjorie Eberts and Margaret Gisler, *Careers for Kids at Heart and Others Who Adore Children*

Your employee handbook should include details about how often the employer conducts performance evaluations. Your employee handbook will also identify what your employer looks for during a performance evaluation and the procedure an employee should follow in responding to the evaluation. During a performance evaluation, an employer may examine such things as the employee's

▶ job knowledge and how the employee applies that knowledge.

▶ willingness to work cooperatively as a team member.

▶ ability to communicate effectively on the job.

▶ positive attitude and workplace ethic.

Performance evaluations are a good opportunity to take a look at your short- and long-term career goals. You can talk about your progress toward your career goals and advancement opportunities with your employer at this meeting.

▼ Honest Conversation

....

A performance review is an opportunity to learn about your strengths and weaknesses as an employee. *What questions might you ask your manager during a performance evaluation?*

Advancing on the Job

Advancement opportunities in early childhood care vary. Advancement may involve a promotion. It also can be at the same job level but with more responsibilities at a higher rate of pay. Advancement may also involve leaving for a better job elsewhere or beginning your own business. Some qualities that will help you advance in your career include:

PhotosIndia.com/Glow Images

- **Show initiative.** The willingness to take on new tasks and levels of responsibility shows initiative. Workers with initiative do not wait to be told what to do next.

- **Show desire to learn.** Continuing your education or training through formal classes, workshops, or independent study shows a desire to learn.

- **Find a mentor.** A mentor could be your supervisor, an experienced coworker, or a retired early childhood professional. A mentor can share his or her experiences with you, answer questions, and give advice on how to progress towards your long-term career goals.

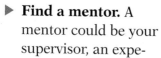▲**Take a Class**

Showing a desire to learn and grow will help you advance on the job. *How can you show your willingness to learn and grow?*

Terminating Employment

Depending on your career goals, there may come a time in the future in which you want to change careers or jobs. When considering a job change, keep the following points in mind:

- Keep your job search to yourself until you have a new job. You do not want to make your work situation difficult with your current employer while you search for a new job.

- Research and list the jobs or careers in which you are interested. Analyze each in regard to your skills, experience, and career goals.

- Set up interviews at times that you will not miss work. If necessary, use vacation time.

- After finding a new job, be sure to give notice to your employer that you are terminating your employment. Check your employee handbook to find out how much notice you must give your employer.

- Until you leave your place of employment, work just as hard as you always have. You want to leave a good impression. How you perform during your last few weeks of work is what people will remember about you.

**READING CHECK** **Contrast** How does a salary differ from an hourly wage?

College & Career READINESS

Continuing Your Education

Is College My Best Option?

This is a very important question that every high school student will ask himself or herself. There is no right answer, but it is a decision that can affect the rest of your life. It is important that you educate yourself before making the decision and give it the serious thought it deserves.

Does college guarantee success?

Having a college degree opens many doors. There are many people who find success and happiness without a degree. However, it is more important to keep in mind that more and more employers want to hire applicants with degrees. You can find work without a degree, but more options are available when you have a degree.

What can I learn if I continue my education?

In college, students read books, have discussions with other students, learn new skills, and learn from experts in their fields. Their experiences encourage students to think, ask questions, explore new ideas, and further develop academically. Students will expand their knowledge and skills, learn how to express themselves more clearly, and increase their understanding of local, national, and global issues.

What are some benefits of going to college?

Going to college creates opportunities. College graduates have an edge in the job market over those who have not experienced higher education. Additionally, a student who attends college usually earns more than a person who does not. According to a recent U.S. Census Bureau finding, a person with a bachelor's degree or higher earned approximately 50 percent more on average than a person with only a high school diploma.

Hands-On

College Readiness Create a list of pros and cons for continuing your education after high school. Think about the long term as well as the short term. Consider all the possibilities, such as community college, vocational school, or a four-year college or university. Go over the list with your parents or guardians, and ask a guidance counselor for his or her input.

Path to Success

Identify Your Goals When considering a college degree, think about what you want out of life and whether or not a degree will help you achieve it.

Explore Your Options Consider community college, trade and technical schools, four-year schools, and distance learning.

Seek Guidance Part of your school guidance counselor's job is to help you with decisions like this.

Think Long-Term Try to think about not only what you want your life to be like next year but what you want it to be like in 20 years.

Be Confident Worrying that college or continuing your education in other ways might be too difficult should not be a factor in your decision.

Employability Skills
Visual Summary

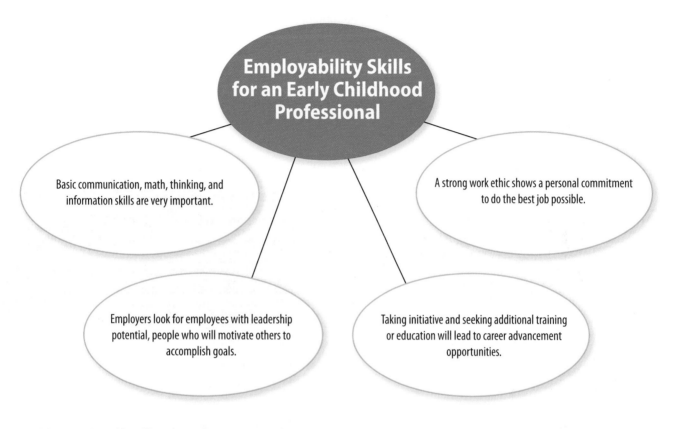

Employability Skills for an Early Childhood Professional

Basic communication, math, thinking, and information skills are very important.

A strong work ethic shows a personal commitment to do the best job possible.

Employers look for employees with leadership potential, people who will motivate others to accomplish goals.

Taking initiative and seeking additional training or education will lead to career advancement opportunities.

Vocabulary Review

1. Write a paragraph using five or more content and academic vocabulary terms.

Content Vocabulary

◇ active listening (p. 22)
◇ body language (p. 23)
◇ work ethic (p. 25)
◇ flexibility (p. 25)
◇ networking (p. 28)
◇ trade publications (p. 29)
◇ service learning (p. 30)

◇ résumé (p. 33)
◇ prioritize (p. 39)
◇ empathy (p. 41)
◇ ethics (p. 42)
◇ workers' compensation (p. 45)
◇ minimum wage (p. 45)
◇ compensatory time (p. 45)
◇ labor union (p. 45)

◇ collective bargaining (p. 45)
◇ discrimination (p. 45)
◇ sexual harassment (p. 45)
◇ probation (p. 45)

Academic Vocabulary

■ foundation (p. 22)
■ responsibility (p. 39)

Review Key Concepts

2. Describe the basic employability skills that applicants need for positions in early childhood care.

3. List the qualities of effective leaders.

4. Outline the steps of the job application and hiring process and the required actions at each step.

5. Summarize the rights and responsibilities of employees and employers.

Critical Thinking

6. **Give examples** of how communication skills are used in a child care setting.
7. **Apply** leadership skills to a child care setting. Write a scenario in which a child care worker demonstrates leadership.
8. **Predict** the potential benefits of professional development activities, including networking with other early childhood professionals, joining professional organizations, and reading trade publications. Is it possible to be truly professional without engaging in such activities? Why or why not?
9. **Explain** why networking is one of the most successful resources in searching for a job.
10. **Analyze** your personal behavior in terms of work ethic and leadership. What can you do to develop these skills while still in school?

21st Century Skills

Leadership Skills

11. **Leadership Styles** There are four styles of leadership: authoritarian, democratic, integrated, and laissez-faire. Use print and Internet resources to learn more about each of these styles. Write a paragraph that describes which leadership style most closely matches yours and how you can effectively utilize your style or a combination of styles in a teamwork situation.

Critical Thinking Skills

12. **Problem-Solving From Experience** Talk to a trusted adult such as a parent or teacher about a problem he or she encountered in the workplace. Ask the adult to describe the problem and how it was resolved. Consider how you would have acted if you were faced with the same situation. In what other ways could the problem have been solved?

Child Care LAB

Use the skills you have learned in this chapter.

Practice Teamwork

13. **Use Teamwork to Solve a Problem** In this activity, you will work in a team of five students to solve a scenario-based problem and to analyze teamwork.

   A. Review the scenario. Your team are staff at a local child care center. The center director has set aside $200 from the budget for the staff to decide how to spend. The money can be spent on anything, such as new technology for the centers or lunch out for the staff.

   B. Assign team roles. Designate a discussion leader, a note taker, and a spokesperson for the team. The discussion leader should lead the group's discussion and ensure that everyone is able to share his or her opinion. The note taker should keep a running list of the team's ideas. The spokesperson will present your team's decision to the class.

   C. Use teamwork to solve the problem. Work with your team to make a group decision about how to spend the $200. While working with the team, observe how your team members demonstrate teamwork.

   D. Share your decision. Have your the team spokesperson share how your team decided to spend the money to the class.

   E. Analyze your group's teamwork. Write a brief report that summarizes your observations on the teamwork experience. Include what your team did well and what teamwork skills could be improved.

Create Your Evaluation

Create an evaluation sheet with these categories:
- Working with Others
- Focus on Task
- Attitude
- Contribution
- Problem Solving
- Leadership

Self-assess your performance in each area and evaluate it on an Always/Sometimes/Rarely/Never scale.

Academic Skills

English Language Arts

14. Interview Dialogues With a partner, write two different dialogues between an interviewer and a job candidate. The first dialogue should show the candidate using poor interviewing techniques and skills. The second should show the candidate using good techniques. Role-play your dialogues for the class.

Social Studies

15. Professional Organizations Professional organizations are a community of people committed to a common cause or interest. Select a professional organization associated with child care from the list in Figure 2.2 on page 29. Access its Web site and research its mission and requirements to become a member. Write a paragraph analyzing the organization's benefit to an individual member and to the community it represents based on its activities and publications.

Science

16. Workplace Comfort Ergonomics is the study of the work environment for comfort and efficiency. It is an employer's responsibility to minimize the risk of employee injury on the job. They can do this by providing an ergonomic environment, from lighting to chairs and computer equipment. If you are working with a computer, improper placement of the monitor can cause strain on your neck and eyes.

Procedure Place a monitor so that you have to look up to see it and type for five minutes. Lower the monitor so that you can look straight ahead and type for five minutes. Raise your chair or lower the monitor even farther so that you must look down to see it and type for five more minutes. Note how your neck and eyes feel after each placement of the monitor.

Analysis Which position places the least amount of strain on your neck? Review your results and write a statement that explains your conclusion.

Certification Prep

Sharpen your test-taking skills to improve your certification program score.

Directions Read each statement. Then read the answer choices and select the best answer.

17. Proper interview behavior includes _____.

    A. asking questions about job responsibilities

    B. avoiding eye contact

    C. wearing casual clothes

    D. chewing gum

18. The amount of earnings after deductions is called _____.

    A. taxes

    B. gross pay

    C. net pay

    D. salary

Test-Taking Tip

When taking a multiple-choice test, glance over the test before starting. See how many total questions there are so that you can figure out how much time you have to answer each question.

CHAPTER 3

Professional Skills

Writing Activity

★ 21st Century Skills

Communication A blog, short for *Web log*, is a Web site in the form of an online journal. Bloggers write their reflections and opinions, as they would in traditional journals. However, as with anything posted online, blogs can be viewed publicly. Write a blog about professional dress codes, including pros and cons of having a dress code in the workplace.

Writing Tips
1. Date your blog.
2. Include your observations and reflections about the topic.
3. Write your blog in the first person.
4. Let your words flow naturally.

Explore the Photo
Working well with others is an important professional skill. *Why is teamwork important in an early childhood setting?*

Upper Cut Images/SuperStock

Reading Guide

BEFORE YOU READ

Understanding Write questions you have as you read. Many of them may be answered as you continue reading. If they are not, you will have a list ready for your teacher when you finish.

Read to Learn

Key Concepts

- **Identify** three ways early childhood professionals communicate with families.
- **Explain** the importance of professional ethics.
- **Describe** the role of advocacy in the early childhood profession.

Main Idea

Early childhood professionals have many responsibilities for their employees and the families they serve. In this chapter, you will learn about communicating effectively. You will also learn about the importance of professional ethics and advocacy skills.

Content Vocabulary

- ◇ open door policy
- ◇ bilingual
- ◇ public relations
- ◇ conferences
- ◇ professional ethics
- ◇ dress codes
- ◇ continuing education
- ◇ confidentiality
- ◇ advocacy
- ◇ advocates
- ◇ constituents

Academic Vocabulary

- ■ interact
- ■ primary

Graphic Organizer

As you read, you will discover that you have professional ethical responsibilities to three different groups. Use a tree diagram like the one shown to help you organize that information.

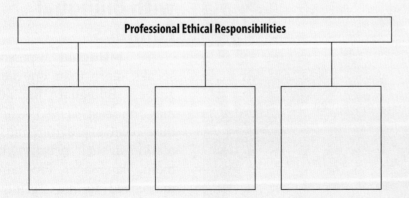

Professional Ethical Responsibilities

Graphic Organizer *Go to* **connected.mcgraw-hill.com** *to print this Graphic Organizer.*

◇**Vocabulary**

You can find definitions in the glossary at the back of this book.

▼ **Communicating**

Communication between family and staff enhances the effectiveness of the program. *How does an open door policy help with communication?*

Professional Communication

Communication is a process of giving and receiving information. In the early childhood profession, there is a wide variety of information to be shared between staff and the people they serve. How well that information is communicated determines a program's level of success. This chapter will explore ways communication helps provide the foundation for a high-quality program.

Communicating Goals and Philosophy

As an early childhood professional, you must be able to communicate well whenever you interact with others, including your supervisor, coworkers, children in your care, and parents. Answering people's questions about your programs, goals, philosophy, and services is an ongoing process. People will want to know what your program offers. You will need to communicate the array of services you provide, as well as where and when these services are provided. For example, parents will want to know what type of learning activities will take place and why. They will have questions about naps, meals, and the program's approach to managing children's behavior.

Families have the right to know how their children are at all times. While admittance to programs may be limited to the public in general, early childhood programs maintain an **open door policy**. This allows parents or approved family members to visit at any time. Such a policy builds trust, encourages communication, and decreases the chance that an unethical staff member would mistreat children.

Communicating with Bilingual Families

A **bilingual** person speaks more than one language. Bilingual families may be best served when they receive program information in their primary, or main, language. Programs may need to have printed materials translated into several different languages. For programs, events, and activities in which oral communication is used, present information in diverse

Ariel Skelley/Getty Images

languages whenever possible. For example, child care professionals should

- ▶ use the language best understood by children to explain safety practices and procedures.
- ▶ provide health and nutrition information to parents and family members in a language best understood.
- ▶ incorporate objects, music, and celebrations that encourage cultural understanding and multiple language use for children.
- ▶ assist parents in locating resources that support multiple language use.
- ▶ maintain routines that include the use of multiple languages in daily activities.

Public Relations

Communicating information about your program to the public is called **public relations**. Getting a program's name out to those who might use its services and establishing a good reputation for services provided are both public relations goals.

Web Site, Brochure, Telephone, and E-mail

A parent viewing a program's Web site is often the parent's first contact with a child care program. Therefore, it is very important to maintain an updated, easy-to-understand Web site. Web sites offer basic program details such as hours, location, and fees. Web sites also communicate information about discipline policies and family involvement.

Small pamphlets called brochures, as well as paid advertisements, provide similar information as Web sites, but in less detail. Telephone conversations help parents determine if they want to use a program's services. Those staff answering telephones should be well acquainted with the program and able to describe services in a clear and simple way. They should be trained in using polite manners so a positive image of the program is conveyed. Those answering e-mail questions about Web site, brochure, or advertisement content must apply proper language use, often called electronic communication etiquette.

▼ **Promote Your Program**

Many early childhood programs provide information about their services online. *If you were setting up a Web site, what information would you include?*

Public Presentations

Some child care professionals give presentations to inform the public about their program's services. In a presentation, you might tell parents and other community members about the services your program provides or give information about child development. Dressing properly for the event is important. Being prepared for your presentation contributes to effective communication. Having good audio-visual aids, such as a PowerPoint® presentation or handouts makes the presentation more interesting.

Family Communications

Children benefit when early childhood professionals share information with family members and work with them as a team. Family members want to know how their children are doing in the program, what they have accomplished, and whether they show signs of special needs. Early childhood staff also need insight into how home life affects behavior. Through regular communication, a trusting relationship is built between family members and staff. The following communication methods are most commonly used in an early childhood program.

Informal Conversations

Arrival and departure times are ideal for brief, informal discussions. At arrival, parents may share helpful information—for example, "Nikki's grandparents visited last night, so we let her stay up a little later than usual." At departure, early childhood staff can tell parents how their child's day went. You might say, "Jeremy tied his shoes without help today." During informal discussions, avoid sharing confidential matters others may overhear. Discuss problems and private matters during scheduled meetings when staff and family members have more time and can focus on an issue.

Written Messages

Sharing information in writing also plays a role in child care programs. A written note, whether on paper or as an e-mail message, helps professionals and families communicate information when a face-to-face conversation cannot take place or when you need to remember to give parents specific information. Sometimes a written note is preferable so a record of the communication can be put in a child's file. Programs set communication policies for staff to follow so confidentiality is maintained at all times.

©Comstock/Alamy

How to . . .

Manage a Meeting

Efficiently managing a meeting is an important professional skill to learn, whether it is a fundraising meeting or a parent meeting. A little planning and preparation will help you accomplish everything that you need to discuss during the meeting. Follow simple procedures and take good notes to keep everyone informed.

▶ **Agenda** *Create an agenda of items to discuss. This will guide your discussion during the meeting.*

▶ **Meeting Notice** *At least one week in advance, send each person attending a notice or an e-mail reminder including the meeting time, location, agenda and directions if needed.*

▶ **Procedures** *The group leader calls the meeting to order and follows agreed-upon rules for discussion if it is a formal community or board meeting. An informal meeting with parents or staff can be more relaxed and conversational.*

▶ **Notes** *The meeting should be summarized soon after it takes place. The summary or minutes of the meeting should be distributed to each member and saved in a common location for future reference.*

Apply It!
Attend a public meeting in your area. Analyze the procedures used to conduct the meeting.

Digital Vision/Alamy

Newsletters

Many child care programs provide regular newsletters to parents. This is a good way to keep all families informed of the program's activities. A typical newsletter might include a list of learning experiences and special events planned for the coming week. It might also suggest activities for families and children to enjoy together at home. See **Figure 3.1** for a sample daily newsletter.

Telephone Usage

Occasional telephone calls can help keep staff and family members in touch. Leaving a voice message for family members is an easy way to share an encouraging message or to explainin how a bump or scrape occurred can prevent a parent from being surprised when they arrive at the end of the day. Family members may also call to check on their children during the day.

Figure 3.1 Sample Newsletter

Share Fun A newsletter is a good way to communicate with families. *What types of information would you share in a newsletter?*

Preschool Daily Newsletter

Class: Toddlers

Weekly Theme: Earth Week

Language Arts: We read a variety of books today dealing with this week's Earth week theme.

Sensory Stimulation: We made a rice cereal "earth" using blue and brown colored rice cereal treat mix.

Creative Art: We went outside and painted pictures of the trees.

Music: We sang our Earth Day song, "Love Our World."

Life Skills: We learned how to sit in our chairs at snack time and not waste our food.

Upcoming Events: We are planning a trip to the zoo on Friday, April 23rd. Please join us if your schedule allows. Let Miss Sue know if you are interested.

Conferences and Scheduled Meetings

Formal **conferences**, or meetings between family members and staff should be scheduled on a regular basis. These conferences allow information to be shared about a child's progress or special needs. They also give family members an opportunity to ask questions and to discuss concerns. The guidelines for conducting conferences or meetings include the following:

▶ Try to find a time that is convenient for the parents.

▶ Prepare for the meeting by reviewing records of the child's behavior and progress. Identify the topics you would like to discuss.

▶ Help family members feel at ease by greeting them in a friendly, respectful manner.

▶ Start by focusing on the child's strengths. Discuss areas in which the child is doing well or has shown improvement. Share specific examples to illustrate your points.

▶ Avoid labeling the child or criticizing the family members when bringing up problems or concerns. If you say, "Paige is a troublemaker who has obviously been allowed to run wild," the parent will probably take offense. It is more effective to say, "Paige finds it difficult to sit and listen quietly during story time."

▶ Suggest ways that parents and staff can work together to help the child improve.

▶ Listen carefully to what family members say. Make sure you understand their concerns.

▶ Take the opportunity to learn more about the client by asking respectful and relevant questions.

▶ End the discussion on a positive note. Be sure to thank the family members for coming.

Staff Communication

Communication and teamwork go hand in hand. Staff members who take the time to communicate with each other during the workday tend to have better working relationships. Informal conversations and staff meetings encourage teamwork. Written and electronic communication also help keep the staff informed.

▶ Having polite and comfortable conversations help staff members develop friendly relationships. These conversations will help build a sense of staff unity and teamwork.

▶ Keeping written records of program details helps a child care center run smoothly. Staff work better as a team if they share details to keep everyone informed.

▶ It is not uncommon for one child care program to have several locations. Staff must find creative ways to maintain communication despite their physical separation.

▶ Regular staff meetings are the most effective way to ensure ongoing communication. Staff can communicate program goals, share ideas, and stay informed about new developments.

Minimizing Conflict

There are times when staff members, or a staff member and a child's parents, do not agree. Communicating in a respectful and professional manner will minimize conflict and lead to better cooperation.

If your supervisor analyzes some aspect of your work, resist the urge to become angry or defensive. Listen carefully and try to understand the reasons behind the comments. If something is not clear to you, politely ask for further explanation. At the end of the conversation, agree on actions that will remedy the situation.

Respectful Discussion

Treat supervisors and coworkers with professional respect, and ask that they treat you in the same way. If a coworker asks for feedback, offer helpful suggestions. Express your thoughts and feelings in a positive, nonjudgmental way. Avoid demeaning or attacking a person if you disagree with his or her point of view. Remember to share compliments when a coworker does an especially good job. A sincere word of praise goes a long way in establishing a good working relationship.

Here are some additional suggestions for minimizing conflict.

▶ Keep the lines of communication open.

▶ Resolve small differences right away, before they can grow into major conflicts.

▶ Keep discussions positive. Address issues, not personalities.

▶ Do not jump to conclusions. Give each person a chance to explain his or her side of the story.

The ability to resolve conflict is important in every job. Most issues require careful thinking and an efficient solution. Before trying to resolve a conflict, be sure you have the authority, knowledge, and experience to make the necessary decisions. If you do not, obtain assistance from a coworker or supervisor.

Documentation

In early childhood programs, information is documented and recorded to help staff provide high-quality service. Child care professionals will document information such as conversations and observations. Information may relate to medical conditions or descriptions of daily behavior.

Individualized Services

Documentation about a child's abilities can guide staff in selecting activities geared to individual needs. The records can be helpful during activity or lesson planning as well as during conferences with family members. Taking time to record items of concern helps care providers decide how serious a concern is. It will also demonstrate how long the problem continues. If concerns persist, the document can be used for a discussion with the child's family member.

Referral Records

There are times when staff members feel they must refer children and families to specialized services. Whether it is a referral for counseling or speech services, documentation provides evidence of how staff members have responded to individual needs and concerns. Documentation also helps staff avoid duplicating a coworker's efforts on a child's behalf.

Recording Information

A number of different methods can be used to record vital documentation in early childhood programs. Making sure that your written correspondence is accurate is key to documentation.

- ▶ **Details to Document** When documenting information, always write the full date of the observation. In addition, write the child's full name, age at the time of recording, and specific details related to the purpose of the documentation. Sign your name so those who review the information know whom to contact for further information.

- ▶ **Checklists** In order to record broad concerns, such as a client's language use or motor coordination skills, checklists are quick ways to record information for future reference. Checklists can also be used to share information about a child's daily schedule and activities with parents.

READING CHECK ✔ **Recall** What are some events that a child care professional should document?

▼**Keep Records**

Documenting information accurately is an important skill for early childhood professionals. *Why is keeping accurate documentation necessary?*

Professional Ethics

Your personal guidelines for distinguishing right or wrong behavior are your ethics. In early childhood careers, ethics relates in particular to a provider's sense of fairness, kindness, and humane treatment of all people.

A sense of purpose is also important in early childhood careers. Child care professionals take pride in being able to make a positive difference in the lives of children and families. They also develop a strong sense of ethical duty to help others.

The standards of right and wrong that apply to your professional behavior are called **professional ethics**. The way you conduct yourself on the job and carry out your responsibilities should be guided by professional ethics at all times. Ethical standards are like road signs. Professionals can look to these guidelines to help them choose the right paths.

Professional Ethics Statements

Many professional organizations create statements to help their members perform ethically. For programs that serve young children, The National Association for the Education of Young Children (NAEYC) has the most widely known child care ethics statement, called the "Code of Ethical Conduct." The code addresses four areas: responsibilities to children, responsibilities to families, responsibilities to colleagues, and responsibilities to community and society. You can find the full texts for these codes at each organization's Web site.

Professionals must assume ethical responsibilities for their own growth, as well as for the well-being of the families and children they serve and the community at large. Your success in child care comes from acting in an ethical manner. As an early childhood professional, you also have responsibilities to your employer.

Employee Responsibilities

In return for your pay and benefits, your employer has the right to expect certain things from you. One expectation is that you will perform the duties of your job to the best of your ability. You are also expected to follow all guidelines and rules, such as those found in an employee handbook. You must also meet certain basic expectations that apply to any job.

Professional Attitude and Conduct

Ethical professionals maintain desirable character traits, such as honesty, dependability, and trustworthiness. Professionals with a strong work ethic are motivated to perform their job to the best of their abilities. Supervisors and coworkers alike value a professional who shows initiative and dedication.

Dress Code

Your appearance on the job also makes a statement. It shows how you feel about yourself and your job. Proper dress and grooming convey a professional image to all in your program. Start with good grooming. You should arrive at work clean, with teeth brushed and hair neatly combed. A well-groomed appearance provides children with a healthy role model. **Dress codes,** or rules for workplace dress, vary from one program to another. In general, clothing should be clean, practical, and in good repair. If T-shirts are allowed, avoid those with inappropriate pictures or slogans. Avoid jewelry that poses a safety hazard, such as a long necklace or hoop earrings that could be pulled out by a child.

Continuing Education

The world changes quickly, resulting in new information and new processes. Keeping up with the latest developments requires continual learning. Through **continuing education,** you can update career knowledge and acquire new job skills. Continuing education takes different forms. Some are single events, and some are ongoing experiences. They may be free of charge or involve costs. Child care professionals look for continuing education opportunities that fit their needs as well as their budgets. A child care professional might participate in some of the following educational opportunities:

▶ Take classes that lead to a related degree

▶ Learn first aid or CPR

▶ Attend training on how to recognize and prevent child abuse and neglect

▶ Observe teachers or care providers in other programs

▲ **Positive Attitude**

Child care professionals should display a positive and professional attitude. *What are some ways that you can display these traits?*

©Ariel Skelley/Blend Images LLC

- ▶ Attend a weekend workshop on guiding behavior, curriculum or activity planning, or administration
- ▶ Travel to another country to visit early childhood programs

Organization Membership and Participation

A simple and inexpensive way to continue education is to join organizations in the professional field and to subscribe to their periodicals, which are a good resource for new ideas and products. In addition, these organizations may offer educational workshops on both regional and national levels.

Conference Attendance

Large gatherings at which members of a specific profession exchange information about the latest findings, developments, and practices in their field are called professional conferences. Professionals often attend conferences to continue their education. A variety of groups host early childhood conferences. For example, the National Association for the Education of Young Children (NAEYC) hosts a yearly conference of early childhood professionals. At this conference, people attend workshops conducted by their peers and listen to experts speak on important topics. Businesses display the latest in early childhood care and education materials and equipment.

▼ **Be a Professional**

It is important to join professional associations in your field. *What are some of the benefits of joining a professional organization?*

Acquiring Credentials

Earning the Child Development Associate (CDA) credential is another type of continuing education. One of the requirements for receiving this credential is the completion of course credit in several subject areas. The subject areas are related to the six CDA competencies. Courses may be offered by colleges and universities or by organizations recognized for early childhood teacher preparation. Pursuing the CDA credential benefits early childhood professionals. It also lets them measure their own skills and knowledge against a national standard. It gives them feedback from peers and authorities in the field. Because the CDA credential is a valued award, it provides incentive to learn new skills or to fine-tune

Purestock/SuperStock

existing ones in order to be accredited. Some states also offer credentials that qualify staff to work with a specific age group. For instance, your state might have an infant caregiver credential or a school-age provider credential.

In many states, colleges or training agencies offer a director's credential for managers of early childhood care and education programs. To earn the credential, program directors complete courses while working as an administrator. Requirements vary by state, but often include classes on the following:

▶ Marketing and Public Relations

▶ Staff Management

▶ Staff and Facilities Management

▶ Program Operations

▶ Curriculum Development

▶ Leadership and Advocacy

▶ Community and Family Relationships

Some states' child care licensing laws require a director's credential in order for an individual to be legally qualified to direct an early childhood program.

Responsibilities to Children and Families

Child care professionals accept ethical responsibilities for the children entrusted to their care and for their families. The following information discusses areas of critical importance for child care professionals.

▼ **Credentials**

Earning a professional credential has many benefits. *How does pursing a credential help an early childhood teacher professionally?*

Protection from Harm

A key responsibility for all early childhood professionals is to protect children from harm. This protection can take place in a number of ways:

▶ Medical Precautions. Child care professionals have an obligation to help keep children as healthy as possible. It is their responsibility to be aware of special health needs and to know how to respond to them. Professionals are ethically bound to obtain training that would help them respond appropriately to a child's health needs.

▶ Environmental Precautions. Maintaining a safe environment protects children from injury and limits safety hazards. Professionals diligently survey program facilities for safety problems. If hazards are spotted, staff members remedy them as quickly as possible.

Respect for Diversity

Americans are guaranteed basic civil rights. It is illegal to discriminate based on race, ability, religion, gender, or any other difference. However, ethical professionals do more than avoid discrimination; they do all they can to respect and value diversity. One way to do this is to include foods, activities, and cultural practices that help all people feel comfortable, accepted, and valued. In addition, staff may be responsible for translating program information into another language for those who use English as a second language.

Developmentally Appropriate Practices

Early childhood professionals do all they can to match program services with a child's individual needs and abilities. For example, many programs encourage children to learn a second language. Staff members organize the environment and plan activities, taking into account each child's personal situation and experiences.

Confidentiality

Confidentiality is the belief that the privacy of others must always be maintained. Early childhood professionals, who often know many private family details, are bound by their professional ethics to maintain confidentiality if they are to maintain the trust and confidence of those they serve.

Maintaining confidentiality means keeping individual family information private. It also means keeping individual staff member and sensitive program information private. Child care providers make it a practice to share information only when family members give written permission. Professionals follow a program's written guidelines as to how confidentiality will be maintained and to whom information may be provided.

Partnerships in Caring

Cooperative teamwork between family and program staff ensures that the needs of children will be met. Regular communication and decision making can take place during arrival and departure times or during scheduled family conferences.

Information Sharing

Information can be shared with clients and family members in a variety of ways. Program brochures, policy handbooks, newsletters, and reports on daily activities are all good methods of sharing information. Monthly family meetings allow families to communicate information to program staff as well.

Family Involvement

Children feel most comfortable and secure when their family members are encouraged to participate regularly in activities. Such involvement can include evening family events or special daytime celebrations. Family members should feel welcome to volunteer time or special talents for these events.

Cooperative Care

There are times when children need services beyond what the program staff can provide. For instance, a child may need special nutritional advice or speech therapy. In such cases, professionals refer families to other service programs to obtain the extra assistance needed.

▲ Get Involved

Family members need to trust that their child care professionals are providing a safe environment. *How does becoming involved ensure that safety practices are being followed?*

Responsibilities to Community and Society

As an early childhood professional, you have a number of responsibilities to families, the community, and society at large. These responsibilities include compliance with laws related to child care, cooperation with other professionals, and community outreach.

Compliance with Laws

Professionals are ethically required to follow laws that apply to their program. If their program is not in compliance, it is their responsibility to bring the problem to the attention of the program director. In severe cases, a professional might need to report legal violations to official authorities such as a state's Department of Human Services. A child care worker should investigate the legal standards for licensing in his or her state.

Ingram Publishing/SuperStock

Working together with other staff members allows early childhood professionals to provide the best possible service. *What are some ways that an early childhood professional can work with other professionals?*

Cooperation with Other Professionals

In some situations, professionals from a variety of fields will work with a client. These professionals may need to share information in order to help the child. For instance, a child with behavior disorders may be visiting a child psychologist. With written permission from the parent, early childhood staff would cooperate with the psychologist as he or she provides treatment to the child. Cooperation might include sharing assessment information or allowing the psychologist to observe the child's behavior in the classroom. Additionally, child care centers may be able to connect parents who need assistance with professionals, such as suggesting a physical therapist for a child who has been injured.

Community Outreach

When families need extra help, such as with utility bills or with groceries, staff members refer families to community services. Some utility companies offer a utility support program. Local health departments offer support as well. A child care center may keep a list of these and many other community resources that can help families in need.

READING CHECK ✔ **Recall** What are some of the specific issues that require professional confidentiality?

© Sam Edwards/age fotostock

Advocacy

The process of pleading a cause to influence change for the best interests of others is called **advocacy.** Organized advocacy efforts can influence change in public policy, allocation of resources, and social justice that affects the lives of all people. People who inform legislators (or policymakers) of their clients' needs and welfare are called **advocates.** Almost everyone has taken action on issues by which he or she is personally affected. Professionals have an ethical responsibility to take action to protect the basic needs and rights of the children and families they serve. What are some basic needs and rights of children?

Advocacy Responsibilities

Whenever conditions or circumstances need to be improved for children, families or program staff, advocacy efforts can be put into action. As an early childhood professional, you assume the responsibility of meeting the needs and rights of the children and families in your care. You also have a responsibility to support the needs of your coworkers. The common issues for children, families, and staff may include the following:

▶ Creating community awareness about the quality of services and rights of children and families

▶ Influencing public policy to include stricter abuse laws

▶ Promoting better licensing laws for early childhood and education facilities

▶ Supporting legislation, such as child care tax credits, to meet the care and educational needs of children better

▶ Promoting issues such as better pay and working conditions for staff members

Protecting Individual Rights

Part of your advocacy efforts as an early childhood professional will involve protecting the individual rights of the children in your care. All individuals have the right to be free from physical or emotional harm. They also have the right to be assured of privacy and protected from fraud. Laws exist to protect such individual rights. An early childhood professional should be aware of these laws and able to use them in advocacy efforts, if necessary.

Laws that apply to clients in child care programs change frequently, even from year to year. Early childhood professionals are obligated to stay up to date on the laws that protect those they serve. Newspapers, radio, television,

SAFETY MATTERS

Advocate for Safety

As an early childhood professional, you are responsible for the safety of the children in your care as well as the safety of everyone who works at the center. You have an ethical as well as a legal responsibility to keep everyone safe and healthy. If you see a safety issue that could harm someone, it is your responsibility to correct it or report it.

What Would You Do? Your child care program lets the older children wait for their parents at pickup time out in the parking lot. You feel that there could be a safer procedure for picking up children. What would you do to advocate for a safer procedure?

and the Internet are media sources early childhood professionals can use to learn about current issues. In addition, licensing and accrediting agencies often distribute updates regarding new laws. Professional journals, magazines, and agency Web sites also provide quick references for new laws.

Legal Acts for Advocacy

In order to protect every person's rights, legal acts such as the Abuse and Neglect Act, Americans with Disabilities Act, Individuals with Disabilities Education Act, and the Family Educational Rights and Privacy Acts were created to ensure fair treatment of all people. These acts protect individual rights by creating laws such as those that protect children from abuse, assist people with disabilities in obtaining education and employment without discrimination, and maintain the privacy of children and families. Laws that apply to clients in child care programs change frequently, even from year to year. Professionals must always operate legally—keeping well informed of changes in laws and how these changes impact their programs.

Becoming an Advocate

It takes work to be an informed and influential advocate, but it is not as difficult as many believe. You can make an advocacy effort once a year, once a month, or once a week, depending on how much time and determination you have. Your advocacy efforts can be short-term or long-term. They can be as quick as writing a letter to a legislator or as committed as serving on a task force or committee. The following shows how you can keep informed about advocacy issues.

▶ Review newsletters and journals of professional organizations or professional advocacy groups so you know when to write letters or to make telephone calls to decision makers who can impact early childhood programs.

▶ Talk with others voters about issues. When people are made aware of the specific needs of others, they tend to support the issues with their votes.

▶ Get on the mailing lists of advocacy groups that deal with issues related to children.

▶ Maintain memberships in professional organizations. Professional organizations—such as the National Association for the Education of Young Children (NAEYC)—often hold advocacy workshops that teach professionals how to promote good laws for children and families.

▶ Write, call, or visit a local agency, such as the health department, that serves the needs of children.

▼ **Become an Advocate**

Becoming an advocate can be very rewarding. *What are some ways that advocating for a cause, such as healthful eating, can be rewarding?*

Design Pics/Monkey Business

▶ Write a letter, call, or visit your local, state, or federal legislators about issues related to early childhood. Specifically target senators and representatives in your voting district. Legislators welcome contact with their **constituents** (kən-stich'-ü-ənts), or the residents of their electoral districts.

Contacting Legislators

An important measure for any advocate is to contact legislators who can influence policy change. Any contact with voters has the potential to influence a legislator's stand on various issues. A personal visit, either at a legislator's state office or Washington, D.C., office, is the most effective way of contacting a legislator. It shows your commitment to an issue. If you want to visit a legislator in person, be sure to call his or her office to make an appointment. You can locate addresses and telephone numbers for local, state, and federal legislators on the Internet.

Personally written letters or e-mails and telephone calls are also effective means of contacting legislators who influence public policy. Use the following guidelines when writing to legislators:

▶ Always write with courtesy and respect.

▶ Neatly type or write your letter so it can be easily read.

▶ Use a formal writing style. To address your letter, always use the formal title "The Honorable," followed by the legislator's name and title. Be sure to use the correct address.

▶ Include your complete name and address in the letter.

▶ Write the clear purpose of your letter in the first paragraph. Address only one issue per letter. If you are writing in regard to a specific bill (or piece of legislation), be sure to include the number and title of the bill. Be sure to state your viewpoint on the bill.

▶ Use concise and clear information to support your viewpoint.

▶ Identify yourself as a constituent if you reside in the legislator's electoral district.

▶ Finish your letter by requesting a direct response regarding the legislator's stand on the issue in your letter. For example, you might say, "I would appreciate hearing from you regarding this matter."

▶ Thank the legislator for his or her time and consideration of the matter.

▶ Follow up your letter with a telephone call to the legislator's office after a reasonable period of time. This will help confirm your stand on the issue.

Whether you choose to become a child care professional or a caring neighbor, there is much you can do in advocacy for the needs and rights of others. What role do you see yourself playing in advocacy for children?

READING CHECK ✔ **Identify** What is one issue for which an early childhood professional might advocate?

Expert *Advice . . .*

"If you don't like the way the world is, you change it. You have an obligation to change it. You just do it one step at a time."

— Marian Wright Edelman, *President of Children's Defense Fund and activist*

College & Career
R E A D I N E S S

Child Care Finance Manager

What Does a Child Care Finance Manager Do?

A finance manager, or accounts manager, for a large child care business oversees the daily financial operations, monitors the budget, and prepares financial reports. The finance manager may also be involved in setting and achieving the long-term financial goals of the child care business. If you have strong math skills, you may want to consider a career in finance.

Career Readiness Skills

In additional to the analytical skills required for financial analysis, a finance manager needs to have good interpersonal skills. He or she needs to have a broad understanding of business and be able to explain how public relations and marketing affect business decisions. A finance manager also needs to have good ethical standards.

Education and Training

Most finance managers have a bachelor's degree in finance, accounting, economics, or business administration. Many have a master's degree, (preferably in business administration, finance, or economics) or a professional certification. Many finance managers have experience in a related industry or have started an entrepreneurial business. An entrepreneur would gain experience managing all aspects of a business, including the financial operations.

Job Outlook

There will always be a need for strong financial managers in larger non-profit or for-profit child care businesses. Those who have additional education, training, or credentials, such as a master's degree or a professional certification such as a Certified Public Accountant (CPA), stand the best chance of obtaining employment as a finance manager.

Critical Thinking Research some of the typical responsibilities of a finance manager. What personal interests, abilities, and skills might draw someone to a career as a finance manager? How do your skills compare to what is needed for this career? What are some short- and long-term goals that will help you prepare for this career?

Career Cluster

Finance Finance managers work in the Business Financial Management pathway of the Finance career cluster. Other jobs in this cluster include:

- Accountant
- Auditor
- Economist
- Controller
- Tax Preparer
- Treasurer
- Financial Analyst
- Tax Examiner
- Investment Advisor
- Bookkeeper
- Cash Manager
- Personnel Manager

Explore Further The Finance career cluster contains four pathways: Banking and Related Services, Insurance Services, Business Financial Management, and Financial and Investment Planning. Choose one of these pathways to explore further.

Professional Skills
Visual Summary

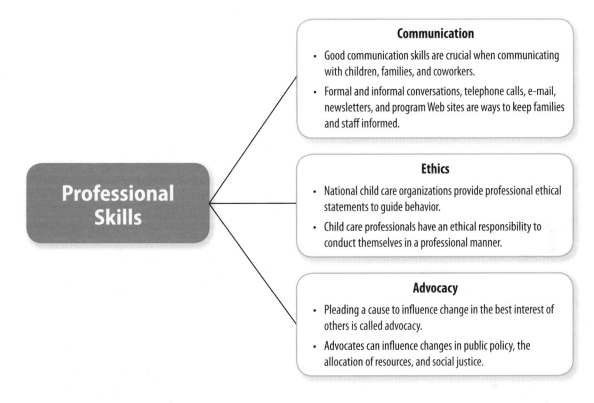

Professional Skills

Communication
- Good communication skills are crucial when communicating with children, families, and coworkers.
- Formal and informal conversations, telephone calls, e-mail, newsletters, and program Web sites are ways to keep families and staff informed.

Ethics
- National child care organizations provide professional ethical statements to guide behavior.
- Child care professionals have an ethical responsibility to conduct themselves in a professional manner.

Advocacy
- Pleading a cause to influence change in the best interest of others is called advocacy.
- Advocates can influence changes in public policy, the allocation of resources, and social justice.

Vocabulary Review

1. Create a multiple-choice test question for each content and academic vocabulary term.

Content Vocabulary
◇ open door policy (p. 54)
◇ bilingual (p. 54)
◇ public relations (p. 55)
◇ conferences (p. 59)
◇ professional ethics (p. 62)
◇ dress codes (p. 63)
◇ continuing education (p. 63)
◇ confidentiality (p. 66)
◇ advocacy (p. 69)
◇ advocates (p. 69)
◇ constituents (p. 71)

Academic Vocabulary
■ interact (p. 54)
■ primary (p. 54)

Review Key Concepts

2. Identify three ways early childhood professionals communicate with families.
3. Explain the importance of professional ethics.
4. Describe the role of advocacy in the early childhood profession.

Critical Thinking

5. Analyze the consequences a staff member's attitude can have on communications with children, children's families, and staff members. How does a positive attitude affect communication? How does a poor attitude affect communication?

6. **Evaluate** the type of personal and family information early childhood professionals may know about the children they serve. Draw conclusions about the consequences of violating ethical confidentiality.

7. **Describe** advocacy opportunities you might have as an early childhood professional. Why are early childhood professionals in a unique position to serve as advocates? Do these professionals have more responsibility than others to serve as advocates? Explain your response.

8. **Compare** how communication at school is similar to workplace communication.

9. **Analyze** how you can apply what you have learned about ethics to the way that you interact with others or behave at school. Give an example of how ethical behavior can be demonstrated at school.

10. **Locate** an online newspaper or magazine article about advocating for children. Make a brief presentation to the class discussing an issue presented in the article. Ask students to share their opinions on the issue.

21st Century Skills

Research Skills

11. **Investigate** There are many legal issues for early childhood educators. Investigate some of these issues. Discuss the ethical implications for early childhood professionals. What do professionals need to know to protect children and themselves? Create a chart to show at least four things that you have discovered.

Critical Thinking Skills

12. **Interview an Expert** Interview an early childhood professional to identify five communications issues that might be encountered when providing services for children. For each issue identified, describe appropriate behavior. Create a multimedia presentation to document your findings. Share your presentation with the class.

Child Care LAB

Use the skills you have learned in this chapter.

Professional Writing Skills

13. **Effective Professional Communication** Compose an e-mail letter to a congressperson regarding an issue concerning early childhood care or education.

   A. Discuss your issue. With a partner, discuss some of the important issues that you think need to be brought to the public's attention. What do you think is the most important issue?

   B. Plan your e-mail. Write some important considerations for this issue, including your position on the issue and why you feel that action needs to be taken.

   C. Compose the text. Write a rough draft of your letter. Have someone else read the letter to make sure it is clear. Include your congressperson's name and appropriate title. Include your name and contact information at the bottom of the e-mail. Check your spelling.

   D. Locate the e-mail address. Find the Web site for your local congressperson. Determine the e-mail address to use when sending correspondence.

   E. Send. Choose a descriptive subject for the subject line. Proofread your e-mail and ask your teacher's permission before you send it.

Create Your Evaluation

Evaluate your e-mail on the quality of what you sent. For your records:

• Write a brief summary of the issues that you considered

• Keep a copy of your correspondence

• Check your e-mail to determine if you receive a response

• If you do receive a response, is it a personal letter or a form letter?

Academic Skills

 ### English Language Arts

14. A Positive Message Think about a time that someone used a positive message to help you succeed. Write a paragraph that describes what that person said or did and how it made you feel. Explain how you could use that experience to help a coworker.

 ### Social Studies

15. Take Action Many citizens show responsibility in their communities by writing letters to government officials to express approval or disapproval of new laws. Do you think these letters can have an impact on the laws that are passed? Why or why not? With permission from your teacher or parents, go online to research specific examples to support your opinion. Write a brief report to explain your opinion.

 ### Mathematics

16. Calculate Network Size Networking can help you achieve greater professional success by alerting you to new opportunities. Imagine you are using your networking contacts to find resources for a job search. You list six people as possible contacts for your job search. Each of those six people suggests two additional people who might help. Half of those people suggest one more person each. How many people will you have in your job search network?

Math Concept **MultiStep Problems** When solving multistep problems, think through each step before starting.

Starting Hint Step 1: Start with 6 people. Step 2: Add 2 people for each of those 6 people. Step 3: Determine half of the total from Step 2. Step 4: Add 1 person for each of the total in Step 3. Step 5: Add the totals from Steps 1, 2 and 4.

 For more math practice, go to the Math Appendix at the back of the book.

Certification Prep

Directions Read each statement. Then read the answer choices and choose the phrase that best completes the sentence.

17. Early childhood educators can continue education by _____.

    A. working extra hours

    B. showing up to work on time

    C. pursuing a professional credential

    D. maintaining confidential records

18. A child care staff member must _____.

    A. share as much information with the team as possible

    B. be a good communicator

    C. be careful about sharing sensitive information

    D. all of the above

Test-Taking Tip

Read and consider every possible answer on a multiple-choice test. Eliminate each choice that is clearly incorrect. Then decide which remaining choice is the best answer.

Education and Training

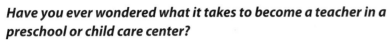

Have you ever wondered what it takes to become a teacher in a preschool or child care center?

A career as an educator in the child care profession may involve teaching children in a variety of roles and settings, such as a teacher's aide or teacher in a child care center or preschool. It may also involve teaching adults about children and how to help them grow and develop in a nurturing environment.

To succeed in education and training, you may need an education, psychology, or social work degree or the Child Development Associate (CDA) credential and a basic understanding of children. You will also need excellent oral communication and organization skills.

Denise Stroman • Preschool Teacher

Q What is your job?

A I work in a private child care facility that provides all-day child care for children as young as two months old. We make sure that the children are learning while we care for them. We work with children until they are ready for kindergarten, at age five or six.

Q What is your typical workday like?

A I work long hours and am always on my feet. We usually have a staff meeting first thing in the morning, and then children start to arrive as their parents go to work.

Q Why did you choose your career?

A I have four children of my own and I love working with preschoolers because they are so energetic. Now that my children are getting older, I wanted to continue working with young children. There are so many influences on children and I feel that it is important to be a positive, caring person for this age group.

Q How did your career path lead to your current job?

A I went to college before I had my own children. I studied to be a teacher and earned my teaching certificate. After a long career as a teacher, I decided that I wanted to work with younger children, so I got a job at the center. I had to apply for the CDA credential, which I received before starting at this facility.

Q Who or what has been your biggest career influence?

A I had a child psychology professor in college who inspired me to use my life lessons to teach young children.

Q What skills are most important in your job?

A I find that I need to have a lot of patience to work with children. You can introduce them to many new things, but they also like to do familiar activities. Preschoolers need to be observed all the time so they do not get hurt. I also need to be very flexible in my job.

Blend Images/Alamy

Career Requirements

Education or Training	Education and training jobs usually require some education beyond high school. Preschool teachers and child care providers often have an associate's degree or the CDA credential. Many trainers and educators have bachelor's and master's degrees in specific areas.
Academic Skills	English Language Arts, Mathematics, Science, and Social Studies
Aptitudes, Abilities, and Skills	Knowledge of children, planning and organizational skills, communication skills
Workplace Safety	Basic first aid certification and CPR certification are recommended.
Career Outlook	Well qualified teachers in child care facilities are always needed.
Career Path	Your career path may vary depending on your training. There are careers in the education and training portion of the child care industry at almost every education level.

Career Pathways

Teacher's Aide	A teacher's aide works with teachers and students to help children in the child care, preschool, or elementary classroom. Sometimes they work with children with specific behavior or physical issues. Most teacher's aides have an associate's degree or a higher level of education.
Special Needs Teacher	A special needs teacher has an education degree, plus additional training in working with special needs students, and often has endorsements and certifications in specific areas such as reading. These teachers work with students, parents, and other teachers to help students who struggle because of physical, mental, or behavioral challenges.
Early Childhood Education Instructor	An early childhood education instructor teaches courses on child development, psychology, and education at the college level.
Parent Educator	A parent educator works with parents at hospitals, early care and education sites, and through social service organizations to help them learn how to care for their children, including handling development and behavior issues.

Critical Thinking   What classes have you taken in school that might help you prepare for a career as a preschool teacher? Propose the possible short-term and long-term career goals that will help you prepare for this career.

Certification Prep

Observe activities for each age level in a child care center. How are they different for each age group? Write two to three sentences that describe your observations.

Competitive Events Practice

Shadow a preschool teacher. Take notes about the kinds of activities that the teacher does during the day. Write a summary of the shadowing experience and the variety of activities that you observed. Include ideas for new activities.

Evaluate your shadowing experience summary on the following points:

• Does your summary describe all aspects of the day?

• Did you include ideas for new activities?

• Does your summary have an introduction and a conclusion?

Job Search Skills

The skills you have learned about in Unit 1 are essential when trying to get a job. You will demonstrate job-seeking skills by using the information you learned about early childhood careers, employability skills, and professional skills.

My Journal

If you completed the journal entry from page 2, refer to it to see how your experiences might influence your role as a child care professional. Add any additional notes that you thought of after reading this unit.

Project Assignment

In this project, you will do the following:

- Research available jobs
- Prepare a job application and a cover letter for one of those jobs
- Determine a list of references
- Create your job portfolio that includes your resume from Chapter 2; your mission statement from Chapter 3; and your application, cover letter, and references
- Conduct a mock interview with a partner
- Discuss the results of your mock interview

Applied Child Care Professional Skills Behind the Project

Your success as a child care professional will depend on your skills. Skills you will use in this project include the following:

▶ Organizing information
▶ Communicating clearly in writing and in person
▶ Determining what information is important and appropriate to share in a professional setting
▶ Demonstrating appropriate dress and hygiene for an interview
▶ Designating acceptable behavior before, during, and after a job interview

English Language Arts Skills Behind the Project

The English Language Arts skills you will use for this project are research, writing, and speaking skills. Remember these key concepts:

Research Skills

▶ Perform research using a variety of resources
▶ Discriminate between sources
▶ Use the information you gathered to narrow your choices

Writing Skills

▶ Use complete sentences with correct spelling, grammar, and punctuation
▶ Consider your audience
▶ Use findings from research to communicate discoveries in writing

Speaking Skills

▶ Speak clearly, slowly, and concisely so that the interviewer can follow your presentation
▶ Be sensitive to the needs of your audience
▶ Adapt and modify language to suit various purposes

©Nova Development

STEP 1 Research Available Jobs

Conduct research to find child care job opportunities in your area using online sources, newspaper ads, and by networking with people you know. Write a summary of your research findings to

- describe the types of jobs available.
- explain what education and job skills are required for the position.
- list specific ways you meet those requirements or can work to meet the requirements.
- identify the next steps you would take to apply for one of those jobs.

STEP 2 Complete an Application

Use the results of your research to contact a child care center and obtain its job application. Complete the application, making sure to include the following:

- Your personal data
- The position you are applying for
- The skills that will help you do the job well
- Your education and work experiences
- A list of people who will recommend you for the job and who know that you are listing them as references

STEP 3 Write a Cover Letter and Organize Your Portfolio

Using a sample cover letter, create a cover letter for the job you identified. Make sure to state the reason for your letter, your qualifications for the job, and request an interview. Review and edit the letter to make sure it sounds professional. Combine your cover letter with your application, resume, reference list, and mission statement to create a portfolio you can bring to the interview.

Child Care Professional Project Checklist

Plan
- ✔ Research and select a job opportunity.
- ✔ Complete a job application.
- ✔ Create a cover letter.
- ✔ Assemble your portfolio.
- ✔ Prepare for your mock interview.

Present
- ✔ Present your professional portfolio.
- ✔ Complete your mock interview.
- ✔ When the interviewer asks you questions, demonstrate your communication skills in a professional manner.
- ✔ Review the results of your interview.

STEP 4 Prepare for and Complete Your Interview

You and a partner will take turns interviewing each other for a job at a child care center. To complete this step, do the following:

- Dress and groom yourself as if you are going on an actual interview
- Review appropriate behavior before your interview. Remember to speak clearly, and to act professionally and respectfully.
- Complete your interview and interview your partner
- Evaluate your performance and your partner's performance

STEP 5 Evaluate Your Child Care Professional and Academic Skills

Your project will be evaluated based on the following:

- Extent of research and information about available jobs
- How well you completed your job application and portfolio
- Proper use of standard English and mechanics in your cover letter and portfolio materials
- Your professional conduct in your mock interview

Ariel Skelley/Getty Images

 Project Worksheet *Go to* **connected. mcgraw-hill.com** *for a worksheet you can use to complete your portfolio project.*

Child Care Basics

Chapters

Project Preview

Interview a Child Care Professional

After completing this unit, you will know more about the basics of caring for children in an early childhood setting. In the Unit 2 child care portfolio project, you will observe and interview a child care professional at work. You will write a report about what you learned from the interview about the child care profession and present the information to your class.

My Journal

Write a journal entry about a day in the life of a child care professional. Describe the day's events, from children's arrival to cleanup at the end of the day.

- What preparation does a child care professional need to do in addition to lesson planning?
- What challenges might a child care professional face on a daily basis?
- What personal traits and abilities help a child care professional deal with these challenges?

Explore the Photo
Caring for children requires learning about health, safety, nutrition, and behavior. *What care basics should a child care professional know about outdoor play?*

CHAPTER 4

Child Development Principles

Writing Activity

21st Century Skills

Planning An outline can help you organize any information you gather before writing. An outline contains the main topics you want to cover and the detailed subtopics that support each main topic. Browse the main ideas that will be covered in this chapter. Create an outline for an essay about child development.

Writing Tips

1. List your main topics in a logical order.
2. Under each main topic, list at least two supporting subtopics.
3. Under each subtopic, list supporting information or details you want to include. Subtopics are indented farther than main topics. Topics of equal importance should be at the same level.

Explore the Photo

This child is learning as he plays. *What kinds of skills do you think children can develop as they play?*

Exactostock / SuperStock

Reading Guide

Stay Engaged One way to stay engaged when reading is to turn each of the headings into a question and then read the section to find the answers. For example, *Factors Affecting Development* might be *What are some factors that affect development?*

Read to Learn

Key Concepts

- **Describe** the four areas of child development.
- **Explain** key findings in child development research.
- **Identify** the main principles of child development.
- **Summarize** the factors that affect a child's development.
- **Describe** potential characteristics of children at risk.

Main Idea

In this chapter you will learn about the stages of development and the factors that affect the proper growth and development of children. After you understand how a child might act or what a child might learn at different ages and stages, you will better know what to expect from a child in your care.

Content Vocabulary

◇ cognitive development
◇ sensorimotor
◇ sensory
◇ temperament
◇ perspective taking
◇ environment
◇ heredity
◇ neurons
◇ synapses
◇ at-risk
◇ prenatal
◇ cesarean section
◇ intervention services
◇ referral

Academic Vocabulary

■ theories
■ factors

Graphic Organizer

As you read, you will discover information about four areas of child development. Use a cluster chart like the one shown to record the four topics. Include notes about the changes and skills involved with each developmental area.

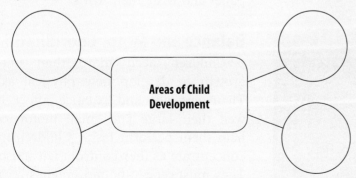

Areas of Child Development

Graphic Organizer *Go to* **connected.mcgraw-hill.com** *to print this Graphic Organizer.*

AS YOU READ

Connect Think about playtime activities that children enjoy. What kinds of developmental skills could they learn from these activities?

◇**Vocabulary**

You can find definitions in the glossary at the back of this book.

▼**Curious Crawlers**

This child's muscles have developed enough for him to begin crawling. *Which type of motor skills does a child need to develop to crawl?*

Child Development Basics

Child development is the pattern of changes that scientists study in how children grow from birth to teen years. Early childhood educators pay attention to children's development by watching and reacting to signs of progress. This allows them to help children grow and learn. These early educators can give extra help to children with developmental delays and tell their parents about special services.

Researchers who study development look at four areas: physical, intellectual, emotional, and social development. In this section, you will learn about how children change at different ages in each of these areas.

Physical Development

Physical development includes the ways a child's body grows and what all the body can do. Growing taller and learning to walk are parts of physical development. The most dramatic changes in growth happen during infancy and the teen years.

Large Motor Skills

As children grow, they gain muscle strength. They learn to move and control their muscles. When they can move and control their larger muscles, they have developed large motor skills. For example, when infants develop large muscles in their upper bodies, they hold up their heads. Later, when they develop large muscles in their lower bodies, they learn to creep and crawl.

Small Motor Skills

Children also develop small muscles, such as moving and controlling their fingers and wrists. For example, an infant who holds a rattle with the thumb and forefinger has developed small motor skills. As they grow, children further develop these skills. In time, they draw on paper and write their ABCs.

Balance and Motor Coordination

Children need more than muscle growth to develop new physical skills. Their eyesight and balance affect how well their large and small motor skills help them perform tasks. Children must concentrate as they control their muscles. They must repeat the movement over and over. For example, children who walk, run, and jump have learned balance. Children who hop, skip, and throw have also learned to coordinate, or use many muscles at the same time. As children move on to even more complex motions, such as bike riding or playing the piano, they must further refine and strengthen their large and small motor skills.

Responsible early educators should make sure children participate in a wide variety of activities that stimulate their physical development. Active playtime should include games that promote large motor skills. Quiet play should involve activities that stimulate small motor skills. As children get older, activities should incorporate balance and motor coordination as well. Keep in mind how activities could be adjusted if a child in your care has special needs.

Intellectual Development

Intellectual development—often called **cognitive development**—includes how children think, communicate, make decisions, and solve problems. Researchers in cognitive science study how people think and learn. They found that infants develop these skills as they make sense of their experiences. Children learn best as they move within their surroundings. They explore through their senses of sight, touch, taste, sound, and smell. This is called **sensorimotor** (sen(t)s-rē-ˈmō-tər) learning.

Sensory Skills

Children use their senses to learn about the objects around them. These are called **sensory** experiences because they involve the senses. For example, children notice if an item is soft or hard, bitter or sweet, loud or quiet. As children gather such information through their senses, their brains explain and store the information.

Language

Language allows children to organize and express their thoughts and ideas. It helps them ask questions to better understand experiences. Children use language to explore what interests them.

Concepts

As children gather information, they gradually develop concepts. Their senses, especially sight and touch, allow them to learn that objects vary. A young child's brain thrives on noticing the differences.

▲ **Baby's First Steps**

This child is learning to walk as part of his physical development. *Which types of physical skills does a child need to develop to walk?*

While playing with colored building blocks, for example, children learn the concepts of size, color, and shape. With further intellectual development, children learn to make more difficult comparisons, such as realizing that some objects are heavier than others.

Thinking Skills

A child's thinking skills and abilities change quickly during the first few years of life. Over time, intellectual development becomes more complex and begins to slow down. This development continues gradually throughout childhood. As children grow intellectually, they learn to analyze, evaluate, and solve problems. They also begin to learn about cause and effect, which helps them understand the consequences of their actions.

Early educators should make sure children participate in activities that encourage their intellectual development. Toys, activities, and games should use objects that stimulate the senses and reinforce concepts. Rhymes, word games, stories, puzzles, and group play encourage language development and thinking skills. Keep in mind how activities could be adjusted if a child in your care has special needs.

▲ **Development Can Be Fun!**

Learning to sort by color and shape is a process children go through in their early years. *What other factors indicate children are developing intellectually?*

Emotional Development

Emotional development takes place as children form feelings about themselves and others. They experience feelings such as happiness, excitement, fear, frustration, and anger. Teachers should learn effective ways to react to children's emotions. This helps children understand their feelings and accept them in positive ways.

Temperament

Research shows that each child is born with an individual **temperament**, or a typical way he or she responds to people and situations. From birth, some children are easygoing and accept change well. Others are anxious and cannot sit still or finish a task. Some children are friendly and look for more ways to play and be with others. Some children are slow to warm up to people and like to play alone. When caring for children, it is important to identify and respect their individual temperaments and to react with sensitivity.

Glow Images

Trust and Attachment

Healthy emotional development begins during the first days and years of life. When children form emotional bonds, or a special attachment, to a small circle of people, they learn trust. If you are consistent and responsive in providing care to infants and toddlers, you will generate and reinforce their trust in you.

Identity and Self-Esteem

Over time, children create individual identities. They form a mental picture of who they are, including whether or not they are attractive, capable, and likable. Self-esteem is the overall feeling children have about themselves. How other people treat a child in his or her early years greatly influences the child's identity and self-esteem. Children learn to think favorably of themselves when care providers show them love, respect, and support.

Self-Control

As children mature, they better understand their emotions and learn to control them. Toddlers have a reputation for temper tantrums. Yet with guidance, they learn to use words to express their needs and wants. When you show children that you know how to control your own feelings, you help children learn how to manage their emotions. Children gain better self-control as they learn and accept that everyone has feelings they must respect.

Social and Ethical Development

Social development builds as children learn how to get along with others, play together, and make friends. They find ways to settle disagreements through the use of words instead of action. Children also learn that society has rules to follow. Getting along with others means knowing and following these rules. For example, children learn to reply when someone speaks to them. They learn to walk rather than run in certain places.

As children master social skills, they gain acceptance from others. This gives children positive feelings about themselves. Without these social skills and acceptance, children feel alone and unworthy. Responsible teachers give children opportunities to work with and socialize with other people to stimulate their social development.

Social development is also linked to children's understanding of ethics. Learning the difference between right and wrong, personal accountability to others, and the importance of telling the truth are vital for developing relationships with family and peers.

Family Relationships

Families influence social development when they talk to their children about their beliefs and values. The practices parents develop for their families over time reveal their values.

Special traditions, for example, introduce children to their heritage and show the love within the family. Family love and values shape the children's values.

Children receive their foundation for morals and ethics from their families. Experiences with parents, siblings, and extended family members give children their first examples of what is right, what is wrong, and how to treat others. Families also help children learn to expect respectful treatment from peers. Teachers can reinforce this foundation by learning about each family's stance and encouraging children to act according to their families' values.

Peer Relationships

As children interact with others, they learn that everyone has different goals, ideas, and ways of doing things. Through play, children in early childhood programs gradually develop skills that allow them to see their play partners' perspectives. This is called **perspective taking**, when children learn to consider and respect other children's points of view as well as their own. Perspective taking allows social skills to develop, such as listening, taking turns, sharing, and solving conflict. As a result, they make friends more easily and become accepted members of a group.

▲ Making New Friends

Group projects and activities allow children to develop and practice social skills. *How can an early educator help children develop their social skills?*

READING CHECK✔ **Recall** How do sensory experiences aid a child's intellectual development?

Child Development Research

In the past, few people realized that children have specific needs and characteristics. As adults grew more concerned about children's issues, they asked more questions of doctors and other scientists . In order to learn more, researchers developed and tested theories, or ideas and principles about a subject that can be investigated, using the scientific method. They watched children, collected data, and drew conclusions. These child development researchers have created a body of knowledge about how children learn and develop skills, which has provided insight on how to nurture and educate children.

The findings of certain researchers have gained wider acceptance among scientists and development experts. **Figure 4.1** summarizes the studies and findings of several major child development researchers.

Figure 4.1 **Researchers Describe Development**

Important Theories and Ideas These are some of the researchers who have made a major contribution to the study of child development. *Which theorist said that people must first meet their basic needs? Why is this important?*

Researcher	Findings or Ideas	Significance
Jean Piaget (psychologist; 1896–1980)	Children develop cognitive skills based on how they mature, interact with others, and react and adapt to their physical surroundings.	Defined the four stages of children's learning. Therefore, children must be given learning tasks appropriate to their level of development.
Lawrence Kohlberg (cognitive development researcher; 1927–1987)	Organized developmental stages by how children learn right from wrong. Said young children choose what seems in their best interests, but teens are influenced by their parents and friends.	Knowing a child's current development stage allows you to understand his or her reasons for a decision and to help him or her learn right from wrong.
Erik Erikson (psychoanalytical researcher; 1902–1994)	Said that a person's identity and self-esteem are linked to how he or she handles life's challenges. If challenge or crisis is met in a positive way, the child develops normally.	Early educators should be aware of, and sensitive to, a child's needs at each stage of development. They should support children through challenges they meet in each development stage.
Howard Gardner (education professor; born 1943)	Proposed that many kinds of intelligence exist. A large range of skills and abilities is tied to intelligence. For example, an athlete has kinesthetic, or bodily movement, intelligence.	The diversity of interests, skills, and abilities among people creates more knowledge for all. Teachers should encourage children's varied interests and skills to support all kinds of intellectual development.
Sigmund Freud (neurologist, psychoanalyst; 1856–1939)	Said that a child's personality develops through a predictable pattern of stages. Freud believed the emotional or psychological problems of adults are connected to how their parents and care providers met their basic needs as children.	Childhood is much more important than previously thought. Experiences in childhood can have profound, long-lasting effects on adult life.
Lev Vygotsky (psychologist; 1896–1934)	Said that social contact is essential to intellectual development. The social interactions children have with others greatly influence their intellectual ability to gain knowledge, think, and learn a language.	Child care professionals should make sure children are given the opportunity for frequent social interaction.
Abraham Maslow (personality theorist; 1908–1970)	Known for his theory on the hierarchy of needs. The lowest and most basic needs are physical, such as food and shelter. Higher levels include safety, love and belonging, esteem, and self-actualization. People must first meet their basic needs before they can focus on higher needs.	Children rely completely on their care providers to fulfill their basic needs. It is important for care providers to consistently monitor a child's basic needs to help him or her advance to higher levels of needs.
Stella Chess and **Alexander Thomas** (psychologists; 1914–2007, 1914–2003)	Studied concept of temperament. Found that children should be nurtured according to their individual temperament needs.	Early educators should identify and respond sensitively to children's temperaments. They should accept that children will respond differently to the same situation, and adjust their responses to the child's needs.
B. F. Skinner (behavioral psychologist; 1904–1990)	Researched how people behave in their environments. Proved that a child learns a certain behavior through positive and negative reinforcement. Actions with positive results will be repeated. Negative results will cause actions to stop.	Early educators can influence a child's behavior through the use of positive and negative feedback.
Urie Bronfenbrenner (developmental psychologist; 1917–2005)	Emphasized that many environments collaborate to influence a child's development. Things such as biology, culture, community, family, and society all affect a child's development.	Because there are many sources of influence on a child's development, early educators should provide a stable and loving relationship for the child.

Understanding and Applying Child Development Theories

Teachers who understand the theories of child development researchers can apply these theories to help them better nurture and educate children.

Procedure With a partner, choose a child development theory to research further. Identify how the scientists conducted their research. Did they observe as children moved through the stages of development, or did they conduct experiments? What significance does this theory have on experts' understanding of child development? Is this theory widely accepted by these experts? How is the theory being applied in child care situations today? With your partner, plan how you could use this theory in a child care setting.

Analysis Use the information you collected to draw conclusions about how this theory impacts educational and child care practices today. Analyze the possible benefits and drawbacks of your plan. Create a presentation to share your findings with the class. Your presentation should include your plans for applying the theory in a child care setting. Explain the benefits of your plan as well as any problems that might occur.

As Figure 4.1 on page 89 suggests, there are many influences involved with child development. The researchers you just read about spent their careers studying the unique combination of aspects that influence development. However, much of their research falls into one of two categories:

▶ A child's **environment** includes the people, culture, and physical and social surroundings in which the child lives. Environments—including family, home, school, and community—surround and influence a person throughout his or her life.

▶ **Heredity** is qualities and traits that are passed from parents to children through their genes at conception. For example, inborn, or natural, temperament of children is a part of heredity. Eye color, blood type, and hair color are a few other characteristics determined by heredity. Can you think of other characteristics that are part of heredity?

READING CHECK ✔ **Relate** Define *environment* and *heredity* as these terms relate to child development.

Principles of Child Development

Children in every part of the world develop in similarly predictable patterns and stages. Many **factors**, or things that contribute to a result, will influence their growth, but the foundation of their development is the brain. The brain coordinates all human development.

As the brain continues to grow and develop, it oversees the sequence of development that occurs in every child. This has led researchers to list five general principles of child development, which include the following:

▶ **Development follows a similar pattern for each child.** All children go through the same stages, in about the same order. For example, the stages of muscle development allow babies to lift their heads before lifting their bodies.

▶ **Development rate depends on the individual.** While most children go through the development stages in the same order, each child will set his or her own pace.

▶ **Development is sequential.** Children follow a sequence, or order of steps, as they develop. They build on the skills they have already mastered to learn new skills.

©Comstock/Alamy

- **Development is interrelated.** Children are constantly changing. Toddlers will improve motor coordination as they practice language skills. Developmental changes occur in many areas at the same time.

- **Development is a lifelong process.** Development does not end with childhood. No matter what an individual's pace is, development does not stop.

Brain Coordination

The brain is the leading player for all development. It records and interprets a child's mental and sensory experiences. Any information that a child's body needs to develop must first go through the brain. All areas of human development are affected by the growth and functions of the brain.

An infant's brain contains billions of nerve cells called **neurons**. But it still has a lot of growing to do! A newborn's brain is about 25 percent of its adult weight. By age six, a child's brain reaches its full adult weight.

The brain continues to grow throughout childhood, but not in neurons. What develops is the number of **synapses**, or electrical connections between the neurons. Some experts say that, by adulthood, the brain has more than 100 trillion such connections. As they increase, neuron pathways develop.

This brain wiring sends information to all parts of the body to tell it how to function. More neuron pathways lead to a greater capacity for thinking and learning. They are actually learning pathways. Scientists say a child's synapse activity is two and one-half times faster than an adult's. As a result, children learn much faster than adults.

Sensory Experiences

A child's early experiences and heredity affect brain development. If children experience a secure, engaging environment from infancy, brain function develops as it should. A child's synapses increase with proper nurturing and plenty of sensory and movement experiences. Sensory experiences, such as squeezing a ball or singing a song, naturally engage children's interests. Because they enjoy such activities, children continue to explore and learn.

SAFETY MATTERS

Basic Toy Safety

Toys that engage children's senses are a great way to aid their development. Child care professionals must make sure all toys are safe for children to use. Here are some safe toy guidelines:

Use only nontoxic art materials such as crayons and paint.

Fabrics should be labeled flame resistant or flame retardant.

Paint on toys must be lead-free.

Toys should not easily break into sharp pieces.

Avoid toys with long cords or strings that could wrap around a child's neck.

Small objects can be choking hazards. Toy pieces should be more than 1.75 inches in diameter.

Watch children carefully to keep nonteething toys out of their mouths.

Be Prepared Spend a half hour examing the toys of a child under age four. Check each toy for safey. Write a description of each toy's safety features or safety hazards.

What Would You Do? You are examining some of the toys in your child care facility. You find that some of the toys in the toddler room are old and slightly broken. You feel that they are unsafe. What would you do?

▲ Let's Play Pretend

This child is copying behavior she has seen as she plays. *How does repeating the actions of others help children learn concepts?*

Repeated and Related Experiences

Children enjoy learning by copying their parents' behaviors. They also love to repeat favorite activities such as listening to nursery rhymes and bedtime stories. This repetition helps the brain retain information.

Babies grasp the concept of cause and effect by playing peek-a-boo or stacking and knocking down blocks. If you plan related experiences for preschoolers, it will help them gain and retain knowledge better. For example, if children watch birds, draw birds, pretend to fly like birds, and later listen to stories about birds, their concept of bird features is more accurate and detailed.

Critical Periods

Scientists have discovered that different parts of the brain develop at different times. Certain types of learning occur only during a child's early years. Each development area has its own "window of opportunity," or time frame for normal development to occur. For example, the part of the brain that controls language develops during the first two years of life. It is important for parents and teachers to talk to infants and toddlers and to respond to children's babbling and attempts to communicate during this time. This helps them develop language skills. The part of the brain that controls social skills begins developing from birth. Activities and routines that encourage a child's attachment to others are very important. The critical period for learning to play an instrument or learning a second language ends by age ten. Children can learn these skills later, but their brains offer the learning pathways in early childhood.

Development Rates

The interesting thing about development—and the challenging part for you as a child care professional—is that every child develops at a different rate and will begin new stages at different times. All children experience growth and develop new abilities at a unique pace.

Researchers have found that developmental stages are predictable, especially during early childhood. The rate at which each child progresses through a stage varies, but the child must pass through all stages to grow and mature. When you notice that a child's progress through a stage is significantly delayed or advanced, plan to give extra help or attention to the child.

Sometimes a child may experience different rates of development in each area. A child with strong intellectual abilities may not have developed age-appropriate social skills. Researchers have found that boys tend to develop more slowly than girls, as much as two to six months behind girls of the same age. Early educators who notice and understand the difference can react and respond more relevantly to both boys and girls.

Sequential Development

The skills children learn develop gradually, building one upon another. As mentioned earlier, development follows a step-by-step sequence. **Figure 4.2** describes the four principles of sequential development. For example, children learn the letters of the alphabet before learning to spell words. Motor skills also progress from simple to complex. For example, when learning to play with a ball:

▶ Children first hold the ball—touching it to sense its shape and texture.

▶ Then they roll, drop, and bounce the ball to experiment.

▶ Eventually a child's brain learns to coordinate eye and hand movements.

▶ In time the child will gain the ability to throw and catch a ball.

Interrelated Development

Connections between developmental areas are very important. Teachers should consider activities that will stimulate development in multiple areas. Growth in one area can affect growth in another.

Figure 4.2 **Principles of Sequential Development**

Step-by-Step As children grow, their skills and abilities gradually develop in a predictable sequence. *Why do you think children must master moving their heads before moving the rest of their bodies?*

From Top to Bottom	Children progressively master body movement and coordination from the head downward. First, children can lift their heads and then the trunks of their bodies. Eventually, they coordinate their whole bodies to walk.
From Center to Outside	Children develop from the center of their bodies outward. Development progresses from the spine to the arms and legs, and then to the fingers and toes. Children can use their shoulders and swing their arms in large circles before they can coordinate and maneuver their wrists and fingers.
From Large to Small	Children develop control over large muscles before small muscles. For example, children can run and jump before they can throw or catch a ball.
From General to Specific	Development progresses gradually from general to specific. Children's attempts to develop new abilities start simple and become increasingly complex. For instance, children jump up and down with both feet before they can hop on one foot. Running comes first, skipping later. Babies make sounds before saying words.

For example, it is easier for a child to work out a disagreement with another child (emotional development) after he or she learns to use words to communicate (intellectual development). Before children can draw or write, they must experience many different play activities that aid in large and small motor development. Early educators must consider the total child when planning activities that will promote growth, development, and learning.

READING CHECK ✔ **Identify** What specific types of experiences assist children's brain development?

Factors Affecting Development

Proper growth and development depends on heredity and environment. Heredity may pass on to children serious diseases or physical or mental disabilities. **At-risk** environments interfere with proper development and well-being. Children who live in at-risk environments may not receive enough nurturing and stimulation from their parents or care providers. This can cause them to fall behind other children their age developmentally.

Heredity and Environment

You have learned that heredity and environment are the two general factors that affect how well children grow and develop. Researchers have debated for decades which of the two have the greater impact. Many scientists today believe that heredity and environment each play a very important part in development.

A child's heredity is set before birth and is unchangeable. Children receive a unique biological set of genes from their parents. These genes decide which of the parents' traits the child will have. Heredity influences how the child will look but also influences a child's physical, intellectual, emotional, and social strengths and weaknesses.

A child's environment after birth changes regularly. Parents and caregivers help give an infant a stable environment. Researchers have found that environmental experiences such as good nutrition and health care, responsive care and nurturing, and an engaging play environment lead to proper growth and development.

▼ **Seeing Double?**

Although heredity strongly influences development (as shown with these twins), it is important to remember that heredity and environment work together to influence how children use their inherited abilities.
Other than physical characteristics, what are some other ways that heredity can influence development?

© Hero/Corbis/Glow Images

Prenatal Development

As you learned earlier, development rates vary with each child for many reasons. For example, a child may experience problems before birth or during delivery. Injury or illness during the earliest years of life may also slow down the typical rate of development.

Maternal Health Before Birth

An unborn infant relies completely on the mother for nutrients during pregnancy. The infant is more likely to be born healthy if the mother is healthy. The mother needs ample nutrition for her own energy and health and for her rapidly developing child. To ensure a healthy child, a pregnant woman must receive proper **prenatal**, or before birth, health care, especially during the first three months of pregnancy. Proper prenatal care is essential to help prevent some birth defects.

Prenatal Drug Use

Abusing alcohol, caffeine, nicotine, and illegal drugs while pregnant may hurt an infant's development. Depending on the drug, the infant may have physical deformities or mental disabilities. For example, infants born with Fetal Alcohol Syndrome may have deformed hearts or faces or slow physical growth. They may also show poor motor coordination. Mothers who use addictive drugs such as cocaine or heroin often deliver their infants early. These babies are usually born addicted to the drug and have very fragile nervous systems. They go through a painful withdrawal from the drug after birth. Many have low birth weight and severe learning disabilities. Even prescription or over-the-counter medication should only be taken after the mother has consulted with her doctor.

The Birth Process

Most births are routine and predictable, but some involve complications. For example, an infant's oxygen flow may be cut off during delivery, causing brain damage. Some infants do not enter the birth canal with their heads down. Their delivery may require a surgical procedure, called a **cesarean section**. Each have higher risks and a possibility of causing further delays.

▲ **Mommy-to-Be**

Pregnant women have an important job. Their health will affect the health of their unborn children. *Why is it important for pregnant women to monitor their nutrition?*

Health and Nutrition

Growth and development move along properly if children are provided with basic health care and proper nutrition. Parents and care providers who make sure that children have well-child preventive and routine health care services help the children avoid a decline in their health. Illness or injury slows growth and learning. Early educators can support families by providing information on local government or nonprofit agencies that support children's health care.

Growing bodies need both exercise and rest. Early educators should give children opportunities to exercise their bodies and muscles to promote physical health. They should also be alert for children who are tired or cranky because their bodies need a nap.

Poor nutrition during pregnancy and during the first few years of a child's life can result in neurological and behavioral disorders. Developing a lifelong habit of proper nutrition is essential to avoid the serious effects of poor nutrition. Well fed children eat food that gives them at least the minimum daily requirements of calories and nutrients such as protein, vitamins, and minerals.

Only when children receive a variety of nutritious foods—such as whole grains, proteins, and fresh fruits and vegetables—can they receive the fuel they must have for growth and energy. Early educators play an important role in providing proper meals and snacks to children and teaching children and their parents about proper nutrition.

▶ Embracing Uniqueness

Every child brings unique family and cultural experiences to the early childhood classroom.
How can you support the individuality of each child and respect diversity in your classroom?

Responsive Care and Nuturing

Children need to be nurtured by their parents, guardians, and other special people around them. An attentive child care professional responds quickly to children's basic needs for comfort, love, and assistance. Early educators who excel at nurturing genuinely enjoy interacting with children. They show enthusiasm and encourage children with each new task. A child care professional's calm dialogue and warm facial expressions communicate love and worth to the child.

Developing routines—such as bathing, feeding, diapering, and dressing—help nurture a child's overall development. For example, when you tickle a baby's tummy during diapering, a foundation for the child's social development begins to build. When you sing lullabies and rock the baby to sleep, the child begins to build trust and a bond with you.

Parents nurture their children within the setting of their family's values and goals. Their ethnicities, cultural backgrounds, countries of origin, religions, and unique experiences affect each family's beliefs, traditions, and other practices. Make it a priority to become familiar with the cultural beliefs of the families and children you serve. It is important for early educators to embrace each child's unique cultural background and support individuality and diversity in a child care program.

READING CHECK ✔ **Recall** What are five factors that affect a child's proper development?

Children at Risk

You have learned that the basic principles of child development apply to all children and that the rate and success of each developmental stage varies with each child. You have also learned about the concept "at risk." Many people are alarmed when they hear an adult call a child "at risk." They believe it is a label that lowers a child's self-esteem.

Children at risk experience conditions that interfere with their proper development and well-being. Children at risk have a greater chance of developmental delays. You must use care to use this term only with other early childhood professionals and parents but not with children.

Risk Characteristics

There is a wide range of characteristics of children at risk. Some children are at risk of learning failure because their language development is slow. Others are at risk because their behavior in groups is unacceptable. Some children are at risk of child abuse or malnutrition because of their environment.

Respond to SPECIAL NEEDS

Chronically Ill Children
Children who are fighting a chronic, or long-lasting, illness may need special care. Children with chronic heart conditions may need physical activities adjusted to meet their needs. Children fighting cancer may need help navigating questions from their curious peers. Teachers must be sensitive to the life changes these children are experiencing. Other family members in your care may need help coping with emotions or stress caused by a chronic illness situation. Teachers must be sensitive to family members in this situation, especially regarding sharing information about the illness with others.

Critical Thinking

Choose a chronic illness to research with a partner and write a summary of the illness. Discuss how a teacher could accommodate a child with this illness, such as adjusting activities, nutrition, or aiding interactions with others. Present your summary and discussion results to the class.

A child who does not feel a sense of safety and security in his or her environment could experience developmental issues as well. As a child care professional, you must be alert to the at-risk indicators for the children in your care. **Figure 4.3** lists examples of some at risk indicators.

Intervention and Prevention

Early childhood professionals help children at risk when they notice signs of potential problems and take action. They must diligently observe each child under their care for signs of slow development. If ignored, developmental problems can become more serious and interfere with a child's life.

Children with at risk characteristics may need special attention or activities adjusted to suit their needs. When creating activities, think about various strategies you can use to meet each child's special needs that encourage physical, intellectual, emotional, and social development.

What should you do if you identify a developmental problem in a child in your care? It is your professional responsibility to help the child's parents understand the problem and seek further help. Resources and specialized help are called **intervention services**. When you help the family pursue such services, you reduce or eliminate the risks for the child.

Figure 4.3	Characteristics of Children At Risk

Factors Affecting Development Early educators should watch for indicators that a child might be at risk for developmental issues. *What is an indicator of delayed emotional development? What would you do if you saw this sign in a child in your care?*

Physical Development
- Drug exposure prior to birth or during breastfeeding
- Premature birth, low birth weight, or birth delivery problems
- Physical disability or other special needs
- Malnutrition, poor overall health, or low energy level

Intellectual Development
- Inability to listen, concentrate, or participate according to expected age and abilities
- Significantly delayed language for child's age and experiences
- Mental disability or other special needs

Emotional Development
- Behavior problems, especially aggression toward self or others
- Signs of childhood depression, such as sleep or toileting problems

Social Development
- Early isolation from others
- Family moves often

Environmental Factors
- Lack of safety or security
- Signs of neglect or abuse
- Untreated mental illness of family member
- Exposure to domestic or community violence

◀ **Learning to Be Moms and Dads**
....
Parent education may be part of an early childhood program and can include topics such as holding a baby properly and changing diapers. How can parent education benefit young children?

Parent Education

You have learned about the importance of prenatal care for proper development. Because of this need, parent education must begin before pregnancy. Parents need to learn how to give safe and proper care to their child. Parents can meet childrearing challenges if they know about developmental needs and how they should respond to them.

Parent education during pregnancy helps parents learn how to balance all the new responsibilities that come with raising a family. Typical parent education programs include topics such as time management, basic first aid, childhood nutrition, and well child check ups. Helping parents learn positive ways of guiding children's behavior lessens child abuse and neglect.

Parent education can take many forms. Some parents like formal classes. Other parents like support group meetings to casually discuss topics with other parents. Many parenting books and DVDs offer information and advice. Good early childhood programs have parent lending libraries, stocked with such resources.

Support Services

Parents usually receive their first information on child rearing from family members, especially from their parents and grandparents. Families may need other resources if their own parents live far away or if their children's needs are unusual. You should give them a **referral**, or send the parent to another resource or support service.

Effective early childhood programs keep a list of local family-centered agencies and parenting Web sites. You should know of local hospitals, health departments, schools, and social service agencies that offer low-cost programs for parents and children with special needs. These programs can help children with issues such as language delays, limited motor skills, and mental disabilities.

READING CHECK **Describe** What are five characteristics of children who may be at risk of developmental delays?

Community College

What Is a Community College?

A community college is a two-year, government-supported college that offers both technical and general-education associate degrees. Community colleges tend to be more affordable than four-year colleges and offer career-oriented degrees such as fashion design, public service, hospitality, and computer certification programs. Community college student bodies are often quite diverse with regard to age, experience, and employment status.

What are some positive reasons for attending community college?

A community college usually costs significantly less than state or private colleges and universities. Also, if you are unsure about what you want to study, a community college can allow you to explore various subject areas before deciding on a particular one. Community colleges also have more flexible schedules, including part-time options and online courses.

What are the benefits of a community college?

Many students use the community college as a bridge between high school and a four-year college or university. It can be a good way to save money and to establish a strong grade point average before transferring. A community college can be a great way for you to take college-level courses while building your academic skills.

Can a degree from a community college help me get a job?

Community colleges are often career-oriented, so they provide opportunities for you to connect with employers. Community colleges communicate with potential employers to learn what fields are hiring and what skills the market currently demands. Community college counselors can help you make decisions about your career path or help you meet transfer requirements.

Hands-On

College Readiness Find the Web site of a community college near you. Find information on the classes and areas of study that this community college offers. Think about which area of study interests you most. Write a paragraph identifying this area of study, and explain why it is the one in which you are most interested. What types of jobs could you get with a degree in this area of study?

Path to Success

Get a Taste Community colleges can be a way to "test drive" a specific career field.

Enjoy Flexibility Community colleges allow you to choose days and times that fit your personal schedule.

Consider Cost and Location Tuition and fees can be less expensive at community colleges than at four-year colleges. And they are often close to home.

Be Career-Focused Community colleges offer many programs leading directly to a career.

Bridge to Success Preparing students to transfer to a four-year institution is one of the purposes of community colleges.

Jupiterimages/Getty Images

Child Development Principles
Visual Summary

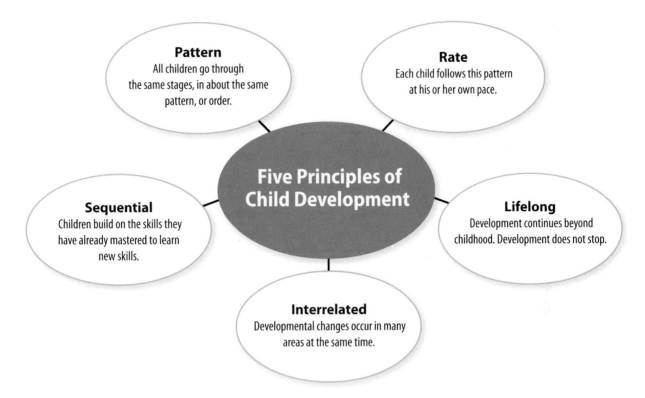

Pattern
All children go through the same stages, in about the same pattern, or order.

Rate
Each child follows this pattern at his or her own pace.

Five Principles of Child Development

Sequential
Children build on the skills they have already mastered to learn new skills.

Lifelong
Development continues beyond childhood. Development does not stop.

Interrelated
Developmental changes occur in many areas at the same time.

Vocabulary Review

1. Arrange these content and academic vocabulary terms into groups of related words. Explain your choices.

Content Vocabulary

◇ cognitive development (p. 85)
◇ sensorimotor (p. 85)
◇ sensory (p. 85)
◇ temperament (p. 86)
◇ perspective taking (p. 88)
◇ environment (p. 90)

◇ heredity (p. 90)
◇ neurons (p. 91)
◇ synapses (p. 91)
◇ at-risk (p. 94)
◇ prenatal (p. 95)
◇ cesarean section (p. 95)

◇ intervention services (p. 98)
◇ referral (p. 99)

Academic Vocabulary
■ theories (p. 88)
■ factors (p. 90)

Review Key Concepts

2. Summarize the four areas of child development. Include key characteristics for each area.

3. Identify a child development researcher who interests you. Examine his or her theory or area of research and apply his or her findings to a child care center.

4. Recall the five principles of child development. Give an example of each, and explain how this knowledge relates to a child care professional.

5. Paraphrase the main factors that affect a child's growth and development. How would children who experience differences with these factors develop differently?

6. Name three local resources for parent education. Describe a situation in which you could refer a parent for each of these resources.

Critical Thinking

7. Examine what you have learned about parents' involvement in child care and development. Analyze how changes in society or demographics could affect the roles of parents or other family members as children develop. How could these factors affect children?

8. Characterize the milestones involved for each area of child development. Analyze development's normal progression to determine when a teacher should raise developmental issues or concerns.

9. Relate development to play time. Describe play activities that also encourage development. For example, describe activities that promote large or small motor skills. What other strategies could you use to encourage children's growth and development?

10. Extend your knowledge of development to define the term *developmentally appropriate*. What do you think this term means? How can you use your knowledge of development to categorize appropriate and inappropriate games and activities for children?

21st Century Skills

Collaborative Skills

11. Encourage Emotional Development Work in teams to brainstorm strategies to build positive self-esteem and identity or self-concept in children. Discuss how teachers can promote individual differences while building identity and self-esteem. Research behaviors in children that reflect negative and positive self-concept to help decide how to respond to those behaviors. Create a list with a variety of strategies for children at various age levels to share with the class.

Critical Thinking Skills

12. Analyze a Case Study With your teacher's help, find a case study that compares normal child development to atypical development. Identify which areas of child development are discussed in the case study: physical, intellectual, emotional, or social. Classify which behaviors are linked to each area of development. Write a summary that compares the subject's development to typical development.

Child Care LAB

Use the skills you have learned in this chapter.

Child Development

13. Research an Area of Child Development Work as a team to research child development and then create a presentation explaining how to apply an area of child development to a child care setting.

A. Choose your topic. Select one area of child development (physical, intellectual, emotional, or social).

B. Research development goals. Define and research development expectations associated with each age group (infant, toddler, preschooler, and school-age child).

C. Think about theories. Research relevant theories in this area of development and relate this to the expectations you discovered above.

D. Organize your research. Organize the information you have discovered on development goals, age groups, and theories. Then use this information to explain how you would apply this information to a child care environment.

E. Present your findings. Create a presentation (such as a poster or Web site) of your research on how children develop and learn in the selected area. Include your explanation for applying your findings to a child care environment. Share your findings with the class.

Create Your Evaluation

Answer the following questions in writing: How well does each team's presentation convey information about an area of child development? Which area is featured? How can their research be applied to a child care setting? Include praise, constructive criticism, and further questions you might have for the presenters.

Academic Skills

English Language Arts

14. Contributing Factors Imagine that you will participate in a panel discussion on Nature versus Nurture. Create notes to use that explain how heredity and the environment can work together to shape a child. Use the information you have learned about the factors that affect proper development to support your claim.

Social Studies

15. Influences on Development How does society affect children's development? How do development goals differ from culture to culture? What role does family, religion, ethnic group, nationality, or gender play in development? What effect does the media have? What do you think has the most influence on children? Explain your conclusion.

Mathematics

16. Calculate Average Marcia, Jamal, and Leslie have spent a total of 12 hours so far working on an assigned child development research project together. Each must keep track of the time he or she spends on the project. What is the average number of minutes each of them has spent working on the project?

Math Concept **Variables and Operations** Translating words into algebraic expressions requires knowing what the verbal descriptions mean. A variable is a symbol used to represent a number. Operations include addition, subtraction, multiplication, and division.

Starting Hint First convert the hours into minutes. If x = the average number of hours each student spends on the project, the algebraic expression for the problem is $3x = (12 \times 60)$. Solve for x.

For more math practice, go to the math appendix at the back of the book.

Certification Prep

CERTIFICATION PREP

Directions Read each statement. Then read the answer choices and choose the phrase that best completes the sentence.

17. Intellectual development includes sensory skills, language skills, thinking skills, and _____.

  A. small motor skills

  B. concepts

  C. temperament

  D. learning society's rules

18. Factors that affect proper development include _____.

  A. prenatal care and development

  B. health and nutrition

  C. heredity and environment

  D. all of the above

Test-Taking Tip

In a multiple-choice test, pay attention to key words in the question and each answer choice. In question 17, the key words are *intellectual development*. Which answer choice specifically refers to intellectual development?

CHAPTER 5

Health, Safety, and Emergency Response

Writing Activity

⭐ 21st Century Skills

Critical Thinking A paragraph is a group of sentences that develop one central idea. Write a paragraph on a health or safety topic that you think would be important in a child care facility. Include a topic sentence, supporting sentences, and an ending sentence.

Writing Tips

1. Focus on the main idea of your paragraph. A topic sentence should introduce or summarize your main idea.
2. Write clear, simple sentences to express your meaning.
3. Make sure your sentences link clearly and logically to one another. Use transition words such as *because* and *also* to link the ideas in the paragraph.
4. Use correct grammar and spelling.

©DreamPictures/Blend Images LLC

Explore the Photo
A field trip can teach children about health and safety. *What safety considerations are needed for a field trip?*

Reading Guide

Vocabulary Create a vocabulary journal. Divide a piece of paper into three columns. Label the first column Vocabulary. Then, label the other two columns What is it? and What is similar to it? Write down each word and answer the questions as you read the chapter.

Read to Learn

Key Concepts

- **Describe** how child care professionals can limit the spread of contagious diseases.
- **Explain** the practices child care professionals use to check for and report illnesses.
- **Define** seven special health conditions that can affect children.
- **Summarize** the rules and procedures in an effective early childhood program safety policy.
- **Identify** procedures to maintain the health and safety of all staff members.
- **List** the emergency skills training needed by staff members.

Content Vocabulary

- ◇ immunizations
- ◇ pathogens
- ◇ universal precautions
- ◇ biohazardous
- ◇ hypothermia
- ◇ frostbite
- ◇ heat exhaustion
- ◇ screenings
- ◇ safety policy
- ◇ risk management plan
- ◇ toxins
- ◇ food service sanitation certificate
- ◇ abdominal thrust
- ◇ cardiopulmonary resuscitation
- ◇ automated external defibrillation

Academic Vocabulary

- ■ sensitivity
- ■ prevention

Main Idea

The health and safety of children and child care staff can be protected by using universal precautions. A safety policy describes policies and procedures for ensuring children and staff safety. Certification and training in first aid and other emergency skills help staff handle emergencies.

Graphic Organizer

As you read, note and describe four different forms that early childhood professionals use to ensure children's health and safety. Use a cluster diagram like the one shown to help you organize your information.

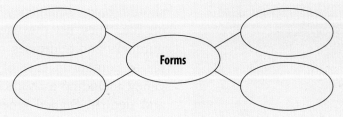

Forms

Graphic Organizer Go to **connected.mcgraw-hill.com** *to print this Graphic Organizer.*

AS YOU READ

Connect Think about the daily routines of children. What safety concerns do they encounter every day?

◇**Vocabulary**

You can find definitions in the glossary at the back of this book.

▼ **Sharing More Than Toys**

Germs can spread easily in a child care center when children play together and share toys. *What is one way child care staff help limit the spread of contagious illnesses among children?*

Promoting Children's Health

Parents of children enrolled in early childhood programs trust that child care staff will do everything they can to keep their children safe and healthy. Positive environmental factors such as good nutrition, daily exercise, regular health checkups, and clean, safe home and school environments contribute to the health and wellness of children. During the early childhood years, illness, injury, and poor nutrition can interfere with children's normal brain and body development. For example, a diet high in calories and inadequate physical activity can lead to childhood obesity. Exposure to harmful substances can impair brain development.

Healthy children have the foundation they need for early learning. Healthy children, however, will experience occasional mild illness. A child's immune system is still developing. The immune system helps resist disease. Until the immune system fully develops and children learn good health habits, early childhood staff must take extra steps to keep children healthy.

Health Records and Emergency Forms

When a new child enrolls in an early childhood program, parents or guardians should submit a copy of the child's health records. Health records list the results of health checks and screenings. These records include a doctor's report of overall health and may include results of tuberculosis testing. Health reports may also include information about known conditions, diseases, or other problems. Records of **immunizations**—vaccines that protect children from certain diseases—should be included. **Figure 5.1** shows what immunizations a child should receive and when. Health records should also include details about a child's developmental growth, allergies, medications, and medical problems or injuries that affect development. Health records are confidential information and should be updated as needed.

Every child and staff member should have emergency forms on file. They list the telephone numbers and addresses of people to contact in case of emergency, including a child's doctor and dentist. Signed emergency treatment waivers allow the staff to obtain emergency care for children, if necessary.

McGraw-Hill Education/Jill Braaten

Figure 5.1 — Recommended Immunizations for Children

Vaccinations The Centers for Disease Control and Prevention (CDC) establishes schedules for children's immunizations. A vaccine exposes a person to a small amount of a disease-causing agent so that a person can build immunity, or resistance, to it. *When should a child receive Varicella (chicken pox) vaccinations?*

Vaccine	Birth	1 month	2 months	4 months	6 months	12 months	15 months	18 months	19–23 months	2–3 years	4–6 years
Hepatitis B	HepB 1	HepB 2			HepB 3						
Rotavirus			RV 1	RV 2	RV 3						
Diphtheria, Tetanus, Pertussis			DTaP 1	DTaP 2	DTaP 3		DTaP 4				DTaP 5
H. influenza type b			Hib 1	Hib 2	Hib 3	Hib 4					
Pneumococcal			PCV 1	PCV 2	PCV 3	PCV 4					
Polio			IPV 1	IPV 2	IPV 3						IPV 4
Influenza					Influenza (Yearly)						
Measles, Mumps, Rubella						MMR 1					MMR 2
Varicella (chicken pox)						Varicella 1					Varicella 2
Hepatitis A						HepA (2 doses)					

Shading indicates range of recommended ages.　　**Source:** Centers for Disease Control and Prevention, 2015.

Limiting Contagious Illness

Children are subject to many infectious diseases. Disease-causing organisms are called **pathogens**, or germs. Bacteria and viruses are two kinds of pathogens. Some infectious diseases are passed from person to person. They include colds, influenza, and strep throat. Some conditions such as diaper rash and ear infections are not contagious. Coughing, sneezing, and physical contact allow illness to pass easily in a child care setting. Everything touched, such as toys, food, and other people, is a possible source of illness. Some pathogens are found in feces, urine, and blood. Contact with these sources can spread disease too. For example, changing diapers and caring for injuries pose a risk when not done properly.

Using Universal Precautions

Universal precautions are infection-control guidelines staff must follow to protect themselves from infectious disease and to limit its spread. They include hand washing, environmental disinfection, wearing gloves, and proper disposal of biohazardous materials. Because some pathogens are present in blood and other bodily fluids such as urine, feces, vomit, and draining wounds, universal precautions must be followed to prevent direct contact.

▶ Sanitized Surfaces

Keeping indoor and outdoor surfaces clean and sanitized helps maintain a safe and healthy learning environment. *How often should toys be disinfected?*

Hand Washing

The best way to limit the spread of contagious diseases is by frequent and thorough hand washing. Children and staff should wash their hands before and after preparing or eating meals and snacks, after handling pets, and after coughing, sneezing, and toileting. Staff members must also wash their hands before and after diapering. Everyone should wash hands after messy activities such as sand play and finger painting.

Environmental Disinfection

Cleaning and sanitizing or disinfecting with a solution of bleach and water limits germs. Sanitizing and disinfecting solutions should be mixed fresh every day. Use a disinfecting solution of ¾ cup of ultra liquid bleach to one gallon of water for disinfecting diapering areas, toys, cribs, walls, and floors. Toys that are mouthed by infants should be disinfected daily. Toys used by older children should be disinfected weekly, or sooner, if dirty. When using disinfecting solution, rinse items thoroughly in clear water, and then air dry. A sanitizing solution of one tablespoon ultra liquid bleach per gallon of water is good for sanitizing hard surfaces such as meal-service tables. Store all cleaning supplies in a locked cabinet.

Wearing Gloves

Wear fresh, disposable latex or vinyl gloves whenever you may come into contact with bodily fluids, such as during diapering, toileting, or treating an injury. Wear disposable gloves when handling blood spills or objects with blood on them. Remove gloves by pulling them off inside out. Wear gloves only once. Thoroughly wash your hands after removing gloves.

Disposal of Biohazardous Materials

Materials that come into contact with bodily fluids are called **biohazardous**. Diapers, diaper wipes, used disposable gloves, and blood-soaked clothes are examples of potentially hazardous materials. Biohazardous materials should be double-bagged and securely tied. Label each bag as biohazardous waste. Contaminated clothing should be double-bagged and sent home with parents. If the clothes cannot be thrown away, they should be washed separately.

How to . . .

Wash Your Hands

The best way to teach children and staff members good health practices, such as hand washing, is through classroom activities and routines. Supervise children and guide them as they wash their hands. Posters, signs, and bulletin boards educate and remind everyone about good health practices. Follow these steps to wash your hands properly.

▶ **Step 1** *Turn on the water and wet your hands and forearms. Warm water is recommended.*

▶ **Step 2** *Apply soap and build up a good lather by rubbing your hands together.*

▶ **Step 3** *Rub your soaped hands together for 20 seconds. Wash the backs of your hands, wrists, between fingers, and under fingernails.*

▶ **Step 4** *Rinse your hands well under running water.*

▶ **Step 5** *Dry your hands with a paper towel or an air dryer. Turn off the water faucet using a paper towel, not your clean hands.*

Apply It!
With a partner, take turns practicing proper hand washing. Did your partner follow all the steps?

▲ Fun in the Sun

Hats and sunscreen help protect children's faces from sunburn. *How can you protect children from the heat on a warm, sunny day?*

Limiting Weather-Related Illness

Diseases are not the only threat to health. Overexposure to extreme weather can also cause illness. As an child care professional, you will need to protect children from the following types of extreme weather illnesses:

▶ **Hypothermia. Hypothermia** (ˌhī-pō-ˈthər-mē-ə) results when the body's temperature gets dangerously low. It can occur if children are out too long in cold weather. Shivering is a clear sign that a child has been in the cold too long.

▶ **Frostbite. Frostbite**, the freezing of body tissue, occurs if parts of the body—especially feet, hands, face, and ears—are not well protected. Even if dressed in warm and waterproof clothing, children may still get frostbite if they are outside for long periods in severely cold weather. Signs of frostbite include numbness and white or grayish-yellow skin.

▶ **Heat exhaustion. Heat exhaustion** is a form of physical stress on the body caused by overheating. It results in dizziness and fatigue caused by the loss of fluid and salt through profuse sweating. Children with symptoms of heat exhaustion should drink fluids and rest in a cool place. Prevent heat exhaustion by not allowing children to play outdoors for long periods during very hot weather. Play areas should be shaded if possible. Encourage children to drink water frequently to replace water lost through perspiration.

▶ **Heatstroke.** Heatstroke is a dangerous condition in which the body loses its ability to cool itself through perspiration. Symptoms of heatstroke include a lack of sweating, extreme body temperatures, and the possibility of collapsing. Staff can help prevent heatstroke by following the same preventative measures for heat exhaustion.

▶ **Sunburn.** Sunburn can be a problem during any season. When playing outdoors, children should wear sunscreen with a 30 SPF level. Parents should supply the sunscreen for their children.

▶ **Air pollution.** Air pollution can pose risks for those with allergies, asthma, or other breathing problems. During an air-pollution alert, keep children indoors until the alert is cancelled.

READING CHECK ✔ **Recall** When should a child care provider wear disposable gloves?

Pixtal/AGE Fotostock

Handling and Reporting Illness

Even in the best of environments, illness occurs. Child care professionals work to limit the spread of disease and care for ill children appropriately. They also record health information to comply with health codes and licensing requirements.

Health Checks and Screenings

Daily health checks help staff spot children's health problems early, when an illness is most treatable and can be kept from spreading. Health checks take place when children arrive. Staff members note children's appearance and behaviors. Healthy children have energy and have good appetites. Their eyes and noses are clear. They are free of coughs and congestion. Physical symptoms of illness include a rash, watery eyes, harsh coughing, inflamed throat, fever, and runny nose. Behavior, such as tiredness and crankiness, may also be signs of illness. **Figure 5.2** provides information about the symptoms of common childhood illnesses and precautionary measures that can be taken to prevent their spread.

Examinations given to a group of children to look for one specific health problem are called **screenings**. Children with an identified problem are referred to a doctor or specialist for special treatment. Vision and hearing screenings usually start at age three—earlier if problems are suspected.

Figure 5.2 **Common Childhood Illnesses**

Symptoms of Illness Children often get contagious illnesses, such as the common cold, that require them to stay home. *What symptoms could signal that a child has an ear infection?*

Disease	Symptoms	Precautions
Pink eye (conjunctivitis)	Redness in one or both eyes. Possible discharge from eyes that forms a crust at night. Eye itchiness.	Child should stay home while symptoms are present. Contagious through hand-to-eye contact.
Ear infection	Infant may pull at ear and cry. Older child will say that ear hurts. Possible temporary hearing loss. Fever.	Child should stay home until fever-free for 24 hours.
Common cold	Stuffy or runny nose, sneezing or coughing, mild fever, sore throat, diminished appetite.	Child should stay home during first three days symptoms are present. Contagious through eye or mouth contact.
Influenza (flu)	Sudden onset of fever, chills, nausea, tiredness, and aching muscles. A sore throat and stuffy nose may occur.	Child should stay home while symptoms are present. Contagious through eye or mouth contact.

▶ Fevers

Most child care centers require that children who are running a fever must stay home until they have been fever-free without medication for 24 hours. *Why is this attendance restriction important?*

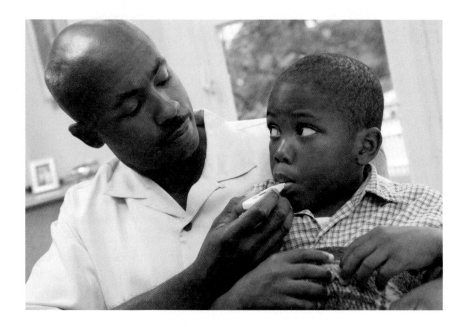

Restricting Attendance

Children with a contagious illness need to be temporarily absent from child care. Restricting attendance protects other children and staff from illness. Programs establish guidelines so that parents and staff know when children should be kept home. For example, a child with a fever should be kept home until he or she is fever-free for 24 hours. A child who becomes ill while in child care should rest in a supervised isolation room until a parent can take him or her home.

Reporting Illness and Informing Parents

Certain contagious diseases such as strep throat should be reported to the public health department for tracking. Parents should also be informed of any outbreaks at the center. Communicate to parents the illness or condition, associated symptoms, suggested treatment, and when a child can return to the classroom.

Medication Procedures

State licensing laws may restrict dispensing medicine in child care settings. Programs that do administer medicine follow a system so children receive the correct dose, or measured amount. Parents complete and sign a medication permission form. The form details the exact time, amount, method of dosage, and any side effects the medication may have on the child. When staff give the medicine, they enter the information on a log and sign the entry. Label and store all medications properly. Store medicines that need to be refrigerated in a locked, labeled container in the refrigerator. Store all other medicines in a locked, dry storage area out of children's reach.

READING CHECK ✓ **Contrast** How does a health check differ from a health screening?

Special Health Concerns

Some children have health conditions that require special attention. Care and medication details should be noted in enrollment records and discussed with parents. When caring for children with health problems, professionals respond to a child's individual needs.

Conditions That Impact Child Health

Every special health condition has its own set of concerns. A few of the conditions you might encounter are described here. The more knowledge you have about these and other conditions, the better able you will be to care for children's individual needs.

Allergies

An allergy is an extreme **sensitivity**, or reaction, to a common substance. The substance causes a reaction when eaten, breathed in, or touched. Many substances, including foods, animal fur, insect stings, dust, pollen, and mold, can trigger allergic reactions. Symptoms of allergic reactions may be mild, such as a rash, itchy eyes, or nasal congestion. Some allergic reactions are treated with medication. Follow parents' directions for treatment of allergic reactions. Some allergic reactions are life-threatening. If an allergic reaction is severe, seek medical assistance right away.

Asthma

Asthma ('az-mə) is a lung condition that makes it difficult to breathe. Coughing, wheezing, rapid breathing, and shortness of breath are signs of an asthma attack. Asthma attacks can be brought on by an allergic reaction or be triggered by dust, air pollution, physical exercise, smoke, and pets. Keeping children away from the causes helps minimize attacks. Children with asthma can take medication to open their airways and breathe more easily. If an asthma attack is severe, seek medical assistance right away.

Diabetes

Diabetes (dī-ə-'bē-tēz) is a condition in which the body does not produce enough of a chemical called insulin. Diabetes is usually controlled through medication and diet. Child care professionals caring for children with diabetes should work with parents to plan how to monitor and maintain a child's blood sugar levels.

Drug Exposure

Drug exposure, either prenatally or during nursing, affects children's health and overall development. The drugs a mother ingests and transfers to her child may affect the child's nervous system, resulting in physical, emotional, and social problems. Drug-exposed children require special care to address possible developmental delays.

Expert *Advice . . .*

"With a toddler on the loose, accidents are bound to happen once in a while. One study showed that the typical toddler has three minor bumps or boo-boos a day."

— Heidi Murkoff, Arlene Eisenberg, and Sandee Hathaway, *What to Expect: The Toddler Years*

Giardiasis

Giardiasis (jē-är-'dī-ə-səs) is a contagious intestinal disease caused by a parasite that results in diarrhea. It can be passed among children when staff do not wash children's or their own hands after diapering or toileting. Proper diapering and hand washing are the best ways to prevent the spread of giardiasis. Because infants and toddlers constantly mouth objects, daily toy disinfection helps prevent spreading the illness.

Head Lice

Head lice are small insects that live close to the scalp on human hair. Lice are usually identified when lice eggs, called nits, are found. Nits are typically spotted at the back of the neck, behind the ears, and on the top of the head. Signs of lice include itching at the roots of the hair and small red bite marks on the scalp. Head lice spread easily. Staff members should alert parents and other staff members as soon as an outbreak of head lice occurs.

Human Immunodeficiency Virus

Human Immunodeficiency Virus (HIV) is a virus that attacks and slowly weakens the immune system. Over time an infected person has frequent illnesses that a healthy person's immune system would easily fight off. This cycle of repeated illness from infectious disease is called Acquired Immune Deficiency Syndrome (AIDS). People with AIDS die from diseases that others usually survive, such as pneumonia and influenza. HIV can be treated with medication, but at this time, there is no known cure for HIV or AIDS.

Enrollment of Children with Health Conditions

The Americans with Disabilities Act (ADA) protects children's rights to be enrolled in child care whenever reasonably possible. When staff members learn of a child's special condition, confidentiality is critical. Information about a child's health is limited to the primary teacher and the program director. Parents must give written permission to staff to discuss the case with the child's doctor. Staff should work cooperatively with parents to receive any training they may need to provide the child with the best care possible.

READING CHECK **Identify** What substances might a child with allergies be sensitive to?

McGraw-Hill Education

Ensuring Children's Safety

The most important safety precaution in group child care is adequate and continuous supervision of children. Children should always be monitored and cared for in safe conditions. Children also need teachers who model good safety practices.

Children learn to practice safety during classroom activities. Field trips such as visiting the fire station emphasize the importance of being careful. Children can help teachers with safety inspections. Here are simple safety rules children can learn:

▶ Walk indoors. Running is for outside.

▶ Give broken toys to a teacher.

▶ Settle conflicts with words, not by hitting, biting, or pushing others or throwing toys.

▶ Stay with the teacher when on walks or a field trip.

▶ Obey safety rules when using art and other project supplies.

▶ Tell a teacher right away if a stranger comes into the classroom or play yard. Do not talk to the stranger.

▶ Tell a parent or teacher if anyone touches you on a private area of your body.

Safety Risks for Children

Children are exposed to hazards in both indoor and outdoor environments. Staff members must make sure the furniture, toys, and play structures are safe. Here are ways to ensure safety:

▶ Avoid toys with long cords or strings to avoid strangulation.

▶ Use only nontoxic items in art and science projects.

▶ Provide only round-tipped scissors.

▶ Make sure electric wires are not frayed and batteries in battery-operated toys are not leaking. Cover all unused electric outlets.

▶ Label potential poisons and lock them out of children's reach.

▶ Select toys that are appropriate for the ages and abilities of children in the classroom.

▶ Avoid toys that have sharp edges. Plastic toys should be shatterproof and nonflammable.

▶ Toys and any removable toy parts must not be small enough to swallow or inhale. For children under three, objects, toys, and toy parts that fit completely into a no-choke testing tube—a tube that measures 1¼ inches wide by 2¼ inches long—are choking hazards.

▼ **Learning Safety**

Teaching a child to use safety scissors properly is a classroom activity that helps children learn about safety. *What are other classroom activities that teach about safety?*

(c) Keith Eng 2007

Developing a Safety Policy

To ensure safe conditions, early childhood program directors develop a safety policy. A **safety policy** states the rules and procedures that protect children and staff. Staff must receive training on the policy. A safety policy addresses facility, transporation, and toy safety and safety inspections. It also covers emergency and evacuation procedures, rules for children's conduct, positive methods of discipline, and dealing with strangers.

Risk Management Plans

When emergency procedures are established in writing, it is called a **risk management plan**. Creating and following such a plan helps staff and children remain calm and respond quickly to any emergency. Risk management plans contain procedures for emergencies such as weather, fire, and bomb and other violent threats. Some emergencies may be community health-related, such as a widespread flu epidemic. Risk management plans also identify emergency survival supplies to keep on hand, such as bottled water and nonperishable foods. The Office of Emergency Services (OES) in your area can help create an emergency plan. Parents and guardians must be informed about the risk management plan and what they should do in an emergency.

Fire Evacuation Drills

Fire evacuation diagrams, with arrows toward exits, must be posted in all classrooms. Evacuation plans will vary depending upon the facility. Every classroom, the kitchen, and the laundry area should have a fire extinguisher. Staff members should be trained on how to use this equipment. Hold fire drills monthly. In the event of an actual fire, sound the alarm at the first sight of smoke or flames.

▼ **Emergency Drills**

Regular drills help children and staff react calmly when severe weather or an emergency occurs. *What should a child care professional do immediately after reaching a safe area with his or her class?*

Comstock/AGE Fotostock

Severe Weather and Disaster Drills

Weather emergencies include electrical storms, tornadoes, hurricanes, blizzards, and floods. Safety procedures vary. The American Red Cross and local safety agencies can provide information on preparing for and responding to emergencies. General rules that apply to weather emergencies include:

▶ Keep battery-operated radios and flashlights on hand.

▶ Post directions to designated shelter areas.

▶ Take shelter at the first sound of an alarm and remain there until the all-clear signal is given.

▶ Take attendance immediately after reaching shelter so you can locate missing children.

Disasters such as earthquakes, mudslides, wildfires, and explosions require an evacuation plan so children and staff can seek shelter quickly. Identify and post the locations in your building that would offer the best protection.

Injury and Accident Prevention

Prevention means taking action to keep something from happening. No child care program is completely free of accidents. With prevention, the number and severity of incidents can be limited. Staff reduce the risk of mishaps by anticipating problem situations. Careful observation is important for accident prevention. Always be alert to safety hazards—items, conditions, and situations that put children in danger. For example, a safe toy for a four-year-old may be hazardous for a one-year-old. Respond quickly and calmly to prevent children from hurting themselves or another child.

Safety Inspections

Indoor and outdoor play areas should be inspected daily for safety hazards. Use a checklist. Check toys, equipment, and facilities for wear and damage. Report hazards such as torn carpeting and exposed wiring for immediate repair. Dispose of litter, especially glass and other hazardous waste.

Transportation Safety

Child care facilities must transport children safely, whether during field trips or daily trips to or from school. To ensure safety,

▶ conduct vehicle safety inspections.

▶ make sure drivers are legally licensed to drive the vehicles.

▶ equip vehicles with age-appropriate safety restraints such as seat belts, booster seats, and car seats.

▶ provide adequate adult supervision.

▶ equip each vehicle with a working two-way radio, a flashlight, a first aid kit, and a fire extinguisher.

Field Trip Safety

When conducted safely, field trips are an opportunity to expand children's knowledge and understanding of the world. Field trip vehicles should be parked in a safe, off-street area when children enter and exit them. Each child should wear a name tag identifying the program's name and telephone number in case a child is separated from the group. Invite parents along to increase supervision. Keep track of children by counting the number of children before leaving on the field trip and by counting them several times during the trip.

▲ **Field Trip**

Careful planning and extra supervision are needed to keep children safe on a field trip. *What are some field trip safety tips?*

Safety Documentation

In following a program's safety policy, staff members need to be familiar with the forms that they have to fill out as they work with children. These forms apply to the following:

▶ **Injuries.** All injuries, no matter how minor, must be recorded on an accident report form immediately after a child is treated. Use the accident report form to record specific information. Include the date and time of injury; witnesses to the injury; the location and equipment or products involved; the cause of the injury; the type of injury and how it was treated; and any action taken by a doctor, dentist, or emergency personnel. This form is placed in the child's file.

▶ **Suspected abuse.** Any suspected cases of child abuse or neglect must be documented and reported.

▶ **Releasing children.** Children may leave a program's care only with their custodial parent or legal guardian. Parents may sign a release waiver giving release permission to someone else. Before a child can be released, staff must see photo identification. In most programs, parents or guardians must sign the children in and out of the center. Special care must also be taken in cases of divorce, separation, or other circumstances in which it is necessary to know who has legal access to a child.

▶ **Emergency treatment waiver.** An emergency treatment waiver form is maintained for each child. This statement, signed by a parent or legal guardian, gives the program permission to secure emergency medical treatment for a sick or injured child. These forms should be carried on field trips in case a child is injured.

READING CHECK **Describe** What areas and items should be checked for hazards during a safety inspection?

Staff Health and Safety

Early childhood programs also must protect the health and safety of the staff. Child care staff can experience a variety of workplace risks. Good programs take steps to reduce the risk of staff members becoming ill or injured while performing their jobs. For example, requiring staff to consistently follow universal precautions reduces their exposure to contagious disease and harmful substances, called **toxins**, that are in certain cleaning, sanitation, and pest-control products. Toxins can cause various illnesses, from rashes to flu-like illness.

Ensuring Staff Health and Safety

All child care centers must follow the health and safety standards issued by the Occupational Safety and Health Administration (OSHA). These guidelines for safety and health program management help employers prevent work-related injuries and illness. OSHA guidelines protect employees from exposure to hazards such as bloodborne pathogens by requiring universal precautions to be followed.

All staff members are required to submit a physician's report verifying their good health. In addition, each staff member must receive a negative result on a tuberculosis test annually. To lessen the risk of contagious disease, staff should get regular immunizations such as influenza, tetanus, and Hepatitis B.

Staff members at child care centers should obtain first aid and CPR certificates. In addition, many states require people who work with children to be fingerprinted and to submit to a criminal background check. Those who do not pass the criminal background check cannot be hired to work with children.

Leave Policies and Staff Substitutes

Employers with generous sick leave policies encourage staff to stay home when they have a contagious disease. In addition to sick leave, the Family and Medical Leave Act (FMLA) allows employees to take up to 12 weeks of unpaid, job-protected leave a year. Employees are required to have documentation and supervisor approval to be granted unpaid leave. Child care centers should keep a list of qualified staff substitutes who can provide good care for children when regular staff must be absent. When a staff member is absent from work, it is the director's responsibility to find another worker to fill the position.

SAFETY MATTERS

Protection Plans

To protect staff members from exposure to contagious diseases passed through blood, early childhood programs must follow a written plan. According to OSHA, the plans must contain the following:

- **Exposure Determination.** A list of job titles or duties that puts staff in contact with blood or blood-containing fluids, such as first aid and diapering.
- **Methods of Compliance.** A statement of how staff will follow the protection plan by limiting exposure to blood; following universal precautions; and cleaning, sanitizing, and disinfecting.
- **Hepatitis B Vaccination.** Hepatitis B is a virus passed through blood. Employers must offer vaccinations within ten days of employment at no cost to the staff.

What Would You Do? A toddler falls on the playground and gets a bloody nose. You need to respond to the injury and clean up the blood safely. What would you do?

Certifying Food Service Staff

Bacteria in improperly cooked or handled food can cause illness. Young children are at a high risk for developing foodborne illnesses. Food service staff must be regularly trained in proper food-handling and sanitation practices. Managers and staff may be required to obtain a **food service sanitation certificate** showing that they passed a state-administered test covering proper food handling practices. Food service staff should also follow the U.S. Department of Agriculture's (USDA) food safety guidelines:

▶ **Clean.** Use universal precautions for hand washing. Sanitize all food preparation surfaces and cooking utensils.

▶ **Separate.** Do not cross-contaminate foods. Keep different types of foods separate during preparation. Sanitize the work space and utensils before preparing another type of food.

▶ **Cook.** Prepare foods to the proper temperature, according to USDA guidelines.

▶ **Chill.** Refrigerate foods promptly at 40°F or below.

▶ **Serve.** Hot foods should be served at 140°F or above and cold foods at 40°F or below.

READING CHECK **List** What are three health and safety requirements for child care staff?

▼ **Bumps and Scrapes**

When minor injuries happen, a child care provider can usually treat them with items in a first aid kit. *What are three items you would find in a first aid kit?*

Emergency Skills

Child care staff must be able to respond to injuries and other health emergencies. If a child requires medical treatment, a staff member should give appropriate first aid and call for emergency medical assistance if needed. Staff need emergency skills training to respond to life threatening injuries and situations. The American Red Cross provides first aid, CPR, and other emergency skills training that can be used with infants, children, and adults.

Treating Minor Injuries

Minor injuries can be quickly treated with basic first aid. First aid is the care that is first given to an injured or sick person. For bumps and bruises, an ice pack lessens swelling. A scraped knee may require cleaning and a bandage. First aid training helps staff treat minor injuries. **Figure 5.3** describes basic first aid procedures.

A child care center should keep basic supplies, such as blankets, towels, and a first aid kit, on hand for minor injuries. First aid kits should

Pixtal/AGE Fotostock

Figure 5.3 First Aid Basics

Get Certified Reading about first aid is not a substitute for getting hands-on training. All child care professionals should be certified in first aid by the American Red Cross. *What should a child care provider do if a child has a splinter?*

Injury	What to Do	When to Seek Medical Attention
Nosebleeds	Have child lean slightly forward. Squeeze lower half of the child's nose with a tissue for about 10 minutes. Repeat if bleeding has not stopped.	If bleeding cannot be stopped after 20 minutes.
Open Wounds	Place sterile gauze pad on cut and apply pressure until bleeding stops. Clean the wound with soap and water. Apply an antiseptic and cover the wound with a bandage.	If wound is very deep, bleeding cannot be stopped, or there is an object in the wound.
Bumps and Bruises	Apply a cold pack for 10 minutes to minor bruises. A hard blow to the head requires immediate medical attention.	If child loses consciousness, complains of a headache, or vomits.
Splinters	If necessary, break the skin with a sterilized needle to expose splinter. Remove splinter with sterilized tweezers. Then apply antiseptic and bandage wound.	If splinter is glass or deeply embedded in skin or the eye.
Burns	For burns that produce just redness (first-degree burn), place burned area under cold water or apply a cold, wet cloth. Do not put ointment on the burn.	If burned area forms blisters (second-degree burn) or has broken or blackened skin (third-degree burn).
Insect Stings	Remove stinger by scraping with a sterile blunt-edged object. Wash area and apply a cold pack.	If child shows any signs of an allergic reaction.

include bandages, gauze pads and strips, adhesive tape, antiseptic wipes, antibiotic ointment, cold compress, scissors, disposable latex or vinyl gloves, and tweezers. Check first aid kit contents regularly and replace missing or expired items.

Treating Serious Injuries

If a child requires professional medical treatment, a teacher should administer first aid while someone else calls for emergency assistance. Then call the child's parents. Retrieve the medical treatment waiver from the child's file.

Choking

Young children are at a high risk for choking because they tend to put all kinds of objects into their mouths. Certain foods, such as hot dogs and grapes, are also choking hazards. Choking victims need immediate attention. For children older than one, use abdominal thrusts. An **abdominal thrust** is a quick, upward thrust with the heel of the hand into the abdomen that forces air from the lungs out to expel an object caught in the throat. This action should not be used on infants because of the possibility of internal injury. With conscious infants, trained staff members use a procedure called back blows and chest thrusts described in **Figure 5.4**.

Rescue Breathing

If a child stops breathing but has a heartbeat, staff must breathe for the child. This is called rescue breathing. The victim's head is tilted back, the chin is lifted, and the nose is pinched shut. The rescuer then seals his or her mouth over the victim's mouth and gives a breath about every five seconds. Staff members must be certified in order to perform rescue breathing.

Cardiopulmonary Resuscitation

Cardiopulmonary resuscitation (CPR) is used when a heartbeat or pulse is not detected for ten seconds. Chest compressions and gentle puffs of air are given to the person to help the heart circulate blood. CPR can keep a person alive until emergency medical professionals arrive. Staff must be certified in CPR before they can apply the technique.

Automated External Defibrillation

Many states now require that early childhood providers be trained in **automated external defibrillation** (AED). This procedure is used when there has been a disruption in a person's regular heart rhythm. AED requires an electrical shock that reestablishes a normal heart rhythm. Early CPR will help circulate oxygen-containing blood to vital body organs while an AED is prepared for use.

Accidental Poisoning

Poisoning is a serious medical emergency. Signs that may indicate poisoning include burns around or in the mouth and throat, nausea or vomiting, burns or rash on the skin, burning or irritation of the eyes or blindness, choking, coughing, headache, or dizziness.

Figure 5.4 Rescue Techniques for Choking Infants

Back Blows and Chest Thrusts Choking infants require immediate attention. *What is the purpose of giving the infant five quick blows to the back?*

Step 1 Place infant stomach-down across your forearm, using your thigh for support, and hold the infant's chest in your hand and jaw in your fingers.

Step 2 Point the infant's head downward and give up to five quick, firm blows to the infant's back with the heel of your hand.

If back blows fail to expel the object that is causing choking:

Step 3 Turn the infant face up. Lay the infant on your thigh or lap, and support the infant's head with your hand.

Step 4 Using your other hand, place two fingers on the middle of the infant's breastbone. Give up to five quick downward thrusts.

Step 5 Continue giving five back blows followed by five chest thrusts until the object is dislodged or the infant loses consciousness.

Step 6 If the child loses consciousness or starts to turn blue, immediate CPR is needed. Have someone call 911, and begin CPR if you have been trained.

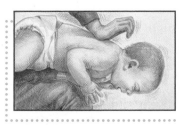

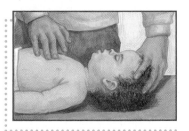

Figure 5.5   Common Household Poisons

Poisonous Substances Most poisonings occur when children eat or drink substances they have found. *What should you do if you think a child has swallowed a poisonous substance?*

Type of Poison	Examples	Type of Contact
Plants	Some wild mushrooms, English ivy, daffodil bulbs, rhubarb leaves, holly berries, poison ivy, poison oak	Swallowing, contact with skin or eyes
Medicines	Painkillers, stimulants, sleeping pills, aspirin, vitamins, cold medicines	Swallowing
Cleaning Products	Ammonia, laundry detergent, bleach, drain and toilet bowl cleaner, disinfectant, furniture polish	Swallowing, contact with skin or eyes, inhaling
Personal Care Products	Shampoo, conditioner, soap, nail polish remover, perfumes, aftershave, mouthwash, rubbing alcohol, lotions	Swallowing, contact with skin or eyes, inhaling
Gardening and Garage Products	Insecticide, fertilizer, insect repellent, paint and paint thinner, rodent poison, acids, gasoline, lighter fluid, antifreeze	Swallowing, contact with skin or eyes, inhaling

If you believe a child has touched, eaten, or inhaled a poison, quickly try to determine the cause. Immediately call a poison control center and follow the directions you receive. You will be asked to describe the poison, how it was taken, and the ingredients on the product container, if possible. **Figure 5.5** gives examples of common poisonous substances.

Handling Emergency Evacuations

When an emergency requires that child care professionals evacuate children from the program facility, staff must act swiftly and calmly. Regular emergency drills will help staff and children know what to do in case of a real emergency. Here are some tips for handling emergency evacuations:

▶ Immediately get children out of the building via the closest exit and to a safe place. Do not stop to get coats or shoes or even finish diapering a baby if you need to evacuate. Toddlers and other children may need to be carried to safety by staff.

▶ Designate one care provider to grab the sign-in sheet so that children can be accounted for when in a safe place.

▶ Put all infants into one evacuation crib that is on wheels to speed evacuation. Infants should always be cared for on the main floor of a facility for ease in evacuation.

Regardless of the emergency, the important thing for staff is to get all children in their care to a safe place. Then, notify families of the emergency relocation.

READING CHECK ✔ **State** What circumstances could require a child care professional to use emergency skills?

Child Nutritionist

What Does a Child Nutritionist Do?

Child nutritionists use scientific information to promote and teach healthful eating habits to children. Nutritionists plan food and nutrition programs, supervise meal preparation, and oversee the serving of meals at schools, early childhood centers, or medical facilities. They also help improve children's health by recommending dietary modifications that meet their specific needs.

Career Readiness Skills

Child nutritionists should be knowledgeable about relationships among science, diseases, and food. They must be good at communicating and teaching about nutrition. Nutritionists need to listen carefully to their clients. They must think independently to plan various dietary programs, and they must understand the federal food guidelines and recommendations. Nutritionists should also have strong math and science skills.

Education and Training

A bachelor's degree in usually required in dietetics, food service systems management, foods and nutrition, or a related area. College students take courses in foods, nutrition, and a variety of math and science classes. Graduate degrees also are available and usually expand job opportunities. Licensing requirements vary from state to state. Nutritionists can also receive a credential or specialize in an area such as diabetic nutrition, which can make them more competitive in the job market.

Job Outlook

Average employment growth is projected for child nutritionists over the next decade. This job growth will result from increasing emphasis on disease prevention through improved dietary habits. Public interest in nutrition and health education will also increase demand for nutritionists.

Critical Thinking Further research the role a child nutritionist would have in an early childhood setting. What early childhood health problems might a child nutritionist help with? Write a paragraph summarizing your findings.

Career Cluster

Health Science Child nutritionists work in the Therapeutic Services pathway of the Health Science career cluster. Other jobs in this career cluster include:

- Psychologist
- Social Worker
- Public Health Educator
- Health Information Coder
- Medical Technician
- Health Aide
- Fitness Trainer
- Patient Advocate
- Geneticist
- Health Care Administrator
- Dietetic Technician
- Registered Nurse
- Art Therapist
- Wellness Coach

Explore Further The Health Science career cluster contains five pathways: Therapeutic Services; Diagnostic Services; Health Informatics; Support Services; and Biotechnology Research and Development. Choose one of these pathways to explore further. Write a paragraph that summarizes your findings.

© Hero/Corbis/Glow Images

Health, Safety, and Emergency Response

Visual Summary

Child care professionals are entrusted with promoting the health and safety of the children in their care.

Promoting Health and Safety

Look for signs of illness during daily health checks when children arrive.

Wash hands frequently to reduce the spread of germs.

Use universal precautions to protect children and staff from contagious disease.

Know and follow program rules and procedures described in the safety policy.

Conduct daily safety inspections to identify hazards in indoor and outdoor play areas.

Take first aid and emergency skills training to learn how to respond safely to health emergencies.

Vocabulary Review

1. Create a fill-in-the-blank sentence for each of these vocabulary terms. The sentence should contain enough information to help determine the missing word.

Content Vocabulary

◇ immunizations (p. 106)
◇ pathogens (p. 107)
◇ universal precautions (p. 107)
◇ biohazardous (p. 108)
◇ hypothermia (p. 110)
◇ frostbite (p. 110)
◇ heat exhaustion (p. 110)

◇ screenings (p. 111)
◇ safety policy (p. 116)
◇ risk management plan (p. 116)
◇ toxins (p. 119)
◇ food service sanitation certificate (p. 120)
◇ abdominal thrust (p. 121)

◇ cardiopulmonary resuscitation (p. 122)
◇ automated external defibrillation (p. 122)

Academic Vocabulary

■ sensitivity (p. 113)
■ prevention (p. 117)

Review Key Concepts

2. Describe how child care professionals can limit the spread of contagious diseases.
3. Explain the practices child care professionals use to check for and report illnesses.
4. Define seven special health conditions that can affect children.
5. Summarize the rules and procedures in an effective early childhood program safety policy.
6. Identify procedures to maintain the health and safety of all staff members.
7. List the emergency skills training needed by staff members.

Critical Thinking

8. Explain how proper nutrition and exercise contribute to a child's health and wellness.

9. Critique your current classroom for safety hazards. If you were to conduct an activity with toddlers in the room, what items might pose potential hazards? Why are these items hazardous? What would you do to ensure the children's safety?

10. Analyze why is it important for a child care professional to protect his or her own health and safety. What are some steps he or she can take to reduce health and safety risks on the job?

21st Century Skills

Planning Skills

11. Plan a Safe Field Trip Taking children on a safe field trip requires detailed planning. Select a field trip destination for toddlers, such as the zoo or a fire station, and create a plan for a safe field trip. Include how you will transport the children, how many parent chaperones you will bring, how you will keep track of the children, what supplies you will bring, and any other safety considerations discussed in the chapter.

Information Skills

12. Investigate OSHA Regulations The Occupational Safety and Health Administration (OSHA) is a federal agency responsible for the regulations that ensure workplace safety and worker health. Explore the OSHA Web site and review the various kinds of regulations the agency enacts. Write a paragraph that describes the history and function of OSHA, and list any regulations that apply to a child care workplace.

Child Care LAB

Use the skills you have learned in this chapter.

Emergency Procedures

13. Plan for Emergency Situations In this activity, you will work in a group of four to plan and practice emergency procedures in a child care center.

A. Assign emergencies to group members. Assign one group member to each of the following emergencies: fire, tornado, hurricane, and earthquake.

B. Create an emergency plan. Research your assigned emergency and determine how the emergency should be handled in a child care center. Outline the actions a child care professional should take in an emergency situation, including how often emergency procedures should be practiced.

C. Practice emergencies procedures. Explain the emergency procedures for your topic to your group members. Lead your group in an emergency drill to practice your emergency plan. Revise your plan, if needed, based on what you learned during the practice drill or from group feedback.

D. Create an emergency procedures display. As a group, create a visual display such as a poster or bulletin board that describes the step-by-step procedures for each emergency. Include evacuation routes, if applicable, and general emergency best practices. Take a photograph of your display for your professional portfolio.

E. Present your display to the class. Share your display with the class and demonstrate one emergency procedure from your display.

Create Your Evaluation

Create an evaluation sheet with these categories:

- Information on emergencies
- Clarity of procedures
- Emergency procedure demonstration
- Display

Have your classmates use the sheet to evaluate your group's display and presentation, rating each category from 1 to 5 (1 = poor, 5 = excellent).

Academic Skills

English Language Arts

14. Children's Health Care Federal and state programs such as the Children's Health Insurance Program (CHIP) offer medical coverage for low-income families that cannot afford regular medical care or health insurance. Using the Internet, locate resources in your state for managing children's health care, such as insurance programs and county health clinics. Create a brochure that describes the programs' services.

Social Studies

15. Immunization Safety Immunizations have become the subject of debate recently. Some parents are deciding not to immunize their children because they believe vaccines are not safe. The medical community claims that immunizations are safe and essential for maintaining public health. Research both sides of the issue and evaluate each side's opinions. Should parents be able to decide not to immunize their children? Why or why not?

Science

16. Analyze Household Items for Safety Common household items such as buttons, cleaning products, and electrical cords can be potentially hazardous to young children. Household items can be choking hazards, poisonous, or potentially cause physical harm to a child.

Procedure Collect 15 common household items. Include a variety of types of items. Test each item for choking hazard using a no-choke testing tube or a tube that measures 1 ¼ inches wide by 2 ¼ inches long. Then determine if each item is poisonous. Examine each object for other potential hazards. For example, could it harm a child if used improperly? Record your test results in a table.

Item	Choking Hazard	Poison Hazard	Other Hazard
button	X		

Analysis Analyze your test results. Can the items be categorized by hazard? Did some objects pose multiple hazards? Summarize your results in a paragraph. Include suggestions for ways to keep children away from hazardous household items.

Certification Prep

Sharpen your test-taking skills to improve your certification program score.

Directions Read the sentence, and choose the best word or phrase to fill in the blank.

17. A(n) _____ is an extreme sensitivity to a common substance.

A. allergy

C. immunization

B. pathogen

D. toxin

18. Cardiopulmonary resuscitation (CPR) is used when _____.

A. a person is choking

B. a person stops breathing but has a heartbeat

C. a person stops breathing and does not have a heartbeat

D. a person has a disrupted heart rhythm

Test-Taking Tip

When answering a fill-in-the-blank question, read the sentence with each possible answer in the blank. The best word or phrase results in a sentence that is factual and grammatically correct.

(tl)©Nova Development; (tr)©Comstock/Alamy

CHAPTER 6

Observation Skills

Writing Activity

★ 21st Century Skills

Creativity When you write, use sensory details to help your reader see, hear, smell, taste, and touch your subject. Write a paragraph about an event or activity you recently observed. Use adjectives that describe the sights, sounds, and smells you observed—and possibly what you touched or tasted—during this event or activity.

Writing Tips

1. Start by writing adjectives that you can use to describe your subject.
2. Do not get too caught up in the details.
3. Do not use too many adjectives. This will confuse the reader.

Blend Images/Alamy

Explore the Photo
This teacher is observing children. *What might she be recording?*

Reading Guide

What You Want to Know Write a list of what you want to know about observing children. As you read, write the headings in this section that provide that information.

Read to Learn

Key Concepts

- **Explain** why early childhood teachers observe and record children's behavior.
- **Identify** five types of methods used for recording observations.
- **Summarize** behaviors that show children's development.
- **Describe** items to include in a child's portfolio that will reflect development.

Content Vocabulary

- ◇ objective observations
- ◇ subjective description
- ◇ naturalistic observation
- ◇ participant observer
- ◇ checklist
- ◇ anecdotal record
- ◇ running record
- ◇ frequency count
- ◇ rating scale
- ◇ authentic assessment

Academic Vocabulary

- ■ evaluate
- ■ bias

Main Idea

Observation of children helps early care professionals assess children's development so they can plan experiences to respond to and nurture that development.

Graphic Organizer

As you read, you will discover information about the types of observations that early care and education professionals use to identify and explain children's development. Use a KWL chart such as the one shown to record your thoughts as you read the chapter.

What I Know	What I Want to Know	What I Learned

Graphic Organizer *Go to* **connected.mcgraw-hill.com** *to print this Graphic Organizer.*

◇**Vocabulary**

You can find definitions in the glossary at the back of this book.

Observing Children

Those who work with children never stop observing. Early care and education professionals systematically record the details of observations and put these details to use in various ways. Early childhood professionals observe and record children's behavior to

▶ know individual children better. Observations help care providers learn about each child's abilities, interests, and level of development.

▶ identify special needs. Observation records help determine whether a child needs special services or programs, such as speech therapy, counseling, or a gifted program.

▶ address specific problems. Observing children helps early educators respond wisely and sensitively to problem behaviors.

▶ guide curriculum development. Observing the play, interests, and abilities of children helps care providers plan more motivating experiences.

▶ document progress and assess skill development. Care providers and parents want to know how children are progressing in their development. When observation records are kept, development can be tracked. This information helps guide activity planning.

▶ **Daily Records**

A lot goes on in an early childhood setting each day. The practice of observing and recording behavior helps focus your attention on details that might otherwise be missed. *What details might you record?*

Paul Burns/Tetra Images/CORBIS

- **evaluate**, or determine the value of, the program. Observations help staff determine whether all the program goals are being met effectively and efficiently.
- learn about child development. Even the most experienced early childhood staff members gain a deeper understanding of children from firsthand observation.

READING CHECK ✔ **Connect** How do child care professionals use observations to guide curriculum development?

Becoming a Skilled Observer

It may seem easy to watch children at play, but developing a keen eye for detail requires effort and practice. Concentration and a good attention span result in better observations. Learning how to observe without interfering takes skill, too. This chapter includes ways to build your observation skills.

Observer Conduct

When you observe children, your goal is to see what would naturally happen if you were not present. Observers should do their best not to influence the activities they observe. It is important to be quiet, courteous, and respectful to children and others you observe. When there is no separate observation booth or room, follow these guidelines for observer conduct:

- Sit in a low chair.
- Position yourself to the side but where you can still observe easily.
- Wear simple, appropriate clothing.
- Do not start a conversation with children or maintain eye contact.
- If a child asks what you are doing, give a brief but honest answer. You might say, "I am writing how children play so I can remember it later."
- Do not interfere in what is going on unless a child is in immediate danger and no other adult is available.

Ethics and Confidentiality

To ensure that the privacy of a child and family is protected, observation records must remain confidential. Do not leave them in open view for others to see. If the records will be shared with people other than the child's program staff, a custodial parent or legal guardian must give written permission. If observations are used in research, consider using false names or initials to identify children who have been observed.

Making Objective Observations

Observations are not useful unless they reflect what really happens. It is important for observers to keep facts separate from

---

A Matter of ETHICS

Parent Relationships

Observing children sometimes requires a child care professional to make interpretations and judgment calls based on the data collected.

Sensitive Issues

When explaining difficult news to parents, consider how they may feel hearing what you are saying. Be sure that your supervisors approve of your interaction with the parents.

Thinking Ethically

After working with a one-year-old girl, you are concerned that she is showing signs of developmental delays, and you believe the parent should have her evaluated by a specialist. The parent disagrees and will not take the child to get help. What do you do? What do you say to the parent?

Objectivity

Make clear unbiased observation statements when recording your observations of children. *What may be the consequences of making subjective rather than objective observation statements?*

personal opinions, preferences, or **bias**, (bī'-əs) a tendency to favor one side. **Objective observations** record facts rather than personal opinion or bias. An objective observation might state: "Shannon walked into the room with her head held down. She was dragging her sweater on the ground behind her." A **subjective description**, on the other hand, is an observation based on personal judgments and might state: "Shannon was depressed as she came into the room." While you observe, your job is to record facts. Later, you can think about your impressions of what took place. Was Shannon depressed, or was she tired, ill, lonely, or disappointed? Do you have enough information to decide? Others may want to read what you have recorded and draw their own conclusions. If your observation does not contain the facts, it is difficult to draw conclusions.

Objective observations require you to record only what you actually see happen, not what you hear about secondhand. Do not record that a child hit another unless you actually saw it happen. You may, however, report that a child told you someone was hit. The difference is small but very important. Recorded observations should include the following:

▶ Your name so that others will know who made the observation
▶ The date and the beginning and ending times
▶ A list of children involved and their ages
▶ A list of any adults involved
▶ Identification and brief description of the setting
▶ Specific behaviors in the order they happen
▶ Specific events in the order they happen

Interpreting Observations

Observations give information that can be helpful when reviewed and interpreted. When interpreting observations, early childhood professionals look for patterns and try to draw conclusions about the causes and meaning of behavior. Interpretations must be made with care. Experienced professionals resist drawing conclusions based on one observation. Instead, they review a series of observations. These may have been collected over several days, weeks, or months. Professionals base their interpretations on facts, experience, and training. They do not base them on personal likes and dislikes.

Early care specialists also make interpretations based on a child's individual culture and past experiences. Behavior that is respectful in one family or culture may not be acceptable in another. For example, wise observers realize that their interpretation is only an educated guess, so before interpreting facts, they consult with a child's family for clearer understanding.

READING CHECK ✔ Connect What should be provided in an observation record?

Observation Style and Methods

Observing is a purposeful, structured task that can be done using a variety of systematic methods. Researchers sometimes place children in special experimental situations to see how they react. However, early childhood professionals are more likely to observe children in their regular daily setting.

Naturalistic Observation

Early childhood teachers in the classroom commonly use a style of observation called **naturalistic observation**. It means the observer watches children and records their natural behaviors as they occur.

With this style, the observer is called a **participant observer**, or someone who interacts with children while observing. The participant observer still talks to the children and leads them in activities. During the activities, he or she notices details about the children's behavior and writes these details on index cards or a note pad. This keeps the children from becoming distracted by the presence of the observer.

SAFETY MATTERS

Activity Safety

Observations can be used to evaluate the environment of a child care facility. It is important to manage the space so that the learning environment is safe and healthy and encourages activity. When observing a physical activity, make sure each participant has enough space to do the activity. If you are leading an activity, you should be able to see each participant.

What Would You Do? While observing a classroom, you notice that the children are tripping on toys and furniture. What recommendations could you make to encourage better safety practices in the classroom? How could you express this in a professional manner?

► **Unseen
Observation**
··

A one-way mirror allows
observers to see into the
classroom without distracting children from their
normal activities. *What are
some possible advantages
and disadvantages of the
style?*

The naturalistic style of observing is convenient, but it also has drawbacks. When you interact with children, you become a part of the situation you are observing. This makes it difficult to step back and to see the situation as an outsider. In addition, thinking about what you are doing can distract you from what you are observing. Finally, you may not have time to record your observations right away or in as much detail as you would like.

It is often better if someone who is strictly an observer makes observations. This ensures that the observer is more likely to be objective. This person might be one of the classroom staff, who is temporarily assigned to observe rather than participate. It might also be a child care student who is visiting the classroom for the purpose of recording observations.

If an observer hovers over children with a clipboard, the children will know that something unusual is going on. Therefore, the observer must make his or her presence felt as little as possible.

Sometimes the observer views children from another room equipped with a one-way viewing window and, sometimes, headphones connected to classroom microphones that pick up speech. More often, the observer has no choice but to sit in the same room with the children. In that case, the observer must take care to stay in the background as much as possible.

Observation Methods

Early childhood staff use several systematic methods for recording observations. The method you choose depends on your purpose for observing. Some commonly used methods are described below.

Checklist

A **checklist** is simply a list of specific information for which an observer is looking. It can be used to study the environment, but more often a checklist identifies children's developmental behavior or skills. When the child demonstrates a behavior or skill, such as drinking from a cup, the observer either makes a check mark or writes the date next to the appropriate item on the list. Additional space may be provided for comments or descriptions. Some early childhood educators update each child's checklist weekly. Others may do so only twice a year. Checklists are useful for parent-teacher conferences because they can give parents a picture of how their children are developing. **Figure 6.1** shows a sample developmental checklist.

Figure 6.1 **Sample Checklist**

Digital Records This is a short example of a developmental checklist. A complete checklist could include a longer list of developmental skils. Many early child care centers are beginning to use digital programs to document their observations. *How is a checklist different from a rating scale?*

Developmental Checklist for Angel G.

Class Level: Infant Room
Collection Period: 1
Academic Year: 20___/20___

Developmental Skill	Not Yet	In Progress	Proficient	NA
Physical Development				
1. Sits alone	●	○	○	○
2. Reaches for objects	○	●	○	○
3. Holds objects	○	○	●	○
4. Rolls front to back	○	○	●	○
5. Rolls back to front	○	●	○	○
6. Imitates actions	●	○	○	○
7. Responds to sounds	○	○	●	○
8. Vocalizes	○	○	●	○
Social and Emotional Development				
1. Smiles	○	○	○	●
2. Recognizes parents	○	●	○	○

SUBMIT

Anecdotal Record

A written description that focuses on a particular incident is called an **anecdotal record** (a-nik-'dō-t°l). Early care and education staff might use an anecdotal record to observe how a child interacts with classroom materials and how his or her development is enhanced. The record includes where and when an incident took place, who was involved, and what was said and done. For instance, you might write an anecdotal record about the interaction among several children in the dramatic play area. You would describe everything the children do and say, including tone of voice, facial expressions, and body language. **Figure 6.2** shows an example of an anecdotal record.

Running Record

With a **running record**, the observer creates a sequential record of anything that happens during a specific period of time. The time period may be as short as ten minutes or may last all day. The observer may write everything that happens during the time period or may observe and record at specific intervals within the time period. For example, a staff member may want to identify a toddler's developmental abilities. The staff member decides to observe for ten minutes. During this time, the staff member writes what the toddler is doing and saying each minute. When completed, the notes provide insight into the child's current skills. **Figure 6.2** shows a partial running record.

Frequency Count

A record of the number of times a particular behavior or situation occurs during a specific period of time is called a **frequency count**. A tally sheet is used for recording this information. The observation may focus on one child or include several children. Repeating the frequency count at a later date can help you see whether the behavior is occurring more or less often than before. For example, to find out how often conflicts occurred on the playground, a preschool teacher

---

Figure 6.2 Sample Anecdotal Record

Written Form This is an example of an anecdotal record. Note that the example gives a short description of the event without drawing conclusions. *How is a running record different from an anecdotal record?*

Anecdotal Record Form

Child's Name _Courtney, age 4_

Date: _9/23_ Time: _11:15 a.m._ Place: _Dramatic Play Center_

Notes: _After Courtney played alone in the play center, she_
started to leave. All of the dress-up clothes she had used
were on the floor. When reminded of the rule for putting
things away, Courtney walked away.

---

made five observations during the day. Each observation period was three minutes long. No notes were made—only a tally mark indicated each episode. Totaling the tally marks gave an indication of how serious the problem was. Later, after further investigation and corrective measures, another frequency count showed that the number of incidents had decreased.

Rating Scale

In a **rating scale**, the observer records a letter or numerical evaluation of listed items. The listed items might focus on children's abilities or behaviors. The items might also focus on the characteristics of the center's environment. For example, the observer might rate a child's skill in performing a certain task on a scale of 1 to 5. As with checklists, rating scales are often used periodically throughout the year to give an overall picture of a child's development and can help determine the rate of progress a child is making. Early childhood professionals may develop checklists and rating scales for their specific use. These items also can be purchased from suppliers of educational materials.

READING CHECK ✓ **Connect** Why should a nonparticipant observer stay in the background?

Assessing Children's Development

As you have read, people observe children for various reasons. Some reasons to observe are to identify a child's skills, needs, and rate of progress. To determine a child's overall development, you should observe him or her in a variety of situations over time. Collect details about all areas of development, including physical, intellectual, social, and emotional. Your knowledge of development will help you learn what to look for. Some of the basics are descibed below.

Observing Development

Clues to physical development include the child's appearance, health, and physical abilities. Observe and record the following:

▶ Signs of health

▶ Changes in napping, toileting, or eating habits

▼ Developmental Basics

Your knowledge of development will help you learn what to look for when observing children. *What specific areas do you focus on when observing physical and intellectual development?*

(t)Comstock/Alamy; (b)IT Stock Free

▶ Evidence of large and small muscle skills

▶ Evidence of eye-hand coordination

To observe intellectual development, note how children think and cope with daily experiences. When observing, pay attention to the following:

▶ Problem-solving ability

▶ Ability to recognize shapes, colors, letters, numbers, sizes, and spatial relationships

▶ Vocabulary development and the ability to communicate effectively

▶ Use of imagination and creativity.

Observation can also give clues to children's social development. Observers should note the following:

▶ Social skills, such as sharing, cooperation, and taking turns

▶ Ability to follow directions

▶ Ability to accept responsibility

▶ Number and types of friendships maintained

▶ Small- and large- group play skills

Children give hints about their current level of emotional development through behavior. Observations should include the following:

▶ Evidence of identity and self-esteem

▶ Methods of dealing with frustration

▶ Evidence of trust and attachment to classroom adults

▶ Ability to express feelings

Becoming a skilled observer takes practice. The more often you observe, the more effective you will become at noting and recording the details of children's behavior. If you continue in the child care field, you will gain the experience required to make sound judgments when interpreting ovservations. Firsthand observation of children will help give you the insight needed by a child care professional.

Maintaining Observation Records

Observation records should be filed for later reference. Several easy systems can be used for keeping observations organized and confidential. All records that pertain to individual children should be placed together under each child's name. Some teachers keep a file folder, accordion file, or tabbed ring binder for each child. Others keep electronic observation records. Care providers and their supervisors should review the records periodically to make sure they are collecting adequate information about each child in the program.

Records that deal with certain situations can be organized and filed in some systematic and secure manner. For example, a study of how often children use a particular toy on the playground might be filed under "active play."

Collecting Samples of Children's Work

Observation is one way to gather details about children's development. Another way is collecting samples of their work and storing them for reference. For instance, samples of children's artwork reveal creativity and ability to use their small muscles to handle art tools. Audio recordings of stories told to a teacher illustrate a child's language, vocabulary, and ability to apply concepts. Videos of children during dress-up play allow observers to witness imagination and emerging social skills. Photos of children's block buildings show their understanding of size, shape, and spatial concepts.

These collections of work—often called portfolios or **authentic assessment**—can be shared during parent-teacher conferences to illustrate children's development. Teachers also use portfolios when preparing either a more challenging—or less challenging—activity for a particular student. See **Figure 6.3.** Child development specialists also review a child's portfolio items when creating individualized lesson plans for children with special needs.

READING CHECK ✔ **Recall** What are two common ways that child care professionals assess children's development?

Figure 6.3 Sample Portfolio Items

Authentic Assessment These two artworks are samples of pieces that would go in a child's portfolio. The teacher can share them with the parents and use them to plan unique lesson plans for the child's further development.

How can these drawings be used to assess the child's development?

College & Career
R E A D I N E S S

Choosing the Right College

How Do I Choose the Right College?

Deciding which college to attend is a very important decision. There are many factors that you must consider when choosing a college. Your life goals, financial concerns, and personal preferences all have a role in your choice. Should you stay close to home or move away? Should you go to a four-year college or a two-year college? Should you go to a college in a big city? Should you pick a college that specializes in a specific area? These are just some of the questions you will need to ask yourself.

What are some things I should consider when selecting a college?

There are many different things you should think about when trying to decide which college to attend. You sould research and consider the following:

- Size of the student body
- Location
- Campus life, including housing, extracurricular activities, athletics, and social clubs
- Cost
- Classes and programs offered

You might also want to find out about the geographic, ethnic, racial, and religious diversity of the students.

Are there different types of colleges?

Yes, and different colleges suit different people. Liberal arts colleges offer a broad base of courses in humanities. Universities are generally bigger than colleges, with larger classes and more class options. Community colleges offer two-year degrees in programs that prepare you for the job market. If you have a clear idea about what you want to do, a specialized college might be a good choice. You will also need to decide between public colleges, which are usually less expensive, and private colleges, which are often smaller. Finally, you might want to consider a special interest college, such as a single-sex or religious college.

Hands-On

Think about what you need to consider when choosing a college. Complete a self-assessment and use it to write a list of qualifications you would look for in your potential college. Then go online to find colleges that match your list. There are many Web sites that allow you to search for colleges by various features.

Path to Success

Tips for Choosing the Right College

Start Early College is closer than you think. Start your decision-making process early.

Talk It Over There are many people you can talk to about this decision, including your friends, school guidance counselor, teachers, and parents.

Do the Research There is information on the Internet and in print about choosing the right college.

Create a List Develop a list of conditions you want to use to evaluate and eliminate colleges.

Write It Down Creating a chart of the pros and cons of each college you are considering can be helpful.

Visit! If you can, visit some of the colleges you are considering.

Observation Skills

Visual Summary

Early childhood professionals can use various methods to record observations and children's development.

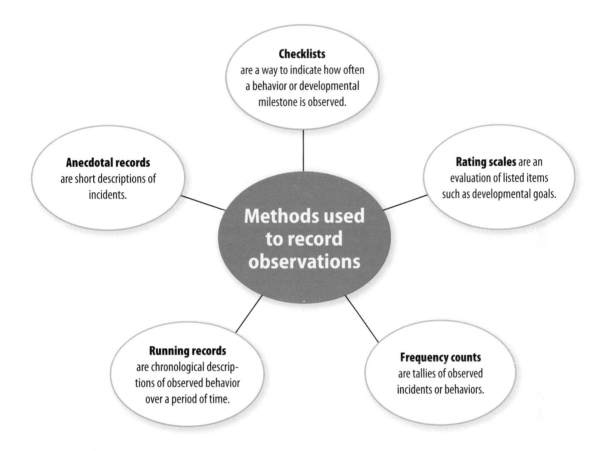

Checklists are a way to indicate how often a behavior or developmental milestone is observed.

Rating scales are an evaluation of listed items such as developmental goals.

Anecdotal records are short descriptions of incidents.

Methods used to record observations

Running records are chronological descriptions of observed behavior over a period of time.

Frequency counts are tallies of observed incidents or behaviors.

Vocabulary Review

1. Use at least six of these content and academic vocabulary terms to write a brief essay about conducting an observation.

Content Vocabulary

◇ objective observations (p. 132)
◇ subjective description (p. 132)
◇ naturalistic observation (p. 133)
◇ participant observer (p. 133)
◇ checklist (p. 135)
◇ anecdotal record (p. 136)
◇ running record (p. 136)

◇ frequency count (p. 136)
◇ rating scale (p. 137)
◇ authentic assessment (p. 139)

Academic Vocabulary

■ evaluate (p. 131)
■ bias (p. 132)

Review Key Concepts

2. **Explain** why early childhood teachers observe and record children's behavior.
3. **Identify** five types of methods used for recording observations.
4. **Summarize** behaviors that show children's development.
5. **Describe** items to include in a child's portfolio that will reflect development.

Critical Thinking

6. **Recall** the type of information included in an anecdotal record. When is an anecdotal record appropriate?

7. **Support** When observing children, consider why appropriate observer conduct should be strictly monitored. Why are the guidelines important to follow?

8. **Appraise** What factors might cause early childhood professionals to interpret the same observation records differently?

9. **Apply** A parent asks whether you think her child is ready to write her own name. What information would you use to help you answer this question?

10. **Extend** Objectivity is important when describing behavior. Is it also important when using other recording methods, such as a checklist or frequency count? Explain.

21st Century Skills

Critical Thinking Skills

11. **Collecting and Analyzing Samples** Collect samples of children's completed art projects, audiotapes of children's stories, videotapes of children during dress-up play, or snapshots of children's block building. Analyze the samples for evidence of the children's levels of development, and recommend goals for the children based on your findings. What are the benefits of using samples to assess children's development?

Management Skills

12. **Appropriate Programs** Observations can be used to evaluate the strengths and weaknesses of an early care and education program. Imagine you are a program director. Create a checklist that you could use to evaluate a classroom in your program. Research your state requirements and use them to create a list of recommendations for classroom goals. Include a plan for storing the records.

Child Care LAB

Use the skills you have learned in this chapter.

Observation Forms

13. **Multiple Observation Options** In this activity, you will create and use appropriate forms for observations.

   A. **Research development.** Investigate a physical, emotional, social, or intellectual developmental skill to determine what signs to look for at a particular age.

   B. **Create a rating scale.** Create a rating scale that might be used in observing a child's developmental level and participation in related activities.

   C. **Create a running record.** Create a running record that could be used when observing the same activity.

   D. **Conduct an observation.** Complete an observation, and use your forms to report the results.

   E. **Evaluate results.** Are the children meeting developmental milestones? Draw conclusions based on the observations. Then analyze how well your forms worked and which one was better for the observation you did. Write the results.

Create Your Evaluation

Create an evaluation sheet with the following categories:

• Appropriate forms

• Observation records completed

• Conclusions

Ask your classmates to use the sheet to evaluate your observation forms and conclusions, rating each category from 1 to 10.

Academic Skills

 ### English Language Arts

14. Objective Writing With a partner, use pictures from magazines to write objective descriptions of what you see. After you both look at the same picture, write separate descriptions. Then compare and analyze what you have each written, looking for any subjective observations. Rewrite these to make them objective.

 ### Social Studies

15. Child Development Around the World
Different cultures have different expectations for when some developmental changes such as toileting, crawling, and walking will occur. Working in a small group, choose a developmental milestone and research the expectations for when children will reach that milestone in the United States and three other countries or regions. Present your findings to the class. Include any differences between cultures that may explain the variation in expectations.

 ### Mathematics

16. Observing Naps Changes in napping habits are one of the basics that childhood professionals look for in a child's overall development. A care provider recorded the daily napping habits of her children for one week. Look at the table below and find the mean, median, and mode for Kristin's data.

Name	Monday	Tuesday	Wednesday	Thursday	Friday
Chad	45 min.	29 min.	39 min.	41 min.	35 min.
Candace	49 min.	40 min.	45 min.	49 min.	43 min.
Kristin	48 min.	43 min.	36 min.	48 min.	45 min.
Miles	42 min.	43 min.	40 min.	39 min.	45 min.

Math Concept **Data Analysis** Mean is the average for a set of values. Median is the middle data value when a set of data is ordered from least to greatest. If there are two middle values, then find the mean (average) of the two numbers. Mode is the value that appears the most in a set of data. If all the values appear the same number of times, then there is no mode.

Starting Hint Locate the data for Kristin and write it on a separate sheet of paper before calculating median, mean, and mode..

 For more math practice, go to the math appendix at the back of the book.

 ## Certification Prep

Sharpen your test-taking skills to improve your certification program score.

Directions Choose the correct answer for each of the questions below.

17. Physical development is assessed by observing all but which of the following?

   A. Small- and large-group play skills

   B. Changes in napping, toileting, or eating habits

   C. Evidence of large and fine motor skills

   D. Signs of health

18. Confidentiality rules for observation mean that you can share your results with which people?

   A. Parents, coworkers, and students

   B. Coworkers and your supervisor

   C. Parents and students

   D. Parents and your supervisor

Test-Taking Tip

In a multiple-choice test, the answers are usually specific and precise. Read the question first and carefully. Then read all of the answer choices. Eliminate answers that you know are incorrect.

CHAPTER 7

Preventing
Abuse and Neglect

Writing Activity

★ 21st Century Skills

Communication Imagine you are a child care center director. Write a memo to your staff explaining the center's position on the seriousness of abuse and neglect, what to look for, and what to do about it.

Writing Tips

1. For the form of the memo heading, follow this sequence: To, From, Date, and Subject.
2. Write concise sentences that clearly state your thoughts and link sentences together logically.
3. Support your position with facts, statistics, and citations.
4. Reread your memo when you are finished, proofreading for errors in spelling and grammar.

Explore the Photo

Individual attention helps a child to build trust. *Why is trust important in a situation involving child abuse or neglect?*

Ingram Publishing

Reading Guide

Pace Yourself Short, concentrated blocks of reading are more effective than one long session. Focus on reading for 10 minutes. Take a short break. Then read for another 10 minutes.

Read to Learn

Key Concepts

- **Identify** the types of child abuse.
- **Describe** five signs of child abuse or neglect.
- **Identify** documenting and reporting responsibilities of early childhood staff.
- **Explain** ways to prevent child abuse and neglect.

Content Vocabulary

◇ child abuse
◇ child neglect
◇ documenting
◇ crisis nursery
◇ resilience

Academic Vocabulary

■ investigate
■ alternative

Main Idea

Child abuse and neglect happen in all neighborhoods and to children of all races and economic backgrounds. Early childhood professionals are among the people who can help prevent child abuse and neglect. Because they see children daily, they are in a unique position to help children who suffer from abuse and neglect.

Graphic Organizer

As you read, look for information about the signs of possible physical, emotional, and sexual abuse. Use a graphic organizer like the one shown to help you organize your information.

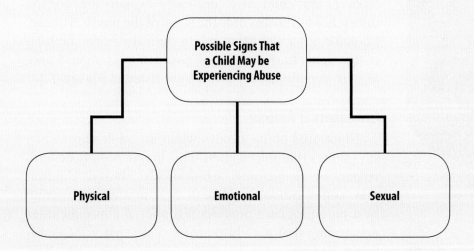

Possible Signs That a Child May be Experiencing Abuse

- Physical
- Emotional
- Sexual

Graphic Organizer *Go to* **connected.mcgraw-hill.com** *to print this Graphic Organizer.*

AS YOU READ

Connect Think about a positive interaction you have witnessed between a parent and a child. What can you learn about parenting from this interaction?

◇**Vocabulary**

You can find definitions in the glossary at the back of this book.

Ways to Help

Social workers often use dolls and toys to help children talk about sensitive issues such as abuse. *Why is it difficult to talk to children about abuse?*

Understanding Child Abuse and Neglect

In the federal Child Abuse Prevention and Treatment Act (CAPTA), research indicates that one million children every year are affected by abuse and neglect. A child is often abused by a family member or trusted friend. Abuse that happens in the home is called domestic violence. Abuse or neglect can have lasting effects on the child and on the family. The impact to society can also be high. Tax dollars are used to support public child welfare agencies, foster care, counseling services, and other programs related to abuse. Any sign of abuse needs to be reported. Families in crisis need to be offered guidance and counseling options. Because child care professionals see children daily, they are in a unique position to help keep children safe.

Types of Abuse

Child abuse occurs when an intentional injury is inflicted on a child. The injury may be physical, sexual, or emotional in nature. Early childhood professionals must recognize the symptoms of each type of child abuse.

Physical Abuse

Physical abuse involves physical contact that is intended to intimidate or cause suffering to the child. Physical abuse often results in visible injury to the child's body. Because children frequently injure themselves through play, how can you tell the difference between abuse and a routine injury? Normal bruising often occurs on bony areas such as the knees, shins, and forehead. Watch for a severe injury, repeated injuries, and indications from the child that something out of the ordinary is occurring. Notice if a parent and child have conflicting explanations for the injury. Some abusers hide the signs of the physical abuse. Look for other signs that might indicate that something is not right. Early childhood professionals should note any, or a combination, of the signs listed in **Figure 7.1**.

Emotional Abuse

Emotional abuse occurs when an adult chronically says things that hurt a child. This language may be foul, vulgar, or demeaning. Emotionally abused children may suffer ridicule, torment, and unmerciful teasing by a parent or care provider. Emotional abuse includes demanding that a child perform tasks that are too difficult. Failing to provide a child with continuing affection and emotional support is also considered abusive. In addition, encouraging children to commit illegal acts such as stealing is emotional abuse. See Figure 7.1 for signs of emotional abuse.

Sexual Abuse

When someone subjects a child to any sexual activity, sexual abuse occurs. This includes showing pornography, taking inappropriate photographs, incest, and rape. This may also include genital exposure, touching personal body parts (either the child's or the adult's), and other inappropriate sexual contact. Sexual abuse most often begins before age seven. The blind trust children have in adults makes them vulnerable to abuse. Abusers often intimidate and scare children to keep them from telling anyone about the abuse. For example, children may fear being physically hurt if they tell about the abuse. See Figure 7.1 for signs that a child may be suffering from (or experiencing) sexual abuse.

Figure 7.1 **Signs That Child May Be Experiencing Abuse**

Signs Many signs of abuse can appear as routine injuries. *How can you tell if an injury is not routine?*

Types	Signs of Abuse
Physical	• Shows sudden change in behavior, at home and at school • Displays unexplained learning problems • Lacks adult supervision • Has unexplained or repeated injuries (bumps, bruises, fractures, burns, welts, cuts) • Has untreated medical conditions • Is always watchful or fearful, as though waiting for something bad to happen • Shows reflexive fear, such as shielding self from a sudden blow • Appears frightened of parent • Is overly compliant, passive, or withdrawn • Displays no desire to go home • Shows evidence of malnutrition or dehydration
Emotional	• Displays low self-esteem or calls self names • Expresses sadness, depression, a sense of hopelessness, or displays extreme shyness • Lacks self-confidence • Demonstrates delayed emotional development • Acts out aggressively, has uncontrollable outbursts, or uses foul, demeaning language • Acts inappropriately for age (infantile or adult) • Displays unusual anxiety or excessive fear of making mistakes • Displays stuttering or other speech difficulties that have not been present earlier • Appears to have trouble sleeping • Shows changes in appetite or has regular complaints of an upset stomach • Displays unwillingness to try new things • Withdraws from activities and other children • Attempts suicide
Sexual	• Displays unusual sexual knowledge for the child's age. • Has soreness, sensitivity, or injury in genital regions • Has nightmares or bedwetting • Displays a change in appetite • Demonstrates very low self-esteem • Creates drawings with sexual themes or advanced sexual play with peers or dolls

Child Neglect

Child neglect is the failure to provide a child with the basic necessities of life, including food, clothing, shelter, and medical care. Because young children cannot care for themselves, they need reliable attention from adults. A child who is neglected may be left without adult supervision for hours, days, or weeks at a time. Neglect puts a child's emotional and physical health and safety at risk.

It is possible to neglect a child both physically and emotionally. Emotional neglect is depriving a child of a basic emotional need such as love or attention. Physical neglect is depriving a child of a basic physical need. A child who routinely lacks good hygiene, nutrition, shelter, appropriate clothing, medical care, or dental care may be suffering from neglect. Neglected children may be deprived of sleep, so they are often tired. Some neglected children develop behavioral problems and demand more of a teacher's attention and time. Others are quiet and shy and often wander aimlessly. A child might have difficulty concentrating or have a limited attention span that could result in learning problems.

▲ Stress

Stress in an adult's life can sometimes lead to abuse. *What are some ways to deal with stress in a positive way?*

Factors That Can Lead to Abuse

Although abuse can occur in any family, there are certain factors that are associated with abuse. Parents and others who abuse or neglect children often suffer from low self-esteem. Many are very young parents or have poor coping skills. They may lack knowledge about parenting and appropriate care for their child. They might have unrealistic expectations for being a parent. Some of these individuals were abused children themselves. Parents may be stressed due to financial difficulties or unemployment and take out their frustrations on the child. A parent who is dependent on alcohol or other drugs is also more likely to abuse or neglect a child. The following are signs that an adult may be abusing a child:

▶ Sees the child as bad, worthless, or a burden

▶ Shows little concern for the child

▶ Makes frequent demands that the child cannot achieve

▶ Asks child care professionals to use physical discipline if the child misbehaves

- Denies child's problems in school or at home
- Rarely looks at or interacts with the child
- Looks primarily to the child for care, attention, and satisfaction of emotional needs
- Blames or berates the child
- Is not concerned with the child's welfare
- Rejects the child emotionally
- Is secretive
- Is overprotective of the child
- Limits contact with other children

Effects of Abuse

Abuse and neglect have short-term consequences in children. A child may have injuries, behavioral problems, or excessive fears. Abuse and neglect also have long-term consequences for the child, the family, and for society. Some children are able to adapt in a positive way but others adapt to abuse in ways that are damaging to themselves. If a child is being mistreated or abused by a family member, his or her concept of what is a healthy, positive relationship can be distorted. A child may have problems developing close relationships with others and as they become adults may also have trouble at work.

If a child is overly fearful or avoids new experiences, he or she may lose the important learning that occurs through this exploration. This could interfere with intellectual development. Problems in school that are caused by reactions to abuse and stress can have the long-term effect of keeping a young adult from pursuing goals such as college or a steady job.

The constant stress caused by abuse can have physical effects on a child. The child could develop reactions such as being overly startled, inattentive, or unemotional. As a child develops into adolescence and adulthood, he or she could seek high-risk behaviors and experiences. High-risk behaviors such as unprotected sexual activity could put his or her health and life at risk.

Abuse can cause stress within a family, which can lead to divorce, substance abuse, or more physical violence. The cost to society can also be high. Public resources such as child welfare services and substance abuse programs are often costly. The high cost of the judicial system that provides for the abusers also has a financial impact on society.

READING CHECK **Understand** What are two signs that a child may be neglected?

Science *for Success*

Effects of Child Abuse and Neglect

Child abuse and neglect negatively affect children's physical, emotional, behavioral, and social development. The impact on children can include death, neurological damage, psychological problems, and high-risk behaviors that endanger children's health and relationships.

Procedure Research the immediate and long-term effects of abuse and neglect. How might the development of the brain be affected? Which mental health issues and disorders may by caused by child abuse and neglect? Which risky adolescent and adult behaviors have been linked to child abuse and neglect?

Analysis Using the information you gathered, draw conclusions about the negative impacts of child abuse and neglect. Share your conclusions in a brief report. If presentation software is available, you might consider creating a multimedia presentation.

©Comstock/Alamy

Responding to Child Abuse and Neglect

Children are put at great risk if suspicions of child abuse and neglect are ignored. Early childhood professionals and other caring adults must act on behalf of children to prevent or limit abuse and to help them overcome its harmful effects. The Victims of Child Abuse Act was developed to improve investigation and prosecution in child abuse cases.

Documenting and Reporting

All states have laws against child abuse and neglect. They also operate agencies staffed with social workers who **investigate**, or look into, suspected child abuse and neglect.

Child-abuse and neglect laws in all states require those who work with children to report suspected abuse or neglect. These people are called mandated reporters. Early childhood staff must file a report even if neglect or abuse is only suspected, not absolutely proven. Reporting suspected abuse is required even when the adult is a parent or a fellow staff member. Because accusations of abuse and neglect are very serious, professionals must act in good faith by reporting only those conditions that cause genuine concern for a child's health or safety.

Documenting is what care providers do when making a confidential, written record of suspected abuse or neglect. It includes recording what the staff member sees and the comments the parents make. Conversations staff members have about their concerns, including dates and information shared, must be recorded. Use photos to record physical injuries.

When reporting suspicious conditions, mandated reporters follow the guidelines set by their state child-abuse and neglect laws. In some states, reports can be made anonymously. Procedures for reporting abuse usually require calling the police or a child-abuse hotline or contacting the child-welfare agency. When calling in a report, you will need to report other facts besides the child's symptoms. Be prepared to provide basic information, such as the child's full name, age and birth date, address, and parents' names and home and work telephone numbers.

▼ **Reporting Abuse**

Physicians are mandated reporters. *What other professionals are considered mandated reporters?*

(c) Custom Medical Stock Photo/Alamy

When a report is filed, it should be documented in the child's file for future reference. Be sure to include the details of the report. Note that any type of documentation can be used in a court of law should the suspected abuse or neglect be found true.

Parent Referrals

Many early childhood programs offer evening workshops for adults on factors that lead to abuse. These programs address parenting topics such as developmental stages of children, **alternative** or other forms of discipline, and ways to cope with stress.

Referring parents to support groups such as Parents Anonymous can help relieve stress and prevent further abuse. Parents can also be informed of community mental health agencies that offer affordable family therapy or family violence prevention programs. These agencies can be found online or in your local telephone book under key headings such as counseling, social services, or behavioral health services.

Some communities have a **crisis nursery** that provides 24-hour child care services to parents who feel they might hurt their child. While at the crisis nursery, a child can be safely cared for while the parent receives support services such as emergency counseling.

▼ Parent Support

Child care professionals can refer parents in crisis to support groups or other resources. *Why is it important for parents in crisis to get help?*

Image Source/age fotostock

Building Children's Resilience

Life events such as child abuse and neglect often make children feel powerless and out of control. Those understandable feelings undermine their coping abilities. When a child has problems, there are things you can do to help build a child's resilience. **Resilience** occurs when children learn to cope with and eventually recover from difficult situations such as the hardships of abuse and neglect.

Children are known for bouncing back from difficult experiences, but they do not often do it alone. Research shows that a resilient child has formed a deep and trusting relationship with at least one adult in his or her life. Extended family and care providers are often those adults who make the difference for an abused or neglected child. Here are some things that early childhood professionals can do to help build resilience in children:

▶ ◢**Childhood Resilience**

Children are sometimes able to bounce back from harmful experiences. *How can a child care professional help a child build resilience?*

▶ Give children individualized attention.

▶ Spend quality time with children to build their sense of self-worth.

▶ Respond warmly to children to help them relax. This also helps children maintain a hopeful attitude even during hard times of life.

▶ Talk with children and listen to them closely. Listening to children's thoughts, fears, and feelings helps them sort out their emotions. Respond meaningfully when children share information or ask questions.

▶ Give children some decision-making power and control over their daytime experiences. Self-confidence is built when care providers encourage children to be independent in developmentally appropriate ways.

▶ Provide children with a consistent daily routine. When children live in fear, classroom routines promote a sense of security and stability. Abused and neglected children need to rely on predictable people and places to help them feel safe and cared for during times of extreme stress.

READING CHECK ✔ **Explain** What does it mean to be resilient?

Preventing Child Abuse and Neglect

Recognizing and reporting suspected child abuse and neglect can put an end to existing abuse. Child care professionals can also help prevent abuse from happening in a child care setting. One way is to screen early childhood staff prior to employment by conducting a criminal background check. This check, which usually involves fingerprinting, identifies people who have been convicted of a crime against children. Such a conviction would prevent employment in an early childhood program. There are other ways to prevent abuse as well.

Limiting Abuse Opportunities

Visibility and continuous supervision greatly reduce opportunities for abuse to occur. In early childhood programs, children should never be taken alone to a private room that can be locked by any staff member. Rooms with doors should have windows so staff may be easily observed at any time. Training on child abuse and neglect—including how to spot it, report it, and prevent it—should be provided yearly to staff members. Other ways to prevent or limit abuse in children include the following:

▶ Teaching children about the danger signs of abuse and how to protect themselves

▶ Providing strategies for resisting uncomfortable situations

▶ Teaching children how to say "no"

▶ Warning children about strangers

▶ Teaching children how to report abuse to a trusted adult

Protecting Staff

Child abuse can occur in any setting. Children need to be protected from child abuse, but early childhood staff members also need to protect themselves from false accusations. To avoid questions about your conduct with children, make sure you always supervise them with another adult present. This is especially important during nap time, toileting, outdoor play, and bus loading. This way a witness can verify that appropriate behavior was used. Be aware of a child's personal boundaries and respect that distance. Encourage parents to drop in and observe program activities in action. Child care professionals can help protect themselves from false accusations by practicing these behaviors. Any accusations of abuse should be documented and immediately reported to a supervisor.

READING CHECK ✔ **List** What are two ways that you can prevent abuse in a child care setting?

A Matter of ETHICS

Society's Role

Each member of society has an ethical responsibility to treat children well and report any signs of abuse or neglect. Child care staff are often the first professionals to see signs of abuse because they see children daily and can notice changes in behavior and mood.

Impact of Abuse

The child, the family, and society are all affected by abuse. Communities provide a variety of public services to respond to abuse and help the victims and their abusers. The cost to provide these services can be very high. Preventing abuse can greatly reduce the overall impact of abuse.

Thinking Ethically

You notice that a child at your center is starting to have trouble concentrating and cannot sleep at naptime. You learn the child's family is going through financial stress and divorce. You suspect abuse. What should you do as a member of society and as a child care professional?

Legal Advocate for Children

What Does a Legal Advocate for Children Do?

A legal advocate for children will provide legal advice or assistance to make sure that the best decisions are made based on a child's needs or legal rights. A legal advocate might also refer parents or children to resources such as counseling and substance abuse programs that can help. Many legal advocates are lawyers but some are paralegals. A paralegal is a nonlawyer with specialized training to assist lawyers.

Career Readiness Skills

Legal advocates must be able to understand complex legal information and explain it in plain language. They need to have strong communication, writing, research, and analytical skills.

Education and Training

A lawyer advocate needs to have a four-year college degree, complete three years of law school, and pass a written bar examination. A paralegal advocate needs to have an associate or bachelor's degree and two years of full-time study beyond high school in a paralegal program. Some states require a specialized certificate to become a paralegal advocate. This certificate is obtained through the state bar association.

Job Outlook

Population growth should increase the demand for this career. Legal advocates offer specialized guidance to children and families. They are an important liason between the legal system and the general public. Some legal advocates work for law firms but others enjoy the independence of being self-employed. A legal advocate for children can work in a paid position or be a volunteer. Law students often volunteer as paralegal advocates to gain valuable experience on the path to becoming a lawyer.

Critical Thinking Research some of the typical responsibilities of a legal advocate and summarize your findings. What personal interests, skills, and abilities might draw someone to this career? What are some short-term and long-term goals that would help you prepare for a career as a legal advocate?

Career Cluster

Law, Public Safety, Corrections, and Security Legal advocates work in the Legal Services pathway of the Law, Public Safety, Corrections, and Security career cluster. Here are some other jobs in this career cluster:

- Child Care Lawyer
- Judges and Magistrates
- Legal Assistant
- Child Custody Mediator
- Investigator
- Security Guard
- Police Officer
- Fire Inspector

Explore Further The Law, Public Safety, Corrections, and Security career cluster contains five pathways: Correction Services, Emergency and Fire Management Services, Security and Protective Services, Law Enforcement Services, and Legal Services Research this career cluster. Then choose a career from this cluster, other than legal advocate, that you would like to learn more about. Research the skills, education, and training required for this career. Write a paragraph that summarizes your findings.

Corbis/SuperStock

Preventing Abuse and Neglect
Visual Summary

Recognizing and reporting suspected abuse and neglect can help prevent and limit the damaging effects of abuse and neglect.

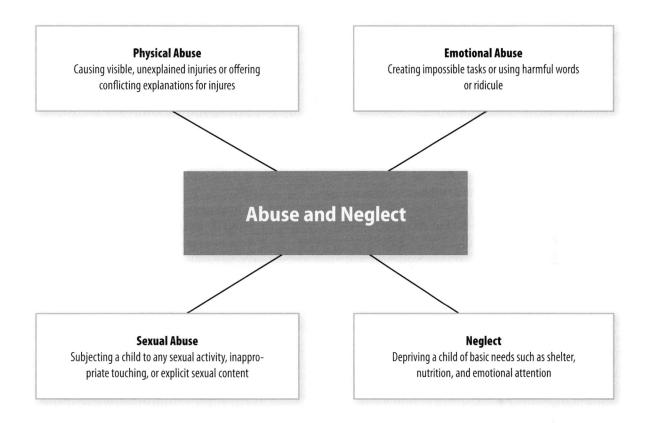

Physical Abuse
Causing visible, unexplained injuries or offering conflicting explanations for injures

Emotional Abuse
Creating impossible tasks or using harmful words or ridicule

Abuse and Neglect

Sexual Abuse
Subjecting a child to any sexual activity, inappropriate touching, or explicit sexual content

Neglect
Depriving a child of basic needs such as shelter, nutrition, and emotional attention

Vocabulary Review

1. Label each of these content and academic vocabulary terms as a noun, verb, or adjective.

Content Vocabulary
◇ child abuse (p. 146)
◇ child neglect (p. 148)
◇ documenting (p. 150)
◇ crisis nursery (p. 151)
◇ resilience (p. 152)

Academic Vocabulary
■ investigate (p. 150)
■ alternative (p. 151)

Review Key Concepts

2. Identify the types of child abuse.
3. Describe five signs of child abuse and neglect.
4. Identify documenting and reporting responsibilities of early childhood staff.
5. Explain ways to prevent child abuse and neglect.

Critical Thinking

6. **Infer** why a young child might falsely accuse an adult of child abuse. What are two ways to protect staff from false accusations?

7. **Analyze** Why might a person who was abused as a child abuse others as an adult? What are some ways to stop this cycle of abuse?

8. **Contrast** voluntary and mandatory reporting of abuse.

9. **Assess** the long-term impact of abuse on a child. What impact does this abuse have on the child's mental health?

10. **Explain** how criminal background checks can help prevent child abuse.

21st Century Skills

Accountability Skills

11. **Reflect** Consider your opinions on reporting abuse and neglect. Do you have any concerns with reporting suspected abuse and neglect? How would you feel if your suspicions were confirmed? How would you feel if your suspicions were unfounded? Consider the information you read in this chapter on abuse and neglect. Summarize how the information you read may have impacted they way you feel about reporting suspected abuse and neglect.

Critical Thinking Skills

12. **Building Resilience** A trusting relationship between a child and a responsible adult can help to build resilience in a child. Work with a partner to discuss other strategies for establishing trust as well as building resilience. After discussing strategies, role play as a child care professional working with a child to build trust and resilience. Implement the strategies with your partner and then discuss your approach.

Child Care LAB

Use the skills you have learned in this chapter.

Community Resource Guide

13. **Create a Community Resource Guide** In this activity you will work in small groups to create a guide of community resources for neglected or abused children and their abusers.

   A. Identify local, state, and national agencies. Research and identify the local, state, and national resources that help neglected or abused children and their abusers in one of the following categories: Social Services, Counseling/Mental Health, Substance Abuse, Education and Training, and Emergency Services.

   B. Research services. What are some of the services provided by each of these resources? For example, a local non-profit group may provide substance abuse counseling to abusers and their families.

   C. Document your findings. Create a spreadsheet identifying each resource and the service provided.

   D. Create a class resource guide. Share your information with other groups. Eliminate any duplicate resources and combine your resource list into one class community resource guide.

   E. Share your information. Contact a local child care center and ask if they would be interested in the resource guide that your class created.

Create Your Evaluation

Create an evaluation sheet with these categories:

- Appropriate category
- Resources for Victims or Families
- Resources for Abusers
- Contact information
- Completeness
- Organization

Ask your classmates to use the sheet to evaluate your database, rating each category from 1 to 10.

Academic Skills

English Language Arts

14. Autobiographical Articles Collect autobiographical articles about people who have overcome abuse or neglect. Analyze each article. What symptoms of neglect or abuse were identified in each case? How did each person deal with his or her situation? What helped them to overcome the effects of the experience? What insights can you gain from studying these accounts of abuse or neglect?

Social Studies

15. Research State Laws Research your state's laws regarding child abuse. What requirements for reporting suspected neglect or abuse are outlined? What are the consequences of failing to report suspected neglect or abuse? What are the provisions for protecting the abused child? What range of punishment is provided for the abuser?

Mathematics

16. Volunteer Hours Karen is a child care professional. She wanted to volunteer in her community to help with children's issues. Last year, Karen volunteered as a legal advocate at a community legal aid center that supports child welfare. Of the 1750 hours that she worked last year, she spent about 1500 hours volunteering. The rest of that time was spent doing paid work. What was the ratio of her paid work to her volunteer work?

Math Concept **Ratios** Ratios are comparisons of numbers that can be represented in different forms. Usually, ratios are represented in simplest form. The ratio 1:2 can also be expressed as 1 out of 2, 1 to 2, or ½.

Starting Hint Calculate the number of paid hours worked. Then set up the ratio as a fraction, with paid hours as the numerator and volunteer hours as the denominator. Your answer should be a fraction in the lowest terms.

 For more math practice, go to the math appendix at the back of the book.

Certification Prep

Sharpen your test-taking skills to improve your certification program score.

Directions Read each statement. Then read the answer choices and choose the phrase that is correct.

17. What is a sign of possible emotional abuse?

   A. A child is overly clean.

   B. A child has untreated fractures.

   C. A child is fearful.

   D. A child has a positive self-image.

18. Examples of mandated reporters are _____.

   A. teachers   **C.** medical professionals

   B. social workers   **D.** all of the above

> ### Test-Taking Tip
> Read and consider every possible answer on a multiple-choice test. Eliminate each choice that is clearly incorrect. Then decide which remaining choice is the best answer.

CHAPTER 8

Promoting Nutrition and Wellness

Writing Activity

⭐ 21st Century Skills

Information Literacy People read articles to learn about a specific topic. It is the job of the article writer to inform readers in a concise yet engaging way. Use your background knowledge to write an article on the basics of good nutrition. Look at a magazine or newspaper article for an example of format and style. Edit your article to adjust information and add facts after learning more about the topic in this chapter.

Writing Tips

1. Write a first draft that outlines at least three main points.
2. Present your topic in a lead paragraph.
3. Cover the journalistic information of who, what, where, when, why, and how.
4. Edit your article at least once after reading the chapter, and do a final proofread.

Explore the Photo
Children need to eat healthful foods that provide enough of all the basic nutrients. *Why do children need good nutrition?*

Stockbroker/Purestock/SuperStock

Reading Guide

Prior Knowledge Look over the Key Concepts in the Reading Guide. Write what you already know about each concept and what you want to find out by reading the lesson. As you read, find examples for both categories.

Read to Learn

Key Concepts

- **Identify** the six nutrients required for good nutrition.
- **Summarize** how to plan balanced menus for young children.
- **Explain** proper food safety and sanitation practices.
- **Describe** factors that contribute to a child's wellness.

Content Vocabulary

◇ wellness
◇ nutrients
◇ nutrition
◇ deficiency
◇ fiber
◇ MyPlate
◇ perishable

Academic Vocabulary

■ restrict
■ exposure

Main Idea

Children develop health and wellness when they eat nutrient-rich meals and snacks, get plenty of sleep, and engage in developmentally appropriate physical activity.

Graphic Organizer

As you read, record the six categories of nutrients. Use a graphic organizer like the one below to organize your information.

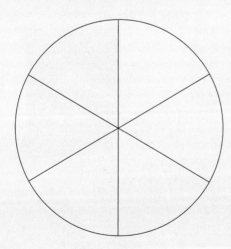

Graphic Organizer *Go to* **connected.mcgraw-hill.com** *to print this Graphic Organizer.*

AS YOU READ

Connect Think about what you do to promote your individual health and wellness. How could these apply to children?

◇Vocabulary

You can find definitions in the glossary at the back of this book.

Good Nutrition Promotes Wellness

Children develop health and fitness when they eat nutrient-rich meals and snacks, get plenty of sleep, and engage in developmentally appropriate physical activities. These three elements combine to promote a child's **wellness**, or overall good health and well-being.

Nutrients are the substances in food that the body uses to function, grow, repair tissue, and produce energy. **Nutrition** is the process through which the body uses the nutrients in food. Nutrients provide energy for activities, such as running and playing, and for essential body processes, such as pumping blood and digesting food. With the right amounts of the many different nutrients, the body can produce the energy it needs. It functions properly and can resist illness.

Good nutrition is especially important in early childhood. It provides the foundation for children's normal physical growth and intellectual development. Most of the brain's growth occurs in the first two years of life. To function properly, the brain must regularly receive important substances from nutrients. Research has shown that well-nourished children learn better. They are better able to stay alert and handle everyday stress. Many children may obtain up to 75 percent of their daily food intake in child care settings, so it is very important that early childhood professionals know and follow good nutrition practices.

▶ **Drinking Water**

Drinking plenty of water throughout the day helps children maintain good health. *Why is water important for good health?*

McGraw-Hill Education/Eclipse Studios

Nutrition for Children

For good health, the body needs six types of nutrients: carbohydrates, proteins, fats, vitamins, minerals, and water. Each plays a unique role in developing and maintaining a healthy body. **Figure 8.1** describes the functions and sources of these nutrients.

Many different nutrients play a role in maintaining good health. These nutrients work as a team. The body needs different amounts of each nutrient. If children have a nutrient **deficiency**, a lack or inadequacy in one or more nutrients, especially over long periods of time, they can develop serious health problems. For instance, a deficiency of vitamin D can lead to rickets, a disease in which bones soften and may become deformed. A deficiency of iron can cause a type of anemia. Children with this condition are tired, pale, and weak and have poor appetites.

The energy is food is measured as calories. Proteins, carbohydrates, and fat provide calories. Getting too many calories from any food and not burning enough calories with physcial activity can lead to childhood obesity and health problems in later life. To maintain good health, children need a variety of nutritious foods and regular physical activity.

Figure 8.1	Nutrient Functions and Sources

Nutrients perform specific functions in the body. *Which nutrients help the body eliminate waste?*

Nutrient	Functions	Sources
Carbohydrates	Body's main source of energy. Help body use proteins and fats. Supplies **fiber**, a plant material that helps the body eliminate waste.	Vegetables, breads, cereals, rice, pasta, sugars, fruits, and vegetables
Proteins	Build, maintain, and repair body cells. Help the body grow and fight off disease. Provide energy.	Meat, poultry, fish, eggs, milk, yogurt, cheese, and plant sources such as peanuts and dry beans
Fats	Provide energy. Carry vitamins that regulate body processes.	Meat, poultry, fish, whole milk, cheese, egg yolks, nuts, oils, margarine, mayonnaise, and salad dressing
Vitamins	Include vitamins A, C, D, E, K, and B-complex. Help body process other nutrients. *Example:* Vitamin D helps build and maintain strong bones and teeth.	Grain products, fruits, vegetables, dairy products, meat, fish, poultry, eggs, dry beans and peas, and nuts
Minerals	Include calcium, phosphorus, iron, potassium, and sodium. Regulate body processes. Build bones. Different minerals have specific functions. *Example:* Iron helps builds red blood cells.	Milk and milk products, meat, poultry, fish, and eggs, whole grains, vegetables, and fruits
Water	Delivers nutrients throughout the body. Helps control body temperature. Helps body eliminate waste.	Water, beverages, soups, fruits, and vegetables

Diabetes is a chronic disease in which a person cannot control the glucose, or sugar, in his or her blood. Type 1 diabetes is usually diagnosed in children and young adults. In type 1 diabetes, the body does not produce insulin, a hormone that controls blood sugar levels. A child with type 1 diabetes has to keep his or her blood sugar levels as normal and even as possible. Staff are trained to help the child follow an individualized care plan that usually involves a specialized diet, monitoring glucose levels, administering insulin, and taking specific action if blood sugar levels are too high or too low.

Critical Thinking

Type 2 diabetes is another form of diabetes. Find a reputable online source and make a list of recommendations for preventing type 2 diabetes. Highlight those that are inexpensive and easy to implement.

MyPlate

MyPlate is a tool developed by the U.S. Department of Agriculture (USDA) to help individuals make healthful food choices and be physically active every day. Child care professionals can use this tool to help plan healthful meals for children. **Figure 8.2** illustrates the USDA's MyPlate, which divides foods into five basic groups. Everyone needs foods from each food group daily. The food groups are:

▶ **Grains** Grains are the richest source of carbohydrates. They provide B vitamins, vitamin E, iron, and fiber. Select whole-grain, enriched, or fortified products.

▶ **Vegetables** Vegetables provide many important vitamins and minerals, including vitamins A and C. They are a good source of carbohydrates and many are high in fiber. Choose fresh, frozen, canned, and dried vegetables and vegetable juice. Eat vegetables raw or cooked.

▶ **Fruits** Fruits provide essential vitamins and minerals, especially vitamins A and C and potassium. They are good sources of carbohydrates and many are high in fiber. Choose fresh, frozen, canned, and dried fruits and 100 percent fruit juices.

▶ **Dairy** Milk is an excellent source of protein. It is rich in calcium, phosphorus, and vitamin A and is fortified with vitamin D to help calcium absorption. Dairy products have varying amounts of fat and carbohydrates. Yogurt and cheese are also nutritious choices.

▶ **Protein** Meat, poultry, fish, eggs, dry beans or peas, nuts, and seeds are part of this group. They are all sources of protein and some B vitamins. These foods also provide, iron, other minerals, and varying amounts of fat.

Although not a food group, some healthy oils are needed for good health and to absorb nutrients. Because they are high in calories, include them in small amounts.

The five main food groups are equally important to health, but they are not needed in equal amounts. MyPlate shows a range of food amounts for each food group based on the calories children two years and older need each day. Calorie levels are based on age, gender, and activity level. The ChooseMyPlate Web site can help you determine a person's individual daily food requirements based on his or her age, gender, and activity level.

MyPlate is not intended for use with infants and children under two years of age because their food needs vary. Early childhood professionals should refer to the USDA's Child and Adult Care Food Program (CACFP) guidelines for feeding infants and younger children.

READING CHECK **Identify** What is MyPlate and how can it be used by early childhood professionals?

Figure 8.2 MyPlate Kids' Place

Choose Healthful Foods The MyPlate graphic shows how much of each food group should be consumed in relation to the other food groups. The MyPlate Kids' Place website offers games and activities for kids to learn proper nutrition. *How many cups of vegetables does MyPlate recommend that children eat every day?*

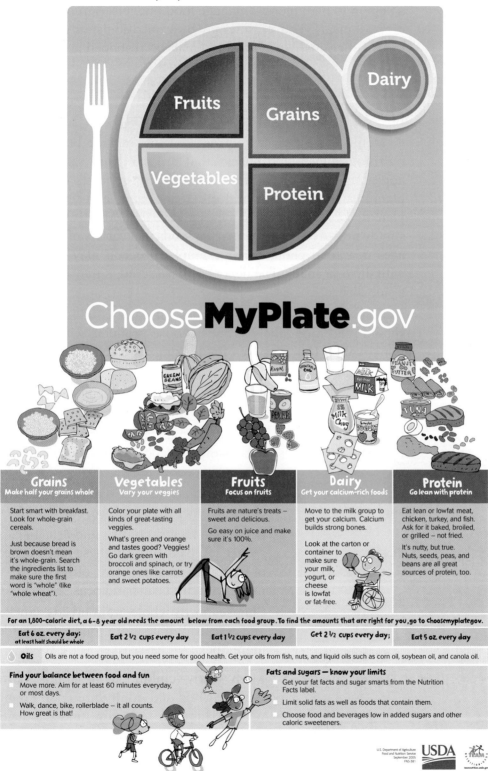

US Department of Agriculture

Menu Planning

Meals provided by a child care program depend on the hours of operation and the age of the children. A full-day program might provide breakfast, lunch, and one or two snacks. Half-day preschools might provide only a snack.

When programs provide full food service, they usually employ a person to plan menus, manage food budgets, purchase food, and prepare meals. This person may be a nutritionist or a dietitian. In other programs, staff members may be responsible for planning, preparing, and serving meals and snacks.

Meet Nutrition Requirements

Menus for a child care program must include budget-friendly, nutritious meals and snacks that are easy and safe to eat and appealing to children. Meeting these requirements takes creative planning. Bright colors and different shapes and textures on the plate make for interesting meals and snacks. Many children prefer simply prepared foods. Preparing foods in a variety of ways encourages new food choices. For example, broccoli may be eaten raw with dip as a snack. The next time it is served, it may be steamed as a side dish.

Staff members who plan menus for early childhood programs should read food labels so they choose products with high nutritional value. Here are tips for making sure the foods served are nutritious:

▶ Choose fruit and vegetable juices that are 100 percent juice with no added sweetener.

▶ Serve a colorful variety of fruits and vegetables. Avoid overcooking to reduce nutrient loss during cooking.

▶ Offer low-fat or fat-free dairy products for children older than age two.

▶ Serve lean meats, poultry, and fish. To reduce fat, bake or broil these foods instead of frying. As an alternative, offer dishes made with dry beans and peas.

▶ Choose mostly whole-grain breads, crackers, and cereals. Whole-grain products provide more fiber.

Many early childhood programs participate in the Child and Adult Care Food Program (CACFP). This is a federally funded nutrition program that helps provide meals and snacks that meet federal nutrition guidelines in child and adult care facilities. **Figure 8.3** shows the meal pattern established by the CACFP.

▼ **Texture and Taste**

Serving foods with different textures, such as soft and creamy or hard and crunchy, helps make food appeal to children. *How can you change the texture of a food?*

Figure 8.3 **CACFP Meal Patterns for Children**

Planning Meals and Snacks The CACFP meal patterns for children help child care professionals plan well-balanced and nutritious meals and snacks. Portions shown are the minimum portion sizes for each meal component. The CACFP recommends not serving juice to meet the fruit/vegetable requirement too many times throughout the day. *If you are serving milk for a snack, what else could you serve to round out the snack?*

	1–2 years old	3–5 years old	6–12 years old
BREAKFAST			
Milk	½ cup	¾ cup	1 cup
Juice or Fruit or Vegetable	¼ cup	½ cup	½ cup
Grains/Breads			
Enriched or whole-grain bread	½ slice*	½ slice*	1 slice*
Cold, dry cereal	¼ cup	1/3 cup	¾ cup
Cooked cereal, pasta, or noodle products	¼ cup	¼ cup	½ cup
MID-MORNING OR MID-AFTERNOON SNACK			
Select 2			
Milk	½ cup	½ cup	1 cup
Juice or Fruit or Vegetable	½ cup	½ cup	¾ cup
Meat or Meat Alternate	½ ounce	½ ounce	1 ounce
Grains/Bread	½ slice*	½ slice*	1 slice*
LUNCH OR SUPPER			
Milk	½ cup	¾ cup	1 cup
Meat or Poultry or Fish	1 ounce	1 ½ ounces	2 ounces
or Cheese	1 ounce	1 ½ ounces	2 ounces
or Egg	½ egg	¾ egg	1 egg
or Cooked, dry beans and peas	¼ cup	3/8 cup	½ cup
or Peanut butter or other nut or seed butters	2 tablespoons	3 tablespoons	4 tablespoons
or Nuts and/or seeds	½ ounce**	¾ ounce**	1 ounce**
or Yogurt, plain or flavored, sweetened or unsweetened	4 ounces	6 ounces	8 ounces
Juice, Fruit, and/or Vegitable (2 or more)	¼ cup total	½ cup total	¾ cup total
Grains/Breads	½ slice*	½ slice*	1 slice*

*Or an equivalent serving of an acceptable bread alternate such as cornbread, biscuits, rolls, or muffins made of whole-grain or enriched meal or flour.
** Nuts and seeds are allowable as only one-half of the total meat/meat alternate serving and must be combined with another meat/meat alternate to fulfill the lunch or supper requirement.

Cultural and Ethnic Diversity

Menus should include foods children are familiar with in their homes as well as new foods that they can learn about. This requires planning meals and snacks that include food from many cultures. Serving such foods broadens all children's food preferences and cultural experiences. Adding ethnic foods—such as tortillas, hummus, scones, and wontons—during snack time is a good start. Lunches that include different pastas, various types of rice and beans, breads, fruits, and vegetables help all children feel represented in a program.

Accommodate Special Needs

Some children may be unable to eat certain foods because of allergies or other medical problems. In addition, religious beliefs may **restrict**, or avoid or limit, certain foods or food combinations. Ask parents about restrictions that may apply to their child. Keep a convenient record of restrictions to refer to when planning meals. Consult with the staff member who plans meals to determine alternatives for children with special needs.

Serving Meals and Snacks

Meal and snack time should be safe, enjoyable experiences for children. Young children have smaller stomachs that cannot hold as much food as an adult. Offer small amounts of food at first, and then let a child have more if he or she is still hungry. Snacks between meals help children get enough of the nutrients they need during the day. **Exposure** to, or experience with, a variety of foods, prepared and served in healthful ways, helps children develop positive attitudes toward eating properly.

▼**Eating Together**

Children build social skills during meals and snacks. *How can early childhood teachers make meal and snack times a learning experience?*

Stockbroker/SuperStock

Serve Easy-to-Eat Foods

Young children are just learning to use eating utensils. Offer eating utensils appropriate for the age of the children. Younger toddlers may need sipper cups with lids or straws. Older toddlers can use sturdy cups. To make eating easier, include finger foods such as carrot sticks or apple slices. Serve children's food in small, bite-size pieces. Large chunks of meat, vegetables, or fruit may be difficult for them to chew and could cause choking. Remind children to eat slowly and to chew food thoroughly, and be a role model for them. Allow plenty of time for children to eat so that they are not rushed.

Avoid serving young children nuts, popcorn, hard candies. Whole grapes and hot dogs must be cut into small pieces. These foods can be inhaled easily and cause choking. For some children, foods such as nuts and peanut butter can also cause allergic reactions.

Building Social Skills

Snacks and meals should be served under pleasant, relaxed conditions. Teachers should role-model good manners so children can learn them. They should also guide children in proper meal conversation and behavior so they learn how to behave respectfully at home or when eating out.

READING CHECK ✔ **Summarize** What qualities make a safe, appealing meal for children?

SAFETY MATTERS

Allergy Awareness

Children can be allergic to many substances, including food, animals, dust, and pollen. Common food allergies include peanuts, milk, eggs, fish, soy, and wheat. When a new child joins a class, the early childhood teacher should review the child's enrollment records for any allergies. If a food allergy is noted, the teacher should alert fellow staff, including team teachers, meal planners, food servers, and cleaning staff so that special accommodations can be made. A child with a severe allergy should wear a medical alert bracelet. If a child has an allergic reaction, call for medical assistance immediately.

What Would You Do? You learn that one child in your class is allergic to strawberries, another is allergic to peanuts, and a third child has an allergy to rabbits. You need to remind everyone about these allergies, including other teachers or parents who are helping in the class. What would you do?

Food Safety and Sanitation

Part of taking good care of children is ensuring that they receive nutritious foods that are safe to eat as well as handled in sanitary ways. Safe food handling standards have been established by the U.S. Department of Agriculture (USDA) and the Food and Drug Administration (FDA).

Food Safety

Food that is spoiled or contaminated with bacteria can cause serious illness in children and adults. Anyone preparing or serving food must be trained in food safety and sanitation practices. Proper temperatures for storing, cooking, and serving food are necessary. Many foods are **perishable**, which means they will spoil if not refrigerated or frozen. That is because bacteria multiply rapidly at room temperature. Cold temperatures limit the growth of bacteria. High temperatures used in cooking food destroy harmful bacteria.

How to . . .

Encourage Positive Food Choices

Eating habits learned in early childhood continue into adulthood. Learning to make wise choices from the food group can help children live healthier lives. To encourage good eating patterns, conduct food and nutrition education activities for children and parents. This helps parents reinforce healthful eating at home.

▶ Teach About Food
Young children can understand basic concepts such as: Food is fuel for the body. It helps people grow and gives them energy. Teach children that food comes from plants and animals and is grown on farms and in gardens.

▶ Cook With Children
Children can learn about nutrition through simple cooking activities. Two-year-olds can spread peanut butter on crackers. Older children can help bake muffins or make soup. While preparing food, talk about the smell, taste, and appearance of the ingredients.

▶ Do Food-Related Activities
Link activities to nutrition education. For example, after reading "Goldilocks and the Three Bears," have children prepare oatmeal (porridge) for breakfast or the morning snack. Field trips to a farm, orchard, farmer's market, or restaurant teach where food comes from.

▶ Involve Parents
Ask parents to join the class for a healthful meal, cooking project, or food-related field trip. Include nutritious snack or meal recipes in center newsletters.

Apply It!
Conduct an activity for preschoolers that incorporates nutrition and food safety information.

©Ariel Skelley/Blend Images/Corbis

Limiting Food Hazards

To maintain proper food temperatures, follow these guidelines:

▶ Store food in properly cooled refrigerators and freezers. Keep refrigerator temperatures at 40°F or below. Keep the freezer at 0°F or below. Use thermometers to check that appliances are at the proper temperatures.

▶ Thaw frozen food in the refrigerator, never at room temperature.

▶ Be sure food is cooked thoroughly. Meats should be cooked to an internal temperature of at least 160°F. Poultry should be cooked to a minimum internal temperature of 165°F. Reheat leftovers to an internal temperature of 165°F.

▶ When serving a meal or snack, keep hot foods hot at 140°F or above and cold foods cold at 40°F or below. Bacteria grows rapidly as the food reaches room temperature.

▶ After a meal, freeze or refrigerate any leftovers promptly. If perishable food has been left sitting out for more than two hours, discard it.

Keeping Records

State laws usually require child care programs to be monitored regularly by the local health department. A health department inspector periodically observes and evaluates a program's health practices, including the food-service area. Health inspectors make sure that meal-service personnel follow proper food safety and sanitation procedures. Child care programs must keep records of health department inspections in an office file.

Sanitation

Sanitation means practicing cleanliness to prevent the spread of illness. Harmful bacteria and other disease-carrying agents can easily spread from unclean hands or equipment to food. Strict cleaning routines and consistent use of proper sanitary precautions help keep food safe for eating.

Food handlers must wear hair restraints while preparing food. If food handlers have a wound, they must wear disposable gloves until it is healed. Food handlers also must wash their hands thoroughly before beginning food preparation, after coughing, sneezing, or blowing their nose, after using the restroom and handling garbage, and after handling raw meat, poultry, fish, or eggs.

Science *for Success*

Nutrition and Brain Development

Nutrition plays an important role in a child's development. Good nutrition not only helps a child develop properly but also can positively affect intellectual and physical development.

Procedure Using reliable print and Internet resources, research the effect of nutrition on children's brain development. What specific nutrients have been scientifically observed to have a positive influence on brain development? Which foods are sources of these nutrients?

Analysis Using the information you found in your research, list the nutrients that are important for brain development and the foods that are sources of those nutrients. Then plan a breakfast and lunch menu for one week for infants, toddlers, and preschoolers. Include a variety of foods that contain nutrients that are specifically beneficial to brain development. How could you modify your menus to address food allergies or include cultural foods? Review your menus to make sure that they also provide children with the balanced nutrition required for overall development. List the nutrients in each meal that contribute to brain development. Share your meal plan with the class.

Clean, sanitary cooking equipment also contributes to food safety. Equipment that touches raw food, such as cutting boards and knives, must be scrubbed in hot, soapy water before being used for other foods. All dishes and utensils must be sanitized after each use. This is usually done in dishwashers, using very hot (170°F) water to kill bacteria. Eating areas and food-preparation areas must be cleaned with a sanitizing solution before and after each use.

READING CHECK ✔ **Explain** When serving meals, why is it important to keep hot foods hot and cold foods cold?

▲ Nap Time

A doll, a stuffed animal, or a special blanket can be a helpful sleep aid to a child. *Why is reducing sources of anxiety at nap time important?*

Promoting Wellness

Good nutrition is only one part of a child's total wellness. Sleep and physical activity are essential to early childhood development. Nutrition, sleep, and physical activity combine to foster a child's mental health. Teachers can create daily schedules and plan curriculum activities that promote overall wellness habits.

Sleep Sustains Health

The average preschooler needs 11 to 12 hours of sleep daily. This includes nap time as well as nighttime sleep. Sleep gives children's brain cells the opportunity to repair and keep learning pathways in good order. With adequate sleep, children have improved short-term memory as well as the ability to follow directions and to remember details. Sleep is also important for children's growth.

Sufficient sleep also improves children's physical health by supporting the body's immune system, which fights off illness-causing germs. It also helps them have energy for physical activities they engage in during play and learning. Children who develop good sleep habits tend to have more patience and self-control as they develop social skills and interact with adults and peers.

Whether napping at child care or sleeping at home, the following tips help children develop good sleep habits:

▶ Create a specific routine to follow every nap time so children can learn what to expect.

▶ Limit caffeine, which can interfere with sleep.

▶ At least 30 minutes before nap time, avoid active play. Create a calming atmosphere with quiet activities.

▶ Reduce sources of anxiety and distraction. Nervous, scared children cannot sleep. A night light casts a cozy glow.

▶ Quiet music can help children relax into sleep. Some like a gentle back rub to calm them.

Active Play Promotes Wellness

One hour of daily active play for children can help prevent long-term health problems—ranging from obesity to diabetes and high blood pressure—as children grow into adulthood. Children need to develop the habit of daily movement to support fitness factors such as muscular strength, flexibility, and cardiovascular endurance.

Early childhood professionals are key people in helping children and families make physical activity a part of daily life. They should provide safe spaces where children can enjoy unstructured active play. They can create opportunities for children to explore how their bodies can move and to develop coordination, flexibility, and balance.

Nurture Good Mental Health

The first factor to a child's good mental health is a secure attachment or emotional bond with a responsive adult—usually a parent—during the first few years of life. From that foundation, children develop an identity and self-esteem. Good nutrition, sleep, and physical activity help the body manufacture hormones and other chemicals that contribute to good mental health.

▲ **Outdoor Active Play**

Children get good physical activity through unstructured outdoor play. *What other outdoor activities provide physical benefit to children?*

Early childhood teachers need to observe children closely so they can adjust experiences to work with a child's temperament, rather than against it. Such cooperation helps reduce children's frustration and supports their emerging self-confidence. Children need to learn to manage age-appropriate stress and anxiety. To help children adopt good mental health habits, early childhood teachers can

▶ plan a daily schedule that meets children's overall wellness needs.

▶ conduct developmentally appropriate activities in which children enjoy successes that build self-esteem and confidence.

▶ use positive discipline strategies that teach while preserving children's sense of self-worth.

▶ be sensitive to events that can cause stress, such as changes in a typical daily routine or familiar environment. Help children anticipate changes and provide ways to respond.

▶ give children opportunity to talk about their feelings and ask questions. Be patient, empathetic, and respect their concerns.

▶ consult with parents if a child's reactions to stress are negatively affecting mental health. If a child's behavior or comments show excessive stress or anxiety, refer parents to a specialist.

READING CHECK ✓ **Understand** Why is it important for a teacher to learn and work with a child's individual temperament?

College Entrance Exams

College & Career READINESS

What are College Entrance Exams?

College entrance exams are tests used to measure students' abilities and are one factor colleges and universities use to select students for admission. There are two major college entrance exams: the SAT and the ACT. Most colleges require either the ACT or the SAT, but you must check to see which exam each specific college accepts. In addition to entrance exams, colleges use grades, scholastic achievements, extracurricular activities, and application essays to evaluate and compare prospective students.

What is the difference between the ACT and the SAT?

Both are national standardized tests that help colleges evaluate students. However, they are different. The ACT has a science section, the SAT does not. Both the SAT and ACT have essay sections, but the essay is optional on the ACT. Some colleges may require the essay portion of the ACT. The SAT is scored out of 2400. The ACT is scored out of 36. Also, there is a penalty for wrong answers on the SAT, but not on the ACT.

How do I know which exam to take?

If the college you are applying to accepts only one, the decision is easy. However, many accept both, and then you must decide which to take. Generally, if you feel relatively comfortable with vocabulary, grammar, and writing essays, you should take the SAT. If your vocabulary is not as strong or if you are more academic than test savvy, you might want to take the ACT. However, the best way to decide is to take a practice test for each and see how you do.

Do I need to study for these exams?

Yes! Studying for college entrance exams, familiarizing yourself with their formats, and taking practice tests can greatly improve your scores. Because your score could be the difference between getting into the college of your choice or not, it is definitely worth the time to prepare.

Hands-On

College Readiness Choose one college you are thinking about applying to, and find out whether it accepts the SAT, the ACT, or both. Based on this information and what you learned on this page, which test do you think you would take? Go online and find out when this test is offered and where. Also, find out if any practice tests are being offered in the near future.

Path to Success

Set a Goal Different colleges require different college entrance exam test scores. Figure out what your goal score is.

Assess Yourself Take a practice college entrance test to see how close you are to your goal score.

Draft a Study Plan Based on your practice test, create a study plan and a time frame for improving your score.

Get Help There are many resources if you need help preparing for the exam, including your teachers, classes, online courses, and test preparation books.

Take Care of Yourself Be sure to get enough sleep the night before the exam. On test day, eat breakfast and wear comfortable clothes.

Promoting Nutrition and Wellness

Visual Summary

Children maintain health and wellness when they eat nutrient-rich meals and snacks, get plenty of sleep, and engage in developmentally appropriate physical activity.

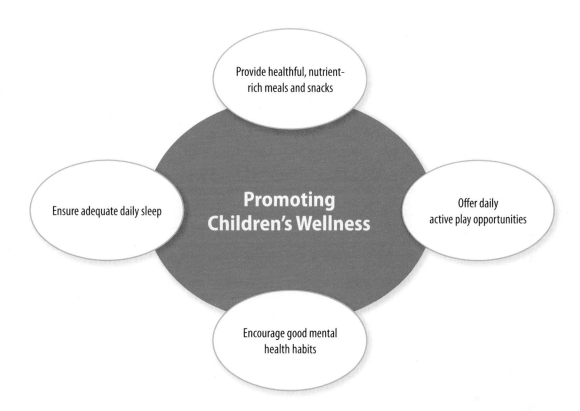

Provide healthful, nutrient-rich meals and snacks

Ensure adequate daily sleep

Promoting Children's Wellness

Offer daily active play opportunities

Encourage good mental health habits

Vocabulary Review

1. Create a multiple-choice test question for each content and academic vocabulary term.

Content Vocabulary

◇ wellness (p. 160)
◇ nutrients (p. 160)
◇ nutrition (p. 160)
◇ deficiency (p. 161)
◇ fiber (p. 161)
◇ MyPlate (p. 162)
◇ perishable (p. 167)

Academic Vocabulary

■ restrict (p. 166)
■ exposure (p. 166)

Review Key Concepts

2. **Identify** the six nutrients required for good nutrition.
3. **Summarize** how to plan balanced menus for young children.
4. **Explain** proper food safety and sanitation practices.
5. **Describe** factors that contribute to a child's wellness.

Critical Thinking

6. **Discuss** the challenges an early childhood professional could face in planning meals and snacks for children.
7. **Describe** a situation that shows how the physical health and the mental health of a child influence one another.
8. **Give examples** of what early childhood educators can do to encourage good eating habits in young children.
9. **Create** a checklist of items that a health inspector might look for in a child care facility's kitchen and meal service areas.
10. **Research** health problems that can result from a poor food handling and sanitation.

21st Century Skills

Research Skills

11. **Seasonal Produce** Child care centers often have the challenge of feeding children nutritional meals and snacks on a limited budget. Fresh fruits and vegetables generally cost less when purchased in season. Conduct research to create a chart showing when various fruits and vegetables are in season. Include fruits and vegetables for each season.

Creativity Skills

12. **Wellness Education for Children** In addition to providing healthful meals and active play opportunities for children, early childhood professionals must also teach children about wellness. Design a fun and interactive activity for either toddlers or preschoolers that teaches them about wellness. List the supplies and time required for the activity in your lesson plan.

Child Care LAB

Use the skills you have learned in this chapter.

Meal Plan for Toddlers

13. **Plan a Toddler Menu** In this activity, you will plan, evaluate, and present a day's meals—breakfast, lunch, and snack—for a toddler classroom.

    A. Select breakfast and lunch menu items Using the Child and Adult Care Food Program (CACFP) guidelines, select breakfast and lunch menu items appropriate for toddlers. Menu items should:
    - meet toddler's nutrition requirements.
    - include a variety of colors and textures.
    - include cultural diversity
    - promote independence skills.
    - be safe for toddlers to eat.
    - Include any special preparation instructions.

    B. Plan a snack Select snack food items that meet CACFP guidelines.

    C. Identify food safety practices List the food handling procedures that you will need to follow while preparing your menu.

    D. Prepare your menu presentation Prepare one menu for your class to sample. Also create a visual aid of your menu for your presentation, using poster board or presentation software.

    E. Share your menu Using your visual aid, present your menu and sample menu item to the class.

Create Your Evaluation

Create an evaluation sheet with these categories:
- Meets nutrition requirements
- Is visually appealing
- Incorporates cultural diversity
- Promotes independence skills

Ask your classmates to use the sheet to evaluate your menu, rating each category Excellent, Good, or Needs Improvement.

Academic Skills

English Language Arts

14. Nutrition and Wellness Newsletter Create a parent newsletter with the theme of nutrition and wellness. Include an introductory article that explains the importance of childhood nutrition and wellness. Also include tips for planning and making kid-friendly healthful meals, wellness tips, and list resources where parents can go for more information.

Social Studies

15. Cultural Food Recipe Collection Research the foods and meal patterns of cultural groups in your region. Collect recipes from the various cultures. What culturally diverse food items could you incorporate into early childhood center meals? Create a lesson plan that teaches about cultural diversity using a food and an activity or game from a culture other than your own.

Mathematics

16. Recipe Conversion David is planning a autumn-themed breakfast menu for his pre-school class. He decided that pumpkin muffins would be a good nutritious and seasonal menu item. He found a healthful recipe online, but all the ingredient measurements are in metric units. The recipe calls for 85.5 grams of wheat bran and 237 milliliters of buttermilk. How many cups of wheat bran and buttermilk does David need to make the recipe?

Math Concept **Metric System** The metric system is a decimal system of weights and measurements. In the system, the main units of weight are grams and kilograms. Liquid is typically measured in milliliters and liters.

Starting Hint Conversion formulas for volumes are specific to what is being measured. For this problem, one cup equals 57 grams and 237 milliliters. To convert grams to cups, divide the grams by 57. To convert milliliters to cups, divide the milliliters by 237.

 For more math practice, go to the math appendix at the back of the book.

Certification Prep

Sharpen your test-taking skills to improve your certification program score.

Directions Read each statement. Then read the answer choices and choose the word or phrase that is correct.

17. What should be consumed in small amounts to help absorb nutrients from foods?

   A. vitamins

   B. milk

   C. water

   D. oils

18. Food hazards can be limited by _____.

   A. thawing frozen foods at room temperature

   B. refrigerating perishable food that has been sitting out for more than four hours

   C. cooking food to minimum internal temperatures

   D. serving hot and cold foods at room temperature

Test-Taking Tip

In a multiple-choice test, the answers are usually specific and precise. First, carefully read the question. Then read all the answer choices. Eliminate answers that you know are incorrect.

CHAPTER 9

Guiding Behavior and Social Competence

Writing Activity

⭐ 21st Century Skills

Interpersonal A dialogue is a piece of writing in the form of a conversation. Write a short dialogue between an early educator and a parent about a child's development and behavior to show what you know about communication. Be sure to use proper voice and tenses as you write.

Writing Tips

1. Let the people in your dialogue express themselves and their purpose through the words you write.
2. Use language that sounds real and appropriate for the people talking.
3. Use quotation marks appropriately.

Explore the Photo
This teacher is practicing her guidance skills. *What skills come to mind when you think of the words guiding children?*

Glow Images

Reading Guide

BEFORE YOU READ

Look It Up Keep a dictionary near you, as well as the glossary at the back of the book, as you read. If you hear or read a word that you do not know, look it up in the glossary or in the dictionary. Before long, this practice will become a habit. You will be amazed at how many new words you will learn.

Read to Learn

Key Concepts

- **Describe** effective social skills and communication skills.
- **Identify** the guidance goals of the early childhood classroom.
- **Describe** basic child guidance techniques.
- **Explain** how to handle inappropriate behavior and consequences and how to aid conflict resolution.

Main Idea

Early educators help children develop essential social skills. Guiding children's behavior requires knowledge of positive guidance techniques and the ability to plan ahead, to adapt quickly, to stand firm with consequences, and to act as a positive behavior coach.

Content Vocabulary

◇ social competence
◇ compassion
◇ guidance
◇ self-discipline
◇ I-messages
◇ redirection
◇ consequences
◇ positive reinforcement
◇ cool-down moment

Academic Vocabulary

■ vary
■ functions

Graphic Organizer

As you read, you will learn about strategies for preventing behavior problems. Use a web like the one shown to record notes about each strategy. Add additional circles to your web as needed.

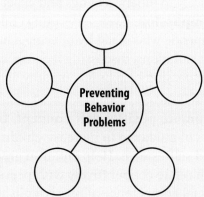

Preventing Behavior Problems

Graphic Organizer *Go to* **connected.mcgraw-hill.com** *to print this Graphic Organizer.*

◇Vocabulary

You can find definitions in the glossary at the back of this book.

▼Learning to Care

This child is comforting her friend. *Is this child displaying empathy or compassion? How can you tell?*

Building Social Skills

People do not live in isolation—we like to be around each other! Starting and maintaining social relationships is a basic human need. Children first develop caring attachments with parents. Then, children form attachments with siblings and extended family such as grandparents. As people grow, they develop relationships with many others in the community. Early educators play an important role in helping children build the skills necessary for social relationships.

Social Competence Goals

Social competence ('sō-shəl 'käm-pə-tən(t)s) is a person's ability to get along with others in acceptable and appropriate ways. It is important to nurture positive social traits in young children. Positive social traits include kindness, courtesy, adapting to peers, honesty, and respect for others. Those traits then foster specific social skills such as cooperation, sharing, and conflict resolution.

Social Skills

The foundation of social skills is respect for self and others. Learning respect helps people to view life from another person's point of view. As children learn to respect others, there is a greater chance they will develop socially acceptable ways of behaving throughout life. The following are ways to build social skills:

▶ **Model respect, acceptance, and positive social skills.** Demonstrate behavior that is caring and nonabusive, which will build self-esteem and responsibility. Plan activities that value people of different cultures, age groups, genders, and abilities. Include children in community connection activities. Your examples can teach children the value of respect, including respecting the rights and property of others.

▶ **Encourage empathy and compassion.** The ability to understand another person's feelings is called empathy ('em-pə-thē). The ability to respond sensitively to others' feelings and experiences is called **compassion**. Even very young children can comfort someone who is sad by offering a hug. Explaining situations, discussing feelings, and displaying compassion help build empathy and compassion in children.

▶ **Promote positive self-concept.** Use positive methods of guidance to increase children's self-concept and self-esteem. Help children gradually learn they can relate cooperatively with peers and adults. That social competence allows friendships to bloom that support children's self-esteem. Guide children by keeping their individual temperaments in mind.

McGraw-Hill Education/Ken Karp

◀ Working Together

These children are developing social skills while working as a team. *What are three activities an early educator can use to nurture cooperation and teamwork?*

Working with a child's nature, age, and development helps the child develop self-control and the ability to express thoughts and feelings constructively. Wise teachers use discipline and guidance techniques that are respectful, relevant, and related to children's specific behavior. They help protect children's self-esteem by refusing to use negative methods of discipline. They know such behaviors undermine children's self-esteem, sense of security, and basic trust in adults.

▶ **Encourage cooperation and teamwork.** The ability to work well with others helps you to be successful throughout life. Children should be given opportunities to practice social skills. Group projects, such as gardening and creating art murals together, nurture cooperation and teamwork. Contributing to classroom routines, such as setting tables for meals, builds pride in teamwork. Teaching children to solve problems together respectfully encourages a cooperative attitude.

▶ **Require self-control.** To work well with others, each person must be able to control his or her own actions. Intense feelings such as anger, disappointment, frustration, and jealousy must be managed appropriately. To get along well with others, everyone must address problems respectfully. Using physical or verbal aggression is not a productive way to solve problems. Use stories, games, modeling, and other strategies to teach children these important concepts and guide behavior.

Fostering Social Development

A variety of activities encourage social development. Early educators should create an environment that encourages group activities and fosters friendships. Card and board games, activity tables, and group storytelling encourage cooperative interactions.

Teachers should coach social skills. If a child has trouble entering a group activity, you might suggest ways to join. For instance, if a child would like to join dress-up play, you may quietly suggest that the child say, "I'd like to play, too. What part can I play?" This support method can also help shy children enter a group situation.

Social Communication Skills

In order to nurture and understand social communication, teachers must observe and carefully respond. Infants communicate through sounds such as cooing and crying. They also use body language. Sensitive early educators learn the meanings of each child's different sounds and motions.

Listening to and speaking with infants builds the foundation for social attachment. Talk to babies frequently, using short sentences and exaggerated facial expressions. Talk more with toddlers as they become more verbal. Language games, silly songs, and rhymes can help support toddlers' language development. Language rapidly develops after age two, allowing children's social attachments to expand.

Children begin more complex verbal communication in the preschool years. Speak to individual children often and use activities that will stimulate conversation among children. Encourage children to take turns talking and listening instead of interrupting each other or adults.

Expressing Feelings

Children experience a wide range of feelings. Their moods change quickly. One minute they may be angry, scared, or frustrated; and the next forgiving, calm, and happy. Learning to manage feelings appropriately is important for a child's lifelong happiness. When children are upset, it helps when teachers respond with understanding.

One method for responding to children is to use active listening, a strategy in which the teacher listens to what the child says and then repeats the message to show that he or she has heard the child.

Using active listening helps children learn to identify feelings and find appropriate ways to express them. For example, if a child's painting is ruined by a spill, a sensitive, active-listening message is, "You seem upset because the paint spilled on the picture. You worked hard on that picture." Responses like these encourage children to maintain self-control within a social environment. Teachers who consistently use active listening can also help children learn to identify and manage their own emotions.

Children can learn to express feelings when using a puppet or by "acting out" problems during dramatic play. Read stories to children with characters who cope successfully with their emotions to give children ideas for coping. Some children like to draw pictures of how they feel. Some prefer to create a make-believe story about a child facing challenges like their own. Dancing to music or active outdoor play can help children run off excess energy that often occurs when children become overwhelmed by emotion. Relaxing activities can also help children calm their emotions.

▼ Active Listening

Active listening involves listening to what the child says and then repeating the message. *What are some examples of active-listening statements?*

JGI/Blend Images LLC

Figure 9.1 **Parenting Styles**

Types of Guidance Children in your care will have experiences with different parenting styles. *Why is it important for teachers to understand various parenting styles?*

Authoritarian style	Democratic style	Permissive style
• Parents who use the authoritarian style are strong leaders. • They make all the decisions concerning their children and expect children to accept their judgments. • They believe in setting standards for behavior that children must meet. • When rules are broken, these parents act quickly and firmly. • Children of these parents feel secure with their parents in charge.	• Parents in a democratic household believe that children deserve a say in matters that affect them. • They allow their children to help set the rules and the penalties for breaking them. • Children are given a certain amount of choice, as long as they stay within the rules. • Children in these families tend to be confident and move easily toward independence.	• Parents who are permissive allow their children to make all the decisions they can handle, offering guidance as needed. • These parents have fewer rules, but the children understand the expectations. • These parents also let children experience natural consequences for behavior, instead of imposing penalties. • Children in these families often learn to solve problems creatively and learn from their experiences.

Parenting Styles

Children in a child care center come from a variety of cultures and family structures. Children's experiences with different parenting styles can affect how they interact with others. These styles can also affect how you communicate with the parents or guardians. **Figure 9.1** above lists the different types of parenting styles. Few parents follow one style exclusively. Parents may also change their parenting styles as children age. No one parenting style is better than another. Only when one is carried to the extreme can it be harmful to a child's development.

Children who are used to different parenting styles will often also be used to different types of guidance. **Guidance** involves behavior modeling and corrective actions by adults, which help children learn about appropriate behavior. Guidance requires both firmness and understanding, and as an early educator, you will need these to adjust to the various types of guidance associated with different parenting styles. It is important for teachers to understand and respect the parenting styles used for the children in their care.

However, teachers must also watch for signs that children may have an unhealthy home life, as in situations of abuse and neglect. Sometimes violence takes place in a child's home. This may be in the form of adults hurting each other (physically, emotionally, or verbally) or adults abusing a child. Teachers have the responsibility of recognizing symptoms of children in family crisis situations or the possibility of child abuse at home.

Family crisis situations and family violence are not the sole cause of behavior issues, but they can be linked to behavior concerns. Staff should also be alert to behaviors that may indicate a child is experiencing violence or emotional trauma in the home.

This will help them respond to children's needs immediately and refer parents to help. Many different behaviors can indicate home violence. Some specific child behaviors include the following:

▶ Having a quick "startle" reflex in response to noise or unexpected sounds

▶ Change in typical personality characteristics

▶ More aggressive behavior with peers

▶ A change in eating or sleeping patterns

▶ An excessive need for attention

Such behaviors should be recorded so staff can determine how to act on behalf of the child's safety. It is wise for child care professionals to post the contact information of local family violence prevention agencies for all parents.

Cultural Sensitivity

A family's beliefs, customs, and culture impact a child's behavior. For example, families differ in how and to whom they express and talk about feelings. Some families prefer not to speak about family issues with early educators; others are eager to do so.

Appropriate nonverbal communication also varies from culture to culture. Some cultures view direct eye contact between children and adults as offensive and disrespectful. However, other cultures, such as locations in the U.S., insist on eye contact to show that a person is listening.

Take time to learn about the values and beliefs of the families who use your program's services so you can practice effective communication skills. When cultural differences are openly discussed among early educators and families, cultural practices are taken into account and respected.

Guidance in Multigenerational Homes

Some children grow up in homes in which children, parents, and grandparents all live together. Multigenerational homes provide children with love, attention, and a sense of belonging. However, it also means many people contribute to childrearing decisions. Child care professionals should encourage these families to discuss cooperatively how they should raise the children. They should agree on behavior expectations, consequences for misbehavior, and who has the final say in behavior guidance.

Considering all the factors involved with each family will set the stage for a positive, collaborative relationship between teacher and parent or guardian. Early educators should demonstrate respect, sensitivity, and a willingness to work through each family member's concerns to promote these important relationships.

READING CHECK ✔ **Identify** List five ways to build social skills in children.

Positive Child Guidance

Children's spontaneous behavior makes for exciting workdays. This unpredictability also requires staff to be adept at guidance. To guide children's behavior, teachers must think before they speak and act. Guidance skills require practice. Listen to and observe experienced teachers in action to develop your skills. They can show you how to build children's self-esteem and to teach them to behave well.

Goals of Child Guidance

Children need guidance so they can learn to share, to take turns, and to resolve conflicts peacefully. Positive guidance helps children develop positive traits such as kindness, courtesy, and respect for themselves and others. Positive guidance also tells children what they can do instead of what they cannot do. **Figure 9.2** gives examples of positive guidance messages to use with children.

The elements of positive guidance should be based on each child's stage of development. Guidance serves the following purposes:

▶ Protects each child's physical safety

▶ Supports children's self-esteem and emotional well-being

▶ Ensures respect for all children's rights and feelings

▶ Teaches appropriate use of classroom materials and property

▶ Promotes independence and the ability to make good decisions

▶ Nurtures a sense of responsibility and accountability

▶ Encourages self-control and **self-discipline**—the ability to guide your own behavior

READING CHECK **Interpret** How can positive child guidance lead to self-discipline?

Figure 9.2 Using Positive Messages

Watch What You Say Positive commands or messages are better received and can give children more knowledge than negative "no" statements. *How can using positive messages support a good relationship between teacher and child?*

Say This . . .	Instead of This . . .
Hold on tightly.	Do not fall.
You may run outside.	Do not run in class!
Chairs are made for sitting.	Quit climbing on the furniture.
Use your paint smock.	Do not get paint everywhere.
Turn the pages gently.	Stop crumpling the pages.
Use your quiet voice.	No yelling!
When the blocks are on the shelf, we will go outside.	Quit dawdling and pick up those blocks right now.
When you use your regular voice, I'll get your ball for you.	Do not whine like a baby.

Child Guidance Basics

Children cannot learn to behave appropriately if they do not understand what behaviors are appropriate. Teachers' expectations must be simple, clear, and age-appropriate. Expectations and rules **vary**, or are different, from one program to another. Staff members must agree on the expectations and consistently enforce them.

Children learn best by watching and imitating the behaviors they see in others instead of being told what to do. This means that families and teachers are essential role models for appropriate behavior.

A long list of rules is overwhelming to children. When children help make classroom rules, they are more likely to follow them.

▶ First agree on general classroom rules.

▶ Then set up guidelines for routine activities and learning areas. For instance, the rules for finger painting might be "Wear a smock, clean up spills, and paint on your own paper."

▶ The chosen rules should be developmentally appropriate.

▶ Children will understand rules better if you phrase them simply.

▶ Be positive and specific. A rule for arrival time might be "Hang your coat on the hook in your cubby." This is clearer than saying, "Don't leave coats lying around everywhere."

▶ Explain the reasons for rules. You might say, "We walk indoors. If we run indoors, someone could fall and get hurt." Younger children will need simpler explanations.

▶ To help children remember the rules, display rules on a poster in each learning center. Use pictures to illustrate the rules.

▶ Use firm and friendly techniques, such as reminding and persuading, when rules are forgotten or disobeyed.

Preventing Problems

Many potential behavior problems can be prevented through careful planning. By structuring the schedule and the environment to minimize boredom, frustration, and conflict, you can reduce misbehavior. A supportive environment that provides physical and emotional security is important. It allows children to learn and practice acceptable behaviors as individuals or in groups.

Providing Balance

Children can lose focus if quiet activities last too long. They can become overtired if they participate for too long in active play. A balanced schedule is important because children who are either overly tired or full of energy find it difficult to behave appropriately. Remember to consider children with special needs when planning active and quiet play. Children with special needs may need to rest more than other children or may need activities adjusted to meet their needs.

Schedules, Transitions, and Routines

Follow a consistent schedule with smooth transitions and routines. Children find security in a predictable schedule. They become confused if a routine is interrupted or changed. This confusion can lead to disruptive behavior. A child who acts out may be responding to a change in a schedule or routine at home as well. A comforting hug and kind words as a child separates from his or her parent helps alleviate the child's stress. Prepare activities and routines that do not make children wait a long time for a turn. Effective transitions help children move between activities smoothly.

Activities

Plan a wide variety and choice of interesting activities. Children who are busy with practical and positive activities are less likely to misbehave. You can plan an interesting curriculum that incorporates project topics, themes, and activities for music, math, art, science, literature, cultural events, social studies, and more.

Plan activities appropriate for children's abilities. To avoid frustration, boredom, and misbehavior, plan open-ended activities, or those without an expected result, for multiple-age groups. Provide developmentally appropriate activities for each child. Activities should help create a positive and pleasant atmosphere, not a stress-filled one. While children enjoy activities, too many choices or rapid changes in activities can cause frustration for children. Learning how many activities to do and how long to do each one with children will help avoid behavior issues.

Environment and Equipment

Arrange the physical environment to promote children's success. When toy shelves are within children's reach, they can easily obey rules about putting away toys. Store materials not meant for use by children out of sight. Provide enough equipment for all students.

Children play more cooperatively when an adequate number of toys and equipment is available. Behavior problems can arise if too many children are playing in the same area or if multiple children want to play with the same equipment. Make sure that children use equipment that matches their abilities, and suggest alternatives if children choose equipment beyond their abilities.

▼ **Just My Size**

This early childhood classroom contains toys and equipment that are easily accessible and the correct size for children. *How does this help prevent behavior problems?*

Fancy/SuperStock

Provide Individual Attention

Plan times when children can interact with teachers one on one or in small groups. This prevents children from misbehaving to get a teacher's attention. Consider each child's special circumstances. Some children may come from homes that are less stable. This lack of stability might affect a child's behavior. Other situations, such as family crises, may have a negative effect on behavior.

Expectations and Limits

Setting limits helps children understand expectations and acceptable behavior. Limits should keep children from hurting themselves, other people, and property. Children will respect and follow reasonable limits. When setting limits, consider whether the limit is fair, age-appropriate, and if the limit still allows the child to learn, explore, and grow. Limits should not be set simply for the convenience of the adults.

To encourage good behavior, provide children with a positive example to follow. Obey the classroom rules just as you would expect from the children. Role-model desirable social skills as you interact with children and adults. For instance, if you would like children to say "please" and "thank you," model that behavior by making it a habit to do so yourself.

Expectations and limits for children's behavior should be clear, simple, and specific. Providing children with understandable directions is critical. **Figure 9.3** has tips for giving effective direction. When choosing a guidance approach, consider the child's age, development level, experience, and inborn temperament. Match expectations and limits to a child's ability to understand and respond appropriately. By keeping a child's individual abilities in mind, you can help them successfully cooperate with classroom expectations and social situations.

Figure 9.3 **Giving Effective Direction**

Speaking Tips Clear, specific directions are essential for setting appropriate expectations and limits for children. *What is one strategy for giving effective direction?*

To give effective direction
- use eye contact and speak at the child's level to make sure you have his or her attention.
- speak politely in a normal voice.
- use positive statements.
- begin your direction with an action word.
- use specific words that the child can understand.
- give a limited number of directions at one time.
- consider the child's age and level of development when choosing your words.

Jason Lugo/Getty Images

However, if too much or too little is expected of a child, he or she is likely to experience frustration and even failure. What do you think is an age-appropriate behavioral expectation for a toddler? For a preschool-age child? For a school-age child?

Clear expectations are often communicated by teaching children the **functions**, or purposes, of play materials. For example, a teacher might say, "Crayons are used for coloring on paper, not on walls." Expectations and limits are also communicated using I-messages. **I-messages** include a specific description of behavior, how it affects you, and your feelings about it. An I-message should follow this basic form: "I feel _____ when _____ because _____.

For example, suppose that at mealtime the teacher is just about to serve himself some peaches when a four-year-old grabs the bowl from his hands. The teacher wants to discourage the child's disrespectful behavior. An early educator who nurtures positive behavior would respond with an I-message: "It hurts my feelings when you grab the bowl away from me without asking. Is there a better way to get the peaches?" The I-message does not attack the child's character. Instead, it helps the child see why the behavior is a problem. It also gives the child a chance to choose a more respectful behavior.

Verbal and Nonverbal Guidance

Teachers can use verbal and nonverbal techniques to guide children. Verbal communication should be simple and clearly stated based on a child's development and age. To avoid confusion, use facial expressions and physical mannerisms that are consistent with your words. Teachers also use nonverbal techniques that help cue children into expected behavior. For instance, a special song might be sung at cleanup time or when children should gather in a specific location. Sometimes teachers use puppets to give directions to help children cooperate more easily with expectations.

Handling Inappropriate Behavior

Many factors can contribute to misbehavior. Children who misbehave are not usually trying to intentionally anger teachers or upset their peers. They may be bored, frustrated, hungry, tired, or ill. If they are experiencing problems at home they may misbehave as a way of asking for more adult attention. This does not mean that misbehavior should be excused. However, if you are aware of these factors, you can guide behavior more effectively.

▲ **Verbal and Non-verbal Guidance**

Teachers can use both verbal and nonverbal guidance techniques when directing children to gather in a specific location. *What nonverbal cues could a teacher use in an early childhood classroom?*

When you respond to misbehavior, choose your words and actions carefully. Negative methods such as spanking, threatening, frightening, shouting, isolating, or shaming children should never be used because they are ineffective at guiding behavior and may harm a child's self-esteem. You simply want the child to understand that the misbehavior is unacceptable and cannot continue. You also want the child to feel like a worthwhile person who is capable of doing better in the future. Your goal is to discourage the misbehavior without discouraging the child.

Handling Biting

Biting is never appropriate and situations involving children biting should be dealt with promptly by a child care professional. However, it is important to understand the reasons why children bite before addressing this behavior. Children bite for many reasons. Biting may be

▶ a response to teething pain.

▶ an experiment in cause and effect.

▶ a way to get a desired toy.

▶ a method of expressing anger and frustration.

▶ a signal of wanting a care provider's attention.

A teacher has to closely observe and consider the circumstances around a biting incident to best determine the cause and follow-up action. For example, if a child bites because of teething pain, chilled teething rings provide temporary relief. Having plenty of toys for children, as well as providing plenty of attention to each child, are prevention methods to avoid biting situations. **Figure 9.4** gives additional strategies for handling biting.

Figure 9.4 **How to Handle Biting**

Why do children bite? Children who are still mastering language skills may resort to biting. This most often occurs among toddlers and two year olds. *What are some factors that could contribute to this type of misbehavior?*

Strategies to Handle Biting

• Separate the children immediately.

• Attend to the hurt child first. If a child's skin is broken, put on latex or vinyl gloves before cleaning the area. Show compassion and empathy. Tenderly comfort the bitten child, and wash the injury with soap and water, even if the skin is not broken.

• Speak privately with the child who did the biting after you have cared for the injured child.

• Make eye contact, and in a firm but calm voice say, "Biting hurts people. We use our teeth only for food. It is unacceptable to bite." Make sure your facial expressions match your serious concern.

• Record the incident and the circumstances under which it occurred. At the end of the day, inform both families of the incident. Seek input from the parents of the child who bites and ask if this occurs at home and, if so, how it is handled.

Ignore Minor Misbehavior

Sometimes children misbehave just to get attention. For example, a child might continually stand and talk during circle time. The best response may be to ignore the misbehavior, as long as it is not harmful to anyone. If minor misbehavior gets attention—even negative attention such as yelling, using demeaning sarcasm, or embarrassing the children—it may increase rather than decrease.

Offer Choices

Some behavior problems are a result of children feeling as if they have little control over choices in their lives. To encourage independence and to build children's self-discipline, frequently offer developmentally appropriate choices. Collaborate with children to include their input on classroom rules and routines.

Allowing children to make age-appropriate decisions prevents needless power struggles with teachers. Offer only real choices. If a child is getting ready to go outdoors on a cold day, asking, "Would you like to put on your coat?" is not appropriate. Instead, say, "Here's your coat. Which arm is going in the sleeve first?" Giving children a choice shows that you respect their opinions and independence, and that builds self-esteem.

Coach Appropriate Behaviors

Young children are forgetful and easily distracted. They need firm but friendly reminders to follow classroom rules. You might say, "Where do we put the costumes when we're finished playing with them?" or "Did you remember to wash your hands before coming to the table?"

Coaching encourages children's progress and expresses confidence in their ability to behave correctly. A smile, a pat on the back, or a hug recognizes children's efforts. Children are encouraged when early educators acknowledge hard work, such as saying to a struggling child, "I'm proud of the time you have put into cleaning up the toys." Early educators should also recognize and reinforce motivation, initiative, and assertiveness.

Distraction and Redirection

With very young children, such as infants, distraction is the best method of reducing dangerous behavior. For instance, distraction is used when a child care professional jingles keys to shift a baby's attention from pulling a plug out of an electric socket.

SAFETY MATTERS

Mouthing

Babies use their mouths to explore tastes, textures, and shapes. Mouthing is normal, but it can be dangerous. A baby can choke on small objects or be poisoned by chemicals. Distraction is a good technique to use if infants find an object they should not play with, but prevention is an even better safety method. Make sure that all infant toys are too large to fit all the way into a baby's mouth. Keep soaps, medicines, and chemicals out of reach. You can satisfy a baby's need to explore by choosing toys and foods with interesting shapes and textures.

Be Prepared

Use the library or the Internet to conduct research on child safety. Describe the characteristics and safety features of developmentally appropriate play toys and activities for infants. Make a safety checklist of twenty common choking hazards for babies, including toys and toy parts, household objects, and foods. Share your descriptions and checklist with the class.

What Would You Do? You examine some of the infant toys in your child care facility. You find that some of the toys in the infant room are unsafe and could be choking hazards if put in a child's mouth. What would you do?

Redirection involves steering a child's disruptive behavior to a different, more acceptable activity that still meets the child's basic needs. This method is more often used with preschoolers. For instance, an early childhood educator would interrupt children throwing blocks by saying, "Remember, blocks are for building, not throwing. If you want to play a throwing game, you may toss these bean bags into the bucket." In this instance, the early educator recognized the children's desire for an active game and provided a safe alternative to throwing blocks.

Establish Behavior Consequences

Allowing children to experience the consequences of their actions is one strategy child care professionals use to guide behavior. **Consequences** are events that occur as the result of a particular behavior. Consequences may be positive or negative. When children realize their actions may have negative consequences, they are motivated to control their own behavior.

Early educators should select consequences that are suitable for the child's age and developmental level. Make sure they are reasonable, respectful, and related to the appropriate or inappropriate behavior.

Encouragement and Positive Reinforcement

Children will respond better to encouragement and praise than negativity. Encouraging the things that a child does right will produce good behavior better than only reminding the child what he or she did wrong. A consequence that rewards a particular behavior, making it more likely to be repeated, is **positive reinforcement**. Praise, attention, and smiles are all examples of positive reinforcement. This type of reinforcement helps children take pride in their actions. It also helps children understand when they are successfully meeting social expectations.

Praise and encouragement should be specific and genuine, such as, "Great job of putting all the blocks on the shelf. You didn't leave a single one on the floor!" or "I like that you shared your crayons with Julie. She is enjoying drawing with you." Remember to recognize the positive behavior right away to help the child link the action to the praise.

While this is an important guidance tool, keep in mind that if children are praised for everything they do, it no longer motivates them. Tailor your encouragement to the needs of the child, such as praising a newly acquired skill or an action the child has struggled with in the past.

▼ **Great Job!**
This early educator is using positive reinforcement to encourage this child's good behavior. *What are some examples of positive reinforcement messages?*

Negative reinforcement, in which children are ridiculed or demeaned as a result of behaviors, should be avoided. Letting children taunt, tease, bully, or call their peers mean names, or teachers using such negative reinforcement, is never acceptable.

Natural Consequences

Sometimes the natural results of an action are enough to discourage the repeated misbehavior. For instance, if a child drops a drawing on the floor and does not pick it up, the drawing will be walked on and torn. Natural consequences can be effective but should be used only if they do not endanger the child or others.

Logical Consequences

By promoting responsibility, logical consequences teach a child to correct a mishap. For instance, if a child spills milk, teach the child how to clean it up. Use the following guidelines for enforcing consequences:

▶ Speak privately to the child. Do not embarrass the child by making him or her—and the misbehavior—the center of attention.

▶ Give the child a chance to correct the behavior, then identify a consequence: "You may play with the puzzle as long as you keep the pieces on the table. If you continue to throw the pieces on the floor, the puzzle will be put away."

▶ After you state the consequences, take action right away so the child understands that the consequences are in response to the misdeed.

▶ If the child cries or sulks, stay calm and use a quiet voice, but remain firm. Giving in only teaches the child to use the same tactics again.

▶ Be consistent. If you enforce rules only some of the time, children can become confused. This can cause unacceptable behavior to continue.

▶ Guidance techniques and classroom expectations should be consistent and fair for all children in your care. Behavior problems can arise if one child is not held to the same standard as others.

▶ Express your trust in the child to behave more appropriately in the future.

Science *for Success*

Sleep, Behavior, and Social Skills

According to the National Institutes of Health, teenagers need only nine hours of sleep per day, while preschoolers need at least 10 to 12 hours of sleep. When children get an adequate amount of sleep, they are better able to learn and practice appropriate behavior and social skills.

Procedure Create a survey as a class that all students will complete. It should ask students to indicate how many hours of sleep they had the previous night. Then students should use a scale of 1 to 10 to indicate their current levels of focus, energy, mood, concentration, and comprehension. Students will fill out the survey every day for one week.

Analysis Use the survey answers to draw conclusions about the importance of adequate sleep. Answer the following questions: How does inadequate sleep affect a person's ability to focus, learn, and relate well to others? Link the information from the surveys to preschool children. What effect would an inadequate amount of sleep have on preschool children? How would this affect aspects of a child care center, such as the daily schedule, activities, or guidance techniques? Then plan a naptime routine that would assist teachers in helping children calm themselves for an early afternoon nap.

Figure 9.5 Cool-Down versus Time-Out

Purpose of Techniques The cool-down moment guidance technique is sometimes called a "time-out" by teachers and parents, however a cool-down moment is different from "time-out." *What is the difference between a cool-down moment and a "time-out?"*

Cool-Down Moments	"Time-Outs"
• The purpose of a cool-down moment is to help the child regain self-control for proper expression of emotions and behavior. • These moments involve a follow up discussion between early educator and child. • The emphasis should be on talking through the problem with a child after he or she has regained composure. This helps the child learn to cope with his or her feelings and then listen and communicate in a clear manner after he or she returns to activities. • This technique helps children learn to problem solve and express feelings productively.	• A traditional "time-out" sometimes focuses too much on a specific chair or time out area. • Incorrect use of "time-out" can lead to a "trouble maker" label if a child is sent to a specific chair or area too often. • This type of label can undermine the child's self-esteem. • A criticism of the traditional "time-out" is that sometimes its purpose is to punish, embarrass, isolate, or emotionally abandon a child.

Withdrawal of Privileges

Another approach is to deny a child a privilege for a short time. The privilege being taken away should directly relate to the misbehavior so the child understands the reason for its withdrawal. For example, if children throw sand, they may be denied access to the sandbox, but should not be denied access to the entire play area. Establish a definite time: "You may not play in the sandbox until this afternoon." Then direct the children to another activity where they may start fresh.

Cool-Down Moments

When prevention and other discipline methods do not work, a child who continues to be very disruptive may be given a **cool-down moment**. This is a short period of time in which the child must sit away from group activities that he or she is interrupting, yet still be in clear sight of the teachers. This may mean sitting at another table or sitting by his or her own cubby. Make sure that the area chosen as a cool-down space is a safe spot. Teachers should explain to a child why he or she needs a few cool-down moments. **Figure 9.5** above explains the difference between a cool-down moment and a "time-out."

When directing a child to take a cool-down moment, encourage him or her to breathe normally and offer a tissue for tears. Explain how the child is expected to behave when he or she returns to activities. Be sure that the same teacher who takes the child to the cool-down area also brings the child back to classroom activities for consistency. The teacher can reinforce that he or she likes the child but did not like the misbehavior.

Cool-down moments should be no longer than three to five minutes. Some teachers use the rule of one minute of cool-down per year of age, so a three-year-old would have a cool-down moment for three minutes. However, this rule is not appropriate for children over the age of six. Due to toddlers' limited ability to understand, calm down periods are not recommended for that age group. A cool-down moment may also not be appropriate for some children with special needs.

Guidance Challenges

Conflict is a natural and common occurrence among children. Learning how to resolve conflicts in a positive manner—without physical or verbal aggression—is a major challenge of childhood. Resolving conflicts involves many social skills: communication, negotiation, cooperation, and the ability to stand up for your own rights while respecting the rights of others. A supportive child care professional can help children acquire these skills.

Avoid Labels

Using labels with children should always be avoided. A child who is labeled "troublemaker" or "bully" tends to confirm the label by giving adults just what they expect. In addition, negative labels such as "stupid" and "clumsy" create stereotypes, which are hurtful and damage self-esteem. Labels do not need to be spoken to have an effect. The labels assigned a child affect your tone of voice, your facial expression, and how you react to misbehavior. Children pick up on these subtle differences.

Conflict Resolution

As an early educator, what should you do when conflict occurs? The answer depends on the situation. If a child is being physically harmed or endangered, immediately take action. Stop the child who is doing the hurting, and then comfort the one who is hurt. If the situation poses no immediate danger, simply move closer and remain observant. This lets children know that you are aware of what is going on. If children seem to need help resolving conflict, provide only as much guidance as necessary. **Figure 9.6** on page 194 lists problem-solving steps teachers can use to help children resolve conflict. Try these ideas as well:

▶ Encourage each child to express his or her point of view. Ask questions such as "What happened next?" and "How did you feel about that?"

▼**Resolving Conflict**

Early educators should encourage each child to tell his point of view and work together to resolve conflicts, such as this one. *What are some examples of questions or coaching techniques that can help a child express his or her point of view?*

© Randy Faris/Corbis

▶ If children find it difficult to express their feelings, you may need to coach them: "Maybe you feel mad because Sonia took the tricycle away from you. It's okay to tell her that it makes you mad." Questions and leading statements such as these guide children to solve problems and make decisions about resolutions on their own.

▶ Coach children through problem-solving steps. Teaching children how to resolve conflicts on their own takes more time than solving the problem for them. In the long run, however, it is much better for the children because it teaches them the important lifelong skill of problem solving. Only as a last resort should a teacher solve a problem. If children cannot resolve the conflict, a teacher might say, "This is a tough one. I'll help you decide this time."

Figure 9.6   Help Children Resolve Conflict

Teachable Moments   Early educators can use the following steps to guide children in resolving a conflict. *What steps should the children repeat if their problem is not solved?*

Two children fighting over a toy is a common conflict in child care centers. Early educators can use this conflict as a teachable moment to help students learn how to problem-solve and to develop their interpersonal skills for resolving conflicts. Early educators can use the following steps to guide children in resolving a conflict.

Assess the situation	If aggressive behavior is taking place, immediately step in and stop the aggression.
Identify	Help children identify the problem. Help children tell their feelings about wanting the toy. Restate what each child says. For example, you might say, "James is angry because you took the toy from him."
Brainstorm	Ask children to think of several possible solutions. You may have to make suggestions for younger children, such as, "Let's take turns. Andy, you play with the toy for a few minutes, then James can play with the toy." A timer may be used to signal the end of a turn. Older children should be asked to offer their own solutions, with the teacher modeling possible resolutions only as necessary.
Evaluate and Choose	Help children evaluate the options and arrive at an acceptable solution. After a solution has been reached, allow the children to follow through with the solution, stepping in only if the conflict continues.
Reevaluate choice	Have the children evaluate how well they solved their problem. If their problem is not solved, repeat the problem-solving steps: Identify, Brainstorm, Evaluate, Choose, and Reevaluate.
Provide positive reinforcement	When children resolve conflicts well, let them know that they have done a good job.

Apply It! The next time you experience two children fighting over a toy, assess the situation and demonstrate the problem-solving steps outlined for resolving conflict. Did the steps work? Share what you learned from the experience with your teacher or a classmate.

Documenting Concerns

Some children have more difficulties than others. If a child's behavior problems last for weeks or months, it may require special attention. To determine if there is a pattern or a specific cause of a problem, early educators should make frequent, objective observations. A child's behavior should be recorded to see how often problems occur and when.

Keep in mind that a child's behavior problems could be linked to an undiagnosed physical, mental, emotional, or social problem. Documenting your concerns about a child's behavior may actually uncover issues such as hearing loss or attention disorders, which can lead to helpful solutions for the child's life.

Unresolved behavior problems require a conference with the child's parent or guardian. Be careful not to use negative labels or sound as though you are placing blame. Speak clearly, courteously, and concisely. Explain that you are concerned about the child's behavior and want to work together to find a solution. Make sure that parents or guardians have realistic expectations of their child. For example, some parents may expect their young toddler to sit quietly at the dinner table, although that is not a developmentally appropriate behavior for a toddler.

You may want to ask some questions: Have there been behavior problems at home? If so, when did they begin? How do you handle them? Is there something in the child's life that might be upsetting? Some problems require parents to seek help. Give them referrals to appropriate agencies.

READING CHECK ✔ **Recall** What are the various types of consequences that can guide children's behavior?

▲ **Family Conference**

This early educator is discussing a child's behavior problem with the child and his parent. *What are some guidelines to follow when speaking with the parent of a child in your care?*

Mental Health Consultant

What Does a Mental Health Consultant Do?

Mental health consultants help early educators recognize, understand, and respond appropriately to the emotional and social needs of children. They answer questions and discuss concerns about children's behaviors. They also provide information and referrals for child care staff working through difficult child care situations or family problems. They can help the teacher sort through the pieces of a difficult situation, including the needs of the child, the parents, and the staff.

Career Readiness Skills

Mental health consultants must have a desire to help others and an ability to relate to various types of people. They should be fair and sensitive to people and their problems and be able to refrain from judging others. They should also have strong communication skills and a keen understanding of emotions and mental, emotional, and social development. Professional ethics are an essential part of this field.

Education and Training

A master's degree or graduate level certificate in a mental health field is the minimum requirement for entry into this occupation. People pursuing this field often receive a bachelor's degree with a major under the counseling and mental health services field. To specialize in consulting with child care centers, a student should also have a strong background in early childhood theory and classroom practices. Specific licensing and credentials vary by state. Most states require that mental health consultants be licensed as qualified mental health professionals.

Job Outlook

Employment opportunities for mental health consultants are expected to grow faster than the national average for all occupations. However, the stability of this field relies heavily on the availability of government-funded grants. Economic conditions that affect government budgets can affect employment in this field.

Critical Thinking There are many career areas available for people interested in mental health. Some occupation examples are social workers, psychiatrists, substance abuse counselors, and career counselors. Choose one specialty and research it. Assess how your personal interests, aptitudes, and abilities would fit into a mental health profession. Propose the possible short- and long-term goals that will help you prepare for this career.

Career Cluster

Human Services Mental Health Consultants work in the Counseling and Mental Health Services pathway of the Human Services career cluster. Here are some other jobs in this cluster:

- Sociologist
- School Counselor
- Personal Trainer
- Clinical and Counseling Psychologist
- Consumer Advocate
- Teacher's Aide
- Community Service Director
- Adult Day Care Worker

Explore Further The Human Services career cluster contains five pathways: Early Childhood Development & Services; Counseling & Mental Health Services; Family & Community Services; Personal Care Services; Consumer Services. Choose one of these pathways to explore further.

Custom Medical Stock Photo/Alamy

Guiding Behavior and Social Competence

Visual Summary

Child Guidance Basics

Prevent Problems	Set Expectations and Limits	Handle Inappropriate Behavior	Allow Consequences
Plan schedules ahead	**Think** age-appropriate	**Stay** calm	**Use** positive reinforcement
Use consistent routines	**Be** a positive example	**Choose** your words and actions carefully	**Monitor** natural consequences
Give simple rules	**Have** clear expectations	**Ignore** minor mischief	**Watch** for logical consequences
Offer variety of activities	**Keep** it simple, specific, and fair	**Offer** choices	**Use** cool-down moments
Keep ages in mind	**Use** I-messages	**Be** a positive behavior coach	**Consider** withdrawal of privileges
Provide enough equipment for everyone		**Distract** unsafe behavior	
Small bodies = small spaces		**Redirect** inappropriate behavior	
Give individual attention			

Vocabulary Review

1. Write each of the content and academic vocabulary terms and their corresponding definition on an index card. Match each of these terms related to child guidance to the correct definition.

Content Vocabulary

◇ social competence (p. 178)
◇ compassion (p. 178)
◇ guidance (p. 181)
◇ self-discipline (p. 183)
◇ I-messages (p. 187)

◇ redirection (p. 190)
◇ consequences (p. 190)
◇ positive reinforcement (p. 190)
◇ cool-down moment (p. 192)

Academic Vocabulary

■ vary (p. 184)
■ functions (p. 187)

Review Key Concepts

2. **Relate** How does modeling respect, acceptance, and positive social skills help nurture a child's social competence?
3. **Describe** some positive child-guidance techniques and strategies for positive classroom management that will create a supportive environment for children.
4. **Demonstrate** You have learned about many strategies for guiding children. Think of a situation in which you would need to use a guidance strategy with a child. Which strategy or strategies would you use? List the steps you would take to guide this child.

Critical Thinking

5. **Evaluate** Think about the parenting styles you read about. Explain how different parenting styles could affect your child-guidance strategies.

6. **Analyze** What message does a child care professional send if he or she hurts, frightens, threatens, or demeans a child? Why is it important to avoid labeling children?

7. **Explain** three ways a child care professional might react when conflict occurs between children.

8. **Infer** How can behavior consequences promote responsible behavior?

9. **Interpret** Why is consistency so important when enforcing consequences?

10. **Assess** Draw conclusions about how collaboration with a parent or family member can help solve problem behavior in children.

21st Century Skills

Collaboration Skills

11. **Promote positive relationships** You have learned that it is important for a child to feel trust, attachment, respect, and security with his or her care provider. With a partner, demonstrate some techniques for building a positive teacher-child relationship. What techniques will foster respect through positive collaborative relationships with children? What interpersonal skills promote positive and productive relationships with children?

Responsibility Skills

12. **Responding to Crisis** Sometimes inappropriate behavior is linked to serious issues at home. Research symptoms of children in family crisis situations and ways to respond to family crises or child abuse. Use library or Internet sources, or interview a child care director. Create a presentation on appropriate ways to respond. Discuss the impact of crises on children, their families, and children's behavior. Provide contact information for local child protective services.

Child Care LAB

Use the skills you have learned in this chapter.

Dealing with Challenging Behavior

13. **Write a Scenario** Select a difficult or challenging behavior such as hitting, shyness, or tantrums. Write a scenario that requires guidance strategies for the behavior you selected. Then script a response about how you would respond and what guidance techniques you would use.

    A. Choose the challenging behavior you would like to research.

    B. Research how to handle such behavior in a positive, caring, and effective manner. If applicable, also search for referral or resource services for extreme behavioral disorders.

    C. Ask yourself the following questions: What factors may be contributing to the behavior? What could be some rules or consequences for this behavior? Is a referral necessary or can the behavior be dealt with in the classroom? How would you communicate with the parent in a constructive, supportive way?

    D. Write your scenario and responses that include positive guidance techniques.

    E. Consider the child's age and stage of development when assessing the behavior and choosing your guidance method.

    F. Discuss your scenario with a partner and evaluate your responses. Were positive or negative methods used? Were they appropriate for the situation?

Create Your Evaluation

Create an evaluation sheet with these categories:

- Age appropriate
- Fair
- Consistent
- Positive
- Developmentally appropriate

Use the sheet to assess the guidance strategies presented for the scenario. Present your responses to another pair, and do the same assessment to gain additional feedback.

Academic Skills

English Language Arts

14. Conflict Resolution Ask parents who have young children if you may observe the behavior of their children. Document situations in which conflict occurred. For each situation, write a dialogue showing how a child care professional might mediate or provide positive guidance to resolve the conflict. Create a flowchart of your observations and share it with your class.

Social Studies

15. Research Effective communication with children, parents, and family members is an important part of guiding children's behavior. Using print, Internet resources, or interviews, investigate ways in which nonverbal communication is used in different cultures. Explain how cultural differences in nonverbal communication will impact early childhood programs.

Mathematics

16. Balanced Schedules A balanced schedule can help prevent behavior problems. Lindsay wants to create a balanced environment that encourages social development and friendship building by creating a rotation schedule for her child care class. She has from 9:45–11:30 A.M. to rotate through 5 group activity stations and must include a 30 minute lunch period. Create a rotation schedule for Lindsay's class. List five activities that could be used for the stations. Create a table to represent the amount of time that can be spent in each station.

Math Concept **Elapsed Time** The amount of time that passes between one event and another is called elapsed time.

Starting Hint Calculate the number of minutes available from 9:45-11:30 A.M. Then subtract 30 minutes for lunch from the total amount of minutes. Divide the remaining amount of minutes by the number of stations (5).

 For more math practice, go to the math appendix at the back of the book.

Certification Prep

Directions Read each statement. Then read the answer choices and choose the one that best completes the sentence.

17. Praise, encouragement, and attention are all examples of _____.

    A. logical consequences   **C.** I-messages

    B. positive reinforcement   **D.** negative reinforcement

18. Guidance techniques and classroom expectations should be _____.

    A. age appropriate

    B. consistent and fair

    C. set simply for the convenience of adults

    D. both A and B

Test-Taking Tip

In a multiple-choice test, the answers should be specific and precise. Read the question first, then read all the answer choices. Eliminate answers that you know are incorrect.

(tl)©Nova Development; (tr)McGraw-Hill Education

Health and Safety

College & Career READINESS

Who takes care of children's mental health?

There are many careers that care and advocate for the health and safety of children in specialized areas. Mental health professionals such as family counselors and play therapists work with children to treat behavioral and emotional difficulties that interfere with normal development. These professionals also work with children who have experienced trauma or family crisis.

To succeed in health and safety positions, you may need an education, psychology, social work, or law degree. You will also need excellent interpersonal and communication skills.

Dr. Connor Walters • Play Therapist

Q What is your job?

A A play therapist works with children and families to help them resolve troubling emotional issues and behaviors. Play therapy might look to the untrained eye as just "play," but it is the application of theory and has been thoroughly researched and found to be very effective.

Q What is your typical workday like?

A There really is no typical day for a play therapist! With some children, you might be using art, but with others, puppets, games, role playing, storytelling, and so much more.

Q Why did you choose to train as a play therapist?

A When I was taking coursework in Marriage and Family Therapy I realized that many techniques that were useful for adults weren't really successful with children because they weren't developmentally appropriate. Because play is the child's language, I was naturally drawn to play therapy.

Q What education and training have you received?

A I have a Bachelor's, a Master's, and a PhD in Child Development and Family Relationships. I also completed a year-long internship in Marriage and Family Therapy. I have to admit that attending or presenting at a conference full of play therapists is a uniquely fun experience!

Q What skills are most important in your job?

A Play therapists need an understanding of children's development. Play therapists also need to understand the theories and research behind play therapy techniques. Otherwise, you can't apply them in a way that uniquely serves that particular child. The most effective play therapists are those who have interpersonal skills that allow children and families to build strong relationships. A sense of humor and fun is helpful too. Good play therapists are keen observers of individual and family dynamics and have the patience to let the child or family heal.

Career Requirements	
Education or Training	Health and safety jobs usually require a bachelor's degree or higher level of education. Play therapists and other mental health consultants have a master's degree or higher. Health and safety workers also must be registered, certified, or licensed and continue their education throughout their careers.
Academic Skills	English Language Arts, Mathematics, Science, and Social Studies
Aptitudes, Abilities, and Skills	Desire to help others, strong sense of ethics, interpersonal skills such as ability to inspire trust and confidence, communication skills, high emotional energy
Workplace Safety	Workplace safety rules must be followed. Toys or props must be age-appropriate and safe for children.
Career Outlook	There is a very high demand for qualified individuals in all health and safety fields.
Career Path	Career paths will vary depending on education level and interests. Some mental health consultants are entrepreneurs and open their own private practices.

Career Pathways	
Family Counselor	A family counselor provides counseling services to individuals and entire families. A family counselor is familiar with issues a family may face, such as financial difficulties or conflicting opinions about raising children, and provides guidance and communication strategies to help families deal with these issues.
Family Mediator	A family mediator works with both parents during a divorce or separation to determine a parenting and care plan for minor children.
Child Care Policy Analyst	A child care policy analyst develops government policies and advises lawmakers and government administration about child care. Policy analysts spend time speaking with child care professionals and related agencies to gather information about important child care issues.
Child Care Employee Advocate	A child care employee advocate works to improve child care staff wages and working conditions through public campaigns and policy lobbying on key issues such as health care and compensation.

Critical Thinking What classes have you taken in school that might help you prepare for a career as a play therapist? Propose possible short- and long-term career goals that will help you prepare for this career.

Certification Prep

Research how play can be used as a form of nonverbal communication. How can children be helped to develop their communication skills through play? Describe an activity that would encourage a child's communication skills development using play.

Competitive Events Practice

Plan a developmentally appropriate communication activity for a group of preschoolers that uses play. Prepare a portfolio that includes your lesson plan and evidence of developmental appropriateness. Assemble the materials for the activity in a resource container.

Judge your work on the following criteria:

• Is your lesson plan complete?

• Does your portfolio provide evidence of the activity's developmental appropriateness?

• Does your resource container have all the materials necessary to do the activity?

Interview a Child Care Professional

Interviewing and observing a child care professional on the job can provide valuable information about the experiences you will encounter in your career as a child care professional. You will learn about the education, training, skills, and abilities needed to be a successful child care professional.

My Journal

If you completed the journal entry on page 80, refer to it to see how you described a child care professional's typical day at work. Add any additional notes about a child care professional's job responsibilities after reading this unit.

Project Assignment

In this project, you will do the following:

- Choose a child care career that you are interested in learning more about
- Develop questions to ask a child care professional
- Interview and observe a child care professional
- Write a report summarizing your experience and what you learned from the interview
- Present the information you gathered during this experience to the class

Applied Child Care Professional Skills Behind the Project

Your success as a child care professional will depend on your skills. Skills you will use in this project include the following:

▶ Interacting with child care professionals in a professional environment
▶ Conducting observations and drawing conclusions about those observations
▶ Determining education, training, skills, and abilities required for the child care profession
▶ Identifying aptitudes and personal interests needed for child care careers

English Language Arts Skills Behind the Project

The English Language Arts skills you will use for this project are interviewing, writing, and speaking skills. Remember these key concepts:

Interviewing Skills

▶ Organize your interview questions in the order you want to ask them
▶ Take clear and accurate notes
▶ Listen attentively and ask follow-up questions
▶ Thank the interviewee for his or her time

Writing Skills

▶ Use complete sentences with correct spelling, grammar, and punctuation
▶ Consider your audience
▶ Use findings from the interview to communicate your discoveries in writing

Speaking Skills

▶ Rehearse what you are going to say before your presentation
▶ Speak clearly so that the audience can follow your presentation
▶ Make and maintain eye contact with your audience

©Nova Development

STEP 1 Choose and Research Your Career

Choose and research a child care career that you are interested in learning more about. Do background research to determine the following general information about the career:

- educational requirements
- job responsibilities
- average salary
- job outlook

STEP 2 Plan Your Interview and Observation

Use the results of your research to write a list of interview questions to ask a local child care professional about his or her career. Your questions should ask about education, personal interests and aptitudes, and skills and abilities needed in the child care profession. Your questions might include:

- Why did you choose your career?
- What education did you receive?
- How did your career path lead to your current job? Where do you see your career path taking you?
- Describe a typical workday.
- What skills are most important for your job?
- What is the most challenging part of your job? The most rewarding?
- What advice would you give to someone interested in this career path?

STEP 3 Connect with Your Community

Identify a local child care professional you can interview. Conduct your interview using the questions you prepared in Step 2. After the interview, observe the child care professional at work. Take notes during the interview and observation and write a summary of the experience.

Child Care Portfolio Project Checklist

Plan

- ✔ Choose and research a child care career that you are interested in.
- ✔ Plan and write your interview questions.
- ✔ Interview and observe a child care professional and write a summary of the information that you learned.

Present

- ✔ Make a presentation to your class to share the results of your interview and observation.
- ✔ Invite students to ask any questions they may have. Answer these questions.
- ✔ When students ask you questions, demonstrate in your answers that you respect their perspectives.
- ✔ Turn in your interview questions and the summary of the interview and observation to your teacher.

STEP 4 Share What You Have Learned

Use the Child Care Portfolio Project Checklist to plan and give an oral report about your interview experience to share what you have learned with your classmates. In your presentation, be sure to describe your interviewee's

- typical workday.
- education.
- skills and interests.
- daily challenges and rewards.
- advice to students interested in pursuing the career path.

STEP 5 Evaluate Your Child Care Professional and Academic Skills

Your project will be evaluated based on the following:

- Content, organization, and completeness of your information
- Depth and detail of your interview and observation
- Use of complete sentences and correct spelling, grammar, and punctuation
- Quality of presentation, including speaking and listening skills

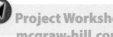 **Project Worksheet** *Go to* connected. mcgraw-hill.com *for a worksheet you can use to complete your portfolio project.*

Managing an Early Childhood Program

Chapters

Project Preview

Money Matters

After completing this unit, you will know more about managing early childhood programs for infants and children. You will learn about the schedules, routines, equipment, and supplies needed to run an early childhood program. In the Unit 3 child care portfolio project, you will research the income and expenses involved in operating a child care center. You will set a financial goal and create a sample monthly program budget.

My Journal

Imagine you are the owner of a child care center. Write a journal entry about the types of reoccurring monthly expenses that your program might have. Do not include expenses such as furnishings, changing tables, and play equipment that would not be replaced each month.

- What kinds of art supplies, toys, and reading materials would your program need?
- What other expenses might you incur each month?
- How might the purchasing choices you make impact the program's budget?

Explore the Photo

Managing an early childhood program involves much more than planning lessons and activities. *What else is involved in running a child care program?*

CHAPTER 10

Quality Early Childhood Programs

Writing Activity

⭐ 21st Century Skills

Brochure A brochure is a persuasive document that advertises a product or service, or conveys information in small amounts. Imagine you are opening a child care center in a small community. Write a brochure introducing the local residents to your center. Include important program information.

Writing Tips

1. Keep the purpose of the brochure on your mind as you write.
2. Develop the text first, then figure out the design.
3. Try to appeal to the customers' emotions as well as their logic.

Explore the Photo This girl is enjoying reading with her teacher. *What can you observe about this interaction?*

Design Pics / Kelly Redinger

Reading Guide

Study with a Buddy It can be difficult to review your own notes and to quiz yourself on what you have just read. According to research, studying with a partner for just twelve minutes can help you learn better.

Read to Learn

Key Concepts

- **Identify** six different types of early childhood programs.
- **Explain** licensing and registration requirements.
- **Describe** the role of the director in managing program services.

Main Idea

A variety of early childhood programs are available that provide children with supervision, care, and education. Program directors have responsibilities to follow legal requirements, to hire and train qualified staff, and to work with boards and parents to provide high-quality early childhood programs.

Content Vocabulary

◇ philosophy
◇ program goals
◇ for-profit
◇ nonprofit
◇ program sponsors
◇ license exempt
◇ registration
◇ accreditation criteria
◇ organizational chart
◇ reference check
◇ board
◇ program governance
◇ advisory board
◇ governing board
◇ financial management

Academic Vocabulary

■ terminate
■ subsidy

Graphic Organizer

As you read, choose six different types of early childhood program options. Use a cluster web like the one shown to help you organize your information.

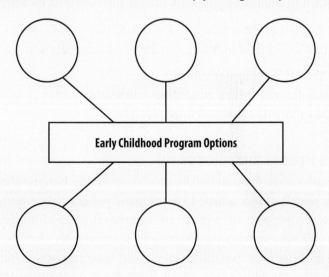

Early Childhood Program Options

Graphic Organizer *Go to* **connected.mcgraw-hill.com** *to print this Graphic Organizer.*

AS YOU READ

Connect How can a family determine which early childhood program is best for it?

◇**Vocabulary**

You can find definitions in the glossary at the back of this book.

Program Types

Early childhood program is the broad term that describes any situation in which children have supervision, care, education, or special lessons by qualified people. This typically occurs outside of the children's homes. The demand for such programs has grown over the last few decades. This chapter will introduce you to a wide variety of early childhood programs.

Program Philosophy and Goals

The defining feature of any early childhood program is its program philosophy. A program's **philosophy** describes the general beliefs, concepts, and attitudes a program has about how children learn. It is sometimes called a mission statement. In addition, it describes how the program should serve and educate children and involve parents. See **Figure 10.1**.

Program goals identify basic skills, concepts, and attitudes to develop and encourage in children. They also address the range of services to be provided. For example, program goals might expect children to

▶ gain high self-esteem and a positive attitude.

▶ learn self-help skills, responsibility, and independence.

▶ develop positive social skills such as cooperation and sharing.

▶ develop large- and small-motor skills.

▶ improve communication skills such as listening, speaking, reading, and writing.

▶ develop curiosity, creative thinking, and problem-solving ability.

▶ learn to respect, accept, and understand the rights and feelings of others.

Program goals for families of the children might include

▶ opportunities for classroom participation.

▶ use of a child development lending resource library.

▶ access to a toy-lending library.

▶ options for parenting education workshops.

▶ involvement in special family events.

Sample Program Philosophy

Programs can vary according to their basic beliefs about how children develop and learn. Curriculums reflect those beliefs, and form the foundation of a program's early childhood guidance and teaching. For instance, the curriculum known as the Montessori Method emphasizes that children should learn basic self-help skills by using objects children find in their daily environment. In this setting at snack time, children will likely be seen using a pitcher to pour their own juice into their own glass.

Figure 10.1 Child Care Center Philosophy

Mission Statement A program philosophy is sometimes called a mission statement. *Why is having a program philosophy important?*

Child Care Center

Mission Statement: Purpose & Services

The Child Care Center provides high-quality, developmental child care services for children aged 2-8 years. The Center serves as a model program for the community and the early childhood profession.

Service Philosophy

The Child Care Center staff believe children and parents are to be respected and treated with courtesy, dignity, patience, and compassion. While in our care each child is nurtured physically, socially, emotionally, and intellectually. Our well-trained teachers and care providers regard early childhood experiences with the respect and commitment they deserve. The staff works to share this attitude with the parents.

We believe children who feel love can love others. We believe children who are guided with patience and gentleness learn to trust.

The curriculum known as the Project Approach is developed from a philosophy that children learn best when they actively investigate topics of interest that emerge during their own play with peers.

Regardless of the curriculum style, there are basic beliefs that reflect developmentally appropriate practices.

Research has shown that the following beliefs work best when teaching and caring for young children:

▶ Children need many sensory, concrete, and hands-on learning experiences.

▶ Children have different learning styles, rates of learning, and developmental levels.

▶ Classroom design should encourage curiosity and exploration.

▶ Children need independent activities and group activities.

▶ Children's interests and needs should guide learning activities.

▶ Activities should encourage physical, intellectual, social, and emotional development.

▶ Activities should encourage problem solving and creativity.

▶ Parent involvement enhances children's overall development.

▲ **Early Childhood Programs**

A variety of for-profit and nonprofit centers exists throughout the country. Both types of centers should offer a high-quality program with appropriate curriculum. *What is the difference between a for-profit and a nonprofit center?*

For-Profit and Nonprofit Programs

Programs that are designed to bring in more income than they spend on their services are called **for-profit**. This extra money goes to the owners or investors, sometimes known as stockholders. Some for-profit programs are owned by individuals. Others are large investor-owned or company-owned businesses, such as KinderCare®. Some programs operate on a **nonprofit** basis. This means there are no owners or stockholders who receive money from the program's income. Money earned by a nonprofit program goes back into the budget or into savings for future use.

Program Quality

Whatever type of care a family uses, they want it to be high quality. When working in early childhood, you will be responsible for quality programming in all these areas:

▶ Program philosophy and goals

▶ Knowledge of child development; appropriate guidance

▶ Basic health, safety, and nutrition; appropriate environment

▶ Developmentally appropriate curriculum and practices

▶ Activities, records, reports, and evaluations

▶ Organized daily schedule

▶ Family involvement

▶ Ongoing staff training

Program Options

Early childhood programs have both similarities and differences. All programs aim to provide a safe and healthy learning environment for children. However, **program sponsors**, the specific groups that fund or manage an early childhood program, vary in their operating purposes. Sponsors range from faith-based groups to social service agencies and colleges. Program philosophies and goals vary according to their sponsor's or owner's individual purposes.

Child Care Centers Child care centers enroll children whose parents or guardians work or attend school. Child care centers are typically open from 6:00 A.M. to 6:00 P.M. To accommodate a variety of work schedules, some even operate evenings or 24 hours a day. Good child care centers provide learning activities, active play, meals, snacks, and nap time. Centers may serve children from 6 weeks to 12 years of age.

Family Child Care Homes

These programs are private child care services offered by individuals in their own homes. Such homes usually enroll three to eight children of varying ages. When care providers in family child care homes take in infants, fewer children can be cared for in these homes. Homes that serve more than eight children are called family child care group homes. Check the licensing or regulation laws in your state for specific guidelines for family child care homes.

Before- and After-School Child Care

These programs provide care for school-age children before and after school. Some programs operate in schools. Other programs transport children to and from school to care for them at another site. Schools sometimes manage the programs but often contract with other agencies, such as the YWCA, to operate them.

Preschools and Nursery Schools

These programs provide educational services to children from three to five years of age. These schools usually operate two and one-half hours or three hours per day, in the morning or afternoon. Preschools and nursery schools emphasize learning skills and social development. Preschools are often used by families to give children extra stimulation and experiences prior to formal education.

▼ **After-School Care**

After-school care programs provide one option for parents of school-age children. *What might be some of the benefits of after-school care?*

Public School Prekindergarten

Prekindergarten programs help prepare a child for success in kindergarten. They usually serve three- to five-year-olds. They provide enrichment activities that help a child succeed in elementary school and beyond. Public prekindergartens usually run half days and are free of charge. Most operate only during the school year. Parent involvement, including teacher home visits, is heavily stressed. Some states fund universal prekindergarten for all age-eligible children in their states. The names of programs vary from state to state. A popular title for universal state prekindergarten is Preschool for All.

Christopher Futcher/Getty Images

Employer-Sponsored Centers

Child care programs that are offered by businesses to employees are called employer-sponsored programs. The center may be on or very near the work site. The employer may operate the center itself or contract with a child care management firm to operate it for the employer.

In-Home Child Care

Some parents or guardians employ nannies, usually through an agency, to provide child care in their own homes. Sometimes a nanny lives with the family and receives a room and food as part of his or her wages. Other times the nanny goes to the child's home each day. Another option for child care is an au pair ('ō-'per). An au pair is a person who comes from one country to live with a family in another country. Au pairs are usually students who exchange child care for room, board, and money for tuition. Au pairs might be subject to federal taxes depending on how long they have been in this country.

Intergenerational Care Centers

These programs offer daytime care for young children and older adults. Young and old participate regularly in activities. The children benefit from the older adults' care and wisdom, and the older adults benefit from the children's energy and enthusiasm. This interaction helps children develop and older adults maintain zest for lifelong wellness and learning.

Child Care for Mildly Ill Children

Staffed with early childhood professionals and nurses, these programs care for mildly ill children while they get better. Only children whose illnesses are not or are no longer contagious can attend. Program activities are slower paced and provide more rest time than a regular child care center.

Back-Up Child Care Centers

Sometimes an employer has a worker whose regular child care option is interrupted. For instance, a working parent may have a nanny or a family child care home provider who becomes too ill to provide child care for a few days. To help employees avoid missing work on those days, employers use the services of a back-up child care center. These programs specialize in providing short-term

McGraw-Hill Education

child care until a working parent can go back to the regular care provider. Unlike most programs, the children who attend a back-up child care center vary greatly from day to day.

Head Start Preschools and Child Care Centers

Head Start was created in 1964 as part of President Johnson's War on Poverty. Its purpose is to prepare economically disadvantaged preschoolers for school success. Free of charge to parents, it offers education, health, dental, and nutrition services. Head Start requires active parent participation. For children under age four, Head Start employs home visitors to teach parents how to educate and care for children. Some Head Start programs operate half days. Others operate full days to accommodate the child care needs of working parents. Head Start programs are required to enroll children with special needs and to include them in regular classroom operation.

Montessori Preschools

These programs are based on the teachings of Maria Montessori. Montessori schools use educational materials designed to help children master specific tasks in a step-by-step sequence. They encourage independent learning, learning by doing, and learning through the senses. For example, during a cooking activity, children may learn all about the ingredients in bread. Then the children would mix and bake the bread and use their senses to smell and taste the bread. Teachers must receive formal instruction in the Montessori Method before they can teach in Montessori schools. Some of these programs operate half days, others operate full days. Some Montessori programs serve infants through third graders. Most serve three- to five-year-olds.

Preschools and Child Care for Children with Special Needs

Most preschools and child care centers try to include children with special needs in their regular programs. However, some children have disabilities that are very complicated. They, too, need safe and developmentally appropriate child care. To provide such care, some social service agencies, such as Easter Seals, operate child care programs designed to meet the specific needs of

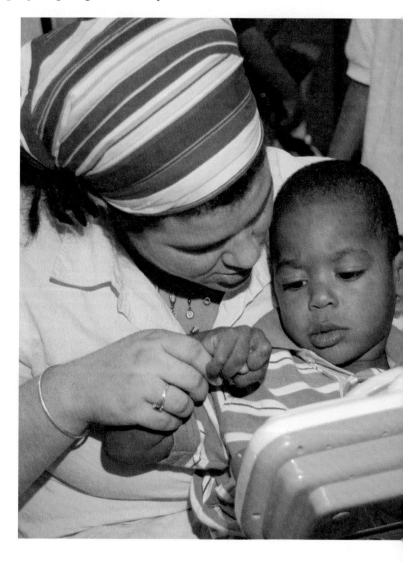

▼ **Specialized Programs**

Children with special needs benefit from extra care. *How can a specialized program help these children?*

Realistic Reflections

children with disabilities. Full- or part-day classes may include children who have birth defects or disabilities such as cerebral palsy, autism, behavioral disorders, Down syndrome, and vision or hearing impairments. Teachers need special certification or courses in order to work in these programs.

Crisis Nurseries

Crisis nurseries help prevent child abuse. Overstressed parents who feel at risk of abusing their children may use a crisis nursery. These programs operate on a 24-hour basis. Children stay at the crisis nursery until the parents feel once again capable of caring for them in a safe manner. Some nurseries care for children for up to three days while parents seek counseling. The United Way or other social service agencies often fund crisis nurseries.

Parent Cooperatives

When parents jointly create a preschool or a child care center, it is called a parent cooperative. In a cooperative, the parents hire a teacher, determine the goals, and set the rules and procedures to be followed. Child care professionals, teachers, and parents work together to influence philosophy and goals. Cooperatives require parents to work in the program a few hours every month. They may assist teachers and do administrative work.

Laboratory Schools

Some universities, colleges, and high schools provide child care or a preschool for students, employees, or community members. These programs often serve as training sites for child development students and those preparing for careers with children. Because lab schools are the training ground for future child care professionals, many are at the forefront of what is going on in the field. Children often receive care, education, and guidance based on the latest research and methods. While the atmosphere may be different from those centers in the "real" world, they make an excellent learning environment for children and students.

Kindergarten

Elementary schools, funded by state and local tax dollars, have a full- or part-day kindergarten that operates during the regular school day. Full-day kindergarten programs are becoming more common. To teach in one of these programs, a four-year degree in early childhood or elementary education is required, along with a state certification. A teacher's aide position in a kindergarten may require less training. Kindergartens offer a developmentally appropriate curriculum for children five to six years of age.

READING CHECK **Explain** Why is it important to establish program goals?

How to . . .

Locate Early Childhood Programs

You may not realize it, but there are many early childhood programs in your own community. There are programs that offer services to children and families in a variety of settings. Locating all these programs can be difficult. The following are some ways to discover what programs are offered in your community.

Image Source/AGE fotostock

Apply It!
Research and create a list of early childhood programs in your community.

▶ **Phone Book or Internet** *Search the telephone book, the local paper, or the Internet. Early childhood programs may be listed under a variety of headings. Search using the key terms day care, child care, preschool, or nursery school.*

▶ **Licensing Office**
Call your local child care program licensing office. Some states call it the Department of Health and Human Services or the Department of Children and Family Services. Ask if they provide a listing of local programs.

▶ **Agencies** *Contact your local United Way office or Cooperative Extension office. Both agencies support community programs. Ask for a listing of early childhood programs near you.*

▶ **Referrals** *Identify a local child care resource and referral agency. These are agencies that keep a current listing of all early childhood programs in the community.*

▶ **Schools** *Find your local public school district office. Ask for a listing of their prekindergarten programs or early childhood programs for children with special needs.*

Licensing, Registration, and Legal Duties

▼ **Safety Standards**

Program inspections, such as fire and health, are part of state licensing standards. *What other criteria do licensing standards address?*

Parents, communities, and state governments have a stake in protecting children's welfare. One way of ensuring that children in child care settings are safe and healthy is to require early childhood programs to meet specific requirements before they are allowed to operate. These requirements are set by local and state laws and regulations, and they vary from state to state.

Licensing and Registration Laws

Each state has its own set of licensing laws for operating early childhood programs. State licensing laws identify programs that must meet minimum requirements for legal operation. Licensing laws vary from state to state and are usually approved by a state's legislature. The legislature assigns a specific state agency to enforce licensing laws. The agency is often called the Department of Human Service or the Department of Children and Family Services.

Meeting a state's licensing laws for operation is a mandatory requirement, not a program choice. After a license to operate has been granted, a program must renew its license regularly to prove that is continuing to comply with the laws. Some states require that the license be renewed on a yearly basis; other states require that it be renewed every three years.

In some states, certain types of programs are **license exempt**. That means they are not required to obtain a license to operate legally in that state. For example, early childhood programs that are associated with parochial schools that are part of places of worship can be license exempt. Family child care homes that care for fewer than three children may also be license exempt. Offices that license programs can tell you which programs are license exempt and which require a license to operate.

Some states require registration, rather than a formal program license. **Registration** requires a care provider to notify city or state officials in writing of the program's name, address, telephone number, and intention to provide services. States vary in these requirements and procedures.

Early Childhood Licensing Requirements

Most early childhood programs, such as child care centers and preschools, require licensing. State licensing standards vary widely. However, they usually address minimum requirements for the following areas of program operation:

▶ Health, safety, and nutrition requirements

▶ Maximum group size of children by age

▶ Square footage of space per child for indoor and outdoor areas

▶ Minimum staff qualifications and in-service training requirements

▶ Minimum amount of equipment and supplies for each classroom

▶ Recommended classroom ratios of teachers to children as shown in **Figure 10.2** below

Legal Duties for Early Childhood Professionals

Laws protect the rights and interests of children and their families from the time of their applications to acceptance and ongoing enrollment in a program. In order for early childhood programs to operate within the law, program directors and staff must be aware of the legal duties of their positions. This helps ensure that children are better served and are well protected. Program staff must keep in mind a variety of legal issues when performing their duties.

Figure 10.2 **Recommended Teacher-Child Ratios**

Recommended Ratios The National Association for the Education of Young Children (NAEYC) provides recommendations for teacher-child ratios for each age group.
Why is it important to have the correct teacher-to-child ratio?

NAEYC Recommendations for Teacher-Child Ratios	
Infants – Birth to 15 months	1 adult to 3 children
Toddlers/Twos – 12 to 28 months	1 adult to 3 children
Toddlers/Twos – 21 to 36 months	1 adult to 4 children
Preschool – 2.5-year-olds to 3-year-olds	1 adult to 6 children
Preschool – 4-year-olds	1 adult to 8 children
Preschool – 5-year-olds	1 adult to 8 children
Kindergarten	1 adult to 10 children

Enrollment Application Legalities

Each state's licensing laws specify the minimum amount of information to be included in a program's application form. Required information typically includes

▶ a child's name, birth date, age, home address, and contact information.

▶ the legal parent or guardian along with his or her address and contact information for home and work.

▶ emergency contact information for at least two other individuals.

▶ names of noncustodial parents and the rights that they been awarded.

▶ a child's health reports, immunization records, allergy information, and state-required medical tests for communicable diseases such as tuberculosis.

▶ signed permission forms if children are to participate in field trips, research studies, or activities that will be photographed or videotaped.

Nonbiased Enrollment Practices

Programs must offer enrollment services on an equal-opportunity basis. Programs that receive government funds cannot reject a potential client for reasons of gender, religion, income, race, or other protected statuses. In addition, the ADA law ensures the enrollment rights of those with special needs. If enrollment ends for any client, programs must provide at least one week's notice and must document suitable reasons for discontinuing enrollment.

Ensuring Privacy and Confidentiality

All children and their families have rights to privacy. Information from their files, or about their behavior while in the program, may be shared only with specific supervising staff. Before information about a child can be shared verbally or in writing with nonprogram staff, written permission from a legal parent or guardian must be obtained. A court of law can also require a program to share confidential records.

A Fun and Educational Trip

Class field trips require signed permission forms. *What other information should a center have for each child?*

Fee Agreement Contracts

In order for families to know what they will need to pay for services, programs develop fee agreement contracts. The written contract states the days and hours of a child's attendance, costs for

services, and payment procedures. These contracts also specify consequences if bills are paid late. Programs keep the signed fee agreement in enrollment files.

Compliance with Laws

Protecting the legal rights of participants and their families requires daily staff attention. When employed in an early childhood program, it will be your legal responsibility to respond if laws are being ignored or incorrectly followed.

First, decide if you can take corrective action on your own. If you cannot solve violations on your own, alert your supervisor. Verbally inform him or her and then provide your concerns in writing. Be clear and specific about the problem and state why it raises concerns. Work cooperatively with the staff to solve problems.

If you have continuing concerns about unresolved problems, you are ethically required to report them to the proper legal authorities. The following violations would require reporting:

▶ Failure to maintain legal records or their confidentiality

▶ Illegal financial practices such as fraud

▶ Biased, discriminatory practices

▶ Licensing and accreditation violations

▶ Health, safety, and fire-code violations

▶ Suspected abuse and neglect

Accreditation Criteria

Accreditation criteria refer to a set of standards that represents high-quality, developmentally appropriate programs. Accreditation is awarded from a professional organization that assures others that the program operates according to recognized professional practices.

There are several accreditation agencies, but the best-known accreditation program for early childhood settings is the National Academy of Early Childhood Programs, sponsored by the National Association for the Education of Young Children (NAEYC). Family child care homes seek accreditation through the National Association for Family Child Care (NAFCC).

Complying with accreditation criteria is voluntary. Programs that are committed to high-quality services work hard to meet as many accreditation criteria as possible. To ensure that programs maintain high quality, they must be reaccredited, usually every three to five years. **Figure 10.3** on page 220 provides the basic areas of NAEYC accreditation. You can find out more information about NAEYC accreditation on the Internet.

READING CHECK ✔ **Identify** What are three legal duties for early childhood professionals?

Figure 10.3 NAEYC Accreditation Criteria

Guidelines Professional organizations provide guidelines for quality programs. *Why are guidelines like these important?*

Samples of NAEYC Accreditation Criteria	
Relationships	• Works in partnership with families, establishing and maintaining regular, two-level communication • Fosters a child's emotional well-being by demonstrating respect and creating a positive emotional climate
Curriculum	• Provides written statement of philosophy and curriculum framework • Allows curriculum framework and daily schedule to be responsive to individual needs.
Teaching	• Works as a team to implement daily and learning activities • Works to prevent challenging and disruptive behaviors
Assessment of Child Progress	• Conducts assessment as integral part of program • Demonstrates sensitivity to family culture, experiences, abilities, disabilities, and home language as part of assessment
Health	• Maintains current health records for the child, emergency contacts, and special health needs • Provides daily opportunities for outdoor play
Teachers	• Knows and uses ethical guidelines in conduct • Recognizes health and safety hazards to protect children from harm
Families	• Ensures that all families are included in all aspects of the program • Provides access to families at any time
Community Relationships	• Maintains current list of child and family support services • Develops partnerships and professional relationships with agencies, consultants, and community organizations
Physical Environment	• Provides equipment and facilities for diaper changing, hand-washing sinks, appropriate chairs, and sleeping areas • Provides individual space for each child's belongings
Leadership and Management	• Program has well-articulated mission and philosophy for program excellence. • Administrator has professional qualifications and personal commitment to program.

Managing Program Services

Program Leadership

A successful program relies on good leadership. Early childhood programs employ directors as administrators and managers. They are usually responsible to a board of directors or an owner; however, some directors own their own programs.

Director as Role Model

The director sets the tone for the entire staff's professional performance. He or she demonstrates commitment to the program's philosophy and goals and helps put respect, cooperation, and teamwork into action. Directors keep staff informed through regular communication, often through weekly staff meetings.

Implementing Philosophy and Goals

Directors work with teachers to plan, apply, and evaluate learning programs and activities based on the program's goals and philosophy. They also work with other employees, such as food service staff, to meet program goals such as good nutrition. Every year, directors should reevaluate program philosophy and goals. They should also look at future needs and trends in early childhood programs and adjust or improve the program's services as needed.

Staff Recruitment and Supervision

Staff performance influences program quality, so it makes sense for directors to maintain the best staff possible. They recruit, interview, and hire the best-qualified employees. Age, education, and work-experience requirements for employees vary according to positions. Most directors hire the following staff members:

▶ **Assistant director:** Assists the director in administrative duties and program operations.

▶ **Teaching staff and substitutes:** Care for and teach children in classrooms.

▶ **Food service staff:** Purchase and prepare food for meals and snacks.

▶ **Transportation staff:** Drive children to and from field trips, and school-age children to and from school.

▶ **Custodial and grounds crew:** Maintain the facility, outdoor areas, driveway, parking lot, and play yards.

▶ **Health care staff:** Perform health checks, especially in infant rooms.

▶ **Family involvement coordinator:** Plans and conducts family activities.

▶ **Curriculum coordinator:** Makes plans for and purchases educational materials.

▲ **Staff**

Early childhood program directors are responsible for hiring staff. *What qualifications might be necessary for a teaching position?*

Staff Qualifications

Programs identify and describe responsibilities for each staff member to offer program services in an effective manner. The number of staff, and their qualifications, is determined by a program's purpose, services, and size. Licensing and accreditation criteria also influence program staffing.

Every staff position has a job description. This is a written list of duties and responsibilities for each staff member. Each job description describes how much decision-making authority a position holds. For instance, a director's job description would allow him or her to hire or **terminate** (fire) employees. A teacher's job description would not include that responsibility. A bookkeeper would have financial job responsibilities that would be unique to that position.

Staff Organization

Quality programs have a specific plan for staffing. An organized staffing plan identifies supervisors for specific positions. Such a plan is called an organizational chart. An **organizational chart** helps staff know to whom they report. For instance, it helps staff know whom they should inform about problems, solutions, or suggestions for program activities. It also reveals who will evaluate their work performance. An example of an organizational chart is shown in **Figure 10.4**.

So program services can be well managed, directors create work schedules and inform each staff member of his or her specific work hours. Work hours for positions vary. For instance, a cook or a van driver might work different hours from a custodian or classroom teacher.

Figure 10.4 **Child Care Center Staff Organization**

Staff Structure A staff organizational chart assists center employees in knowing to whom they report. *Why is it important to establish these reporting relationships?*

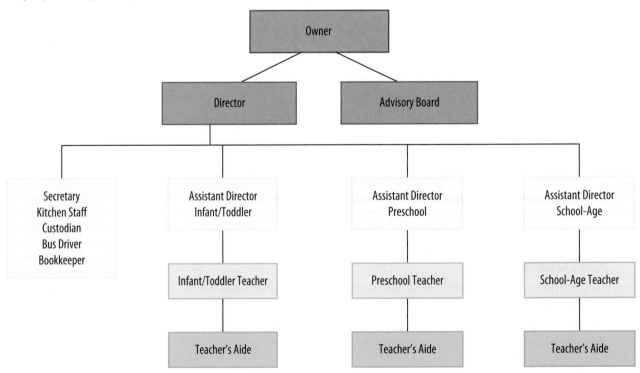

Screening Staff

Directors are responsible for employing program staff. Before hiring, directors screen potential staff to make sure they hire only the best-qualified employees. Directors review employment applications to make sure candidates meet minimum requirements for state licensing laws and, if applicable, accreditation criteria. They review each applicant's work history, educational background, and résumé. **Reference checks** are made by contacting people who know the applicant's character, job performance, and employment skills. Staff must also pass any medical tests such as a TB test or drug screening. Many states also require directors to conduct criminal background checks on potential employees. Such checks would identify persons who had been convicted of a crime, specifically one involving abuse or neglect.

Staff Development

Directors provide the following useful tools to help staff members perform their jobs to the best of their abilities:

▶ **Personnel Policies and Handbooks** Handbooks provide basic program information to introduce new staff to the policies and procedures they will be expected to follow. These materials provide employee job descriptions as well as conditions for employment. They outline requirements for continued employment as well as causes for dismissal.

▶ **In-Service Training** Directors must ensure that staff members receive yearly job training. Required training topics include identifying and reporting suspected child abuse and neglect, providing positive child guidance, and limiting the spread of illnesses.

▶ **Continuing Education** Motivated staff members will often seek ways to further their job-related education. Directors encourage continuing education by paying part of an employee's conference attendance expenses or the cost of a seminar or college course. Many states require that all early childhood professionals receive a certain amount of continuing education each year.

▶ **Performance Evaluation** Every staff member should have a yearly performance evaluation. This evaluation gives valuable feedback on strengths and skills that need improvement. Evaluations should be objective and based on direct observation of an employee's performance. Directors should make sure that all evaluations remain confidential in employees' personnel files.

▼ **Evaluation**

One of a director's responsibilities is to evaluate employees on a yearly basis. *How can a performance evaluation benefit the employee and the director?*

Quality Facilities

A quality facility creates a nurturing environment for all. Its design should support the program philosophy and goals. For instance, if a program's philosophy states children should learn in small groups, the facility should meet this need. One way would be to create learning centers for four to six children to use at a time.

Good facilities are comfortable and useful for staff, clients, and clients' family members. Good storage allows staff to have supplies within easy reach, whether they are changing a child's diaper or conducting an art activity. Children need areas to learn, to relax, and to feel at home. Parents feel welcome in spaces that encourage them to sit and linger.

Licensing laws set minimum standards that facilities must meet. For instance, good facilities are clean and safe and offer several ways to escape from fire or severe weather. Accreditation criteria require that physical environments are well designed and equipped for those who use them.

▲ Upkeep

Daily upkeep applies to all areas of a child care program, including centers, toys, art supplies, and books. *Why is this important?*

Maintenance and Upkeep

Human service facilities house a large number of people for long hours each day. All the traffic that creates poses a constant challenge. Facilities must remain in good shape so quality services can be provided. Daily maintenance and upkeep applies to the whole environment, including facility, equipment, and supplies. Everything, from toys to floors, requires regular cleaning, sanitizing, and repairing, if necessary.

Year-round facilities need routine care and upkeep indoors and out. For instance, buildings may need painting every five years. During the summer, playgrounds must be mowed and air conditioners repaired. During the winter, snow must be removed and furnaces maintained.

Program Governance

In many programs, directors do not manage programs on their own. It is a cooperative effort between the program sponsor and a director. Program operations can also be influenced by a **board**, a group of individuals who supports the program's purpose but are not employed by the program. When a director and a board make decisions about a program's policies and procedures, the process is called **program governance**. The board helps make a variety of decisions, including budget, finances, and fund-raising; enrollment policies; employing staff; and setting fees for services.

Organizational Structure

Not all programs require boards. It depends on the wishes of the program's sponsors. Programs that operate on a nonprofit basis usually have boards. Programs that are sponsored by a public organization, such as a social service agency, are more likely to have a board.

Some boards have members who are elected, by either program clients or board members themselves. Other boards merely ask for volunteers. People who serve on boards are not paid. They usually serve on the board because they want to make sure the program succeeds.

Advisory Boards and Governing Boards Some boards only give directors recommendations on decisions to be made. This is called an **advisory board**. Other boards have full decision-making power, meaning they tell directors what actions to take. This is a **governing board**, because they have final authority for decisions. Whether it is an advisory or a governing board, all boards assign leadership positions to lead work. Typical positions are president, vice president, treasurer, and secretary.

Board Responsibilities Boards meet regularly to discuss program developments. They help plan activities that promote a positive image of the program to the community. Boards help ensure that many different people have input into a program's operation. They make sure policies and procedures are fair to staff and to clients. They also help ensure that those policies and procedures apply fairly to everyone.

Board Committees To conduct their work well and in a timely manner, boards divide into separate work groups called committees. Assignment to a committee gives a board member a clear idea of how he or she can serve the program. So they can perform well, committee members should be given a written job description. Typical committees include finance, fund-raising, personnel, and public relations.

Governance Handbooks

Governance materials are written statements that help guide program operation. Handbooks help guide decision making for directors and boards. They also help staff understand program procedures so they can be followed more easily.

▶ **Constitution and by-laws.** This document states the program's purpose and establishes conduct rules for the board. For instance, it states how often board meetings should be held. It spells out term limits for board members. Committees are also established.

▼ **Handbooks**
Written policies that help guide program operation can be the responsibility of the program director and the board. *Why are handbooks valuable for staff and families?*

- ▶ **Governance handbook.** All of a program's policies and procedures are listed in this in-depth handbook, from enrollment to staffing. It details emergency routines staff must follow, such as medical emergencies or evacuation in case of fire or severe weather.
- ▶ **Personnel handbook.** This states personnel policies, such as employment qualifications, job descriptions, evaluation procedures, dress code, salary range and benefits, and causes for suspension or termination of employment.

Administration

As you have learned, many people influence how a program runs. Those people who have a say in program operations make up a program's administration. Sponsors, or those who provide funding for a program, usually have the final say in administration decisions.

Wise sponsors will often utilize a team of people to guide good program operation. For instance, board members can contribute legal, accounting, or public relations advice to sponsors and directors depending upon their special skills. Directors may ask board members to help recruit and interview job applicants. Directors can help sponsors determine if program goals are being met.

▼ Program Operations

Board members will often provide assistance with accounting or other program operations. *How might this benefit a program?*

Client Services

Early childhood programs frequently interact with the public. Directors must have skills in managing public and client relations to be able to serve children and families.

Program Enrollment

Directors advertise program services. It is their job to attract and maintain steady enrollment according to the program's licensed capacity. After children are enrolled, it is the director's responsibility to maintain good relationships with the family to meet the child's needs and family's expectations.

Parent or Family Handbooks

These handbooks give families an understanding of program policies and procedures and if well-written, are handy parent references. Handbooks address many topics but most often include information on hours of operation, billing policies, health and immunization requirements, daily schedules and routines, courses or classes, guidance policies, illness policies, and guidelines for celebrating birthdays. Most states require programs to inform parents of these policies in writing.

Family Involvement

Directors have frequent opportunities to talk with parents as parents drop off and pick up their children. In addition, directors use newsletters, individual progress reports, postings on parent bulletin boards and Web sites, as well as e-mail to communicate with families. They make sure parent-teacher conferences and family events are conducted. Many directors invite family members to serve on advisory boards so they have input on program operations. All parents should feel welcome to visit the program at any time.

Community Referrals

Many families have needs that cannot be met by an early childhood program. Good directors are well acquainted with community services, and they can refer families to help. Referrals may be in response to a child's disability, a housing problem, health insurance coverage for a child, or a question about applying for a state's child care **subsidy** or financial assistance program.

▲ **Family Involvement**

Directors have many opportunities to talk with families. *Why is family involvement crucial to a program's success?*

Financial Management

Balancing income and expenses to ensure that a program's doors remain open to children and families is called **financial management**. Good management allows a program to meet the costs of daily operation.

Financial management requires preparation of a yearly budget. A budget is a detailed listing of program expenses for services and an account of how much money the program expects to receive for services. A budget should be reviewed monthly and requires an organized bookkeeping system. The director is responsible for making sure income meets or exceeds expenses. Otherwise, programs cannot continue to offer services.

Managing Income

A program earns income by charging an hourly, weekly, or monthly fee for its services. Directors make sure the fees cover the cost of the services they provide. If the fees are too low, directors find other ways to bring in money. The program might host a fundraising event or write an application to receive money through a government grant or from a private funding agency.

Managing Expenses

Costs that are a result of program operation are called expenses. Program expenses include building costs; monthly utilities such as gas, water, electricity, and telephone; indoor and outdoor facility upkeep and repair; staff wages and training costs; vehicle purchase and routine care; equipment and supplies for all program services; advertising; and printing and postage fees.

Public Relations

Directors recruit a qualified staff, maintain full enrollment, and increase donations by building a good reputation for their programs. They do all they can to present a positive image of the program to the community. These efforts are called public relations.

▼ **Outreach**

A program's involvement with the community is part of the director's public relations efforts. *What other things can a director do to reach out to the community?*

Community Outreach

Directors should be actively involved in the community. This involvement can be serving on local boards or helping plan and conduct community events with other agencies. Directors place information about their programs where potential clients might see it. For instance, they may place flyers or brochures at a doctor's office or other service that caters to children. Directors also make sure their programs are listed with a local child care resource and referral agency that helps parents find care to match their needs.

Being a Reliable Source of Information

By keeping current on new child-related laws and research, directors can inform local government, city offices, and media of valuable information. When a program director and staff are known to share accurate and current information about children and families, community members respect their program.

Professional Organization Membership

Active participation in professional organizations also conveys a positive image to the community. For instance, local chapters of the National Association for the Education of Young Children hold an annual Week of the Young Child. During this week, many program directors and staff plan activities to raise community awareness of children's needs.

kali9/Getty Images

Quality Assurance

Maintaining quality standards is an ongoing process. Programs routinely undergo a variety of inspections and evaluations to confirm that quality is achieved. An outside person or agency often conducts health, fire, or building inspections. This assures an objective evaluation of quality. Inspections often check to see if a program meets specific laws for operation. An audit—or a review of a program's records, practices, and procedures—also assures quality. Programs whose meal service is partially funded by the federal Child and Adult Care Food Program are audited. The review assures that programs serve appropriate meals and maintain proper financial records such as grocery store receipts listing food purchases.

Programs hire accountants to audit their financial records such as budgets, bill payments, and receipts of income. Sometimes state or federal agencies audit programs to make sure they are following fair employment practices.

SAFETY MATTERS

Licensed Programs

A license is a registration with the state that indicates child care professionals meet health and safety standards. Licensing guidelines and state laws are passed to keep children safe. These laws mandate safety requirements, staff-to-child ratios, training requirements, emergency procedures, as well as many other aspects of the program. It assures parents that the center is following stringent guidelines for health and safety

What Would You Do? Imagine that you work at a child care center and you notice several violations of the safety guidelines needed to meet state licensing requirements. The fire extinguishers are no longer charged and there is a bookshelf blocking the fire door. What would you do to address these violations?

Reporting Licensing Violations

Early childhood staff must know and follow the licensing laws that apply to their programs. When a licensing violation occurs,the first people to become aware of it are often staff. If you observe a violation, you should write the date, time, location, and situation surrounding the violation. Any information you record should remain confidential and be shared only with those legally involved. This is considered an ethical duty of every early childhood professional.

Some violations must be immediately reported to authorities outside the program, such as violations involving child abuse or neglect. However, most often a violation concern should first be reported to your supervisor or the program director. Then, all those involved in the violation should cooperatively create a corrective plan of action to restore licensing compliance.

If a program continues violating licensing requirements, despite efforts to remedy the problem, further action is needed. An agent from the licensing office should be notified by telephone or in writing. That person will then investigate the violation and decide upon further action. In most states, staff can report concerns to licensing agents anonymously. This protects staff members from punishment for making a formal report. Many states also have labor laws that protect the jobs of staff who in good faith report a violation.

READING CHECK **Analyze** How does a program maintain quality assurance?

The Application Process

What You Should Know About Applying to College

The only way to get into college is to apply. The college application process is complicated. There are many parts of a college application besides grades and test scores. Many colleges also require letters of recommendation, essays, financial aid forms, and interviews. It is important to start early and to stay organized.

Does applying early give me a better chance of getting in?

There is no easy answer to this question because this varies from year to year and from school to school. The best way to answer this question is to do research on a school-by-school basis. One advantage of applying early is that you get the process over with sooner. One potential disadvantage is that many schools that accept early admission require you to attend the school if you are admitted, limiting your options.

What is the Common Application?

The Common Application is an application accepted by certain colleges in place of their own application. You fill it out once and then submit copies of the same application to any school that participates. Some schools have a supplement that must be submitted along with the Common Application. This option can be a great time saver, but not all schools accept it, so be sure to check first.

When will I find out if I got in?

Although it varies from school to school, college applicants usually receive letters informing them if they are accepted, rejected, or put on the waiting list in April of their senior year. Some arrive as early as March. Early-decision responses usually arrive in December and January of the applicant's senior year.

Hands-On

College Readiness It is crucial to keep track of all the tasks necessary to complete your college applications. Create a checklist with all your required tasks, a column for each college, and any deadlines. If more information is needed, get permission from a parent or teacher and research online what needs to be done to complete the application process.

Path to Success

Talk to Your Counselor He or she will play a big role in the process, so be sure to keep your counselor informed.

Start Early You do not want to have to rush through your applications.

Focus on the Essays Be sure to schedule enough time to write and proofread your college essays.

Get Letters of Recommendation Think carefully about whom you want to ask, and ask early.

Send Applications in Early Mail applications as soon as possible for colleges with rolling deadlines.

Double-Check Thoroughly review your college applications and confirm they are received.

Alejandro Rivera/Getty Images

Quality Early Childhood Programs
Visual Summary

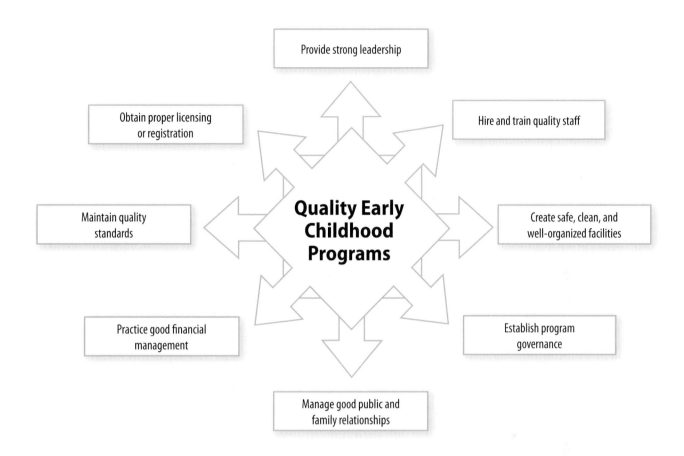

Provide strong leadership

Obtain proper licensing or registration

Hire and train quality staff

Maintain quality standards

Quality Early Childhood Programs

Create safe, clean, and well-organized facilities

Practice good financial management

Establish program governance

Manage good public and family relationships

Vocabulary Review

1. Use each of these content and academic vocabulary terms in a sentence.

Content Vocabulary

◇ philosophy (p. 208)
◇ program goals (p. 208)
◇ for-profit (p. 210)
◇ nonprofit (p. 210)
◇ program sponsors (p. 210)
◇ license exempt (p. 216)
◇ registration (p. 216)

◇ accreditation criteria (p. 219)
◇ organizational chart (p. 222)
◇ reference check (p. 223)
◇ board (p. 224)
◇ program governance (p. 224)

◇ advisory board (p. 225)
◇ governing board (p. 225)
◇ financial management (p. 227)

Academic Vocabulary

■ terminate (p. 222)
■ subsidy (p. 227)

Review Key Concepts

2. **Identify** six different types of early childhood programs.
3. **Explain** licensing and registration requirements.
4. **Describe** the role of the director in managing program services.

Critical Thinking

5. **Explain** When should an early childhood program's philosophy and goals be determined? Why?

6. **Contrast** Choose three different types of child care programs. What factors should parents consider when deciding between your chosen types of programs?

7. **Draw Conclusions** How can good public relations efforts influence the success of an early childhood program?

8. **Apply** What are some good business practices that could be applied to a child care program?

9. **Identify** What are some of the benefits of handbooks? What could happen if handbooks are not provided?

10. **Predict** What might happen if there were no legal guidelines for child care programs?

 ## 21st Century Skills

Leadership Skills

11. **Teamwork** Most teams function better when one person takes on the role of team leader. In a small group, role-play a scenario in which a team lacks leadership. What challenges might a team face without leadership? Role-play a second scenario in which the team has a strong leader. How does a team benefit from leadership? Discuss both role-plays with the class.

Information Skills

12. **Investigate** Determine the minimum standards, licensing requirements, regulations, and codes in your state for each of the child care options listed in this chapter. Be sure to include both home-based and center-based program options. Create a spreadsheet that details the requirements for each and share it with your class.

Child Care LAB

Use the skills you have learned in this chapter.

Business Plan

13. **Develop a Business Plan** Imagine you are starting your own child care business. Create a mission statement like the one shown on p. 209. Keeping your statement in mind, develop a business plan, including job descriptions, staffing procedures and policies, and an advertising strategy. Share your business plan with the class, a small group, or a partner.

   A. **Description.** Create a description of your child care program. Include your vision for the program and the services you plan to provide. What will make your program unique?

   B. **Advertising Strategy.** Design advertising, marketing, and recruitment materials. Be sure to include ways that you plan to grow your business.

   C. **Operational Information.** Describe your location, the facilities, and equipment needed.

   D. **Policies.** Create a one-page outline of the child care center's policies.

   E. **Organizational Chart.** Determine all the jobs that are needed for your child care center and create an organizational chart. Include job descriptions for each position.

   F. **Financial Plan.** Develop a start-up budget for the child care center. How much money will you need to start your business? What sources of funding might be available to you?

Create Your Evaluation

Create an evaluation sheet with these categories:

- Description
- Advertising
- Operations
- Policies
- Job Descriptions
- Finances

Ask your partner or your classmates to evaluate your business plan based on the categories listed, rating each category from 1 to 10.

Academic Skills

English Language Arts

14. Research Read a biographical article or book about Maria Montessori. Look for information about her stance on children's education. How did she develop the Montessori Method? What research or events influenced her philosophy as she built and implemented her method? How has her philosophy influenced early childhood education? Write a paragraph summarizing your findings.

Social Studies

15. Government Connection Choose a local, state, or national government law that affects child care programs. What is important about this law? What does a child care center need to do to follow this law? How does it affect the quality of care in a child care program? How do laws like this one affect society as a whole? Prepare a brief oral report detailing your findings.

Science

16. The Scientific Method You can use the scientific method to answer specific questions related to a child care center. The steps in the scientific method are as follows:

1. Ask a question.
2. Conduct research to collect information.
3. Form a hypothesis.
4. Test the hypothesis by doing an experiment.
5. Study the results.
6. Draw conclusions that others can evaluate.
7. Communicate the results.

Procedure First, ask the scientific question: How would making environmentally friendly improvements affect a child care center? Second, research some environmentally friendly changes and choose one to test in a child care center. Third, form a hypothesis about the change. Your hypothesis could be that making this change would save the center money. Fourth, plan an experiment to test the hypothesis. Collect data to support your hypothesis.

Analysis Summarize the results of your experiment and form a conclusion based on your results. Was your hypothesis proved or disproved? Support your conclusion with examples. Share your findings with the class.

Certification Prep

Directions Read each statement carefully. Then read the answer choices and choose the phrase that best completes the sentence.

17. A Montessori Preschool _____.

    A. is based on the teachings of Jean Piaget.

    B. encourages independent learning.

    C. is only for children with special needs.

    D. operates only on the weekends.

18. _____ could be involved in program operations.

    A. Board members   **C.** Teacher aides

    B. Sponsors   **D.** All of the above

Test-Taking Tip

In a multiple-choice test, read the question before you read the answer choices. Try to answer the question to yourself before you read the answer choices. This way, the answer choices will be less confusing.

(t)©Nova Development; (tr)©Comstock/Alamy

CHAPTER 11

Schedules and Routines

Writing Activity

★ 21st Century Skills

Self-Management Planning daily tasks and events can help keep you productive and manage stress. Early educators need daily planning skills when managing the tasks and events for the children in their care. Create a personal schedule for one day this week to practice this skill.

Writing Tips

1. Organize your schedule from waking up to going to sleep.
2. First, insert the events or tasks with preassigned times into your schedule.
3. Next, consider any other tasks or activities you must complete. Include time to fulfill your basic needs. Assign these tasks or events to spaces on your schedule.
4. Keep in mind how much time you will need to move between each task and activity.

Explore the Photo
Children feel secure when they have a regular daily schedule. *How is this child experiencing a daily routine?*

Grady Reese/age fotostock

Reading Guide

BEFORE YOU READ

Adjust Reading Speed Improve your comprehension by adjusting reading speed to match the difficulty of the text. Slow down, and when needed, reread each paragraph. Reading slower may take longer, but you will understand and remember more.

Read to Learn

Key Concepts

- **Explain** the importance of a daily schedule as a tool at a child care center and how one is developed.
- **Discuss** how a balanced schedule creates a secure, stable environment for children and staff.
- **Describe** how predictable routines and transitions contribute to a calm, dependable classroom atmosphere, and identify staff responsibilities in daily routines.

Content Vocabulary

- ◇ schedule
- ◇ self-directed
- ◇ routine
- ◇ transition
- ◇ transition techniques
- ◇ chore board
- ◇ job jar
- ◇ choice time

Academic Vocabulary

- ■ individual
- ■ major

Main Idea

Many activities and small events occur throughout the day in an early childhood program. In this chapter, you will learn how a thorough plan, including daily schedules, routines, and transitions, help make both the child and early educator's day go smoothly.

Graphic Organizer

As you read, you will discover information about planning a schedule. Use a tree organizer like the one shown to record the five categories a child care professional should consider when making a schedule. Include notes about each topic.

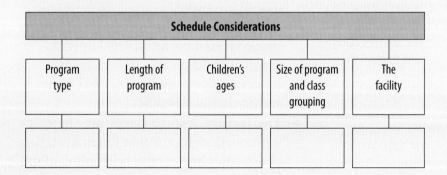

Schedule Considerations				
Program type	Length of program	Children's ages	Size of program and class grouping	The facility

Graphic Organizer *Go to* **connected.mcgraw-hill.com** *to print this Graphic Organizer.*

AS YOU READ

Connect Think about all the needs and activities a child requires each day. What are some strategies for keeping all these needs and activities organized?

Vocabulary

You can find definitions in the glossary at the back of this book.

Daily Schedule Needs

Many different experiences take place in one day at an early childhood program—for children as well as staff. When you carefully plan a day, you help ensure that children will be happily engaged in beneficial activities. A structured day helps children behave appropriately. Staff also benefit from a well-planned day because they can perform their duties in a relaxed, enjoyable setting. A well-planned day provides enough structure so that teachers can cope with emergencies.

Schedule Considerations

A **schedule** is a plan for how time will be used. No single schedule works for every child care program. Although some patterns may be similar, each schedule is planned according to the program's characteristics. All of the following affect schedules:

▶ **Program type** The main goals of a program determine how a schedule is arranged. A program emphasizing active investigation and independent learning provides ample time for small-group, self-chosen activities. If a program emphasizes creativity, then scheduling of art and music may be given a high priority, along with longer play periods for deeper exploration.

▶ **Length of the program** A full-day child care program allows for a longer time period for each activity than a half-day program. A full-day schedule will likely include more varied activities as well.

▶ **Children's ages** Infants have very different needs than older preschoolers. Infants' schedules may vary considerably so that each baby's biological needs can be responded to individually. Toddlers and younger preschoolers need more assistance with self-help skills. Older preschoolers typically have longer attention spans and need shorter rest periods. Those factors affect the length of time needed for activities.

▶ **Size of the program and class grouping** A large program requires several groups of children, so activities and meal times must be staggered to create relaxed routines. The larger the group of children an early educator has to supervise, the more time needed for each activity in the schedule.

▶ **The facility** A small center may have multipurpose rooms that require rotation of activities and careful scheduling of different classrooms for efficient use.

READING CHECK ✓ **Recall** What is a schedule?

Financial *Literacy*

Hourly Wages

Jordan has two part-time job offers at a child care center. Each job is 3 hours a day, 4 days a week. The first offer pays $15 an hour. He would have to take the bus, which costs $2 each way. The second job pays $12 an hour and is much closer—Jordan could walk. Including transportation costs, which job will have the highest weekly wage?

Math Concept **Multistep Problems** When solving problems with more than one step, think through the steps before you start.

Starting Hint To calculate a weekly wage, first figure the daily wage. Multiply the number of hours a day (3) worked by the dollars paid per hour. Multiply by the number of days worked a week (4), and then subtract transportation costs.

 Math For more math practice, go to the Math Appendix at the back of the book.

McGraw-Hill Education

Balancing a Schedule

A schedule plans events in the order they will occur and indicates how long each event will last. Schedules bring order to daily needs and events. In an early childhood program, the schedule is the guideline that assists children with daily activities. It tells how the hours will be spent from the time children arrive until they leave at the end of the day.

A predictable daily schedule creates a secure, stable environment for children and staff. Both rely on the familiarity of a set schedule. A predictable schedule helps guide children's behavior and allows children to anticipate a change from one activity to another. When teachers provide a consistent daily schedule, children become more **self-directed**. This means they learn to cooperate in class activities in an independent fashion with less physical or verbal direction needed from the teacher. **Figure 11.1** gives an example of a daily schedule. How might you adapt this schedule to meet the needs of infants and toddlers? Of school-age children?

Figure 11.1 **Planning the Day**

Sample Schedule Schedules provide a reliable order to meet children's daily needs. *How much time is devoted to snacks or meals in this schedule? How much time is devoted to rest periods?*

Time	Activity
7:30 to 9:30 A.M.	• **Families Greeted.** Children store belongings and hang up coats. • **Self-Directed Play.** Children play at indoor and outdoor learning centers.
9:30 to 9:50 A.M.	• **Snack.** Children wash hands and eat nutritious foods.
9:50 to 11:40 A.M.	• **Morning Meeting.** Children and teachers discuss the day's activities. • **Project Work/Activity Time.** Children explore activity areas within the indoor or outdoor classroom. Activities may include art, science, math, dramatic play, language arts, physical activity, creative movement, water/sandplay, block play, and table games.
11:40 A.M. to 12:00 P.M.	• **Music Time.** Children sing songs while taking turns washing hands for lunch. This activity serves as a transition to lunchtime.
12:00 to 12:40 P.M.	• **Lunchtime.** Children eat in small groups to promote conversation about the day's experiences.
12:40 to 1:00 P.M.	• **Prepare for Rest or Quiet Time.** Toileting, hand washing, and teeth brushing after lunch followed by a story, quiet play, or a movie prior to rest time helps children settle down. Older children who do not need naps often enjoy quiet time for relaxation.
1:00 to 2:30 P.M.	• **Rest Time with Calming Music.** Early risers play quietly.
2:30 to 5:30 P.M.	• **Gradual Wake Up** • **Toileting, Hand Washing, and Snack** • **Self-Directed Play.** Children play indoors or outdoors. • **End-of-Day Cleanup.** Children help clean up by sorting toys and straightening areas before returning home.

Pacing the Day

Early educators plan schedules so children's days can be interesting and engaging. They are also careful not to overstimulate or overwhelm children. For example, teachers avoid introducing activities for holidays and other special days too early because weeks of anticipation for these activities can tire and overexcite children. Children's daily home routines, such as sleep, meals, and family playtimes, can become irregular. A dependable, unhurried routine at child care centers can help children maintain health and energy.

The pace of the daily schedule should be active enough to keep children's attention but not so rushed that children become frustrated or cannot enjoy the activities. Early educators should track their time during the day, either mentally or with a watch. Tracking time helps make sure the pace of the day is appropriate. Daily schedules require a delicate balance of activities, taking into consideration the following factors.

Include All Developmental Areas

A daily schedule allows for experiences that address all developmental areas to help children reach their full potential. Staff should plan activity times to nurture children's intellectual, physical, social, and emotional growth.

Active and Quiet Play

Young children have lots of energy, so they need daily opportunities for active play. A number of activities fulfill children's need for active play, such as building with blocks, playing dress up, singing silly songs, dancing to fun music, playing outdoor games, and climbing on outdoor equipment.

Balancing active play with quieter play options is important so children do not become exhausted. Some examples of quieter pursuits include playing board games, completing puzzles, looking at or reading picture books, and playing alphabet and letter games. Scheduling quieter activities before nap time is also a good way to help children relax and to prepare for a period of rest.

▼ **One-on-One Time**

This early educator is giving individual attention to this child. *How does individual attention contribute to a child's development?*

Glow Images

Give Individual Attention

Opportunities for **individual**, or separate and personalized, attention contribute to children's emotional and social growth. When children receive friendly, individual attention from adults, attachment and respectful relationships are formed. Children know staff care when they respond to them individually. Playing, reading a story, or singing songs together provides children with individual attention.

Large- and Small-Group Activities

Young children learn best in small groups. However, they also enjoy the sense of community that comes from large-group activities. Children should have chances to participate in both small- and large-group activities each day.

Large-group activities can be extra-stimulating to children, so they should be scheduled when children can most easily focus in an area free of distractions. Large-group activities scheduled before routine meal, snack, or nap time may result in behavior problems if children are tired or hungry during the activity. Morning meetings, music time, and story time work well as large-group activities.

Art and science activities and playing with blocks are good small-group activities. This is an ideal time for early educators to focus on supporting specific developmental areas for individual children or to reinforce certain concepts with a smaller group. Organizing groups of children with similar developmental levels or related interests can help keep children engaged and focused on the activity.

Indoor and Outdoor Play

Children need chances for fast-paced active play as well as more reserved, quiet indoor play. A daily schedule that balances indoor and outdoor play meets both needs and allows children to develop large and small muscle control. Children enjoy nature experiences that outdoor play provides. Fresh air and sunlight promote children's mental and physical health.

READING CHECK ✔ **Summarize** What are five factors a child care professional should consider when planning the pace of a program's day?

SAFETY MATTERS

Routine Sanitation

Disinfecting Play Equipment Keeping play equipment clean and as free of germs as possible should be part of every child care center's daily schedule.

- Indoor and outdoor play equipment must be disinfected on a regular basis. Indoor toys and climbing equipment and outdoor playground equipment should be sanitized thoroughly if an accident involving blood occurs. This can help protect children from blood-borne pathogens.
- Toys that are frequently handled, such as toys that infants put in their mouths, should be disinfected daily.
- Toys used by toilet-trained toddlers and by older children can be disinfected weekly.
- Use a fresh disinfecting solution of ½ cup liquid bleach to 2½ gallons of water daily.

What Would You Do? The director of your child care center recently brought in new cleaning supplies for the classroom because "they were a great deal!" After inspecting the bottles' labels, you realize that these cleaning supplies are not meant for disinfecting equipment. How would you approach the director with your concerns about these products?

Daily Routines

Schedules give the structure and order needed for daily classroom activities. Clear, predictable routines put the schedule into action. A **routine** is a regular, expected procedure that is followed to accomplish something. It provides orderliness and discourages conflict, which helps save valuable learning time. Predictable routines contribute to a calm, dependable classroom atmosphere. A routine may be short, such as washing hands, or long, such as eating lunch. When routines are consistent, children learn what to expect in a daily schedule and when to expect it.

Down Syndrome

Down syndrome is a genetic condition present at birth that usually causes developmental delays and certain kinds of health problems. It is caused by an abnormality on the twenty-first chromosome.

Most children with Down syndrome have low muscle tone. As a result, the development of physical skills may be delayed. They are also likely to be slower to develop speech and self-help skills. Health problems that often affect people with Down syndrome include heart defects and impaired hearing and vision.

It is important for teachers to recognize that each child with Down syndrome develops and learns at his or her own pace.

Critical Thinking

Use print or online sources to learn about two individuals with Down syndrome. For example, you might read interviews with parents of children who have Down syndrome. Compare what you learn about the development of the two individuals. Record your comparison in a Venn diagram.

Staff Responsibilities in Daily Routines

Children rely on early educators to fulfill their needs and to make each day run smoothly so they can focus on their own development. Because of this, teachers have responsibilities and routines they must follow throughout each day.

▶ **Arrival** Teachers should greet children and parents warmly when they arrive. In many programs, the arrival routine begins by taking attendance. Parents or children might sign an attendance sheet or log in on a computer. Use arrival routines as an opportunity to build trusting relationships and to develop effective communication with children and families. Include time during arrival to store children's personal belongings in cubbies and hang coats on hooks. Children learn independence as they do these tasks on their own. Some children respond to a conversation with the teacher that bridges home to school. Others prefer to play independently while adjusting to the new setting.

▶ **Health Check** As children enter the classroom, take an informal health check. Pay attention to the appearance of children to spot early signs of illness, such as watery eyes or runny noses. Note any unusual markings that could indicate a child was maltreated or suffered an injury that needs treatment.

▶ **Daily Kick-Off** An arrival routine can end with teachers and children gathered in a group to discuss the upcoming day's activities. Telling children the schedule for the day and having the schedule posted in picture form at children's eye level helps them feel secure at the center.

▶ **Playtime** Early educators should provide children with a choice of developmentally appropriate activities. They should reduce distractions and interruptions so children can focus on and enjoy the activities. Consider including culturally diverse materials and activities in playtime as well to help children develop their cultural awareness. Teachers should always provide appropriate supervision for all playtime activities.

▶ **Mealtimes** Early educators are responsible for making sure each child's nutritional needs are fulfilled each day. Some child care centers prepare and serve food at mealtimes, while others serve food provided by parents. Developing strategies for creating a relaxed mealtime routine helps make the feeding process run smoothly. Consider age appropriateness when planning meals, snacks, and mealtimes. Encourage age-appropriate self-help skills by asking students to help set tables and to use utensils and lunch kits. Teachers should record the food children eat as well as the number of meals and snacks served daily.

▶ **Nap Times** Teachers should arrange nap mats or cots and get blankets and pillows ready prior to nap time. It is important to help children ease into sleep. Lower lights, read a story, and distribute stuffed toys for easier resting. Soft music, mobiles, and back rubs can also help lull young children to sleep.

Figure 11.2 Staff Responsibilities

Health, Hygiene, and Dressing Routines can help children learn skills for taking care of their own needs. *Why would a hand-washing routine be important in a child care center?*

Routines	Staff Responsibilities
Health and Hygiene	• Plan for hand washing or sanitizing for children and staff. • Plan time to brush teeth and assist children with brushing teeth and storing toothbrushes. • Help children learn the location of tissues, assist them with nose blowing, and teach them to wash their hands after blowing. • Respond to children's personal schedules for toileting and diapering, encourage children's self-help skills, teach health routines, and properly dispose of soiled items.
Dressing	• Encourage self-help skills for dressing. • Dress for outdoor play. • Teach responsibility for belongings. • Dress after soiling and toileting accidents.

▶ **Departure** Children will react differently at the end of the day. Most will be excited to see the family member at the door, but some will be upset to leave an activity unfinished. Early educators can help facilitate this by keeping an eye on schedules and ending activities prior to a family member's arrival. Teachers should also share information with parents or guardians about their child's day. Make sure that children get their belongings and projects to take home so that nothing is lost between the child care center and home.

As a child care professional, it is also your responsibility to make sure the center is ready for the following day by putting away toys and taking care of any cleaning or sanitization required after children leave. **Figure 11.2** lists other staff responsibilities that occur throughout the day when caring for children.

Encouraging Self-Help

Clearly stated routines help children understand what is expected of them. As they adapt to routines, such as getting coats on for outdoor play, children gain confidence and become more independent and organized.

To be effective, routines are organized according to children's ages and developmental abilities. Early educators need to know each child's abilities and identify children with special needs. Children with special needs might need more flexibility in their routines. Flexibility gives them more time to learn self-help skills. Over time, children's independent self-help skills, such as hand washing, putting on shoes, and brushing teeth, develop and improve.

▼ **I Can Do It!**

Routines help children develop their self-help skills. *What are some examples of self-help skills?*

Eric Audras / age fotostock

Employee Absenteeism

Employee absenteeism has a negative impact on workplace schedules and routines, especially at child care centers. If the early educator assigned to their care is not a consistent face at the center, children will take longer to develop a sense of trust with this teacher. They might also experience more stress during the day if a familiar face is missing.

Taking Time Off

Teachers should plan ahead when taking a day off. Children should be told when their teacher will not be there but should be reassured that he or she will return soon. Sometimes this notice is not always possible, especially in case of contagious illness, but chronic absenteeism, without just cause, should be avoided.

Thinking Ethically

You are the director of a child care program. One of your teacher aides has been consistently absent on Monday mornings for the last three weeks. This is hard on the children as they start their week at the program. How would you handle this situation with your employee?

Handling Transitions

A **transition** is a short activity or procedure used to guide children smoothly from one activity, routine, or event to another. Transition activities provide children with something to focus on so they make it from one place to another without becoming distracted. As transitions become familiar, they help children adjust to the child care routine. Smooth transitions prevent crowding and keep the classroom atmosphere relaxed but organized.

One **major**, or very important, transition occurs when children first arrive. Some children have difficulty separating from their parents, and teachers should assist this transition. You can make arrival time happy and positive with a friendly greeting. Bend or kneel at the child's level and smile warmly. Use the items children bring, such as a favorite stuffed animal, to start conversations. A good way to begin this conversation time is to sing a familiar greeting song.

You can show interest and respect by asking questions and listening attentively. Your interest helps children adjust to the child care setting each day. For children who speak other languages, this serves as a good time to talk, sing, or read stories in other languages.

Transition Times

Transitions take place throughout the day, particularly when children move between learning activities and daily routines. A transition takes place as children leave a large group to play in small-group activities. Transition time can be hand washing before sitting at a table to eat a snack or lunch. After children return from outdoor play, a transition takes place as they use the toilet before starting an indoor activity. Children picking up toys between activities or at the end of the day are other examples of transition times.

Transition Techniques

Signals or short activities that prompt children to move from one place or routine to another are called **transition techniques**. They often include sounds and visual cues that alert children to what is coming next. Transition techniques help guide children's behavior without repeating detailed directions. When choosing a technique, be sure to evaluate various transition techniques for their appropriateness in helping children adjust to the early childhood setting. Here are some examples of transition techniques:

▶ Sing a simple tune when it is time to pick up toys.

▶ Jingle chimes to gather the group in a circle for music.

▶ Flicker the lights off and on to signal story time.

▶ Play a recording of a drumbeat to lead children to outdoor play.

▶ Ask children to move like gorillas, rabbits, frogs, or robots as they go to wash hands.

▶ Use puppets, fingerplays, or props to focus children's interest during group discussion times.

- Add surprise to capture curiosity. At music time, use cards with the title of a different children's song on each. Children randomly pick a card, and the class sings the chosen song.

- Play thinking games. Rather than moving children in one large group, play games to move them in smaller groups. Ask children wearing red shirts to leave first, then children with blue shirts, and so on. Many themes can be used, such as patterns on clothing or first letters in children's names.

- Give advanced warning. Tell children how much time they have left to finish an activity. This will allow children to prepare themselves to move on to new activities and to avoid possible behavior issues if a child is abruptly told to stop their play before they have had a chance to finish.

Children should be expected to help clean up the center as part of the end-of-day routine, but teachers should make sure their expectations are developmentally appropriate. Child-friendly storage equipment allows children to organize learning center supplies, to put away toys and games, and to store personal belongings. Making a cleanup routine fun and allowing children to do a variety of jobs help build self-help skills.

A **chore board** features pictures of different cleanup activities, such as washing paintbrushes and putting away tricycles, in various sections of the board. Children use the board to select a classroom chore to perform. The board is laid flat on the floor. A child tosses a beanbag onto the board and then completes the task indicated by the beanbag's position.

A **job jar**—a container filled with pieces of paper that show pictures of activities—serves the same purpose as a chore board. Each child draws a piece of paper from the jar and completes the job indicated. Some early educators include special "jobs," such as "hug a friend."

Choice time is a transition technique that lets children decide which activity they would like to participate in next. Early educators handle choice time in a variety of ways. Most begin by gathering children into a group. Then each child is given a nametag, often with a photo on it for easier identification. Teachers then provide a poster board or clipboard that has sections squared off and pictures of different classroom play areas in each section. Children make a choice by placing their nametags in their desired play areas, such as art or block building. A daily schedule should always include time for children to choose an activity or activities that interest them.

▲ **Classroom Chores**
Early educators should involve children in age-appropriate and safe classroom chores. *What are some strategies for organizing children's classroom chores?*

READING CHECK ✔ **Define** What are *transitions* and *transition techniques*?

M. Constantini / PhotoAlto

College & Career
READINESS

Child Care Licensing Inspector

What Does a Child Care Licensing Inspector Do?

A child care licensing inspector is an occupational health and safety inspector that has specialized knowledge of child care licensing and regulation requirements. These inspectors work to prevent harm to workers and to children. They make sure that child care employers follow all federal and state health and safety laws by evaluating workplaces and reporting any violations.

Career Readiness Skills

Child care licensing inspectors must be knowledgeable about the child care industry and related laws, rules, and regulations. They have good writing and verbal communication skills in order to report and explain health and safety violations. Child care licensing inspectors must also be prepared to travel to and visit different kinds of child care work environments.

Education and Training

Most jobs require a bachelor's degree in occupational health, occupational safety, or a related field. Some positions will require a master's degree. Child development knowledge and child care experience is helpful for a child care licensing inspector. On-the-job experience is also important, so look for degree programs that offer internship opportunities. Child care licensing inspectors can become certified by taking a certification exam. Continuing education is necessary to stay up to date on changing technology and laws and regulations.

Job Outlook

Employment is expected to grow at the average rate for all occupations over the next ten years. Having knowledge and experience in more than one health and safety specialty will lead to the best job prospects. Licensing inspectors are often government employees. Some inspectors work as consultants. They advise managers on how to make a workplace safer and healthier.

Critical Thinking Research the different kinds of child care facilities a child care licensing inspector might visit. Describe the differences and explain how the inspector's job may vary at each location. What skills does a child care licensing inspector need to have for each location?

Career Cluster

Government and Public Administration
Occupational Health and Safety Inspectors work in the Regulation pathway of the career cluster. Other jobs in this career cluster include the following:

- Election Supervisor
- Senator
- Child Support Officer
- Fire Inspector
- Ambassador
- Census Clerk
- Tax Auditor
- Border Inspector
- City Council Member
- Child and Adult Care Food Program Auditor
- Health Inspector

Explore Further The Government and Public Administration career cluster contains seven pathways: Governance, National Security; Foreign Service; Planning; Revenue and Taxation; Regulation; and Public Management. Choose one of these pathways to explore further. Write a paragraph that summarizes your findings.

OJO Images/SuperStock

Schedules and Routines
Visual Summary

Schedules

Consider the program goals and the length of time included in the day when creating a schedule.

Think about children's ages, class size, and space limitations when planning time for activities.

Organize a balanced schedule that includes all developmental areas to provide daily variety.

Provide opportunities for active and quiet play, large- and small-group activities, and indoor and outdoor play.

Routines

Use routines to create a calm, dependable classroom atmosphere.

Encourage self-help skills through developmentally appropriate routines.

Guide children smoothly from one activity, routine, or event to another by using transitions.

Prompt children to move from one place or routine to another with signals or short activities called transition techniques.

Vocabulary Review

1. Create a fill-in-the blank sentence for each of the content and academic vocabulary words. The sentence should contain enough information to help determine the missing word.

Content Vocabulary
◇ schedule (p. 236)
◇ self-directed (p. 237)
◇ routine (p. 239)
◇ transition (p. 242)
◇ transition techniques (p. 242)
◇ chore board (p. 243)

◇ job jar (p. 243)
◇ choice time (p. 243)

Academic Vocabulary
■ individual (p. 238)
■ major (p. 242)

Review Key Concepts

2. **Explain** what a schedule is and why is it an important tool at a child care center.
3. **Discuss** How does a balanced daily schedule create a secure, stable environment for children and staff?
4. **Describe** how predictable routines and transitions contribute to a calm, dependable classroom atmosphere.

Critical Thinking

5. **Assess** Why is it important to encourage self-help through the routines provided for young children?
6. **Contrast** planning schedules for infants and older children. Would it be more difficult to plan schedules for infants or for older children? Why?
7. **Interpret** How can an organized schedule help children learn how to function in a group situation?

8. **Explain** how teachers can use routines to teach children proper safety, health, and sanitation habits.

9. **Relate** Multiple adults are often involved with the care of a child. How can using schedules and routines consistently with children at home and at a child care program help manage the multiple adult roles in a child's life?

10. **Model** How do transitions help move children smoothly between activities or learning spaces? Plan and demonstrate an original transition technique with a partner.

21st Century Skills

Time-Management Skills

11. **Getting Ready** Follow your teacher's instructions to form into pairs. Working with your partner, imagine that you are the two early educators for a child care center that opens at 7:00 a.m. Brainstorm a list of tasks you must complete before the first child arrives. Then discuss how much time you will need to complete each task. Write a schedule showing when you arrive and the time you spend on each task. Remember to allow extra time for unexpected developments.

Adaptability Skills

12. **Be Flexible** It has been raining for days and suddenly the sun comes out. Roberto would like to finish his block tower tomorrow. Lucy is easily overstimulated and is showing signs she may be overwhelmed. All these situations are examples of when a routine might need to be altered. Use these situations, or select three of your own, and write a paragraph for each, explaining how you could modify a routine to support children's changing needs or respond to unexpected events.

Child Care LAB

Use the skills you have learned in this chapter.

Plan a Schedule

13. **Daily Events** You and a partner are team teachers for an infant, toddler, or preschool program. Choose an age group and plan a detailed schedule of a day's activities that are developmentally appropriate for your selected age group.

    A. Program Type Think about the type of program you would like to run and what activities you would want to emphasize.

    B. Timing Will your program be half day or full day? Create a detailed schedule with a time line for how you will divide the day. Allow time for arrival, active and quiet play, group activities and individual attention, snacks or meals, nap or rest periods, cleanup, and departure.

    C. Ages Consider your students' ages when adding activities to the schedule. Activities should include all developmental areas and be age-appropriate.

    D. Size and Facility How many students will you allow in your program? How will this affect your schedule? Consider how you will plan for large- and small-group activities. What kind of indoor and outdoor spaces will you need to complete activities?

    E. Balanced Pace Consider whether the pace of the day is active enough to keep children's attention, but not so rushed that children cannot enjoy activities.

    F. Routine Discuss how routines and transitions can help the pace of your schedule go smoothly.

    G. Share Trade schedules with another pair and analyze whether the schedules include all the characteristics of a good schedule.

Create Your Evaluation

Work in groups to assess your schedules. Create an evaluation sheet with the following categories:
- Timing
- Age-appropriateness
- Balance of activities
- Range of developmental activities
- Consideration of basic needs (meals, rest, hygiene)

Use the sheet to evaluate the schedules. Rate each schedule on a scale of 1 to 10 for each category.

Academic Skills

English Language Arts

14. Step-by-Step Instructions Choose a consistent daily event that would benefit from a routine, such as arrival, mealtimes, hand washing, transitions between activities, nap time, or departure. Write a step-by-step routine that a child care professional could use to make this event run smoothly.

Social Studies

15. Meeting Individual Needs It is important for teachers to know how to adjust their plans for the day to meet the individual needs of each student in their care. How could you adjust daily routines or schedules to meet needs of students whose first language is not English or of students with special needs?

Science

16. Research Computer Use Children are learning to use computers at a much earlier age than in previous years. Many child care centers have computers in learning centers or media areas. Child care professionals can encourage children to use computers and other media as part of the daily scheduled activities.

Procedure Research the various ways computers are used for learning in child care centers and early childhood classrooms.

Analysis Write a one-page report that discusses the impact computer use might have on child development. What issues might a child care professional face when using technology with children? Hypothesize some safeguards a child care professional might take to prevent misuse or abuse of technology with children. Discuss your report and possible safeguards with a small group.

Certification Prep

Sharpen your test-taking skills to improve your certification program score.

Directions Read each sentence, and choose the best term to fill in the blank.

17. A _____ is a regular, expected procedure that is followed to accomplish something.

- **A.** plan
- **B.** schedule
- **C.** transition
- **D.** routine

18. A _____ is a container filled with pieces of paper that show pictures of activities.

- **A.** job bag
- **B.** chore board
- **C.** job jar
- **D.** chore hat

Test-Taking Tip

When answering a fill-in-the-blank question, silently read the sentences with each of the possible answers in the blank space. This will help you eliminate wrong answers. The best term results in a sentence that is both factual and grammatically correct.

CHAPTER 12

Environments, Equipment, and Supplies

Writing Activity

⭐ 21st Century Skills

Communication Imagine that you work in a child care center that is making changes to its outdoor area to better meet the needs of the infant room. Write a memo to parents explaining the changes that are being made, and why.

Writing Tips
1. State the purpose of your memorandum.
2. List the author and the recipients of the memo.
3. Explain your changes clearly and briefly.
4. Organize the paragraphs in a logical way.
5. Review what you have written to make sure you used correct grammar, spelling, and punctuation.

Explore the Photo
Equipment should be appropriate for the children's age. *What makes this swing age-appropriate?*

Ingram Publishing

Reading Guide

BEFORE YOU READ

Be Organized A messy environment can be distracting. To lessen distractions, organize an area where you can read this chapter comfortably.

Read to Learn

Key Concepts

- **Identify** how environments can respond to all areas and levels of child development.
- **Name** the criteria for supplying and equipping early childhood environments.
- **List** sensory considerations in the classroom climate.
- **Describe** the types of learning centers and activity areas.
- **Explain** the role outdoor design plays in health, recreation, and overall learning for children.
- **Summarize** the ADA requirements that allow children with disabilities to use play areas.

Content Vocabulary

- ◇ developmentally appropriate
- ◇ toxic
- ◇ inventory record
- ◇ sanitized
- ◇ learning centers
- ◇ traffic pattern
- ◇ nontoxic
- ◇ fall zones
- ◇ dehydrated

Academic Vocabulary

- ■ designated
- ■ adequate

Main Idea

Classrooms, outdoor spaces, toys, and materials should be designed and chosen according to children's ages and stages of development. Children with special needs may have specific space and equipment needs.

Graphic Organizer

As you read, look for six types of outdoor play areas found at child care centers. Use a fishbone organizer like the one shown to help you list the areas.

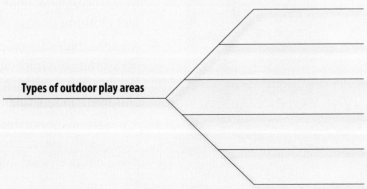

Types of outdoor play areas

🖱️ **Graphic Organizer** *Go to* **connected.mcgraw-hill.com** *to print this Graphic Organizer.*

◇**Vocabulary**

You can find definitions in the glossary at the back of this book.

▼**Nurturing Environments**

When children work and play in interesting environments, their sense of enjoyment increases. *How can displaying art at children's eye level increase enjoyment?*

Appropriate Indoor Environments and Equipment

Early childhood programs need caring professionals to create places where children will grow and develop safely. Most importantly, children need a warm and engaging environment that is fun to explore with friends. Early childhood staff must be able to maintain environments that are interesting, yet not over stimulating. That's a big challenge, but this chapter will illustrate ways you can meet it.

There are many details to consider when designing early childhood classrooms. For example, state licensing laws are used to guide the design process. In addition, accreditation criteria list desirable features that are considered part of high-quality early childhood programs. These criteria are developed by various professional organizations, such as the National Association for the Education of Young Children (NAEYC). In addition to these resources, consider the following factors when planning environments that serve children and families.

Program Services and Goals

Program services, including hours of operation, determine the variety and size of areas in an environment. For example, a part-day program may not need the space for napping that a full-day program needs. Kitchen size will also vary with the number of meals served daily.

The environmental design, and well-chosen equipment and supplies improve a staff's ability to meet program goals, too. Items and activities that fit children's abilities and ages are **developmentally appropriate**. Wisely chosen supplies can support that goal. The following practices help promote program goals in the classroom:

▶ Smocks in the painting area help children learn to be responsible and protect clothing during play.

▶ An area that offers plentiful storage at children's heights helps nurture children's independence.

▶ A program supporting strong self-esteem displays children's art at eye level.

▶ Toys such as puppets encourage language use.

© Paul Bradbury / age fotostock

- Equipment and activities that require the use of the whole body support large-muscle development.
- Supplies such as connecting blocks encourage small-muscle development.

Developmental Needs

All areas of child development need to be considered when designing space for children. Because developmental abilities of children vary, classrooms must be set up to meet a variety of needs. The first step in meeting these needs is to look at the classroom from a child's level when arranging space. What do you see?

General and Preschool Program Needs

Meeting basic care needs in a safe and sanitary manner is a high priority. These needs include napping, toileting, hand washing, eating, and teeth brushing. Each element requires specialized space. Early childhood classrooms should have the following:

- Child-size toilets and sinks in toileting and hand-washing areas. They should be mounted low enough for children to reach. Mirrors should be placed at children's eye level.

- Low tables with child-size chairs. For older preschoolers, meal service is provided on low tables that can be used for play activities during the rest of the day. Chairs that fit small children should be available, and utensils should accommodate their smaller hands and mouths. Using age-appropriate equipment will help children learn to eat independently. Cleanup and sanitation is easier with hard-surfaced floors, such as tile or wood.

- Storage for cots in full-day programs. Full-day programs provide cots and sheets for naptime. Stacking cots on a rolling cart makes it easier to move them into the classroom.

- A separate isolation room for children who become ill. This helps prevent the spread of illness and gives children a comfortable place to rest until their parents arrive.

- First aid and emergency supplies. Each classroom and each transportation vehicle needs a first-aid kit and emergency supplies such as a flashlight, a battery-operated radio, and a fire extinguisher. The first-aid kits should be stored out of reach of children. Portable first-aid kits should be on hand when children play outdoors and take walks.

Most centers are set up to meet the needs of preschool children. Understanding what a child is like at each stage of development enables you to provide a program that is satisfying and safe for children and provides opportunities for growth. Special considerations must be made when planning the space needs for infants, toddlers, school-age, and special needs children.

A Matter of ETHICS

Handling Violations

Child care facilities are legally obligated to maintain state and local codes to ensure the health and safety of children and staff.

Fire Codes

Fire codes require that buildings have smoke detectors, fire extinguishers, and evacuation plans and that items being stored are kept away from aisles and ceilings.

Thinking Ethically

You are concerned about continuing fire code violations in the location where you work. You have reported these violations to your immediate supervisor and the program director. Your supervisor has told you that this is not your concern. However, the exits continue to be blocked with boxes and equipment on a regular basis. What would you do?

Infant and Toddler Program Needs

Infant, toddler, and preschool environments differ. Infant diaper changing areas require proper ventilation, easy access to diaper disposal, and easily washed flooring surrounding the area. Changing tables must be the proper height to limit caregiver back injuries. Hand-washing sinks should be close by to limit the spread of disease. Low windows allow toddlers to see the outside world. A warm room adds to children's comfort. Because times for eating, sleeping, and playing may vary for each infant, separate areas with cribs for napping must be available throughout the day. Infants and young toddlers eat in special feeding chairs that keep them secure in their seats. Bibs help protect the clothing of these children while they learn to eat.

School-Age Program Needs

After a long day at school, the school-age child may be ready for either action or time to rest. Peer relationships are very important to school-age children. Their environment needs lots of room for group games and interaction. School-age children also need **designated**, or set apart for a specific purpose, space away from younger children. Privacy is especially important to this group. A semi-secluded area allows these children to relax with a good book, to listen to music, or to chat with friends. Private storage for their belongings, such as jackets and coats, school books, and supplies, is also important. Space should be planned for activities that interest school-age children, such as

▶ hobby areas for activities.

▶ homework areas that are quiet and well lit.

▶ computer areas for doing homework, playing computer games, or exploring the Internet.

▶ a play yard built for the size and abilities of school-age children.

Adapting for Children with Special Needs

Early childhood programs also serve children with special needs. An environment should be planned with features that allow easy access to children with special needs. For example, early childhood classrooms should have the following:

▶ Wider classroom pathways to accommodate wheelchairs and devices that aid walking

▶ Ramps that provide access to classrooms.

▶ At least one toilet stall to accommodate wheelchairs or walking devices. Stalls should be at least 69 inches deep and have grab bars mounted between 18 and 27 inches from the floor.

▶ At least one accessible restroom sink and mirror

▶ Accessible tables in eating and activity areas with clear floor space for wheelchairs

By working closely with families, early childhood professionals can also meet the needs of children with special needs. Understanding the specific needs of each child allows the classroom staff to make further plans and adaptations to meet the child's needs.

Storage Needs for Children

Children arrive each day with an assortment of belongings. They may bring coats, hats, extra sets of clothing for toileting accidents, and special items to share in class. Cubbies hold children's personal items. A cubby resembles a small locker, but without doors. Each child needs a personal cubby identified by his or her name and photo, and possibly a symbol or color. Parents can also tape a family photo inside the cubby to help children feel more at home. Placing cubbies near an entrance makes them convenient and encourages children to be responsible for their possessions. Children's labeled toothbrushes or diapers should be stored in a sanitary, organized fashion in their rest room.

▲ **Personal Storage**

Children need a place to store the personal belongings they bring to daycare. *What other sorts of storage may be needed in a child care center?*

Family-Friendly Environments

An entrance that is inviting and convenient for parents and children helps get every day off to a better start. For personal safety, programs increasingly provide an electronic security system for parents to use when entering the center. This usually requires parents to enter a password into a keypad or swipe a center-issued security card through a sensor. After entering a facility, a space is needed for parents to sign children in and out on a daily attendance sheet or a computerized sign-in system. Display space in this area is useful for posting items, such as parenting articles, notices, menus, and newsletters. Some programs have digital slideshows of children taking part in play and learning activities in the center.

Because family involvement is so important in early childhood programs, centers should include some adult-sized seating in classrooms so parents can stay for periods of time. For instance, rockers, gliders, chairs, or love seats and end tables are provided so adults and children can comfortably interact.

Many programs have an observation space for parents or child development students to use. These classroom and observation spaces are equipped with audio equipment that allows observers to hear children's discussions. The observation space has a one-way window that allows observers to watch children without interrupting activities.

Figure 12.1　Space Needs for Staff

Physical Space While the primary focus of the environment of a child care center is the children, the adults who use the building need designated spaces to do their jobs. *How does having appropriate space for adults benefit children?*

Director's Office	Directors need a private office for conducting confidential business and storing important files and financial records. The director's office is usually placed near the entrance for viewing who enters and leaves the center.
Staff Training Room	A training room allows the director to provide on-site professional development for staff. The same room can be used to conduct parent advisory board meetings or parent education programs.
Staff Workroom	Teachers and classroom aides need storage space for instructional materials, such as art supplies. A staff lounge for work breaks is also helpful. Staff members also need space for storing personal belongings and teaching materials.
Kitchen	The kitchen staff needs space and equipment for food preparation and storage.
Custodial and Grounds Storage Room	Custodians keep cleaning equipment and supplies in a locked closet because many cleaning supplies can be **toxic** (poisonous) to children. Likewise, staff caring for outdoor play spaces need space for tools and ground treatment chemicals or facility supplies, such as paint or de-icer.

Staff Space Needs

Staff members also need environments that help them do their jobs effectively and efficiently. A good working environment helps keep staff morale high. In turn, their attitudes toward the children are more likely to be positive. See **Figure 12.1.**

READING CHECK ✔ **Identify** How should a center be equipped to meet program goals?

Indoor Equipment and Supplies

Use good judgment, knowledge of children, and creativity when selecting equipment. Good choices promote learning. Poor choices can create safety hazards and increase behavior problems. When selecting toys and equipment, the following guidelines will be helpful:

▶ Supply items that are safe and appropriate for children's ages and abilities. When care providers plan for children's developmental abilities, children are more likely to experience success. Injuries are reduced when staff avoid toys that could choke young children or puncture older ones.

▶ Provide a variety of materials. Children need variety and novelty to keep their interest and to allow them to develop at their own pace. Include items to develop physical, intellectual, social, and emotional skills. Rotate items regularly, maintaining a balance between familiar items and new ones.

▶ Include sensory, or experienced through the senses, materials that encourage hands-on play. Children need items to look at, to touch, to listen to, to smell, and sometimes even to taste.

- Materials should reflect diverse cultures. Children's books, puppets, dolls, musical recordings and instruments, dress-up clothes, pretend cookware, and posters should reflect the practices of different ethnic groups.

- Provide enough materials so children can comfortably share. Having too few materials frustrates children and sets the stage for conflicts. The younger the children, the more important it is to have duplicate toys.

- Provide a balance of commercially purchased and homemade toys. Creativity is encouraged when children learn they are not dependent on costly items to have fun. Teachers can make easy games with stickers and tagboard. Children can help make doll clothes.

- Include items adaptable to special needs. Materials in a classroom should respond to the varying needs and abilities of those enrolled. For instance, puzzles with knobbed pieces help children succeed despite small-muscle coordination challenges. Sensory play items can be stored in a raised table that allows a child in a wheelchair to use them.

Quality Equipment and Supplies

Programs are required to have **adequate**, or enough or sufficient, equipment and supplies available. Those requirements are listed in licensing laws and accreditation criteria. Of course, potentially hazardous equipment and supplies should be stored away from children in a locked storage area. Likewise, the web site of the U.S. Consumer Product Safety Commission should be checked monthly for recalls of dangerous or defective children's toys, equipment, or supplies.

When purchased, equipment and supplies should be listed on a sheet, called an **inventory record**. An organized inventory should include the following: item, date of purchase, place of purchase, cost, and warranty date, if any.

Inventory records have several uses. Staff can easily see what resources they have available. It allows a program director to see what materials are on hand, as well as what new materials need to be purchased. An inventory also allows staff to determine if broken appliances are still under warranty. If program theft occurs, an inventory helps police and insurance agents determine the extent of loss.

Financial *Literacy*

Property Insurance

Daniel recently experienced a break-in at his child care center. Three computers worth $850 each and a television worth $125 were stolen. The thieves also broke a window and ripped carpet, doing a total of $1,200 in damages to this property. Daniel has a $1,000 deductible on his property insurance policy. How much money will Daniel's insurance provider pay to cover the losses and damages?

Math Concept **Deductible** The deductible in an insurance policy is the portion of any claim that is not covered by the insurance provider. It is usually a fixed amount that must be paid by the insured before the full benefits of a policy can apply.

Starting Hint Calculate the total value of the stolen property and damages ($(3 \times \$850) + \$125 + \$1,200$). Then subtract Daniel's deductible ($1,000) from the total damages.

 For more math practice, go to the Math Appendix at the back of the book.

Evaluating Quality

Careful thought pays when choosing equipment and educational toys. Selections will be better when you ask questions like these before making selections:

▶ Is the item safe? Metal, wood, and plastic edges should be rounded rather than sharp. Paint should be non-toxic. Some paints and other finishes contain ingredients that are toxic, especially to young children who may chew on the toys or equipment.

▶ Will the item withstand heavy or rough use by large groups of children? Is it durable?

▶ Will the toy be easy to clean? Can it be **sanitized**, or cleaned in a way that will kill the organisms that can cause illness?

▶ Can children of different ages use the toy?

▶ Does the toy encourage cooperative play rather than aggressive or even violent play?

▶ Can more than one child use the item at a time?

▶ Does your classroom have storage space for the item?

▶ Can the item be used in more than one way? Will it encourage creativity?

▶ Does the item encourage children's active involvement rather than passive observation? Will it hold a child's interest?

▶ Will children learn basic concepts while playing with the toy? Will it support program goals? Will it reinforce curriculum themes and objectives?

▶ Will the toy allow for sensory learning?

▶ Will both girls and boys enjoy the toy? Is the toy free of racial, cultural, and gender stereotypes?

▶ Are children likely to have fun with the toy?

▲ Selecting Toys

Children with special needs do not always need different toys. *What toys could children at different developmental levels share?*

READING CHECK ✓ **Describe** What should an inventory record include?

The Classroom Climate

Early childhood classrooms must meet children's needs for stability, curiosity, and delight in anything sensory. Sensory means experienced through the senses—sight, smell, sound, taste, and touch. Keeping sensory environments interesting requires balancing basic room arrangements with appealing items that are easily changed. The classroom sound level should be neither too loud nor too quiet. Instead, a continuous hum of activity should dominate the room as children learn through play. A sensory-effective classroom engages children without overwhelming them with too much change.

Realistic Reflections

Creating Atmosphere

Elements, such as sound, color, lighting, patterns, and textures, have a large impact on the behavior of children. Creative staff members can use these elements to enhance the classroom atmosphere. Classroom organization and decoration should be simple and displayed in an organized way to avoid a cluttered look. A classroom that appears crowded and busy with too much displayed at once distracts children, instead of helping them focus and notice details and patterns. Calm but engaging sensory surroundings can be achieved by occasionally rotating play and learning materials as well as wall displays and decorations. This is especially important for children with learning challenges.

Sound

Rooms with a consistently high noise level can make children tired. This limits their ability to concentrate and to learn. To soften the noise level, designers use features such as carpeting, upholstered furniture, sound-absorbing ceiling material, and lined draperies. Tabletop water fountains can filter noise and produce sounds children enjoy. Using play lofts or sunken play spaces also helps limit excess noise.

Color

The use of color in early childhood settings also affects children's activity level and behaviors. For example, the colors red and orange increase children's activity level and appetites. Cool shades of blue and green promote relaxation. Of course, children enjoy color variety, but too many colors at once will impact their ability to focus. Natural colors such as the tans of wood furnishings help calm children. Walls painted with a warm white color are perfect for showcasing children's artwork. Shelving on light-colored walls showcases children's three-dimensional creations.

Lighting

Healthful lighting conditions must also be considered when creating children's spaces. Because children spend so much time indoors, harsh fluorescent lighting can cause fatigue and eye strain. Research shows that adequate amounts of daily sunlight play an important role in good mental health. All classrooms should have windows at children's eye level. Creative use of skylights and mirrors also helps reflect sunlight on play and learning spaces.

Glow Images

Pattern and Texture

The use of soft textures and muted patterns helps create a cozy, homelike atmosphere. A variety of textures may be featured in pillows, rugs, quilts, tapestries, and wall hangings. Fabrics from around the world can be used on a rotating basis to help children understand the diversity in other cultures. Hanging plants, floor plants, and terrariums all help create a homelike atmosphere. Aquariums with tropical fish fascinate children. The colored patterns of the fish and the rhythms of their movement capture children's attention and help them relax.

READING CHECK ✔ **Reflect** What elements enhance the atmosphere of environments for children?

Learning Centers

The well-planned classroom is divided into **learning centers**. Learning centers are clearly defined spaces for specific types of play and investigation. See **Figure 12.2**. Each learning center is organized around a specific type of curriculum, or learning area. Areas for block play, art, science, or dramatic play are each suited to the age and number of children who will use them. When

Figure 12.2 Learning Centers

Multiple Activities Learning centers allow students to engage in active learning and should be adjusted as children's interests change. *What are the benefits of offering multiple activities at one time?*

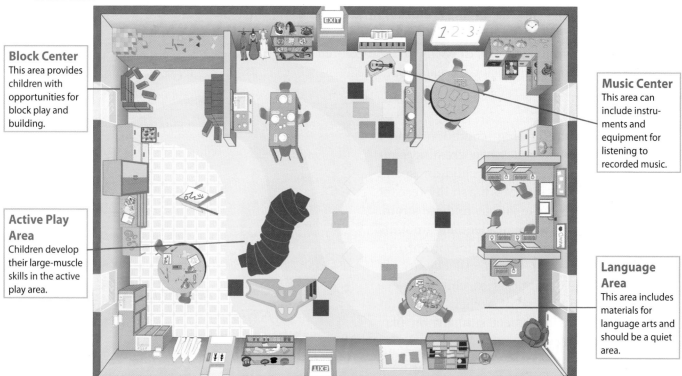

Block Center
This area provides children with opportunities for block play and building.

Active Play Area
Children develop their large-muscle skills in the active play area.

Music Center
This area can include instruments and equipment for listening to recorded music.

Language Area
This area includes materials for language arts and should be a quiet area.

planning learning centers, consider the direction, or **traffic pattern**, children take as they go from one learning center to another.

Learning centers provide an organized way to arrange space and manage the activity. Specifically, they

▶ direct children to activities and focus their attention.

▶ allow children to learn by doing, while working at their own pace.

▶ provide opportunities for independent and small group play.

▶ distribute children throughout the classroom.

▶ minimize conflicts and noise in any one area.

A program may not be able to offer every type of learning center at one time. Budget and space can be limiting. Most programs, however, do try to include certain core learning centers. These include centers for art, language arts, dramatic play, music, science, math, blocks, and active play. Other learning centers, such as cooking, woodworking and computers, can be added as space and resources allow.

A learning center should engage children's participation. It should also allow children to see where to get and return the materials they use. This promotes independence, organization, and critical thinking and encourages decision making.

Supplying Learning Centers

Teachers create learning centers for their specific age group. For instance, a woodworking center is appropriate for preschoolers, but not for infants. Suggestions for supplying typical learning centers follow.

Art Center

Provide an easel with paints and brushes; smocks; storage shelves for supplies; scissors for left- and right-handed children; crayons; markers; a variety of paper and scrap materials for cutting, painting or pasting; paint drying rack; play dough and modeling tools; art cart; and a locked storage cabinet for teacher supplies.

Sensory Play Area

Include a water and sand table, which can also be filled with other sensory items, such as cotton balls; plastic animals; tools such as plastic buckets, shovels, sand and water wheels, plastic measuring cups, funnels, and sifters for sand or water play; science discovery items such as mineral, rock, shell, and other nature collections; bug cages; color paddles; aquarium, terrarium, and other plants; pinwheels; wind chimes; magnifying glasses; balance scales; and magnets.

Woodworking Area

Supply a woodworking bench, child-size quality tools, carpenter's apron, safety goggles, scrap wood, nails, and screws.

Block Center

Provide shelving; wooden unit blocks (for a classroom of 20 preschoolers, provide 400 blocks of various shapes); toy vehicles; plastic zoo, circus, forest, and farm animals; and a train set.

Cooking Center

Supply aprons and hats and basic cooking items such as unbreakable bowls, measuring cups, cookie sheets, and muffin pans.

Dramatic Play and Puppetry Center

Provide pretend home furniture such as table with chair, refrigerator, and range; dress-up clothes; and dolls, stuffed animals, and puppets. Make sure supplies reflect the cultures of all children enrolled in the program.

Language and Relaxation Area

Include a library bookstand with books that allows the front covers to be displayed; relaxing seating, such as a love seat, a rocking chair, a glider, or large pillows; and a CD player with books on CDs (headphones optional).

Music Center

Supply multicultural musical instruments; basic rhythm instruments such as tambourines, finger cymbals, triangles, and drums; compact disc player and discs; items for dancing and creative movement, such as scarves, streamers, tutus, grass skirts, magic wands, and even tap shoes.

▼ **Proper Supplies**

Equipment and supplies in all learning centers must be able to be used by all children, even those with special needs. *How can you make sure that all children can participate in learning centers?*

Image Source/AGE fotostock

Media Stations

Include at least one computer and printer, computer table, and computer games; a DVD player and DVDs; and a handheld camcorder. You may wish to provide digital bookmarks or a list of Web sites with topics related to the curriculum and appropriate educational games.

Manipulatives Center

Include items that help build small-muscle coordination skills, such as stringing beads, Peg-Boards, and snap-together toys; items that build concepts related to color, size, and shape, such as colored table blocks for stacking and making patterns; items for counting, such as teddy-bear counters and number bingo; age-appropriate board games; and matching games such as memory, concentration, color bingo, and shape bingo.

Large-Movement Area

Provide bean bags, streamers, a balance beam, a low climber over padding, a parachute, expandable fabric tunnels, a classroom slide, scooters, balls of all sizes—from beach balls to sponge balls—a plastic bowling-ball set, hula hoops, flags, wheel toys, and a thick mat for rough-and-tumble play. Provide plenty of space free of fall hazards, such as tables, chairs, or toy shelves.

READING CHECK **Connect** What guidelines should be kept in mind when creating and arranging learning centers?

▲ **Appropriate Technology**

Children often begin to use computers at a young age. Media stations provide an opportunity to teach them to use computers safely. *How can you use technology to foster healthy child development?*

How to . . .

Plan a Learning Center

A typical child care classroom is a large rectangular room. Deciding how to arrange the learning centers within the room can be a challenge. You want each area to be distinct from the others, yet for safety reasons they all need to be visible to supervising teachers. When space is limited, combining or rotating learning centers works well.

▶ **Boundaries** *When learning centers are well marked, children understand the limits for play. Most areas need at least three boundaries. For instance, a block center can be placed in a corner of the room. A block storage unit can serve as a third "wall."*

▶ **Arrangement** *Learning centers should provide for children's exploration, discovery, creativity, and development.*

▶ **Privacy** *Learning centers can be arranged so that children have a degree of privacy when needed. Lofts— platforms raised a few feet off the ground—allow children to get away from loud activities when they feel like being alone or with a friend.*

▶ **Traffic Pattern** *Well-planned traffic patterns limit congestion as children enter or leave a learning center. They also help children move more easily during routines, such as hand washing before meals or getting ready for a nap.*

Apply It!
Plan the learning centers for an early childhood classroom. Draw your plans to scale on graph paper.

Image Source/AGE fotostock

Sensory-Appropriate Outdoor Environments

Children often spend more time indoors than outdoors. Safe and appealing outdoor spaces help capture the interest of children This can lead to better health and enjoyment of nature and outdoor activities.

Children and adults alike have an inborn sense of wonder about the outdoor world. The fun and excitement of outdoor life is good for the mind and body. Outdoor play areas today are rich in natural green space, trees, native flowers and shrubs, and exposure to natural elements such as dirt, sand, fresh air, and wind and water.

Color, texture, and aroma are introduced into outdoor play areas by including trees, shrubs, and other types of **nontoxic** (not poisonous) plants. Children can learn about animals and insects that make trees, shrubs, and plants their homes. When birdhouses and feeders are hung, children can observe bird habits and natural cycles, such as nesting time and migration. While outside, children can see and hear the effects of moving air on leaves and branches. Hanging wind chimes or colorful windsocks from trees shows air movement. Trees and shrubs also provide much-needed cool shade.

When seasons change, plants and trees show the effects of weather and climate. Aromas from trees and shrubs, such as pines and lilacs, offer more sensory experiences. Herbs and flowers have aromas that attract butterflies and hummingbirds.

As well as providing sensory experiences, outdoor areas should be made accessible to all program participants. The Americans with Disabilities Act (ADA) is a civil rights law that offers specific guidelines for providing safe, accessible play yards for all participants.

Outdoor Play Areas

Good outdoor play environments nurture children in all areas and stages of development. Good design also responds to varying abilities, including those of children with special needs. For example, sand and water play offered in raised tables allow for independent

Agnieszka Kirinicjanow/Getty Images

use by children in wheelchairs. Because children have a wide range of physical and intellectual needs, separate outdoor play yards are necessary for infants and toddlers, preschoolers, and school-age children. (Some states do allow preschool and school-age children to use the same play yard.) Separate outdoor play areas protect the safety of each age group. State licensing laws and the ADA set standards for outdoor play yards.

Accreditation criteria, such as those of the National Academy of Early Childhood Programs, also address play yard features. Play yards need a variety of areas and surfaces to allow for different types of play. Such play variety ensures children's development of fine- and gross-motor skills.

Climbing and Sliding Areas

Large spaces must be allowed for climbers and low slides. These items should be no higher than 4 feet off the ground and must have at least 9 inches of shock-absorbing material under them to cushion falls. Raised platforms need railings to prevent falls. Placement of swings and climbers must allow ample space for **fall zones**. These zones help keep children from walking into swings, and help ensure children fall onto soft, rather than hard, surfaces.

▼ **Play Yard Safety**

Separate play yards should be provided for toddlers and preschoolers and school-age children. *What equipment differences might there be for each age group?*

McGraw-Hill Education/Eclipse Studios

Hard Surface Areas

Hard surfaces are needed for tricycle and wagon paths, and for games with balls, balance beams, or hoops. Shock-absorbent rubber coverings are often used to soften hard surface areas.

Grassy Areas

Soft, grassy areas are ideal for playing group games, discovering nature, and reading stories. Small grassy slopes allow for sledding in winter, and rolling in summer.

Sensory-Rich Areas

Sensory-rich areas such as sand and water areas or gardens are attractive to children. Sand can be packed in many ways, while playing with water cools and relaxes children. Outdoor water play may include a shallow stream or pool. Vegetable and flower gardens let children explore the natural world, such as worms, butterflies, and plants with a variety of textures. Choose nontoxic plants for children. Again, state licensing laws will dictate what types of water play can be offered in programs.

Art Areas

Art areas can be created on concrete walkways. Colorful wall murals can be made with chalk or water-soluble, nontoxic paint. Children can also sit at picnic tables to draw on paper with markers, crayons, and watercolor paints.

Dramatic Play Areas

Playhouses or small stage areas encourage dramatic play outdoors. Children like to "play house" outdoors, too. They also enjoy pretending to be firefighters and police officers.

Equipping Play Areas

Items offered in outdoor areas vary among programs. If a center believes the play yard should be an outdoor classroom, rather than just a recess area, it often includes areas for art activities or dramatic play. Outdoor play areas generally allow 75 square feet of play area per child. The following are suggestions for equipping typical outdoor play areas. Keep in mind that the suggested items must be adjusted to the size and needs of the group they serve and the available storage.

- ▶ Climbers: ramps, slides, swinging bridge, and firefighter poles
- ▶ Swings: individual swings or porch-style swings for multiple seating

SAFETY MATTERS

Safe Play Yard Equipment

Teeter-totters, merry-go-rounds, swinging exercise rings, trampolines, and high slides have been associated with many injuries to preschoolers. These and other similar items should not be included in the play yard. Be sure to arrange play yard equipment to allow for large fall zones around climbers, slides, and swings. In addition, adequate depth of padding, such as sand, pea gravel, or shredded tires, should be under climbing equipment to absorb shocks from falls. State licensing standards provide requirements for fall zones and surface padding. The arrangement should also allow for care providers to easily view and supervise all children while they play.

What Would You Do? The child care center you work at does not have a set of safety rules and regulations for the playground. What would you do to address this problem?

- ▶ Sand play equipment: sandbox or table with buckets, shovels, scoops, plastic dishes, molds, measuring cups, and plastic zoo, farm, or dinosaur animals
- ▶ Wheel toys: scooters, wagons, tricycles, push-pull toys, and large strollers for infants and toddlers
- ▶ Balls: rim ball with basketballs, soccer balls, soft foam balls, T-balls, and other types of balls
- ▶ Garden toys: flower or vegetable garden space, water source, hose, watering cans, and gardening tools
- ▶ Dramatic play toys: play house, log cabin, tree house, tepees, and tents. Include equipment and supplies that might go with each of these items

▲ Safe Equipment

Safety is a high priority when choosing toys and planning activities. *What evidence do you see that safety concerns are met in this activity?*

Outdoor Storage

Lockable outdoor storage is used to maintain the condition of outdoor recreation materials, and to reduce theft or vandalism. Storage areas should have adequate floor space for wheeled toys and garden chairs. Wall shelving for items, such as sand toys and hand-held gardening tools, should be secure and easily reached. Outdoor storage can be placed near activity areas when the main building doesn't have enough storage space.

Outdoor Safety

Outdoor safety for children requires careful planning and maintenance. Shaded areas with drinking fountains help keep children from becoming **dehydrated**, ill from losing water or body fluids. Constant staff supervision is required when children participate in water activities such as water play, swimming, and fishing. Fences around these outdoor areas help reduce safety risks.

Equipment and surface materials should be routinely checked for breakage, splintering, rusting, or jagged edges that could cause injury. Solid buildings such as playhouses and decks should be placed over concrete or asphalt. This helps keep wildlife, such as skunks, from building homes beneath the structures. Daily safety checks should be performed for all outdoor activity areas to ensure safety.

READING CHECK ✔ **Reflect** How would you determine if a program's outdoor area was engaging as well as safe?

ADA Playground Requirements

The ADA states minimum accessibility requirements for new or altered play areas. These requirements ensure that children with disabilities are able to access a variety of components in a play area. The ADA describes requirements for routes, ramps, landings and wheelchair-accessible platforms, transfer systems, and play opportunities. The ADA accessibility guidelines for play areas are very

Realistic Reflections

complex. When planning, building, or renovating play areas, be sure to obtain the complete ADA requirements. Designing spaces to meet ADA codes is the responsibility of a building or landscape firm's staff. A program's owner and/or director is responsible for insisting ADA requirements are strictly followed. The following information gives a brief overview of the ADA requirements:

Accessible Routes

Specifically designed pathways that provide access to children with disabilities—such as those who use wheelchairs or other mobility devices—are called accessible routes. These routes must connect all entry and exit points to accessible play components.

Ramps, Landings, and Transfer Systems

In providing access to elevated play components, ramps, landings, and transfer systems must meet specific requirements. For instance, hand-rails are required on both sides of ramps that connect to elevated play components.

The level surfaces at the top and bottom of each ramp run are called landings or platforms. Landings must be as wide as the ramps they connect to and must be at least 60 inches in length. Barriers are required along landing or platform edges to keep wheelchairs from falling off.

Transfer Systems

In order to provide access to elevated play components without wheelchairs or mobility devices, a transfer system is used. Transfer systems consist of transfer platforms, transfer steps, and transfer supports. A transfer platform is a landing that allows a wheelchair or mobility device user to lift onto a play structure and leave the mobility device on the ground. Transfer supports include handrails, handgrips, and custom-designed handholds.

Accessible Play Opportunities

In order to make play areas more usable for children with disabilities, additional considerations should be made. These considerations include maneuvering space; knee clearance when sitting at a table; reachable surfaces, cubby storage, and storage shelving for children's toys and supplies.

READING CHECK ✔ **Summarize** What is the purpose of the ADA regulations for play equipment?

▲ **Play for All**

The ADA requires that play yard components be accessible to all children, including those with disabilities. *Why is it important to allow children with disabilities to access play yard components?*

Realistic Reflections

The College Essay

Why Are College Essays Important?

Like any part of your college application, your college essay can be the difference between acceptance and rejection. Your college essay is your chance to show the admissions committee who you are and how you are different from all the other applicants. It allows you to provide information about yourself besides your test scores, grades, and extracurricular activities.

What are typical college essay questions like?

Generally, there are three main types of college essays. The first, sometimes called a personal statement, is an open-ended question looking for information about you. The second requires you to explain your choice of school or career. With this question, colleges are looking for information about your goals and commitment level. The third type explores your creativity by giving you a specific topic to write about.

Does the topic of my college essay matter?

Absolutely. Your essay topic reveals your interests and preferences. For example, if you are passionate about art, you might choose to write about a painting that inspired you. Also, what you choose to write about reflects your values and what is important to you. Lastly, your essay provides a window into your thought process. Think carefully about your topic because what you choose to focus on says a lot about you.

What is the point of the college essay?

There are three main purposes of the college essay. First, it showcases your technical writing skills, including grammar, spelling, and punctuation. Next, it demonstrates your ability to organize your thoughts into structured, logical writing. Finally, and perhaps most importantly, it allows you to paint a clear picture of your unique character and personality.

Hands-On

Imagine you are applying to college, and the essay topic is "Write an essay about a person who has significantly influenced you. Describe the person and how he or she has influenced you." Brainstorm ideas for how you would write this essay. Pick a person, and write a brief outline of your ideas for this essay. Share this with your teacher.

Path to Success

Tips for Writing a College Essay

Answer the Question If you do not answer the question, it does not matter how well your essay is written.

Be Specific Avoid predictable, general, or clichéd writing.

Make It Short and Sweet Eliminate unnecessary words, and do not go over the word limit.

Proofread Carefully Typos, spelling errors, and grammatical mistakes will count against you.

Do Not Repeat Information Make sure your essay is not just a summary of the rest of your application.

Be Yourself Write about your feelings and thoughts.

Environments, Equipment, and Supplies

Visual Summary

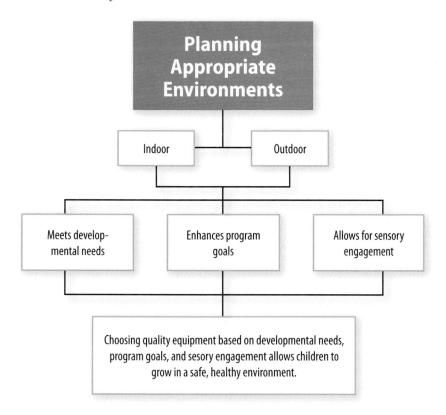

Planning Appropriate Environments

Indoor — Outdoor

Meets developmental needs

Enhances program goals

Allows for sensory engagement

Choosing quality equipment based on developmental needs, program goals, and sesory engagement allows children to grow in a safe, healthy environment.

Vocabulary Review

1. Create a multiple-choice test question for each content and academic vocabulary word.

Content Vocabulary

◇ developmentally appropriate (p. 250)
◇ toxic (p. 254)
◇ inventory record (p. 255)
◇ sanitized (p. 256)
◇ learning centers (p. 258)
◇ traffic pattern (p. 259)
◇ nontoxic (p. 263)

◇ fall zones (p. 264)
◇ dehydrated (p. 266)

Academic Vocabulary

■ designated (p. 252)
■ adequate (p. 255)

Review Key Concepts

2. Identify how environments can respond to all areas and levels of child development.
3. Name the criteria for supplying and equipping early childhood environments.
4. List sensory considerations in the classroom climate.
5. Describe the types of learning centers and activity areas.
6. Explain the role outdoor design plays in health, recreation, and overall learning for children.
7. Summarize the ADA requirements that allow children with disabilities to use play areas

Critical Thinking

8. **Apply** How can a well-planned environment help children learn through their senses?
9. **Contrast** the environmental features needed for infant/toddler and school-age programs.
10. **Analyze** How can equipment or supplies support program goals?

21st Century Skills

Financial Literacy Skills

11. **Choosing Supplies and Equipment** Review at least two catalogs of early childhood equipment and supplies to determine the items you would use to equip a learning center. You can use online or print catalogs.
    • Calculate the total cost of all the supplies.
    • Suggest alternatives that may reduce the cost.
    • Explain how the materials meet the needs of children.
    • Write statements to explain any benefits of using more expensive equipment.

Research Skills

12. **Playground Research** Research outdoor playground equipment for young children. Use print and Internet resources for your research. Determine the age-appropriateness of the equipment. Does it meet ADA requirements for accessibility? Why or why not? Develop safety guidelines for equipping a safe play yard for young children. What differences are there in equipment for young children versus equipment for school-age children? Visit a local play yard and write a brief evaluation based on your guidelines.

Child Care LAB

Use the skills you have learned in this chapter.

Activity Centers

13. **Design an Activity Center** In this activity, you will work with a group to design indoor activity centers and outdoor play areas for a child care center.
    A. **Make a plan.** Work with your group to decide which age group to focus on and which center each of you will design. Each person in your group should work on a different center or play area.
    B. **Describe your center.** Describe the purpose, function, and features of the area.
    C. **Illustrate your center.** Sketch—setup and photograph—your area. Consider using graph paper to draw your floor plan.
    D. **Add features.** Make sure your design includes safety features, traffic patterns, items of visual interest, and characteristics for meeting special needs.
    E. **Evaluate your plan.** Consider possible maintenance issues and how your area will benefit children. Research equipment and supply costs online. What kind of budget would be needed to equip the center fully?
    F. **Combine your designs.** Work with your group to determine how the centers you designed will fit in a classroom space.
    G. **Share your design.** Share your classroom plan with your class.

Create Your Evaluation

Create an evaluation sheet with these categories:
• Safety
• Maintenance Requirements
• Budget
• Appropriate Design
• Appropriate Features
• Teamwork

Ask your classmates to use the sheet to evaluate your design, rating each category from 1 to 10.

Academic Skills

English Language Arts

14. Supply Blog Blogs have become a popular way to rate and review a variety of products, including those for children. Many people use these blogs to decide which products to purchase or whether to purchase an item at all. Choose a toy or other item that might be used in a child care setting. Write a blog entry to share your opinion about the product. Would you recommend it? Why or why not?

Social Studies

15. Multicultural Toys Children benefit from playing with toys from a variety of cultures. Study a catalog of equipment for children. For five typical learning centers, list what could be used to enhance children's understanding of other cultures. Explain how they build children's developmental skills and interest in the world.

Science

16. Benefits of Environmental Education Children use their senses to explore the world. This is particularly important as children explore the outdoors. This exploration enhances their development and scientific understanding of the world around them. Because many children do not spend as much time outdoors as they used to, scientists are researching the benefits of outdoor experiences.

Procedure Conduct research to learn about the benefits of outdoor exploration and play. Make sure to use reliable sources when you research.

Analysis Write a summary of your findings. What sources did you use? Include recommendations for how to make sure that children in a child care center gain these benefits. What activities, environments, and equipment would a child care center need? How could this be implemented when there is limited space?

Certification Prep

Sharpen your test-taking skills to improve your certification program score.

Directions Read each statement. Then read the answer choices and choose the phrase that best completes the sentence.

17. Dehydration can be prevented during outdoor play by _____.

  A. keeping children indoors

  B. having a drinking fountain outside

  C. sitting in the sun

  D. running and playing on accessible equipment

18. The first thing to consider when preparing an environment for children is _____.

  A. ADA requirements

  B. child safety

  C. center rules

  D. state regulations

> **Test-Taking Tip**
> In a multiple-choice test, read the question before you read the answer choices. Try to answer the question before you read the answer choices. This way, the answer choices will be less confusing.

CHAPTER 13

Family Program Partnerships

Writing Activity

⭐ 21st Century Skills

Interpersonal Fiction is an invented story. Think about some of the rewards of being a parent. Then write a short story about a parent experiencing the rewards of parenting. The characters and events in your story may be based on people you know, but remember that this is fiction, so you should make up the details and dialogue.

Writing Tips

1. Make sure your story has a beginning, a middle, and an end.
2. Plan your plot, characters, and setting before you begin writing your story.
3. Introduce the plot in the opening paragraph to help grab your reader's interest.
4. Have your characters use realistic dialogue.

Explore the Photo
Family involvement in a child care center has many positive benefits. *How does a child benefit from family involvement?*

Ingram Publishing

Reading Guide

Preview Understanding causes and effects can help clarify connections. A cause is an event or action that makes something happen. An effect is a result of a cause. Ask yourself, "Why does this happen?" to help you recognize cause-and-effect relationships in this section.

Read to Learn

Key Concepts

- **Discuss** needs and opportunities for family involvement in the child care setting.
- **Explain** types of family referrals.
- **Describe** the basic steps of problem solving with families.
- **Identify** legal responsibilities of working with families.

Content Vocabulary

◇ family relations philosophy
◇ support groups
◇ custody rights

Academic Vocabulary

■ jeopardy
■ consensus

Main Idea

Good relationships with families help early childhood professionals provide quality care. Parents should be involved in planning, applying, and evaluating the care given to their children. Child care professionals provide referrals based on specific needs of a child or family.

Graphic Organizer

As you read, look for six ways that an early childhood program can involve families in the program. Use a wheel graphic like the one shown to help you organize your information.

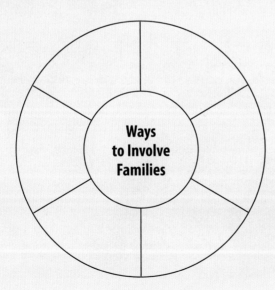

Ways to Involve Families

 Graphic Organizer *Go to* **connected.mcgraw-hill.com** *to print this Graphic Organizer.*

AS YOU READ

Connect Think of specific examples of how your family was involved in your early childhood education.

◇ Vocabulary

You can find definitions in the glossary at the back of this book.

▼ Dropping In

An open door policy builds trust and encourages communication with families. *How does good communication build family program partnerships?*

Building Partnerships

Good relationships with families help early childhood professionals provide quality care. Family members should be involved in planning, applying, and evaluating services that children need. As an early childhood teacher, you should involve family members in the total program that you provide. In preparing to serve families, early childhood program management should identify the program's **family relations philosophy**. This means deciding on a common approach to how families should be treated and included in the program. A family relations philosophy gives program staff clear guidance on a wide variety of issues, including the following:

▶ Recognize that parents are children's first teachers.

▶ All parents deserve respect and patience.

▶ Fathers and mothers are equally important in children's lives.

▶ Nonbiased practices must be used with all families, including non-traditional families, teen parents, and non-English-language speakers.

▶ Parents have the right to ask questions and to make suggestions about their child's program and development.

▶ Family confidentiality must be maintained at all times.

Family Involvement in Child Care Centers

The first step in building good partnerships with children's families is to welcome them warmly. Frequent, positive interactions help build supportive relationships. This makes communication easier. Meeting children's needs is a team effort, and family members are critical team members.

Fancy/Alamy

Family members need to feel included in every area of the early childhood program. In many cases, family members want to be involved, but they may not know how to do so. Effective communication techniques that promote parental involvement can encourage family members to use their knowledge and skills in the program.

Communication with Families

To encourage family and program partnerships, child care staff communicate with families regularly in multiple ways. Information shared by family members helps teachers meet the needs of all children in their care. Staff should seek parent input about their parenting styles when trying to understand and guide a child's behavior. They can ask for parental assistance as a valued, informed partner. For example, ask parents how they think each of you can nurture developmental skills such as toilet training and independent dressing.

Once or twice a year, early childhood professionals schedule a 30- to 60-minute parent-teacher conference with parents to privately discuss children's development and behavior. More frequent meetings should take place for parents of infants. Conferences help staff and parents make decisions together on the care and guidance of each child. During conferences, teachers should suggest ways parents can nurture children's development at home, too.

Face-to-face conversations are best, but early childhood professionals can reach out to parents through technology. A program Web site is a great communication asset. Send out announcements or newsletters as hard copy, but you can also e-mail them and post them on your Web site. A parent bulletin board in a prominent location can help communication, too. When you use many ways to communicate opportunities for family involvement, you will more likely reach all parents in the program.

Open Door Policy

An open door policy means that all family members approved by the child's legal guardian can visit the program anytime. An open door policy encourages families to visit often and builds trust. It also gives them many chances to be active in program activities. During visits, family members are better able to check on service quality. Allowing siblings and other family members such as grandparents to visit also builds a sense of community for children in the program.

Family Engagement Opportunities

Because every family is different, programs plan various ways for families to be involved. Families can be involved in child care centers according to their own interests and schedules. Here are some ways to include families in program services.

▶ **Offer a parent orientation program for newly enrolled families.** Make sure you include time for relationship building as well as for addressing the most important program policies.

▶ **Create a parent buddy or mentor system.** Pair a current parent with a newly enrolled family. The parent mentor helps the new family feel comfortable and welcomed and become familiar with program procedures. It also gives them a chance to ask questions they might be hesitant to ask program staff.

▶ **Distribute surveys to determine parents' hobbies, skills, cultural traditions, and talents.** Ask responders if they would share their unique interests in the classroom. For example, invite musical parents to play their instruments in the classroom weekly. Other parents may wish to be guest readers during story time. Be prepared to help them gear activities to children's developmental levels.

▶ **Include parents in program curriculum and routines.** Working together toward a common goal allows staff and parents to build a good working partnership. Inform parents about each new classroom project or theme. At least one parent or sibling will likely be able to make a contribution to the learning process. **Figure 13.1** is an example of how to involve parents in the curriculum outside the classroom.

▶ **Invite family members to chaperone field trips.** Programs can almost always use extra hands when taking children on field trips. Family members can share the field trip experience with each other and with their children.

▶ **Hold family events.** Many family members work during the day, so they need evening or weekend opportunities for program involvement. Potluck meals allow families to get to know one another. In addition, programs may host an evening performance, hold a children's concert, or plan craft activities as a fun way for families to share in program activities. Many programs like to bring families together to explore the community. Weekend events held at zoos, family theaters, and museums are great group events.

▼ **Family Events**

Family events such as center plays or recitals involve child care staff, all the children, and their families. *Why are family events beneficial for all involved?*

Ariel Skelley/Blend Images LLC

Figure 13.1 Engaging Families in Curriculum Investigations

Involve Families in Class Curriculum Families can be included in the learning process at home by having children and parents complete a simple activity such as this survey that can then be shared with the class. *What are other ways families can be engaged in curriculum in the classroom?*

Dear Parents,

We're learning about flowers! We wish we could see everyone's flowers at home, but we don't have time. So could you and your child please answer these questions about your flowers and bring them back to child care by Friday, July 2nd? Thank You!

1. Do you grow flowers at home?

2. What kinds of flowers do you grow?

3. How many kinds of flowers do you grow?

4. What color flowers do you have?

5. Which flower is the shortest and which is the tallest?

6. What shapes are your flowers?

7. Did you plant the flowers with seeds?

8. Do your flowers have leaves?

Cerebral Palsy

The term cerebral palsy refers to a number of neurological disorders that affect body movement and muscle coordination. Most signs of cerebral palsy occur in infancy or early childhood. The most common signs are lack of muscle coordination, stiff or tight muscles and exaggerated reflexes, and muscle tone that is either too stiff or too floppy. There is no cure for cerebral palsy, but treatment can help a child manage the disorder. Children with cerebral palsy may need therapy, medicine, movement aids such as wheelchairs and walkers, and communication aids depending on the severity of the condition.

Critical Thinking

What must you consider when buying toys for children with cerebral palsy? Make a list of your own ideas. Then, research the question using reliable Internet sources. Compare your findings to your list and edit your list as necessary.

▶ **Add features in classrooms for family comfort.** Parents do not feel welcome in classrooms if they cannot find a comfortable place to sit. To encourage parents to linger in classrooms, provide some adult-scaled furniture parents may use.

▶ **Accept parents' assistance.** Ask parents how they would like to help the program. For example, a parent skilled at working with computers might help maintain a program's Web site. Another parent might be willing to help with safety checks. Some parents may be willing to serve on committees to handle specific projects. For example, some programs form a committee to plan play yard improvements or a fundraiser.

▶ **Include families in program evaluation.** Yearly ask parents to rate and comment upon overall program quality.

▶ **Create opportunities for parents to share or trade family resources.** Seasonally, host a family swap of children's clothing, toys, or books. A lending library for toys, children's books, or parenting books or videos helps families learn more about developmentally appropriate practices.

▶ **Identify community family support agencies.** On a family or parent bulletin board, post brochures of family services that address typical family needs such as health care, nutrition, children's insurance, dental health, family counseling, and child care subsidy options.

▶ **Help parents keep children safe at home.** Sponsor a car safety seat demonstration on site at a convenient time for parents. Invite parents to obtain CPR and first aid training with program staff each time they renew their certifications.

▶ **Work very closely with parents of children with special needs.** Parents of children with disabilities should be asked to train staff or direct them to appropriate community resources for training on their child's special needs and how to meet them.

▶ **Organize an advisory board.** Family members are more supportive of programs that give them a say in how the programs are run. Having families serve on early childhood advisory boards allows them to influence program quality. They can also offer specialized help such as advice on managing program finances.

▶ **Sponsor support groups.** People with similar needs can often help each other by sharing information or advice. Some programs create support groups for this purpose. **Support groups** are groups that meet regularly to discuss common concerns and needs. For example, support groups may exist for single parents, grandparents raising grandchildren, or parents raising children with special needs.

READING CHECK ✔ **Recall** What topics are addressed in a family relations philosophy?

How to . . .

Include the Family in Bilingual Development

Children more easily develop first and second language skills when early childhood teachers and family members work cooperatively. Teachers should meet with parents before a child's first day to determine the extent of the child's language skills and how parents would like their child's language development to be handled in child care. These suggestions can help teachers plan how to include families in a child's bilingual development.

me llamo maria

yotengo ocho Anos

yo quiero a mi perro

©Ariel Skelley/Blend Images LLC

Apply It!

Create a plan for children's development of a second language at a child care center.

▶ **Translate Program Information** *Translate program information into parents' first language. Provide translators at evening parenting workshops so parents who speak a second language can be more involved in discussions.*

▶ **Use Children's First Language** *Communicate with children to some extent in their first language. Ask parents of non-English-speaking children to complete a home language survey that provides translations and phonetic spellings of common words and phrases. The survey should include important phrases such as "Do you feel sick?" "Do you need to use the toilet?" and "Are you hungry?"*

▶ **Invite Families into the Classroom** *Encourage families of non-English-speaking children to share customs, books, cultural toys, songs, and recipes.*

▶ **Use Bilingual Signage** *Use bilingual labeling for signage at the child care facility.*

Providing Parent Referrals

Some families need services beyond those offered by early childhood programs. Staff that is well informed of community services can connect families to the assistance they need. This is called providing a referral. A referral is based on staff observations and is not a diagnosis. A child care staff member cannot diagnose behavioral, health, or other issues.

Deciding If a Referral Is Needed

Early childhood staff should learn to assess a child's or family's need for a referral. They can determine if a referral is needed by reflecting upon the following questions.

▶ Is the child's mental, emotional, or physical welfare and development in **jeopardy**, or danger?

▶ Does a healthy parent-child relationship seem in jeopardy?

▶ Does the parent's own mental or physical health, financial status, or housing resources limit his or her ability to adequately or safely parent a child?

▶ Is the child's behavior frequently harmful to self or others?

▶ Is the child's ability to learn or his or her classmates' ability to learn impaired by the problem?

▶ Is the classroom's social environment frequently disrupted and tense due to the problem?

▶ Have other teachers or professionals noted the same concerns and behaviors?

▶ Has the concerning situation continued despite multiple attempts to cope with and solve the problem without outside help?

▶ Is the child's behavior or problem significantly unusual compared to typical child development?

If the answer is yes to even one of these questions, giving a parent a referral to a community resource would be helpful. Providing such a referral is one way early childhood teachers advocate for children's and families' well-being. Referrals should be made in a private, culturally sensitive manner and in a way parents can easily understand. Teachers should help parents identify their options. Seeking help is a parents' decision, but child care staff can make finding community support an easier task for parents.

Science for Success

Parenting Roles and Family Life Cycle

Parents have many responsibilities, including feeding, sheltering, and nurturing their children. Over the course of the family life cycle, children grow up, become independent from their families, and may start families of their own. Parents and children play various roles during the different stages of the family life cycle.

Procedure Conduct research on parenting roles and responsibilities and the different stages of the family life cycle. Use reliable print and Internet resources to find answers to the following questions: What are the stages of the family life cycle? What happens in each stage? What skills do parents and children develop and use during each stage? How do the roles of various family members change over the life cycle of the family?

Analysis Use the information you have gathered to create a presentation that shows the changes that occur in each stage of the family life cycle. Be creative. You might choose to make a chart, a collage, a multimedia presentation, or a short play. Show your presentation to the class, explaining the family members' roles and responsibilities throughout the family life cycle.

©Comstock/Alamy

Types of Referrals

Staff members make referrals after identifying specific needs or in response to a family question. Referrals are often made to those who specialize in specific types of care, such as pediatricians or speech-language pathologists. The following are typical referrals made by child care staff:

▶ **Nutrition education.** Referrals to nutrition education programs can help promote good health. In some cases, referrals are made for problems such as undernourishment, obesity, and eating problems.

▶ **Family therapy.** When families are under stress, they can benefit from family therapy. Referrals for family therapy may be made in response to a concern about suspected neglect or abuse. Families may need extra help in learning how to solve conflicts without violence.

▶ **Financial assistance.** Families with limited income or those who experience a job loss may require income assistance. Staff can refer these families to financial assistance programs. For example, many states provide monetary assistance to low-income families to help pay the cost of quality child care.

▶ **Child development services.** If children have delayed development, they may benefit from extra help. For example, a physical therapist can help a child with delayed motor skills develop muscle strength and motor coordination appropriate for his or her age.

▶ **Medical referrals.** Families often need help with finding medical care. A family may need a referral for required immunizations. Parents of a child who has trouble listening and following directions may be referred to a hearing specialist.

In order to give families timely referrals, many early childhood care programs create a community service directory. The directory is a quick reference guide for staff members in making referrals. It consists of a detailed list of helpful referral agencies or organizations. A community service directory should including the following information about each referral agency: description, eligibility requirements, contact information, application procedure, location, and costs for services.

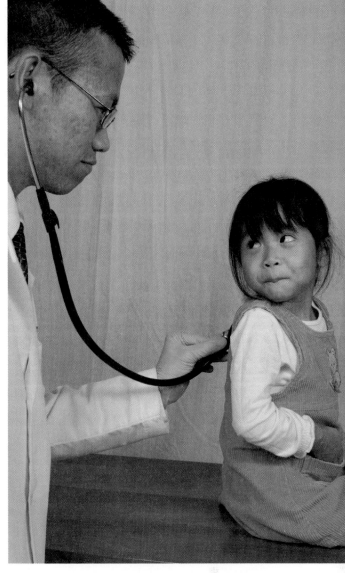

▲ **Medical Referral**

An early childhood teacher may refer a family to a health care professional when a child has a continuing health problem. *What other kinds of specialists might families be referred to?*

READING CHECK ✓ Define What is a referral?

Problem Solving with Parents

Even in the best of family program partnerships, concerns or disagreements can occur. Parents might have a concern about a child's eating or napping habits. Or they might feel their child is being unfairly disciplined. Staff members also sometimes have concerns about parent attitude or behavior. For example, they may be concerned when they see a child being brought to child care in a car without a child safety seat.

No matter what the issue is, there are basic steps that promote productive problem solving between families and program staff. Staff should use the following steps to solve problems.

▶ Identify the problem. Make sure both parties (child care staff and parents) agree on what the problem is. If there are multiple problems, agree to prioritize the order for addressing concerns.

▶ Objectively gather information about the problem. Make sure you get information from everyone's perspective and viewpoint.

▶ List several possible ideas that might solve or reduce the problem. Think creatively and avoid making snap judgments on solution ideas.

▶ Together, parents and staff should decide on a specific plan. Seek **consensus**, or mutual agreement, rather than a majority vote. Put the plan in writing.

▶ Mutually decide what results will be considered indicators of the plan's progress.

▶ Put the plan into action.

▶ At an agreed-upon time, evaluate the progress or results of the plan, including all parties in the evaluation. Revise the plan as needed until everyone is satisfied with the results.

▶ **Putting a Plan into Action**

....

When problem solving with parents, agree on an action plan to solve the problem, such as providing an on-site specialized therapist for a child with special needs. *Why is it important that everyone agrees to an action plan, not just the majority?*

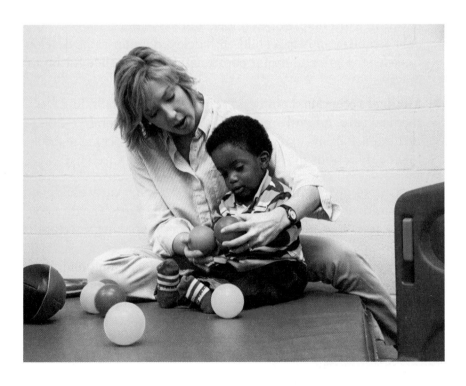

Professional Ethics with Families

As an early childhood professional, you will never be able to predict every topic of disagreement or misunderstanding that can arise between program staff and parents. If you are in doubt on how to respond to a new challenge, the National Association for the Education of Young Children's (NAEYC) Code of Ethics for working for families can guide your decision making as you create an action plan that is respectful to parents, children, and staff.

READING CHECK ✔ **Review** What should parents and staff do after a problem-solving plan is put into action?

Legal Duties to Families

In order for early childhood programs to operate within the law, program directors and staff must be aware of the legal duties of their positions concerning families. This helps ensure that children and their families are well served and protected.

Family Licensing Laws

Licensing laws in each state address specific legal issues related to child care services. Some states require a copy of a child's actual birth certificate to determine parentage. If a court of law has decided on child **custody rights**, the rights to care and guardianship of a child, programs must follow them. For example, custody rights determine who may enroll a child, who may make decisions about the child's medical treatment, and who staff may allow to leave with a child. Changing demographics and non-traditional families complicate custodial issues, making it more important for child care staff to know who has legal guardianship to a child.

Referral Legal Issues

Providing referrals is also affected by legal issues. The type of referral and the reason it was given, including incidents that lead to the referral, must be recorded in a child's file. Conversations and meetings concerning the referral should also be kept in a child's file. Parents have a right to view any of the documents maintained in a child's file. They also have the right to ignore the referral or get a second opinion.

Ethically and legally, early childhood professionals must keep referrals confidential. Only custodial parents and legal guardians have the right to referral status. Only those directly involved in caring for the child have the right to be informed of decisions related to giving referrals. Reporting suspected child abuse and neglect also requires documentation and is subject to confidentiality and privacy laws.

READING CHECK ✔ **State** What are the legal considerations of providing referrals to families?

College & Career READINESS

Child Care Referral Specialist

What Does a Child Care Referral Specialist Do?

Child care referral specialists help parents locate quality child care. They can provide information on financial assistance for child care services, education on what to look for in a quality child care, and other information that will help parents in their search. Child care referral specialists can also help families and child care professionals identify other referral services such as specialized health or counseling services.

Career Readiness Skills

Child care referral specialists need to have strong active-listening and problem-solving skills. They must be able to communicate with a diverse group of parents, guardians, and child care professionals about private or sensitive issues and maintain confidentiality. Child care referral specialists must also be able to keep track of and reference a large amount of print and electronic resource information.

Education and Training

Child care referral specialists have a background in childhood development. Some positions require an associate's or bachelor's degree in early childhood education, human development, or a related field. Referral specialists participate in regular training to stay up-to-date on referral resources and services. The ability to speak and write another language fluently is highly desirable.

Job Outlook

Child care referral specialists are usually employed by a government or nonprofit agency. Employment is expected to experience average growth over the next ten years. Demand may increase as private firms such as health insurance companies hire child care referral specialists to provide information resources for their clients.

Critical Thinking Think about the diverse group of people a child care referral specialist may talk with on a daily basis. What communication challenges might a referral specialist encounter? What could he or she do to prepare for those challenges?

Career Cluster

Government and Public Administration
Child care referral specialists work in the Public Management and Administration pathway of the Government and Public Administration career cluster. Other jobs in this cluster include the following:

- Subsidy Specialist
- Grant Administrator
- County Clerk
- Program Administration Officer
- Policy Advisor
- City Council Member
- Child Care Licensing Inspector
- Social Worker
- Foundation Director
- Charitable Organization Secretary
- Family Advocate

Explore Further The Government and Public Administration career cluster contains seven pathways: Governance, National Security, Foreign Service, Planning, Revenue and Taxation, Regulation, and Public Management and Administration. Choose one of these pathways to explore further.

Family Program Partnerships
Visual Summary

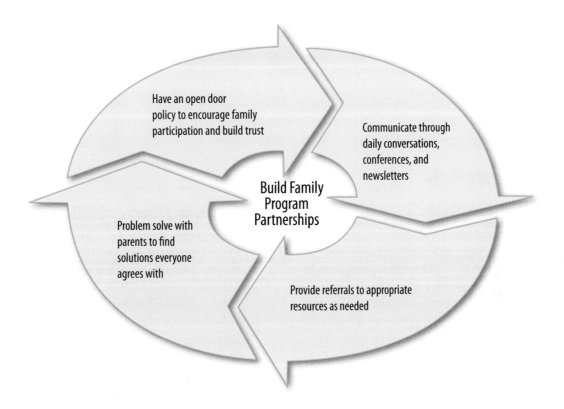

Have an open door policy to encourage family participation and build trust

Communicate through daily conversations, conferences, and newsletters

Build Family Program Partnerships

Problem solve with parents to find solutions everyone agrees with

Provide referrals to appropriate resources as needed

Vocabulary Review

1. Use these vocabulary terms in a short essay about child care family program partnerships.

Content Vocabulary

◇ family relations philosophy (p. 274)
◇ support groups (p. 278)
◇ custody rights (p. 283)

Academic Vocabulary

■ jeopardy (p. 280)
■ consensus (p. 282)

Review Key Concepts

2. Discuss needs and opportunities for family involvement in the child care setting.
3. Explain types of family referrals.
4. Describe the basic steps of problem solving with families.
5. Identify legal responsibilities of working with families.

Critical Thinking

6. **Research** parenting styles and skills. Why is it important for early childhood professionals to be familiar with the parenting styles of the parents of children in their care?

7. **Analyze** the impact of changing societal patterns and demographics on parents, children, and family members. How can a child care professional support the changing roles within the family? How does this affect parent-teacher communication?

8. **Compare** How does a child care professional's legal responsibilities to a child differ from a parent's the legal responsibilities to his or her child?

9. **Devise** ways to involve a parent or a family member who is reluctant to participate in program events. What could you do or say to positively influence the person to participate?

10. **Determine** three different ways to approach a family with a referral to a community agency.

21st Century Skills

Communication Skills

11. **Create a Checklist** Create a checklist that a parent could use to evaluate the quality and service received at a child care program. Include items that cover bonding with staff, parent-staff communication, parent involvement at the center, and problem warning signs. For example, the first item on your checklist could be "My child has bonded with a teacher."

Information Literacy Skills

12. **Changing Families** According to the U.S. Census Bureau, there were 18,824,000 nuclear families living in the United States in 1950. This number rose to 25,129,000 in 2009. The number of single-parent families rose from 1,500,000 in 1950 to 10,505,000 in 2009. Record this information using a line graph or a bar graph. What can you conclude from the information?

Child Care LAB

Use the skills you have learned in this chapter.

Parent/Guardian Handbook

13. **Develop a Parent Handbook** In this activity, you will work in a group of four to create a child care program handbook for parents/guardians.

   A. Discuss the handbook sections. With your group, discuss your ideas for the handbook sections. The handbook should include the following elements:

   - Introduction
   - Communications
   - Conferences
   - Family Involvement

   Assign each group member to write one section. Consider your audience when writing your section and use proper grammar.

   B. Write the introduction. Summarize the child care program's family relations policy in the handbook's introduction.

   C. Explain program communications. Describe how the program communicates with parents, both formally and informally.

   D. Determine a conference schedule. Explain the program's conference schedule and list general conference topics of discussion.

   E. Outline family involvement. Describe volunteer opportunities and other program family involvement activities.

   F. Assemble the handbook. Combine all four sections into a final parent/guardian handbook.

Create Your Evaluation

Create an evaluation sheet with these categories:

- Introduction
- Communications
- Conferences
- Family Involvement
- Grammar/punctuation

Have your teacher use this sheet to evaluate your handbook, rating each category on a Detailed and Complete/Adequate Information/Needs Improvement scale.

Academic Skills

 ### English Language Arts

14. Parent's Perspective Understanding a parent's perspective on parenting issues is important for maintaining consistency between home and child care. Read a book about parenting skills. What issues would be important for an early educator to discuss with parents? How could an early educator learn about a parent's preference on these issues?

 ### Social Studies

15. Family Crisis Families can experience crisis for many reasons, including financial stress, divorce, and domestic violence. Select two organizations that provide support for families in crisis and research the services they provide. What do these organizations identify as symptoms of children in crisis situations? How do these organizations contribute to society's role in the protection of families?

 ### Mathematics

16. Two Child Discount Jenna and Jason are trying to decide whether to place both of their children in child care. One factor in their decision is cost. Kelsey is an infant and Garrett is in 3rd grade. At the child care program that Jenna and Jason like, full-time child care for an infant costs $700 a month. It costs $500 a month to enroll a child in the afterschool program. A family with more than one child enrolled in care receives a 5% discount. How much will it cost per month to have both children in child care?

Math Concept **Percent** A percent is a part of a whole expressed in hundredths. To find the percent of a number, multiply the number by the percent written in decimal form. For example, 5% is 0.05.

Starting Hint Calculate the total cost of child care for both children per month. Multiply the total by 0.05. This will give you the discount amount. Subtract the discount amount from the total.

 For more math practice, go to the math appendix at the back of the book.

Certification Prep

Directions Read the sentence, and choose the best phrase to fill in the blank.

17. A family relations philosophy states that _____.

  A. parents should be treated differently based on family structure

  B. parents should trust early childhood teacher decisions without question

  C. parents are children's first teachers

  D. parents do not deserve respect or patience

18. A parent with custody rights to a child _____.

  A. cannot make decisions about a child's medical care

  B. has legal guardianship of the child

  C. may not enroll a child in child care

  D. does not decide who may pick up a child from child care

> **Test-Taking Tip**
> If two options in a multiple-choice question both appear to be true, carefully examine the differences between them. Then select the choice that best answers the question.

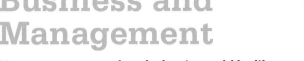

Business and Management

College & Career
R E A D I N E S S

Have you ever wondered what it would be like to own a child care center?

A career as a child care center owner involves many different roles. An owner oversees all aspects of program operations, including establishing program goals, working with children and families, maintaining licensing standards, developing curriculum, hiring and managing staff, managing the program budget, and marketing the program to the community.

To succeed in business and management, you will need management and financial skills. You will also need excellent communication and organization skills. A child care owner should have an understanding of early childhood care and education and enjoy spending time with children.

Steve Thomas • Child Care Center Owner

Q What is your job?

A I co-own a private child care center with my parents. We work with children from eight weeks until they are ready to go to school. We also offer before- and after-school programs for school-age children.

Q What is your typical work day like?

A I work long hours and am at the school before the children and staff arrive. I am typically the last one to leave every day. I help teachers with their classes and I meet with parents. I was even the project manager for our recent building renovation.

Q Why did you choose your career?

A I have always enjoyed working with children. I started as a teacher's aide at a child care center. I decided that I wanted to own a small business, and owning a child care center made sense because of my experience in early childhood education. I like being able to manage both the operations of the center as well as the financial side of things.

Q How did your career path lead you to your current job?

A I have a bachelor's degree in communications. I took quite a few business classes after I graduated from college and worked for several large corporations in the area. This experience taught me the business skills that I need to own and manage a child care center.

Q Who or what has been your biggest career influence?

A Both of my parents have been involved in early childhood education for most of their lives. Their enthusiasm for children's education made me to want to participate in the child care center.

Q What skills are most important in your job?

A I need to have a lot of patience with the children and my staff. I am managing so many things at once that I can't get too stressed or I will pass that stress on to my staff. I find that I need to be very organized and able to manage many tasks at the same time.

McGraw-Hill Education/Ken Cavanagh

Career Requirements	
Education or Training	Business and management jobs usually require education beyond high school. In many child care centers, an owner must have a bachelor's degree, experience in early childhood care, and training in child development. Some owners may have advanced degrees in business management.
Academic Skills	English Language Arts, Mathematics, Science, and Social Studies
Aptitudes, Abilities, and Skills	Knowledge of children, planning and organizational skills, communication and financial skills
Workplace Safety	Basic first aid certification and CPR certification are recommended.
Career Outlook	The demand for quality child care continues to rise, creating opportunities and market need for new child care centers.
Career Path	Career paths may vary depending on training. Many child care center owners begin their careers as early childhood teachers or teacher's aides.

Career Pathways	
Bookkeeper	A bookkeeper keeps all the financial records for a business and prepares any necessary reports. He or she needs to have strong financial skills. Sometimes a bookkeeper is employed by a small business, but often they are self-employed, keeping records for many businesses.
Indoor Play Center Manager	An indoor play center provides a safe space for children to be able to play actively on indoor equipment all year round. A manager for an indoor play center needs to be a strong leader and be able to communicate well with staff and parents. He or she must be able to manage many tasks.
Business Analyst	A business analyst analyzes the organization and functions of a business and makes strategic decisions about how to improve business. He or she needs to have strong problem-solving skills and the ability to communicate and collaborate with others.
Marketing Director	A marketing director promotes a business to the community in order to create new customers. A marketing director would have a bachelor's degree and usually a Master's of Business Administration (MBA) degree.

Critical Thinking   What classes have you taken in school that might help you prepare for a career as the owner of a child care center? Propose the short- and long-term career goals that will help you prepare for this career.

Certification Prep

Shadow a child care owner for a day. Take notes about the kinds of activities that the owner does during the day. How involved is he or she in program operations? How does he or she interact with the staff? Use your observations and your notes to create an organizational chart that includes each staff position.

Competitive Events Practice

Imagine that you are the owner of a child care center. Write a list of all of the possible jobs and job descriptions that you would need to run your center. Consider teaching staff and other support staff positions such as transportation workers.

Does your list

• consider a variety of jobs?

• include descriptions for each job?

• include a description for your job as the owner?

Money Matters

An important skill for a child care professional is to be able to make sound financial decisions regarding a business. A child care center owner or director must manage the income and expenses of the program in order to run a business successfully. In this project, you will use your research and the information in the chapters in this unit to create a monthly program budget for a child care center.

My Journal

If you completed the journal entry from page 204, refer to it to see what kinds of expenses are involved in managing a child care program. Add any additional notes about expenses that you have after reading this unit.

Project Assignment

In this project, you will do the following:

- Set a financial goal for a child care center
- Determine child care program income and expenses
- Create a sample monthly budget with estimated income and expenses for a child care center
- Analyze your sample budget in relation to your financial goal for the child care center
- Present your financial goal, budget, and budget analysis to your teacher for evaluation

Applied Child Care Professional Skills Behind the Project

A business like a child care center needs to create a budget in order to manage expenses and to meet financial goals. Skills you will use in this project include the following:

- ▶ Researching the income a child care center receives for tuition and fees per child enrolled in the program
- ▶ Identifying monthly child care program expenses such as rent, staff salaries, and art supplies
- ▶ Creating a monthly budget for a child care center.
- ▶ Analyzing income and expenses in order to make business decisions about the program's financial goals

English Language Arts Skills Behind the Project

The English Language Arts skills you will use for this project are research and writing skills. Remember these key concepts:

Research Skills

- ▶ Perform research using a variety of print and nonprint resources
- ▶ Discriminate between reliable and unreliable sources
- ▶ Take clear notes on your research, and keep them organized for future reference
- ▶ Use the information you gathered to narrow your choices and make reasonable estimates

Writing Skills

- ▶ Write in complete sentences
- ▶ Use correct spelling, grammar, and punctuation
- ▶ Consider your audience
- ▶ Organize your information in an easy-to-understand format

STEP 1 Set a Financial Goal

Imagine that you own a child care center. Set a financial goal for your business. For example, your financial goal might be to make a profit or to purchase a van for field trips. Write a summary of your financial goal that

- describes your goal and reasons for setting this goal. Is the goal short- or long-term?
- outlines a plan for reaching the goal. How much money will you need to earn or save?

STEP 2 Calculate Your Monthly Income

A child care center's primary source of income is the tuition collected per child enrolled in the program. Research how much programs in your area typically charge per child per week. Decide on the number of children and age groups your program with serve. How much tuition will you charge per child per week?

STEP 3 Estimate Your Monthly Expenses

Estimate your program's expenses for the following:

- **Staff.** Based on the number of children in your program, how many staff members will you need? Total all staff's monthly salaries.
- **Building Costs.** List estimated monthly costs for rent, utilities, and building maintenance.
- **Equipment.** List estimated monthly costs for program equipment such as art supplies.
- **Marketing.** Determine how much you will spend per month marketing your program.

STEP 4 Prepare Your Monthly Budget

Use your income and expense estimates to create your budget. Create a table with four columns labeled as follows and complete the table.

Blend Images/SuperStock

- **Income/Expense.** Add a line item for your program's income and each expense.
- **Budget.** Enter your estimates for each income and expense line item. Enter expenses as negative numbers.
- **Actual.** Enter the actual income and expenses for each item. If you do not know the actual numbers, enter reasonable estimates.
- **Difference.** Subtract the actual amount from the budgeted amount.

STEP 5 Analyze Your Monthly Budget

Analyze your budget to determine if you can reach your financial goal. Consider the following:

- Subtract total expenses from total income. Is your business breaking even or operating at a loss? How could you adjust your budget to make a profit?
- Look at the Difference column. Did you budget too much or too little for a particular line item? How would you adjust your budget estimates for the next month?
- Does your monthly budget help you meet your financial goal? If it does not, what changes can you make to reach your goal?

STEP 6 Evaluate Your Child Care Professional and Academic Skills

Your project will be evaluated based on:

- Thoroughness of income and expenses list
- Clarity of budget table and calculation accuracy
- Depth and detail of your budget analysis

 Project Worksheet *Go to* **connected.mcgraw-hill.com** *for a worksheet you can use to complete your portfolio project.*

Providing Early Care and Education

Chapters

Project Preview

Games and Activities for Learning

After completing this unit, you will know more about caring for children at various ages and the kinds of activities that promote a child's development. In the Unit 4 child care portfolio project, you will research and create your own game or activity that encourages a child's physical, intellectual, emotional, and social development for a specific age group. You will assemble or create the materials needed for your activity and then present your research and demonstrate your activity for the class.

My Journal

Write a journal entry about games or activities that promote children's development for each of the age groups you will study. You can refer to games and activities you have experienced on your own or with children you know, or you can research activities that are discussed in your text.

- What kinds of games or activities did you choose?
- Why did you choose them, and where did you find information on them?
- How do you think these games or activities help a child's intellectual, emotional, and social development?

©Nova Development

Jj jaguar Kk Ll lion Mm
iguana koala moose

Explore the Photo

Providing care involves helping children learn and develop new skills. *How are educational goals met in a child care setting?*

CHAPTER 14

Nurturing Infant Development

Writing Activity

★ 21st Century Skills

Decision Making Many parents will rely on alternate care for their children at some point in time. This is a big decision that should not be taken lightly. Write a short essay to compare and contrast what you already know about different types of child care, such as child care centers, family child care homes, nannies, and after-school care. Consider how a parent's career decisions might impact child care.

Writing Tips

1. Use a graphic organizer to map your ideas.
2. Organize your essay by comparing subjects or features.
3. Use appropriate transition words and phrases.
4. Address both the similarities and differences in your essay.

Explore the Photo Infants need constant care and attention to grow and develop properly. *How do caregivers meet the needs of infants?*

Sasha Haltam/Getty Images

Reading Guide

Use Notes When you are reading, keep a notepad handy. Whenever you come upon a section or term that is unfamiliar to you, write the word or a question on the paper. After you have finished the section, look up the terms or try to answer your questions based on what you have read.

Read to Learn

Key Concepts

- **Summarize** the stages of prenatal development, as well as infant physical, intellectual, emotional, and social development.
- **Identify** the responsibilities of infant caregivers and three components of a successful infant care program.
- **Describe** four strategies for nurturing the developmental areas in an infant.

Main Idea

In this chapter you will learn about prenatal development and how infants change as they develop physically, intellectually, emotionally, and socially. You will also learn about the key components of an infant program, including staff responsibilities. Finally, you will learn strategies for nurturing development in infants.

Content Vocabulary

◇ prenatal development
◇ reflexes
◇ perceptual motor skills
◇ eye-hand coordination
◇ sensorimotor period
◇ object permanence
◇ vocalizations
◇ attachment behavior
◇ egocentric
◇ stranger anxiety
◇ staff turnover
◇ on demand
◇ caregiver report form
◇ parent or guardian report form

Academic Vocabulary

■ sequence
■ process

Graphic Organizer

As you read, you will discover information about infant reflexes. Use a graphic organizer like the one shown to record six types of reflexes. Include notes about each type of reflex.

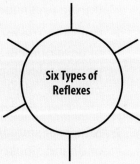

Six Types of Reflexes

🧭 **Graphic Organizer** *Go to* **connected.mcgraw-hill.com** *to print this Graphic Organizer.*

◆**Vocabulary**

You can find definitions in the glossary at the back of this book.

▼ **Watch Me Grow!**

Infants experience remarkable changes and fast growth during the first 12 months of life. *What three things do infants need to have the best possible start in life?*

Development and Care

Most experts define infancy as the time between birth and 12 months of age. This is the beginning of a child's progress through the developmental stages. This age is known as a time of remarkable changes. Infancy is the most intense period of accelerated growth and development in a person's life. Good health services, sound nutrition, and loving care allow infants to have the best possible start in life.

Prenatal Development

The foundation for lifelong development starts at conception. Humans have their most rapid period of physical development in the womb. Changes that occur to humans during the nine months of pregnancy are referred to as **prenatal development**. Prenatal development includes three distinct stages: the zygote stage (month 1), the embryo stage (month 2), and the fetus stage (month 3 until birth). **Figure 14.1** on page 297 lists important changes that occur during each stage of prenatal development.

As with all life stages, the rate of prenatal development varies slightly from one person to another. Many factors contribute to healthy prenatal development. Good maternal nutrition and mental health are important. Pregnant women need proper nutrients for the growing baby, appropriate exercise, sleep, and additional vitamins and minerals to support the fast growth of a fetus.

There are many factors that can harm typical prenatal development. Some factors are genetic, or inherited. Some are linked to the mother's condition or behaviors. Proper prenatal care is essential to prevent birth defects such as spina bifida and cerebral palsy. The following tips for pregnant women can help provide children with a good start in life:

▶ The pregnant woman should be in good physical condition.

▶ Well-balanced nutrition is essential.

▶ Be aware of any mental health problems of the mother, including depression or disabling stress.

▶ Use caution to prevent physical injury during pregnancy.

▶ Consider the mother's age and stage of development. Teens are still experiencing development themselves, so pregnancy during adolescence can affect typical prenatal development.

▶ Maternal smoking, or exposure to secondhand smoke, should be avoided.

▶ Avoid drug use, whether medical prescriptions, alcohol, or other drugs.

Corbis/age fotostock

Figure 14.1 **Stages of Prenatal Development**

Our first growth spurt Humans grow and develop extremely fast while in the womb. *In which month of development are all organs present? During which month do breathing movements begin? Discuss the development that occurs during the zygote, embryo, and fetus stages.*

First Trimester

Month	Developmental Characteristics
1 (four weeks) zygote stage	• Size of a pinhead at two weeks. 4 to 6 millimeters at four weeks. • Egg attaches to uterus lining. • Internal organs and circulatory system begin to form. • The tubular heart begins to beat at 28 days. • Small bumps, called limb buds, are the beginnings of arms and legs.
2 (eight weeks) embryo stage	• About ¼ inch long as month begins • Face, eyes, ears, and limbs take shape. • Cartilage is replaced as bones begin to form.
3 fetus stage	• About 1 inch long as month begins, 2 ½ to 3 inches long as month ends • Nostrils, mouth, lips, teeth buds, and eyelids form. • Fingers and toes are almost complete. • All organs are present, although immature.

Second Trimester

Month	Developmental Characteristics
4	• About 3–4 inches long, 1 ounce as month begins • Can suck its thumb, swallow, hiccup, and move around • Facial features become clearer.
5	• About 6½–7 inches long and 4–5 ounces as month begins. • Hair, eyelashes, and eyebrows appear. • Teeth continue to develop. • Organs are maturing.
6	• About 8–10 inches long and 8–12 ounces as month begins • Fat deposits are under skin, but fetus appears wrinkled. • Breathing movements begin.

Third Trimester

Month	Developmental Characteristics
7	• About 10–12 inches long and 1½–2 pounds as month begins • Periods of activity are followed by periods of rest and quiet.
8	• About 14–16 inches long and 2½–3 pounds as month begins. • Weight gain continues rapidly. • May react to loud noises with a reflex jerking action • Moves into a head-down position
9	• About 17–18 inches long and 5–6 pounds as month begins • Weight gain continues until the week before birth. • Skin becomes smooth as fat deposits continue. • Movements decrease as the fetus has less room to move. • Acquires disease-fighting antibodies from the mother's blood • Descends into pelvis, ready for birth

Early Brain Development

The first year of life is an important time for brain development because the foundation for all future development is formed. Learning pathways are created in the brain when caregivers respond to infants appropriately. Children's brain function develops best in a secure environment. Consistent and calm caregivers are most important to a secure environment.

Infant brains are very responsive to positive experiences. Different sensory experiences stimulate the brain, which then organizes and makes sense of the information. Interesting and repeated experiences strengthen infants' learning power. An infant's brain is also vulnerable to negative experiences. Physical or emotional harm can interrupt normal brain function. Such harm can delay or limit an infant's learning potential in all developmental areas.

Physical Development

Rapid growth requires energy. To help sustain them, very young infants sleep up to 17 hours a day and need frequent feedings. Older infants may sleep less but still need frequent naps.

Generally, infants weigh between six and ten pounds at birth. On average, they are about 20 inches long. By the end of their first year, most infants weigh about 22 pounds and are 30 to 32 inches long. Inherited qualities from a mother and father influence this growth.

An infant's head grows rapidly. Open spaces in the bones of the infant's skull, called fontanels, allow for the growth of the brain. The bones of the skull gradually grow together, and the open spaces are usually closed by 18 months of age.

All humans are born with **reflexes**, or instinctive, involuntary bodily reactions to a stimulus such as a noise or a touch. Some reflexes are used by humans throughout life. Infants, however, have certain reflexes that function only during the first months of life. After that, intellectual and physical growth allow for voluntary action. Infants have the following reflexes:

- **Moro reflex** This is also known as the "startle reflex." The infant throws out the arms and legs in response to a loud sound or sudden movement.

- **Rooting reflex** Infants turn their heads toward a touch on the cheek or lips. This is linked to the following sucking reflex.

- **Sucking reflex** When something is put in the infant's mouth, the baby begins to suck. This allows a newborn to feed.

- **Grasping reflex** The infant automatically closes a hand when the palm is touched.

- ▶ **Babinski reflex** An infant's toes fan out when the bottom of the foot is stroked.
- ▶ **Movement reflexes** Infants make a walking or stepping motion when held up with the feet touching the floor. Infants also appear to swim when held horizontally in water.

Sensory Development

At birth, infants are equipped with all five of their senses. Newborns hear well enough to tell the difference between the voices of those who spend the most time with them. Infants will turn their heads toward a noise. They may cry when startled by a loud noise or can be lulled to sleep with a soothing rhythm.

Vision is not clear at birth, but it improves within weeks. After their vision clears, infants prefer to look at a human face, or pictures of faces. They enjoy brightly colored objects and patterns with contrasting colors. Caregivers can place infants under floor mobiles to promote sensory development.

Infants also sense differences in taste and smell. They prefer sweet over plain tastes. Within the first two weeks, infants know the unique scents of their mothers. Infants feel differences in texture. Some infants will cry if dressed in clothing made of a texture they dislike.

Motor Development

At birth, infants are completely dependent on others. They cannot lift their own heads, roll over, sit up, or stand. Physical strength and movement improve quickly, however, especially as motor actions are repeated. The repetition also increases infants' flexibility and coordination.

Muscular development eventually gives infants mobility, allowing them to move from one place to another. **Figure 14.2** on page 300 lists major motor developments during infancy. This development follows a **sequence**, or order, as earlier development helps to encourage new skill growth.

As infants progress physically and intellectually, they acquire **perceptual motor skills**—skills that require the coordination of vision, intellect, and movement. Climbing up a step is a perceptual motor skill. The child must see the step, judge the height, and lift his or her hands and knees.

▼ **Reach for It**

This infant is reaching for a colorful toy. *What skill does an infant need to develop to be able to reach for and grasp an object?*

McGraw-Hill Education/Jill Braaten

Figure 14.2 Motor Development During Infancy

Constant Changes Infants are developing and learning new ways to use and move their bodies every day. *In which month can an infant walk with the help of an adult?*

Age	Motor Development
2 months	Lifts head and chest when lying on stomach
4 months	Sits erect in arms of adult; reaches for objects
6 months	Grasps objects; rolls self over
8 months	Thrusts arms and legs out and squirms to push self forward; pulls self up
10 months	Crawls on hands and knees; walks with help of adult
12 months	Stands; sometimes walks alone; picks up small objects between thumb and forefinger; begins self-feeding

A related skill is **eye-hand coordination**—the ability to move the hands and fingers precisely in relation to what is seen. Infants begin to develop eye-hand coordination around three or four months of age. They can see a toy, reach for it, and grasp it successfully. Caregivers can influence motor development by using toys and activities to encourage infants to move, reach, and grasp.

Intellectual Development

The work of cognitive theorist Jean Piaget has provided insight into how children learn to think. He identified four periods that people go through as they develop intellectually from infancy through adulthood. The first one, the **sensorimotor period** (ˌsen(t)s-rē-ˈmō-tər ˈpir-ē-əd), applies to infants and describes the time frame during which infants develop their intellect.

During this period, from birth to age two years, infants and one-year-olds learn by using their senses and motor abilities to gain information about the world. They learn through sight, touch, taste, smell, and sound. For instance, the idea of cause and effect is learned when an infant sees that pulling a string on a toy will make the toy move. This and similar types of learning usually begin between seven and eight months of age.

Piaget found that at around nine months most children acquire an intellectual ability called **object permanence**, which is the understanding that an object continues to exist even when out of sight. Children discover that although a person or an object disappears from view, it will be back. Before object permanence develops, you can cover a child's toy with a blanket, and the child's interest shifts to something else. After object permanence develops, the child deliberately removes the blanket to find the toy.

As intellect increases, children begin to analyze, make associations, and form predictions. At one year, for example, an infant can learn that the rattle of keys in the front door lock means that someone has come home. Caregivers and the environment greatly influence a child's intellectual development. To nurture intellectual development, it is essential for caregivers to make sure that infants have a safe environment with developmentally appropriate materials available to explore.

Language Development

Language plays a large role in developing intellectual abilities. Children understand language long before they can speak it well themselves. They listen closely to inflections and how adults use their hands with certain words. By six months of age, children can understand some spoken words, such as *no, up, more, mommy, daddy,* and their own names. Children can usually speak several words by one year. Two-word sentences are common by 18 months, and complete sentences can be formed by age two years.

Even very young infants benefit when you talk to them. Although they do not understand the words, they soon make **vocalizations**— sounds that imitate adult language. When adults respond, infants begin to learn that their wants and needs can be expressed through language. Eventually, they learn specific ideas, and understandable spoken language is not far behind.

Emotional Development

Infants experience emotions such as fear, discomfort, and happiness. As children develop, feelings become more specific. Excitement, joy, frustration, and anger are evident. These emotions are much easier to identify and manage after an infant learns language skills.

Bonding and Attachment

Throughout a baby's first year of life, an important emotional development called bonding is taking place. Bonding is forming a strong attachment to, and preference for, a specific person. This is usually a parent, both parents, or guardians. Secondary bonding can take place with other caregivers.

Bonding is necessary for development of good self-esteem. According to theorist Erik Erikson, children develop a sense of trust or mistrust based on the quality of early experiences with care providers. Infants will develop a sense of trust if their needs for food, warmth, and comfort are met.

▼ **Comforting Care**

This infant is comfortable with this infant caregiver and is developing a sense of trust. *How do infants develop a sense of trust?*

Design Pics/Kristy-Anne Glubish

If these needs are not satisfied, infants develop a sense of mistrust. They see the world as a threatening and unpredictable place. In contrast, the infants who develop a sense of trust become children who trust in others and in their environment, with better emotional health. Responsive and reliable caregivers influence the development of trust. When children experience warmth and caring, they are more likely to be resilient throughout life.

A sign that bonding has occurred is **attachment behavior**, or when the infant shows signs of pleasure when a preferred person appears—and signs of distress when that person leaves. Infants who smile and gurgle with delight when their caregivers enter the room and cry or fuss when these individuals leave are showing signs of strong attachment.

Personality Development

Personality development also begins during infancy. Inherited traits form the basis for personality. But personality is also influenced by an infant's experiences with the environment. Reactions from care providers affect personality. Interactions with people and the environment, however, do not completely explain how personality develops.

From birth, every child has a different way of approaching the world. A person's inborn style of reacting to the environment is known as temperament. Temperament has a strong impact on personality.

▶ **Identifying Temperament** An infant's temperament is affected by a combination of temperament traits. Every person exhibits these traits in varying degrees with a broad range of behaviors. Some children may strongly exhibit trait characteristics, while others reflect traits more moderately. **Figure 14.3** on page 303 explains these traits in detail.

▶ No child is completely one temperament or the other. However, children do show a general pattern of behavior that is consistent with one category more than another.

▶ It is a care provider's job to respond to the intensity of traits revealed by each child's unique attitude and behavior. It is important to work with a child's temperament rather than ignore it or try to change it because a child's temperament is constant throughout life.

©Comstock/Alamy

Figure 14.3 Temperament Traits

Temperament Mix A child's temperament is a combination of different temperament traits. Each person has these traits in different amounts. *Do you recognize these traits in any infants or children you know?*

Trait	Description
Activity, or energy, levels vary in children.	High-energy children are constantly moving. For infants, they may kick or swing their arms more often and may even move in their sleep. Low-energy children are less active and seem more relaxed.
Intensity involves the power of a child's emotional response.	Very intense children will have stronger responses, such as crying or screaming loudly. Less intense children are calmer and have quieter responses.
Sensitivity includes how children notice their own feelings, and those of others.	Children with high sensitivity may have their feelings hurt more easily. They may notice sights, sounds, or smells more easily than others. Children with lower sensitivity are not concerned with people's opinions of them, but also may not easily recognize emotions in others. Sensitivity also affects how easily children adapt to occasional changes in routine or even food choices.
Adaptability involves how well a child accepts change.	Surprises or changes in plans do not upset adaptable children. Less flexible children resist change. Adaptable children often seem more patient, while less adaptable children seem to need to follow a more rigid routine.
Mood involves a child's general outlook.	Children with a positive mood are upbeat and expect the best from others. They tend to be able to control their emotions and behavior more easily. Children with a negative mood may typically be more down or suspicious of others. They may feel—and express—anger, frustration and disappointment more often and more persistently than their positive peers. Such children may also take longer to spring back from conflict with others.
Persistence, or determination to complete a task, varies in children.	Some children are eager to take on challenges. They do not like to leave a project uncompleted. Less persistent children are willing to move on to other activities. They more easily accept *no* as an answer. Extreme persistence sometimes hinders a child's ability to cooperate with adults or peers as quickly as other more flexible children.
Regularity involves a child's tendency to follow a daily pattern.	Highly regular children are comfortable with a routine. They may become upset if they must eat, sleep, or play outside their normal routine. Children with lower regularity are comfortable with a different schedule each day.
Approach includes how a child faces new people, places, or events.	High-approach children are often outgoing and open to trying new activities or foods. Low-approach children are more cautious when faced with a new experience. However, when given time to become familiar with change, they warm up and adjust to change quite well.
Perceptiveness, or awareness of the surroundings, also varies.	Very perceptive children can be extremely sensitive to sights and sounds around them, making them more easily distracted. Children less alert to surroundings do not notice as much of what is going on around them. However, most children have very keen senses but gradually develop the ability to focus and "tune out" distractions. Levels of perception can affect how well a child can focus on completing an activity and cooperate with adult requests. It is important that highly perceptive and sensitive children not be overwhelmed by too much classroom stimulation at once.

By taking into account a child's individual temperament, caregivers are better able to plan a schedule and to present learning activities that will be most comforting and engaging to an individual child. Responding sensitively to temperament will help you plan for each child's need for active play, quiet activity, and rest. It will also help you guide children in developing coping skills best suited to their unique temperament and style of interacting with others.

Social Development

The foundations of social development—the ability to form relationships with others—are laid during infancy. Piaget believed that during the first year of life, children's thinking is **egocentric** (ˌē-gō-ˈsen-trik). They see everything only from their own points of view. During infancy, for example, children do not play cooperatively with each other. They may show interest in another infant but only as they would another object. They do not perceive the infant as another person. It is impossible for them to understand how anyone else thinks or feels.

It takes several years of social experiences to help children grow beyond egocentrism. Emotional development is linked to this **process**, or series of changes. Caregivers influence children's social development. When infants learn to trust caregivers, they learn to value a social relationship. They discover that they can depend on others for assistance. They become secure in their relationships. Positive social skills are further developed when routines such as feeding, diapering, and bathing are pleasant experiences.

An infant's fear of unfamiliar people, usually expressed by crying, is called **stranger anxiety**. It becomes common as object permanence develops, usually around nine months of age. By then, children distinguish between strangers and familiar loved ones.

Children usually grow beyond stranger anxiety by 12 or 15 months of age. If possible, parents should avoid placing an infant in a new child care center between 8 and 15 months of age as a strategy to help reduce separation anxiety.

▼ **All About Me**

Infants do not perceive another infant as another person. *What does the term* egocentric *mean?*

READING CHECK ✔ **Analyze**
Why is it important to understand a baby's temperament?

Managing Infant Programs

Many families are headed by single parents or dual-earner couples. This often makes seeking full-time infant care a necessity. The result is a great demand for high-quality infant care services. This is an important reason to recruit and train enough talented people to meet this growing need. Keep in mind that parents may want to compare their options for child care. With children as young as six weeks old in full-time child care, excelling at the basics of infant care could put a program at the top of a parent's list.

Infant Care Basics

They may be tiny, but infants require a lot of physical care! Infant caregivers must know how to take care of all basic needs promptly, effectively, and quickly, especially if there are several infants in the room. While attention and playtime are vitally important to an infant's development, the essential basic needs include sleeping, diapering, feeding, and general cleanliness.

Helping Infants Rest

Sleep is essential for an infant's growth, development, and brain function. You have learned that very young infants sleep up to 17 hours a day, but not all babies sleep at the same time or even the same amount. Babies who are very active need more sleep than babies who are more sedate. A change in a family schedule will also affect when and how well an infant sleeps at a child care center.

Figure 14.4 shows the average amount of sleep an infant will need throughout his or her first year. Child care professionals must work with parents to develop a sleeping schedule for infants that will provide consistency and the rest needed for little growing bodies.

Figure 14.4 **How Much Do Babies Sleep?**

Little Bodies Need Lots of Rest Babies up to a year old sleep more than half the day. *Why do infants need so much sleep?*

Age	Hours of Sleep (Approximate)	Description
Newborn	16	• Takes four or five naps a day, each about three to four hours
3 months	14 to 15	• Total amount of sleep decreases but takes longer—four-to-five-hour-long—naps • Longer sleeping periods at night
4 months	12 to 14	• Takes a midmorning and a late afternoon nap • Sleeps at night
6 months	12 to 14	• Sleeps about six hours at night • Takes two long naps in the day
1 year	12	• Sleeps about nine to ten hours at night • May take one or two naps during the day

Sudden Infant Death Syndrome

Sudden Infant Death Syndrome (**SIDS**) is the unexpected death of an infant with no obvious cause. The baby dies during sleep, with no crying and no evidence of struggle. The majority of infants who die of SIDS are between one and four months old, but SIDS can affect infants up to a year old. SIDS happens to about 2,000 infants each year in the United States. The cause of SIDS is unknown.

Researchers have identified some groups who are more at risk, such as male babies with low birth weights. Smoking during pregnancy and smoking while living with an infant causes a risk for SIDS. Premature babies and babies who sleep on their stomachs also have a greater risk of SIDS. Infant caregivers should be aware of SIDS and check on sleeping infants often, especially very young infants, during nap times. Infants should always be placed on their backs for sleeping.

What Would You Do? Imagine you work in an infant room at a child care center. A fellow child care professional places an infant on her stomach to sleep. How do you respond?

However, infant caregivers must keep in mind that the needs and activities of a family will change, and they may have to adjust an infant's daily sleep routine at the center to help support the family.

Putting an infant to sleep should be a relaxed and pleasant experience. A consistent sleeping schedule carried out in a warm manner will help the caregiver accomplish this goal. It will also help infants anticipate what will be happening so they can more easily cooperate with rest time. This helps infants experience a greater sense of control as well.

The process of helping infants transition to sleep helps build good sleep habits for life.

▶ A quieted room, softened lighting, and gentle rubs on arms or legs calm most infants.

▶ Quietly reading to an infant or gently rocking the baby can help lull him or her to sleep.

▶ Singing a lullaby or humming may also help infants reach a restful state. This also supports the attachment bond between baby and caregiver.

When holding infants, especially newborns, it is important to support their heads and necks until they have the strength to hold up their own heads. Practice this skill on an infant doll.

An infant's safety must be monitored even while sleeping. Because they are still developing muscle strength, infants are not able to move themselves easily if something in their cribs blocks their breathing. Pillows, fluffy blankets, puffy crib pads, and stuffed toys should not be placed in an infant's crib as they can cause suffocation. Infants should be placed faceup on their backs in cribs to prevent SIDS, sudden infant death syndrome. All cribs must meet the government minimum safety requirements regarding hardware, head- and foot-boards, slats, and corner posts.

Diapering Infants

It may not be the most glamorous part of the job, but changing an infant's wet or soiled diaper promptly is an important part of keeping baby healthy and shows you value the baby's comfort. Very young infants may need diaper changes every two or three hours. Babies should always be checked for changing needs before and after a nap. Older babies will not need quite as many diaper changes, but they are more likely to cry when they feel uncomfortable in a wet or dirty diaper. Always change a soiled diaper regardless of how long the child has been wearing the diaper.

Infant caregivers will create a routine for checking diapers regularly, such as before and after every feeding and nap or checking every half hour throughout the day. Wet or dirty diapers should be changed immediately to avoid diaper rash, patches of rough, red, irritated skin in the diaper area.

As you diaper, use facial expressions and words to explain to the baby what is happening. Take advantage of diapering time to name baby's body parts, to sing songs, or to chant nursery rhymes. The following are specific steps to sanitary diapering:

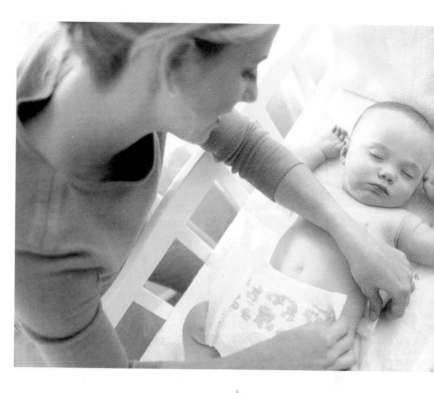

Francisco Cruz/Purestock/SuperStock

1. Wash your hands thoroughly with soap and water before beginning.
2. Put on disposable gloves and sanitize the diapering surface.
3. Securely strap the diapering area's security belt around the baby's stomach. This will prevent an infant from falling.
4. Remove the diaper and clean the infant. Thoroughly clean the baby's diaper area with a disposable wipe.
5. Put on a fresh diaper. Hold the baby's ankles and lift the body gently to slide the diaper underneath. Make sure the adhesive tabs of the disposable diaper are on the back side of the diaper. Fasten the diaper together with the adhesive tabs.
6. Throw away used supplies. Dispose of all used gloves, wipes, and disposable diapers in a trash container with a secure lid that is out of reach of children.
7. Wash your hands and the infant's hands in case they have come in contact with the soiled diaper.
8. Gently lift and return baby to his or her play area or crib. Never leave an infant unattended on a changing table. Work in small groups to practice these skills on a life-size infant doll.

▲ Caring for Baby

Changing diapers is a significant part of an infant caregiver's responsibility. *Why is regularly changing diapers important?*

Feeding Infants

Most babies under the age of six months eat only breast milk or formula. Even if a baby is breast-fed at home, you will need to use a bottle to feed him or her, unless a mother decides to come to the center to feed her baby. Parents or guardians should bring pre-filled bottles to the center each morning to use during feedings.

Infant caregivers are responsible for feeding each infant the amount appropriate for individual needs. Foods, and their quantity eaten, should be recorded at each feeding for parents' review. Most infants prefer their bottles at room temperature or warm.

To warm a bottle, place it in a container full of warm water or heat it in a bottle warmer or slow cooker full of water. Never warm a bottle in a microwave because the uneven heating can be a safety hazard for the baby. Always test the temperature of the liquid by dripping a small amount on your arm or wrist before feeding the baby. Work with a partner to practice these skills.

At about six months, infants will start to eat "solid" foods, which are not really that solid. Watery rice cereals and pureed fruits and vegetables can be fed to infants using smaller baby spoons. Infants will continue to consume breast milk or formula as they transition to solid foods. Caregivers need to be flexible and patient as each infant gradually adjusts his or her individual eating habits and diet. Never force food into infants, as it may cause choking. Serve foods to infants in a warm, calm manner. A predictable feeding routine helps build trust and attachment between caregiver and baby.

Staff Responsibilities

Caring for infants requires a wide variety of skills and personal qualities, as well as a lot of energy! Your success as an infant caregiver starts with understanding the basics of infant development. Infant caregivers must be warm, gentle, and responsive to development. You must be able to relate to and understand infants' needs and feelings. It is also important to understand each child's unique temperament. You should also respect each family's cultural beliefs and traditions.

Attention to Emerging Skills

Successful child care professionals take interest in infants' emerging skills. Caregivers praise each new accomplishment of an infant with enthusiasm. In addition, they are able to spot delays in development that may need extra attention. Infant caregivers should be mindful of presenting too many new activities to infants all at once. It is important to meet the developmental need for new experiences without overwhelming the child.

▶ **More Than Just a Job**

A successful infant care teacher has special qualities, such as a warm and gentle nature. *What other skills and personal qualities contribute to an infant caregiver's success?*

Interpret Infant Cues

Skilled child care professionals can interpret the cues infants give them. They can distinguish a "hungry" cry from a "change-me" cry and attend to both quickly. You should quickly respond to an infant's cry for help or attention with comforting arms and reassuring words. Responding promptly to an infant's cry reinforces feelings of trust.

When an infant is crying, first assess whether he or she is asking for a basic need to be met. If he or she does not need to be fed, changed, or rocked to sleep, he or she may simply want to play or cuddle with you. Never shake a baby to get their attention or to attempt to control them. Their necks are very fragile and severe injury, or even death, can be caused from any kind of shaking. You will begin to recognize the cries of infants in your care as you gain experience in the field.

Observing and Recording Behavior

Infant care professionals must be careful and exact about observing and recording behavior. This is time consuming but necessary for monitoring children's well-being and development. Observing and recording early behaviors may actually uncover developmental issues, such as hearing loss, which can lead to helpful solutions for the child's life.

Management Responsibilities

Infant care requires a surprising amount of paperwork. Detailed records must be maintained daily. This paperwork requires good organizational skills and attention to detail. Activities planned for and conducted with children must be recorded. Copies of communications with fellow staff, parents, or social workers must be maintained in confidential files.

Child care professionals must also manage classroom resources. An infant room requires more equipment than the average classroom. Early care professionals must maintain the areas for infant feeding, sleeping, and diapering as well as play areas. Regular inspection records must be maintained and an inventory of equipment and supplies, and their condition, should be updated regularly. Such tasks remind staff to request additional supplies or to repair or replace broken toys or equipment.

Child care center directors should make sure that their infant care staff has the appropriate materials for a sanitary infant environment. The feeding area should have appropriate refrigeration for infants' bottles and food as well as a heat source for preparing this food. Staff will also need appropriately sized child and adult chairs for feedings. It is also important for an infant room to have easy access to a sink for hand washing to allow for sanitary food preparation and diapering.

A Matter of ETHICS

Developmental Delays

Rate of Growth For some infants, development does not keep pace with most of their peers. When development is significantly slower than an average infant's growth, assessments called developmental screenings may be used to determine if a child is experiencing a developmental delay. These screenings usually measure intellectual and language growth as well as motor and behavioral abilities.

Caregiver Response

Infant caregivers can inform parents if they notice developmental delays. They can plan activities to stimulate growth in a specific developmental area. This lets infant caregivers help prevent early delays from growing into bigger problems.

Thinking Ethically

You observe that one infant is lagging behind others of the same age in motor development. While the other infants are pulling up or crawling, one makes no attempt to move on his own. How would you express your concern to his parents?

Teams of individuals provide infant care, often with a lead caregiver and an assistant. In this approach, each child is assigned a specific staff member as his or her primary caregiver. This requires staff members to co-plan, to delegate, and to share responsibilities with others.

Program Components

Infant care programs must follow rules established by state licensing laws. Infant programs must be well managed to provide quality care. Infants thrive on adult attention. They also keep their caregivers very busy. For these reasons, there are fewer children per child care professional in an infant care program than in a program for older children. In addition, the maximum number of infants in the group is smaller than with older children. A typical group may have six to eight infants with two or three care professionals. State requirements vary.

To promote bonding and attachment, each child is often assigned one primary caregiver to respond to all of the child's basic needs. Managers of infant programs must work hard to limit frequent staff turnover. **Staff turnover** is the rate at which employees leave their jobs, creating the need for hiring new employees. When staff turnover is high, infants do not have a chance to bond with one caregiver. Infants need familiar and predictable care. Too much change is upsetting to them and can hinder their emotional and social development.

Infant and preschool programs differ in the way daily routines are managed. In a preschool program, a schedule is set and maintained by the teachers. For instance, all the children eat lunch at a specific time. In infant care, routines should be conducted **on demand**, or according to each child's individual needs. Each child requires food, sleep, diapering, and play activities at different times.

Child care professionals must be alert for each infant's signals and give proper care. For example, it is essential for infant caregivers to know appropriate and sanitary diapering procedures and to respond quickly when an infant needs to be changed.

▼ **Responding to Basic Needs**

An infant is usually assigned a primary care provider to attend to his or her needs. *What does the term* on demand *mean in regards to an infant's needs?*

Infants are especially vulnerable to illness because their immune systems are not fully developed. Their tendency to put items in their mouths increases their chances of illness. Staff members will clean and sanitize toys and equipment throughout the day and frequently wash their hands and the infants' hands, feet, and mouths.

Staff and Parent Communication

As a child care professional, it is very important to establish a friendly relationship with parents. Child care professionals and parents or guardians should speak daily to discuss the infant's overall health and well-being. You should share important information with parents by providing them with a copy of the daily **caregiver report form**. This form is used to organize and record the routine care provided each day. This form includes information such as

▶ the amount of liquid and solid food served and consumed.

▶ the number of diapers changed and the consistency of bowel movements.

▶ the length and quality of naps.

▶ any accidents and the treatment provided.

▶ any signs of illness and any medicine given.

▶ the infant's overall mood and activity level.

▼ **Caregiver Report Form**

It is important to keep track of how an infant's basic needs are met throughout the day. *How much total time did Emma spend sleeping, according to this report?*

Caregiver Report Form

Child's Name **Emma**   Date **8/18/___**

Teacher's Name **Katie**

Feedings	Naps	Diapering			
		Time	**Dry**	**Wet**	**BM**
10:05 A.M. Bottle–all	7:50 A.M. to 9:55 A.M.	10:00 A.M.		X	
12:15 P.M. Cereal–all	12:30 P.M. to 1:10 P.M.	12:20 P.M.			X
1:30 P.M. Bottle–half	3:10 P.M. to 4:25 P.M.	2:30 P.M.		X	
		4:25 P.M.		X	

Comments ___Emma seemed extra tired today. She took her usual 3 naps, but also wanted to be rocked and held more than is normal for her. We adjusted her schedule to allow for this extra rest.___

Parents can also fill out a **parent or guardian report form** each morning. This form details the infant's activities and behavior before arrival at the center. They may include information on the child's last feeding, notes on medications, and diapering information. They may also include notes about the child's mood from the previous evening, such as if the child slept well or was restless or if the child was happy, out of sorts, or not feeling well. Having this information can help staff members provide the best care possible.

Early educators can effectively communicate with parents in other ways too. They can show parents photos of their children at play. Parents should be encouraged to visit frequently. Early educators can share parenting information from articles, DVDs, or books. Together, parents and early care professionals can think of new experiences to offer infants. Regular contact with parents is one way of providing stability between the home and infant care center.

READING CHECK ✔ **Explain** Why is it important to respond to a baby's cries?

Nurturing Development

You have learned that humans experience their most intense period of growth and development during infancy. New skills and abilities emerge daily as children progress through developmental stages. Development in one area affects development in another. Successful child care professionals can determine the developmental differences of children at various ages. Quality infant programs address children's changing developmental needs.

As a child care professional, you have an important responsibility to nurture each child's physical, intellectual, emotional, and social development. New abilities are signs of good health. You will get to know each infant on an individual basis. If you believe an infant is lagging in an area of development, provide activities to help the child develop and refine skills. When typical growth and development are significantly delayed, refer the family to special services.

Nurturing Physical Development

During the first year of life, muscle growth and coordination and the development of perceptual motor skills are major goals for physical development. Caregivers should plan an environment that allows the infants to develop these skills at their own rate. Child care professionals must also adjust their strategies for aiding development if a child in their care has special needs.

For example, an infant who is visually impaired will need extra attention to develop perceptual motor skills and to learn to crawl and walk without injury. **Figure 14.5** on page 313 lists actions a early care professional can take to respond to an infant's emerging development.

Figure 14.5   Responses to Physical Development

Help Me Grow   It is important for early care professionals to provide a nurturing response to an infant's emerging development. *What is an appropriate response to a 10-month-old infant who is learning to stand, to balance, and to take initial steps?*

Age	Emerging Development	Early Care Professional's Responses
Birth to 4 months	• Muscle growth • Motor development • Improved vision • Development of perceptual motor skills • Awareness of body parts	• Place brightly colored pictures or family portrait near crib. Hang mobiles over crib. • Encourage gazing by holding objects about 8 to 12 inches from the baby's face. • Play vision-tracking games by moving objects slowly from side to side. • During routines such as changing clothes, bathing, and diapering, name baby's hands, feet, and facial features.
4 to 8 months	• Increased muscle strength • Muscle control • Motor coordination	• Provide toys that infants can use to bang, hit, shake, and squeeze. • Offer toys with handles that can be easily grasped. Make sure toys do not have any small loose parts that could be a choking hazard. • As babies begin to roll over by themselves, provide open space on carpeting. • Provide toys that roll, such as soft sponge balls, so infants crawl for them. • Encourage crawling and creeping by placing toys just outside baby's reach. Let them crawl on materials of different textures.
8 to 12 months	• Learning to stand and balance • May take steps • Picking up items with thumb and forefinger • Improved perceptual motor skills	• "Dance" together by holding onto both of baby's hands. • Provide low, soft chairs or sofas to allow baby to practice walking skills. Sturdy handrails mounted securely to walls encourage cruising. Make sure that baby will not encounter any electrical outlets or other safety hazards along the way. • Provide open space as baby tries to walk. Allow infants to go barefoot for better footing. • Avoid walkers that can interfere with muscle and joint development. • Allow babies to feed themselves small, soft pieces of healthful cereal. • Provide stacking and nesting toys to support small-motor skills.

Nurturing Intellectual Development

Intellectual development occurs as infants notice details about their environment and try to make sense of them. Experiences with caregivers, especially verbal and nonverbal interactions, help infants understand their world. Child care professionals should work with parents to nurture an infant's intellectual development.

Child care professionals must also adjust their strategies for aiding development if a child in their care has special needs. For example, an infant who is hearing impaired will need extra nonverbal interactions that stimulate other senses to support intellectual development.

Emerging Development

Infants begin to show the early development of language and communication skills. Their first language skill is babbling, which they will later use to form words. Babies also learn cause and effect and object permanence, two crucial skills in development. Some infants in child care have parents or guardians who are English language learners. Caregivers also need to understand bilingual language development as well as ways a specific family communicates nonverbally.

Infant Caregiver Responses

Child care professionals can respond in many ways to nurture intellectual development. Infants learn by using their senses. Provide interesting objects to look at, touch, taste, smell, and listen to as well as grasp, push, pull, and kick. To stimulate language and cognitive development, caregivers can

▶ use the same sounds in response to an infant's vocalization.

▶ use language frequently with three- or four-word sentences. Explain what you are doing: "We turn on the water. We fill up the tub." Comment on things the baby is seeing or hearing.

▶ use facial expressions and a lively tone of voice to convey word meanings. Name your feelings as you talk, so infants understand how the words, facial expressions, tone of voice, and feelings are connected. Keep in mind that different cultures express feelings in different ways. Infants from other cultures may not express their feelings in ways that you may expect.

▶ look at pictures and read books together. Name the objects in pictures as you point to them. Let the infant turn the pages.

▶ use voices as you play with puppets and stuffed animals.

▶ sing to infants. Repeat songs often so infants become familiar with the tune and the words.

▶ adapt activities to the surroundings. Carry infants around frequently until they are old enough to sit up or crawl on their own. This gives them new views of their surroundings. Vary the direction that infant chairs face so that babies can see what is happening in the room.

▶ take infants on frequent strolls and name objects outside. Infants enjoy outdoor sights and sounds.

▶ play games, such as peek-a-boo or hide-and-seek with objects.

▶ offer toys with different shapes, colors, and textures.

▶ provide toys infants can manipulate and investigate, such as plastic blocks, nesting toys, and stacking rings. Noise-making toys teach cause and effect. Make sure that all toys are age appropriate to avoid safety hazards.

▶ provide opportunities for sensory experiences. Infants learn by using their senses. Any activities you plan should engage one or more of the five senses.

How to . . .

Introduce Babies to Different Cultures

You can use infants' interest in their environment to inspire appreciation for cultural variety. Add a multicultural twist to the usual items and practices found in the program. For example, babies enjoy pictures of other babies. Find drawings or pictures showing infants of varied ethnic backgrounds. Hang them up at children's eye level and above the changing table for infants to view. Cultural and environmental influences are important to consider when assessing development. Search catalogs and online retailers that sell cultural items and identify items you could purchase for an infant room.

▶ **Visual** *Keep sensory details in mind, such as incorporating colors and textures. Choose brightly colored curtains, floor pillows, and wall hangings made of batik and other ethnic fabrics.*

▶ **Stories** *Read books that include diverse people and settings.*

▶ **Listen** *Sounds add to sensory development. Play peaceful music or lullabies from around the world. The soothing voices and melodies can add variety and culture to nap routines.*

▶ **Action** *Introduce a variety of activities from other cultures, such as dances, music, finger plays, and age-appropriate active games.*

▶ **Play** *Provide dolls of different ethnic backgrounds and other ethnic toys.*

▶ **Interact** *Encourage families to include their infants in interactions with friends of other ethnicities or from other cultures.*

Apply It!
List cultural items you could include in an infant room. Make sure to include books, toys, and music recordings.

McGraw-Hill Education/Jill Braaten

Nurturing Emotional Development

The foundation for lifelong emotional well-being begins at birth. Nurturing infants' emotional development helps children grow into confident, well-balanced adults. Child care professionals should work with infants' families to optimize emotional development. If an infant is failing to show attachment behaviors, then early care professionals should set up a conference with the parents or guardians to discuss strategies and possible referrals needed if necessary.

Emerging Development

Safe, secure environments and nurturing caregivers support infants' emotional development. Infants form trusting bonds with caregivers, which is necessary for the development of good self-esteem. Developing a sense of trust is essential to infants' emotional development. Infants begin to express attachment behaviors when bonding has occurred. Infants also experience new emotions during their first year of life and begin to express their feelings.

Infant Caregiver Responses

Child care professionals are responsible for nurturing infants' emotional development. Some ways to promote healthy development include the following:

▶ A primary caregiver should provide feeding, diapering, dressing, and all other basic routines for an infant. This encourages caregiver and infant bonding.

▶ Respond immediately to crying infants.

▶ Hold, cuddle, and rock infants frequently to nurture the feelings of caring, closeness, and security.

▶ Show affection and interest to infants by talking to them, reading or telling them stories, and playing with them.

▶ Vary the music tempo and volume to help calm anxious, fussy, or crying infants.

▶ Plan challenging activities, but within infant's developmental capabilities. Adapt these activities to the surroundings to keep infants engaged as well as safe.

▶ Be enthusiastic when infants develop new skills. Praise builds a sense of self-esteem.

▶ Establish a regular pattern of routines and rituals to give infants a sense of comfort and security.

▼ **Promoting Emotional Development**

Showing affection and interest nurtures an infant's feelings of caring and security. *What are some other strategies for nurturing infants' emotional development?*

John Lund/Drew Kelly/Blend Images LLC

Nurturing Social Development

Learning how to respond and behave appropriately with others begins during infancy. Infants' first steps toward social development begin with their families and caregivers. From that beginning, children are gradually prepared for social experiences that will later develop with peers.

Emerging Development

Infants' social development begins with special relationships with parents, guardians, and primary caregivers. These relationships, when consistent and interactive, provide infants with opportunities to learn about others.

Sometimes the physical needs of an infant with a serious disability or special need can overshadow the importance of other developmental areas. Early care professionals who care for infants with special needs should remember to keep intellectual, emotional, and social development in mind as they are focusing on a child's specific physical needs.

▲ **Stimulating Social Development**

Talking to infants helps them to develop socially. *What are some other strategies for nurturing infants' social development?*

Infant Caregiver Responses

Early care professionals help infants develop socially. To optimize social development, successful caregivers can

- ▶ make feedings social times. Hold infants when feeding and talk quietly to them. When feeding from a high chair or eating at the table, allow time for friendly conversation.
- ▶ talk and sing to the infant while diapering.
- ▶ smile back when the infant smiles.
- ▶ snuggle in a soft chair together to read a book. Talk about what you see.
- ▶ use a puppet or soft toy to tickle baby's arms and legs.
- ▶ play give-and-take games, such as pat-a-cake. Hand objects back and forth to each other.
- ▶ reinforce imitation by playing copycat.

READING CHECK ✔ **Explain** Why should caregivers choose toys that are age appropriate?

Blend Images/SuperStock

College Majors

What is a college major?

Your college major is the specific academic subject or professional field that you focus on at college. Your major should be a topic that interests you and be related to a field that will help you reach your career goals. Depending on your college, you might be able to major in two fields, have a major and a minor, or even create your own major.

How do I choose my major?

During the first and second years of college, students often take general education courses such as English, math, and history while trying to decide on a major. During this period, you can take different types of classes to figure out which best suit your interests and which ones you find the most enjoyable. It is also very important to think about the long term. Classes that are fun may not necessarily lead to the career that is right for you, so keep future employment in mind as you start to narrow your major choices.

When do I have to declare a major?

At many colleges, you are not required to declare a major until the end of your sophomore year. If you are attending a two-year program, however, you will likely select your major at the beginning. Keep in mind that not all colleges are the same. It is very important that you frequently communicate with your academic advisor to make sure you are on track.

By choosing my major, am I choosing my profession?

For most students, picking a major is not the same as picking a career. If you major in something very specific, such as nursing or accounting, you are learning a specific trade that will likely lead to a specific career. Most majors, however, such as English and history, help prepare you for a variety of careers.

Hands-On

College Readiness Think about academic topics that currently interest you. Write a self-assessment that summarizes your interests. Then go to a college's Web site and print a list of all the majors offered. Use your self-assessment as you review them and research what jobs are associated with specific majors. Then choose a major in which you might be interested. Write a brief report explaining why you are interested in that specific major.

Path to Success

Get Information When considering a major, talk to students in that major. Meet with professors. Read about the available classes.

Think Ahead Find out which majors are recommended for a specific career that interests you.

Take It Seriously Choose your major carefully. You will invest several years studying this specific subject.

Do the Research Keep an open mind and look into all your options before deciding.

Take Your Time Choosing a major is not a decision that should be made in an hour, a day, or a week.

Get Advice Picking a major is usually done with the help of an academic advisor.

Neustockimages/Getty Images

Nurturing Infant Development
Visual Summary

Nurturing Development

Physical	Intellectual	Emotional	Social
• Plan an environment that allows infants to develop perceptual motor skills at their own rate. • Provide activities and toys that support muscle growth, control, and coordination.	• Offer a variety of visual and auditory experiences to help infants understand the world around them. • Provide opportunities for sensory experiences. Infants learn by using all five senses.	• Bond with infants by promptly and affectionately attending to their needs in a safe, secure environment. • Form trusting bonds with infants to promote good self-esteem.	• Develop a special relationship with infants by talking, smiling, and playing games to prepare for social experiences. • Adjust strategies for aiding development if an infant has special needs.

Vocabulary Review

1. Write your own definition for each of the content and academic vocabulary terms.

Content Vocabulary

◇ prenatal development (p. 296)
◇ reflexes (p. 298)
◇ perceptual motor skills (p. 299)
◇ eye-hand coordination (p. 300)
◇ sensorimotor period (p. 300)

◇ object permanence (p. 300)
◇ vocalizations (p. 301)
◇ attachment behavior (p. 302)
◇ egocentric (p. 304)
◇ stranger anxiety (p. 304)
◇ staff turnover (p. 310)
◇ on demand (p. 310)

◇ caregiver report form (p. 311)
◇ parent or guardian report form (p. 312)

Academic Vocabulary

■ sequence (p. 299)
■ process (p. 304)

Review Key Concepts

2. Summarize the stages of prenatal development, as well as infant physical, intellectual, emotional, and social development.

3. Identify three responsibilities of infant caregivers and three components of a successful infant care program.

4. Describe four strategies an infant caregiver can use to nurture the four developmental areas in an infant.

Critical Thinking

5. Compare and Contrast how heredity, or genetics, and environmental influences such as prenatal care affect prenatal development.

6. Describe three strategies or activities you can use to help promote the development of large- and small-motor skills in infants.

7. **Explain** the importance of play on the physical, intellectual, emotional, and social development of infants.

8. **Analyze** how fulfilling the needs of infants affects their growth and development. What can you do as a child care professional to promote this growth?

9. **Describe** characteristics of developmentally appropriate play toys, activities, and equipment for infants. Include any safety issues you should consider for these when caring for an infant.

10. **Draw Conclusions** about the qualities a program director should look for when selecting an infant care provider.

21st Century Skills

Problem Solving Skills

11. **Generate Solutions** Imagine you are a child care professional caring for a six-month-old infant. You have put her down for a nap, but she begins to cry. How would you identify the cause of the crying? What strategies would you use to comfort the baby? How would you assess her basic needs? Write a list of suggested techniques to use in this situation.

Collaborative Skills

12. **Work in Teams** Follow your teacher's instructions to organize into groups. Practice undressing, diapering, and dressing baby-sized dolls. As team members take turns, offer comments about their techniques. Make sure that your comments are constructive and not critical. Then, as a group, create a list of tips for undressing, diapering, and dressing an infant.

Child Care LAB

Use the skills you have learned in this chapter.

Infant Program Staffing Plan

13. **Setting Up a Program** Work with a partner or small group. Imagine you are the directors of a new infant care program. Adequate planning of staff requirements and program elements helps ensure a quality program.

    A. Research Review your state's requirements for infant-to-caregiver ratios, classroom size, caregiver qualifications and responsibilities, and desired knowledge and qualities in an infant care provider.

    B. Search Write a job advertisement describing the qualities desired in an infant caregiver.

    C. Prepare Write a description of an infant care program that incorporates the rules established by your state's licensing laws. Include the number of infants to be cared for, the size of the group, the number of care providers, and their responsibilities. Refer to professional guidelines to help enhance your design.

    D. Communicate Create examples of the forms that will be used to facilitate staff and parent communication.

    E. Plan Develop a list of appropriate themes that staff members can use to begin creating lesson plans for an infant room.

    F. Share Present your plan to the class or a small group.

Create Your Evaluation

Work with a partner to assess your program plan using the following categories:

- Organization
- Accuracy of requirements
- Level of detail
- Accuracy of job ad
- Completeness of communication forms
- Appropriateness of themes

Evaluate each category on a scale of 1 to 10.

Academic Skills

English Language Arts

14. Infant Activities Form into groups of four. Assign each person in your group one of the four developmental areas: physical, intellectual, emotional, or social. As a group, brainstorm ideas for age-appropriate infant activities that support development. Then write step-by-step instructions for completing the activity for your assigned development area. Share all four activities with the rest of the class. If possible, practice using your activity with an infant.

Social Studies

15. Social Development Brainstorm actions that an infant caregiver can take to aid a baby's healthy social development. Group your ideas into major topics such as "play" and "modeling positive behaviors." Create a table of information by listing three activities under each of your major topics.

Mathematics

16. Budget Management Stacey was given a budget of $2500.00 to purchase furnishings, equipment, and supplies for the new infant care program at her child care center. She found cribs for $249.50 each, changing tables for $385.99 each, and diaper organizers for $203.53 each. She wants to purchase five cribs, one changing table, and one diaper organizer. About how much money will she have left to spend on additional supplies?

Math Concept **Estimation** When the word *about* is used in a word problem, it means you are looking for an estimate, not the actual answer. Estimation is the approximate result of a calculation.

Starting Hint Round the prices to the nearest dollar; for example, $249.50 would round to $250.00. Add how much she will spend for the needed items. Subtract the total from her budget to get an estimate of how much she has left for additional supplies.

 For more math practice, go to the math appendix at the back of the book.

Certification Prep

Sharpen your test-taking skills to improve your certification program score.

Directions Read each sentence, and choose the best term to fill in the blank.

17. Bones begin to form and the face, eyes, ears, and limbs take shape during the _____ stage of prenatal development.

   A. zygote stage

   B. big stage

   C. fetus stage

   D. embryo stage

18. The _____ is the time frame during which infants develop their intellect.

   A. temperament

   B. sensorimotor period

   C. attachment

   D. perceptual motor skills

> **Test-Taking Tip**
> When answering a fill-in-the-blank question, silently read the sentences with each of the possible answers in the blank space. This will help you eliminate wrong answers. The best term results in a sentence that is both factual and grammatically correct.

(tl)©Nova Development; (tr)McGraw-Hill Education

CHAPTER 15

Nurturing Toddlers

Writing Activity

★ 21st Century Skills

Articulate Ideas Think of an art activity you would like to do with a toddler. For example, you might want to finger-paint, mold play clay, or paint at an easel. Write a step-by-step guide for this activity, beginning with setting up materials and ending with clean-up.

Writing Tips
1. Include each step in the project. Do not leave out anything.
2. Explain each step simply and clearly. Do not include unnecessary information.
3. Arrange the steps in sequential order, from beginning to end.

Explore the Photo
This toddler is playing at a child care center. *What can you observe about the way he is playing?*

Ingram Publishing

Reading Guide

BEFORE YOU READ

Use Diagrams As you are reading through this chapter, write the main idea. Write any facts, explanations, or examples you find in the text. Start at the main idea and draw arrows to the information that directly supports it. Then draw arrows from these examples to any information that supports them.

Read to Learn

Key Concepts

- **Summarize** the signs of physical, intellectual, emotional, and social development in toddlers.
- **Identify** the information toddler programs need from parents to develop individualized care and activities.
- **Describe** the key features of successful toddler programs.

Main Idea

During the toddler years, from ages 12 to 36 months, children develop new skills that help them move toward independence.

Content Vocabulary

- ◇ toddler
- ◇ self-help skills
- ◇ attention span
- ◇ symbolic thinking
- ◇ preoperational period
- ◇ concept
- ◇ assimilation
- ◇ accommodation
- ◇ autonomy
- ◇ solitary play
- ◇ parallel play
- ◇ receptive language
- ◇ productive language
- ◇ separation anxiety
- ◇ temper tantrum

Academic Vocabulary

- ■ resort
- ■ consistent

Graphic Organizer

As you read, you will discover information about two kinds of motor skills that toddlers develop. Use a pie chart like the one shown to record the two kinds of motor skills. Include notes about the accomplishments related to each kind of motor skill.

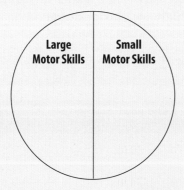

Large Motor Skills | Small Motor Skills

✈ **Graphic Organizer** *Go to* **connected.mcgraw-hill.com** *to print this Graphic Organizer.*

AS YOU READ

Connect Think about activities you have seen toddlers enjoy. What do you think they were learning from those activities?

Vocabulary

You can find definitions in the glossary at the back of this book.

Development and Care

An exciting time for learning takes place during the toddler stage. **Toddler** is the term given to a child between the ages of 12 and 36 months. Older toddlers are often called twos. Children at these ages are ready to absorb all the information they can. Toddlers are in a transitional stage. No longer infants, they eagerly increase their skills to become more independent.

Physical Development

Watch a 15-month-old walk and you will see why children this age are called toddlers. When learning to stand erect, they often appear a bit bowlegged. Their stomachs stick out, and they toddle from side to side. By 18 months, a toddler's balance is much improved. When they reach age two, toddlers' bodies begin to slim down and take on the appearance of more mature children.

After infancy, growth in height and weight slows for toddlers. Early childhood educators should keep in mind that because less fuel is needed for growth, toddlers' appetites decrease. Teeth come in rapidly between 18 and 24 months of age. Body proportions gradually change along with height and weight. An infant's head is relatively large compared to the rest of the body, and his or her arms and legs are short. As children grow, they achieve more mature proportions. **Figure 15.1** shows average heights and weights for children from ages one to three. Remember, these numbers vary from child to child.

Motor Development

Toddlers' motor development and coordination advance quickly. Improved large motor skills that use the larger muscles of the back, legs, shoulders, and arms let children achieve new physical abilities. Learning to walk gives children greater independence.

Between 12 and 18 months, children begin to climb. At first, climbing up stairs is easier than climbing down. By age two, this skill is mastered. Older toddlers love to climb over, on top of, and through items in their way. Their skills in running, hopping, and jumping increase, which are all signs of good health.

Figure 15.1 Average Heights and Weights of Toddlers

Rapid Growth
Between the ages of one and three years, an average toddler will increase in height by more than 25% and in weight by nearly 50%. *How do you think this rapid growth affects a toddler's sense of self?*

Age	Height	Weight
One Year	30 in.	22 lbs.
Two Years	34 in.	28 lbs.
Three Years	38 in.	32 lbs.

Children begin to push themselves on wheeled toys between 18 and 24 months of age. By the end of their second year, they are able to pedal tricycles or other vehicles with pedals.

Toddlers are also refining their small motor skills, those that require use of muscles in the fingers, wrists, and ankles. These skills contribute to improved hand/eye coordination and other perceptual motor skills. Children learn to stack blocks, string beads, and put together simple puzzles. Children 12 to 18 months old can stack two to four blocks and join a two-piece puzzle. Between 18 and 36 months, they can put together six-piece puzzles and stack about eight blocks.

Self-Help Skills

Greater physical control allows toddlers to develop more **self-help skills**. These are skills that allow children to help take care of their personal needs. Self-help skills for toddlers include getting dressed, washing hands, eating with utensils, brushing teeth, passing out supplies for an art activity, and putting away toys. Toddlers can also assist in household chores, such as dusting or feeding a pet. Using self-help skills helps toddlers feel competent and this optimizes their physical development. That feeling leads to pride and confidence.

Independent Toileting

At about age two, most children have achieved control of the muscles of elimination. They are ready to begin toilet training. Toddlers can recognize the bodily sensations that precede elimination and understand the use and purpose of a toilet or potty chair. Girls tend to master toileting skills earlier than boys. Early childhood educators can assist toddlers with toileting by providing easy access to toilets and hand-washing sinks. They can also help toddlers with buttons and zippers but should be aware that some toddlers prefer to dress independently.

When children are developmentally ready, the learning process usually takes only a few weeks or even days. However, newly trained children usually do not stay dry when sleeping. Provide diapers or a rubber sheet as long as necessary. Even during waking hours, occasional accidents occur. Accept these in a calm, matter-of-fact way.

▲ **More than Just Fun**

This toddler is clearly having fun stacking the blocks. *What physical skills is he developing while he has fun?*

How to . . .

Toilet Train Toddlers

Toilet training is an essential part of developing self-help skills for toddlers. Toddlers who show signs of body awareness are usually ready to begin training. Children may gesture when their diapers need to be changed. Their facial expressions may show an awareness that elimination is about to occur. Toilet training is most successful when parents and early educators work together.

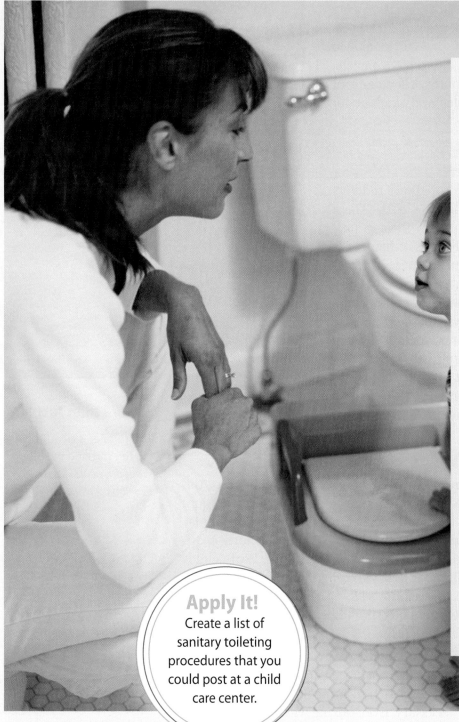

▶ **Signs** *Be alert for signs that children need to use the toilet. For example, they may tug at their pants.*

▶ **Reminders** *Remind children of the feelings that signal it is time to use the toilet.*

▶ **Frequency** *Take children to the toilet as often as needed. Before long, children will associate the toilet with the need to eliminate.*

▶ **Clothing** *Parents should dress children in elastic-waist, pull-down pants for easy removal.*

▶ **Time Limits** *If the child does not urinate or have a bowel movement within five minutes of sitting on the toilet, allow the child to resume play.*

▶ **Sanitation** *Have children wipe themselves and wash their hands after using the toilet. Show toddlers how to wash their hands effectively.*

Apply It!
Create a list of sanitary toileting procedures that you could post at a child care center.

Exactostock/SuperStock

Intellectual Development

Discovery is a big part of intellectual development. Toddlers learn by doing and by using their senses. They need many hands-on experiences. Toddlers continue to grow intellectually through sensorimotor development. They have a keen sense of wonder and are fascinated by the simplest things. Toddlers need freedom and time to explore a safe environment to satisfy their curiosity. Children become enthusiastic learners when early childhood professionals patiently respond to multiple questions, such as "Why?" and "What's that?"

Toddlers learn in other ways, too. They use trial and error, repetition, and imitation. They closely observe adults and copy their behavior. They adopt attitudes that adults have. Early educators are powerful role models.

Attention and Memory

Toddlers develop an increased **attention span**, the time spent focused on one activity. It generally increases with age. A child's interest in an activity and the activity's developmental level can also affect attention span. Children tend to continue activities that are challenging without being boring or frustrating. These positive experiences encourage learning.

Increased memory also helps intellectual development. Memory is the ability to recall images and information. Without memory, there would be no learning. Memory begins to develop in infancy and grows rapidly during the first two years. Toddlers begin to have memories of actual events. Two-year-olds can remember a parent who has been absent for several weeks. They can repeat favorite rhymes and stories and tell about experiences after returning from an outing.

Symbolic Thinking

With increased attention span and memory, children develop a more advanced thought process—symbolic thinking. With **symbolic thinking**, children understand that one thing can stand for something else. They learn to use images, art, and language as symbols to represent objects, events, and concepts.

Symbolic thinking occurs during Piaget's second period of intellectual development—the **preoperational period**. This period covers ages two to seven. In this period children start to think symbolically and imaginatively. Because they can think symbolically, older toddlers enjoy make-believe play. It is not unusual to see a two-year-old holding "conversations" with the use of a wooden block "telephone" or sitting inside a cardboard box that has become a vehicle. Playing "dress-up" can help encourage imagination and symbolic thinking. A child care professional can provide props like boxes, blankets, or blocks to encourage imaginative play.

A Matter of ETHICS

Helping Children Succeed

Successful toilet training gives children an important sense of confidence and an awareness of their growing independence.

Readiness

Children must be physically ready for successful toilet training. They should have control over their muscles of elimination. They should also be able to recognize physical signals that they are ready to eliminate.

Thinking Ethically

One of your coworkers at a child care center is impatient with toilet training. She makes the toddlers sit on the toilet every thirty minutes, leaves them sitting on the toilet for long periods, and punishes those who have accidents. She says that you should follow the same procedures. What will you do?

Climbing Safety

Climbing is an especially exciting skill for many toddlers. However, toddlers cannot judge where it is safe to practice this skill. It is important to provide safe climbing equipment, both indoors and outdoors. The equipment should be stable and sturdy, and it should have handrails toddlers can reach. It is also important to prevent toddlers from trying to climb on unsafe items. Be alert for toddlers creating "stairs" from chairs, tables, shelves, or even drawers.

What Would You Do? During an indoor playtime, you turn around and see a toddler standing on a low table, preparing to climb onto a shelf. No other teachers are close to the child. What would you do?

Imagination and creativity are natural products of symbolic thought. With symbolic thinking, children can create their own ideas. This is a significant milestone in a child's development.

Language Development

Vocabulary and language skills advance greatly from ages one to three. Although a twelve-month-old may speak two to eight words, a 24-month-old knows about 50 words. Babbling continues as children learn the meanings of their native languages.

Eighteen-month-olds can respond with "yes" or "no" to questions. They identify parts of the body by pointing to them when named. They follow simple commands, such as "Hand me the ball." Nonverbal signals using the hands, arms, head, or face—gesturing—begin at this age.

Many two- to three-year-olds have vocabularies of 50 to 300 words. They can name familiar objects and understand three- and four-word sentences. They can follow increasingly complex directions, such as "Put the ball inside the box."

Conceptual Development

The ability to understand concepts increases rapidly with emerging language skills. A **concept** is a general idea formed from other information. A child's first concepts may be that all toys are called balls or all plants are called flowers. Concept development and language development build on each other. The more concepts children encounter, the more words they need to label them. The more words children understand, the more concepts they are able to identify and label.

When first labeling concepts, children use broad generalities. To them, one word has many meanings. As their experiences increase, they gradually learn that concepts have limits. Piaget explained how children absorb information and attempt to make sense of it. He used two terms—assimilation and accommodation—to describe this skill.

▶ During **assimilation** (ə-ˌsi-mə-ˈlā-shən), children take in new information and try to make it fit with what they already know and understand. For example, a child might see a red cup on the table. Although the cup might be new, the child understands that it is similar in shape to other cups. It also is on the table, where cups usually sit. The child assumes that the cup holds a drink because what the child observes fits with the information the child already has about cups.

▶ During **accommodation** (ə-ˌkä-mə-ˈdā-shən), children change their thinking to make the new information fit. Intellectual development involves balancing new information with existing concepts to achieve better understandings. For instance, two-year-olds may think all four-legged animals are called dogs. Given time and experience, they learn to see other important features that distinguish four-legged animals from each other. Through accommodation, children alter their concepts to make better sense of new information.

Toddlers learn to notice many similarities and differences. They match and sort items that look alike. They begin to recognize shapes and sizes. For example, many toddlers can work a simple puzzle. This ability is critical to learning to read letters.

Toddlers also begin to understand opposites. They start to see the relationship between hot and cold, hard and soft, and up and down. Cause and effect also fascinates toddlers. When playing hide-and-seek, toddlers are more logical than random. They think about where and how to look for a hidden person or object. This problem solving reveals complex intellectual abilities.

▲ Same or Different?

As toddlers begin to recognize similarities and differences, they enjoy sorting items by size, shape, and color. *What is this toddler comparing while sorting blocks?*

Respond to SPECIAL NEEDS

Autism Spectrum Disorders

Autism Spectrum Disorders (ASD) are a category of developmental disorder that affects social interaction and communication. A child with autism is often diagnosed at about age three. Signs may appear as early as infancy when verbal-skill milestones such as babbling and speaking are delayed. There is a range of symptoms within the family of ASD. For example, people with Asperger's Syndrome often have better language and cognitive skills. Children with ASD may have difficulty understanding social cues or nonverbal communication. This can make it hard for them to interact socially with other children in a child care or school setting.

Critical Thinking

Research Autism Spectrum Disorders. What strategies could you use to help a child with autism in an early childhood setting? Share your findings in a one-page essay. Be sure to cite your sources.

Emotional Development

Toddlers are still beginning to develop emotional control. They are still prone to impulsiveness and quick mood swings. Toddlers may be happy one minute and screaming the next. Working with toddlers is easier when you understand child development and know that a stage will pass.

When the basic needs of toddlers are met, they are very pleasant and cooperative. Sudden shifts in mood and behavior are more a result of individual temperament. Problems may stem from frustration. Toddlers struggle to learn and do more, but not all their abilities are yet present. When their grasp of language is inadequate, toddlers **resort** to, or use, whining and crying. As language improves, toddlers are better able to communicate their wants, needs, and feelings. They gradually learn to appropriately identify and express their feelings. Language advances help children gain greater control over their behavior.

Independence and Autonomy

According to Erik Erikson, toddlers develop a sense of **autonomy** (ö-ˈtä-nə-mē), or independence. They start to see themselves as separate from loved ones. Toddlers assert their independence and make their own decisions. They frequently exclaim "No!" They often resist cooperating in routines, such as eating and bathing. Toddlers are sensitive about being shown, helped, or directed. They frequently do the opposite of what an early childhood educator wants. With patience, and by offering limited choices, early educators help toddlers move toward autonomy.

Emerging Fears

Having specific fears is common for toddlers. Their fears may include things such as storms, birds, and being alone in a room. Healthy fear contributes to children's safety. Children should be afraid of jumping from a high wall or petting a wild animal. Some fears often develop from lack of experience or from misconceptions. For a young child who has never been in a wading pool, stepping into water may cause fear. Getting a haircut for the first time might cause fear. Some fears are learned from other children and adults. When fears arise, early childhood professionals should:

▶ Stay close to calm the child.

▶ Use simple language to explain the experience.

▶ Be patient.

▶ Talk about the child's fears. If a toddler fears storms, explain that rain is needed for flowers to grow.

▶ Do not push children to overcome fears all at once. This results in more fearful children. Most fears pass with time and experience if handled in an understanding manner.

Importance of Security

A toddler's sense of security is a primary emotional need. Stable routines help fulfill this need. Toddlers are more secure and relaxed when their daily schedules and environments are reliable and predictable. They feel free to explore and pursue learning through trial and error.

The importance of reliable care for toddlers cannot be overemphasized. Attachments to and secure relationships with specific people set the foundation for children's future emotional and social development. Children experience greater trust and security when caring and dependable adults provide their care.

Social Development

Social development progresses slowly for toddlers. It takes time for them to develop social relationships with their peers and new adults.

Beginning at age two, children can take part in activities with groups of up to eight children for short time periods. They may enjoy group singing for five minutes or listening to a short story with others. Their main social interactions, however, continue to be with parents, siblings, and other early childhood educators. Toddlers are most at ease sharing time with a teacher or two or three children.

Children begin making friends at age two. They often show kindness when someone is hurt or crying. At this age, children like to snuggle with a buddy in a cozy space. Children develop stronger friendships after the age of three.

Play and Social Development

Throughout the early childhood years, play is the best method of learning. Through play, toddlers stretch their abilities and expand concepts. They spend hours poking, prodding, and manipulating objects. They engage in delightful conversations with early childhood professionals. These are all signs of good developmental health.

From 18 to 24 months, children still engage mostly in solitary play. **Solitary play** means they play alone, rather than with other children. They are interested in other children, but more out of curiosity than a desire to form friendships. Between about 24 and 36 months of age, children engage in parallel play. In **parallel play**, children play near each other, but not with each other. Two children at this age might investigate a toy together at the same time, but each acts independently of the other. A small group of

▲ **Overcoming Fears**

Reassuring early educators can help toddlers begin to overcome their fears. *Why is it important for early educators to be patient when children feel fearful?*

toddlers might all play with the same adult at once. The interaction, however, is taking place primarily between the adult and each separate child, not among the children.

As they approach age three, children begin to interact more with other children, but for limited time periods. Parallel play continues to be their main style of interaction.

Independence and Responsibility

Even at this early age, a sense of responsibility develops. You can foster independence and responsibility by promoting the use of self-help skills. Setting limits also helps toddlers become responsible. Toddlers understand very simple limits and rules. Rules should relate primarily to safety. Very brief explanations for rules help children understand their purpose.

Toddlers can also learn social skills, such as using table manners, sharing, and cooperating. Early childhood educators should give toddlers plenty of chances to develop these skills. The best way for early educators to teach positive social behavior is to model appropriate behavior.

READING CHECK ✔ **Connect** What is the relationship between toddlers' fears and their safety when trying new experiences?

Nurturing Development

Programs for toddlers should be designed around their developmental needs and growth. To better understand and meet these needs, many programs ask parents for information about their children's development. This information helps the program provide individualized care and activities that nurture all areas of development. The information may be collected on a form or through an interview. The parents provide information about the children's:

▶ Extent of vocabulary and the primary language spoken at home.

▶ Small motor, large motor, and toilet skills.

▶ Napping habits.

▶ Typical behavior and recent experiences that might affect behavior.

▶ Experiences with other children.

Nurturing Physical Development

Large motor skills develop quickly in toddlers, and playtime offers many options for aiding this physical development. Children just learning to walk enjoy noisy push and pull toys. Smaller wheeled toys and wagons are good choices. Older toddlers need plenty of chances to run, jump, and climb. Promote coordination skills with low swings, climbers, or obstacle courses. Toddlers also like balls that they can safely kick, roll, or toss.

◀ **Outdoor Activities**

Outdoor activities help toddlers develop large motor skills. *What options should be provided when outdoor play is not possible?*

To develop small motor skills, early childhood teachers should supply manipulative toys, such as nesting cups, simple puzzles, sewing cards, snap beads, small blocks for stacking, and large beads for stringing. Inexpensive household objects can also be used as manipulative toys. For example, let toddlers practice twisting and untwisting the covers on plastic jars. Toddlers can also use metal tongs to put cotton balls into empty oatmeal boxes. During outdoor play in warm months, children can squirt water from empty dish detergent bottles to strengthen muscles while having fun.

Creative activities also encourage small motor skills. Toddlers enjoy scribbling, finger painting, painting with brushes, cutting with scissors, and molding play clay. For practical experience with self-help skills, let children practice working zippers, buttons, and snaps. Sandboxes and sensory tables provide opportunities for learning to pour and scoop.

Nurturing Intellectual Development

Toddlers learn best by using their senses. They develop an understanding of concepts by experimenting with hands-on materials. Teachers can encourage intellectual development by using the following:

- ▶ **Matching Games** When toddlers begin to notice similarities and differences, they are ready to play matching games. Begin with basic colors and shapes. Provide safe objects to sort, such as large colorful shapes.

- ▶ **Blocks** All kinds of blocks stimulate learning through trial and error. Toddlers can explore concepts related to balance, size, shape, and weight. Light cardboard and plastic floor blocks are best for beginning builders.

- ▶ **Nature Experiences** Nature items trigger curiosity. Let children handle pinecones, flowers, leaves, and seashells. Have them use magnifying glasses to capture interest. An aquarium at toddlers' eye level can be exciting and physically relaxing.

- ▶ **Sensory Activities** Include items and activities that allow toddlers to use all their senses—sight, smell, touch, taste, and hearing. Encourage sensory learning with things such as shaving cream mixed with food coloring, sensory tables filled with cornmeal or colored water and ice, and colorful and tasty snacks.

Toddlers learn by watching and doing. Do not be distressed if a child spends a lot of time watching others play. He or she may be gathering new information before participating.

▶ **Take a Look!**

Common objects in nature are new and exciting for toddlers. *How can early childhood professionals encourage toddlers' curiosity about the natural world?*

Hoby Finn/Getty Images

Language Development

Language plays a large role in intellectual development. Toddlers understand much more language than they can speak. The ability to understand spoken words is called **receptive language**. The ability to use words to express oneself is called **productive language**. Toddlers have more receptive language than productive language. Nurture all language by modeling. Some strategies include using language to:

▶ Label, describe, count, and explain objects that are part of everyday life.

▶ Read books, tell stories, and invent dialogue for puppets and dolls,

▶ Call the children by their names, and have them address staff members by name, too.

Although your sentences should be short and simple, avoid "baby talk." Gradually make your language more complex, using more adverbs and adjectives. Be aware that children whose parents do not speak English are learning two languages at once. Encourage children to speak—and allow them to practice words—in both languages.

Nurturing Emotional Development

Toddlers can undergo difficult emotional times. They are experiencing new feelings that they may not understand. They are coping with fears. They are struggling with the unfamiliar practice of self-control.

As they help children adjust to the care environment, effective teachers assist with emotional development. They help toddlers identify their feelings—both positive and negative—and deal with them in appropriate ways. To help toddlers deal with fears, for instance, teachers show empathy and understanding and gently encourage children to overcome their fears. Many children's books are written for just this purpose. See **Figure 15.2** on page 336 for more tips on helping toddlers cope with fears.

Building self-esteem is another high priority. Early childhood teachers can plan positive play experiences that give toddlers chances to succeed. Encouraging self-help skills and offering developmentally appropriate toys, play activities, and tasks help toddlers feel good about their accomplishments. This optimizes their emotional development.

Most importantly, care and education providers who are warm, loving, and comforting can help children become emotionally secure as they adjust to early childhood care routines.

Science *for Success*

Exploring Simultaneous Acquisition

Toddlers who are exposed to two languages at the same time tend to learn both languages. This learning process is called simultaneous acquisition.

Procedure With a group of classmates, create a parent survey to estimate a toddler's language skills in English and in his or her home language. This information can help child care professionals with curriculum planning and assessment. As you write your questions, think about where toddlers learn to speak. Who is involved when children learn language? Then consider what other information would help you learn about simultaneous acquisition. Be sure to write with proper voice and use correct tense and syntax as you create this parent communication.

Analysis When your survey is complete, share it with other groups in the class. Review all the surveys and determine which questions you could use to get the most useful information.

Figure 15.2 Responding to Toddlers' Fears

Helping Fearful Toddlers Remember that it is natural for toddlers to feel fearful sometimes. *What are some ways toddlers might express their fears?*

Don't . . .	Do . . .
• Make fun of fears. • Become angry or scold the child. • Shower the child with too much sympathy—"You poor thing. That big mean dog scared you!" You will just convince the child that there really is something to fear. • Try to explain too much. Toddlers will not understand. • Force the toddler to confront the fear.	• Stay calm and confident. • Avoid the fearful object or situation, if possible. If a child is afraid of a dog on your daily walk, explore a different route. • Distract the child. Try singing a song or talk about an activity the child enjoys. • Help the child role-play whatever is causing the fear. • Follow a child's lead. Gradually introduce children to objects or situations they fear.

As toddlers grow emotionally, they learn to face separation from loved ones and to grow beyond the tendency to say "no" and to have temper tantrums.

Separation Anxiety

A child's fear of separation from familiar people is called **separation anxiety**. It may occur when a child first begins child care. Separation anxiety also occurs in times of stress, such as when a sibling is born. It is a sign of positive emotional development and it shows development of a strong emotional bond to parents or early educators. Separation anxiety usually lasts a few weeks. Patient educators help children learn to cope.

Negativism

Toddlers often show negativism, a tendency to refuse to do or do the opposite of what is asked. Saying "No!" is a way for toddlers to rebel. Negativism does not mean a child is "bad" or will grow up to be defiant. It is simply a healthy sign of growing independence. To reduce negativism, give toddlers many chances to make choices and to practice self-help skills.

Temper Tantrums

A **temper tantrum** is an episode in which a child shows anger or frustration in an aggressive or destructive way. Toddlers do not yet have the coping skills to handle frustration. A tantrum may occur when a want or privilege has been denied. During a temper tantrum, a child may scream, kick, or hold his or her breath. Early childhood professionals offer age-appropriate activities so toddlers experience success with minimal frustration. They give reasonable choices and let toddlers do as much as possible for themselves. If a tantrum occurs:

- ▶ **React calmly.** Some children need to be held and comforted until they calm down. Others simply want to be left alone.

- ▶ **Keep an eye on the child at all times.** Tell the child you understand the child's anger. Naming feelings helps children recognize and deal with their feelings. Then offer a tissue to signal it is time to end the tantrum.

- ▶ **Provide a place to rest.** Some children become exhausted from tantrums.

- ▶ **Communicate with parents.** Ask parents how tantrums are handled at home. Be aware that different cultures express emotions differently. Allow the parents to give you input on how to deal effectively with the tantrums. Frequent tantrums could be a sign of emotional difficulties or other problems, such as illness.

Nurturing Social Development

During the toddler stage, children move from solitary play to parallel play. As children approach age three, they begin to interact with one another in cooperative play. Carefully arrange the environment for cooperative play. For instance, encourage children to cooperate by pulling each other in toy wagons.

Toddlers can understand simple rules for behavior. As they get older, these rules can become more specific. Always state rules positively. Say, "When you're angry with people, tell them," instead of "Don't hit people when you're angry." Guide children by telling them what to do.

Toddlers are just beginning to learn to share. Introduce this concept in small groups. Toddlers share more easily in groups of two or three. Teachers should also model sharing. Toddlers who see adults cooperating are more likely to behave the same way.

Disputes are bound to occur among toddlers. When conflicts arise, teachers can distract, divert attention, or redirect the child to a different, acceptable activity. Conflicts that include hitting—and even biting—can occur among toddlers.

Children who bite or hit usually do it out of frustration or anger. They may want a toy but have not learned to express their feelings in words. Others may do it for attention. In other cases, children are copying another child's behavior. If a child has acted aggressively, follow these steps:

1. If one child bites or hits another, first attend to the victim with comfort and first aid if necessary. Directing your attention first to the aggressive child teaches that biting or hitting is a good way to get an adult's attention.

▼ **Growing Up**

Saying "no" to adults is part of growing and establishing independence for toddlers. *Why is it important to be calm and pleasant when responding to a toddler's negativity?*

2. Firmly tell the aggressive child that hurting others is not permitted. If necessary, remove the aggressor from the group.

3. Biting and hitting are serious behaviors. Parents should be contacted as soon as possible.

As with any discipline problem, observation may give you clues to a guidance solution. Take steps to reduce or eliminate situations that could lead to conflict. The child may need to be redirected to quiet, solitary activities at certain times of day. Children who are ill, tired, or hungry are also more prone to conflict. If your solution does not work, try an alternative guidance solution.

READING CHECK ✔ **Recall** Why is it important to provide activities that appeal to all five senses?

Managing Toddler Programs

Toddlers tend to have a sense of competence and a spirit of adventure. They delight in new accomplishments. They require proper adult guidance to safely and successfully explore their expanding world. Successful toddler programs work with children's parents to ensure that toddlers have the necessary spaces and daily routines needed for development in all areas. The leadership of the child care professional and collaborative teamwork by all care providers is essential to a program's success.

Age ranges in toddler classrooms vary. It is important to keep in mind child care options for this age level when providing care. Although state requirements vary, an ideal program might have eight toddlers and two adults per classroom.

▼ **Just Right**

The furniture in this toddler classroom is just the right size for the children. *How does this kind of furniture help children develop both physical and emotional skills?*

Digital Vision/Alamy

Classroom Spaces

Early childhood programs strive to promote positive physical, emotional, social, and intellectual development of all children. Toddler spaces are designed to help them develop new abilities and gain independence.

▶ **Furniture and Toys** Toddlers need age-appropriate furniture and toys. Serve snacks and meals at low tables with small chairs. Toddlers should nap on small cots. Play equipment helps children practice their increasing physical skills.

▶ **Security Items** A secure atmosphere with soft sofas and rockers allows toddlers to relax with a book. Pillows, stuffed toys, or beanbag chairs help create a comfortable environment.

▶ **Learning Centers** Toddler classrooms are divided into learning centers. The equipment should fit a toddler's size and abilities. Most toddler rooms have a manipulative center instead of a math center. This area is stocked with items—such as pop beads, puzzles, and snap toys—that require hand/eye coordination and small motor skills.

Daily Routines

In toddler programs, routines provide structure for daily events. Children choose from several individual or small-group activities. Some activities come directly from children's play with classroom materials. Others are planned and led by teacher aides or teachers. A typical daily routine followed in toddler rooms includes:

▶ Arrival

▶ Playtime in learning centers, including outdoor play

▶ Diapering, toileting, and hand washing

▶ Meals and snacks

▶ Napping

▶ Story time and music

▶ Departure

Following a **consistent**, or continually the same, schedule and routine helps toddlers feel secure. When handled well, routines allow children to develop self-help skills, such as hand washing.

READING CHECK ✔ **Identify** Explain why routine and consistency are important for toddlers.

College & Career READINESS

Speech-Language Pathologist

What Does a Speech-Language Pathologist Do?

Speech-language pathologists diagnose, treat, and help prevent language disorders related to speech. They help people who cannot produce speech sounds, have speech problems, have voice disorders, or have problems swallowing. In an early childhood or other educational setting, a speech-language pathologist might work with a child after school or in the classroom to integrate speech activities into his or her daily routine. They may also offer training classes for parents who want to nurture language development at home.

Career Readiness Skills

Speech-language pathologists need to understand anatomy, physiology, and the causes of language disorders. They need to have patience, be able to communicate effectively, and keep track of details as they develop a long-term treatment plan for each patient. Some speech-language pathologists develop expertise with certain age groups such as preschoolers or adolescents.

Education and Training

A speech-language pathologist must have a bachelor's degree and usually a master's degree as well. Most states also require a certification or a license. Licensing requirements vary from state to state. The need for entrepreneurs interested in private practice will grow as hospitals and other settings try to control costs by hiring independent speech-language pathologists.

Job Outlook

About half of speech-language pathologists are employed by educational services. Others are employed by hospitals, nursing care facilities, outpatient care centers, or child care centers. The field of speech-language pathology is growing rapidly.

Critical Thinking Speech-language pathologists can choose to work with difference age groups in a variety of settings. Research different settings available to a speech-language pathologist. Write a brief paragraph identifying which environments would best fit your interests. What short-term and long-term goals will help you prepare for this career?

Career Cluster

Health Science Speech-Language Pathologists work in the Therapeutic Services pathway of the Health Science career cluster. Here are some other jobs in this career cluster:

- Dentist
- Pharmacist
- Nurse
- Physician
- Optometrist
- Microbiologist
- Medical Scientist
- Medical Biller
- Health Educator
- Medical Transcriptionist

Explore Further The Health Science career cluster contains five pathways: Therapeutic Services, Diagnostic Services, Health Informatics, Biotechnology Research and Development, and Supportive Services. Choose one of these pathways to explore further.

McGraw-Hill Education/Ken Cavanagh

Nurturing Toddler Development
Visual Summary

Toddler programs should be designed and managed with all of these developmental needs in mind.

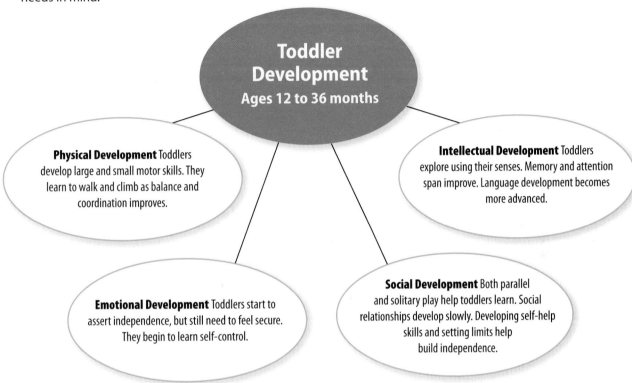

Toddler Development
Ages 12 to 36 months

Physical Development Toddlers develop large and small motor skills. They learn to walk and climb as balance and coordination improves.

Intellectual Development Toddlers explore using their senses. Memory and attention span improve. Language development becomes more advanced.

Emotional Development Toddlers start to assert independence, but still need to feel secure. They begin to learn self-control.

Social Development Both parallel and solitary play help toddlers learn. Social relationships develop slowly. Developing self-help skills and setting limits help build independence.

Vocabulary Review

1. Use these content and academic vocabulary terms to create a crossword puzzle on graph paper. Use the definitions as clues.

Content Vocabulary

◇ toddler (p. 324)
◇ self-help skills (p. 325)
◇ attention span (p. 327)
◇ symbolic thinking (p. 327)
◇ preoperational period (p. 327)
◇ concept (p. 328)
◇ assimilation (p. 328)
◇ accommodation (p. 329)
◇ autonomy (p. 330)
◇ solitary play (p. 331)
◇ parallel play (p. 331)
◇ receptive language (p. 335)
◇ productive language (p. 335)
◇ separation anxiety (p. 336)
◇ temper tantrum (p. 336)

Academic Vocabulary

■ resort (p. 330)
■ consistent (p. 339)

Review Key Concepts

2. **Summarize** the signs of physical, intellectual, emotional, and social development in toddlers.
3. **Identify** the information toddler programs need from parents to develop individualized care and activities.
4. **Describe** the key features of successful toddler programs.

Critical Thinking

5. **Infer** what might be the result of leaving a child on the toilet for an extended time.
6. **Determine** why offering a toddler a choice of two specific snacks is a better way to promote independence than asking, "What do you want for a snack?"
7. **Give examples** of three specific situations in which a toddler might have a temper tantrum.
8. **Evaluate** this suggestion for the schedule at a toddler center: Let's provide variety by having snacks at a different time each day.
9. **Apply** what you have learned about toddlers' fears. Give an example of a specific fear a toddler might show and describe how you would respond to that fear.
10. **Compare** the social needs of toddlers with those of infants.

21st Century Skills

Research Skills

11. **Investigate Piaget** As toddlers develop symbolic thinking, they enter into Piaget's second period of intellectual development, the preoperational period. Use print or online resources to learn more about this period of development. Write notes about the most significant intellectual changes children make during the preoperational period. Create a chart to share at least five facts that you discover.

Communication Skills

12. **Interview an Expert** Interview a toddler care provider to find out his or her experiences with toilet training. What toddler fears about toileting has the care provider encountered? How did he or she help children cope with those fears? Did the care provider use children's books to help with the learning process? If so, which ones? Write a summary to share what you learned about successful toilet training.

Child Care LAB

Use the skills you have learned in this chapter.

Classroom for Toddlers

13. **Design a Toddler Classroom** In this activity, you will work with a partner to design your ideal classroom for toddlers.

   A. Discuss your design. With your partner, discuss your ideas for the classroom. Your design should include the following elements:
   - Floor plan
   - List and illustrations of furniture
   - List and illustrations of equipment
   - List and illustrations of essential toys

   B. Draw the floor plan. Use graph paper or a computer-aided design program to plan the layout and design of the toddler room. Be sure to design it to scale.

   C. Add furniture. Place furniture pieces in the floor plan. Also create a portfolio with pictures of the furniture you will use. Include pictures from catalogs or Web sites, or draw your own pictures. Be sure to get accurate measurements of the furniture so it is the proper scale in your floor plan.

   D. Add equipment. Draw the chosen equipment in the floor plan. Add pictures of the equipment pieces to your portfolio.

   E. List essential toys. In your portfolio, include a list of what you believe the most important toys will be for your classroom. Add pictures of the toys.

   F. Share your design. Share your floor plan and portfolio with your class.

Create Your Evaluation

Create a sheet with these categories:
- Appropriate Space
- Appropriate Furniture
- Appropriate Equipment
- Appropriate Toys
- Completeness
- Neatness

Ask your classmates to use the sheet to evaluate your design, rating each category from 1 to 10.

Academic Skills

 English Language Arts

14. A New Experience Imagine you are a two-year-old in a new situation. For example, you might be meeting a friend's dog, going to a friend's house for a play group, or visiting a child care center for the first time. What do you see and hear? What fears and other emotions do you feel? Write a paragraph describing your experiences from the toddler's point of view.

 Social Studies

15. Toddlers Around the World How do families and communities in other cultures nurture their toddlers? Are toddlers typically cared for in families, in child care centers, or in other settings? If child care centers are common, how do they compare to the centers in your community? Is there a growing need for early childcare? Select a country, and use print and online resources to answer these questions about your chosen country. Prepare an oral presentation to share your findings.

 Mathematics

16. Staffing a Toddler Center Suppose a large child care center limits its toddler classes to a maximum of eight children. It also has two adult care providers in every classroom. The center has a total enrollment of 38 toddlers. It has 8 care providers to work with the toddlers. Does the center need to hire more adult care providers? If so, how many? If not, why not?

Math Concept **Solving Multistep Problems**
Consider what you already know and what you need to find out. In this case, you know how many toddlers and how many care providers there are. You need to find out whether more adult care providers are needed. That means you need to find out how many toddler classes the center will have.

Starting Hint Begin by dividing the total number of toddlers (38) by the maximum number of toddlers per class (8). Remember to round up your answer, because no classroom can have more than 8 toddlers. Then multiply your answer by the number of care providers needed for each class (2).

 For more math practice, go to the Math Appendix at the back of the book.

Certification Prep

Sharpen your test-taking skills to improve your certification program score.

Directions Read each statement. Then read the answer choices and choose the phrase that best completes the sentence.

17. A toddler is a child _____.

    A. who can walk independently

    B. over the age of 15 months

    C. who is ready for toilet training

    D. between the ages of 12 and 36 months

18. Offering reasonable choices helps a toddler develop _____.

    A. assimilation

    B. autonomy

    C. temper tantrums

    D. accommodation

Test-Taking Tip
Read and consider every possible answer on a multiple choice test. Eliminate each choice that is clearly incorrect. Then decide which remaining choice is the best answer.

CHAPTER 16

Nurturing and Teaching Preschoolers

Writing Activity

⭐ 21st Century Skills

Creativity Have you ever spent time caring for a preschooler? Write a short personal narrative about a memorable experience you had with a preschool-age child. Describe the child and the event or the activities you did together, and give sensory details about the experience.

Writing Tips

1. Freewrite to gather ideas.
2. Ask yourself questions to help fill in details of the narrative.
3. Construct an outline or other graphic organizer to help organize your narrative.
4. Be as descriptive as you can.

Explore the Photo
Preschoolers can create detailed artwork with their improved small motor skills. *How else do preschoolers use small motor skills?*

Ariel Skelley/Getty Images

Reading Guide

BEFORE YOU READ

Use Color As you read this chapter, try using different colored pens to take notes. This can help you learn new material and study for tests. Use red for vocabulary words, blue for main ideas, and green for examples.

Read to Learn

Key Concepts

- **Describe** the physical, intellectual, emotional, and social development of preschoolers.
- **Identify** features of preschool programs.
- **Explain** how preschoolers develop literacy.

Main Idea

Preschoolers, children ages three to five, have increased mobility, improved motor skills, and expanding vocabulary and language skills. Preschooler social development includes making friends, cooperative play, and dealing with conflict.

Content Vocabulary

◇ centration
◇ seriation
◇ rote counting
◇ one-to-one correspondence
◇ rational counting
◇ conservation
◇ cooperative play
◇ sociocultural theory
◇ literacy
◇ cooperative learning

Academic Vocabulary

■ subside
■ stable

Graphic Organizer

As you read, you will learn how early childhood teachers can nurture preschoolers' physical, intellectual, emotional, and social development. Use a chart like the one shown to list activities that nurture each area of development.

Physical	Intellectual	Emotional	Social

Graphic Organizer *Go to* **connected.mcgraw-hill.com** *to print this Graphic Organizer.*

AS YOU READ

Connect Think about an activity you enjoyed as a preschooler. What made the activity fun?

Vocabulary

You can find definitions in the glossary at the back of this book.

Development and Care

Children three, four, and five years old are referred to as preschoolers. Preschoolers are eager and ready to learn and interact with others in larger group settings such as child care and preschool. Growth in the preschool years is dramatic and exciting. As preschoolers become more mobile, their vocabulary grows, and they learn to play with others, their overall development and learning advances by leaps and bounds.

Physical Development

Physical growth during the preschool years is slow and gradual, which keeps the appetite small. **Figure 16.1** shows the average heights and weights of children at different preschool ages. Because preschoolers eat small amounts of food, it is essential to make sure that what they eat is healthful and contains adequate nutrients. Regular and adequate sleep routines nourish the body, too.

As preschoolers grow, their bodies appear less babylike. Body fat is reduced, and most growth occurs in the muscles and bones. The neck lengthens, the shoulders widen and flatten, and the once protruding stomach flattens as well. Legs become proportionally longer.

Motor Development

Preschoolers play energetically, and new physical and motor abilities rapidly emerge. Both small and large motor skills gradually become refined and complex. By age five, preschoolers can run fast and can walk on a balance beam. Three-year-olds ride tricycles. Five-year-olds can usually ride bicycles. At three, children move and sway to music. By five, they can learn specific rhythms and dances. A three-year-old can throw a ball. A five-year-old can also catch a ball.

Preschoolers master greater control of their bodies, so they can move in a variety of ways. They hop, gallop, and run. They zigzag while running and change directions with increasing ease. Climbing is a favorite activity of preschoolers. The older they become, the more challenging the structures they try to climb.

Figure 16.1 **Average Heights and Weights of Preschoolers**

Growing Taller
Children grow taller and leaner during the preschool years. *How many inches does an average preschooler grow from ages three to five?*

Age	Height	Weight
Three Years	38 in.	32 lbs.
Four Years	41 in.	36 lbs.
Five Years	44 in.	41 lbs.

Perceptual Motor Development

Preschoolers become more skilled in hand-eye coordination and small motor skills. Three-year-olds learn to use crayons and paintbrushes to create pictures. By five, they can draw and paint shapes and write letters. These are important first steps in learning to read and write. Other activities that develop perceptual motor skills include simple cooking tasks. For example, they can help spread peanut butter on crackers.

Intellectual Development

During the preschool years, children's intellectual abilities also become more refined. Attention span lengthens. Curiosity leads them to observe, analyze, problem-solve, and note cause and effect. Preschoolers' memory and ability to anticipate events increase. As a result, they can make more complex decisions and improve their game-playing skills.

Although Piaget's preoperational period begins during the toddler years, by the time children are preschoolers, the characteristics of this period are much more evident. With the increasing ability to think symbolically, children readily understand new concepts.

▲ **Climbing High**
....
Motor control emerges rapidly during the preschool years. *How can early childhood teachers encourage motor control and development?*

Classification and Centration

Preschoolers begin to learn classification—grouping objects into categories according to similarities. For example, they can separate a mixed set of cards with pictures of cats and dogs into two smaller groups of just cats and just dogs. Preoperational thought, however, limits preschoolers' focus to one characteristic at a time. Piaget called this **centration**. Younger preschool children, for example, can sort objects by color alone. They can find all the red items in a group of toy cars, trucks, and airplanes. Not until children are almost six can they pick out only the red cars. Considering two qualities at once is a difficult task for preschoolers.

Seriation

Around age five, children learn **seriation**, the ability to organize objects according to increasing or decreasing size. As with classification, a preschooler's understanding is very limited. If you give a three-year-old six blocks and say, "Line these up from biggest to smallest," the child may put a large block beside one of the smallest. It will be a couple more years before children can see the relationship between the sizes of all six blocks.

Dave and Les Jacobs/Blend Images LLC

Numbers, Counting, and Time

Children in the preoperational period begin to understand numbers and counting. Two-year-olds are capable of **rote counting**, or reciting numbers in order, but they do not understand that each number represents a specific amount. When rote counting, preschoolers may count some objects more than once. Or, they might not count some objects at all. **One-to-one correspondence** is counting each item once. Children must comprehend this math concept before they can count accurately. **Rational counting** is the understanding that the last number counted in a group represents the entire number of objects. By age five, most children are capable of rational counting to at least the number 10.

Preschool children also have difficulty understanding time. They can understand the difference between *now* and *later* but not the passage of time according to a clock or calendar. By the end of the preschool years, children are able to grasp time terms such as *yesterday, today,* and *tomorrow,* but they still do not understand the concept of minutes versus hours or weeks versus months.

Conservation

Preschoolers' understanding is limited by what they see, making some concepts difficult to grasp. When determining amounts, they do not consider varying features such as size, shape, and volume. For example, preschoolers do not understand that the amount of a liquid stays constant, regardless of the shape of its container. They assume that a shorter glass holds less water and that a taller glass holds more. Piaget termed the understanding that an object's physical weight and properties remain the same even when its appearance changes as **conservation**.

▼ **Learning New Words**

Reading to preschoolers helps encourage vocabulary development. *What other activities encourage language development in preschoolers?*

©Jose Luis Pelaez Inc/Blend Images LLC

Language Development

The human brain is specially designed to learn language. With proper brain development, children learn language from their environment. Adults reinforce language development by praising them for first making sounds, then words, and finally sentences.

With reinforcement, language blossoms during the preschool years. Preschoolers notice that writing on paper, such as in books, magazines, or in cookbooks, represents specific language. The average three-year-old has a vocabulary of 300 words. Four-year-olds speak about 1,500 different words. By age five, an average child speaks 2,200 words. As with most age groups, preschool children understand more words than they can speak. Their language becomes more expressive. Children use facial expressions, tone of voice, and a variety of gestures to show meaning.

With good examples, children develop their language ability more quickly. Talking and reading to children daily helps them expand their language use and grasp its meaning. For example, a three-year-old may simply say, "My ball." An adult can encourage more complex language development by saying, "Yes, that is your big red ball. Show me how you can bounce the ball." Early childhood teachers should encourage children to ask questions and to tell stories or jokes.

Grammar and Pronunciation

Gradually, children learn rules for grammar and pronunciation. With experience, they also learn exceptions to rules. For example, three-year-olds first notice that plurals are formed by adding *s* onto the ends of words. This leads them to make incorrect plurals, such as saying *foots* or *gooses*. As they hear correct language used, preschoolers gradually become aware of the exceptions to plural rules. They will learn that in English, *feet* is used instead of *foots*, and *geese* is used instead of *gooses*. When children are first developing language, early childhood teachers should focus on content rather than on grammar or speech mechanics.

Stuttering

During the preschool years, most children speak clearly. However, you can expect children to say some sounds incorrectly. Some preschoolers have problems with stuttering. They may leave long pauses between words or repeat a sound or word many times before continuing a sentence. This is not "true" stuttering. It is the natural result when thinking ability exceeds speaking ability. It does not mean a child has a special need or disability. When speaking abilities catch up with thinking abilities, this speech pattern usually will **subside**, or lessen in frequency. By not emphasizing it, early childhood teachers preserve a child's self-esteem. If children stutter past age six or seven, they are usually referred to a speech-language pathologist for evaluation.

Bilingual Development

Sometimes the language spoken at child care is different from a child's first language, or the language spoken in a child's home. Such situations provide opportunities for children to become bilingual, or able to speak more than one language. Because of unique early brain development, preschoolers can master multiple languages more easily than adults. When a language is used in meaningful ways, children learn to use different languages in their appropriate setting.

When children speak a different first language, early care teachers should make it a point to learn words and phrases in the child's language. It helps them respond to children warmly and appropriately. Whenever possible, teachers should speak to the child in both English and the first language, such as during mealtimes and activities. To encourage bilingual development:

▶ **Use names correctly.** Names are often linked to culture and are a vital part of identity. Greet children at arrival time by name, making sure that you pronounce their names correctly.

▶ **Use cultural greeting songs.** Add variety to the greeting songs each morning by learning some songs in children's first languages. Parents can be a helpful resource.

▶ **Label learning centers.** Identify learning centers with photos and labels written in both English and children's first languages.

▶ **Use languages at snack time.** During snack time, use both languages for discussion.

▶ **Play ethnic music at nap time.** Nap time can be a time to play lullabies in languages other than English.

▶ **Use first languages at departure time.** At departure, speak with parents and say good-bye in the children's first languages.

Emotional Development

Preschoolers experience an increasing range of emotions, including loneliness, disappointment, curiosity, anticipation, and sympathy. With more developed language skills, preschoolers are able to identify feelings and vent their emotions with words, rather than with physical outbursts such as hitting or pushing. Preschoolers may still have a variety of fears. For example, children may fear a specific type of animal, be afraid of the dark, or frightened by storms. Most of these fears will pass with time and experience.

Though often egocentric, or engrossed in their own point of view, preschool children are not always self-centered. Gradually they begin to develop empathy and compassion. This is the ability to recognize and understand the feelings of others. Preschoolers learn to regret actions that hurt others. They begin to help others without expecting a reward. This emotional development paves the way for making friends and further developing social skills.

Self Esteem

During the preschool age, feelings of self-esteem become more distinct. Preschoolers' self-esteem comes from their pride in performing physical and intellectual tasks. They often ask for attention when climbing, running, or hopping or after naming colors, counting, or reciting the alphabet. "Teacher, see what I can do!" is frequently heard in a child care center.

Self-esteem also increases as preschoolers develop self-help skills. They like to take care of themselves and their personal needs. You will often hear preschoolers say, "I want to do it myself." Three-year-olds can begin lacing shoes. With practice, five-year-olds can tie them. By age four, children can dress themselves, eat neatly using a spoon and fork, and use proper manners.

As the list of accomplishments grows for preschoolers, the resulting feelings of independence and self-worth excite children. According to Erikson, these feelings give rise to a sense of initiative, or motivation to accomplish more. Children feel proud about what they learn to do and try to accomplish more to increase the good feelings. As a result, preschoolers are very willing to be helpful. They especially like contributing to the group. In the classroom, they can pick up toys, set the table, feed classroom pets, and help pass out name cards.

◀ Little Helpers

Preschoolers like to help in the classroom by cleaning or taking care of a pet. *How does helping build a child's self-esteem?*

Gender Identity and Roles

Around age three, children begin to notice that boy and girls are physically different. Preschoolers learn who they are as males and females by watching adults and mimicking some of their behaviors. For example, a little girl might hand a parent tools while he or she fixes the family car or set the table while her dad or mom prepares a meal. A little boy might help a parent do yard work or bake cookies.

Early childhood professionals are careful to show the full potential of both genders in the work setting and at home. They promote diversity by including children in all activities, according to their interests and abilities. This action helps encourage self-esteem development as children learn and grow as males and females.

Building Resilience

As during other developmental stages, early childhood professionals can promote preschoolers' resilience, meaning their ability to develop and thrive in times of hardship and crisis. Events that cause children stress, such as experiencing a natural disaster or enduring a parents' divorce, are times when children need extra care and attention at child care.

Consistent, reliable routines help preschoolers feel relaxed, secure, and better able to cope with changes or challenges their families face. Stable relationships and a strong attachment to one child care teacher help build children's self-esteem, confidence, and resilience despite adversity.

▶ **Learning About Gender**

Preschoolers learn about gender roles from the adults in their lives. *How can a teacher provide exposure to nontraditional gender roles?*

© Hero/Corbis/Glow Images

Social Development

Before the preschool years, most social interactions for children are with adults. By age three, peers increase in importance. When given many chances to play, children become skilled in forming relationships.

Forming Friendships

Three-year-olds like to play in small groups of two or three. By five, children enjoy playing in groups of five to eight. Through play, preschoolers develop social skills. They learn to get along and to share with each other. They learn to compromise to please playmates. They can also bargain for what they want. Preschoolers become more comfortable joining in activities with others and suggesting their own play ideas. They engage in **cooperative play**—playing together with other children and agreeing on play activities and themes.

By four, children can form close friendships with one or two other children, whom they may call their "best friends." Preschoolers often "bribe" other children into friendship. A child might offer to let another child play with a favorite toy on the condition that they become best friends. These friendships are usually temporary. Preschoolers may have a different "best friend" every day of the week. By age five, children form close-knit groups of preferred playmates. They can be extremely blunt in their rejection of anyone who is not in their "group." After age six, friendships become more stable, or more firmly established.

Dealing with Conflict

When conflicts arise between preschoolers, it is often over toys or personal property. Child care staff should ask children and parents to bring only personal items from home the child is willing to share. Children who have trouble sharing are asked to keep personal items in their cubbies.

Around four or five years of age, some children engage in name-calling. They may direct silly, crude, or hurtful names at others. Some of this can be ignored. If it becomes too frequent, however, teachers should firmly tell children that name-calling is not allowed because it hurts people's feelings. When dealing with conflict, teachers should help a child recognize and accept their feelings by naming and describing them for the child.

▲ **Best Friends**

During the preschool years, children form closer friendships with one or two other children. *Why might conflicts arise between preschoolers?*

Realistic Reflections

Influence of Social Play

According to Vygotsky, cooperative play has a great influence on children's intellectual and social development. His **sociocultural theory** states that children learn their culture's beliefs, customs, and skills through social interactions with skilled peers and adults. For example, when children talk to people with a strong command of language, children expand their language skills. As children cooperatively play with others who are socially competent, they learn to act according to their culture's specific rules. In addition, children increase their thinking and problem-solving skills.

READING CHECK ✔ **Recall** What is usually the cause of a preschooler's stuttering?

Managing Preschool Programs

Preschoolers' abilities build on the achievements of all previous developmental stages. Early childhood programs must offer preschoolers many chances to refine their skills so that children may reach their full learning potential. As their skills develop, they require more freedom to make independent choices during play and learning times. As with services for other ages, safety, nutrition, and good sanitation are also important parts of the preschool program.

SAFETY MATTERS

Evacuation Pathways

There are times when adults and children must evacuate classrooms for safety reasons, such as severe weather, fire, earthquake, individual or group violence, or a civil defense emergency. Evacuation directions help everyone find safe shelter. Near the entrance and exit of every classroom and common area, post escape directions. Evacuation pathways should be identified for each type of emergency. Some programs color-code pathways for different emergencies. For fire emergencies, primary and secondary escape routes should be posted. Laminate the evacuation sheets so they remain in readable condition.

What Would You Do? Your child care program has clearly identified safety procedures. There are fire doors, alarms, and evacuation routes posted throughout the building. You have been a teacher at the center for more than two years and you have never participated in a center safety drill. What would you do?

Managing Daily Schedules and Routines

Regular routines are important to preschoolers. Include routines in a balanced schedule. Depending on the length of day, schedules and routines should include the following:

▶ Arrival

▶ Meals, including snacks

▶ Personal hygiene such as hand washing and toileting

▶ Morning group meetings at which children and teachers greet each other and cooperatively plan the day's events

▶ Group times for large-group experiences; activity times for individual and small-group learning; extended periods of free time for self-chosen activities either indoors or outdoors

▶ Monthly or quarterly field trips that relate to classroom curriculum

▶ Toy cleanup times and nap or rest time

▶ End-of-day group activity and departure

Glow Images

Nurturing Physical Development

The preschool years are a time of rapid development in all areas of growth. Observable changes take place in terms of children's increased physical size. Preschoolers love to expand their skills in all areas. Using more complex small and large motor coordination skills allows preschoolers to enjoy a wider variety of games and physical activities. Whether indoors or outdoors, preschoolers enjoy vigorous large-muscle play and challenges to their new abilities, such as using safe climbing equipment. Outdoors, preschoolers do not just want to run, but enjoy greater challenges, such as maneuvering an obstacle course or playing chasing games with peers.

Small-muscle development, such as coordination of small finger muscles, allows preschoolers to do more complicated art activities. They eagerly use new art materials that teachers supply. They experiment with new writing instruments such as markers, crayons, and pencils, and even computer mouses. The ability to hold crayons and markers leads children to the ability to handle pencils for future writing. Preschoolers' refined coordination paves the way for making large block buildings or detailed constructions with small manipulative blocks.

▲ Expanding Skills

Preschoolers love to expand their skills in all areas. *How is drawing helping this preschooler expand his motor skills?*

Nurturing Intellectual Development

As the brain develops, preschoolers are capable of increasingly complex thinking skills. Teachers nurture intellectual development by providing children with many meaningful hands-on experiences that encourage children's thinking skills, such as using a magnifying glass to view a caterpillar up close. Daily encounters with sensory materials in both indoor and outdoor environments stimulate brain development. They set the stage for children to learn to observe, describe, and make sense of new shapes, textures, sounds, and even tastes. Asking children timely questions prompts them to explain, compare, and contrast their experiences and also nurtures intellectual development.

The ability to speak and listen to language is mastered during the toddler years. Preschoolers' greater intellectual capacity allows them to recognize and understand abstract symbols that represent spoken words. That process includes the beginning steps toward achieving the ability to read and write language, often referred to as **literacy**. Preschoolers develop literacy skills rapidly. They increasingly put their expanding language skills to good use. For example, during pretend play, preschoolers use more detailed and expressive language. They begin to ask more questions about other's activities rather than only making simple statements about their own play. **Figure 16.2** describes ways teachers can help develop preschoolers' literacy skills.

| Figure 16.2 | Emerging Literacy |

Learning to Read Child care teachers can foster preschoolers' emerging literacy by providing access to literacy materials. *How can a child see written words used in meaningful ways?*

- Offer many daily opportunities for listening and speaking. For example, encourage creative use of language through music and storytelling.

- Read books to children—in groups and individually—daily. Let children look at or listen to books on CD independently.

- Give children easy access to literacy materials such as markers, books, and paper. Have children make and illustrate their own books.

- Show children how literacy relates to real life, such as reading a recipe during cooking or reading directions to put together a new toy.

- Include printed materials in learning centers such as toy traffic signs in the block center and menus in a pretend restaurant.

- Allow children to see written words used in meaningful ways, such as writing thank-you cards to field trip hosts or labels on common items such as tables and chairs.

Glow Images

◀ **Expressing Emotions**

Helping a preschooler put feelings into words can nurture a child's emotional development. *How can teachers be role models for dealing with emotions?*

Nurturing Emotional Development

Preschoolers begin to handle their emotions more maturely. Greater language mastery helps them deal more effectively with frustrations. They increasingly use their words to cope with emotions, rather than having emotional outbursts. Preschool children often face new emotional realities. For example, during these years, children first encounter a feeling of jealousy when new siblings are born. During short separations from parents, they learn to deal with a sense of loss. Many preschoolers must learn to cope with the sorrow when a close family member or pet dies.

Child care teachers can help children cope with emotional events by empathizing with them rather than distracting them from their discomfort. For example, after a pet's death, a teacher can help put a child's probable feelings into words: "It can feel very lonely when a favorite pet dies. It's sad when it happens." Teachers can also read books to children that feature characters dealing with similar emotional challenges. Children's librarians can suggest book titles for most events preschoolers find emotionally confusing or challenging.

Teachers also encourage preschoolers' emotional development by giving them many opportunities to express their emotions and ideas. This communication can take place during pretend play or during mealtime conversations. When children experience conflict, teachers support children's emotional development by coaching them through the steps for problem solving and resolving conflict. Teachers can also be good role models for dealing with emotions. Setting a good example for self-control and calmly handling difficulties are very helpful teaching tools when working with preschoolers.

Nurturing Social Development

Toddlers most often engage in solitary and parallel play. Preschoolers enjoy playing together and agreeing on play activities and themes, making cooperative play possible. Through cooperative play, preschoolers refine social skills such as listening and sharing ideas with others. During cooperative play, preschoolers are more inclined to take turns making plans with peers and create play themes together. The give-and-take of these play experiences increases children's social skills and stimulates greater peer learning.

Teachers can be great coaches for social development. Sometimes conflict occurs during preschoolers' play. By gently stepping in to help children look at things from each other's point of view, teachers help children learn self-control, empathy, and a peaceful ways to resolve disagreements. By offering activities that require cooperation, such as setting up a pretend car wash for play vehicles, teachers create opportunities for children to work together and to form friendships. Teachers also help children practice teamwork and feel like an important part of the group when they allow children to complete classroom chores in pairs, such as passing out napkins for snack time and feeding classroom pets.

▼ Learning Together

Preschoolers can successfully engage in cooperative learning. *What skills have preschoolers developed that make cooperative learning possible?*

© IT Stock Free

Cooperative Learning

A preschooler's ability to cooperatively investigate a specific topic of interest with other children expands greatly and is called **cooperative learning**. As a result of greater experience with peers and a greater command of language, children can work well in groups. To encourage preschoolers' cooperative-learning skills, child care teachers can

▶ create more detailed, elaborate learning centers that encourage group play. Introduce a wider variety of play materials that require more advanced thinking skills.

▶ provide more intricate play materials that require more refined perceptual motor skills. Include more toys that require cooperative play, such as board games.

▶ plan projects that require teamwork, such as making murals or cardboard cities. Encourage children to suggest topics to investigate.

▶ conduct activities that allow children to plan together and to make decisions, such as creating and putting on a play.

Community Awareness

With their expanding ability to grasp new concepts and information, preschoolers enjoy learning about the community. They benefit from seeing how many different people it takes to make communities operate. Learning about the many jobs and services a community needs helps children see how they can participate in communities when they become adults. To encourage preschoolers' community awareness, early childhood professionals can

▶ plan field trips to introduce children to the diversity in their communities.

▶ use community resources to expand the curriculum. For example, visit the local humane society when studying pets.

▶ invite community members to share their skills and knowledge with children.

▶ include children in community service projects such as picking up litter or donating toys.

▶ draw children's attention to basic rules communities set for behavior. Help them identify rules and laws that protect everyone's safety and wellness.

READING CHECK ✔ **List** What routines should be part of a preschool program?

College & Career
R E A D I N E S S

Letters of Recommendation

What is a Letter of Recommendation?

Many colleges request letters of recommendation so that the admission committee can learn more about you. They have data on your test scores, classes, and grades. Now they want to know how others see you. An application usually states the number of letters required, and may also request letters from specific people such as a teacher in a certain subject. These letters should be written by adults who know you well, who respect your abilities, and who are interested in helping you.

Whom should I ask for letters of recommendation?

Think about teachers whose classes you have enjoyed and in which you have worked hard. Also think about a counselor with whom you have discussed your college plans, an adult who supervised a volunteer project you participated in, an employer, or a leader of your extracurricular activities. It is important that these adults write about you honestly and sincerely. Do not ask a relative to write a letter of recommendation.

When should I request the letters?

Remember that the adults who write your letters of recommendation are busy. Try to request a letter of recommendation a month before you need it sent or delivered. Two weeks' notice is a minimum. If possible, discuss letters of recommendation well in advance. Try to determine whether each adult you are considering asking is actually interested in offering you this kind of help.

What happens to my letters of recommendation?

The letters of recommendation may be sent directly to the college to which you are applying, via e-mail or through the post office. In some cases, they may be delivered to you in sealed envelopes. The letter writers may or may not discuss their letters with you. You should not expect to read the letters.

Hands-On

No matter how close you are to applying to college, think about the people whom you might ask for letters of recommendation. Make a list of possible letter writers. After each name, note your reasons for choosing that person. If possible, discuss your ideas with a relative, friend, teacher, or a counselor. Keep your list, and add to it as you get closer to applying to college.

Path to Success

Do Not Be Shy To get letters of recommendation, you have to ask people to write them.

Make It Easy Provide your letter writers with an addressed and stamped envelope for each letter.

Provide Deadlines Make sure your letter writers know when the letters are due

Trust Your Letter Writers Waive your right to view the recommendation letters. This gives more credibility to the recommendations.

Follow Up Check with your letter writers before the deadline to make sure they have sent the letters.

Thank Them Write thank-you notes to everyone who provide you with a letter or recommendation.

Nurturing and Teaching Preschoolers

Visual Summary

Early childhood activities nurture the physical, intellectual, emotional, and social development of preschoolers.

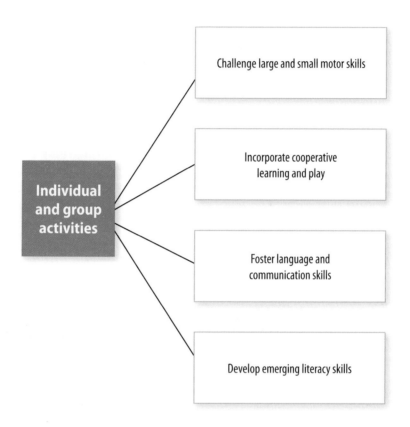

Individual and group activities

- Challenge large and small motor skills
- Incorporate cooperative learning and play
- Foster language and communication skills
- Develop emerging literacy skills

Vocabulary Review

1. Write your own definition for each content and academic vocabulary term.

Content Vocabulary

- ◇ centration (p. 347)
- ◇ seriation (p. 347)
- ◇ rote counting (p. 348)
- ◇ one-to-one correspondence (p. 348)
- ◇ rational counting (p. 348)
- ◇ conservation (p. 348)
- ◇ cooperative play (p. 353)
- ◇ sociocultural theory (p. 354)
- ◇ literacy (p. 356)
- ◇ cooperative learning (p. 359)

Academic Vocabulary

- ■ subside (p. 349)
- ■ stable (p. 353)

Review Key Concepts

2. **Describe** the physical, intellectual, emotional, and social development of preschoolers.
3. **Identify** features of preschool programs.
4. **Explain** how preschoolers develop literacy.

Critical Thinking

5. **Draw** conclusions about the importance of providing a variety of activities for preschoolers.
6. **Compare** a preschool program to a toddler program schedule. In what ways are they different? What are the reasons for those differences?
7. **Describe** the relationship between preschoolers' self-esteem and their physical and intellectual accomplishments.
8. **Explain** Vygotsky's sociocultural theory in your own words. Give examples.
9. **Develop** ideas for two different activities that use print material other than a book to help develop preschoolers' emerging literacy skills.
10. **List** three examples of outdoor safety to discuss with preschoolers. Why is it important for children to understand outdoor safety?

21st Century Skills

Communication Skills

11. **Tying Shoes** Learning to tie shoelaces is a big accomplishment for a preschooler. Plan how you would teach a five-year-old to tie shoelaces. Demonstrate your plan with a classmate. Be sure to use words a five-year-old will understand.

Creativity Skills

12. **Learning Through Play** Design an original board game out of common materials such as cardboard or clay that helps preschoolers learn social skills. Demonstrate your game to the class and explain how it teaches social skills.

Child Care LAB

Use the skills you have learned in this chapter.

Bilingual Development Plan

13. **Develop a Plan for Bilingual Development** A comprehensive early childhood program should include a curriculum plan for all children's bilingual development. In this activity, you will create a developmentally appropriate curriculum plan for preschoolers.

    A. Write a Goal Statement. Write a short paragraph that describes your preschool bilingual program curriculum goals. What language(s) will be taught? What do you want preschoolers in your program to learn? How often will bilingual development be incorporated into the overall curriculum?

    B. Outline the Curriculum Plan. Create an outline of your curriculum plan. List activities that target each area of preschooler development: physical, intellectual, emotional, and social.

    C. Create an Example Activity. Create an example bilingual development activity. Describe how the activity meets the goals of your bilingual curriculum plan.

    D. List Supplies and Expenses. Create a list of any supplies and expenses, if any, needed to implement your bilingual curriculum plan not included in typical child care program budgets.

    E. Peer Review the Plan. Exchange plans with a classmate. Use the evaluation sheet to review his or her plan and provide suggestions on how to improve the plan.

Create Your Evaluation

Create an evaluation sheet with these categories:

- Goal Statement
- Curriculum Plan Outline
- Example Activity
- Supplies and Expenses

Have your classmate use this sheet to evaluate your plan, rating each category on a Detailed and Complete/Adequate Information/Needs Improvement scale.

Academic Skills

English Language Arts

14. Encourage Language Development Teachers can encourage language development during all daily activities such as art. If a four-year-old is drawing a picture of her family and where they live, what questions could you ask the child to encourage language development? Write a list of five questions and explain how these questions encourage language development.

Social Studies

15. Piaget's Influence The research of child psychologist Jean Piaget has had a major influence on how children are taught today. Research the experiments Piaget used to develop his definitions of the preoperational period. Describe these experiments and draw connections to today's preschooler curriculum. What influences of Piaget do you see?

Science

16. Television and Behavior Scientists have established links between exposure to visual electronic media, such as television and video games, and violence, obesity, and consumerism, even in young children. Moderation in visual electronic media use helps limit its effects. For example, one source recommends limiting television viewing to one or two hours a day. Another source recommends no more than four hours of television viewing per week.

Procedure Watch two hours of children's television programming. As you watch, keep track of the number of violent incidents, number of advertisements for foods with low nutritional value, and number of advertisements for toys.

Analysis Use the information you gather to create a bar graph. Draw conclusions about what messages are being conveyed to children in the television program. How could you use this information to evaluate children's programming? Provide recommendations for parents of young children for television viewing based on your findings.

Certification Prep

Sharpen your test-taking skills to improve your certification program score.

Directions Read the sentence, and choose the best word or phrase to fill in the blank.

17. By age five, a preschooler can _____ .

 A. tell time on a clock

 B. throw and catch a ball

 C. understand that weight and properties of an object remain the same when appearance changes

 D. consistently use correct grammar and pronunciation

18. The ability to organize objects according to increasing or decreasing size is called _____ .

 A. centration

 B. seriation

 C. one-to-one correspondence

 D. conservation

Test-Taking Tip

In multiple-choice questions, do not go back and change an answer unless you made an obvious mistake the first time, such as misreading the question.

Comstock/Alamy

CHAPTER 17

Teaching School-Age Children

Writing Activity

⭐ 21st Century Skills

Cooperative Learning The first draft of a piece of writing usually needs improvements. Examine your first draft of a writing activity from an earlier chapter. Work with a partner to edit it for spelling and grammar errors. If needed, revise sentences for clarity and add details you may have forgotten. Read aloud your writing to your partner. Then help your partner revise and edit his or her writing.

Writing Tips
1. Edit your sentences for clarity. Proofread closely to find errors.
2. Ask a friend to look for errors.
3. Review your paper a final time.

Explore the Photo
School-age children expand their language and literacy skills. *How can early educators promote this development?*

©William Pollard/age fotostock

Reading Guide

Prepare with a Partner Before you read, work with a partner. Read the headings and ask each other questions about the topics that will be discussed. Write the questions you both have about each section. As you read, answer the questions you have identified.

Read to Learn

Key Concepts

- **Describe** the overall development of school-age children.
- **Explain** the need for school-age child care programs.
- **Describe** an appropriate environment for school-age children that promotes growth, development, and interpersonal skills.
- **Identify** ways to nurture overall development of school-age children.

Main Idea

School-age children refine their motor skills and problem-solving abilities and encounter new challenges related to social skills and peer interactions. It is important for these children to have a safe place to interact and learn in between school and home.

Content Vocabulary

◇ growth plateau
◇ puberty
◇ hormones
◇ depth perception
◇ concrete operations period
◇ industry
◇ inferiority
◇ diversity
◇ latchkey children
◇ specialized lessons

Academic Vocabulary

■ abstractly
■ refine

Graphic Organizer

As you read, you will learn about managing school-age child care programs. Use a web like the one shown to record information. Include notes in the large box about the basics of a school-age program. Add details in the smaller boxes about an ideal program's environment, daily routines, and activities.

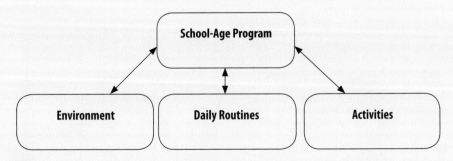

Graphic Organizer *Go to* **connected.mcgraw-hill.com** *to print this Graphic Organizer.*

AS YOU READ

Connect Think about caring for school-age children. What can an early educator do to promote growth and development for school-age children?

Vocabulary
You can find definitions in the glossary at the back of this book.

Development and Care

To work well with school-age children, you need to understand their unique stage of development. Children ages six to twelve are considered school-age children. Because children change so much during these years, this textbook divides the ages for discussion. This chapter refers to children ages six to ten as school-age children. References to older children apply to children ages eleven and twelve years. Both school-age children and older children are still experiencing changes across all areas of development.

Physical Development

Younger school-age children are in a **growth plateau**, which means their growth is slow and steady. They continue to build muscles and bone, giving them a longer, leaner appearance.

Figure 17.1 shows approximate heights and weights for children ages six to eight. Throughout this period, boys are a little heavier than girls. By age eight, however, girls catch up with boys in weight.

Signs of Puberty

Children experience a surge of growth around age twelve (slightly younger for girls). They begin **puberty**—the transition stage at which children undergo a series of physical changes and begin to look like adult men and women. Puberty is triggered by an increase in **hormones**, or chemical substances carried in the blood that impact growth and development. Puberty leads to adulthood. Girls may begin puberty at younger ages than boys, usually six months to a year earlier. These changes can sometimes be confusing, embarrassing, or awkward for the children involved, but these changes are important signs of good health. Here are some changes that come with puberty:

▶ Hormone changes cause girls to begin to menstruate, usually between ages ten and fourteen. Body fat increases in girls, so they may weigh slightly more than boys. This is normal and healthy for girls during puberty.

▶ It is also not unusual for girls to surpass boys in height. When boys are well into puberty, their height and weight surpass that of girls.

Figure 17.1 **Average Heights and Weights of School-Agers**

Slow and Steady
Younger school-age children grow at a steady rate that is slower than earlier years of development. *How many inches will an average six-year-old grow in two years?*

Age	Height	Weight
Six years	46 in.	45 lbs.
Seven years	48 in.	50 lbs.
Eight years	50 in.	55 lbs.

- Boys develop more muscle, which adds weight. Facial hair appears. Male hormone production causes boys' voices to gradually lower.
- The high level of hormone production can cause mood swings in both boys and girls.

Motor Development

School-age children perfect the skills they need for body control. Large muscles now work together, improving coordination. By age ten, children are capable of all types of large-motor movement and like to challenge their bodies with physical activities. They can ride a bike, swim, jump rope, climb fences and trees, and play a variety of sports.

Control over small muscles is most often fully achieved by age seven or eight. The ability to control muscles in the wrists, hands, and fingers enables children to develop their handwriting, to play a musical instrument, and to increase drawing or other art skills.

Both genders experience increased muscle strength and coordination and improved perceptual motor skills. They become more skilled in team games and sports. These activities require quick movements, coordination of the body, and **depth perception**—the ability to judge distance and to see objects in perspective. Many new skills come with perceptual motor development. Younger school-age children can learn to skate, to play T-ball, and to snow-ski. By ages eight to ten, many can play hockey, soccer, and baseball.

◀**Perfecting Skills**

School-age children experience an increase in coordination and control of motor skills. *What activities might a teacher offer to help children refine motor skills and optimize their development?*

Intellectual Development

According to Piaget, children are not capable of truly logical thought processes until the teenage years. However, school-agers are quickly developing the ability to create, analyze, and evaluate ideas. This ability progresses rapidly during the school-age years.

According to Piaget, school-age children are no longer bound to learning through their senses like preschool children. They are now at the developmental stage that Piaget called the **concrete operations period**, which is when children (ages seven to eleven) learn to think more rationally, and less magically. They use valid reasoning to problem-solve and relate more accurate cause-and-effect relationships to actual objects and experiences. For example, during the concrete operations period,

▶ children can grasp the idea of conservation, or the act of considering several variables at one time. This allows them to classify and order different categories of objects, also called seriation. These are skills used in math and science.

▶ children have a much greater grasp of reality versus fantasy and real versus pretend. Their imaginations can be as rich as a preschooler's, but they understand what it means to "make up" things, while preschoolers often do not.

▶ this age group still benefits from active learning with hands-on materials. However, their ability to think **abstractly**, or separately from any specific object or occurrence, is increasing. For instance, school-age children can understand and calculate the passage of time. They can remember the past, consider the present, and anticipate and plan for the future.

▶ curiosity about a wide variety of topics is characteristic of school-age children. By age ten, they have mastered the basic language skills of speech, comprehension, reading, and writing. **Figure 17.2** lists the language and literacy skills that school-age children develop.

Figure 17.2　Expanding Language and Literacy Skills

Learning to Read　School-age children are learning to master basic language skills. *At what age do children begin to read aloud fluently?*

Age	Skill Development
Six to Seven Years	• Learns to print capital and lowercase letters • Learns short vowel sounds and common consonant and vowel blends • Reads a simple book alone • Recognizes common word endings, such as *-er* and *-ing*
Eight to Nine Years	• Prints all letters and begins to learn script (cursive handwriting) • Reads aloud fluently • Writes a simple story alone
Ten Years and Older	• Adept at writing in script • Reads for information and writes a simple factual report • Learns to use prefixes and suffixes to identify meanings of words

- As school-age children gain a greater command of language, they often develop an interest in keeping a journal or a diary. This practice allows for self-expression. It is a constructive way for children to explore their growing sense of individuality and separate identity from parents.

- Many school-age children like the challenge of creative writing. As language skills increase, they can develop complete story plots with details. Often they create story characters that cope with the same issues, feelings, and dilemmas the child is facing.

- Children at this age can also understand basic math concepts and can apply them in solving problems. Their abilities help school performance and allow children to pursue hobbies such as chess, crafts, and creating computer graphics and cartoons.

Emotional Development

School-age children have a wide array of emotions. Increased language skills allow them to express their emotions frequently and more clearly. School-age children understand the viewpoints of others better; however, they do not always agree with others. True discussions and debates begin to surface.

With improved empathy, these children better recognize, understand, and sympathize with the feelings of others. School-agers can be very sensitive and sentimental. Their compassion inspires them to want to make a difference in the world. They increasingly become interested in broader socially responsible world issues such as environmental conservation, limiting pollution, and promoting recycling.

SAFETY MATTERS

Responding to Bullying

Children with low self-esteem may become bullies who may taunt and threaten their classmates. Cyberbullying is when these taunts and threats are made online. Deep down, these children lack confidence and fear that they will not be liked. Early educators must treat bullies firmly but with compassion.

- **Make** it clear that bullying behavior is not acceptable.

- **Manage** the classroom environment to reduce opportunities for conflict and bullying. Focus on practices that will keep all children safe and secure.

- **Establish** and follow through with developmentally appropriate child guidance practices and consequences.

- **Teach** positive conflict resolution skills that are nonviolent. Encourage students to use words to resolve conflict.

- **Talk** with these children's parents to learn how they handle bullying.

- **Look** for chances to praise and encourage positive behavior.

What Would You Do? You are a teacher for a school-age child care program. Two of the children in your program are often in conflict. One is showing signs of emerging bullying behavior. How can you respond to this behavior and teach positive methods for solving problems and resolving conflicts?

Self-Esteem Development

By age six, most children have established clear gender and role identities. They have strong ties to their families and cultural backgrounds. This helps children form a stable and secure self-concept.

According to psychologist Erik Erikson, school-age children strive to develop a sense of **industry**, the desire to perform skills, to succeed at tasks, and to make social contributions. School-age children want to put their energy to use. Erikson claimed that if school-age children do not feel productive, they will develop a sense of **inferiority**, a feeling of not having met expected standards. Feeling inferior greatly damages self-esteem.

School-age children develop self-confidence and pride when they achieve new physical accomplishments. They need successful experiences with peers—through games, sports activities, and group projects—to prevent feelings of inferiority from developing.

Competition

School-age children begin to compare themselves to other people. As they grow, children encounter more competition in sports and school. Healthy competition can motivate children to try hard and helps them assess their individual abilities as compared to the group. Competition can **refine**, or perfect, skills and talents.

Comparing their skills to those of others is natural, but it can also present challenges. Placing too much emphasis on competition—focusing on winning rather than enjoying the activity—can be harmful. Some children may focus more on their weaknesses than on their strengths. This damages self-esteem. Children may avoid activities for fear of failure, which can slow their development.

Teachers should help children avoid excessive comparison with others. Teachers can encourage school-agers to try to achieve their own "personal best" in any activity—whether it is in sports, chorus, or theater. Research has shown that focusing on gradually improving one's own skills is a better motivator for accomplishment than when children focus only on surpassing others' performance.

To promote a spirit of teamwork rather than only competition, teachers may emphasize cooperative games over competitive games. Participating in a team rewards children for cooperating with others and recognizes their contributions. Confidence builds when children identify their strengths, gradually build upon them, and take pride in their personal best. Teachers can also suggest activity groups to parents that promote noncompetitive teamwork.

Typical Fears

When children reach school age, they usually let go of preschool fears. They are not as likely to be afraid of things such as dogs and storms. Instead, their increased reasoning skills allow for more abstract fears. For example,

▶ school-age children may fear not belonging to a group. They often worry that they will not have friends. They may fear being different and not being accepted.

▶ they may fear being teased and criticized. School-age children may imagine that others talk about them behind their backs.

▶ many school-age children fear failure. They dislike the thought of disappointing parents, teachers, and other respected adults.

▲ Personal Best

School-age children build confidence when they succeed as a team without worrying about surpassing others' performances. *What activities could a child care professional offer to help children take pride in their personal best?*

School-age children tend to be less egocentric, or seeing things only from one's own point of view. Instead, they worry about events they cannot control, such as earthquakes, severe weather, homelessness, and the unknown. School-age children's greater cognitive skills allow them to be aware of news events that portray violent acts against others. They begin to understand that bad events may affect their world. This can lead to increased fears about bullying, getting hurt, neighborhood violence, terrorism, and war.

Fears are very real to school-age children. Adults should take these fears seriously by giving children frequent opportunities to openly discuss them. Children need reminders that many adults care about and do their best to protect them. Adults can reassure school-agers about their fears by including them in emergency response plans for home, child care, or school. Being prepared for a crisis can help children feel less fearful.

School-agers with fears that interfere regularly with daily life may benefit from the help of a mental health professional. Such a decision would be made by parents or guardians, but early educators are often asked to help parents decide when fears are too great for school-agers to handle alone.

School-Age Stressors

Stress is present at every stage of life. Children reveal stress in many ways. They may develop fatigue, indifference, poor school performance, physical illness, and even depression. Some children become easily angered, aggressive, or disobedient. Nonverbal cues, such as fingernail biting, frequent stomachaches, headaches, and withdrawal from activities can also signal stress.

Early educators should watch for these signs and consult with parents and mental health professionals when necessary. Possible stressors for school-age children include the following:

▶ Energy expended to develop new intellectual and physical skills

▶ Excessive emphasis on competition with others

▶ Bullying or rejection by peers, in person and online

▶ Concerns about body image and changes to their bodies

▶ Less relaxation and leisure time at home with family and friends

▶ Family changes or problems, such as new siblings or divorce

Social Development

School-age children handle friendships differently from preschoolers. Their friendships are more lasting and meaningful. Feelings and beliefs are shared. Children tend not to form friendships for personal gain but because they sincerely appreciate the characteristics of another person. Younger school-age children have many friends of both genders. By age seven or eight, children tend to prefer friends of the same gender.

A Matter of ETHICS

Keeping Children Safe
As an early educator, you are obligated to protect the safety and welfare of all children. Center guidelines and, in some cases, laws are in place to protect children, families, and programs and to prevent safety hazards and accidents. For that reason, many schools and school-age programs have a zero-tolerance policy for weapons, including items that may seem harmless, such as cutlery and camping tools.

Thinking Ethically

While checking in a child upon his or her arrival, a small knife falls out of the child's lunch box. You are the only person who sees the knife. Your center has a zero-tolerance rule in regard to weapons. What would you do?

When boys play together, they tend to be a bit more physically active than girls. They are also more likely to base friendships on common physical skills they find in peers, especially of their own gender. Girls often base friendships on common interests.

All school-age children can be impulsive. School-age boys, however, tend to be more impulsive and are sensitive to rises in noise level or other sensory stimulation. Sometimes this means they push limits for classroom behavior more often than girls. Impulsiveness, along with slightly slower language development than girls, means that boys sometimes engage in physical confrontation with peers more often than girls. However, girls can be more verbally aggressive, such as name-calling, with peers.

During the school-age years, both genders take longer than preschoolers to forgive others after disagreements or confrontations. With sensitive guidance and coaching from a teacher, both genders readily develop positive social skills that will aid them throughout life.

▲ Buddies

School-age children develop strong bonds and can become lifelong friends. *How can early educators encourage children to nurture good friendships?*

Building Friendships

School-age friendships remain fairly stable despite periodic conflicts. Verbal disagreements can be another part of being friends. When children work through squabbles they have a chance to learn constructive ways of solving conflicts. Responsible teachers should still stay nearby to coach children through the steps of peaceful resolution. Socially competent school-age children know how to maintain friendships by giving as well as receiving. They become skilled at negotiating and finding solutions to conflict that feel fair to everyone involved.

An attitude of "us versus them" sometimes exists among school-age friendships. School-agers have the capacity for great sensitivity. Their growing concern for peer acceptance can lead them to exclude those not considered friends. School-age children are still adjusting to similarities and differences among individuals. Good adult role models can help discourage them from forming stereotypes of others outside their "group." Name-calling and teasing may grow during this period of childhood. However, with sensitive and caring teachers, these children can consistently treat others respectfully and with compassion and empathy.

Younger school-age children are very concerned about rules. They continue to obey them to earn rewards and to avoid penalties. Gradually school-agers see that rules are needed for people to live together peacefully. Awareness of rules and their purposes allows children to participate more fully in group games. Playing fair takes on great importance to school-age children.

How to . . .

Prepare School-Age Children for Peer Pressure

As school-age children form stronger peer relationships, they are more likely to feel peer pressure when making choices. Especially when they try to decide between right and wrong. The behavior and beliefs of school-agers can be highly influenced by peers. Sometimes this is good, sometimes not. Family members and early educators can help children meet appropriate expectations, despite peer pressure. Discuss the role of the teacher and how building self-esteem and self-image relates to that role.

© Image Source/Alamy

Apply It!
What advice could you give a school-age child who is dealing with peer-pressure? Share your advice with a partner.

▶ **Listening** *Regularly take time to listen to school-age children—their hopes and their concerns. Provide meaningful and respectful feedback during discussion.*

▶ **Decision Making** *Show trust in children's ability to make good, independent decisions. Remind them that they can think for themselves and still be liked.*

▶ **Consequences** *Guide children to anticipate positive and negative consequences for behavior.*

▶ **Valuing Others** *Help children value friends who do not pressure them to engage in questionable activities.*

▶ **Self-Esteem** *Provide ways to help build children's self-esteem so they are not driven to find love and attention only from others.*

▶ **Environment** *Maintain an environment in which children feel safe and loved.*

▶ **Safety** *Remind children that some secrets are not safe to keep. Encourage them to seek help from a trusted adult when someone makes them feel unsafe or uncomfortable.*

Stuttering is a communication disorder in which the flow of speech is broken. It affects roughly 5 percent of children at some period of their lives. Stuttering may have different causes in different children. Factors that can contribute to the development of stuttering include genetics, other physical developmental delays, and brain chemistry. Most children affected recover by late childhood, but seeking an evaluation by a speech and language pathologist is advisable.

Critical Thinking

List the steps you would take to get information about a child who has delayed speech and language. Is the child receiving speech therapy? If so what can you do to support the speech therapist? With a partner, discuss how teachers can best assist children who show signs of language disorders.

Diversity Awareness

Diversity refers to the individual qualities people have that make them different from one another. School-age children are aware of differences and similarities. They see differences in gender, race, culture, and physical and mental abilities. They need role models who hold positive attitudes about diversity. Diversity should be discussed openly and honestly. Programs that include children from many economic, social, and cultural backgrounds help children accept and celebrate diversity. A diverse environment helps school-age children become compassionate, tolerant, and accepting. This type of environment also helps children avoid stereotyped and prejudiced behavior.

READING CHECK ✔ **Analyze** How do the abilities and needs of school-age children affect their growth and development?

Managing School-Age Programs

The need for school-age care programs is great. Many children who need care outside school hours are left without adult supervision. Children who stay home alone before and after school are sometimes called **latchkey children**. This is because they carry a house key to let themselves in when no one else is at home. Children who are unsupervised can become bored and aimless, which can lead to more serious issues. And in the event of an accident or emergency, they may confront real danger.

School-Age Programs

School-age programs offer children a safe place to interact and learn until they can go to school or return home with an adult family member. These programs also bring peace of mind to parents who know their children are in a safe place. Families should compare their options when deciding on a child care program.

Most children in school-age programs are between ages six and ten. However, some may be as old as twelve. A typical program operates before school, from 6:00 A.M. to 9:00 A.M., and after school, from 2:00 P.M. to 6:00 P.M. On school holidays and during the summer, programs might be open all day.

Many school-age programs are part of a child care center. A bus or van takes children from the center to school in the morning and returns them in the afternoon. It is also becoming more common for elementary schools to offer before- and after-school care programs.

Ideally, a school-age group includes no more than twenty children, although some states allow more. Many states require one teacher per twenty children. However, one teacher for every ten children is most desirable. School-agers deserve to receive personal attention. Being able to share the day's events with an adult helps them build self-esteem and cope with academic and social pressures.

After-school care enhances the growth and development of school-age children but in a less structured manner than in the classroom. Quality programs provide school-agers chances for fun and for learning. They are safe but not stifling, stimulating but not stressful.

Learning through Play

Like younger children, school-agers love to learn by doing. Active play that includes a sense of fun and relaxation is very important. It also provides an important opportunity for exercise. Child care programs can provide school-age children with leisure time to pursue interests that cannot be fit into the regular school day, while still promoting all four areas of development. **Figure 17.3** explains several types of play that school-age children find engaging.

No matter what activity is offered, safety comes first for all children. School-agers often have a daring, sometimes impulsive nature. This makes it important for teachers to anticipate how they might use equipment and supplies during play. School-age children's greater strength and coordination requires sturdy equipment that will adequately support them.

Figure 17.3 **Play Promotes Development**

Learning Is Fun School-age children learn from a variety of experiences and activities.
What are some playtime activities you could create to promote a school-age child's development?

Type of Play	Activity	Development
Project-based Activities	• School-agers often want their play to have a "purpose." They find project-based activities engaging, such as gardening, class experiments, and building birdhouses for their homes. • School-age children can have fun working together to create their own newspaper or mock television station.	• Fun and active projects support children's quickly developing intellectual and physical skills. • These activities give them opportunities to apply math, reading, and science concepts they learn in school. • Projects also build their literacy, communication, and teamwork skills.
Games	• Cooperative games are very popular with school-agers, along with more advanced board and computer games. • Students enjoy active games such as races outside, team sports, and climbing activities.	• Cooperative games help children refine social skills and cement friendships. • Active games stimulate large and small muscles and motor skills, which support physical development.
Imagination and Pretend Play	• This age group enjoys using their imaginations and pretending. However, their dramatic interests are more detailed and structured than younger children. • These children love to write plays and then act them out together for other children or parents. • More extroverted children like to put on performances in which they improvise or stage dances and music.	• Imaginative play stimulates intellectual development. • Working together on a performance reinforces social skills and allows children to display their skills for peers, teachers, and parents. • Playing and working with art materials, and even blocks, is a great way for school-agers to stimulate creativity.

School-age supplies might have more intricate and complex pieces because of these children's greater dexterity and intellectual abilities. However, smaller pieces could be a choking hazard for younger children. These supplies must be maintained and stored properly to keep all children safe, especially if younger children will also play in the same area.

As with all program equipment, regular safety checks for indoor and outdoor resources is needed. School-agers can be included in these safety checks and help fix minor issues when age-appropriate. This helps children learn responsibility and builds their sense of pride as they contribute to everyone's well-being.

Environment

Classrooms in school-age programs should be casual and comfortable. A relaxed atmosphere helps children get the day off to a good start. It also helps them unwind after a long day at school. A well-planned child care classroom includes learning centers that offer interesting activities. There are also quiet areas in which children can read quietly, listen to music, or talk with a friend. Furnishings could include soft sofas or beanbag chairs and tables or desks for doing homework.

Learning centers for school-agers must be designed to meet these children's specific needs, with age-appropriate materials and activities. An arts and crafts area could include materials for drawing, painting, weaving, jewelry making, and photography. A science area provides for safe exploration. Ideally, programs should provide indoor and outdoor areas for active play. On-site elementary programs usually have access to the school gymnasium, playing fields, and sports equipment.

▼ **Engagement**

School-age children have diverse interests. *What learning center environments should be provided to engage school-age children?*

Daily Routines

School-agers need some predictable daily routines, but they also need variety and choices. Older children do not need all activities planned for them. Programs for school-agers strike a balance between routines and the freedom of unstructured time.

Daily routines include arrival and departure time both in the morning and in the afternoon. The arrival routine includes a greeting and a health check. After arrival, most programs schedule a planning time. Children hear the day's activity options so they can make choices. One or more group activities may be offered.

©KidStock/Blend Images LLC

Blocks of time are set aside for children to do activities they enjoy, such as playing checkers with a friend, reading for pleasure, or climbing on outdoor play equipment. Leisure time is especially necessary in the afternoon, after children have spent the day in school.

Meals are a large part of daily routines. Breakfast gets the day off to a good start. A healthful snack in the afternoon satisfies a child's hunger after school and helps meet nutritional needs. During the summer and on holidays, many programs serve breakfast, lunch, and two snacks. Meal routines should be calm and leisurely. To build skills and a sense of responsibility, children can help set tables and clear dishes.

All-day programs generally provide a rest time, especially for children six and seven years old. It is important for active, growing bodies to have ample rest for proper development.

Grooming and hygiene are other regular routines that are important for personal health. Basic hygiene such as washing hands frequently and brushing teeth after meals is important. The school-age years are a good time to help children realize they maintain better physical, dental, vision, and hearing health by cooperating with regular medical checks and attending to personal hygiene.

▲ **Healthful Snacks**

Child care programs monitor school-age children's nutrition by providing healthy meals and snacks. *What are some healthful options that early educators could offer as an after-school snack?*

Planning Activities

School-age programs are similar to programs for younger ages because teachers must continue to plan activities for all areas of development. The program should provide a reasonable balance between quiet, active, indoor, outdoor, large-group, and small-group experiences. Teachers must also know how to adapt activities to the space provided and time allotted.

Compared to teachers in preschool programs, teachers in school-age programs create less structured activities. Preschool teachers might plan for young children to make collage pictures of farm animals. School-age children would find this too restrictive. They need the freedom not only to decide whether to make a collage but also to determine the type of collage to make and how to make it. School-age children need stimulating options.

Creative child care professionals enjoy sharing their own hobbies such as cooking, computers, yoga, or dance. They discover new interests along with the children. They expand on the activities that children find most appealing. Teachers must also consider the wide age range of children in a school-age child care program. The needs, interests, and abilities of a six-year-old are very different from those of a twelve-year-old.

Community

School-age programs can be an ideal environment to help children learn about and participate in the world around them. *What types of activities can early educators create to help achieve these goals?*

Accommodating all ages can be a challenge. Sometimes organizing groups by age or separating groups into younger and older children works best. However, children also benefit from mixed-age groupings. Younger children look up to older ones and enjoy learning from them. Older children gain a sense of responsibility by watching out for younger ones and helping plan activities for them. Many experiences, such as a nature walk, can interest both younger and older children if early educators are sensitive to the needs of each age group.

Community Participation During school vacations, when children attend all-day child care programs, field trips can stimulate interest and provide new experiences. Invite parents to attend field trips whenever possible for increased supervision and to keep parents involved. Explore your community for good resources.

▶ Museums, aquariums, parks, and zoos are natural choices that allow for exploration.

▶ Children may also enjoy visiting an ethnic restaurant, an airport or train station, a recycling center, a bank, a plant nursery, or a bicycle shop.

▶ Participate in a class volunteer activity, such as picking up trash in a park or collecting food for a shelter.

▶ A swimming pool or other recreational facility is a fun choice.

▶ Field trips to parents' workplaces are also a good way to encourage parent involvement in the program.

Clubs and Special Activities Some programs for school-age children form clubs around a special theme. Clubs foster interests and build friendships. Clubs for children may include creative writing, photography, collecting trading cards, drama, and art. A survey of children's interests can help you decide which clubs to offer. Many programs also offer on-site **specialized lessons**, which are similar to clubs in that they allow children to apply skills, to expand interests, and to form friendships. Usually parents must pay an extra charge for these activities. Some examples of specialized lessons include gymnastics, piano lessons, and a foreign language.

READING CHECK **Recall** Define the term *latchkey children*.

Nurturing Development

School-age children do not need the constant supervision required for younger children. However, early educators play an important role in keeping up with their developmental needs. Teachers must also recognize and report to parents any delays in development. Children this age need chances to be active and to investigate their world. They need support from caring adults as they mature and expand their knowledge.

Physical Development

Early educators have the responsibility to give children opportunities to participate in physical activities. This helps with physical fitness. Large motor skills are needed when children

▶ play tag and other active games.

▶ hold relay races.

▶ play team sports such as T-ball and volleyball.

Noncompetitive activities also aid development. Children enjoy jumping rope, skating, using outdoor play equipment, and engaging in creative movement. Small motor skills and eye-hand coordination are strengthened through arts and crafts such as needlework, pottery, basket weaving, woodworking, and model building.

Another important aspect of physical development is helping school-age children learn responsible ways to groom themselves and to maintain hygiene. Appearance during this stage of childhood has a great impact on children's self-confidence. School-age girls and boys are concerned about their physical appearances. Asking school-agers to help preschoolers or younger siblings develop good hygiene habits is one way to reinforce them in school-agers. It gives school-agers a sense of responsibility as they learn they are role models for younger children.

▲ **Physical Activities**

School-age children enjoy participating in a variety of after-school activities. *What are some physical activities early educators can provide for children even if outdoor or indoor space is limited?*

Intellectual Development

School-age programs can provide enjoyable, interesting activities that promote intellectual development. School-agers like group games that challenge them to think and to solve problems. Many popular card, board, and computer games are fun and stimulate thinking skills. Microscopes, magnets, magnifiers, and prisms can encourage children to explore the natural world. Children's reference books help them identify native trees, flowers, butterflies, and birds.

School-agers often question adults more thoroughly about topics that interest or confuse them. Using language and communication skills to better understand the broader world is one of the key pursuits for this age group.

Optimize intellectual development and nurture language skills by creating quiet areas for leisure reading. Provide a library of paperback books for children to exchange. Keep in mind students who speak a language other than English. Provide various language experiences at different levels for these children.

Learning Styles

Scientists have studied learning styles, which are different ways of learning. Studies have shown that people learn more when they use a learning style or styles that work best for them. The most common learning styles are visual, auditory, and kinesthetic or tactile.

Procedure Use resources to research various learning styles. Form small groups and design a skill-based activity for school-age children. Create adjustments to the activity that would benefit several different learning styles. For example, you could teach children about gravity by posting notes for copying. You also could explain this concept verbally, show pictures or diagrams of the effects of gravity, or have children test gravity by dropping objects from different heights.

Write instructions for the basic activity and its variations. Explain how the variations help different learning styles. Test your activity on other groups in your class. Display the instructions for all the variations, and ask students to choose the method that they think would best help them learn.

Analysis Ask students to record their impressions of your group's activity. Did they thoroughly learn the concept, or would another learning style have benefitted them more? After all the groups have tested their activities, participate in a class discussion. Can you draw any conclusions about learning styles? How could you incorporate what you know about learning styles into the curriculum of a school-age child care program?

Creative Development

Encourage children to apply creativity and imagination to all areas of life and learning. Let them experiment with art materials and help decorate the classroom. Encourage them to make new types of structures with building blocks. Give them opportunities to write stories, poems, songs, and plays. Older children might put on a puppet show for the younger ones, using a script they write themselves and puppets they make.

Emotional Development

It is not always easy for school-age children to sort through their emotions. Early educators should be available to listen to school-age children's thoughts, feelings, and fears. They may help children recognize their emotions by naming them for the children. In particular, teachers can be a valuable resource for children who are confused about peer relationships. Providing this emotional security is an important responsibility of child care professionals.

Teachers can give school-agers opportunities to examine their emotions. One way is through drama and other creative activities. School-agers may also keep a diary or record their feelings by audio. (Ensure privacy when this is done.) Teachers can supply good books about dealing with school-age emotions. Children from different cultures might express feelings in different ways. When selecting books, consider the different cultures of the children and offer books that accurately portray different ethnic groups.

Building Self-Esteem

School-age children are capable of making more decisions and assuming greater responsibilities. Chances to do so build their self-esteem. Younger school-age children may be given a choice of snacks from a selection of nutritious foods. An older child may be responsible for organizing books in the reading area.

Encouraging pride in children's cultural background is another way to boost self-esteem. Invite children to share foods, celebrations, history, and other aspects of their cultural heritage. Display posters made by students that depict their families and cultures. Children who are secure in their cultural identity tend to be more accepting of other cultural groups.

©Comstock/Alamy

Social Development

Cooperative projects help children develop social skills. Children might work together to paint a mural, to construct a papier-mâché dinosaur, or to prepare a meal. Planning parties is a good exercise in cooperation and teamwork. Field trips expand children's awareness of their community, as can special classroom visitors. Include parents as guest speakers—not only can they share information about their work, but they will also enjoy visiting their children's classroom.

▲ **Working Together**

These children are working together to complete a science project. *How do cooperative projects promote social development?*

Guiding Behavior

Early educators' guidance techniques will vary. Some teachers are permissive and leave most decisions up to children without giving feedback. Authoritarian discipline involves adults setting rules and enforcing them with punishment. Most states outlaw physical punishment of any age child in a child care settings.

Clear, specific guidance expressed consistently in a respectful but assertive manner is most effective with school-agers. A caring but firm teacher helps children feel more secure with adult authority. Teachers should be assertive about expectations and developmentally appropriate consequences.

The principles of positive guidance apply to all age groups, but teachers must consider each child's level of development. School-agers need fewer restrictions than preschoolers. They also have greater expectations for responsible behavior. All children can be taught to respect the property of others. Older children can see how this principle requires them to take care of the program's equipment so that all can enjoy it.

As children move toward independence, they may still test the limits set for them. School-agers may begin to challenge adult authority with their growing language and communication skills. Teachers must establish clear, firm boundaries for acceptable behavior. During this stage of childhood, adults have to consistently enforce rules and consequences more often.

School-age children are more likely to follow rules when they help create them. Discussing and voting on rules teaches children to consider the needs and wishes of others. They also learn to compromise to reach an agreement. Teachers show respect for children by speaking courteously when discussing rules. This allows teachers to model appropriate discussions while building students' self-esteem.

READING CHECK ✓ **Paraphrase** What are some strategies a teacher can use to optimize emotional development and to build self-esteem?

Corbis/AGE Fotostock

College & Career READINESS

Playground Engineer

What Does a Playground Engineer Do?

Playground engineers work to meet safety requirements for children's playground products. They use science to test products for things such as strength and durability, as well as test how the products will be affected by general use. They also conduct research to predict how weather, such as lots of sun or rain, will affect playground products. This research allows playground engineers to find solutions to problems with equipment and to make sure it is safe for children to use.

Career Readiness Skills

Playground engineers should be creative, inquisitive, and detail oriented. They need to have a strong interest in and aptitude for science and mathematics. Strong analytical skills and the ability to communicate both orally and in writing are also important. They should also have good teamwork skills.

Education and Training

A bachelor's degree in engineering is required for many entry-level jobs. Engineers trained in one branch often end up working in related branches, allowing engineers to shift to fields with better employment prospects or in which they are more interested. Shifting fields also gives a well-trained engineer more opportunities such as consulting work or starting his or her own firm.

Job Outlook

Employment of engineers is expected to grow much faster than the average for all occupations. New construction and a growing population contribute to the demand for engineers. However, in places that face a decline in construction, fewer jobs may be available. Opportunities will be best for those engineers who are able to distinguish themselves.

Critical Thinking Think about your personal interests, aptitudes, and abilities in the field of science and technology. Write a paragraph explaining how your characteristics would or would not fit well with this field. Consider the educational requirements for a career in this field and then propose the possible short- and long-term goals that will help you prepare for this career.

Career Cluster

Science, Technology, Engineering, and Mathematics Playground engineers work in the Engineering and Technology pathway of this career cluster. Here are some other jobs in this career cluster:

- Experimental Psychologist
- Child Development Researcher
- Zoologist
- Research Technician
- Anthropologist
- Biomedical Engineer
- Communications Engineer
- Geneticist
- Science or Math Teacher
- Cognitive Engineer

Explore Further The Science, Technology, Engineering, and Mathematics career cluster contains two pathways: Engineering and Technology and Science and Math. Choose one of these pathways to explore further.

Teaching School-Age Children
Visual Summary

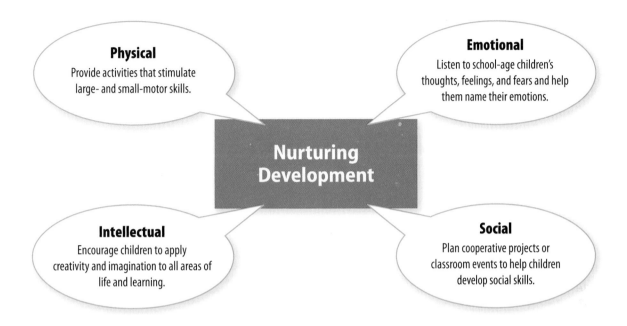

Physical
Provide activities that stimulate large- and small-motor skills.

Emotional
Listen to school-age children's thoughts, feelings, and fears and help them name their emotions.

Nurturing Development

Intellectual
Encourage children to apply creativity and imagination to all areas of life and learning.

Social
Plan cooperative projects or classroom events to help children develop social skills.

Vocabulary Review

1. Create flash cards for the content and academic vocabulary terms. Review them with a partner.

Content Vocabulary

◇ growth plateau (p. 366)
◇ puberty (p. 366)
◇ hormones (p. 366)
◇ depth perception (p. 367)
◇ concrete operations period (p. 368)

◇ industry (p. 369)
◇ inferiority (p. 369)
◇ diversity (p. 374)
◇ latchkey children (p. 374)
◇ specialized lessons (p. 378)

Academic Vocabulary

■ abstractly (p. 368)
■ refine (p. 370)

Review Key Concepts

2. Describe the overall development of school-age children.
3. Explain the need for school-age child care programs.
4. Describe an appropriate program for school-age children that promotes growth, development, and interpersonal skills.
5. Identify ways to nurture the overall development of school-age children.

Critical Thinking

6. Explain how improved motor and perceptual motor skills influence school-age children's activities.
7. Discuss considerations in planning schedules, routines, and activities for school-age children.

8. **Compare** how the options for child care for a school-age child might differ from the options for an infant, a toddler, or a preschooler.

9. **Contrast** friendship among preschoolers to that of school-age children. How does a child's level of social development change at this age?

10. **Draw Conclusions** about the ideal environment for an after-school program for school-age children. Include details about the facility, any food provided, center activities, and staffing.

⭐ 21ˢᵗ Century Skills

Civic Responsibility Skills

11. **Volunteer** Citizens have a responsibility to contribute to their community. As a child care student, you are developing abilities that will help you work effectively with young children. Find a school-age child care program in your community, and contact the director. If possible, arrange to volunteer with a school-age class. Be sure to use developmentally and age-appropriate activities as you interact with these students. Write a brief report to share your experiences and explain how you implemented your activities.

Media Literacy Skills

12. **TV Programs That Teach** Think about a favorite educational television program you viewed as a child. What did you enjoy about the program? What do you remember learning from it? Watch an educational television program for young school-age children. Divide a paper into two columns to take notes about the program. In the left column, summarize what is taking place in each segment of the show. In the right column, identify the development skills each segment is teaching.

Child Care LAB

Use the skills you have learned in this chapter.

Planning a School-Age Program

13. **Program Basics** Learning to plan a school-age program that broadens children's experiences will contribute to your success as a child care professional.

   A. Plan an after-school schedule for a school-age child care program. Include time for arrival, snack, homework, and guided and free-choice activities in your schedule.

   B. Create two developmentally appropriate activities for school-age children that support physical, emotional, intellectual, or social development. Keep in mind the importance of play in promoting development.

   C. Consider school-age children's need for routine, as well as freedom and flexibility when planning your schedule and activities. Make sure your schedule and activities allow for active and quiet time, as well as individual and small-group experiences.

   D. Think about any other factors that should be considered when providing programs for school-age children, such as classroom management strategies or cultural considerations for activities.

   E. Share your plan for the schedule and activities with a small group. If possible, implement your plan with a school-age child you know.

Create Your Evaluation

Work with a partner to assess your program plan using the following categories:

- Organization of schedule
- Developmentally appropriate
- Completeness of activities
- Consideration of other classroom factors

Evaluate each category on a scale of 1 to 10.

Academic Skills

English Language Arts

14. Classroom Guests Child care centers may invite special guests to a classroom. For example, a teacher may invite a local animal expert to teach children about animals in a fun, engaging manner. Make a list of special guests you could invite to a school-age classroom. Prepare a letter or an email inviting a guest to your classroom. Then prepare an introduction for this resource person to tell students when he or she arrives. Finally, write a sample thank-you letter to this person to express your gratitude for the visit.

Social Studies

15. Promote Social Skills Teachers play an important role in promoting social development in children. Think about how you could teach social skills and interpersonal skills to a school-age child. How could you help him or her communicate with peers and feel accepted in a group? Develop two activities that can promote this development. Also consider how you might need to adjust these strategies for a child with special needs.

Mathematics

16. Pricing a Field Trip Field trips are excellent tools for child care professionals. They allow students to gain knowledge and new experiences. A child care center wants to set up a field trip for children to an art museum. The price of the tour is $5 for children and $10 for adults. The museum requires one adult per five children. Forty children have permission to attend the field trip. If the center takes the required number of chaperones plus two extra teachers, how much will this field trip cost?

Math Concept **Mathematical Operations** An operation in math is a procedure that generates a new value. Addition, subtraction, multiplication, and division are examples of mathematical operations.

Starting Hint Divide the number of children by 5 to find the total number of chaperones required by the museum. Add 2 to this number for the extra teachers. Then multiply by $10 to find the total cost for the adults attending the field trip. Use this information after you determine the cost for the children.

 For more math practice, go to the math appendix at the back of the book.

Certification Prep

Sharpen your test-taking skills to improve your certification program score.

Directions Read each sentence, and choose the best term to fill in the blank.

17. Children learn to think more rationally and to solve problems during the _____.

- **A.** preoperational period
- **B.** concrete operations period
- **C.** sensorimotor period
- **D.** recess period

18. If school-age children do not feel productive, they will develop a sense of _____, a feeling of not having met expected standards.

- **A.** wonder
- **B.** industry
- **C.** depth perception
- **D.** inferiority

Test-Taking Tip
If you do not know the answer to a question, first cross off on another sheet of paper any choices you know are wrong. This will make it easier to evaluate the remaining ones.

CHAPTER 18

Inclusion of Children with Special Needs

Writing Activity

⭐ 21ˢᵗ Century Skills

Responsibility Many things affect the care of children with special needs. Write a descriptive paragraph about the factors you should consider when caring for special needs children. Edit your paragraph to add or adjust information and facts after learning more about the topic in this chapter.

Writing Tips

1. Use descriptions to bring your subject to life.
2. Write a strong topic sentence.
3. Think about your senses as you choose details. The sentences in your paragraph should support your main idea.
4. Edit your work at least once after reading this chapter.

Explore the Photo Children with special needs often require accommodations. *What skills allow you to meet the needs of these children?*

©Ariel Skelley/Blend Images LLC

Reading Guide

Two-Column Notes Two-column notes are a useful way to study and organize what you have read. Divide a piece of paper into two columns. In the left column, write main ideas. In the right column, list supporting details.

Read to Learn

Key Concepts

- **Identify** and define the three areas of development in which special needs occur.
- **Describe** some specific needs of children with disabilities and gifted children.
- **Explain** the meaning of inclusion and why it is practiced.
- **Outline** ways to adapt a child care program to meet special needs.

Main Idea

Children with special needs can learn in regular classrooms with other children their age. They can be taught and helped by adapting the classroom and curriculum to be more appropriate for their needs.

Content Vocabulary

◇ special needs
◇ accommodations
◇ learning disability
◇ aphasia
◇ dyslexia
◇ dyscalculia
◇ learning specialists
◇ attention deficit hyperactivity disorder
◇ autism spectrum disorder
◇ inclusion
◇ Individualized Family Service Plan
◇ Individualized Education Program
◇ accessible

Academic Vocabulary

■ prohibits
■ encounter

Graphic Organizer

As you read, you will learn about plans for the education of children with special needs called Individualized Education Programs. These documents have six areas of discussion. Use an idea wheel like the one shown below to record the areas and your notes about each area.

Individualized Education Program (IEP)

Graphic Organizer *Go to* **connected.mcgraw-hill.com** *to print this Graphic Organizer.*

AS YOU READ

Connect Think about the characteristics of an early childhood professional that would be especially important for working with children with special needs.

Vocabulary

You can find definitions in the glossary at the back of this book.

Meeting Needs

When planning an early childhood center, plans should include accessibility requirements for children who use wheelchairs and other mobility devices. *What environmental qualities would make a center user-friendly for children?*

Development and Care

The unique development and abilities of children vary. In any classroom, some children may be developmentally ahead, and some may take longer to develop. Some children with special needs require extra attention. Sensitive early care and education professionals respond to them with these needs in mind. They plan activities so all children can participate to the best of their abilities.

Defining Special Needs

The term **special needs** refers to circumstances that cause a child's physical, cognitive, or behavioral development to vary significantly from the norm. Some children with special needs have disabilities such as vision and hearing problems, limited mobility, mental retardation, or learning difficulties. Other children who learn and develop more quickly than others may be gifted. As an example, a child who is physically disabled may be a gifted writer or artist.

It is important to think of children with special needs as children first and as people with disabilities second. Like all children, those with special needs have the same basic desire to be loved, accepted, and respected. Each child requires a secure, nurturing, and stimulating environment.

Laws Impacting Special Needs

As a means to help parents, teachers, and other advocates ensure that children with disabilities have their needs met, certain laws exist that offer safeguards in obtaining a free and appropriate education. The key laws concerning children with special needs include:

▶ **Individuals with Disabilities Education Act (IDEA).** IDEA guarantees free special education and related services to all children with disabilities, ages 3 to 21. An individualized program of goal-oriented instruction is designed to meet the needs of each child. Parents must be included in the planning process. Related services may include speech, physical, and occupational therapies.

▶ **Americans with Disabilities Act (ADA).** This civil rights law prohibits discrimination on the basis of a disability in public services, accommodations, and employment. The ADA requires that all children be eligible for child care services. This law provides for equal access to public and private services and facilities. For example, a ramp may need to be installed for wheelchair access to a child care center.

▶ **Rehabilitation Act, Section 504.** Like the ADA, this law **prohibits**, or forbids, discrimination against persons with disabilities. This law states that people with disabilities should have an equal chance to be successful. The services and protections of this law extend beyond IDEA to cover people from birth to death and are not related to specific categories of disabilities.

READING CHECK ✔ **Recall** What laws impact the care and education of children with special needs?

Specific Disabilities

In order for children with special needs to participate more fully, sometimes changes are made in a classroom. Such changes are called **accommodations**. The information that follows identifies characteristics and accommodations for those with special needs or disabilities.

Hearing Impairments

Difficulty in hearing ranges from mild impairment to total deafness. Hearing problems interfere with language development and other areas of learning. Social relationships can be more challenging for those who have hearing problems. Here are some ways that children with hearing impairments communicate:

▶ **Hearing aids and cochlear implants.** Some children have limited to almost full hearing with the use of hearing aids or cochlear implants. Child care professionals should ask parents to teach them how to handle the device properly. Hearing aids have limitations. A child who uses one cannot be expected to hear a teacher who is at the other end of the room. Hearing aids make all sounds louder. Early childhood teachers should reduce distracting background noise whenever possible.

▶ **Sign language.** Some hearing-impaired children use American Sign Language to communicate with others. Teachers should become familiar with sign language to communicate with the hearing-impaired child. The child care program may also provide an interpreter skilled in sign language to help with a child's communication skills.

▼ **Helping the Hearing Impaired**

A hearing-impaired child may use various methods of communicating, such as lipreading or American Sign Language. *How can all child care professionals benefit from learning sign language?*

▶ **Lipreading.** When a child lip-reads, make sure you face the child when you speak. Communicate with the child at eye level and face the light if possible. Lipstick helps draw attention to a female care provider's lips. Male teachers should be clean-shaven so that lips can be easily seen. Lip movement should be distinct but natural. Children who read lips should sit directly in front of the teacher during group activities. Facial expressions and frequent gestures help convey meaning.

▶ **Visual helps.** Props, pictures, and hands-on experiences help children with hearing impairments learn. You might illustrate a story's plot as you read it, for example. During music time, let a child with a hearing impairment feel the vibration of the musical instrument. Clapping along with music lets the child sense a song's rhythm. Use visual cues—such as turning the lights on and off—to signal transitions between activities.

▼**Adapting Curriculum**

. . . .

Tools, like this Braille type-writer, allow many children with disabilities to partici-pate in the same activities that other children enjoy. *What reading activities could this child participate in with his or her classmates?*

Vision Impairments

Vision impairments range from mild loss to total blindness. Children with severe vision impairments need consistent physical arrangements in the classroom. They memorize room setups to help identify clear pathways. High-contrast color tape along the edges of the furniture gives visual cues to children with minimal vision loss. Always provide consistent storage for all classroom materials. Cubbies can be marked with bows, feathers, or large buttons. To help children with severe vision loss, use plastic labels with raised print or Braille labels. Braille is the system of writing for the blind that uses characters made of raised dots.

Encourage children to use their other senses to move around the classroom. For example, point out that paints and clay make the art center smell different from other areas of the room. Mark different parts of the room with items that can be felt, heard, or smelled. Vision impairments interfere with learning by limiting cognitive associations. Child care professionals must use the child's other senses to motivate learning.

To adapt activities, use words and hands-on experiences as much as possible. For example, during a garden activity, let the child touch and smell the soil and the seeds. Guide the child's hand as you dig with the spade, while describing what is happening. Let the child hear and feel the drops from the watering can. In the classroom, provide toys of many different shapes, textures, and weights, especially ones that move or make sounds. Provide safe, open areas for small and large motor activities, such as creating a mural or running outdoors.

Many books and games are available in large-print versions to benefit children with impaired vision. Early childhood teachers can enlarge some classroom materials for easier viewing. Children who are blind can listen to recorded stories or music.

Physical and Motor Impairments

Some children have physical conditions that affect their large or small motor abilities. They may use crutches, a walker, or a wheelchair to get around. They may have poor muscle control or be missing part of an arm or leg. All of these conditions create challenges, but none should prevent a child from participating in a program.

The first step in making accommodations is to ensure that the building is accessible. If a child uses a wheelchair, doors and pathways need to be wide enough for easy access. Toilets, sinks, towel dispensers, and drinking fountains must be reachable from a wheelchair. If a child has limited use of his or her hands, faucets in hand-washing areas must be easy to operate. Remember that the goal is to provide all children in the classroom with the same level of independence.

Classroom routines, play equipment, and activities may also need adaptations. Many solutions do not require much time or expense— just some creative thinking. For example, you may need to provide

▶ double-handled cups to use at mealtime.

▶ puzzle pieces and toys fitted with large knobs for easier handling or suction cups that help hold them steady.

▶ raised sandboxes to accommodate children in wheelchairs, and beanbags attached to long pieces of string to make them easier to retrieve when playing target games.

▶ chairs with seat straps for children who cannot easily sit upright.

Cognitive Impairments

Like physical impairments, cognitive disabilities may be mild, moderate, or severe. Children who are cognitively challenged develop intellectual abilities more slowly than others. These children may have shorter-than-average attention spans. Motor skills and eye-hand coordination are often affected. Some show less emotional control and have fewer social skills than other children.

Children with cognitive impairments may be placed in a classroom according to their developmental abilities. These children respond well when given short, clear directions. You may need to break down activities into simple steps. You may also need to guide these children more closely. Demonstrate and repeat activities as often as needed. Give children many chances for success.

Learning Disabilities

A disorder that affects the way the brain processes information is called a **learning disability**. It is not the same as a mental impairment. In fact, many children with learning disabilities have above-average intelligence. However, because they cannot interpret and use information in a typical way, learning may be hindered. Learning disabilities can be caused by errors in fetal brain development, alcohol and drug use during pregnancy, problems during birth, or toxins in the environment. The cause of many learning disabilities is unknown. Many specific types of learning disabilities exist. Here are some examples:

▲ **Learning Disabilities**

Children with learning disabilities often need extra help when working on specific learning areas. *What resources could you use to help a child with a learning disability?*

▶ **Speech and written language disorders.** Children may have difficulty understanding spoken and written language or have difficulty speaking. A disorder called **aphasia** (ə-ˈfā-zh(ē-)ə) is a language impairment that affects a child's use of speech and understanding of language.

▶ **Reading disorders.** With the common reading disorder **dyslexia** (dis-ˈlek-sē-ə), a child may have trouble learning to recognize letters of the alphabet and difficulty reading. With dyslexia, the letters may appear backwards or jumbled or seem to move around on the page.

▶ **Math disorders.** A disorder related to math skills is called **dyscalculia** (dis-ˈkal-kyə-ˈlē-ə). The child may be unable to count objects or recognize basic shapes.

▶ **Reasoning and memory disorders.** These disorders are often caused by severe head injuries. Children with a reasoning disorder may have difficulty organizing learned facts or organizing and integrating thoughts. Children with a memory disorder may have trouble remembering instructions and what they have learned.

Mental Retardation

Mental retardation may be characterized by less-than-average intelligence and limited adaptive skills such as self-care skills and social skills. Mental retardation is a permanent condition. It appears sometime during early childhood and must be carefully diagnosed by a team of people, such as a psychologist, a physician, a learning specialist, and the child's parents. When parents suspect their child may have a problem, they often seek outside assessment before the child starts preschool or elementary school. Children with mental retardation have varying levels of skills, but all can learn.

Professionals trained to identify learning disorders and those that help children overcome them are called **learning specialists**. They can help children learn to use various ways of gathering, organizing, and interpreting information. Counselors can help children deal with behavioral and self-esteem problems associated with learning disabilities. Child care professionals work closely with parents and specialists to determine how best to teach the child.

Behavioral and Emotional Disorders

All children occasionally have trouble relating to others or coping with their emotions. Their behavior may be aggressive or overly active at times. With some children, however, emotional or behavioral problems are frequent and extreme. Their behavior interferes with learning. These children may be diagnosed with a behavioral or emotional disorder. For example, children may be withdrawn, depressed, anxious, unusually fearful, or violent. Children with behavioral and emotional disorders require professional help. Medication may be prescribed by a medical doctor to control the symptoms. Psychological therapy can also be helpful. The classroom atmosphere should be a calm, consistent, and nurturing one. Teachers should also make sure they understand the child's culture and assist the child in expressing feelings in culturally appropriate ways. Two of the most common examples of such disorders follow.

▲ **Early Diagnosis**

Parents or child care professionals may notice that a child has a learning difficulty or developmental challenge at an early age. *What are the benefits of early diagnosis?*

Attention Deficit Hyperactivity Disorder

A disorder of the central nervous system that is caused by a lack of certain brain chemicals is called **attention deficit hyperactivity disorder** (ADHD). Some children with ADHD have difficulty paying attention and following instructions. Others are aggressive, impulsive, and overly active. Some show a combination of these symptoms. ADHD is not a learning disability; however, sometimes children with a learning disability may have ADHD. Children with ADHD can learn appropriate behavior and may be treated with certain medications.

Autism Spectrum Disorder

Typically affecting communication and social interaction, **autism spectrum disorder** is a brain disorder that impacts normal development. Children with autism can vary in language

skills and intelligence and may show a variety of characteristics. Some children may repeat actions, such as rocking or playing with a favorite toy, and may become upset when routines change. Autistic children may be very sensitive to touch, sound, light, or smell. Some people with autism display exceptional skills in one particular area, such as art, music, or completing complex puzzles.

Diagnosing autism is not easy. Several conditions can mimic autism. The parents and pediatrician must rule out these other disorders before a team of specialists begins the process of identifying autism. Specialists must observe clear evidence of poor social relationships, underdeveloped communication skills, and repetitive behaviors, interests, and activities. Early intervention and special education can help autistic children learn, communicate, and have productive social relationships.

Health Conditions

Some children have health conditions—such as asthma, epilepsy, or diabetes—that may affect how they participate in activities. Some health conditions require medications to be administered while a child is in group care. When medications are administered, teachers should discuss a child's health profile with the parents and the child's doctor.

Accommodating Health Conditions

Accommodating children's individual health conditions sometimes requires child care staff to make adjustments in how activities are conducted. Accommodation may require a teacher to be prepared to cope with an unpredictable health emergency. A child highly allergic to bee stings needs to be included on outdoor walks. However, an alert provider would avoid walking in areas where bees may visit. If applicable, the teacher would include the child's bee sting medication in a first aid kit taken along during the walk.

Gifted and Talented Children

Gifted children are those who have extraordinary talent in one or more areas. Some children are intellectually gifted. Others excel in some form of artistic expression, such as music or art. Exceptional athletes have physical talents and abilities. Signs indicating giftedness include

▶ a good memory and advanced vocabulary and language skills.

▶ ease in grasping new concepts and ideas.

- developmental skills—such as walking and talking—that are acquired earlier than usual in infancy than most peers.
- creativity in inventing and problem solving.
- intense curiosity and advanced attention span with an ability to concentrate on and persist in complex tasks.
- an unusual attention to detail.
- a preference for the company of older playmates and adults.
- a good sense of humor.
- talent for making plans and organizing tasks.

Gifted children need programs that challenge them at their advanced developmental levels. Otherwise they lose interest and do not bother to do their best. They may misbehave out of boredom. Care staff can respond to gifted children in many ways. They may, for example,

- plan enrichment activities that explore concepts in more depth.
- plan group projects and involve gifted children in the planning and organizing.
- include field trips and special visitors to help satisfy a gifted child's intellect, as well as stimulate and motivate other children.

Because they pay close attention to detail, gifted children often take longer to complete projects to their satisfaction. Allow them large blocks of time to thoroughly investigate topics. Avoid rushing them through projects.

Children who excel in a particular area, such as dance or music, should be given adequate opportunity to develop their skills. If lessons or experiences outside the program are not available to the child, recruit a volunteer talented in that area.

READING CHECK ✓ **Identify** What characteristics may indicate a child is gifted?

▲ **Specific Talents**

Some children are gifted or talented with certain abilities in one or more areas, while at the same time they lose interest in other areas. *What should care providers do to accommodate the needs of children with special gifts and talents?*

Pixtal/AGE Fotostock

Inclusive Programs

Research shows that children with special needs learn best when they learn from positive role models in the natural environment. The Individuals with Disabilities Education Act (IDEA) is a federal law that states that children with disabilities must be educated with children who are not disabled whenever possible. This is called **inclusion**, or integrating children with special needs into regular education classrooms. The Americans with Disabilities Act (ADA) further ensures equal access opportunities for people with disabilities in all public areas.

These laws mean that children with disabilities cannot legally be excluded from public child care programs. Private programs have the same obligation, unless the cost of including such children is financially impossible.

Providers can explore many resources to locate the items they need for serving children who have disabilities. The Easter Seals organization is one source of information, assistance, and referral. Volunteers, training programs, and special funding may also be available through community resources.

▼**Additional Training**

Successful inclusive programs begin with early childhood educators who understand special needs and focus on the abilities, rather than the disabilities, of children. *Investigate the requirements to be a special education teacher.*

Realistic Reflections

Supportive Early Childhood Professionals

Successful inclusion begins with positive attitudes among child care staff. Those who accept and respect children with special needs serve as models for others. Staff attitudes set the tone for the classroom, helping create a comfortable atmosphere for everyone. Effective early childhood educators focus on abilities of these children, not their disabilities. They find out what children with disabilities can do and encourage them to work to their potential.

As much as possible, treat a child with special needs as any other. Expect no more or less than the child is capable of doing. Show patience and understanding. As with all children, avoid labeling. Children should not be defined by their disabilities.

Acceptance and Understanding

When children **encounter**, or first see or meet, something new, they are usually curious about it. They may also be fearful at first. Meeting someone who has a disability is no different. A person who wears leg braces, or someone whose speech is slurred because of a mental disability, may seem strange and puzzling to many young children. Early childhood staff can minimize these natural reactions by helping children better understand disabilities. For example, a teacher could show a hearing aid and explain how it works, or could invite a sign language interpreter to speak to the class.

Teachers can promote understanding in many ways. Books are available to help children of various ages understand differences. Special puppet programs feature characters who talk about their disabilities. In one outreach project, dolls with special needs are sent home with children without disabilities. The dolls come with letters that describe their special needs and suggest things the family can do to make their stay more pleasant.

In addition to learning about disabilities, children need to see that people who are different are part of everyday life. Display posters and pictures that show children of varying abilities playing together. Provide stories that affirm disabilities without making them the focus of the plot. In the dramatic play area, include dolls, puppets, and dollhouse figures that represent children with special needs. Invite adults with special needs to the program as guest speakers. Ask them to talk about their hobbies, talents, or careers. This helps children see that people with varying needs can lead independent and successful lives.

Benefits of Inclusion

Inclusion encourages children to value diversity. They learn to be compassionate, respectful, and appreciative of those different from themselves. By

▼ **Inclusion**

All children benefit when children with special needs are a part of the class. *How could inclusion benefit the parents of children with special needs?*

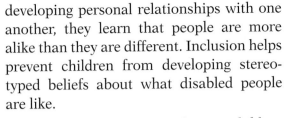

developing personal relationships with one another, they learn that people are more alike than they are different. Inclusion helps prevent children from developing stereotyped beliefs about what disabled people are like.

By attending regular classes, children with special needs learn to function as normally as possible in the world. They can attend a school or child care facility in a convenient location rather than traveling long distances to a special school. In the past, many children with special needs did not have the opportunity to attend any type of educational program until school age. Including those children in infant, toddler, and preschool care programs provides them with enriching experiences they might otherwise miss.

Managing Inclusive Programs

The education of children with special needs has changed greatly in recent decades. In the past, children with special needs were automatically assigned to special education classes or special schools. For some, that remains the best option. However, people are recognizing the value of including children with special needs in regular classrooms.

Goals of Inclusive Programs

Research shows that children with and without disabilities benefit from inclusion. Goals of inclusive programs should

▶ provide all children with enriching experiences they might otherwise miss.

▶ encourage compassion, respect, and appreciation for all to help all children value diversity.

▶ help all children recognize and cope with their strengths and limitations.

▶ encourage children to be comfortable with, rather than fearful of, disabilities.

▶ allow children with special needs to participate in an everyday setting.

▶ provide ways for parents of children with special needs to interact with other parents.

▶ refer parents of all children to needed support services.

McGraw-Hill Education

▶ **Supporting the Family**

Child care professionals do their best to support parents of children with special needs by listening and connecting them with resources. *What agencies and organizations might you recommend to a parent looking for help?*

Staffing and Group Size

Depending on the type and extent of a child's disability, some individual instruction and assistance may be required. Some children may need extra help during basic care routines such as dressing, feeding, and toileting. Others may need assistance moving throughout the classroom or the building. For these reasons, the number of children in the classroom may be fewer.

In addition, an extra caregiver, assistant, or trained volunteer may be needed to give extra individualized help and guidance. To make sure a child is well cared for, many programs assign a primary caregiver to a child with special needs. It is the primary caregiver's responsibility to make sure the child participates in all routines and activities in a meaningful way. This person also assists the child with self-care tasks such as toileting, diapering, and hand washing, if necessary.

Children with severe impairments may need to be assisted or taught by someone with specialized education and training. Many colleges have courses and degree programs relating to children with special needs.

Working with Parents

Parents of children with special needs are a valuable resource for early childhood professionals. They can provide specific information about their child's disability, individual needs, medications, habits, and day-to-day changes. In return, classroom teachers must keep parents informed. Parents naturally want to know what the program is doing for their child and how their child is progressing. They also have a right to take part in decisions regarding their child's care and education. Encourage parents to observe the program on a regular basis. After observation times, a conference

Onoky/SuperStock

allows parents and teachers to ask questions and to share insights.

Parents of children with special needs have many concerns. They may worry about their child being rejected by others or whether they are doing everything they can to help their child. These parents must make difficult decisions about care, educational programs, and medical treatment. Sensitive child care staff are supportive as they listen and respond to parents' concerns. They also refer parents to appropriate sources of help and information.

READING CHECK ✔ **Discuss** How do children benefit from an inclusive program?

▲ **IFSPs**

Individualized Family Service Plans allow teachers, parents, and specialists to work together to best meet a child's needs. *What is covered in an IFSP?*

Serving Children with Special Needs

Like all children, those with special needs benefit from activities and experiences designed to nurture their physical, intellectual, emotional, and social development. When children are younger than age three, they may be enrolled in early intervention programs, which are sponsored by local public schools. In such programs, staff and parents cooperatively create an **Individualized Family Service Plan** (IFSP). This is a plan created to make sure goals are set to meet a child's overall needs. It includes an assessment of a child's development, goals for development, and specific ways to promote and support a family's involvement. It is particularly focused on the family and how providing support for the family allows for greater support of the child. An IFSP also includes plans for creating environments and routines in the home and in community settings.

For children with special needs who are age three or older, public school administrators, parents, teachers, and specialists work together to create an Individualized Education Program for each child. An **Individualized Education Program** (IEP) is a written document that outlines how to encourage development in a child who has special needs. It is focused on the child's educational needs and is required by the IDEA law and must include the following information:

▶ Current level of the child's abilities

▶ Annual goals for the child's development

▶ Short-term educational goals

Realistic Reflections

- Educational services to be provided
- The procedure for determining whether the program's goals are being met
- Degree to which the child will be included in a regular classroom. Some children may need to spend part of the day receiving special services from a therapist.

Adapting the Environment

The most enriching program will not benefit a child who cannot attend because of physical barriers. Making the physical environment **accessible**, or easily used by those with disabilities, is important. Teachers, children, parents, and others should work together to identify and remove barriers and safety hazards so children with special needs can explore the environment safely.

Adapting the Curriculum

To make sure children are not isolated, avoid planning separate activities for children with special needs whenever possible. Creating separate activities emphasizes differences in the children, rather than similarities. Instead, plan activities in which all children can participate.

To accommodate individual children, modify the activity, the equipment, or the teaching method, as needed. For instance, all children enjoy and benefit from playing with puzzles. However, the degree of difficulty of the puzzle and how it is made can vary. A child with a mental impairment might work on a four-piece puzzle, while peers work on puzzles with eight pieces. A child with poor small motor control may be able to do an eight-piece puzzle but would need knobbed puzzle pieces that could be picked up and moved more easily.

Adapting Schedules and Routines

Routines such as eating, dressing for outdoor play, toileting, and transitions can be especially time-consuming for children with disabilities. Allow for extra time when planning the schedule. As with all children, encourage independence and self-help skills. Other children in the classroom may try to be helpful by doing things for the child who has a disability. Remind them that people like to do as much as possible for themselves.

Some children require special health care in their daily routines. This may include medicine, emergency treatment, or some form of therapy. Child care staff should request specific written instructions from parents to meet these needs.

READING CHECK **Describe** What does it mean for a program to be accessible?

A Matter of ETHICS

Workplace Attitudes

Many people are uncomfortable around children with special needs. Because most people do not have to learn about child development and special needs, they may not understand why a child with a disability behaves or looks the way he or she does.

Professional Responsibility

As a child care professional, you can help educate others on disabilities. This can involve your actions and talking with coworkers, parents, children, or others in the community.

Thinking Ethically

Your coworker refuses to work with people who have disabilities of any kind, and he openly comments that people with physical impairments should not participate in the center's activities. You disagree with your coworker's behavior. What would you do?

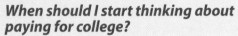

Paying for College

How Do I Pay for College?

It is one thing to decide what kind of education or training you need, but it is another to figure out how you are going to pay for it. Education costs can be expensive. You have to pay for tuition, books and supplies, room and board, and transportation. It is important to think about where the money is going to come from.

When should I start thinking about paying for college?

It is a good idea to start saving money as soon as you begin thinking about going to college. Consider taking a part-time job after school and a full-time job during school breaks. Start a savings account for college expenses, and do not use this money for any other purpose. Talk to your family. Depending on their income, they may be able to set aside money for your education in a special, tax-free account.

What are the possible sources of money for college?

Many students receive financial aid in the form of scholarships, grants, or loans. Scholarships are available from many organizations to help pay tuition costs. They often require you to prove financial need, but some are granted based on academic, athletic, or artistic talents. Grants are usually given on the basis of need and do not have to be repaid. Loans, which are offered by colleges and banks, must be repaid over a period of time. Education loans are usually offered at a lower interest rate than most other loans.

What can I do to learn more?

Each college has its own financial aid policy, and this information may or may not appear in the materials sent to you. It is a good idea to schedule a face-to-face or phone interview with a member of the financial aid staff who will be able to answer specific questions about costs, the financial aid process, and options for financing your education. Your high school guidance counselor will also have information on scholarships and grants that you can apply for.

Hands-On

Imagine you called a school and scheduled a meeting with someone in the financial aid office. To prepare for this meeting, come up with a list of questions you want to ask the financial aid officer. Make sure your questions cover everything you need to know about financial aid.

Path to Success

Start Early The sooner you start saving for college and doing research, the better prepared you will be.

Consider All Options High tuition is not a requirement for good education.

Apply for Financial Aid The majority of federal aid is based on financial need and not on grades.

Over-Apply The more aid you apply for, the higher the chances you will get the money you need.

Get Help There are many sources of assistance, including college financial aid offices, your guidance counselor, your parents, books, and Web sites.

Invest in Your Future Generally, the more education and training you receive, the more money you will be able to earn in the future.

Blend Images/SuperStock

Inclusion of Children with Special Needs
Visual Summary

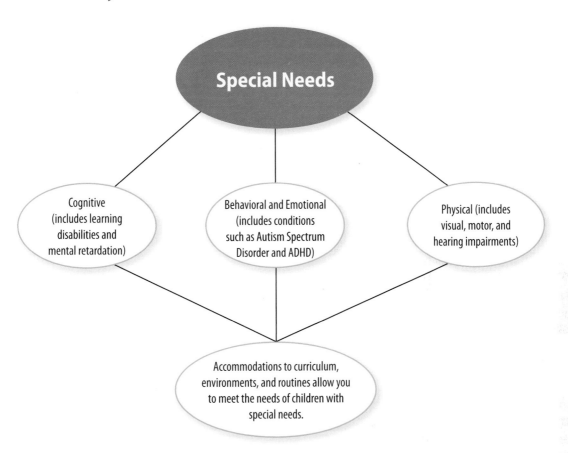

Vocabulary Review

1. Write your own definition for each content and academic vocabulary term.

Content Vocabulary

- special needs (p. 388)
- accommodations (p. 389)
- learning disability (p. 392)
- aphasia (p. 392)
- dyslexia (p. 392)
- dyscalculia (p. 392)
- learning specialists (p. 393)
- attention deficit hyperactivity disorder (p. 393)
- autism spectrum disorder (p. 393)
- inclusion (p. 396)
- Individualized Family Service Plan (p. 400)
- Individualized Education Program (p. 400)
- accessible (p. 401)

Academic Vocabulary

- prohibits (p. 389)
- encounter (p. 397)

Review Key Concepts

2. **Identify** and define the three areas of development in which special needs occur.
3. **Describe** some specific needs of children with disabilities and gifted children.
4. **Explain** the meaning of inclusion and why it is practiced.
5. **Outline** ways to adapt a child care program to meet special needs.

Critical Thinking

6. **Recall** How should care providers treat children with special needs as compared with other children?
7. **Focus** In what way can parents of children with special needs help care providers? In what way can care providers help parents?
8. **Analyze** How does the Individuals with Disabilities Education Act protect and support people with disabilities?
9. **Contrast** What is the difference between a mental disability and a learning disability?
10. **Examine** What modifications best challenge gifted children? Explain.

21st Century Skills

Media Literacy Skills

11. **Children's Characters** Find three children's books that feature characters with disabilities. Then look for three children's television shows that feature characters with special needs. Analyze the books and television shows for how the characters are portrayed and the roles they fulfill. Do the characters function independently and successfully? Record your feelings about the way in which persons with disabilities are characterized in each book and television show.

Technology Skills

12. **Monthly Activity Newsletter** Imagine that you are in charge of program activities for gifted students at your child care center. Use a word processing or desktop publishing software to create a monthly activity newsletter that describes the upcoming activities for gifted students that correspond with the center's monthly theme. Be creative in your selection of activities, and include activities for preschoolers and school-age children.

Child Care LAB

Use the skills you have learned in this chapter.

Inclusive Early Childhood Program

13. **Write an Inclusion Program Description** In this activity, you will work with a partner to write an inclusion program description for an early childhood center.

   A. **Research licensing laws.** Research your state's licensing laws for inclusion in child care programs. In your program description, explain how your program will meet the state requirements for children with special needs.

   B. **Determine child-teacher ratios.** In your description, include the number of children with special needs along with the total number of children to be cared for, the number of teachers, and their responsibilities.

   C. **Plan parent involvement.** Outline ways the program will work with parents of children with special needs. What resources will you provide? What connections can you make between parents and other organizations?

   D. **Assemble resources.** List resources available to teachers and parents that would provide support and information for an inclusive program. Include copies of an example IFSP and an IEP so that you are familiar with the forms.

   E. **Share your work.** Share your program description with your teacher and get suggestions for improvement.

Create Your Evaluation

Create a sheet with these categories:

- Licensing laws
- Child-teacher ratios
- Teacher responsibilities
- Parent involvement
- Inclusion resources

Ask your teacher to use the sheet to evaluate your program description, marking each category as Fully Meets, Meets, or Needs Improvement.

Academic Skills

English Language Arts

14. A Parent's Perspective Interview the parent of a child with disabilities, special health care needs, or signs of giftedness. What challenges has the parent faced in meeting the needs of his or her child? What are some of the influences the parent sees on the physical, emotional, social, and intellectual development of his or her child? Write a report summarizing your interview.

Social Studies

15. Modifying Activities Show how an activity might be adapted to meet the needs of children with special needs. Describe the activity as originally planned. Then explain how you would modify the activity for a child with a specific need. List the equipment needed, and explain the teaching method you would use. Demonstrate the activity and the adaptations to the class.

Science

16. Adapting to Disabilities Having a physical disability requires resourcefulness. Much of the world is not set up for people with physical disabilities. As a result, disabled individuals must develop solutions for performing tasks that others do without thought or take for granted. For example, a hearing-impaired student may need to sit in the front of a classroom in order to read lips or to see the hands of a signer.

Procedure Ask an adult with a physical disability if you could spend several hours with him or her. Observe how this person adapts to everyday activities. What things does this person do differently now than when he or she was younger? What things has he or she always done to compensate for his or her differences?

Analysis Write one or two paragraphs summarizing any modifications in daily routine this person makes to accommodate his or her disability. Explain how the person has modified his or her daily routine as he or she has gotten older, as well as the adaptations that he or she has always used. How would you use this knowledge when planning for a child with a similar disability?

Certification Prep

Sharpen your test-taking skills to improve your certification program score.

Directions Choose the phrase that best completes the sentence.

17. Special needs include _____.

    A. hearing and vision impairments

    B. behavioral disorders

    C. gifted and talented

    D. all of the above

18. Dyslexia is a _____.

    A. language impairment

    B. reading disorder

    C. math disorder

    D. memory disorder

Test-Taking Tip

In multiple-choice questions, do not go back and change an answer unless you made an obvious mistake the first time, such as misreading the question.

Growth and Development

Have you ever wondered what you can do to help children with developmental delays work toward meeting their goals?

Careers monitoring and ensuring the health, growth, and development of children include pediatricians, dentists, physician's assistants, social workers, and occupational therapists. In addition to medical care, these careers include those involving therapeutic services, support services, and research. People in all of these fields work to help children reach developmental milestones physically, emotionally, socially, and academically.

To succeed in growth and development careers, you may need a specific degree in your career field. These degrees can range from an associate's degree to a Ph.D.

Beth Bosak • Occupational Therapist

Q What is your job?

A I provide therapeutic interventions, adaptations, equipment and training to help support children with special needs to succeed in their educational setting as independently as possible.

Q Why did you choose your career?

A I chose my career at a young age. As an elementary student, I volunteered with special education students in my elementary building. Those experiences and the encouragement I received from the teachers there led me to pursue an occupational therapy career.

Q Who or what has been your biggest career influence?

A The clients or patients themselves. I have met all kinds of people, and I learn something that affects me and my character from each and every one of them. Seeing people meet their goals and progress in their abilities is very rewarding and keeps me going even when some days or periods of time can be very trying.

Q What education and training have you received?

A I received my Bachelor's of Science in Allied Medicine - Occupational Therapy. After I received my degree and completed the fieldwork requirements, I passed the National Board of Certification for Occupational Therapists examination. Later, I received my Master's of Health Sciences in Occupational Therapy.

Q What skills are most important in your job?

A Occupational therapists must be highly professional, possess excellent communication skills in speaking and in writing, have strong time management skills, and must be extremely flexible and adaptable. When working in educational settings, an occupational therapist must be patient, knowledgeable about the setting, willing to celebrate even small and slow successes, communicate effectively and respectfully with highly varied families and teachers involved in a child's environment.

Corbis/SuperStock

Career Requirements	
Education or Training	Growth and development careers generally require specific coursework in the field. Often, this means earning a master's degree or beyond. Careers such as a dental hygienist or a physician's assistant require at least an associate's degree.
Academic Skills	Science, Mathematics, and Language Arts
Aptitudes, Abilities, and Skills	Knowledge of health and child development, communications skills, and critical-thinking skills.
Career Outlook	There is currently a high demand for well-trained health science professionals including researchers, nurses, and primary-care physicians, especially in rural area.
Career Path	Your career path will vary depending on your training. Most health sciences careers require you to maintain professional credentials. Moving into higher-level careers often requires additional training.
Career Pathways	
Nursing Assistant	A nursing assistant works directly with patients, including children, under the supervision of nursing or medical staff. He or she helps to feed, bathe, dress, groom, or move patients.
Physical Therapist	A physical therapist could work in a hospital or a medical office to help children who have medical problems, health conditions, illnesses, or injuries that limit their ability to move.
Nurse Practitioner	A nurse practitioner has additional medical training, and can treat illnesses and prescribe medication. A child care center or school will sometimes hire a nurse practitioner to treat sick children.
Public Health Educator	A public health educator will work with child care professionals and teachers to help them learn better health and safety practices. He or she may also work to plan, monitor, and evaluate public health programs.

Critical Thinking   What classes have you taken in school that might help you prepare for a career as an occupational therapist? Propose the possible short- and long-term career goals that will help you prepare for this career.

Certification Prep

Research child development milestones and ways to help children who are behind the developmental guidelines for their ages. Write two to three paragraphs that describe your research.

Competitive Events Practice

Prepare an oral report describing the work of an occupational therapist or other health science or child development specialist. Include details on the daily activities of someone in that career and the requirements to obtain a job in the field. Consider interviewing a professional already in the career.

Judge your oral report on the following:

• Did your summary describe all aspects of the career?

• Did you speak clearly, with appropriate pitch, volume, and tempo?

• Did you use proper grammar and pronunciation?

UNIT 4   Child Care Portfolio Project

Games and Activities for Learning

Some important tools in the child care profession are developmental games and activities. Using your research, the chapters in this unit, and a child care center observation visit, you will create a game or activity that encourages a child's physical, intellectual, emotional, or social development.

My Journal

If you completed the journal entry from page 292, refer to it to see what games or activities you researched or have used in the past. Add any additional notes about children's developmental games and activities after reading this unit.

Project Assignment

In this project, you will do the following:

- Choose an age group to be the focus of your project
- Plan and conduct an observation visit to a child care center. If possible, discuss how to ensure the age-appropriateness of an activity with one of the child care professionals at the center.
- Develop a game or activity for the age group you chose. Be sure to include research that shows how your activity will support a child's physical, intellectual, emotional, or social development.
- Create a resource container and assemble or make the materials needed
- Present your research and demonstrate your activity to the class. Be prepared to discuss why this activity is appropriate for the age group.

Applied Child Care Professional Skills behind the Project

Your success as a child care professional will depend on your skills. Skills you will use in this project include the following:

▶ Identifying children's games and activities
▶ Distinguishing developmental levels between age groups
▶ Knowing how to support a child's physical, intellectual, emotional, or social development
▶ Determining how to develop a game or activity appropriate for a child's age or development
▶ Identifying the materials needed to perform the developmental activity

English Language Arts Skills behind the Project

The English Language Arts skills you will use for this project are research, writing, and speaking skills. Remember these key concepts:

Research Skills

▶ Perform research using a variety of resources
▶ Discriminate between sources
▶ Use the information you gathered to narrow your choices

Writing Skills

▶ Use complete sentences with correct spelling, grammar, and punctuation
▶ Consider your audience
▶ Use findings from research/interviews to communicate in writing

Speaking Skills

▶ Speak clearly, slowly, and concisely so that the audience can follow your presentation
▶ Be sensitive to the needs of your audience
▶ Adapt and modify language to suit different purposes

©Nova Development

STEP 1   Research Developmental Games or Activities

Conduct research, online and using your textbook, to find different children's games and activities that encourage development. Choose an age group to narrow your focus. Consider this age group when researching games. Write a summary of your research findings to:

- describe the types of games and activities used for your chosen age group.
- explain how games and activities selected for your chosen age group encourage physical, intellectual, emotional, or social development.
- list specific items or categories that are often used in these activities that promote development.
- identify the training and experience a child care professional needs to implement these games or activities.
- identify facts you need to know before creating an activity, such as the objective, age range, setting, and available supplies.

STEP 2   Plan Your Observation

Use the results of your research to write a list of questions that you might have before you observe a child care setting. Your questions may include the following:

- What are some examples of games that promote a child's physical, intellectual, emotional, or social development?
- What are some of the standards or guidelines that help you select an age-appropriate game or activity?
- What are some safety considerations for my chosen age group?
- What skills do I need to create these games?

Comstock Premium/Alamy

Child Care Portfolio Project Checklist

Plan
- ✔ Select and research your topic and summarize your findings.
- ✔ Plan your observation visit.
- ✔ Conduct a child care observation visit, and write a summary of the information that you collected.
- ✔ Create a game or activity and assemble the resources necessary to complete it.

Present
- ✔ Make a presentation to your class to share the results of your research and observation, and to demonstrate your game or activity.
- ✔ Invite students to ask any questions they may have. Answer these questions.
- ✔ When students ask you questions, demonstrate in your answers that you respect their perspectives.
- ✔ Turn in the summary of your research, your observation plan and results, an explanation of your game or activity, and the summary of how it promotes a child's development.

STEP 3   Connect with Your Community

Identify a local child care facility that you can visit and observe children playing. Use the plan that you created in Step 2. Take notes during the observation, and write a summary of your findings.

STEP 4   Share What You Have Learned

Use the Child Care Professional Project Checklist to plan and create an age-appropriate developmental game or activity based on your research and observations. Share what you have learned with your classmates.

STEP 5   Evaluate your Child Care Professional and Academic Skills

Your project will be evaluated based on

- the extent of research and information about children's developmental games.
- how well your activity meets its learning goal or objective.
- the age-appropriateness of the content, structure, setting, and supplies.
- the quality of presentation.

 Project Worksheet *Go to* connected. mcgraw-hill.com *for a worksheet you can use to complete your portfolio project.*

Developmentally Appropriate Activities

Chapters

Project Preview

Plan a Thematic Unit

After completing this unit, you will know more about how children learn and the kind of curriculum and activities that promote development in each of the subject areas. In the Unit 5 child care portfolio project, you will research and plan a thematic unit that integrates art, music, movement, language arts, math, and other curriculum areas. You will observe a child care classroom and present your research and thematic unit plan to the class.

My Journal

Write a journal entry about a possible theme that you could use to promote children's learning for each of the age groups you have studied. Refer to theme ideas that you have experienced on your own or with children you know, or research theme ideas that are discussed in your text.

- What theme did you choose?
- Why did you choose it, and where did you find information on this theme?
- What activities would support the theme?

©Nova Development

Explore the Photo

There are many kinds of activities that promote a child's development. *What skills and development does this art activity encourage?*

CHAPTER 19

Approaches to Teaching and Learning

Writing Activity

⭐ 21ˢᵗ Century Skills

Initiative An explanation is a description of how or why someone does something or how or why something happens. Write a paragraph explaining why you might consider a career in early childhood education. What steps would you need to take to reach that goal?

Writing Tips

1. First, plan the points you want to make in an outline or list.
2. Use helper words and phrases such as *because* and *since*.
3. Organize the paragraph by addressing each reason one at a time.

Explore the Photo
Music can make learning fun. *What can you observe about the girl's interest in this activity?*

Reading Guide

Think of an Example. Look over the Key Concepts for this chapter. Think of an example of how or when you could apply one of these concepts. Thinking of how you might apply knowledge can help motivate your learning by showing you why the information or skill is important.

Read to Learn

Key Concepts

- **Describe** the characteristics of different learning styles.
- **Summarize** the concept of multiple intelligences.
- **Contrast** the project and the theme approaches to teaching.
- **Explain** the impact of teaching style on learning.

Main Idea

Children have many different styles of learning and intelligence. A child is able to learn new skills best by having lessons adapted to his or her unique learning style or intelligence. Detailed lesson plans are important to deliver appropriate practices for all children.

Content Vocabulary

◇ manipulatives
◇ core learning skills
◇ intelligence quotient
◇ multiple intelligences
◇ teachable moments
◇ open-ended materials
◇ close-ended materials
◇ curriculum
◇ developmentally appropriate curriculum
◇ intentional teaching
◇ scaffolding
◇ objectives
◇ Bloom's Taxonomy
◇ project approach
◇ Reggio Emilia Approach
◇ theme
◇ lesson plan
◇ open-ended questions

Academic Vocabulary

■ facilitate
■ outcome

Graphic Organizer

As you read, you will discover six ways that children learn. Use a diagram like the one shown to record the ways.

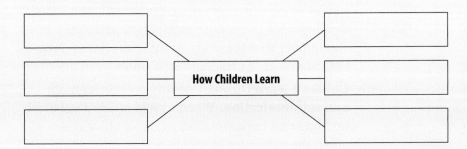

How Children Learn

 Graphic Organizer *Go to* **connected.mcgraw-hill.com** *to print this Graphic Organizer.*

Teaching Children

The better you understand children, the better able you are to help them grow and develop. Experiences you plan for children must take into account how they learn. This chapter will explore how to plan for activities with the learner in mind. Such planning is the backbone of implementing appropriate practices with young children.

How Children Learn

Children learn differently than adults. At birth, only about 25 percent of the brain's learning pathways are developed. As a result, children's vocabularies remain limited for several years. Attention spans are short and motor skills are still developing. Many concepts are not fully understood. For these and similar reasons, early childhood professionals must plan children's activities carefully. Keep the following principles in mind when planning:

▶ **Children learn best by doing.** They do not learn best by listening to explanations. Children need hands-on experiences. For this reason, teachers should provide many **manipulatives**, or toys and materials that children can handle and change with their hands. Play clay, sand, and snap beads are examples. Manipulatives help children develop small motor skills as they learn concepts. Objects of many shapes, sizes, and colors also stimulate thinking.

▶ **Children learn best when using their senses.** Sensory experiences—seeing, touching, hearing, smelling, and tasting— capture children's attention and maintain their interest. Children learn about the world by exploring concepts with their senses.

▶ **Children learn through trial and error.** Children actively explore and experiment when interacting with their environment. They learn what works and what does not work. Making mistakes and learning from them is a natural part of the learning process.

▶ **Children learn best when all areas of development are nurtured.** Children need activities that aim at intellectual, physical, emotional, and social development to become well-balanced adults. Remember that these areas are interrelated. Progress in one area usually means progress in another.

▶ **Children learn through positive reinforcement and self-motivation.** When a child builds a tall block building that remains standing, he or she learns about the principles of weight and gravity. When children learn something new, a modest amount of encouragement and recognition from early childhood care teachers builds children's confidence.

However, excessively praising children can lead to them focusing too much on pleasing others rather than on the joy of learning and accomplishment. Experiencing success stimulates children's inner motivation to learn. When they feel proud of new accomplishments, they are encouraged to keep learning and trying out new ideas. Challenging themselves to master increasingly difficult skills is how children contribute to their own development and learning.

▶ **Children acquire and experiment with new behaviors through imitation and role modeling.** The significant people in children's lives provide them with examples of how people use words and actions to get along with others and to succeed in life. Children often model their behavior after their parents and early childhood teachers. Siblings, close friends, and peers also heavily influence young children's behaviors and attitudes toward learning and classroom behavior.

Core Learning Skills

Researchers have discovered evidence that all learning is supported best when children develop **core learning skills**. Sometimes these skills are referred to as "life skills," because they affect learning not just during childhood but also throughout the life span.

In her book *Mind in the Making*, Ellen Galinsky groups learning skills scientists have identified into seven categories. Following are the seven core skills needed for effective learning:

▶ **Skill 1: Focus and Control** Before children can acquire new information, they must be able to focus on a topic by ignoring distractions and controlling impulsiveness. Being able to consistently give full attention to a specific task is a skill teachers can help children develop. For instance, when a teacher uses a focused transition by asking children to move quietly from the snack table to the restroom to wash hands, children learn to focus as well as to maintain control over their bodies and the amount of sound they make.

▶ **Skill 2: Perspective Taking** Being able to understand other's intentions, as well as their unique point of view is called perspective taking. This skill helps children build good social relationships and avoid conflict through better communication.

McGraw-Hill Education

▶ **New Challenges**

It takes confidence to try a new skill. *What are some other core learning skills?*

During conflict resolution and positive discipline, teachers help children understand other perspectives as they encourage a child to consider another child's viewpoint. Perspective taking is the foundation for empathy, compromise, negotiation, and mutually satisfying problem solving throughout life.

▶ **Skill 3: Communication** Using language competently is just the first step toward communication. Child or adult communicators must be aware of how their message is being interpreted by others. Being able to adjust conversation and communication based on other's perceptions is critical if true intentions are to be expressed and understood by others. When a teacher asks a child about his or her work, the child is encouraged to express himself or herself creatively.

▶ **Skill 4: Making Connections** Understanding how things relate to each other is at the heart of making connections. Children begin this process by noticing patterns in their environment. They notice similarities and differences and are able to sort objects or ideas into logical categories. For example, while singing "Old MacDonald" at music time, toddlers can learn to make connections between animal names and the sounds the animals make.

▶ **Skill 5: Critical Thinking** When children observe and then analyze information it is called critical thinking. Experimenting through trial and error often leads children to make breakthroughs in understanding concepts. Creativity and inventiveness are often the result of critical thinking. Whenever teachers include children in problem solving, such as figuring out how to balance a stack of blocks, critical thinking is encouraged.

▶ **Skill 6: Taking on Challenges** Having the confidence to try a new skill and the persistence to keep trying is the foundation for achievement in learning and life. For example, if a child is building a house with construction toys, asking "How do people inside your house see outside?" motivates a child to take on the challenge of figuring out how to build windows into the structure.

▶ **Skill 7: Self-Directed, Engaged Learning** Children must have a sense of attachment, security, and safety before they feel relaxed enough to satisfy their curiosity fully and to begin exploring. When children pursue engaging topics that interest them, learning becomes satisfying and personally rewarding.

Helping children learn more from books, magazines, field trips, and classroom visitors gives them ample tools for pursuing learning at their own pace.

No matter the activity, early childhood teachers can nurture core learning skills by intentionally providing children with chances to apply them to life and learning throughout the daily schedule.

Learning Styles

There is no single right way to learn. Everyone has his or her own style. Some children are more verbally expressive, others more quiet. Some children are visual learners. They learn best by observing others, looking at pictures in a book, or watching a video. Others learn through listening and language activities. These learning preferences are called perceptual styles of learning and are detailed in **Figure 19.1**.

Teachers should get to know children as individuals so they can gear activities to children's preferred learning styles. Working with a child's natural learning tendencies and preferences is the best way to individualize children's learning based on developmental needs. Avoid a "one style fits all" teaching method.

Figure 19.1 **Characteristics of Different Learning Styles**

Styles of Learning Children have many different styles of learning. *What kind of activity could you plan for an auditory learner?*

Learning Style	Characteristics
Visual	• Learn by observing and looking at pictures and images
Auditory	• Learn by listening and hearing the words spoken • Follow oral directions well
Tactile	• Learn by sense of touch • Enjoy hands-on learning and opportunity to manipulate objects
Kinesthetic	• Learn by moving their bodies • Pairing body movements with music or chants is helpful • Need frequent breaks while learning a new skill
Social	• Learn through teacher and peer-group interaction • See "big picture" and do not focus on the details • Thrive in larger groups and enjoy performing
Independent	• Learn best in individual and small-group settings • Focus on the details of new activity • Can focus for longer periods of time with few distractions

Figure 19.2 Gardner's Multiple Intelligences

Types of Intelligence Children learn better when lessons are geared toward their type of intelligence. *Give an example of an early childhood play activity that would be geared toward a child with spatial intelligence.*

Type of Intelligence	Characteristics	Careers
Linguistic	• Use language to express thoughts	Writers, speakers, lawyers
Logical-mathematical	• Understand underlying principles of systems • Use logic to manipulate numbers, quantities, and operations	Scientists, mathematicians, inventors
Spatial	• Mentally comprehend spatial relationships • Think in three-dimensional terms	Architects, sailors, pilots, sculptors
Bodily-kinesthetic	• Use the whole body or body parts to solve problems, to make something, or to put on some kind of production	Athletes, dancers, actors
Musical	• Think in musical terms • Hear, recognize, remember, and manipulate musical patterns	Composers, singers, musicians, orchestra conductors
Interpersonal	• Understand the intentions, desires, and motivations of others • Work well with other people	Teachers, salespeople, public relations specialists, counselors, therapists, politicians
Intrapersonal	• Understand personal abilities, strengths, and limitations • Find help or delegate when needed	Business owners, managers of organizations
Naturalistic	• See differences among living things such as plants and animals • See features of natural world in terms of patterns, shapes, and colors	Ecologists, biologists, botanists, insect specialists

Multiple Intelligences

At one time, there was thought to be just one type of human intelligence. It was believed that the relative intelligence of a person could be measured by a standardized test and scored to reveal a person's IQ, or **intelligence quotient**. This is the ratio between mental age and chronological age. These IQ tests assessed language, logic, and academic potential. However, they ignored other types of intelligence or talent, such as musical ability or physical competence.

In contrast, Dr. Howard Gardner, a professor of education, believes people vary in terms of intelligence and learning strengths. He believes individual intelligence varies, just as learning styles do. His theory is referred to as **multiple intelligences**.

Gardner believes children understand concepts better when child care professionals and teachers plan activities that allow children to engage their own unique intelligences. For instance, children highly skilled in language can learn about food and nutrition by talking to a cook or listening to a recording. Gardner identified eight types of human intelligence outlined in **Figure 19.2.**

Grouping and Peer Learning

When planning learning activities, early childhood teachers must think about the mix of children in the class. The number of children, their age ranges, and their ability levels affect teaching and learning. Grouping begins with how children are placed in classrooms.

▶ **Same-age grouping.** This grouping occurs when children of the same approximate age are placed together. This is also called chronological grouping, meaning a child's specific age determines classroom placement. However, keep in mind that even children the same year of age can have up to 11 months difference in age depending on their birth month.

▶ **Developmental grouping.** This grouping places children in classrooms according to developmental abilities. If a child varies significantly in mental or physical ability, he or she may be placed in a classroom with children a year or more older or younger than the child's chronological age.

▶ **Mixed-age grouping.** Children of a certain age range are put in the same classroom in mixed-age grouping. For example, three- to five-year-olds might be grouped together. This grouping is similar to how children's ages are staggered with siblings in the family—meaning some are younger than siblings and others older.

When children of the same age or ability level make up the classroom, it is easier to plan activities that will be suitable for all. However, children miss the opportunity to relate to other ages and abilities. Mixed-aged grouping can be a challenge because child care teachers must consider a wide range of developmental needs.

▼ **Mixed-Age Grouping**

Children are sometimes placed in a group with children of different ages. *What is the benefit of mixed-age grouping? What is the drawback?*

Blend Images - Ariel Skelley/Getty Images

Managing Stress

A career in early childhood education and care can be stressful. Child care professionals have to handle many different responsibilities and demands on their time each day. It is important for early childhood professionals to identify sources of stress and to learn ways to manage stress. Managing stress in a positive way will improve job satisfaction and performance. To help staff manage stress, child care centers often provide training that includes time-management strategies and relaxation techniques.

What Would You Do? You are working in a child care center and are finding it stressful to handle all your daily responsibilities. You are afraid that you are not going to be an effective teacher if you do not find ways to manage your stress. What could you do to manage your stress when handling daily responsibilities?

An inappropriate activity will leave older or younger children in the age range feeling left out or bored. On the other hand, mixed-age grouping gives older children the chance to relate positively with younger ones and increases their self-esteem. Younger children learn from slightly older peers, who can be role models for advanced skills.

Often early childhood teachers divide the class into smaller groups for specific activities. They determine group size according to how much personal attention an activity requires. During some parts of an activity, especially when children are learning new skills, teachers may divide the class into smaller groups to give more one-on-one attention to each child. Later, when children are more confident and competent in their abilities, the teacher may have them work in larger groups.

Some activities are better suited to a certain group size. Most outdoor games are more fun with more players. Some art, science, or cooking projects, on the other hand, are best conducted in small groups. Generally, groups should be small enough to prevent overcrowding. A child can feel overwhelmed or lost in a group that is too large. Some children misbehave under the same circumstances. Usually, the younger the child, the smaller the group size should be.

Learning Through Play

Learning is play for young children. Living and learning are inseparable. Many experiences are new to them, so learning is a continual process. Early childhood specialists agree that play has a major role in learning and development. Playful interactions with peers, adults, and materials in the environment add to a child's knowledge about the world.

Because children learn through play, teachers need to handle play activities carefully. Classroom teachers should **facilitate** play, or help bring it about without controlling it. This skill comes with experience. For example, a teacher who tells the children to make a train with the empty boxes controls play. A teacher who puts out the boxes and says, "What can be done with these?" facilitates play.

Teachers can also add richness to play and introduce new concepts to play by offering accessories to play activities. For example, children enjoy playing in a sandbox. By adding buckets of water and shovels to the sand play area, children soon discover they can dig trenches in sand to make rivers with water. Making play more complex encourages a greater attention span, creativity, and cooperative play.

Effective teachers interact with children while they play. By interacting with children in play situations, they spot opportunities for growth and learning. By observing and participating in natural play situations, teachers assess children's growth and development in many different areas. This is called authentic assessment. For example, teachers observe and take note of language growth, social development, and or physical and motor coordination skills.

During play, teachers serve as role models for proper language while also encouraging children's use of complex language use with peers. While facilitating and observing play, teachers recognize **teachable moments**, unplanned opportunities for learning. With experience, they also become skilled at interpreting the thoughts and feelings children express through play. When teachers interact with children, they give children the opportunity to share their experiences from home. This sharing helps build a trusting relationship between the teacher and child.

Some toys and play materials promote learning better than others. When analyzed as teaching tools, play materials are said to be either open-ended or close-ended. Effective teachers make sure that they offer both types during classroom activities.

▶ **Open-ended materials.** Items that can be used in a variety of ways, with no single correct outcome or result, are called **open-ended materials**. In other words, the child decides what to do with them. These materials allow children to creatively develop independence, language skills, decision-making and problem-solving skills, and imagination. Many art materials, such as paint and dough, are open-ended. Water, sand toys, and blocks can be used in an open-ended manner. Because they can be used in many different ways, open-ended materials are very suitable for successful learning in mixed-age groups.

Blocks or manipulatives allow a child to make decisions about what to create. *What are some other examples of open-ended materials?*

▶ **Close-ended materials.** Structured materials, or **close-ended materials**, are items that are to be used primarily in one way, with an expected result. These materials are less open to input from the child. They help children learn how to follow directions. They also help develop sensory perception and motor skills. Examples include puzzles, matching games, snap beads, stringing beads, and sewing cards. Close-ended materials provide a specific and known outcome. These types of materials stimulate and enhance the learning process.

READING CHECK ✔ **Recall** How does a teacher's interaction during play activities help a child learn?

©Jade LLC

Expert *Advice . . .*

"Tell me and I forget. Teach me and I remember. Involve me and I learn."

— Benjamin Franklin, *American Statesman*

Curriculum Planning for Children

By nature, children are eager to explore and make discoveries. They need opportunities to grow and learn. Without them, development suffers. As a child care professional, an important part of your job is to promote child development through learning activities.

The experiences and activities that support and guide children's learning are called the **curriculum**. Learning activities are carefully developed as part of the curriculum framework, giving children relevant educational experiences.

The Intentional Teacher

One of the first challenges for teachers is deciding what, when, and to whom to teach. Early childhood classrooms require a **developmentally appropriate curriculum**. That means curriculum activities teachers offer need to be geared to the varying abilities and levels of development of a whole group of children. When teachers plan activities that are responsive to individual children's abilities and needs, they are using a strategy called **intentional teaching**. They offer activities that encourage children to stretch their skills slightly to build upon knowledge and skills already mastered. Vygotsky called this **scaffolding** children's learning, or building the support needed for emerging concepts or skills. It requires teachers to design and conduct activities carefully that gradually build onto the foundation of information or skills children already have. It takes intentional planning to make sure learning is correctly suited to a child's temperament, learning style, abilities, and interests. If a concept or experience is offered too soon, it can overwhelm a child. If it is offered too late, children's development may lag. Likewise, when activities are geared too far below children's developmental levels, children become bored and restless. They may turn to disruptive behavior. If activities are too difficult, children become frustrated. They begin to believe they cannot learn and then self-esteem suffers. The ideal curriculum challenges children, yet enables ongoing success.

Building a Strong Curriculum

The key to a strong curriculum is well-planned activities. They should be stimulating and varied, not repetitive and boring. They should capture children's interest, giving them information and encouraging them to think.

A strong curriculum is balanced. In other words, it includes activities that address all areas of development, as well as different subject areas. The curriculum also integrates cultural diversity and bilingual development with the various subject areas. Typically, the curriculum is divided into subject areas that correspond to the learning centers in the classroom. The chapters in this unit describe learning centers that are typically included. Remember, however, that activities can also be created for any other learning centers a program might have.

Setting Goals and Objectives

Curriculum is planned to meet all program goals. For example, fostering creativity and imagination is a goal of many programs. To meet this goal, early childhood teachers plan activities in art, music, creative movement, dramatic play, and other subjects that encourage children's creative expression.

After a curriculum topic and associated activities are selected, teachers keep in mind activity objectives. **Objectives** are outcomes for children to achieve or to experience through participation in a specific curriculum activity. Objectives support goals that relate to all areas of development, including social, intellectual, emotional, and physical development. Lesson objectives often begin with the phrase "The ability to…" When teachers identify learning objectives, they always keep in mind what skills, abilities, knowledge, or attitudes they expect children to develop or to master during an activity. The abilities will vary depending on the specific developmental area the activity focuses on.

Dr. Benjamin Bloom, a developmental psychologist, established a ranking of educational objectives for intellectual development. The system ranks mental abilities, from very basic to more complex thinking skills. It is called **Bloom's Taxonomy** (tak-ˈsä-nə-mē). By keeping Bloom's Taxonomy in mind, teachers set objectives and plan activities that will allow children to put all levels of thinking skills to use. **Figure 19.3** on page 424 identifies the key levels of Bloom's Taxonomy and suggested ways to apply the thinking skills to preschool teaching.

▲ Creative Play

Fostering creativity and imagination is a goal in many early childhood programs. *What types of activities promote creativity and imagination?*

Approaches to Teaching

Early childhood teachers vary on how they make curriculum decisions. In some early childhood programs, all classrooms must follow the same curriculum and approach to teaching to meet the program philosophy and goals. Others allow teachers individual choice in planning for classroom learning. In either case, teachers must demonstrate developmentally appropriate teaching methods and techniques in their classrooms.

Teachers in charge of classrooms do most of the curriculum planning. Because early childhood classrooms have a variety of staff, such as teachers and teacher aides, team planning is the common. Team planning requires cooperative, respectful relationships among the staff. Teacher collaboration requires all staff members to work together to meet children's developmental needs. Wise programs include parents in curriculum planning, too.

Image Source/age fotostock

Figure 19.3 **Bloom's Taxonomy**

Levels of Thinking This ranking of objectives helps a teacher develop appropriate learning strategies for each level. *What other questions could you ask a child to help analyze new information?*

Level	Skills	Teaching Strategies
Level 1: Remembering Ability to remember and recall information	List, name, remember, show, recognize	Ask intentionally chosen questions to encourage memory skills. • "Can you tell me the names of three flowers?" • "What do we have to do before we go to lunch?"
Level 2: Understanding Ability to understand information and explain or summarize	Discuss, describe, restate, express, explain, review	Ask questions to promote understanding. • "Can you explain to me how you baked the carrot bread?" • "What is your favorite part of the story we just read?"
Level 3: Applying Ability to apply information in a different way	Collect, classify, sort, choose, show, group	Choose activities to apply knowledge. • Matching games • Sorting objects • Classifying objects according to characteristics.
Level 4: Analyzing Ability to understand isolated parts of information and to discover relationships between them	Explain, combine, describe, compare, contrast, distinguish, examine, organize, give reasons, explain relationships	Ask questions that require analysis. • "What do you think happens in the oven to make the bread rise?" • "How are puppies different from their mother and father?"
Level 5: Evaluating Ability to create an opinion by using specific information to form a judgment	Choose, select, rate, recommend, judge, state an opinion	Ask questions that require an opinion. • "Vote for your choice of song to sing at music time." • "Choose your favorite snack."
Level 6: Creating Ability to combine ideas, information, or objects to create a new pattern or solution	Create, develop, invent, construct, design, assemble, problem-solve	Choose open-ended activities that allow children to apply individual style or interpretation. • Sand and water play • Molding clay • Puppet play

For example, teachers find ways for parents to reinforce classroom activities at home. Or they suggest low-cost family activities that would help extend children's classroom learning. Some programs form a committee of parents who meet regularly with teachers to give suggestions on topics they would like their children to investigate or to experience at child care.

Larger programs may have a curriculum coordinator, or an educational coordinator, who leads and supervises classroom planning. Regardless of how the curriculum and activities are selected, all selections require the program director's final approval. The following includes some of the most popular approaches to planning and teaching in early childhood classrooms.

Project Approach

In the **project approach** to teaching, child care professionals conduct projects that allow children to explore in developmentally appropriate ways. A project refers to children's in-depth investigation of a specific topic. The project topic is chosen both by children and teachers. The teachers make sure projects allow children to investigate topics of value that benefit them as people and learners. Effective topics stem from children's own interests and questions. The topic generates children's enthusiasm and curiosity. If a topic is particularly interesting, teachers will allow children to repeat activities, introducing new activities when the children are ready. Teachers should keep the following points in mind when using the project approach:

▲ **Project Approach**

The project approach involves in-depth investigation on a topic chosen by the class of children. *What are some examples of project ideas that this activity could fulfill?*

- ▶ **Grouping children.** Some projects involve all children; others may involve small groups. Project learning continues as long as children's interest is maintained and the teacher believes the learning is useful.

- ▶ **Project goals.** The main goal of the project is for children to learn how to find answers to their own questions and hypotheses about a topic. A hypotheses is a guess about how something works or what causes something to occur. During project work, teachers help children state what they know about a topic. Through investigations, children discover if their hypotheses are correct or not. If not, teachers help children observe and investigate so their concepts and understanding is modified to become more accurate, based on newly gathered information.

- ▶ **Selecting topics.** Project topic investigations usually revolve around familiar objects, people, or events in children's daily lives. After a topic is selected, teachers and children think of activities that will help them answer their questions. Teachers plan experiences that offer many different opportunities for hands-on learning. Some projects may last a week, some a few months.

- ▶ **Using resources.** A variety of resources can help children learn more about chosen topics. For instance, children learning about pets might look at books on the topic, bring photos of their pets, or ask parents to bring pets to the classroom for a visit. The teacher may also invite a special visitor, such as a veterinarian, into the classroom to explain pet care.

- ▶ **Field trips.** Field trips allow children to see how their topic and the knowledge they learn about it relates to the real world.

In the project approach, field site visits usually occur early so later activities can reflect learning that occurred on the visit. Depending on children's interests, a project about pets might include a trip to a pet store or a rescue shelter. Teachers compile a list of children's questions to ask experts working at the visit and take photographs of children engaged in the experience. Posting the photos after the visit helps children remember the details of the experience better.

▶ **Gathering, organizing, and representing information.** During a project, children learn to gather, organize, and represent information in different ways. Explorations are integrated across curriculum areas as appropriate. During a pet project, children use language skills to make a list of typical household pets. They use math skills to conduct a survey of pets owned by classmates and graph the results on a poster. In the art area, children may draw pictures of pets or make clay sculptures. They may write stories about pets, put on a puppet show, or create a pretend pet shop for dramatic play. The field trip and other investigations allow children to add rich, realistic detail to all those play activities.

▶ **Assessing project learning.** To assess and record project learning, teachers frequently record children's actual dialogue and photograph children during classroom activities. This type of documentation allows children to refer back to experiences to help them gain greater understanding. Documentation also helps teachers keep parents informed about children's progress. It also helps teachers note and keep track of children's developmental delays or advances.

Reggio Emilia Approach

A town in northern Italy, Reggio Emilia, has become internationally known for its unique approach to teaching young children. Its early childhood programs have been a strong inspiration for using the project approach around the world. The core features of the **Reggio Emilia Approach**, or style of teaching associated with Reggio Emilia school, include the following:

▶ Children are considered competent, capable, and motivated learners, full of potential.

▶ Collaborative learning is stressed. Children, teachers, parents, and community members explore and learn together.

▶ The physical environment is purposefully designed and organized. It is considered a very important influence on the learning process.

▶ Curriculum is project based, so children independently and cooperatively investigate topics.

▶ Children construct projects and represent learning in a variety of creative ways across curriculum areas, such as language, art, science, and movement.

Theme Approach

In some classrooms, curriculum activities are based on a theme approach, which is sometimes called a thematic unit approach. A **theme** is one central topic, or theme, selected by the teacher. The theme is not chosen primarily on children's interests, but teachers pick themes they believe will entice children. Teachers think of, plan, and conduct activities that relate to the theme for one or two weeks. The teacher gathers all the resources prior to conducting a theme activity.

There are many different types of themes for early childhood teachers to choose. However, themes are often used to teach specific concepts, such as colors, shapes, numbers, or letters. Themes are usually broad topics, rather than specific topics as used in the project approach. For instance, a theme may include all types of community helpers. In contrast, a project would focus on a specific type of community helper such as firefighters. **Figure 19.4** on page 428 contrasts the different approaches of theme-based versus project-based learning. Whether teachers develop thematic units or teach through project-based learning, many curriculum areas are included to show children how knowledge overlays in real life.

Teachers develop theme activities for each curriculum area. A field trip isn't necessarily included in every theme a teacher selects. However, if a field trip is included, it is usually the final step in the theme approach, rather than a beginning step, as in the project approach.

▲ **Theme-Based Approach**

A theme-based approach is one central topic chosen by the child care professional. *What are the benefits of a theme-based approach?*

Figure 19.4 Approaches to Teaching

Theme or Project
Theme-based lessons are chosen by the teacher. Project-based lessons are chosen based on the interests of the children. *Would weather be an example of a theme or a project-based lesson?*

Differences between Theme-Based and Project-Based Approaches	
Theme-Based Approach (Broad Focus)	**Project-Based Approach** (Narrow Focus)
Ocean	Seashells
Safety	Fire Truck
Clothing	Shoes
Insects	Butterflies
Nature	Trees
Transportation	Buses
Dinosaurs	Fossils
Toys	Balls
My Body	Eyes

Implementing Curriculum

In the United States, most early childhood teachers use a variety of curriculum approaches. They select approaches based on a variety of issues such as the resources that are available, developmental abilities, interest of children, and even special interests of the teacher (such as environmental education).

No one approach is either right or wrong but should be a good match for both the teacher and children. For example in the fall a teacher-selected theme on Friendship might work best. As teachers observe, a strong interest in a specific topic may emerge in children's play, leading teachers to use the project approach for a topic investigation. Sometimes teachers borrow bits and pieces that they especially like from a variety of approaches. In such cases, curriculum may be called "Montessori-inspired" or "Reggio Emilia-inspired."

Regardless of the curriculum approach used, curriculum is implemented to encourage children's basic learning skills. All children need to learn gradually how to focus, to pay attention, and to concentrate. These skills help them learn to follow directions and to cooperate. They need experiences in which they can learn to listen to others' ideas and to express their own ideas clearly. Teachers foster listening skills by reading stories and introducing longer stories as children's attention spans grow. Learning how to work individually and in groups is also necessary. Practice in maintaining a positive learning attitude helps children persevere in the face of challenges.

Children need many different chances to show their understanding of concepts and topics. In early childhood, paper and pencil tests are not used to evaluate children's learning. Instead, learning is encouraged creatively through art construction, drawing, modeling with clay, building with blocks, dictating stories, making books, and putting on plays and puppet shows.

How to . . .

Reflect Diversity Throughout the Classroom

To become comfortable with diversity, children should see it reflected in the classroom in many different ways. From staff to materials, expose children to variety so they can appreciate life's richness. The following are ways to put this concept into practice:

©Jose Luis Pelaez Inc/Blend Images LLC

Apply It!
Create a culturally diverse social studies or language arts activity for preschoolers.

▶ **Staff** *Employ both qualified male and female teachers. Include staff and volunteers of varying ages, different cultural backgrounds, and different teaching styles.*

▶ **Language** *Provide opportunities for children to speak in their native language. Include books and music in a child's native language as well.*

▶ **Music** *Provide instruments from different cultures to play during music time. Sing songs from different cultures. Play lullabies from different cultures during naps.*

▶ **Cultures** *Include dolls of diverse gender and ethnicity in the dress-up area. Learn about cultural resources in the community, and help support parents' use of two languages in the home.*

▶ **Activities** *For dramatic play, provide a variety of multicultural cooking utensils for pretend cooking. Give children cultural-style clothing for playing dress up.*

▶ **Abilities** *Read children's books and hang posters that include characters of varying abilities and backgrounds. Make all classroom areas accessible to those with different abilities.*

Scheduling Curriculum Activities

As activities are planned, they are incorporated into the daily schedule. Regular routines—including arrival, meals, snacks, naps, toileting, and departure—form the core of the schedule. The remaining time is reserved for activities.

Timing affects when activities will be included in the schedule. What is the best time of day for the children to do this activity? Will the activity interfere with anything else going on in the center? Answering questions such as these ahead of time will help the schedule flow more smoothly.

Developing Lesson Plans

It takes more than just an idea to make an activity happen in the classroom. Each activity must first be developed into a lesson plan. A **lesson plan** is a detailed, written explanation of an activity, including the purpose, any materials needed, the step-by-step method for carrying out the activity, evaluation of the activity, and possible related follow-up activities to reinforce the learning objectives.

Lesson plans are an organizational tool. They enable teachers to work through their ideas mentally and on paper before they conduct them. By doing so, they have a clear understanding of the purpose and the objective behind each activity. Teachers apply major learning theories when planning developmentally appropriate learning experiences for children. Teachers identify stimulating learning environments and set up logical learning procedures with orderly steps. This helps implement developmentally appropriate lessons more clearly and calmly.

Teachers often use a preprinted form for preparing lesson plans similar to the one shown in **Figure 19.5**.

Teaching Styles

It is important for teachers to be aware of their teaching styles and to know how to adapt them when necessary. Lesson plans may have to change to meet children's temperaments, developmental needs, or abilities. A versatile teacher does what is necessary when a situation demands it.

Just as personalities are different, teaching styles differ, too. Some teachers have theatrical energy, and others are calm and relaxed. Some teachers prefer structure and orderly lessons. Other teachers are more spontaneous.

▼ **Teaching Styles**

Child care professionals use many different styles for teaching. *Why is it important to introduce children to many different types of teaching styles?*

Figure 19.5 Lesson Plan 431

Preparing a Lesson Preparing detailed lesson plans help child care professionals have a clear understanding of the purpose and the objectives behind each activity. *How does having clearly defined objectives help with evaluating the lesson?*

Age Group
Record the age or level of development of the children.

Objectives
Briefly state the purpose of the lesson. List concepts and skills to be developed.

Introduction
Begin with a short introduction that motivates children. Ask a question or show an object to create interest.

Closure
Conclude with a question that generates thought and provides a transition to the next activity.

Activity Title
Give the lesson an appropriate title.

Materials
List all materials needed, including quantities.

Activity Procedure
Outline the steps for conducting the activity. Calculate and record the time needed to complete.

Evaluation
Assess the effectiveness of the lesson. How many children were successful? How could the lesson be improved?

Follow Up
Brainstorm other related activities that would reinforce skills and concepts addressed.

Sample Lesson Plan
Age Group: Four- and five-year-olds
Activity Title: Touch and Tell

Objectives:
Students will be able to:
• Develop the sense of touch, language, and vocabulary skills.
• Become aware that objects vary in size, shape, and texture.

Materials Required
• Empty, clean, decorated oatmeal container
• Large box filled with familiar toys, plastic fruit, blocks, etc., that will fit individually inside the oatmeal container
• Blanket to cover box of items
• Carpet squares

Activity Procedure
1. Have eight children sit in a large circle on carpet squares.
2. **Introduction.** Ask the children to touch some items around them, such as their hair, clothing, or shoes. Then ask them to describe how these items feel.
3. Tell children they are going to learn how to gather information using just their sense of touch.
4. Using the blanket to keep children from seeing items you select, place an object from the box into the oatmeal container.
5. Invite one child at a time to play the game as follows:
   • Have the child reach into the container and feel the object without looking.
   • Ask the child to describe what he or she is feeling without telling what it is. You might need to prompt younger children with questions to encourage the descriptions, such as asking, "Is the object round? Is it smooth or bumpy?"
   • The class then tries to guess what object is in the container.
6. Once the object is identified, repeat Steps 4 and 5 until all the children have had several turns. Allow 20 minutes for this activity.
7. **Closure.** Remind children that many objects around them are interesting to touch. Can they name any items that they especially like to touch? What objects are not safe to touch?

Evaluation
Six of the eight children were successful with this activity. Be sure to include a few less familiar objects to challenge the more developmentally advanced children. Begin activity with easier objects to identify. Allow 30 minutes the next time the activity is used.

Follow Up Activity
Go outside in the play yard to touch objects of different textures, such as tree trunks, leaves, grass, and flower petals. Encourage children to observe closely and find different ways to describe the textures. Write down children's comments to post for parent viewing.

Integrating Style

When working with children, a teaching style becomes integrated with the activity. In fact, a teacher often plans the activity to fit with his or her teaching style. For example, after reading a story about a monkey, an outgoing teacher may join the children as they all walk around the room like monkeys. A quieter teacher might show pictures of different kinds of monkeys and lead a discussion or help the children write a group story about going to the zoo.

Beliefs of Teachers

Beliefs can affect teaching style. What a teacher believes about children and how they learn can have an impact on children's learning. Suppose two teachers are working with children who are shy and afraid of making mistakes. One teacher might believe that a gentle approach is the best way to build their self-confidence gradually. Another may believe the children need to be drawn out by taking an outgoing approach using humor. Carefully observing how the children react to a teaching style may give the most reliable information regarding how these children will learn best.

Benefits of Different Styles

One teaching style is not necessarily better than another. Children can benefit from all types of styles. Some children may relate better to one style than to another. A child who likes action, for example, might love to run around like a monkey but will become impatient with talk about the zoo. On the other hand, the need to sit still and to practice listening as others talk about the zoo may help the energetic child learn self-control. When teachers with different styles interact with children throughout the day, children have opportunities to learn in different ways and to develop respect for diversity.

Encouraging Creativity

A child care professional's style and behavior can either encourage or discourage children's creativity. Interacting with children in ways that show children that creativity is valued will encourage creativity. Additional strategies to foster creativity and resourcefulness are as follows:

▶ Providing the freedom to explore materials without the risk of being judged or graded

▶ Accepting creativity

▶ Offering a variety of learning materials for independent use and a creative space in which to use them

▶ Encouraging the use of children's own ideas rather than copying those of a teacher

▶ Allowing children time and support for problem solving to find new ways to accomplish goals

▶ Building self-esteem

◀ **Open-Ended Questions**

....

Open-ended questions are an excellent way to get children to express their thoughts and feelings. *What questions might this teacher be asking the child?*

Questions that cause children to think and problem-solve encourage creativity. For instance, the way in which a question is asked can either encourage or discourage creativity. **Open-ended questions** are those that require more than a yes or no answer. These questions often begin with how, what, when, where, and why. Open-ended questions encourage children to express feelings, to explain ideas, and to relate experiences. They stimulate both the creativity and the intellectual skills needed for language development. An example of a meaningful question might be, "What is happening in your drawing?" A question to encourage problem solving would be, "What's another way to stack the blocks so your building will not fall?"

Many people think creativity is used only in an art or music curriculum. However, children can apply creativity in all curriculum areas. It can be applied whether learning indoors or out. For example, sand play allows for creative sand sculptures as well as a variety of ways to apply science concepts. Children can also learn to express themselves creatively through storytelling, puppetry, dramatic play, writing, and movement. Alert early childhood teachers never miss an opportunity to let children apply creative thinking during activities.

READING CHECK ✓ **List** What details should be included in a lesson plan?

College & Career READINESS

Curriculum Coordinator

What Does a Curriculum Coordinator Do?

A curriculum coordinator, or educational coordinator, for a child care center leads and supervises all classroom curriculum and planning. He or she plans, directs, and coordinates lesson plans and activities, making sure they meet guidelines and goals for developmental appropriateness. Coordinators often help teachers organize the classroom learning environments.

Career Readiness Skills

A curriculum coordinator for a child care center needs a strong understanding of children's developmental needs. Often a curriculum coordinator starts his or her career as a child care professional to gain teaching experience. A curriculum coordinator should have good communication skills and planning abilities. Strong interpersonal skills are important because a curriculum coordinator works closely with teachers, children, parents, and volunteers.

Education and Training

A bachelor's degree is usually required along with a CDA credential or some early childhood experience. A curriculum coordinator typically needs prior experience teaching and planning activities at a child care center. If a curriculum coordinator is going to work with a specialized group such as children with special needs, additional training would be needed.

Job Outlook

Employment opportunities continue to grow for curriculum coordinators as the need to meet educational standards grow and change. As the need for specialized programs increases, such as programs for children with special needs or programs for bilingual children, the need for curriculum coordinators with experience in those areas will also increase. Technological advances also contribute to the need for curriculum coordinators with the knowledge to plan lessons that integrate technology.

Critical Thinking Assess the interests, characteristics, and skills that would make someone a good curriculum coordinator. How do your personality and skills compare? Write a paragraph examining why this career might interest you. Propose the possible short-and long- term goals that will help you prepare for this career.

Career Cluster

Education and Training Curriculum coordinators work in the Teaching and Training pathway of the Education and Training career cluster. Here are some other jobs in this career cluster:

- Special Education Teacher
- Adult Educator
- Staff Trainer
- Staff Development Manager
- Administrator

- Principal
- Counselor
- Child Care Worker
- Superintendent
- College Faculty
- Assessment Specialist
- Education Researcher

Explore Further The Education and Training career cluster contains three pathways: Administration and Administrative Support, Professional Support Services, and Teaching and Training. Choose one of these pathways to explore further.

Westend61/Glow Images

Approaches to Teaching and Learning
Visual Summary

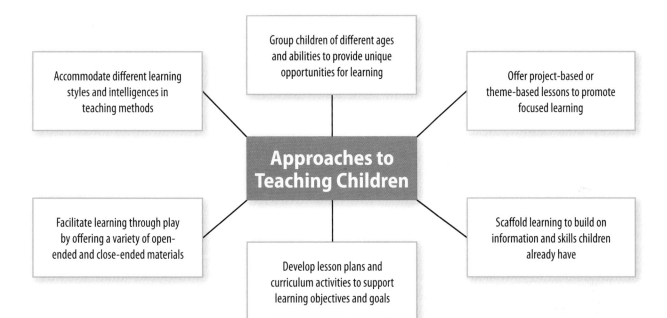

Accommodate different learning styles and intelligences in teaching methods

Group children of different ages and abilities to provide unique opportunities for learning

Offer project-based or theme-based lessons to promote focused learning

Approaches to Teaching Children

Facilitate learning through play by offering a variety of open-ended and close-ended materials

Develop lesson plans and curriculum activities to support learning objectives and goals

Scaffold learning to build on information and skills children already have

Vocabulary Review

1. Write each content and academic vocabulary terms on an index card. On the back of each card, write the definition of the word.

Content Vocabulary

◇ manipulatives (p. 414)
◇ core learning skills (p. 415)
◇ intelligence quotient (p. 418)
◇ multiple intelligences (p. 418)
◇ teachable moments (p. 421)
◇ open-ended materials (p. 421)
◇ close-ended materials (p. 421)
◇ curriculum (p. 422)

◇ developmentally appropriate curriculum (p. 422)
◇ intentional teaching (p. 422)
◇ scaffolding (p.422)
◇ objectives (p. 423)
◇ Bloom's Taxonomy (p. 423)
◇ project approach (p. 425)
◇ Reggio Emilia Approach (p. 426)

◇ theme (p. 427)
◇ lesson plan (p. 430)
◇ open-ended questions (p. 433)

Academic Vocabulary

■ facilitate (p. 420)
■ outcome (p. 421)

Review Key Concepts

2. **Describe** the characteristics of different learning styles.
3. **Summarize** the concept of multiple intelligences.
4. **Contrast** the project and theme approaches to teaching.
5. **Explain** the impact of teaching style on learning.

Critical Thinking

6. **Contrast** intelligence quotient with the theory of multiple intelligences. Why is it important to consider different types of intelligence?
7. **Analyze** methods early educators can use to assess developmental levels of children during planned activities. Write a summary of your analysis.

8. **Explain** why play is an important part of learning.
9. **Reflect** on a teachable moment that you have observed. Why is a moment like this valuable? How can a child care professional create more teachable moments?
10. **Describe** at least two approaches to curriculum development. Why is it important to have a variety of ways to develop curriculum? How does an approach to curriculum development relate to a child care center's program goals?

21st Century Skills

Analytical Skills

11. **Importance of Play** You have learned that playtime activities can have an impact on a child's development. If possible, observe children in a play setting. Record their activities and determine which areas of development are impacted. Analyze how the activities are building physical, emotional, intellectual, or social development based on your observations. Create a chart that details your findings.

Technology Skills

12. **Media Safety** Media such as television, music, movies, and the Internet can be used to foster learning. Educational computer software and online games can help children learn basic reading and math skills in a fun way. Media, however, may contain safety risks for children. Research media safety guidelines. Create a poster that outlines safeguards to prevent the abuse and misuse of that medium with children.

Child Care LAB

Use the skills you have learned in this chapter.

Project-Based Lesson Plan

13. **Design a Project-Based Lesson Plan** A lesson plan is a detailed, written explanation of an activity that helps a teacher plan and evaluate. Create a lesson plan that utilizes a cross-curricular project approach to teaching. How could this project be incorporated into a broader theme/unit-based approach to curriculum planning?

   A. **Choose Age Group.** Indicate the age group or the developmental level of the children.

   B. **Name the Project.** Select a project that is appropriate for the age group. Also consider the children's interest when selecting a project.

   C. **Write Objectives.** Briefly state the purpose of the project. When writing objectives, consider what concepts and skills you want the students to learn or to demonstrate. How will you be able to measure the outcome of the lesson? Be as detailed as possible.

   D. **Materials.** List all materials, including quantities, that will be required.

   E. **Procedure.** Outline the steps needed in order and with as much detail as possible. Allow the activity to be repeated. Include the estimated time necessary for the entire project. Begin with a short introduction, and end with a closing.

   F. **Evaluation.** Include an evaluation that allows other staff members to determine the effectiveness of the project.

   G. **Follow-Up Activity.** Include an activity or thought-provoking question to reinforce the lesson.

Create Your Evaluation

Create an evaluation sheet with the following categories:

- Cross-curricular Learning
- Age Appropriateness
- Detail
- Materials Used
- Organization
- Effectiveness
- Follow-up Activity

Have your teacher use the sheet to evaluate your lesson plan, rating each category from 1 to 10.

Academic Skills

English Language Arts

14. An Activity Resource Research five developmentally appropriate activities that might be used in a project-approach curriculum and five activities that might be used in a thematic-approach curriculum. Create a document that lists each of the activities and a brief description of each one. Include developmentally appropriate adaptations for children with special needs for each activity, if needed.

Social Studies

15. Multicultural Interactions Research activities that can be used in the classroom to create multicultural awareness and understanding. Ask parents from multicultural families how they share their culture at home with their children. Create a document that lists each activity and a brief description for each. Include as many different cultures as you can. Share this information with the rest of the class.

Science

16. Observe Children Children learn using many different styles. These styles are detailed in this chapter and include visual, auditory, tactile, kinesthetic, social, and independent learners. Learn about each child's learning style by watching them during play activities.

Procedure Conduct the activity detailed in the sample lesson plan for this chapter with a small group of children. Conduct several other activities with this same group of children so that you can observe the different styles of learning. Create an observational checklist for each activity that details the activity and then lists each learning style with a brief description. Toward which learning style is each activity geared? Record what you observe each child's learning style to be. What behaviors did you observe that might indicate a particular learning style?

Analysis How does each child learn differently? Are some activities easier for some of the children? What is the relationship between each activity and the learning style of the student? What behaviors lead to your conclusions? How could each activity be adapted to other learning styles

Certification Prep

Sharpen your test-taking skills to improve your certification program score.

Directions Read each statement. Then read the answer choices and choose the word or phrase that best completes the sentence.

17. Close-ended materials include _____.

A. paints

B. play clay

C. puzzles

D. blocks

18. The Reggio Emilia approach is _____.

A. named after a child development theorist

B. a theme-based approach

C. a project-based approach

D. primarily based on science activities

> **Test-Taking Tip**
> In a multiple-choice test, the answers are usually specific and precise. First read the question carefully first. Then read all of the answer choices. Eliminate answers that you know are incorrect.

CHAPTER 20

Literacy and Language Arts

Writing Activity

★ 21st Century Skills

Articulate Ideas When you think about a child care professional or a preschool teacher, what qualities come to mind? Write a character analysis of a child care professional. Be sure to include specific details about the person.

Writing Tips

1. Describe his or her words and actions.
2. Analyze how his or her behavior shows the qualities you believe are ideal for this profession.
3. Describe how you think parents or guardians and children would react to this person.

Explore the Photo Early educators can prepare children for school and for life by encouraging literacy. *What activities encourage literacy?*

© Gaetano Images Inc. / Alamy

Reading Guide

Helpful Memory Tools Successful readers use strategies to help them remember. For example, the acronym HOMES is a memory aid in which each letter stands for one of the five Great Lakes. Some students may try to create a song using the information. As you read the section, look for opportunities to make up your own memory aids.

Read to Learn

Key Concepts

- **Identify** the four areas of the language arts curriculum.
- **Explain** how a language arts learning center can promote development of language skills.
- **Describe** an example activity for each of the main language arts areas.
- **Define** the terms *English language learner* and *bilingual* and explain how they relate to language development.

Content Vocabulary

◇ language arts
◇ emergent literacy
◇ print-rich environment
◇ whole language
◇ auditory discrimination
◇ finger plays
◇ visual discrimination
◇ invented spelling

Academic Vocabulary

■ period
■ require

Main Idea

Child care professionals play a vital role in supporting a child's language development. Teachers can provide activities that promote children's reading, writing, listening, and speaking skills. A language arts learning center is designed for this purpose. Teachers also have the responsibility of supporting English language learners as they develop literacy skills.

Graphic Organizer

As you read, you will discover information about the setup of language arts learning centers. Use a web organizer like the one shown to record the four areas of the center. Include notes about the setup and materials needed for each area.

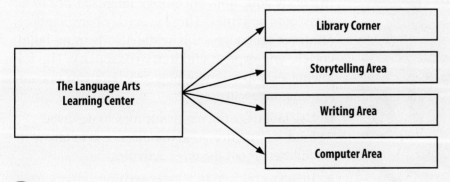

Graphic Organizer Go to **connected.mcgraw-hill.com** *to print this Graphic Organizer.*

◆**Vocabulary**

You can find definitions in the glossary at the back of this book.

▼**Literacy Readiness**

Early educators play an important role in supporting a child's early interest in language arts. *What is emergent literacy?*

The Language Arts Curriculum

From infancy, children begin learning language as they hear sounds on a daily basis at home. They first learn their native languages, or the language spoken in the home. During infancy, children understand much more language than they can speak. Their use of language increases during the toddler years. Preschoolers' vocabulary expands greatly. Interested adults who listen to children and respond with conversation encourage language development.

Child care professionals encourage this development by offering a language arts curriculum. **Language arts** includes activities that teach children to listen, speak, read, and write. The goal is to help children learn to communicate well with others. Children need approximately two years of experience making the sounds of a language and listening to others make sounds before their speech is understandable. The ability to read and write language takes even longer. Time to master language is particularly important for bilingual children who understand and speak two languages.

Encouraging Literacy

Literacy refers to the ability to use language through reading and writing. Children's gradual development of literacy skills over time is called **emergent literacy**. *Readiness* is a key word when speaking about language and literacy development. Although some adults take great pride when a child speaks, reads, or writes at an early age, rushing development too quickly is not the goal of a child care or preschool program. Early educators who create language arts interest in children instill confidence and help them develop coordination. Small motor skills build children's readiness to master language skills.

Effective early childhood classrooms are filled with language opportunities. Child care professionals model proper language usage throughout the day. Teachers should talk with each child every day and call him or her by name, regardless of the child's age or current language abilities. Effective early educators encourage language use in all classroom activities. These everyday conversations reinforce language skills while also helping build, enrich, and expand children's vocabulary. The following examples show how teachers can encourage language learning:

▶ Use language during mealtimes to describe food, to practice good manners, and to talk with children about the day's activities.

▶ Involve children in a letter-writing activity to an ill classmate or writing a thank-you note to a guest speaker.

- Place toy telephones in the dramatic play center to encourage conversation.

- Demonstrate communication skills such as active listening and open-ended questions when speaking with individual children or small groups.

- Encourage listening skills by telling stories, reading books aloud, and asking comprehension questions about the story.

- Explain procedures to children, such as how to tie shoes, clean the classroom, or wash hands after toileting.

- Observe and listen to children. Expand their language by asking questions while children work. For example, when working on tying shoes, ask, "What other kinds of shoes have you seen?" "Who wears them?" and "Why do they wear them?" This encourages children to use verbal skills and increases their vocabulary.

- Encourage children to ask their own questions and to talk about their own experiences and observations.

Early childhood teachers further encourage language skills by creating a **print-rich environment**, which uses printed materials throughout the classroom in meaningful ways. A print-rich environment encourages constructive play. For example, when playing restaurant, children use a telephone book to look up a telephone number to make reservations. Menus in the play restaurant help children understand why reading is helpful. Books in the dramatic play center allow children to read as their parents do. Classroom objects and areas can be labeled. The science center should be stocked with accessible nature books. Including reading and writing in various classroom activities in this manner is known as practicing **whole language**.

The Language Arts Center

Although language skills can be practiced in all learning centers, the language arts learning center is specifically designed for this purpose. This center promotes the process behind creativity. Each child's creative expression is unique and should be supported by early educators as he or she develops literacy skills.

The center should be quiet and well lit. It should include a library corner, a storytelling and puppet area, a writing area, and a computer or media area.

Expert *Advice . . .*

Every child, to be educationally successful, needs a language-rich environment, one in which adults speak well, listen attentively, and read aloud every day.

— Ernest L. Boyer, educator, *Ready To Learn*

Financial *Literacy*

Saving for Library Supplies

Deanna wants to buy new books, literacy games, and three computers for the library and media center at her child care center. The total cost for these supplies is $2,500 plus $200 for shipping and installation fees. The retailer has an installment payment plan but offers a 15 percent discount (on the entire cost, including shipping and installation) if the customer pays in full at the time of purchase. Deanna wants to take advantage of the discount. She can budget $225 a month for savings. For how many months does Deanna need to save before she will have enough money to purchase the library supplies?

Math Concept **Order of Operations** To solve an equation you must use the correct order of operations. First, simplify within the parentheses, and then evaluate any exponents. Multiply and divide from left to right, and then add and subtract from left to right.

Starting Hint Before solving the problem, write an equation using x as a variable for the number of months. Remember that 15 percent off means Deanna will pay 85 percent (0.85) of the price.

 For more math practice, go to the Math Appendix at the back of the book.

Library Corner

A library corner should be a quiet spot with few distractions. Rugs or carpeting, child-size rocking chairs, and stuffed animals all help make reading an enjoyable experience. Displaying book jackets on low bulletin boards and hanging character mobiles helps build interest in reading. Books should also be prominently displayed with front covers visible and eye-catching.

The focal point, of course, is a well-stocked bookshelf. **Figure 20.1** provides tips on how to select good children's literature. Story recordings and audio books are also helpful, especially for children with visual impairments.

Storytelling Area

Here children should find items for acting out stories. These include puppets, a stage for puppet plays, and dollhouses with dolls of different ethnic backgrounds and both genders. Pictures that stimulate ideas and a recording device encourage children to invent stories and to tell about personal experiences.

Some teachers enjoy using a video camera to record children's stories. These can be fun to play back for parents to help them see their children's language development in use with peers.

Figure 20.1 Selecting Good Children's Literature

Quality Reading Not all children's books are of good quality. Early educators can use these tips to make excellent selections for a library corner. *How can you tell whether a book is worthwhile for children?*

Look for the following qualities when choosing children's literature:

- **Characters** that interest young children—such as children, families, and animals—or to whom they can easily relate. Avoid stereotypical characters relating to gender, race, or ethnicity.

- **Plot** A simple, understandable plot

- **Themes** that are appropriate for and understandable by young children, such as friendship or pets

- **Illustrations** Pictures that clearly show the plot and the characters' actions. Illustrations should accurately reflect the story's main concepts.

- **Topics** A focus on familiar topics that build on a child's firsthand knowledge of the world, such as home life

- **Vocabulary** No more than five sentences per page. The story should include basic, but descriptive, vocabulary.

- **Appropriate Tempo** Predictable phrases, repetition, and rhymes that encourage children to read along

- **Engaging** Humor and suspense to maintain interest; make-believe themes that do not frighten or confuse young children

- **Accuracy** Current, accurate information in nonfiction books

Writing Area

Children can practice their emerging writing skills at a writing area. They can "write" their stories as scribbles or with rough words. Listen as a child dictates a story and write the words for him or her exactly as spoken. Stimulate interest in words with alphabet books, magnetic letters, and writing toys such as letter stencils. Offer a variety of writing tools of various thicknesses, such as pencils, crayons, chalk, colored pencils, markers, and pens. Rubber stamps and stamp pads add fun to writing.

Various papers also motivate writing, such as lined and unlined, cardboard, postcards, message pads, graph paper, journals, and outdated business stationery. Include envelopes and play stamps for letter writing. A chalkboard, white board, and clipboards with paper can be used by children. A chart showing numbers and upper- and lowercase letters is another handy resource.

Children love to draw pictures for books they have written— even if the words they write are scribbles. They also like illustrating books they dictate to a teacher. Encourage children to label their drawings, or help them create labels as they explain their work verbally. This shows children the relationship between spoken and printed words. To encourage young authors, provide paper connectors, such as tape, stapler, paper punch, yarn or string, and paper clips, which allow children to create their own books.

The writing area should include many samples of the written word, such as magazines, greeting cards, catalogs, calendars, coupons, and newspapers. Children enjoy making items in the writing area that they can use in the dramatic play center. For example, if children are pretending to run a movie theater, they can make play money or tickets in the writing area for "customers" to use.

▲ Writing Skills

The writing area should include a variety of writing tools and paper as well as many samples of the written word. *What are some strategies a teacher can use to encourage writing practice?*

Computer Area

Computer programs with developmentally appropriate word games may also be provided to build and reinforce children's literacy skills. Computer desks and chairs should be child-size and at the correct level to avoid neck or eyestrain.

Small-motor, verbal, and problem-solving skills as well as basic concepts can be developed through computer play. Computers can also help prevent bias toward children with special needs because some of these children perform as well as their peers on computer tasks. The How To feature on page 444 provides guidelines for using computers effectively with children.

MBI/Alamy

How to . . .

Use Computers Effectively with Children

Like other play materials, computers can benefit children. They should enrich learning by working with other play activities, such as pretend play, art, or music, to support active engagement. Children's software programs and online educational games can stimulate learning and support development. Evaluate software programs and online games before offering them to children. The following are guidelines for the effective use of computers with young children:

▶ **Visual** *The software uses pictures, colorful graphics, and spoken instructions, rather than written ones, to promote independent learning.*

▶ **Control** *Children control the level of difficulty, the pace, and the direction of the program.*

▶ **Variety** *The software offers variety; children can explore a number of topics on different levels.*

▶ **Feedback** *Children receive quick feedback, so they stay interested and experience success.*

▶ **Appealing** *The software appeals to children by using interesting sights and sounds.*

▶ **Developmentally Appropriate** *The product is appropriate for a child's current level of development and skills.*

▶ **Engaging** *The software engages children's interest by encouraging children to laugh, to explore, and to use their imagination.*

▶ **Safety** *Keep the rules of safe Internet use in mind to prevent misuse of technology.*

Apply It!
Preview a selection of children's software programs. Which ones offer more interactive learning? What makes them more interactive?

©JGI/Jamie Grill/Blend Images LLC

Internet Safety When children go online, you are welcoming the world into your child care program. This can be an excellent learning opportunity, but there are some visitors you do not want. That is why filtered search engines are important.

Computers should always be visible in the classroom for teacher monitoring. And young children should never be alone to view Web sites on their own. Many things can pop up on the Internet that children should not see and that could even frighten them. An adult must be nearby to screen content.

Sometimes preschoolers view Web sites with older school-age children, so tips on Internet safety should be shared with both age groups. Children should be taught and always use the following basic rules for children's safe Internet use:

▶ Never give out personal information such as name, address, age, or password.

▶ Never agree to meet anyone they have met on the Internet or invite them to your program or their homes.

▶ Never use an adult's credit card without permission to purchase an item online.

▶ Do not keep secrets from adults such as teachers or parents. If a scary, violent, vulgar, or sexual message or photo appears on the screen, children should tell a teacher immediately.

▶ If cyberbullying occurs, children should tell a teacher immediately.

READING CHECK ✔ **Recall** What is the goal of a language arts curriculum?

Language Arts Activities

Language arts activities offer children opportunities to use language in many different and engaging ways. These activities involve children in the basics of language, including listening, speaking, reading, and writing.

Reading to Children

Hearing good children's books read aloud motivates children to want to learn to read and eventually write. They like to look at books independently and practice early reading skills, such as turning pages and looking at books from front to back. Reading books to children helps them develop a love for language.

Hearing stories is a special pleasure that captures children's imaginations, introduces them to new knowledge, and helps to form a bond with teachers. Board books with sturdy cardboard pages hold up best to wear and tear from toddlers. Preschoolers enjoy picture books. They have large, often full-page, illustrations. The pages may have no words or a few simple sentences.

Respond to SPECIAL NEEDS

Dyslexia

Dyslexia is a learning disability in which children have difficulty learning to decode written language. This leads to problems with reading and spelling. An estimated 3 to 6 percent of school-age children have dyslexia. Reading is central to many areas of learning, so these children often struggle in other subjects. Dyslexia is not related to intelligence. Students with dyslexia can score high on learning ability tests when the tests are not reading-based. When reading to a child with dyslexia, look at and talk about an entire book, including pictures, before reading the text.

Critical Thinking

Select a picture book with a child. Without reading, look at the illustrations and briefly discuss the story page by page. Write key words that the child predicts will appear in the story. Read the story aloud. Listen and look for the words. Did the illustrations reveal the plot and characters? Make a list of the things you will consider before selecting a book for a child with dyslexia.

The plot of a good children's book is simple, so it can be told in pictures. The words and pictures are matched carefully. This shows children that words can create images to tell a story. Big books are oversized picture books, sometimes as large as 24 by 36 inches. This enlarged format enables groups of children to see the pictures better. When choosing books, be sure to think about the interests of each age level:

▶ **Infants and toddlers** enjoy picture books with large illustrations and bright colors. Books for toddlers should emphasize words they already know. Toddlers enjoy stories about others their own age. Animal and vehicle books that emphasize sound words are other favorites. Rhythm, rhyme, and repetition make story time fun and encourage creativity in language.

▶ **Preschoolers** like books about familiar characters and experiences. Stories about other children, family, and community workers, such as police officers and doctors, appeal to them. They also enjoy make-believe and the world of talking animals. Preschoolers love books with funny situations, surprises, and exaggeration. Teachers should introduce longer storybooks gradually as children develop their interest in reading and can focus their attention for a longer period, or length of time.

▶ **School-age children** have various reading tastes depending on their interests. Books and children's magazines about nature, science, and community life are popular. School-age children like fantasy and humor.

▲ Capture Their Imaginations

Preschoolers love to hear stories about familiar characters and situations. *What are some ways an early educator can make reading activities fun and engaging for children?*

Reading Stories to Children

What do you like when you listen to a story? An expressive reader? Humorous characters? Gradual suspense? A surprise ending? Children like the same things. It takes practice to keep children's interest while reading aloud, but the effort is well worth it. Here are suggestions for success:

▶ Prepare by selecting an appropriate book and reading it aloud several times to yourself.

▶ As children seat themselves, do a simple hand game or chant or sing songs until they settle down.

▶ Be certain that all children can see the book.

▶ Introduce the story with an interesting technique or prop to capture interest.

▶ Show children the jacket cover. Ask them if they can guess what the story will be about.

▶ Read the book title and the name of the author and illustrator before beginning to read.

- Hold the book open beside you, facing the children as you read.
- Read with expression and enthusiasm. Use different voices for story characters.
- Whisper, talk louder, or include a child's name in the story to keep the entire group's attention.
- Occasionally move back and forth from the book to children to maintain eye contact.
- Find ways to include children in the story reading. For example, when a horse predictably steps over a bridge, children could provide sound effects by tapping two music rhythm sticks together.
- Whenever possible, encourage children to chant along with predictable words or phrases in the book.
- Have fun with the story by dressing up like one of the characters in the book. For example, if reading a fairy tale, wear a homemade cape, a crown, or a princess hat while reading.

With just a little creativity, children's attention will be captured and they will catch your enthusiasm. Story time can be even more exciting when a teacher can share a story from memory. **Figure 20.2** provides tips on sharing an oral story in an engaging and memorable way.

Figure 20.2 **Succeeding at Storytelling**

Tell Me a Story Children often enjoy being read to, but story time is even more interesting when an adult tells a story from memory. *How does varying your voice help tell a story?*

When telling stories, use the following tips:

- **Identify Your Audience** You will likely tell your story differently to a group of older children than to a group of young toddlers. Use vocabulary, visual aids, and props that will be easily understood by your audience.
- **Use Props** Puppets, pictures, hats, eyeglasses, noisemakers, and other items will help you tell your story. Make sure your props are close by before you begin.
- **Practice** Make sure your story will be heard and understood by practicing. Use a mirror to rehearse speech, facial expressions, actions, and timing.
- **Begin and End** Before you start your story, use an introduction to give listeners a hint of what is to come. Then wrap up your story with an exciting ending.

- **Vary Your Voice** Keep listeners interested by using different voices, especially as you change characters. Different voice tones, volumes, and speeds will help you identify character changes.
- **Stop the Clock** Do not limit yourself to a set amount of storytelling time. You will not want to rush through your story, nor will you want to drag it out to fill time. Use pauses to collect your thoughts or to build suspense.
- **Surprise the Audience** If you are telling a story that may have been heard before, surprise your audience with a different high point or ending.
- **Listen** Although you are the one telling the story, you will want to listen as well. Feedback can help you determine if your story is being told in a way that interests your audience.

APPLY IT! Prepare an age-appropriate story to share with a group of preschoolers or school-age children. Whether you make up your tale or talk about something that actually happened, start out by writing your story on paper. Then use the above tips to tell your story. Make sure the content you choose is appropriate.

Listening and Speaking Activities

Although some children are more talkative than others, all children need practice with talking and listening. Along with having books read to them daily, there are many other ways to promote children's listening and speaking skills. The following activities help children learn to hear similarities and differences in sounds and words, a skill called **auditory discrimination**.

Sound-Matching Games

These games **require**, or need, children to match sounds they hear. To make a sound game, provide pairs of plastic eggs (all one color) that contain identical materials. You might use rice, pebbles, and beans. When children shake the plastic eggs, they match the pairs by sound. You can also find ready-made sound-matching games. Toy catalogs sell games that have animal noises recorded. Children match an animal picture with the sound the animal makes. Music activities are also great ways to encourage children to listen to sounds.

Finger Plays, Nursery Rhymes, and Songs

The playful rhythms, patterns of repeating phrases, and rhyming of words make language fun. Children hear the parts of words (syllables) as they are stressed and stretched to the rhythm of the song or rhyme. **Finger plays** add a visual element to the words by accompanying a song with specific hand motions.

Sharing Time

Children, especially preschoolers, love to talk about themselves—their pets, families, culture, and activities. By encouraging children to share information during group conversations, teachers promote self-confidence, self-esteem, and communication skills. They also encourage children to take an interest in others. With open-ended questions, children give more complete answers.

Puppetry and Dramatic Play

When groups of children play with puppets, they learn to listen and talk. Participate with students in these make-believe activities to promote language and creativity. Dramatic play themes that promote language skills include characters such as news reporters, weather and radio announcers, and restaurant servers. Try to choose plays and puppet shows from children's languages and cultures. Ask parents to participate, if possible.

▼ **Constructive Play**

When teachers participate in puppetry and dramatic play, they are also promoting language and creativity development. *What skills do a group of children practice when playing with puppets?*

Peer Conversations

Children's conversation skills get natural practice when teachers work to make group times, such as mealtimes, relaxed for socializing. Encourage children to listen to and respond to each other by using subtle prompting. For instance, if a child comments on a sight seen at the zoo, ask others if they have questions about the zoo they would like to ask. Build conversations around children's common experiences. If several children visit the same park or see the same movie, suggest children comment about what happened.

If children begin to talk mainly to a teacher, gently remind them that the other children like to listen to them as well. Facilitate children's conversations whenever possible. Children who take a vacation or have extended family visiting have lots of news they can learn to communicate verbally to peers. Remind them to call each other by name and to take turns to let everyone have a chance to share.

Flannel Board Play

Children and teachers can tell stories by using flannel boards. These are large pieces of cardboard or wood covered with flannel or felt. They range in size from 12-inches square to those as large as a bulletin board. Small figures, such as people or animals, are cut from flannel or felt of different colors. These figures stay in position when placed against the flannel board but can be easily repositioned. The storyteller moves the figures on the board as the story progresses. These can be bought from retailers or easily made at home.

Writing Activities

Preschoolers love to pretend to write. They may "write" a letter that contains zigzag markings that represent words. These early steps prepare children for real writing. Children gradually learn **visual discrimination**, or to notice similarities and differences in shapes and alphabet letters. This is a necessary reading and writing skill.

As children learn to write, they have to concentrate to control the writing tool. Writing requires strength in the thumb and fingers. These muscles must be fully developed to easily control writing tools. As small-motor skills develop, the hand gains better control of a pencil. Playing with dough or clay and manipulative toys, such as connecting blocks, helps this skill develop. Using safety scissors, crayons, markers, and paintbrushes also prepares children to use writing tools.

Eye-hand coordination is another skill needed for writing. To form letters and words, children must make the hand and eye work together. Stringing beads and working puzzles develop this skill.

▼ **Learning to Write**

Writing requires strength and coordination. *What are some activities early educators can offer to help children develop small-motor skills?*

▲ Practicing Printing

Learning to write requires a lot of practice. *What are some strategies early educators can use to help children practice writing?*

As with other developmental skills, not all children begin to write at the same time. When children are ready for writing, provide them with examples that show how to make printed letters. Several manuscript systems, or methods for printing letters and numbers, are used successfully with children. Find out which one is used in your program and follow it. Practice your own printing skills to provide a good model.

Generally, the first word a child prints is his or her own name. Help children recognize their names by printing them on paintings, nametags, and cubbies. Use both upper and lower case letters. Provide children with printed copies of their names and encourage them to practice copying the letters. Children need patient support. Gather children's writing in a portfolio and show it to parents so they can see their children's literacy progress.

The need to communicate motivates children to learn to write. Young children can express ideas through writing by dictating their thoughts to a teacher, who writes their words on a poster board or a language chart. Children five years and older enjoy writing words themselves. They often begin by copying words others write for them.

The rules of spelling can be confusing and difficult for children to remember. Early writers often use **invented spelling**, spelling a word the way it sounds. Be patient with children's invented spelling. If you do not understand what a child writes, ask the child to read it to you. The more children write, the more they will want to learn to write accurately. When asked, help children with spelling and writing. You can reinforce writing efforts by asking children to share their writing during group times.

READING CHECK ✔ **Identify** What are the six types of listening and speaking activities?

English Language Learners

Today's diverse society is creating schoolrooms across the country in which children may be learning English as a second language. These students are often called English language learners. This is also not unusual for an early childhood classroom. In fact, some preschoolers enter child care already bilingual, meaning they speak both their families' language spoken at home as well as English.

Contrary to popular belief, a child who is bilingual is not at risk for language delays. In fact, all children are born capable of learning two or more languages. The young brain is "hard-wired" to be especially skilled in learning languages. Children will speak the languages they hear put to use most often in their immediate environment. In many countries, it is very common for children to speak two or more languages. Research has shown that being bilingual has long-term intellectual, social, and economic benefits for children.

Children can build good speaking and listening skills no matter what language they use to communicate. The development of children's language skills in their first language also supports learning English.

While it is helpful to have bilingual teaching staff in classrooms with young English language learners, it is not required for children to learn English. However, to help children maintain their first language as well as learn English, it is important that monolingual or bilingual teachers work closely with parents. These parents can best help children preserve their first language. The parents' attitude can also help, or hinder, children understand the importance of learning English. This is why positive parent and teacher interactions and communication is important to successful child care professionals.

Child care professionals can support English language learners and bilingual children by using the following strategies:

▶ Provide consistent language models for both languages when selecting materials.

▶ Use lullabies, songs, games, stories, books, and finger plays from both languages. Include parents by asking them for examples from their childhood.

▶ Use real objects and everyday experiences to help children learn language and to make connections to word meanings.

▶ Support children's attempts to use the second language with patience and respect.

▶ Encourage and praise children's use of words in both languages to help them feel good about themselves as speakers of each language.

▶ When appropriate, allow children to express themselves in the language of their choice.

▶ Give all children in the class the opportunity to learn by providing whole-group activities that involve dance, music, art, literature, celebrations, and active games from the bilingual students' cultures.

▲ **English Language Learners**

Teachers play an important role in supporting English language learners' literacy skills. *How can parents support English language learners' language development?*

READING CHECK ✔ **Describe** What are three strategies that early educators can use to support English language learners?

OJO Images Ltd/Alamy

The Transition to College

College & Career READINESS

What Can I Do to Make the College Transition Easier?

The jump to college is exciting, but it can also be quite stressful. You are leaving behind what you are comfortable with and going to explore a new place. Many students overlook the stress involved in making so many changes so quickly. The more prepared you are, the easier the transition will be.

What is the biggest change?

College involves more independence and increased responsibility. These can be exciting and enjoyable changes, but they need to be handled carefully. You likely will not have as strong a support system as you do now. For example, you will probably have to start managing your own money. You need to start learning how to make smart decisions and to think about long-term results.

How do I deal with the academic challenges of college?

College courses will be more difficult, and you will probably have more reading, writing, and problem sets than you are used to. Most first-year college students experience an adjustment period, so if you are struggling at first, do not think you are going to fail. Give yourself a chance to adjust gradually by choosing a course load that includes some challenging classes and some that are less intense.

How can I learn to manage my time?

In high school, you probably had a lot of help with time management. At college, the responsibility of managing your schedule will largely be your own. This includes going to class and doing assignments. Write when and where your classes meet, when assignments are due, and when tests will take place. Give yourself time to study rather than waiting until the last minute.

Hands-On

College Readiness One transitional problem that new college students experience is learning how to stay organized. Between living on their own for the first time, choosing and taking classes, learning a new place, and developing a new social life, students have their hands full. With all these changes, it is easy to get overwhelmed. Think of some things new college students can do to get and stay organized. Put these suggestions into a list.

Path to Success

Set Up a Schedule Find a daily routine that works for you, and stick to it.

Go to Class Skipping class can be tempting, but it is a sure way to fall behind.

Be Patient Remember that making new friends takes time and will not happen immediately.

Go to Office Hours Take advantage of the time that professors are available outside of class.

Rest Do not cut back on sleep because you are busy.

Ask for Help If you are falling behind, seek help from your college's resources, including tutors, academic advisors, and writing centers.

Comstock Images/Getty Images

Literacy and Language Arts
Visual Summary

Reading
Read board books, picture books, and big books.
Consider age-appropriate reading levels and themes.
Use expressive reading and characterization.
Engage children in oral storytelling.

Writing
Promote small-motor skills development and eye-hand coordination.
Support children's gradual development from scribbles to letters to words.
Print children's names on paintings, nametags, and cubbies.

Building Language Arts Skills

Listening and Speaking
Encourage listening and speaking skills with the following:
Sound-matching games
Puppetry and dramatic play
Finger plays, nursery rhymes, and songs
Sharing time
Peer conversations
Flannel board play

Vocabulary Review

1. Create a fill-in-the-blank sentence for each of the content and academic vocabulary words. The sentence should contain enough information to help determine the missing word.

Content Vocabulary

◇ language arts (p. 440)
◇ emergent literacy (p. 440)
◇ print-rich environment (p. 441)
◇ whole language (p. 441)
◇ auditory discrimination (p. 448)
◇ finger plays (p. 448)
◇ visual discrimination (p. 449)
◇ invented spelling (p. 450)

Academic Vocabulary
■ period (p. 446)
■ require (p. 448)

Review Key Concepts

2. **Identify** the four areas of the language arts curriculum.
3. **Explain** how a language arts learning center can promote development of language skills.
4. **Describe** an example activity for each of the main language arts areas.
5. **Define** the terms *English language learner* and *bilingual*. How do these terms relate to language development?

Critical Thinking

6. **Summarize** What are two appropriate strategies that help promote the development of children's emergent literacy?

7. **Understand** What is a print-rich environment? How can it support literacy skills?

8. **Produce** Create a plan for two activities that can help increase listening and speaking skills in children.

9. **Describe** the characteristics of a good children's picture book. Create a checklist of these characteristics and use it to evaluate eight children's picture books.

10. **Apply** What are some Internet safety procedures you could use in your classroom to prevent the misuse and abuse of technology with children while online?

21st Century Skills

Communication Skills

11. **Presenting Literature** Use the tips you read in this chapter to select and read a good children's book to a small group of students. Then describe three suitable follow-up activities a child care professional could conduct with children after reading the book. Ask the group to identify strengths of your presentation and to offer suggestions for improvement.

Leadership Skills

12. **Volunteer Project** Develop a proposal for a volunteer project that involves literacy. Possible projects include setting up an after-school reading program between older and younger students or organizing a book collection drive to benefit a local youth program. Use your leadership and teamwork skills to plan and implement this project with fellow classmates.

Child Care LAB

Use the skills you have learned in this chapter.

Create a Language Arts Learning Center

13. **Language Arts Activities** With a partner, plan a language arts center for two different age groups that encourages children's exploration, discovery, and development. Identify the items you would need for a library corner, a storytelling area, a writing area, and a computer area.

   A. Layout Plan the layout for the four areas of the learning center. Where would you place furniture, such as bookcases, chairs, and desks for the best use of space?

   B. List Create a list of items you would need in each area. Think about the number and type of books you might need for the library. What kinds of supplies are needed for the storytelling and writing areas? How many computers are appropriate for this age group?

   C. Create Develop an example learning activity for each area of the center. Use your computer skills to combine all the elements of your activity into a PowerPoint or online presentation.

   D. Appropriateness Consider how to make your activities age- and developmentally appropriate. What development skills would a child need to succeed at this activity?

   E. Present Share your learning center layout, plan, and learning activities with another group. If possible, conduct your learning activity with a child you know.

Create Your Evaluation

Create an evaluation sheet with these categories:

• Appropriate layout
• Appropriate supplies
• Completeness of activity
• Age-appropriate
• Developmentally appropriate

Have another group use the sheet to evaluate your learning center, rating each category from 1 to 10.

Academic Skills

English Language Arts

14. Integrating Curriculum Work in teams to write a lesson plan that combines an element of language arts with another curriculum area such as math, science, creative art, or social studies. Each group must develop three to four activities so its lesson plan could work for different age groups. Consider how children learn differently and choose a variety of teaching methods. Present your lesson plan to the class.

Social Studies

15. Meeting Individual Needs English language learners and bilingual students need special consideration when planning language arts-based activities. Develop a language arts activity that appeals to English language learners by incorporating other cultures. For example, think about how you could use another culture's music, art, literature, dance, celebrations, or games in a language arts activity that would appeal to all learners. Present your activity to a partner.

Science

16. Observe Teaching Styles There are many different methods for integrating language arts topics, such as reading, writing, listening, and speaking, into other curriculum areas. Individuals learn differently so it is important to use a variety of teaching methods. For example, you may learn a science concept best by reading information and writing a report. Your friend may learn better by listening to a teacher explain the concept and then giving an oral report.

Procedure During each of your classes, note if and how the teacher integrates language arts into the lesson. Is the course reading-based with opportunities for writing? How does the teacher support these reading and writing efforts? Are there opportunities to interact with the teacher or other students to practice speaking and listening skills?

Analysis Use your notes to create a table that shows the teaching methods used, the subjects of the classes, and the number of teachers who use them. Write a summary of your findings.

Certification Prep

Sharpen your test-taking skills to improve your certification program score.

Directions Read each statement. Then read the answer choices and choose the option that best completes the sentence.

17. The ability to hear similarities and differences in sounds and words is a skill called _____.

  A. auditory discrimination

  B. acute listening

  C. visual discrimination

  D. restricted listening

18. Spelling a word the way it sounds is called _____.

  A. creative spelling

  C. invented spelling

  B. phonetic spelling

  D. incorrect spelling

> **Test-Taking Tip**
> Be sure to read the directions carefully. If you are asked to choose the best answer, there may be more than one *correct* answer from which to choose.

(t)©Nova Development; (b)©Comstock/Alamy

CHAPTER 21

Math and Science Explorations

Writing Activity

⭐ 21st Century Skills

Initiative Consider what you have learned about child care careers so far and think about your personal career goals. Choose a job in the child care industry in which you are interested and write a cover letter as if you were applying for that job. Use proper grammar, punctuation, and voice as you write, and explain why you are qualified for the position.

Writing Tips
1. Use a standard cover-letter format and type your letter.
2. Explain your employment goals clearly.
3. Reflect your attitude and communication skills.
4. Proofread carefully to correct errors in grammar, usage, spelling, and punctuation.

Explore the Photo
Children build their understanding of science by exploring their world. *What activities encourage learning about science?*

Tetra images/SuperStock

Reading Guide

How Can You Improve? Before starting the section, think about the last exam you took on material you had to read. What reading strategies helped you on the test? Make a list of ways to improve your strategies in order to succeed on your next exam.

Read to Learn

Key Concepts

- **Explain** how math activities benefit children.
- **Describe** the goals of a science curriculum.
- **Analyze** what can be learned from studying the natural world.

Main Idea

Understanding of math and science begins early. To help children develop intellectually, child care and education professionals plan and lead math and science activities that promote learning, and make the subjects interesting and enjoyable.

Content Vocabulary

- ◇ mathematics
- ◇ mathematical vocabulary
- ◇ numerals
- ◇ science
- ◇ sensory table
- ◇ light table
- ◇ rebus recipe
- ◇ nature education
- ◇ field guide

Academic Vocabulary

- ■ highlight
- ■ resources

Graphic Organizer

As you read, you will discover many math and science activities you can do with children. Use a Venn diagram like the one shown to organize the listed activities into categories and see where they overlap.

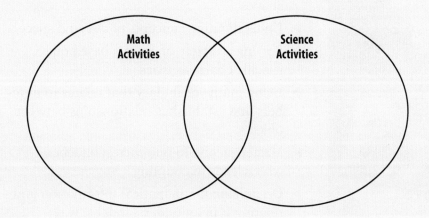

Math Activities | Science Activities

Graphic Organizer *Go to* **connected.mcgraw-hill.com** *to print this Graphic Organizer.*

AS YOU READ

Recall Think about the math and science activities you have enjoyed. What made them entertaining? What did you learn?

◇**Vocabulary**

You can find definitions in the glossary at the back of this book.

▼**Educational Materials**

Many toys and educational materials are designed to teach math principles to young children. *What math skills would these toys help develop?*

Math for Young Children

Math is part of everyone's daily life. As children become competent and comfortable with math, they will see math in everyday life. For example, math is used in determining how much of the family budget can be spent on food. Career opportunities, from construction to computer programming, require good math skills. Effective early childhood educators can help children discover meaningful applications of math skills in daily life.

Helping children develop a positive attitude toward math as a helpful tool begins in preschool or earlier. **Mathematics** is the study of shapes and numbers and the use of numbers. Children experience math concepts daily without realizing it. For example, they may see many flowers in a field or discover that an object is heavier than it looks. All these general ideas become part of their **mathematical vocabulary**, or words that express numbers, quantities, shape, size, and volume. For example, children might say, "We make a sandwich with two slices of bread and one square slice of cheese." This exposure to concepts of measurement, shape, and comparison is a lesson in math. Children who frequently speak and hear these terms become fluent in math.

Math Curriculum Goals

True understanding of math occurs between ages five and seven. At this age, children are in the middle to later part of Piaget's preoperational stage of intellectual development. The goal of a math curriculum for young children is to provide an environment that encourages the awareness and development of math skills. Math program objectives include the following:

▶ Identifying, describing, and classifying shapes

▶ Understanding concepts of size and space

▶ Sorting a variety of objects based on specific characteristics

▶ Using math vocabulary that relates to numbers and establishes relationships between objects

▶ Mastering one-to-one correspondence, which leads to counting

▶ Organizing mathematical information and relating it in an understandable way

▶ Establishing relationships between objects by comparing them

▶ Using math concepts and applying them to everyday life

©moodboard/Corbis

Math Activities

As in other curriculum areas, hands-on experience with real objects is the best way to lead children to math mastery. When children group, sort, measure, weigh, and compare objects, they see how math skills apply to daily life. Children use math as a way of organizing and communicating information.

Child care professionals **highlight,** or bring attention to, math concepts in classroom activities, regardless of the topic the children are investigating. For instance, children learning about supermarkets will learn about math. While at a supermarket, children can learn about shapes, sizes, color, and quantity of foods. Back in the classroom, a teacher may help the children create a pretend supermarket in the dramatic play center. There they can play with cash registers and pretend money. They may weigh plastic vegetables on scales to determine weight and cost. Integrating math awareness and learning into play activities helps children see why math skills are needed in real life. **Figure 21.1** lists suggestions for how to reinforce math skills during snack time and cooking activities.

Figure 21.1 **Reinforce Math Skills**

Food Preparation Design a food-preparation activity that reinforces math skills for a preschool age child. *How many math concepts could be reinforced? Try the activity with one child or a group of children.*

Teach children about fractions when dividing foods such as fruits, sandwiches, or pizza into equal parts. Move the pieces around to show how fractions combine to make a whole, such as putting two of four pieces back together to make one-half.
The concepts of equal and unequal can be illustrated by cutting pieces of food into equal and unequal portions or giving equal and unequal quantities of a snack such as pretzels.
Teach children about sequence by asking them to recall what they did first, second, and third in a recipe.
Children can practice counting by counting aloud the number of times a food is stirred or by counting ingredients such as raisins.
Have children identify the shapes of food, such as round, square, and triangle. Slices of cheese or bread work well for cutting into shapes. Older children may try more complex shapes, such as octagons.
Reinforce measurement by selecting recipes with ingredients children can measure. Show children how to use a ruler or measuring tape to measure a pan's size.
The concept of time can be introduced with recipes that require foods to sit, chill, or bake for a period of time.

Child care professionals can also observe children as they play to determine each child's level of readiness for new concepts. They can also spot any learning problems children might have when teachers are involved in children's activities. Early childhood teachers use the following types of activities to encourage children to use math skills with confidence.

Recognizing Shapes

Children begin to notice different shapes as infants. By the preschool years, they are ready for activities that help build this skill. During block play, provide different shaped blocks so children can discover how different shapes can be put together—a triangular roof on a rectangular house with square windows. Encourage them to see relationships between shapes by giving them colorful paper shapes to use in creating their own designs and patterns. Shape-matching games also help children recognize shapes.

Sorting

Matching shapes is one way of sorting, or classifying, objects according to one or more characteristics. Children notice similarities and differences in objects, a valuable reasoning skill for both math and science. They can sort colors of clothes when "doing the laundry" during dramatic play. Have them sort tableware for meals. Give children small animal figures and have them create barnyards and zoos by including those animals appropriate to each setting.

Seriation

Identifying size relationships between objects is called seriation. It is organizing objects according to increasing or decreasing size. While children look at a picture book about farming, the teacher might ask, "Which is taller—the farmer or the barn?" In the dramatic play center, the care professional could instruct, "Put the dishes away, with the smaller ones on top of the bigger ones." Lining up blocks from shortest to longest is another seriation activity. Anytime a child can make a comparison, you can help children understand the concept of seriation.

Patterning

As children work with blocks, beads, or pegs of different shapes and colors, they begin to create predictable patterns. Children can continue patterns of repeated shapes or colors as they learn to observe, count, and sequence. For instance, stringed-bead necklaces can be made using a red, blue, red, blue pattern. Gradually, children will notice many other types of predictable patterns such as designs in tiled floors or artistic paintings. Patterns can also be used in physical activity by having children clap, stomp, snap, or move in particular ways.

Rote Counting

Many complex mental processes are used in learning to count. By age three, most children are capable of rote counting. That means they can memorize and recite numbers in order, but they have no real understanding of the quantity the numbers represent. Use activities to teach counting skills. Fill a basket with small items and ask each child to pick out a different quantity. Make counting a physical activity by having children clap their hands, stomp their feet, or jump in place a certain number of times. Make a paper-chain calendar, adding a link at the beginning of each day. Have the children count the number of links.

Rational Counting

To truly understand what numbers and their names represent, children must master rational counting, or learning to recognize the numerical symbols that represent quantities and place them in sequential order. Rational counting requires the understanding of one-to-one correspondence. Children learn to assign one number to each object counted. Care providers encourage this skill by counting objects with the child as each object is touched. You can count steps as the class goes up or down them. You can count graham crackers as the child places them on a tray at snack time. This is double reinforcement—the child realizes that the number of crackers corresponds to the number of students.

Recognizing Numerals

When children understand rational counting, they can learn to recognize **numerals,** or written symbols that represent numbers. Teachers can help them make this association through simple activities. Mark bushel baskets with a numeral and have children place the corresponding number of apples in each one. Have children shape numerals from clay and then roll small bits of clay into the matching

▼ **One-to-One Correspondence**

Children begin to understand the numbers they say when rote counting as they match the numbers to a quantity of objects. *What activities can you do to help children build number skills?*

number of balls. Take photographs of the children in groups of different sizes. Provide them with numeral cards and have them pair the cards with the pictures showing the same number of children. When children build with blocks, talk about how many were used, and then write the numeral on an index card in front of the blocks.

Ordering Numerals

As children advance intellectually, they combine their ability to count with their recognition of numerals. They order numerals, or place them in the correct sequence. Many activities help strengthen this skill. For instance, you could paint numerals on toy cars and have the children race the cars, finishing in numerical order. Children could place leis, each with a different number of flowers, around each other's necks in sequential order. Children can draw cards with numerals on them and then line up according to the number shown.

Making Charts and Graphs

After children learn how to count correctly, they can gather information and organize it so it can be communicated. Charts and bar graphs allow children to relay mathematical information they gather. For instance, children can conduct a class survey of favorite pets. To do this, the teacher gives the children a sheet of paper with columns on it. At the top of each column is a photo or drawing of a typical childhood pet, such as dog, cat, or hamster. Children ask each classmate to pick his or her favorite pet. A tally mark is then made in the appropriate column. After responses are gathered, children count the tally marks in each column and write the total at the bottom. By comparing the column totals, children can announce which pet was picked as the class favorite. By ordering the column totals, they can also determine second-place and third-place favorites. Displaying this information on a poster board lets children refer back to results as they share their learning with parents.

Math Materials

Many materials are available for children to use to explore math concepts. The materials can be used in a variety of learning centers, from block play to art. The following are materials early childhood teachers should have on hand for children's creative use:

- ▶ 1-inch square table blocks in many colors
- ▶ Wood pattern chips and pegs and pegboards in many colors
- ▶ Colored stringing beads of different shapes and interconnecting plastic blocks or bricks
- ▶ Nesting toys and measuring spoons and cups
- ▶ Containers that hold from a half-pint to 1 gallon of liquid
- ▶ Balance and weight scales

- ▶ Height charts and tape measures and rulers
- ▶ Counters—such as buttons, shells, or acorns—and counting table games
- ▶ Shape and number bingo, matching card games, and puzzles
- ▶ Play cash register and play money
- ▶ Clocks, kitchen timers, stopwatches, and plastic hourglass timers

READING CHECK ✔ **Apply** How can building with blocks help children develop math concepts?

▲ **Capturing Interest**

When math materials such as coins capture children's interest, they are more likely to work toward developing their math skills. *What other materials could children use to practice their counting skills?*

Science for Young Children

Children learn to appreciate the wonders of the world at a young age. Young children have unending curiosity. They are full of questions and eager to explore. That curiosity naturally leads them to science.

Science is a process of collecting knowledge about the physical world and how the world works. Active discovery and investigation are the basics of science for children. Hands-on experiences let children witness and experiment with basic science concepts.

Topics for science are endless. They range from using magnets to caring for a classroom pet. Teachers need to guard against doing too much for children as they explore. However, showing children how to use some pieces of equipment and how to carefully treat animals and plants is necessary. Ethical treatment of all forms of life teaches compassion and respect.

Guiding Science Learning

Children discover science best when adults set the stage for safe exploration. As children explore, teachers guide children's learning by asking questions to encourage observation, analysis, and problem solving. Teachers might ask the following questions as children explore:

▶ How does it look?

▶ How does it feel?

▶ What is happening?

▶ Why do you think this is happening?

Child care professionals make the most of teachable moments to spark children's interest in science. If a butterfly is spotted on the play yard, an alert teacher gives children magnifying glasses for closer observation. Children's books on butterflies will be displayed. Art materials will be provided so children can create butterfly drawings or paintings. Teachers might help children plant flowers that will feed the butterfly and provide shelter. Early educators know that children's active participation makes learning more meaningful.

▼ **Teachable Moments**

Child care professionals take advantage of children's interests by building opportunities to explore science. *What questions could you ask this child to help him learn more about what he is looking at?*

KidStock/Getty Images

Science Curriculum Goals

The science curriculum helps children satisfy their curiosity. Science encourages children to wonder and ask questions. It also helps children see that all things on Earth are interrelated. Weather and landscape affect how we live. The ways humans use land can impact other living things, such as plants and animals. There are also basic scientific laws that await children's discovery, such as the effect of temperature on objects, the effects of gravity, and how the sun and water help plants grow.

Regardless of the specific science topics children investigate, teachers pursue certain general science goals. Goals for a science curriculum include

▶ fostering children's appreciation of nature and themselves.

▶ encouraging curiosity and providing chances to explore the world.

▶ allowing children to investigate the world using their senses.

▶ providing children with hands-on experiences that develop basic science concepts.

▶ increasing children's ability to observe, to describe, to classify, to see relationships, and to solve problems.

Science Activities

Before you can develop science activities for children, you need to find ways to make the concepts simple and understandable. You want to spark interest, not overwhelm children with complicated, abstract lectures. A hands-on approach does this best. Relate science principles to everyday life. Some favorite science topics are Earth and its environments; properties of air, soil, and water; characteristics of foods and how they are cooked; and characteristics of plants, animals, and humans.

Early childhood educators organize learning opportunities in response to children's questions or immediate experiences. For instance, if a child went fishing with her grandfather and wondered about the fish in the lake, a study of fish might begin. There are endless other topics that include trees, birds, insects, and seasons; animals—ocean, desert, or forest; colors and how they are made; rocks and minerals; how the body works; and types of transportation.

©Comstock/Alamy

Young children can practice many skills through science activities. They like to collect, observe, and touch objects, plants, and animals. As they do, have them describe what their senses discover. Encourage them to question and to think. Through exploration, they can compare and classify materials. They also note relationships such as cause and effect. In addition, they notice similarities and differences in objects, plants, and animals. They use experimentation to test and retest scientific principles, such as what sinks and what floats.

Science activities need not be long-term projects. Some require little planning or preparation, yet they are rich with learning potential. Think of the science concepts you could explore through the following activities:

▶ Show children how to feel their pulse and heartbeat. Have them do this before and after a vigorous physical activity.

▶ Give children magnets of varied shapes, sizes, and strengths. Have them experiment with objects to find out what the magnets can and cannot pick up.

▶ Make a rainbow by spraying water in the sunshine.

▶ Place a bird feeder just outside the classroom window. Experiment to see what foods the birds prefer.

▶ Use objects to make shadows with a flashlight in a darkened room. Move them closer to and farther from the light. Hold the flashlight at different angles to the objects.

▶ Make static electricity. Rub an inflated balloon with a woolen cloth. Under some conditions—such as in dry weather—static electricity can also be produced by running a comb through your hair. Darken the room for the maximum effect.

▶ Hide a ticking timer in the classroom while children are not looking. Have the children find it by tracking the sound.

▶ Hide objects in a sandbox or sand table for children to find as "fossils" or artifacts.

▲ Observation

Science activities allow children to practice skills such as observation. *What might this girl be observing as she looks at the leaves in the net?*

Science Materials

Many classrooms for young children have a science learning center. The center includes at least one table and a set of chairs. Science collections, such as shells, fossils, or seeds, may be displayed on a low table or shelf. If live animals are included in the program, they may be housed in this learning center.

Because science activities sometimes require a group effort, provide enough materials for at least four children to use at the center at once. Providing more than one set of materials eliminates conflicts over the materials. It also encourages children to work together to develop their social skills. When looking for science materials, include items from nature, such as leaves and twigs, nuts and seeds, shells, fossils, rock and mineral kits, and ant farms. Aquariums, terrariums, kaleidoscopes, prisms, and color paddles also encourage science discovery.

Sometimes a **sensory table** is placed in the science learning center. This is a table with a box-like, hollow top that can hold water, sand, beans, cotton balls, or other substances for children to explore. The substance contained in the table can be changed periodically. Pitchers, funnels, rust-proof spoons, shovels, pails, measuring cups, boats, and trucks are among the equipment children might use at the sensory table.

A **light table** may also be found in a science area. This is a low, lighted table with a white plastic cover. Beneath the cover are low-wattage lightbulbs. Children can place items, such as leaves or colored plastic connecting blocks, on the light table for close inspection. When these items are lit up, they are very enticing to children. Veins on tree leaves can be traced or secondary colors made by laying two colored plastic shapes on top of each other. When creating a science area, be sure the space allows children to work and concentrate without distraction. For example, you might place the science area at the back of the room, away from the door and other learning centers.

▲ **Hands-On Learning**

Some materials lend themselves to dozens of different activities. *What do children learn about the world from science experiences?*

Cooking with Children

Though surprising to many, cooking is a science activity in itself. Recipe contents and the chemical processes that occur during cooking and baking reflect science. The equipment and tools used to cook with children are the results of scientific inventions. Most children are familiar with at least some of the equipment and procedures used in cooking. They can carry out many tasks with appropriate supervision. Cooking is a highly sensory experience, with many opportunities to observe, taste, smell, and handle ingredients and utensils. Children's interest and enjoyment peaks when the science project also produces a tasty snack.

Cooking activities lend themselves easily to topics that relate to vegetables, farming, or family traditions and home life. An activity for a unit on farm animals might include making cream into butter. To learn about vegetables, children might visit an outdoor farmers' market to purchase some vegetables. Then they can use the vegetables and mix the dressing ingredients for a tossed vegetable salad. Cooking activities are also perfect opportunities for parents to share their own expertise. Invite parents to join the class during cooking activities.

When cooking with children, print the recipe in large, bold letters on poster board. You may wish to make a **rebus recipe,** a recipe that illustrates ingredients and directions with picture symbols, to help the children follow the steps. See **Figure 21.2** below. For a successful cooking experience, remember these guidelines:

▶ Look for simple recipes that illustrate the concept to be taught. For children whose first language is not English, try to find recipes in their first languages. Encourage them to speak their own languages and to share names for ingredients while working.

▶ Choose cooking activities that relate to other activities. For example, make a recipe after reading a story that mentions it during story time.

▶ Make cooking activities a cultural experience by preparing simple foods enjoyed in other parts of the world, such as baked plantain.

▶ Use foolproof recipes with children. Test them yourself before having children prepare them.

Figure 21.2 Recipes for Pre-Readers

Rebus Recipes   Even though most preschoolers cannot yet read, they can follow recipe directions that include drawings and symbols. *Why would it be better to use such a recipe rather than just telling the children what to do?*

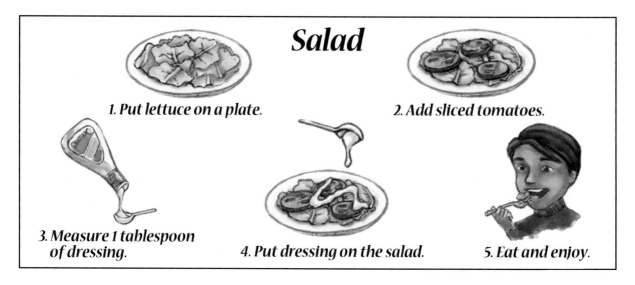

Salad

1. Put lettuce on a plate.

2. Add sliced tomatoes.

3. Measure 1 tablespoon of dressing.

4. Put dressing on the salad.

5. Eat and enjoy.

- Prepare foods over an easily cleaned surface, such as a tile floor.

- Limit group size to no more than six children and supervise them at all times.

- Avoid using kitchen appliances, if possible. Without them, there are more chances for hands-on learning and fewer safety hazards.

- Make sure everyone follows the rules of safety and sanitation. Wear aprons to keep clothing clean.

- Allow plenty of time. Hurrying can lead to carelessness and accidents, and can also hinder learning.

- Let each child participate in some way, adapting the activity or materials for children with special needs.

- Understand that the process of cooking is more important to learning than the finished product. Allow children to take their cooked treat home, if possible.

READING CHECK ✓ **Consider** What characteristics of preschoolers lead them to science discovery?

Exploring Natural Wonders

One of life's special pleasures is experiencing direct contact with nature. Daily experiences with natural elements are relaxing and rewarding for children and teachers alike. Studying nature helps people be in tune with the life cycles of things on earth. Teaching about the environment and life on Earth is called **nature education.**

Here are some ways to help children get the most out of nature education:

- Savor the scents. Smell flowers and blooming shrubs or trees. Notice smells after a rain or after grass is mowed.

- Notice patterns and designs. Patterns can be found in almost any natural object, such as ripples widening in puddles. Rainbows, tree leaves, bird feathers, seashells, or spider webs offer intriguing designs to admire. These patterns may inspire children's drawings, too.

- Trace textures. Gently touch nature items. Discuss textures, such as satiny tree buds, mushy mud, and rough tree bark. Talk about how the breeze feels on the skin and hair.

- Tune into sounds. Sit quietly and listen to nature sounds, such as birds calling, wildlife rustling, and rain falling on a roof.

- Observe the behavior of wildlife. Observe a bird building a nest, caterpillars feeding, or a spider spinning a web. Find animal tracks. Notice what different animals eat and how they catch their food. How do they raise their young? Which animals have colors that blend with nature and help them hide? Notice basic characteristics of wildlife, such as body covering and number of legs.

▶ Notice effects of climate and weather. Observe sun and shadows and notice how wind affects pinwheels, wind chimes, banners, kites, and windsocks. Talk about the different types of clouds. Watch it rain and observe its effects. Enjoy snow activities such as sledding or finding animals tracks in the snow.

▶ Visit various nature areas. Visit a lake or walk a woodland path. Parks and wildlife preserves have many natural objects to investigate. Discover what creatures live in each habitat.

▶ Examine various types of plant life. Learn about seeds, stems, leaves, and roots. Find plants that grow in different types of soil, such as sandy, wet, clay, or dry soil.

▶ Locate animal and insect homes. Observe animals in their homes. What are the homes made of? How are they made?

▶ **Exploring the Outdoors**

Learning about science and how the world works should not be confined to the classroom. *What learning opportunities do the outdoor environment and natural world offer?*

© Image Source Pink / Alamy

Tools for Nature Exploration

Nature items can be explored safely, and in greater detail, when simple tools are provided. These tools may include

- ▶ a magnifying glass to look closely at flowers, moss, or bird tracks.
- ▶ a pair of binoculars to see distant wildlife.
- ▶ paper bags, grocery bags, or backpacks in which to collect nature items for art projects.
- ▶ bug cages for looking at insects or worms.
- ▶ a hand-held recorder for recording nature sounds.
- ▶ sketch pads and some colored pencils for drawing nature sights.
- ▶ cameras or a camcorder to record nature experiences.
- ▶ a **field guide**—book for identifying natural items, such as flowers, insects, birds, or trees.
- ▶ a first aid kit for any nature field trip.

SAFETY MATTERS

Health Precautions and Classroom Pets

Caution and good judgment are part of having animals in the classroom. The animals must be healthy. A veterinarian should certify that classroom pets are in good health. Be sure none of the children are allergic to the pet.

Mature, well-trained pets are best to have around children because children are often unpredictable and could upset or frighten an animal. Older animals are often calmer and less likely to frighten children.

What Would You Do? A parent offers to get a pet for your preschool classroom. What type of animal would be best suited to your room? What questions should you keep in mind when considering this offer?

Classroom Pets

Typical classroom pets include fish, rabbits, gerbils, hamsters, chameleons, and hermit crabs. Pets offer many lessons in science. They allow children to witness basic facts of the natural world up close. A pet's texture and color of body covering provide clues about the natural world. How an animal moves and eats is a great topic for investigation. How an animal communicates and plays is fun to observe as well.

Pets also respond to a human's social needs. Children practice compassion and responsibility as they care for pets during feeding or cleaning. People feel important and needed when they know a pet is depending on them.

When using pets with children, consider the following factors:

- ▶ The value of interaction between children and pets.
- ▶ The energy levels of children. Choosing a more mature pet may be better in many instances. For example, the high energy of a young puppy may overwhelm children. An older, well-trained dog will likely be calmer around children.
- ▶ The limitations of people with disabilities. Will the pets interfere with mobility?
- ▶ Health conditions and allergies in children and staff.

Bird Watching

Learning to identify birds is an enjoyable pastime for people of all ages. As well as being entertaining, bird watching refines skills in concentration, observation, and reasoning.

Birds can be found almost anywhere. To attract birds offer trees and shrubs, a birdbath, and a food source. Bird books and DVDs are good **resources,** or sources of information, for learning about birds, too. Children can observe the following bird traits as they learn to identify birds: feather color, design, and shape; body size and shape; bill shape, size, and color; wing shape; eye color; flight pattern; bird songs and calls; nest site and materials; and foot details.

Gardening Adventures

Activities with plants and gardening are also great ways to connect people with the natural world. Gardening introduces children to the diversity of plants. Plant growth can be quick and dramatic. Eating plants grown in a garden makes learning rewarding.

Gardening also illustrates the life cycle, or the stages that living things go through during a lifetime. It shows what things are necessary for growth, including good soil, sun, and water. Children can also explore the different parts of plants, including seed, roots, stem, leaves, flower, and fruit.

Gardening shows how plants and insects depend on each other. Bees pollinate flowers as they feed. Caterpillars feed on plants before they turn into butterflies, which helps plant pollination. Birds eat flower seeds as well as carry them to new places. The flowers of plants attract insects, on which birds can feed. In those ways, gardening brings science concepts to life.

Gardening also provides good exercise. Motor control is put to use during raking, weeding, digging, planting, watering, and harvesting plants. Raised garden beds allow those in wheelchairs to participate in gardening, too. **Figure 21.3** lists ideas for indoor gardening.

READING CHECK ✔ **Recall** What are some examples of tools for exploring nature?

▶ **Growing Plants**

Gardening extends the concept of a natural cycle and introduces children to the idea of a food chain. *What sorts of science experiments could you do with plants in a garden?*

Alistair Berg/Getty Images

Figure 21.3

Indoor Gardening

Other Options Many child care centers may not have the space or conditions for an outdoor garden. This should not prevent children from learning about the natural world by growing plants. Activities with plants and gardening can take place indoors, too. *What are some benefits of having an indoor garden instead of an outdoor garden?*

The following are indoor gardening activities for children.

Growing houseplants	Provide clay pots, soil, and seeds or nursery plants. Place near a good light source, such as a window. Children can water regularly and trim them when needed.
Experimenting with celery	Place a stalk of celery in a jar of colored water. Children then can see how plants "drink."
Observing blooming buds	Find a branch with buds on it that are about to bloom. Place the branch in a vase of water. Children can watch the buds blossom.
Growing green-haired funny faces	Fill a coffee can with potting soil. Plant grass seed on top and keep it moist. Tape construction paper around the coffee can and draw a funny face on it. As grass grows, it becomes green hair!
Creating a mini-greenhouse	Fill sections of an egg carton with soil. Plant marigold or alyssum seeds. Carefully wet soil using an eye dropper. Put the seeded carton in a plastic bag, seal it, and put in a sunny spot.
Making ivy sculptures	Plant two small ivy plants in a large pot. Use a wire hanger to create a climber for the ivy. Hold the hanger upside down by the hook. Then bend into any shape, such as a circle, an oval, or a heart. Put the hook in the soil so that the hanger shape stands vertically. Gently train the vine to twine around the hanger as it grows.
Growing a pineapple	Twist off the stem of a fresh pineapple. Remove the lower leaves to reveal two inches of stem. Put the stem in a glass and fill with water until the water reaches the bottom leaf. Maintain the water level until the glass is half-filled with strong roots. When that happens, transplant to a pot of soil with good drainage.
Growing a sweet potato vine	Poke four toothpicks around the middle of a fresh sweet potato. Letting the toothpicks rest on a clean jar of water, submerge half the potato. Observe as roots and a vine develop.
Sprouting seeds	Place a mustard seed, lentil, or lima bean on moist paper towels or a jar of water. Children can observe the seed as it sprouts, and then plant them to witness the rest of the growth process.
Forcing bulbs	Place an amaryllis bulb in a pot or vase with light soil or rocks. Water the bulb and place in a sunny spot. Keep the plant watered when the soil gets dry. Children will be able to enjoy watching flowers grow in the winter.

College
& Career
R E A D I N E S S

Camp Counselor

What Does a Camp Counselor Do?

A camp counselor leads and directs activities for children at a day camp or an overnight camp. Because camps can be designed around specific topics, counselors may need skills in areas such as sports or fine arts. Camp counselors plan activities and support the needs of the children in their care. Recreation workers often work outdoors and in a variety of weather conditions, so you must be adaptable to a variety of conditions.

Career Readiness Skills

Camp counselors are often young adults and teenagers working at an entry-level position. Camps may look for people with experience working with children or who plan to work with children in the future. They also consider skills with outdoor and recreational activities helpful. Maturity and the ability to keep children safe is particularly important. Because there are many camps for people with specialized interests, experiences and hobbies related to those interests can help you find a position at a camp.

Education and Training

While the position of camp counselor is often entry-level, additional training and education is helpful when looking for higher-level positions such as a camp administrator. Many camp organizers and those who run public recreation systems have a degree in parks and recreation or leisure studies. Supervisor positions usually require a minimum of an associate's degree. A lifesaving certificate and first-aid training are also common requirements.

Job Outlook

Most camp counselor positions are temporary and seasonal. These positions can be very plentiful. However, the field is highly competitive for year-round, full-time positions.

Critical Thinking Research local summer camps that hire young adults. How does your personality and your skills compare to their job requirements? Write a paragraph examining why you think you would or would not be a good fit as a camp counselor. Propose the possible short-term and long-term goals that will help you prepare for this career.

Career Cluster

Hospitality and Tourism Camp counselors work in the Recreation, Amusements, and Attractions pathway of this career cluster. Here are some other jobs in this career cluster:

- Chefs
- Restaurant server
- Hotel sales managers
- Concierge
- Tourism assistant
- Museum director of membership development
- Group sales manager
- Special events producer
- Interpreter
- Travel agent
- Park ranger
- Resort instructor
- Animal trainer

Explore Further The Hospitality and Tourism career cluster contains four pathways: Restaurants and Food/Beverage Services; Lodging; Travel and Tourism; and Recreation, Amusements, and Attractions. Choose one of these pathways to explore further.

Hero Images/Getty Images

Math and Science Explorations

Visual Summary

Math and science activities can be based on children's natural creativity and curiosity.

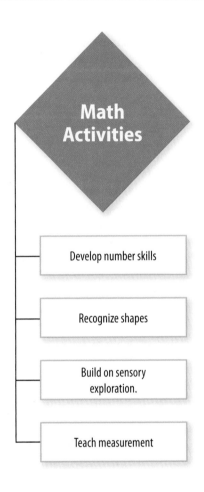

Math Activities
- Develop number skills
- Recognize shapes
- Build on sensory exploration.
- Teach measurement

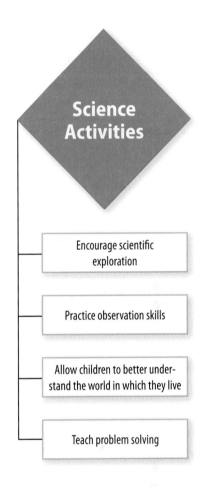

Science Activities
- Encourage scientific exploration
- Practice observation skills
- Allow children to better understand the world in which they live
- Teach problem solving

Vocabulary Review

1. Use these content and academic vocabulary terms to write a short essay about math and science activities.

Content Vocabulary

◇ mathematics (p. 458)
◇ mathematical vocabulary (p. 458)
◇ numerals (p. 461)
◇ science (p. 463)
◇ sensory table (p. 467)
◇ light table (p. 467)
◇ rebus recipe (p. 468)
◇ nature education (p. 469)
◇ field guide (p. 471)

Academic Vocabulary

■ highlight (p. 459)
■ resources (p. 472)

Review Key Concepts

2. Explain how math activities benefit children.
3. Describe the goals of a science curriculum.
4. Analyze what can be learned from studying the natural world.

Critical Thinking

5. **Identify** three ways in which science and math activities benefit children.
6. **Describe** the materials and organization of a science and a math learning center. What activities will children complete?
7. **List** two advantages of keeping classroom pets to teach science concepts.
8. **Apply** How might plants be used to illustrate the life cycle?
9. **Develop** an activity that teaches each of the following math skills: recognizing shapes, sorting, rational counting, recognizing numerals, and ordering numerals.
10. **Focus** What are three examples of the early childhood professional's role in teaching math and science activities?

21st Century Skills

Planning Skills

11. **Transition Times** Transitions are often difficult for young children. Moving from active science and math activities to quiet times can be additionally challenging. Determine five activities to use between an active activity and a quiet activity. Describe each of the transition activities and how you would implement them successfully. Can any of them be planned to reinforce math and science skills? Demonstrate your transition activities for your classmates.

Information Literacy Skills

12. **Locating Resources** Research local organizations that provide resources for children. What museums, companies, and outdoor locations could students visit? Which sites could be used as field trips to stimulate interest in science and math? Choose three locations to visit. Explain how a field trip to those locations will benefit your students. Plan a pre-visit activity to prepare children and a follow-up activity to reinforce what children will learn on the field trip.

Child Care LAB

Use the skills you have learned in this chapter.

Bulletin Boards

13. **Celebrating Themes** Create a math- or science-themed bulletin board for toddlers, preschoolers, or school-age children and an activity associated with the bulletin board content. Photograph the board and include in your portfolio.

   A. Choose a theme. Decide on a math or science theme you could use for a bulletin board or display. Consider how you can integrate this math or science theme with other subject areas and activities.

   B. Choose an age group. Think about what age group would best be able to enjoy the theme.

   C. Create a lesson plan. Write a lesson plan that would allow children in the age group you've chosen to explore the theme through multiple activitities and subject areas. Remember that the children need to create at least one product or project that can be displayed on the bulletin board.

   D. Conduct an activity. Have children complete at least one of the activities you planned for your lesson.

   E. Display the results. Create your math or science themed bulletin board, featuring the children's work.

   F. Photograph the project. Record your work for your portfolio. Include your lesson plan as well.

Create Your Evaluation

Create an evaluation sheet that includes the following headings:

- Theme choice
- Appropriate activity
- Organized display
- Correct spelling and grammar

Ask your classmates to use the sheet to evaluate your design, rating each category from 1 to 10.

Academic Skills

English Language Arts

14. Brainstorming With a partner, make two lists, one of simple adjectives such as *big, round,* and *long,* and one of simple nouns such as *triangle, corner,* and *side.* Use words that would be understandable and interesting to young children. Then discuss with your partner how you might use several words from each list to teach math lessons to preschoolers.

Social Studies

15. Dramatic Play Links Suggest two science-related play themes that students can use for dramatic play. For each theme, list three related pieces of suitable props props. Reflecting on the activities, analyze how science and technology influence children and how their understanding will shape scientific and technological change.

Mathematics

16. Math and Gardening Ms. Payton's class is planting a vegetable garden to explore how plants grow. They will be planting lettuce, toma-toes, and carrots. The whole garden has an area of 42 square feet. The area used to plant carrots is 24 square feet smaller than the total size of the garden. What is the area of the carrot garden in square inches? If another preschool class plants a flower garden that is 10 feet by 4 feet, what is the area of the garden? What is the difference in size between the vegetable garden and the flower garden?

Math Concept **Area** To find the area of a rectangular space multiply the length times the width. Formula $A = LW$

Starting Hint Subtract 24 from 42 to find the area of the carrot garden. Multiply this amount by 12 to find the area in square inches. Use the formula for area to calculate the area of the second garden.

For more math practice, go to the math appendix at the back of the book.

Certification Prep

Directions Choose the appropriate answer to each question.

17. Rote counting is when children _____.

   A. put items in order

   B. recognize numerals

   C. name quantities

   D. name numbers

18. Nature activities provide which benefits to children?

   A. Sensory exploration

   B. Developing scientific understating

   C. Physical activity

   D. All of the above

> **Test-Taking Tip**
> Re-read the question and read all the answers before choosing the correct answer. Tests often include answers with key words but the wrong information to distract you from the correct answer.

CHAPTER 22

Dramatic Play and Cultural Awareness

Writing Activity

⭐ 21st Century Skills

Media Literacy Advertising can influence consumers' decisions. Imagine that you are in charge of marketing for a child care center. Create a script for a radio or print advertisement for a newspaper, magazine, billboard, or Web site to attract new customers.

Writing Tips
1. Decide which features of the center to emphasize.
2. Use language and factual information that will appeal to your target audience.
3. Use short, attention-grabbing statements that will focus the consumer on your message.
4. Use action verbs, descriptive adverbs, and adjectives.

Image Source/AGE fotostock

RESCUE

Explore the Photo Children explore and learn through pretend play. *What is this child learning about his community?*

Reading Guide

Partner Up for Success One advantage to sharing your notes with a partner is that you can fill in gaps in each other's information. You can also compare notes before you start quizzing each other.

Read to Learn

Key Concepts

- **State** how dramatic play promotes development.
- **Explain** how child care professionals encourage dramatic play.
- **Identify** goals of an early childhood social studies curriculum.
- **Describe** methods of helping children become socially responsible citizens.

Content Vocabulary

◇ dramatic play
◇ spontaneous dramatic play
◇ props
◇ prop box
◇ social studies
◇ social responsibility

Academic Vocabulary

■ inanimate
■ acquaint

Main Idea

Dramatic play helps children experience and practice different roles. Dramatic play learning centers and prop boxes use themes to stimulate pretend play. Early childhood social studies focus on studying self, family, and community. Children also learn about diversity, the environment, and social skills.

Graphic Organizer

As you read, note the six areas of the early childhood social studies curriculum described in the text. Use a chart like the one shown to help organize your information.

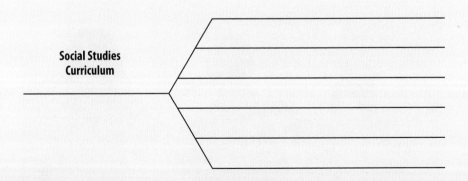

Social Studies Curriculum

![Graphic Organizer icon] **Graphic Organizer** *Go to* **connected.mcgraw-hill.com** *to print this Graphic Organizer.*

AS YOU READ

Connect Think about children's make-believe play. What are some common roles children take on in pretend play?

◇Vocabulary

You can find definitions in the glossary at the back of this book.

Development Through Dramatic Play

When children create realistic or fantasy situations and act them out, it is called **dramatic play**. Dramatic play is also referred to as make-believe or pretend play. Complex development occurs through dramatic play. It enhances children's ability to learn and stimulates creativity. While having fun and being engaged in dramatic play, children learn to express their thoughts, ideas, and feelings. They gradually develop self-control and the ability to focus, all while learning how to get along well with their peers.

Types of Dramatic Play

In dramatic play, children often imitate adults and act out situations they observe or imagine. They may even take on the roles of animals or inanimate, or non-living, objects such as a car and a refrigerator. Dramatic play allows children to safely explore what they are too young to experience in real life. It also gives children opportunities to act out everyday experiences as they work to understand the world around them.

As part of dramatic play, children role-play, or assume the identity of someone else. They "become" fascinating characters, such as parents, community helpers, and cartoon heroes. This most often occurs as **spontaneous dramatic play**, meaning that children engage in dramatic play without the suggestion or direction of adults.

Dramatic play can take place anywhere. Children may prepare and serve "dinner" in the family living center or build a train and take a "vacation" in the block center. Sandboxes, water tables, and outside playgrounds are other common sites for dramatic play.

▶ **Pretend Play**

With dramatic play, children can practice dealing with emotions and developing their imaginations. *What are other benefits of dramatic play?*

©KidStock/Blend Images LLC

Benefits of Dramatic Play

Like real-life experiences, dramatic play helps children develop skills in all areas.

▶ **Physical.** Children use motor skills in all aspects of dramatic play. For example, when children button dress-up clothes, they develop small motor skills. Pretending to be jungle animals hunting food uses large muscles.

▶ **Intellectual.** Children use language skills to suggest and plan their dramatic play scenes. They develop problem-solving skills and use imagination and symbolic thinking—using an item to represent something else—as they create plots and characters. They use memory skills as they reenact events they have witnessed or experienced.

▶ **Emotional.** During dramatic play, children can confront and try to understand their feelings and fears. Dramatic play allows children to try out different emotions, which is a good rehearsal for dealing with them later. They also learn about empathy for other people.

▶ **Social.** In dramatic play, children work together to create and carry out a story. They follow each other's lead as the play progresses and sometimes compromise to work out small problems. They assume social and employment roles by pretending to be a sister or a grandfather or a firefighter or sales clerk. This helps children begin to view others' perspectives, such as being a parent versus a child in the family or a doctor versus a patient. They also learn to appreciate the clothes and customs of other cultures.

Early Childhood Professionals' Involvement

Because dramatic play involves lots of preparation and action, early childhood professionals must allow ample time for it in the daily schedule. Children need at least a 45-minute block of time to decide on a theme and their roles, to put on costumes or dress-up clothes, to enact the scene, and then to put away the equipment and materials.

Children like to have teachers join in their play. Teachers should follow the children's lead and resist taking over. Teacher participation allows teachers to model appropriate play skills for children who have trouble cooperating with others. Teachers can also help other children join a dramatic play scene by suggesting roles they can play.

SAFETY MATTERS

Conflict Resolution

Whether a fight over shared toys or a disagreement about pretend play, children's play can often erupt into conflict. Early childhood educators can help prevent conflict by observing children at play. Frustration or difficulty sharing can be warning signs of potential conflict. When conflict does occur, early childhood educators must first stop it. Then they can work with the children to help them verbalize what they were trying to communicate through aggressive behavior. Acknowledge each child's feelings and offer alternative solutions to resolve the conflict.

What Would You Do? Three preschoolers are playing in the block center. A conflict starts about the curved blocks. One child has them all, but the other two children need some for their buildings. The child with all the curved blocks starts yelling and pushes over another's building. What steps would you take to help the children settle this dispute nonviolently?

By observing dramatic play, teachers gain understanding of children's physical development, thinking abilities, and personal interests. Early childhood professionals look for the following during dramatic play:

▶ Does the child participate regularly and easily in dramatic play? Are there recurrent themes?

▶ How does the child solve conflicts in dramatic play? Can the child be a leader and a follower? Does the child accept the ideas of others?

▶ Does the child use verbal and nonverbal communication skills effectively?

▶ What attitude does the child display? How does this compare with the child's usual attitude?

▶ Do other children choose this child as a playmate? Does the child play with peers or adults?

▶ How involved does the child become in the play's plot?

▶ Are there behaviors that cause concern for the child's physical or emotional well-being?

Teachers often use dramatic play observations to record children's development. By putting notes in a file, teachers document skills they have observed in action. Teachers can identify curriculum projects or themes that are of specific interest to children in their care by paying attention to children's spontaneous interests during dramatic play. Observations that indicate a concern may lead a teacher to provide parents with a referral to local services.

Dramatic Play Learning Center

Although drama happens everywhere, the dramatic play learning center is designed with specific furnishings to help children act out scenarios they see in real life. For example, a child-sized kitchen set allows children to pretend to cook. Dolls and stuffed animals quickly become characters in whatever drama is taking place. Play telephones, cash registers, grocery carts, baby strollers, and doll beds are all examples of items children use in dramatic play.

What you see going on in this center one day may not be the same on another. Teachers set the stage for play by creating different themes throughout the year. For example, the center could be equipped as a post office, bank, campsite, florist shop, jewelry store, or supermarket. By regularly rotating play themes, teachers encourage creativity and keep the learning center interesting for children.

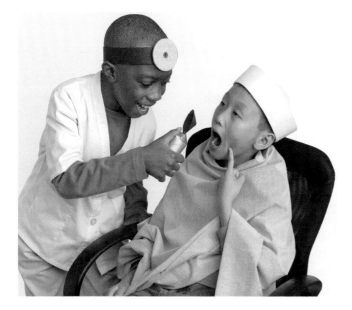

▼ **Props for Play**

With a few realistic, hands-on materials to set a scene, children create their own actions and words to tell a story. *What items would you include in a dramatic play learning center?*

McGraw-Hill Education/Ken Karp

Dramatic Play Prop Boxes

Early childhood professionals create collections of **props**, or items that suggest or support themes for dramatic play. Children use props to add realism, detail, and interest to pretend play. For example, how might you emphasize that firefighters need oxygen to stay alive when working in smoke? One way is to provide face masks (from old diving gear) and make-believe air tanks (oatmeal boxes covered with aluminum foil and strapped on with elastic). Children quickly see that these are important safety items for firefighters.

A **prop box** is a container for storing items used in a specific play theme. Using prop boxes to follow up a story or to help children explore a particular concept is a way to encourage dramatic play. After reading a book about astronauts, a teacher can pull out a prop box with helmets (made from cardboard boxes) and other space-related items. Using props, children develop a deeper understanding of the information in the story. Community helper prop boxes help children learn about jobs in society. These boxes might focus on helpers such as medical professionals, police officers, judges, and veterinarians.

When creating prop boxes, make sure the contents are safe, clean, and durable. Items should be easy to use and familiar to the children. Choose real props, rather than toy ones. Secondhand stores and garage sales are possible sources for props—just be sure to thoroughly check items for safety. Put duplicate props in each box. This encourages cooperative play.

Puppetry

Preschool children love using puppets, with or without a puppet stage. They can use puppets to act out nursery rhymes and folktales. They also enjoy using puppets to act out the lyrics of songs during music time or to make conversation with another child. Playing with puppets develops skills such as:

▶ **Physical.** Children use both the large muscles in the arm and the small muscles in the fingers when playing with puppets. They also practice hand-eye coordination.

▶ **Intellectual.** Puppets encourage children to listen, talk, and share. Children try to give their puppets personality, calling for imagination and creativity.

▶ **Emotional.** Children can express their feelings through puppets. Negative emotions, especially, are more easily shown through the safety and security of a puppet's character.

▶ **Social.** Puppets encourage cooperation and teamwork. The use of puppets may help shy children gain confidence in talking to others. Puppet play allows children to act out acceptable and unacceptable behavior.

READING CHECK ✔ **Recall** List the physical, intellectual, emotional, and social benefits of dramatic play.

A Matter of ETHICS

Imitating Behavior

Children's dramatic play themes are inspired from what they see and hear in their daily lives. Children might imitate the speech of adults or peers or copy behavior they see on television or in a video game. For these reasons, it is important for teachers to model appropriate behavior in the classroom.

Appropriate Play Themes

Children will sometimes engage in pretend play that may not be appropriate for a child care center, such as violent or aggressive play themes. This behavior cannot be completely prevented, but a teacher can make it clear that he or she does not approve of play that involves hurting others and redirect play toward more appropriate classroom themes.

Thinking Ethically

A parent of a child at your center approaches you with the concern that her son is turning every object he can find at home into a weapon. She says her child has not been exposed to weapons at home, so this must be something he has learned at school. How would you respond?

Make Puppets

Puppets come in all shapes and sizes. They can easily be made with common art and craft supplies. Making a puppet is a great creative activity for children. Any home-made puppet should be well-made with no detachable or sharp parts that might cause choking or injuries. Here are some examples of puppets you could make.

▶ **Stick Puppets** *Glue a cutout character to a craft stick. Children can hold and move the stick to act out a story. To create a puppet-in-a-cup, push a stick puppet through the bottom of a decorated paper cup. The stick can be moved up and down, and the cup becomes the puppet stage.*

▶ **Sack Puppets** *Use a small brown paper bag. Decorate the flap with paper, fabric, ribbons, and other trims to make a character.*

▶ **Glove Puppets** *Attach a face to each fingertip of a child's knit glove. Or, make a face on the back of the hand. The glove's fingers become legs or hair.*

▶ **Sock Puppets** *Sock puppets are made by decorating a sock with buttons, felt, yarn, moveable eyes, and other craft items.*

▶ **Hand Puppets** *Made from a simple pattern and fabric, these puppets can be sewn by hand or machine or glued with fabric glue. Attach a face directly to the puppet.*

▶ **Finger Puppets** *Color and decorate small pieces of felt or construction paper that are folded to slip over a finger.*

Apply It!
Create a puppet for a common children's story character using one of the puppet types described.

©Image Source/Corbis

Developing Social Responsibility and Cultural Awareness

As a child care professional, you will influence how children think and behave. Research shows that attitudes form at an early age. During the preschool years, children learn self-respect as well as appreciation for others. Through positive learning activities and cultural and social experiences, children develop attitudes of respect and acceptance.

The Social Studies Curriculum

Social studies is a curriculum area that teaches children about themselves, their families, communities, and the world. Through social studies, children gain cultural awareness and discover that the world is a fascinating place. By learning how people live around the world, they realize there are many similarities and some differences. A social studies curriculum helps children develop skills for getting along peacefully with people from all backgrounds. The goals of a preschool social studies curriculum are to help children

▶ develop a positive attitude toward themselves and others.

▶ understand their roles within the family unit.

▶ recognize and appreciate how individuals and families are alike and different.

▶ learn about their community.

▶ explore how people in their community work and live.

▶ acquire positive behaviors for living happily within the family, community, and society.

▶ see that people of all backgrounds bring special qualities and contributions to the world.

▶ become aware of climates and environments on Earth and how they affect lifestyle.

▶ learn about Earth's resources and how to use and conserve them.

Glowimages RF/age fotostock

▼ **Learning About the World**

Social studies teach children about Earth and its resources. *What are other goals of a social studies curriculum?*

Social Studies Activities

Like all learning, social studies should start with what is most familiar to children. Effective early childhood teachers begin their social studies curriculum with activities that help children learn about themselves, families, the community, diversity, and the environment.

Learning About Self

Children are very individualistic. Gradually they learn to act as members of families, neighborhoods, and communities. Understanding and liking oneself is the first step toward developing a well-rounded personality. It is also the first step to being able to function well in society. People who have high self-esteem—people who accept and value their own traits and abilities—tend to participate more fully in life and to get along better with others. Early childhood teachers help children become good community members by building their self-esteem. They do this by planning activities in which children can succeed. They acknowledge strengths and positive traits, and provide activities that explore children's likes, abilities, and interests.

Showing respect and appreciation for children's heritage helps develop self-pride. You can include items from different cultures in the classroom environment and curriculum. For example, respect for ethnic groups can be promoted with a collection of dolls that have different skin tones, features, and hair and eye colors. Dolls should have hairstyles and clothing that are typical of what people wear in everyday life, not costumes that are outdated or stereotypical.

▶ **Learning About Me**

Children develop self-esteem by acknowledging their strengths and positive traits. *Why is learning about self an important part of the social studies curriculum?*

McGraw-Hill Education/Ken Karp

Learning About Families

After self, family is the next most familiar social concept to children. Through social studies activities, children learn about different families. Nuclear families have two parents and their children. Extended families may include grandparents, aunts, uncles, and cousins. Other family structures include blended families, single-parent families, or a child being raised by a grandparent or other family member or foster parent. Some children have siblings; others do not. Increasingly, adoptive families are international and interracial. Sharing experiences of their own family life with each other teaches children about the diversity of families.

Possibly the most important thing children can learn about families is that strong families are the foundation of society. Family members take care of each other physically and emotionally. Families assume the responsibility of providing children with love, basic care, and education.

Children can also learn that family roles vary among various cultures. Through pictures, stories, and guest speakers, they can see that family members have different jobs and expectations according to their cultures and individual family beliefs. For example, most prepare food, provide education, work in some manner to support family needs, and celebrate traditions, but how they go about these tasks depends on the culture.

Learning how a family functions is also important for children to investigate. For example, children are assigned different chores as they learn to contribute to family life. Family culture often dictates what chores are assigned and at what ages. Birth order in family often determines privileges as well as responsibilities among siblings. Whether pets are kept and how they are fed and cared for are also appropriate family life topics for children.

▲ **Family Time**

Children learn about the basics of family life in a social studies curriculum. *What can children learn about family diversity?*

Henglein and Steets/Getty Images

Learning About Community

Thinking abstractly is difficult for young children. For this reason, learning about people and places beyond their own family and homes is more difficult. The progression from home to neighborhood to city to state to country is very hard for children to grasp.

Exploring community life with children should begin with their home and immediate neighborhood. Take walks around the neighborhood. Discuss what makes a neighborhood strong and why this is important. Next, introduce children to neighborhoods beyond their own. As a class, ride the bus on community routes. Point out businesses where parents and neighbors work. Notice libraries, museums, parks, places of worship, fire and police stations, and schools. Visit these places on field trips to see what happens inside them. These activities gradually introduce children to the world and how it works.

People whose jobs involve helping others within the community are called community helpers. Police officers, firefighters, doctors, nurses, and lifeguards are just a few examples. As part of the social studies curriculum, child care teachers plan experiences for children to investigate the jobs, duties, and skills of community helpers. They use a variety of activities, such as books, special visitors, dramatic play prop boxes, field trips, puppets, and stories.

▼ **Community Helpers**

Teaching about community helpers gives children an opportunity to learn about the world immediately around them. *What types of activities help children to learn about their community?*

©image100/Corbis

Cultural Diversity

Today's children live in a diverse world. They routinely see similarities and differences in people's music, dress, food, celebrations, art, and appearance. Creative teachers make learning about other people and their customs an exciting adventure. They encourage a positive attitude as children notice differences and identify similarities among all people.

Because learning about the familiar is easiest for children, explore diversity among varying cultures represented in your own classroom. Parents of enrolled children can help make experiences authentic. For example, parents may loan the classroom home decorations or visit the classroom to play music enjoyed by their culture.

Include diversity throughout the curriculum. Make it part of every day's curriculum experiences, rather than focusing on different cultures one separate week at a time. Address how varying cultures live today rather than focusing only on their historical experiences or achievements. The following ideas will help you introduce children to a world of diversity. When putting them into practice, help children notice the similarities as well as the differences between peoples.

▲ **Age Diversity**

Older adults can read to children or help them with projects at a child care center. *What do children learn from regular interaction with older adults?*

► Read books that include children from a variety of cultures, ethnic backgrounds, and races.

► Invite special visitors with different cultural backgrounds to visit the classroom. Ask them to talk about and demonstrate some of their customs or family traditions.

► Serve ethnic or traditional foods regularly as part of meals, snacks, and cooking activities.

► Provide instruments from different cultures in the music center. Teach children simple cultural songs and dances.

► Offer dramatic play props from various styles of ethnic cooking. For example, a steamer and a wok are common kitchen items in Asian cultures.

Children also need to develop good attitudes toward aging. Misconceptions about aging occur when children have little opportunity to interact with older adults. Given information and closer contact, children learn to be comfortable with and sensitive to older adults. They discover that aging can mean wisdom, patience, and tenderness. Teachers can arrange visits to retirement homes and senior citizen centers. Also, with parents' permission, invite grandparents to participate regularly in the classroom.

Learning About the Environment

Children enjoy learning about the environment. **Acquaint** preschoolers, or make them familiar, with the characteristics of their local environment. When children reach school age, they can learn about distant climates, such as tropical rain forests.

Children like to investigate land characteristics, plants, and animals. Social studies concentrate on how these impact people's lives. To begin a study with children, take a walk around your facility. What kinds of trees, plants, and animals live there? Are there mountains or flatlands? What is the weather like? How do all these affect children's lives? For example, can they go sledding in your climate? Do children need to use umbrellas often? These questions help children analyze how location and climate affect how they live.

Young children can learn to respect and conserve community resources. Reduce, reuse, recycle—the three "Rs" of conservation—are appropriate concepts to explore. As a class, watch a garbage truck making its rounds. Explain that garbage is buried in the earth. As children learn that trash does not just disappear, they will understand the purpose of practicing the three Rs. Here are other ways to teach respect for resources:

▶ Use both sides of paper for coloring activities.

▶ Conserve electricity by turning off classroom lights and computers when not in use.

▶ Reuse clean computer paper, egg cartons, and packing materials in art or math projects.

▶ Reuse clean paper or plastic bags.

▶ Create classroom recycling centers.

▼ **Environmentally Friendly**

Children can learn about their environment by exploring it. *How can you teach children respect for resources?*

Encouraging Social Skills

When people make a positive contribution to the community and obey community laws, they practice **social responsibility**. To become productive members of society, children should learn from an early age to accept basic social skills and responsibilities. These range from respecting property to voting regularly in elections.

Through daily classroom routines, children learn attitudes and behaviors that prepare them to be responsible citizens. By following these practices, early educators show children that social responsibility is vital to a fair, orderly society:

▶ **Expect children to obey rules.** Include children in making classroom rules that protect individual safety as well as classroom property. Require children to put away toys after they are finished playing with them. Have them help clean up after activities.

▶ **Include children in classroom tasks.** Children develop pride when they participate in routine classroom chores. They can water plants, feed pets, and set tables for snack time.

▶ **Give children opportunities to make decisions.** Allowing children to vote on some classroom matters shows them that by expressing their preference, they can make a difference. Classroom voting opportunities may include choosing a class mascot, a favorite video, or an afternoon snack.

▶ **Teach children to settle conflicts without violence.** Children can follow basic rules related to self-respect and respect for others. Insist that children settle problems with words, rather than by hitting. Help children develop positive social skills to use instead of aggression or violence. Such skills include expressing feelings; calmly discussing differing ideas; sharing, trading, or taking turns with toys; and compromising and negotiating. Be a positive role model for children by always speaking in a courteous manner to children and adults.

▶ **Talk about the importance of fairness for everyone.** Help children learn how to apologize after hurting another child physically or emotionally. Never allow bullying or teasing. Expect children to share classroom toys and supplies fairly.

READING CHECK ✔ **State** What must children learn to become socially responsible?

Financing a Minibus

In order to provide transportation for her child care center's community field trips, Hannah is planning to buy a minibus that costs $42,000. She can afford to pay a $15,000 down payment but needs to finance the remaining $27,000. The bank offered her a loan with 10 percent interest with three different payment options:

Loan A (3 years): 36 payments of $999
Loan B (4 years): 48 payments of $824
Loan C (5 years): 60 payments of $725

What is the total interest of each loan? Which loan is the best deal?

Math Concept **Loan Terms** When borrowing money, the period of the loan matters as much as the interest rate. The principal is the amount of money borrowed.

Starting Hint Multiply the amount of each payment by the number of payments to determine the complete cost for each loan option. To calculate the amount of interest paid for each loan, subtract the principal ($27,000) from the total cost of each option.

 For more math practice, go to the Math Appendix at the back of the book.

Money Management

How Can I Learn to Manage Money?

While you might have had to manage your own money in some ways in high school, your parents were probably still involved in your finances. In college, you most likely will be in charge of managing your own finances. One of the most important skills you need in college and in your adult life is to know how to manage your finances wisely. This involves learning how to keep track of the money you spend it and what you are spending it on.

What do I need to consider when creating my budget?

List all sources of income, including job earnings, savings, and parent support. Then list what you think you might spend in a month. Consider the cost of books and school supplies, meals not covered by a meal plan, entertainment, personal care items, laundry, telephone and Internet service, transportation expenses, and clothes. If your expenses are higher than your income, you need to either increase income or reduce spending.

Should I get a credit card?

Building credit is an important step in adult life, and it is also a good idea to have a credit card for emergencies. However, credit cards can also be major pitfalls for college students. For some, access to a credit results in overspending. You need to weigh the pros and cons and be honest with yourself about how you will respond to having credit. If you decide to get a credit card, never charge more than the amount you can comfortably afford to pay each month.

Do I need a checking account?

It is a good idea to open a checking account in the area your school is located. Find a bank that offers free or low-fee checking for students, a debit card, and convenient ATM locations. This reduces out-of-network ATM fees. You should also know how to balance a checkbook so that you do not incur overdraft or returned check fees.

Hands-On

After your first few months in college, you start to realize you are going through money much more quickly than you planned. When you sit down and come up with a budget, you recognize that you are spending too much. You do not want to cut out your social life all together, but you are worried about your rate of spending. Come up with at least five small things you could do or changes you could make that would save you money.

Path to Success

Practice Discipline Demonstrate self-control with shopping and spending money.

Save Saving in college is difficult, but saving will ensure you have money in case of emergency.

Be Careful with Credit Have only one major credit card, and use it sparingly.

Be Car-Free Most college campuses are pedestrian- and bike-friendly, and cars can be very expensive to maintain and operate.

Try Cooking Dining out can be expensive. If you have access to a kitchen, try cooking sometimes.

Picturenet/Getty Images

Dramatic Play and Cultural Awareness

Visual Summary

Children explore what they learn about culture in their daily dramatic play.

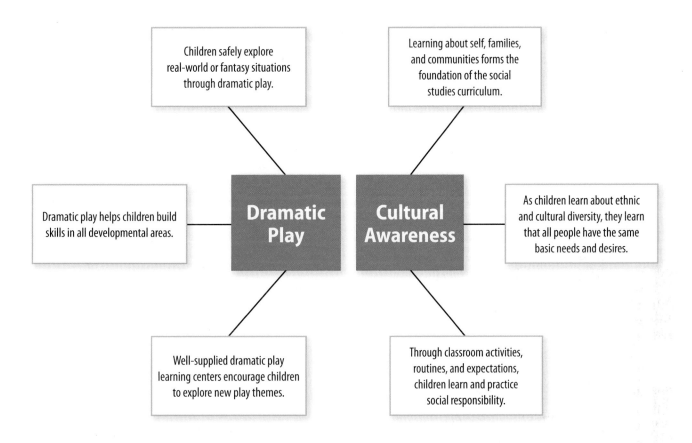

Children safely explore real-world or fantasy situations through dramatic play.

Learning about self, families, and communities forms the foundation of the social studies curriculum.

Dramatic play helps children build skills in all developmental areas.

Dramatic Play

Cultural Awareness

As children learn about ethnic and cultural diversity, they learn that all people have the same basic needs and desires.

Well-supplied dramatic play learning centers encourage children to explore new play themes.

Through classroom activities, routines, and expectations, children learn and practice social responsibility.

Vocabulary Review

1. Create a multiple-choice test question for each content and academic vocabulary term.

Content Vocabulary

◇ dramatic play (p. 480)
◇ spontaneous dramatic play (p. 480)
◇ props (p. 483)
◇ prop box (p. 483)
◇ social studies (p. 485)
◇ social responsibility (p. 491)

Academic Vocabulary

■ inanimate (p. 480)
■ acquaint (p. 490)

Review Key Concepts

2. **State** how dramatic play promotes development.
3. **Explain** how child care professionals encourage dramatic play.
4. **Identify** goals of an early childhood social studies curriculum.
5. **Describe** methods of helping children become socially responsible citizens.

Critical Thinking

6. **Contrast** dramatic play and spontaneous dramatic play.
7. **Explain** why early childhood teachers should participate in dramatic play but should not take over a leadership role during play.
8. **Discuss** why the study of community begins with a child's own neighborhood.
9. **Draw conclusions** about how the social studies curriculum prepares young children to become socially responsible citizens.
10. **Give examples** of symbolic thinking that may be used by two five-year-olds having a tea party for their dolls and stuffed animals.

21st Century Skills

Cooperative Learning Skills

11. **Conflict Resolution** In a group of three students, describe a conflict scenario that might occur regularly at a child care center. As a group, decide upon the best approach for resolving the conflict that is appropriate for the conflict and the children's ages. Write a dialogue for the conflict resolution. Then role-play the scene for your class.

Creativity Skills

12. **Prop Box Materials** Brainstorm prop box ideas for three different dramatic play themes. Where would you source the items? If you did not have the budget to purchase props, how would you acquire the props? Could you make the props or repurpose common household items? Create one prop from your list and share with your class.

Child Care LAB

Use the skills you have learned in this chapter.

Encourage Appreciation of Differences

13. **Diversity Activity** In this lab, you will plan a developmentally appropriate activity for young children that encourages appreciation of personal or cultural differences, such as likes and dislikes or different family structures, as part of a social studies curriculum.

   A. **Select an age group.** Decide whether your activity will be for toddlers, preschoolers, or school-age children. Make sure your activity is developmentally appropriate for your selected age group.

   B. **Determine the activity objectives.** Describe the learning objectives of the activity. What specific information or skills do you want the children to take away from the activity?

   C. **Outline the activity procedure.** Write step-by-step instructions for completing the activity. Include an activity introduction and a conclusion.

   D. **Write guided questions.** Create open-ended questions that can be used during the activity that will help guide the children toward the activity objectives.

   E. **List required materials.** Create a list of supplies or equipment required to complete this activity.

   F. **Peer review the activity.** Exchange activity plans with a classmate. Use the evaluation sheet to review his or her plan and provide suggestions on how to improve the plan.

Create Your Evaluation

Create an evaluation sheet with these categories:
- Activity Objectives
- Procedure Clarity
- Guided Questions
- Supply List

Have your classmate use this sheet to evaluate your plan, rating each category on a Detailed and Complete/ Adequate Information/ Needs Improvement scale.

Academic Skills

English Language Arts

14. Self-Esteem Library One way to help children learn about self and self-esteem is reading books with children that introduce and develop these concepts. Visit your local library and find five books that could be used to support a child's learning about self. Provide a short summary of each book and describe how it could be used as part of early childhood social studies curriculum.

Social Studies

15. Community Helper Visit Identify a community helper you would like to have visit your classroom. Create a proposal for the visit for your child care center director's approval. What are the social studies objectives of the visit? What activities might occur during the visit? What would you need to do to prepare for the visit?

Science

16. Observe Dramatic Play Observing children engaged in dramatic play can provide an early childhood teacher with a greater understanding of children's development and personal interests. Work with your teacher to arrange to observe preschoolers at play at a local child care center.

Procedure Observe the children at play and track all instances of spontaneous dramatic play. Note how the play was initiated, the theme of the play, and the duration of the play. Also record the involvement level and emotions of each child involved in the play.

Analysis Create a table to present the information you collect. In the first column of the table, list the themes of dramatic play observed. Across the top of the table, create columns for your corresponding observations. Write a paragraph summarizing your findings. What can you conclude about the spontaneous dramatic play you observed and child development?

Certification Prep

Directions Read the sentence, and choose the best word or phrase to fill in the blank.

17. Items that suggest themes for dramatic play are called _____.

   A. paraphernalia

   B. drama toys

   C. make-believe toys

   D. props

18. Respecting property and voting in elections are examples of _____.

   A. environment conservation

   B. social responsibility

   C. self-esteem

   D. community involvement

> **Test-Taking Tip**
> If you do not know the answer to a question, first cross off any choices you know are wrong. Evaluate the remaining choices and choose the best answer.

(tl)©Nova Development; (tr)©Comstock/Alamy

CHAPTER 23

Art, Music, and Movement

Writing Activity

⭐ 21st Century Skills

Critical Thinking Write a persuasive essay that convinces your audience that art and music experiences are important parts of education. Give examples of evidence to support this view. If you do not agree with this view, give examples and information as to why not.

Writing Tips
1. Write an opening that will capture the reader's attention.
2. Clearly express your view on the topic.
3. Provide specific reasons why the reader should consider your view.
4. Support your position with facts, statistics, and citations.

Explore the Photo
Art activities encourage children to be creative and express their feelings. *What creative skills is she displaying?*

©KidStock/Blend Images LLC

Reading Guide

Get Your Rest The more well rested and alert you are when you study, the more likely you will be to remember the information later. Studying in the same state of mind as when you are likely to take a test—fully rested and mentally sharp—will help to ensure your best performance.

Read to Learn

Key Concepts

- **Explain** appropriate methods for guiding children's art experiences.
- **Describe** how basic intellectual skills and concepts are reinforced through music activities.
- **Determine** the effects of children's motor development and fitness.
- **List** the six elements that make up creative movement activities.

Main Idea

Art and music provide children with many opportunities for growth in all development areas. Creative movement and body awareness activities provide physical exercise and promote a healthy lifestyle.

Content Vocabulary

◇ proportion
◇ process versus product
◇ three-dimensional
◇ collage
◇ lyrics
◇ tempo
◇ pitch
◇ melody
◇ rhythm instruments
◇ call-and-response songs
◇ creative movement
◇ locomotion
◇ active play
◇ maze

Academic Vocabulary

■ inhibit
■ expand

Graphic Organizer

As you read, look for six examples of art and music activities. Use a table like the one shown to organize your information.

Art Activities	Music Activities

Graphic Organizer Go to **connected.mcgraw-hill.com** *to print this Graphic Organizer.*

AS YOU READ

Connect Think about the ways that art, music, and movement activities enrich children's lives. How do you think these activities enhance children's learning in other areas?

◆ **Vocabulary**

You can find definitions in the glossary at the back of this book.

▼ **Art Centers**

A safe, well-equipped art center allows children to explore art creatively. *What are some important elements of an art center?*

Developing Artistic Expression

Art is the use of skills and imagination to produce something that expresses thoughts, ideas, or emotions. Art provides children with many opportunities for growth in all developmental areas.

Art Curriculum Goals

At first glance, a toddler's scribbles and a preschooler's drawings seem unimportant. With a closer look, you will notice that much learning is taking place. Well-planned art activities develop the following:

▶ **Physical skills.** Children practice eye-hand coordination and small motor skills through coloring, cutting, and pasting.

▶ **Language skills.** As children participate in art and explain their ideas to others, they build their vocabulary skills. Children also learn to observe and listen to others' ideas.

▶ **Thinking skills.** Creating art requires children to make decisions about their projects. They use creativity, imagination, and thinking skills as they work with art materials.

▶ **Emotional skills.** Increased self-esteem and confidence result when children succeed at creating their own projects.

▶ **Social skills.** Art activities often are cooperative efforts. Children work together and see how each child's contribution adds to the final product. This builds respect for others' ideas.

▶ **Appreciation of diversity.** Cultural art activities allow children to discover the use of art in cultural traditions. These activities explore art techniques and help children value the creativity of all people.

▶ **Basic concepts.** Art experiences give children a hands-on method of learning about color, shape, size, and other basic concepts. Skills from many curriculum areas are used in art. For example, mixing paint for different colors is science in action.

Stages of Children's Art

Children go through predictable stages in learning to create art. **Figure 23.1** describes these stages. Remember that each child works through these stages at an individual rate. Physical maturation and how often art activities occur impact how children work through the stages.

©KidStock/Blend Images LLC

Figure 23.1 Stages of Children's Art

Artistic Development Children go through predictable stages as they develop their art skills. *What are the differences between the art of a three-year-old and the art of a five-year-old?*

Stage	Ages	Description
Scribble and Mark Making	One to Three	• Children gain control of shoulder muscles before the wrist and finger muscles. • Early drawings tend to sprawl in wide loops over a piece of paper. • Children first use many different types of scribbles. They progress from scribbling to patterns such as zigzags or spirals.
Symbolic and Design	Three to Five	• There is very deliberate placement of lines and geometric shapes. • Children frequently repeat shapes. • Specific marks begin to represent real objects to children. • Objects may not be recognizable to others. • One shape may represent many things. • A circle might represent a whole body before children learn how to draw body parts.
Representational	Four to Seven	• Drawings and symbols are more accurate and recognizable to others. • Children give greater attention to detail. • Details such as eyelashes and earrings may appear on drawings of people.
Realistic	Five to Ten	• Children make increasingly complex designs. • Children are concerned about making people and objects look real. • Drawings reflect features of people and differences in gender and skin tone. • Children increasingly use perspective and **proportion**, or the size relationship of the parts.

The Art Center

A well-stocked art center invites children to select art activities on their own according to their interests and abilities. Store art materials on shelves with labels. The best location for the center is in an uncarpeted area. Having a sink nearby is very helpful for cleanup. Shelves, tables and chairs, easels, and drying racks should be easy to clean.

Some art materials are hazardous and require caution. Substances such as spray paints can trigger allergic reactions or asthma attacks. Supervise activities continuously when using objects small enough to put in the nose, ears, or mouth. Other safety tips include:

▶ Buy water-based, nontoxic glues, pastes, markers, and paints.

▶ Do not let children use paints or markers on their skin. Wash hands promptly after activities.

▶ Make sure the art center has good ventilation. Use a fan to circulate air, if needed.

▶ Use a vacuum or a wet mop to clean up dusty debris.

Guiding Art Experiences

Children enjoy working on their own in the art center. They also enjoy art activities that are teacher-led. Use the following principles as you plan and guide children's art experiences:

▶ **Value the process.** Children learn through the process of creating art. What they learn while making art is more important than the product they create. This teaching principle is referred to as **process versus product**. When the emphasis is on the process, art experiences are less likely to aim for a specific result—allowing children to make decisions about their projects.

▶ **Encourage creativity.** Activities that require children to assemble products that look exactly like an example of artwork leave no room for creativity. Open-ended art activities encourage creativity and imagination.

▶ **Respond sensitively.** When children proudly show you pictures or paintings, it is tempting to ask, "What is it?" This question can disappoint children who think, "Can't you tell?" An encouraging response is "You've been working hard. Please tell me about your picture." This recognizes children's efforts and encourages language, confidence, and self-esteem.

▶ **Accept and appreciate children's art.** It is important to view art objectively. Teachers should avoid grading children's art or labeling it as bad or good. These practices lower self-esteem and can **inhibit**, or discourage, interest and creativity. They can also lead children to become dependent on pleasing others, rather than creating art for their own satisfaction.

▶ **Respect children's art.** Teachers should not redraw or complete children's creations. Completing projects for children only sends the message that they cannot do it themselves, and self-esteem suffers in these instances. Help children take pride in their accomplishments.

▶ **Display children's art.** Displaying children's art increases their sense of accomplishment, pride, and self-esteem. When displaying art, write the artist's name in an upper corner, using capital and small letters, and hang the art at children's eye level. Rotate items often to show appreciation for every child's effort. Whenever possible, draw parents' attention to the skills and concepts revealed in children's art.

Art Activities

Many art activities can be available daily for children to use in the art center such as drawing and easel painting materials. Provide other materials such as sponge painting tools occasionally. Some activities require more supervision than others, which affects when and how often they occur.

Drawing and Coloring

Provide paper of different sizes, shapes, and colors on which children can draw and color. Supply plenty of crayons, chalk, colored pencils, and markers, including duplicates of each color. In addition to primary colors, provide colors that include different skin tones.

Avoid using coloring books with children. Experts believe that overexposure to coloring books can limit creativity. It is better for children to use their memory and observation skills to create their own drawings.

Painting

Young children with limited vocabularies may be able to "speak" or express emotion through their artwork. Through painting, they learn to blend primary colors into secondary colors. The art center should include the following painting supplies:

▶ **Paint.** Water-based tempera paint is inexpensive, washable, and nontoxic. To help prevent spills, pour only small amounts of paint into individual containers. For younger children, provide only two colors at a time. As children develop, provide more colors. Store paint in labeled, sealed containers out of children's reach.

▶ **Easels.** These slanted boards hold paper for painting at children's height. Use easels that allow two to four children to paint at once.

▶ **Paper.** Newsprint, the paper used for newspapers, is good for easel painting. For variety, use papers with different textures such as wallpaper or poster board.

▶ **Painting tools.** For easel painting, use long-handled brushes ½- to 1-inch wide. Younger children may need wider brushes. Place one brush in each paint container and remind children to put each brush back in its own container. Experiment with using other items as painting tools such as feathers and cotton swabs.

▶ **Smocks.** Plastic aprons and old shirts can be used to keep children's clothes clean during painting.

▶ **Drying area.** Do not leave paintings on an easel to dry. Instead, use a drying rack, a clothesline, or a spare table.

▲ **Planning an Artwork**

Children practice decision making as they plan how to use the space on a canvas or piece of paper. *What other skills do children use as they create drawings and paintings?*

Finger Painting

The sensory experience of finger painting can be very soothing to children. Finger-paint paper is slick and glossy. You can buy ready-to-use finger paint or make your own. Create finger-paint substitutes by adding food coloring to hand lotion, shaving cream, or mild liquid soap. Before using any of the substitutes, be sure to ask parents if children have skin allergies that may be triggered by the solutions.

Modeling and Shaping

Playing with dough or clay is relaxing and fun. Using dough or clay, children can create objects that are **three-dimensional**, having height, width, and depth. Doughs, which are softer and easier to handle than clays, can be made from flour or cornstarch, salt, and water. As they mold and shape the dough or clay, children practice small motor skills and eye-hand coordination. Provide objects and utensils for cutting, shaping, and creating patterns the dough. School-age children can attempt more complex projects because their small-motor skills are more developed.

Cutting and Tearing

Cutting activities develop small-motor skills and eye-hand coordination. Toddlers can develop these skills by simply tearing pieces of paper. For cutting activities, provide safety scissors for children. Right- and left-handed scissors should be available. Magazines and flower catalogs are colorful favorites to cut and tear.

▼ Skill Building

Art helps children build small motor skills and eye-hand coordination. *What types of activities help build these skills?*

Pasting, Gluing, and Attaching

Children like to attach objects to each other. They may use glue, tape, staples, paper clips, string, or hook-and-loop tape to attach objects to paper or poster board. Supervise these activities carefully.

Children can practice cutting, pasting, making decisions, and problem-solving by creating a collage. A **collage** (kə-ˈläzh) is a picture or design made by gluing or pasting different materials to a backing. Many materials work well in collages, such as pictures, paper, fabric scraps, string, small objects like buttons, and different types of beans or seeds. Varying the sizes, shapes, colors, and textures of materials enhances this sensory experience. Label and store items for collage in separate containers in the art center.

READING CHECK ✔ Apply Why is it important to plan a variety of art activities?

How to . . .

Plan Art for School-Age Children

School-age children enjoy more challenging art activities. They are ready to use smaller brushes—⅛- to ¼-inch wide—for easel painting. They can use clay or dough to make more intricate projects such as necklaces or vases. Weaving, photography, woodworking, and assembling model kits are all developmentally appropriate activities school-age children might enjoy.

▶ **Mobiles** *These are a collection of items suspended on wire by string. After all items are attached to the mobiles, they are hung from the ceiling.*

▶ **Origami** *Origami (ȯr-ə-'gä-mē) is a Japanese art form in which squares of paper are folded into representational forms, such as birds.*

▶ **Dioramas** *Dioramas (dī-ə-'ra-mə) are three-dimensional pictures made with small cutout designs. Making a large detailed diorama can be a group effort.*

▶ **Weaving** *A woven item is created by interlacing strands of materials such as paper, reeds, or yarn. Creations can be made using simple, recycled materials.*

▶ **Photography** *Digital cameras allow children to experiment with shooting different subjects from various perspectives. Encourage children to try different lighting and compositions such as close zoom.*

▶ **Clay** *Clay projects that require more developed small-motor skills can be a creative outlet. Traditional earthen clay or newer, "plastic" clays produce interesting projects.*

Apply It!
Work with a group of school-age children to complete one of the projects described.

PhotoAlto/Alamy

Developing Musical Expression

Children enjoy singing and playing simple instruments, as well as moving and dancing to music. They find it especially enjoyable when their teachers play along. Children who acquire an appreciation of music from an early age enjoy it throughout life.

Music Curriculum Goals

Musical enjoyment and expression begin early. Infants eagerly respond to music during basic routines such as diapering or nap time. As children grow in early childhood, their musical interest expands further. During music activities, children learn to recognize and enjoy all kinds of music styles and instruments. Music activities benefit development in many areas.

▶ **Physical Development.** As children move to music, they develop their large muscles and refine their motor coordination skills. Hopping, wiggling, swaying, bouncing, and twirling to music are beneficial ways to release energy. To play basic instruments, such as drums or tambourines, children use small-motor skills and eye-hand coordination.

▶ **Intellectual Development.** Memory and language skills develop as children learn **lyrics**—words to songs—and follow directions to musical games. Vocabularies grow and concepts become clearer as children sing songs about shape, color, and size. Listening skills and concentration develop as children listen carefully to the sounds, words, and music. In addition, children learn about music itself. They identify **tempo**, the speed at which a song is sung, as well as beat, the recurring pulse that gives a song rhythm. To sing in tune, children must be able to recognize **pitch**, the highness or lowness of a sound. They also need to listen for the **melody**, or tune, of a song. Putting all these together to make music helps children learn how to use reasoning skills.

▶ **Emotional Development.** Through music, children express and cope with their emotions. Music can calm frustration and provide an outlet for anger. Children gain self-confidence with success in musical activities. Sharing songs from family backgrounds affirms cultural heritage.

▶ **Social Development.** During music activities, children learn to obey rules and share materials. Playing instruments and singing in harmony require cooperation.

Science *for Success*

Music and Math Comprehension

Asking children to play patterns of beats on rhythm instruments helps children better understand patterning, which is a basic concept in mathematics. Research has shown that when teachers incorporate music into math lessons, children are better able to comprehend and remember the math concepts being taught.

Procedure Using reliable print and Internet sources, research the connections between music and math comprehension in young children. Then create a musical activity that will introduce young children to a math concept such as patterning, addition, or subtraction. For example, a song such as "B-I-N-G-O" teaches children about patterning. Teach the math concept to your classmates without using any music. Then ask them to explain the concept to you. Teach the concept again, this time with music. Test your classmates' comprehension.

Analysis Draw conclusions about your activity and summarize your findings in a short essay.

©Comstock/Alamy

The Music Center

A music center is a classroom area set aside just for music experiences. Teachers conduct small-group activities in the music center and use materials from the center for large-group activities. The music center should also be available to children during playtime. There they can explore the sounds that instruments make and listen to recorded music. A well-stocked music center has recordings suitable for group singing, musical games, dancing, and other movement activities.

Children understand beat and tempo before they master following a melody or singing on pitch. Therefore, the music center should have child-size versions of **rhythm instruments**, musical instruments that allow children to experiment with making their own rhythms. Maracas and drums are two simple rhythm instruments that children can play. Most programs also have musical instruments for teachers to use as they lead activities, such as a piano, a guitar, a tambourine, or a ukulele.

Guiding Music Experiences

Many early childhood professionals are not musically inclined. This does not have to limit their students' musical experiences. Most songs can be sung without instrumental accompaniment. CDs are helpful to teachers who do not play an instrument.

When guiding music experiences, be sure to follow many of the same principles for guiding art. Consider the children's process of making music more important than their final performance. As children participate, educators encourage creativity and reinforce independence as they allow children to experiment and express themselves. Some children take longer than others to feel at ease in group music activities. Avoid pressuring children to perform alone in front of others. Some children feel more secure and confident when they have an instrument to play—they focus on the instrument instead of themselves.

▲ **Learning About Rhythm**

Working with different musical tempos helps develop thinking skills. *What specific skills are these children developing as they play their instruments?*

Music Activities

Singing and playing instruments are not the only ways for children to enjoy music. Music can also be related to other curriculum areas. For example, prop boxes for dramatic play can have a musical theme such as a ballet dancer or orchestra conductor. Field trips—such as visits to high school band rehearsals, radio stations, and dance studios—allow children to see community music in action. Teachers may invite musicians to perform for children. Other music experiences include the following:

▶ **Exploring familiar sounds.** Before learning specifics about music, children need to learn about sounds in general. Then children can enjoy creating new sounds through music.

▶ **Going on listening walks**. What nature sounds can children identify? Are there birds, frogs, or crickets? What city sounds do they hear? How does a train's whistle differ from a truck's horn? Listen for quiet sounds, harsh sounds, pretty sounds, and scary sounds.

▶ **Exploring sounds in daily life.** Clock buzzers wake them up or alarms warn of fire and storms. What other sounds can children remember hearing?

▶ **Exploring the sounds of the human body.** Children should experiment making sounds with their own bodies. They can slap, clap, snap, hum, or stamp to a tune.

▶ **Identifying the uses of music.** Music is used in cars, in places of worship, in elevators, in baby nurseries, on television programs, and in movies. Can children guess why music is used in these ways?

▶ **Singing with children.** Young children love to sing and make up their own songs. They sing as they bathe, dress, eat, and play. The ability to sing in tune develops slowly. Children have a limited singing range that gradually **expands**, or increases, as they grow older. They learn to sing by imitating others.

▶ **Singing in groups.** When choosing songs for group singing, consider developmental level and interests. Select a simple melody. Make sure songs have an identifiable beat or rhythm. Children enjoy songs that have an interesting story to tell. Look for songs with verses that repeat and have understandable vocabulary. **Call-and-response songs**, in which an adult sings questions and children sing back the answers, are popular. Children also enjoy using hand or body motions with songs.

▶ **Moving to music.** Action songs, those for which children act out the motions in the lyrics, require children to use their minds and their bodies. Pairing music with action helps increase attention span and helps children make connections so they learn more quickly. Songs such as "London Bridge" and "Hokey Pokey" allow children to explore body movements. Use short games with very simple rules. Small groups are easier to manage and to motivate than larger ones.

Playing Instruments

Children love to play simple rhythm instruments such as triangles and wood blocks. Simple instruments can be made using the ideas found in **Figure 23.2**. Multicultural rhythm instruments can be exciting additions to music centers. Introduce instruments a few at a time. Demonstrate how to use each instrument appropriately so it does not break. Show children where and how to store instruments. Set basic rules for playing with instruments. Here are some ways to include instruments in the music curriculum:

▶ Use instruments in a marching parade.

▶ Give children instruments to use as sound effects during stories. Before the story begins, explain when each child should play an instrument. Give cues as needed.

▶ Play a tune on an instrument. Have the children guess the song.

▶ Create a pattern of beats with a drum. Have the children repeat your pattern, using their own instruments.

▶ Experiment with tempo and volume by asking children to follow your lead. Can they play loud, soft, slow, and fast?

Music Throughout the Day

Early childhood educators find ways to incorporate many types of music into classroom routines. Greeting and farewell activities are good times to include music. Songs may be used as a calming transition from outside play. At nap time, children are eased into sleep with lullabies and other soft music.

READING CHECK ✔ **Connect** Sound and music connections can be made everywhere. What are two activities that explore everyday sounds?

Figure 23.2 Homemade Rhythm Instruments

Recycled Rhythm Many simple containers can be used as rhythm instruments. *What other items can be recycled to create instruments?*

Instrument	Materials	Procedure
Shakers and Rattles	Plastic eggs, salt and pepper shakers, film canisters; buttons, raw rice, or dried beans	Fill containers with varying amounts of buttons, rice, or beans; secure lids or seams with tape.
Sandpaper Blocks	Two wooden blocks, about 3-by-5-by 2 inches; two 3- by-5-inch rectangles of coarse sandpaper	Glue sandpaper onto blocks.
Drum	Cylinder-shaped snack container, oatmeal canister, smooth-edged coffee can with plastic lid; strip of sturdy fabric	Attach fabric strip to can; sling over shoulder to carry drum and play it with both hands.
Tambourine	Embroidery hoop, paper plate, or pie tin; small bells; string or pipe cleaners	Attach bells to hoop, plate, or pie tin with string or pipe cleaners.
Cymbals	Two pie tins; two empty thread spools	Glue spools to center of insides of pie tins; use spools as handles.

Motor Development and Fitness

Physical fitness, body tone, and good coordination are important components throughout life. Developing and maintaining these attributes promote a healthful lifestyle and allow individuals to participate in activities of their choice.

Motor Skill Development in Children

Developmental skills and abilities increase rapidly in healthy, growing children. Regardless of a child's level of development, the role of a teacher is to aid in the progression of those skills. Activities should be planned for areas of small and large motor coordination.

Over time, large and small motor development increases. Young children learn to coordinate their muscle movements and to increase their motor skills. Through movement activities, children learn to make their bodies do what they want them to do. For example, children first learn to touch an object purposefully, such as a ball. Next, they learn to pat the ball and then to roll it. Within a couple of years, they begin tossing and throwing the ball. They ultimately learn to throw and catch with greater accuracy. Large motor activities, such as walking, must come before running and skipping. From a basic foundation, children can later learn more complex skills. For example, they can dance in different styles, such as tap, folk, or ballet. They can also participate in sports that are more physically demanding, such as tennis or gymnastics.

▼ Jumping Rope

Movement activities help children learn to coordinate their body movements and develop motor skills. *What physical activities help develop children's coordination?*

Exploring Creative Movement

Active participation is the key to children's mastery of motor skills. Early childhood professionals can encourage participation by conducting creative movement activities. **Creative movement** is responding to music or a mental image through physical movement. A teacher may ask children to move across a room as if they were butterflies looking for flowers on which to feed. The children show their interpretation of this idea by how they move their bodies. With creative movement, children should be allowed to interpret the idea in any way they choose.

When conducting creative movement activities, use safe, large, open spaces with flat areas that offer safe footing. Keep children away from window areas to avoid injuries. Teachers often supply materials and props for children to use when participating in movement activities. Sometimes a simple musical instrument is used, such as a drum. The goal of a creative movement activity is to help children become comfortable with their bodies and to enjoy creative movement.

PhotoAlto/Alamy

The elements that make up creative movement are body awareness, force and time, space, locomotion, weight, and moving in groups.

▶ **Body awareness.** Body awareness activities familiarize children with the parts of their bodies and their range of movement. Play music with different tempos. Have children move parts of their bodies to the beat—first the head, then arms, legs, fingers, toes, and finally the entire body. Encourage expression and creativity in movement by having children dance with props. Streamers, scarves, grass skirts, leis, boas, pom-poms, veils, and hats are a few examples.

▶ **Force and time.** Force describes strength of movements. Time refers to how quickly or slowly children move. Have children respond to music with varying tempos, such as a wedding march, an Irish jig, or popular music. Notice how their movements change. Adjust the volume of the music. How do children respond to louder music? To softer music?

▶ **Space.** These activities encourage children to explore the use of physical space. In a large open area, play a steady drumbeat. Encourage children to move to the beat—forward, backward, sideways, and in circles. Play circus music while children move through a safe obstacle course.

▶ **Locomotion.** With **locomotion**, or the act of moving from place to place, children experience different ways to move. Have children mimic animal and human movements. Ask them to gallop like ponies, to slither like snakes, or to march like a bandleader. Play appropriate music for each movement.

▶ **Weight.** In these activities, children learn how weight affects body movements. Tell children to imagine they are carrying heavy backpacks. How would they walk going up a steep hill? Have children participate in a simple musical game, first holding streamers and later holding plastic bottles filled with sand. Ask them to compare their movements in each case.

▶ **Moving in groups.** This requires personal coordination and coordinating movements with others. Playing music with a rapid tempo, have groups of children form themselves into a type of food, such as a bunch of bananas. Play musical Follow the Leader. Have children take turns setting a beat with a tambourine or drum. The leader also selects the movements the others make to the beat.

▲ **Moving Together**

Moving in groups helps children learn to coordinate their body movements. *How do these activities improve social development?*

READING CHECK ✔ **Recall** How can motor development be enhanced through movement activities?

Active Play and Recreation

Boundless energy and enthusiasm are hallmarks of childhood. Children are fueled by the excitement of discovering how fast they can run and how far they can jump. Effective child care professionals plan and conduct appropriate and enjoyable physical activities for everyone. Teachers plan play activities that consider the type of play for which a child is developmentally ready. See **Figure 23.3** for the types of play development.

Benefits of Active Play

Activities that engage children in fun, physical participation are referred to as **active play**. Including active play in the daily curriculum promotes children's overall health and wellness. Active play helps children maintain energy and stamina needed for learning. Regular physical activity has long-lasting benefits. It helps develop the immune system so the body can fight off diseases and strengthens the heart and lungs. It also helps control weight. Establishing good exercise habits during early childhood increases the chances that children will maintain a healthful lifestyle. Here are other ways active play promotes children's development:

- ▶ **Physical development.** Children's small and large muscles in the arms and legs become stronger during active play. They improve small- and large-motor coordination and perceptual motor skills.

- ▶ **Intellectual development.** Remembering and following rules in active play games require thinking. Many games put language skills to use as children sing chants and talk to each other. Games that require strategy and purposeful action develop children's problem-solving and goal-setting skills.

- ▶ **Emotional development.** As children master physical skills, self-esteem and self-confidence grow. Active play offers them a constructive outlet for excess energy, which relieves stress.

- ▶ **Social development.** When children play games, they learn to work well with others and to follow the rules. Team games help children develop a sense of unity and belonging. They learn to cooperate with others to achieve common goals. Older children who play team sports learn positive character traits, such as fairness and teamwork.

Figure 23.3 Types of Play

Stages of Play

Before age six, children will go through predictable stages in their play. *What can you observe about how play changes at each stage?*

Age	Play Type	Explanation of Stage
0–2 years	Solitary	Plays alone
2–2 ½ years	Spectator	Observes other children
2 ½–3 years	Parallel	Plays alongside others
3–4 years	Associate	Starts to interact in play
4–6+ years	Cooperative	Plays together with others

Outdoor Active Play

Having separate, fenced play areas for infants and toddlers, pre-schoolers, and school-age children is ideal. Play yards should have plenty of climbing equipment scaled appropriately to children. Equipment and supplies should be versatile. Except for swings and slides, equipment should accommodate more than one child at a time. This gives more play opportunities for everyone. Teeter-totters, merry-go-rounds, swinging exercise rings, and high slides have been associated with injuries to preschoolers. These should not be included in the play yard. Adequate staff should always be present to supervise outdoor play.

Indoor Active Play

Some programs have a separate room for indoor active play, often large enough to allow for riding toys. This area may include small-scale climbers with mats placed underneath for safety in case of falls. Programs without separate indoor facilities depend on clever teachers who can conduct active play experiences in limited space. By moving classroom furniture to room edges, space can be made for active play. Using soft, flexible, active play props—such as sponge toys—prevents damage to classroom materials.

Guidelines for Safe Play

Safety considerations are especially important for active play areas. Whether indoors or outdoors, children need plenty of open space to move freely with appropriate adult-to-child ratios. Play areas should also be free of items that could hurt children. Make daily checks for dangers such as broken glass, splintered climbing equipment, and tacks on the floor.

Teachers need to help children follow rules that help prevent accidents and injuries. State rules simply and clearly in positive terms. Focus on what children can do. Always keep a close eye on children during active play and remind them of rules when needed. Here are sample safety rules for active play equipment:

▶ **Climber rules.** Only one person at a time may be on each part of the climber. Play on the climber only when it is dry. Hold on with both hands when climbing.

▶ **Swing rules.** Only one person at a time may use a swing. Hold on with both hands while swinging. Sit in the middle of the swing with knees bent and feet down. Only an adult may push a child in a swing. Stop the swing before getting off. Stay away from the swing area when other children are swinging.

▶ **Slide rules.** Only one person at a time may slide. Hold on to the sides with both hands until ready to slide. Check that no one is at the bottom of the slide before going down. Slide in a sitting position with feet first. Move away from the bottom of the slide when you reach the ground.

Respond to SPECIAL NEEDS

Asthma

Asthma is a lung condition that is common among children and can be life threatening. Asthma causes airways to swell and to produce mucus. Symptoms include difficulty breathing, coughing, and wheezing. Triggers include:

- **Exercise-induced asthma.** This occurs after strenuous physical activity. Taking medication prior to physical activities can help prevent a flare-up.

- **Allergy-triggered asthma.** This occurs when environmental allergens such as dust mites and secondhand smoke aggravate a child's condition. Identifying a child's specific allergies and avoiding those substances is the best solution.

Critical Thinking

Research asthma to answer the following questions: Which asthma attack triggers can you control? What are the warning signs of an asthma attack? What is an appropriate procedure to follow when a child has an asthma attack?

Active Play Materials

The best active play materials are safe and encourage children to develop a whole range of physical skills. They should be fun to play with and allow children to experience success alone or while playing in a group.

Many toys and games meet these criteria. Rubber balls, beach balls, sponge balls, and beanbags all help refine eye-hand coordination, perceptual motor skills, and large-motor skills. Scarves, streamers, and crepe paper strips encourage running and creative movement. Pinwheels and kites add variety to active play. Wheel toys—such as tricycles, scooters, and two-seater riding toys—build strong leg muscles. Games such as hopscotch, rim ball (a basketball hoop placed low for preschoolers), and bowling with plastic balls and pins also help develop large-motor and perceptual motor skills. Balance beams, hoops, and obstacle courses help develop balance and coordination.

Active Play Activities

Playing the same games repeatedly is not fun for children. They like new experiences. Start with simple activities and then gradually include more challenging ones as skills develop. Active play activities use a variety of materials, skills, and environments.

Parachute Play

With parachute play, a group of children use a large circle of nylon fabric for active play. The parachute is between six and twelve feet in diameter. Some have handles. Parachute play is good for developing muscles in the arms and shoulders. Parachute activities include the following:

▶ **Bounce the balls.** Have the children firmly grip the parachute edges and pull it tight. Toss sponge balls in the middle of the parachute. Have the children make the balls jump.

▶ **Catch.** With children holding the parachute on all sides, ask them to reach as high as possible toward the sky. Call out the name of a child, who runs under the parachute from one side to the other. As the child crosses, the other children pull the parachute toward the ground, trying to catch the child under it. Repeat until all children have had a turn.

▼ **Active Play**

Using large hoops for play can offer fun, active play activities. *What motor skills can hoop play help children develop?*

Beanbag and Balloon Play

Beanbags are inexpensive play materials that can be used in many ways, indoors and outdoors. Some simple games that use beanbags include the following:

- ▶ **Target toss.** Children toss beanbags into empty coffee cans or plastic buckets.

- ▶ **Moving target.** Using a sturdy rope, suspend a tire from a tree limb. Push the tire gently. Children try to toss the beanbag through the hole of the moving tire.

Balloons are another inexpensive choice for active indoor play. An adult should inflate the balloons. Broken balloon pieces should be thrown away immediately. Consider safety concerns such as choking or latex allergies. Explain the safety issues of playing with balloons to children before starting any balloon activity. Games using balloons include the following:

- ▶ **Balloon volleyball.** Stretch a string across the room. Divide children into two teams. Have them bat balloons to each other over the string.

- ▶ **Balloon catch.** In a circle, toss a balloon in the air and call out a child's name to catch the balloon. If the child catches the balloon, he or she tosses the balloon in the air and calls out the next name.

Rope and Hoop Play

Jumping rope is a longtime favorite activity, especially for school-age children. Ropes, however, also have other uses in active play. Safe rope activities include the following:

- ▶ **Long jump.** Lay two ropes parallel and close to each other. Allow children to jump over the ropes. Gradually make a larger space between the ropes.

- ▶ **Follow the wavy line.** Attach long pieces of rope together. Lay the rope throughout an area in a wavy design. Challenge children to follow the wave in different ways. Can they slither along the wave? Slide? Walk backwards?

Large plastic hoops can be used as originally intended, which is to swivel the hips and abdomen to keep the hoop revolving around the waist. Also use hoops for the following:

- ▶ **Hoop hop.** Place six to ten hoops on the floor or playground. Children must hop from one hoop to the next.

- ▶ **Hoop walk.** Provide each child with a hoop. Call out directions for them to follow. For example, "Walk or skip around your hoop." "Hop on one foot in and out of your hoop."

SAFETY MATTERS

Active Play Safety

School-age children love group games and sports. However, some contact sports, such as rugby, boxing, and football, are not recommended for school-age children in a child care setting. These sports can cause serious injuries that interrupt normal bone and muscle development. Offer alternative activities, such as skating, T-ball or softball, soccer, volleyball, badminton, or basketball.

What Would You Do? During an outdoor play session, you notice children starting to play a game of football. What would you do?

Balance Beams, Obstacle Courses, and Mazes

A balance beam should be no higher than four inches off the ground.

▶ **Reverse walk.** Have children first walk forward, then backward, then sideways along the beam.

▶ **Two-level walk.** Have children walk with one foot on the beam and one foot on the ground.

▶ **Bucket toss.** Have children stand in the center of the beam and toss a bean bag into a bucket or a bowl.

During the following activities, children learn to problem-solve and to control carefully all body parts.

▶ **Obstacle course.** Arrange items so children can crawl under tables, creep through tunnels, step in and out of tires, and hop over teacher-built block walls.

▶ **Maze it.** Draw a large **maze**—a deliberately confusing series of pathways—on a concrete area, using chalk. Mark a beginning and an end to the maze. Children then walk, skip, and hop through the maze or, if there is enough space, drive through it on riding toys. For added fun, make the maze as challenging as space allows by including twists, turns, and dead ends.

Games

Games offer mental as well as physical exercise. These games are especially good for developing eye-hand coordination and perceptual motor skills:

▶ **Simon Says.** Challenge children with directions that focus on parts of the body and positions. For example, "Put your hand beside your ear." "Put your elbow on your knee." For school-agers, you can increase the difficulty by asking them to do the opposite of what Simon says. It requires them to control impulses as well as to think quickly.

▶ **Mirror game.** Two children face each other. Choose one child as the leader, or the person who will move first. The other child tries to copy the exact movements of the leader. Have the children take turns being the leader.

▶ **Freeze tag or statue tag.** This is similar to regular tag, except that when touched by the person who is "it," children must freeze their body position (or turn into a statue). The game continues until all children are frozen or until the care provider asks another child to be "it."

▼ **Balance Beams**

Teachers might have children walk on a jump rope to practice balance before moving up to a balance beam. *What games might help children work on balance and coordination skills?*

McGraw-Hill Education/Lars A. Niki

◀ **Water Play**
....
Snow play activities
engage children's senses.
*What are some safe snow
play activities teachers can
plan for children?*

Active Water and Snow Play

Children enjoy water play during very warm weather. They can keep cool while having fun.

▶ **Water tag.** Provide plastic squirt and spray bottles so children can spray each other.

▶ **Car wash.** Set up a car wash for riding toys by providing a hose, sponges, and rags.

In cold climates, winter snow can provide opportunities for outdoor play experiences. As with water play, make sure children are properly dressed.

▶ **Snow people and animals.** Children can express their creativity, learn about shape and size, practice memory skills, and strengthen muscles by building snow people and animals.

▶ **Treasure hunt.** Have children make tracks in newly fallen snow. Give them each a treasure to hide at the end of their tracks. Let children track down each other's treasures.

READING CHECK ✓ **Remember** What are three active play activities that you learned about in this chapter?

Comstock Images/Jupiter Images/Alamy

Children's Entertainer

What Does a Children's Entertainer Do?

Children's entertainers like being with children and have an interest in drama or music. An entertainer might be part of a big stage show that travels to many different cities or he or she might be a storyteller at a local library. If you have talent as a singer or an actor and like to perform, you might want to consider being an entertainer for children.

Career Readiness Skills

Being a children's entertainer usually requires some performing arts talent and a willingness to perform in public. Performance skills can be developed by attending classes or by hiring a talent coach. People in this profession can also work "behind the scenes." These technicians may be responsible for building sets, creating costumes, or completing administrative tasks. Regardless of which role you want to pursue, you need to be organized with your time and able to learn new things quickly.

Education and Training

While a college degree is not necessarily required for a performer, a children's entertainer often attends acting, singing, or dancing classes. A degree in a performance area such as musical theater or dance may also help you with your career path. Some universities offer graduate programs in Children's Entertainment. You can train to begin a successful career as a writer, a content producer, or a production manager.

Job Outlook

Children's entertainment is a multibillion dollar industry around the world and employment in this industry is expected to keep up with the growth rate in other occupations. Jobs in entertainment fields such as multimedia development will explode as new forms of technology and entertainment evolve. Children's performers will always be needed.

Critical Thinking Assess the interests, characteristics, and skills that make someone a good children's entertainer. How do your personality and skills compare to those skills? Write a paragraph examining why you think you would or would not be a good fit as a children's entertainer.

Career Cluster

Arts, Audio/Video Technology, and Communications Children's Entertainers work in the Performing Arts pathway of the Arts, Audio/Video Technology, and Communications career cluster. Here are some other jobs in this career cluster:

- Make Up Artist
- Costume Designer
- Puppeteer
- Children's Theatre Director
- Children's Dance Troupe Director
- Dance Teacher
- Stagecraft Designer
- Composer

Explore Further The Arts, Audio/Video Technology, and Communications career cluster contains six pathways: Performing Arts; Visual Arts; Printing Technologies; Audio and Video Technologies; Telecommunications Technologies; and Journalism and Broadcasting. Choose one of these pathways to explore further. Write a paragraph that summarizes your findings.

(c) Lars A. Niki

Art, Music, and Movement
Visual Summary

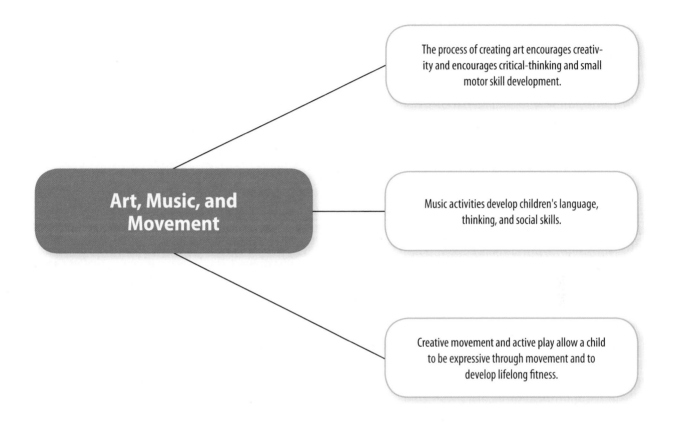

Art, Music, and Movement

The process of creating art encourages creativity and encourages critical-thinking and small motor skill development.

Music activities develop children's language, thinking, and social skills.

Creative movement and active play allow a child to be expressive through movement and to develop lifelong fitness.

Vocabulary Review

1. Create or find a visual example that illustrates each of the content and academic vocabulary words.

Content Vocabulary

◇ proportion (p. 499)
◇ process versus product (p. 500)
◇ three-dimensional (p. 502)
◇ collage (p. 502)
◇ lyrics (p. 504)
◇ tempo (p. 504)

◇ pitch (p. 504)
◇ melody (p. 504)
◇ rhythm instruments (p. 505)
◇ call-and-response songs (p. 506)
◇ creative movement (p. 508)
◇ locomotion (p. 509)

◇ active play (p. 510)
◇ maze (p. 514)

Academic Vocabulary

■ inhibit (p. 500)
■ expand (p. 506)

Review Key Concepts

2. Explain appropriate methods for guiding children's art experiences.
3. Describe how basic intellectual skills and concepts are reinforced through music activities.
4. Determine the effects of children's motor development and fitness.
5. List the six elements that make up creative movement activities.

Critical Thinking

6. **Decide** If art or music were not included in center activities, would a child's development be affected? Support your answer.

7. **Predict** what effect a child care professional's negative comments regarding a child's artwork could have on a child's future art creation.

8. **Analyze** how musical activities stimulate a child's creativity.

9. **Consider** how active play helps a child develop intellectually, emotionally, and socially.

10. **Describe** why safety is an important concern when planning creative movement and active play activities for young children.

21st Century Skills

Decision Making Skills

11. **Analyzing Artwork** Collect artwork from children of different ages. Analyze the artwork to determine each child's stage of artistic development. What can you notice about each art piece? Compare your analyses with those of your classmates. Do you agree on the stages of artistic development?

Creativity Skills

12. **Active Play** Common objects can be used in active play activities. Work with a classmate to create an active play activity using a common object found at a child care center or on a playground. How many different activities can you plan using the same object? Share your ideas with your class.

Child Care LAB

Use the skills you have learned in this chapter.

Creative Movement Activity

13. **Plan a Movement Activity** Creative movement is responding to music or a mental image through physical movement. In this activity, you will work with a partner to develop a creative or active movement activity for toddlers or preschoolers.

    A. Select an activity focus. Decide on the age group for your activity—toddlers or preschoolers. Then, choose an activity focus from the following creative movement elements:

    - Body awareness
    - Force and time
    - Space
    - Locomotion
    - Weight
    - Moving in Groups

    B. Select music or theme. Select an appropriate song or concept that will illustrate the element that you plan to use.

    C. Write your activity. Write a description of your activity. List the space requirements and props it will require. Will a toddler or preschooler be able to understand it? Is your activity safe?

    D. Describe the objectives. List the learning objectives of your activity. What skills and development areas does your activity target?

    E. Plan for different abilities. Have you planned for children of different abilities? Have you planned for children with special needs?

    F. Share your activity. Share your movement activity with your class.

Create Your Evaluation

Create an evaluation sheet with these categories:

- Music or Theme
- Safety
- Developmentally Appropriate
- Learning Objectives
- Accomodation

Ask your classmates to use the sheet to evaluate your activity, rating each category from 1 to 10.

Academic Skills

English Language Arts

14. Encourage Creativity Imagine that a four-year-old is drawing a picture of her family and pets. Write a list of six comments that you could make or questions that you could ask the child to encourage learning, enhance creativity, and promote positive self-esteem. Explain why you feel these comments or questions would be encouraging.

Social Studies

15. Multicultural Music Select a variety of songs from other cultures or countries and create an activity for preschoolers. Think about how preschoolers could learn about other cultures or countries through music. Present your activity to your class. Write a description of the activity that includes a list of the activity objectives and required materials.

Mathematics

16. Active Water Play In preparation for warm weather and outdoor water play, Janna purchased fifty-six 16-ounce spray bottles for her child care center. On an average day of water play, Janna must fill up each spray bottle two times. How many gallons of water will Janna use to fill all of the containers twice?

Math Concept **Customary System** The customary system of weights and measures is used in the United States. Length is typically measured in inches and feet and liquid is measured in ounces, cups, quarts, and gallons.

Starting Hint One gallon is equal to 128 ounces. Multiply 16 by 56 to calculate the total number of ounces in 56 bottles. Divide that number by 896 to determine total gallons need to fill the bottles. Then, multiply by 2 to figure how many gallons are needed to fill the spray bottles twice.

 For more math practice, go to the math appendix at the back of the book.

Certification Prep

Directions Read each statement. Then read the answer choices and choose the phrase or word that best completes the sentence.

17. A collage is a _____.

    A. collection of items suspended on wire

    B. square of paper folded to make an object

    C. three-dimensional picture

    D. picture made by gluing or pasting materials together

18. The tune of a song is called the _____.

    A. tempo

    B. melody

    C. pitch

    D. beat

> **Test-Taking Tip**
> Read and consider every possible answer on a multiple choice test. Eliminate each choice that is clearly incorrect. Then decide which remaining choice is the best answer.

Research and Design

Have you ever wondered what it takes to design children's toys?

A career as a designer or researcher for children's toys, manipulatives, educational games, and literature involves creativity, technical skills, and knowledge of the developmental stages of a child. It may also involve researching or testing how a toy or game is used by a child.

To succeed in a research and development career, you may need a degree in art or design and knowledge of child development. Some designers have a child development background and work with other professionals who have the technical skills necessary to create the toys, games, or literature.

Karen Woodley Thompson • Educational Toy Designer

Q What is your job?

A I am an educational product developer for an educational toy company. I develop educational toys, teaching tools, and books for the preschool classroom.

Q What is your typical workday like?

A When I am in the design and development stage of a new manipulative or toy, I research the latest educational trends in the preschool toy market. I also research the competition to see what they have available. I have the most fun at my job when I visit preschools, Head Start centers, and child care facilities to observe young children at play. This helps me understand how my idea will actually help children learn.

Q Why did you choose your career?

A I think my career chose me. I have always loved the preschool classroom and would spend hours developing new ideas, designing lessons, and creating projects.

Q How did your career path lead to your current job?

A My minor is psychology, and I became fascinated with child psychology and child development courses. It was after several child development courses in college that I realized that I wanted to teach. I taught for several years before becoming a toy designer. My child development classes are invaluable as a toy designer.

Q Who or what has been your biggest career influence?

A My children have been a huge influence on how I design and develop toys. My biggest career influences were my teachers who inspired me to want to teach.

Q What skills are most important in your job?

A Knowledge of child psychology and child development is important. Being able to think outside the box and to be innovative are important skills as well. Thinking like a child and knowing that play has a developmental function is also helpful.

Career Requirements	
Education or Training	Research and design jobs usually require some education beyond high school. A bachelor's degree is typically required. Children's toy designers take coursework in industrial design, child psychology, and early child development.
Academic Skills	English, Language Arts, Mathematics, Science, and Social Studies
Aptitudes, Abilities, and Skills	Knowledge of children and how they learn, planning and organizational skills, communication skills, and interpersonal skills
Workplace Safety	Toy safety for children must be considered.
Career Outlook	Qualified children's toy researchers or designers are always in demand to meet the need for children's products.
Career Path	Careers path may vary depending on education level and training. There are careers in the research and design fields for almost every education level and area of interest.

Career Pathways	
Children's Librarian	A children's librarian works with teachers, parents, and children to share literature appropriate for children at each age and stage of development. He or she usually works for the children's department of a library and plans activities appropriate for children of all ages. A children's librarian needs to have a thorough knowledge of literature appropriate for children.
Children's Multimedia Author	A children's multimedia author is a computer programmer who creates Web sites for children. Knowledge of child development is necessary to create visually appealing, developmentally appropriate sites for children.
Computer Animation Artist	A computer animation artist is a professional artist who has specialized training in the software applications used to create animations. Animation can include movies, video games, Web sites, and advertisements. Animation artists need to have a strong visual arts background.
Children's Illustrator	A children's illustrator creates images for Web sites, toy packaging, advertisements, and children's books. A children's illustrator needs to have a strong visual arts background and creativity skills.

Critical Thinking What classes have you taken in school that might help you prepare for a career as a children's toy designer? Propose the short- and long-term career goals that will help you prepare for this career.

Certification Prep

How do project-based lessons and theme-based lessons address different learning styles? Create a chart that compares the two approaches to lesson planning. List learning styles in one column and describe how each lesson planning approach relates to each learning style.

Competitive Events Practice

Create a resource box of items that can be used for creative activities. Include a variety of items such as empty containers and ribbons. What are two activities that you could conduct using some of the items?

Evaluate your resource box using the following criteria:

• Does your resource box contain a variety of items?

• Can all the items in the box be used for creative activities?

• Were you able to think of two activities that would use items from the box?

Plan a Thematic Unit

A thematic unit teaches children about a broad topic using related curriculum activities over a period of one or two weeks. Using your research and information in the chapters in this unit, you will plan a developmentally appropriate thematic unit that integrates several curriculum areas.

My Journal

If you completed the journal entry on page 410, refer to it to see what themes you researched or have used in the past. Add any additional notes about theme-based activities for children after reading this unit.

Project Assignment

In this project, you will do the following:

- Choose an age group for which to develop your thematic unit
- Research and select an age-appropriate theme for your unit
- Outline concept and skill development objectives for the thematic unit
- Plan activities for each curriculum area in your thematic unit
- Determine ways the theme can be reinforced inside and outside the classroom, such as bulletin boards, guest speakers, family involvement, and field trips
- Create a resource and supply list for items you will need to carry out your thematic unit activities
- Observe a classroom using the thematic teaching approach
- Present your thematic unit plan to the class

Applied Child Care Professional Skills Behind the Project

Your success as a child care professional will depend on your skills. Skills you will use in this project include the following:

▶ Selecting age-appropriate themes
▶ Identifying learning objectives and skill development goals for a thematic unit
▶ Planning curriculum activities that support a thematic unit
▶ Extending themes into all parts of a child care center and routine and beyond the classroom
▶ Determining the materials and resources needed to for a thematic unit

English Language Arts Skills Behind the Project

The English Language Arts skills you will use for this project are research, writing, and speaking skills. Remember these key concepts:

Research Skills

▶ Perform research using a variety of resources
▶ Discriminate between sources
▶ Use the information you gathered to narrow your choices

Writing Skills

▶ Use complete sentences with correct spelling, grammar, and punctuation
▶ Consider your audience
▶ Use findings from research to communicate discoveries in writing

Speaking Skills

▶ Be sensitive to the needs of your audience
▶ Adapt and modify language to suit different purposes

©Nova Development

STEP 1 Research a Developmentally Appropriate Theme

Select an age group (toddlers, preschoolers, or school-age children) for your thematic unit project. Conduct research to find different themes that are appropriate for your selected age group. Write a summary of your research that:

- describes the themes that are often used for your chosen age group.
- explains why the themes are developmentally appropriate for this age group.
- explains how the themes encourage learning and development.

STEP 2 Plan Your Thematic Unit

Use the results of your research to choose a theme and create a thematic unit plan. Your plan should include the following:

- Unit title, age group, and length (1 or 2 weeks)
- **Objectives.** Detail the learning and skill development objectives for the unit. Be specific about the outcomes you wish to achieve.
- **Activities.** Describe suggested activities for each of the following subject areas: math, music, art, science, social studies, dramatic play, indoor/outdoor play, and literacy. State how each activity relates to the theme and meets a learning objective.
- **Theme extensions.** Describe how you will integrate the theme into all parts of the child care program. Be creative. For example, will you create a themed bulletin board or plan a field trip related to the theme? How could you involve families in the theme?
- **Required materials.** Create a list of all the materials and resources that will be needed to conduct all the thematic unit activities.

Child Care Portfolio Project Checklist

Plan

- ✔ Research developmentally appropriate themes and summarize your findings.
- ✔ Select a developmentally appropriate theme for a chosen age level.
- ✔ Outline learning and skill development objectives for the thematic unit.
- ✔ Plan activities for each curriculum subject area and theme extensions.
- ✔ Prepare a visual aid for your presentation.

Present

- ✔ Make a presentation to your class to share your research and your thematic unit plan.
- ✔ Invite students to ask any questions they may have. Answer these questions.
- ✔ Turn in the summary of your research, your thematic unit plan, and your visual aid.

STEP 3 Connect with Your Community

Visit a child care classroom and observe how the teachers implement a thematic unit. Make notes about where you see the theme in the facility and how the teachers meet the thematic unit's learning objectives. After your visit, evaluate your thematic unit plan. Revise your plan based on what you learned during your observation.

STEP 4 Share What You Have Learned

Use the Child Care Portfolio Project Checklist to plan and present your thematic unit plan to your class. Your presentation should include visual aids created using presentation software or poster board. Share what you have learned from your research and observations with your classmates.

STEP 5 Evaluate Your Child Care Professional and Academic Skills

Your project will be evaluated based on the following:

- Depth and detail of research about themes
- Thoroughness of thematic unit plan
- Age appropriateness of the thematic unit plan
- Quality of presentation, including visual aid and speaking skills

 Project Worksheet *Go to this book's Online Learning Center at for a worksheet you can use to complete your portfolio project.*

Math Skills Handbook

Number and Operations

▷ **Understand numbers, ways of representing numbers, relationships among numbers, and number systems**

Fraction, Decimal, and Percent

A percent is a ratio of a number to 100. To write a percent as a fraction, drop the percent sign, and use the number as the numerator in a fraction with a denominator of 100. Simplify, if possible. For example, $76\% = \frac{76}{100}$, or $\frac{19}{25}$. To write a fraction as a percent, convert it to an equivalent fraction with a denominator of 100. For example, $\frac{3}{4} = \frac{75}{100}$, or 75%. A fraction can be expressed as a percent by first converting the fraction to a decimal (divide the numerator by the denominator) and then converting the decimal to a percent by moving the decimal point two places to the right.

Comparing Numbers on a Number Line

In order to compare and understand the relationship between real numbers in various forms, it is helpful to use a number line. The zero point on a number line is called the origin. The points to the left of the origin are negative, and those to the right are positive. The number line below shows how numbers in various forms can be compared.

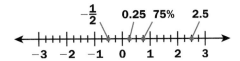

Percents Greater Than 100 and Less Than 1

Percents greater than 100% represent values greater than 1. If the weight of an object is 250% of another, it is 2.5, or $2\frac{1}{2}$, times the weight.

Percents less than 1 represent values less than $\frac{1}{100}$. In other words, 0.1% is one-tenth of 1 percent, which can also be represented in decimal form as 0.001, or in fraction form as $\frac{1}{1,000}$. Similarly, 0.01% is one-hundredth of 1 percent, or 0.0001, or $\frac{1}{10,000}$.

Ratio, Rate, and Proportion

A ratio is a comparison of two numbers using division. If a basketball player makes 8 out of 10 free throws, the ratio is written as 8 to 10, 8:10, or $\frac{8}{10}$. Ratios are usually written in simplest form. In simplest form, the ratio 8 out of 10 is 4 to 5, 4:5, or $\frac{4}{5}$. A rate is a ratio of two measurements having different kinds of units—cups per gallon, or miles per hour, for example. When a rate is simplified so that it has a denominator of 1, it is called a unit rate. An example of a unit rate is 9 miles per hour. A proportion is an equation stating that two ratios are equal. $\frac{3}{18} = \frac{13}{78}$ is an example of a proportion. The cross products of a proportion are also equal. $\frac{3}{18} = \frac{13}{78}$ and $3 \times 78 = 18 \times 13$.

Representing Large and Small Numbers

In order to represent large and small numbers, it is important to understand the number system. Our number system is based on 10, and the value of each place is 10 times the value of the place to its right. The value of a digit is the product of a digit and its place value. For instance, in the number 6,400, the 6 has a value of six thousands, and the 4 has a value of four hundreds. A place-value chart can help you read numbers. In the chart, each group of three digits is called a period. Commas separate the periods: the ones period, the thousands period, the millions period, and so on. Values to the right of the ones period are decimals. By understanding place value, you can write very large numbers like 5 billion and more, and very small numbers that are less than 1, like one-tenth.

Scientific Notation

When dealing with very large numbers like 1,500,000, or very small numbers like 0.000015, it is helpful to keep track of their values by writing the numbers in scientific notation. Powers of 10 with positive exponents are used with a decimal between 1 and 10 to express large numbers. The exponent represents the number of places the decimal point is moved to the right. So 528,000 is written in scientific notation as 5.28×10^5. Powers of 10 with negative exponents are used with a decimal between 1 and 10 to express small numbers. The exponent represents the number of places the decimal point is moved to the left. The number 0.00047 is expressed as 4.7×10^{-4}.

Factor, Multiple, and Prime Factorization

Two or more numbers that are multiplied to form a product are called factors. Divisibility rules can be used to determine whether 2, 3, 4, 5, 6, 8, 9, or 10 is a factor of a given number. Multiples are the products of a given number and various integers.

For example, 8 is a multiple of 4 because $4 \times 2 = 8$. A prime number is a whole number that has exactly two factors: 1 and itself. A composite number is a whole number that has more than two factors. Zero and 1 are neither prime nor composite. A composite number can be expressed as the product of its prime factors. The prime factorization of 40 is $2 \times 2 \times 2 \times 5$, or $2^3 \times 5$. The numbers 2 and 5 are prime numbers.

Integers

A negative number is a number less than zero. Negative numbers like –8, positive numbers like +6, and zero are members of the set of integers. Integers can be represented as points on a number line. A set of integers can be written {..., –3, –2, –1, 0, 1, 2, 3, ...} where ... means continues indefinitely.

Real, Rational, and Irrational Numbers

The rea-number system is made of the sets of rational and irrational numbers. Rational numbers are numbers that can be written in the form $\frac{a}{b}$ where a and b are integers and $b \neq 0$. Examples are 0.45, $\frac{1}{2}$, and $\sqrt{36}$. Irrational numbers are nonrepeating, nonterminating decimals. Examples are $\sqrt{71}$, π, and 0.020020002....

Complex and Imaginary Numbers

A complex number is a mathematical expression with a real-number element and an imaginary-number element. Imaginary numbers are multiples of i, the imaginary square root of –1. Complex numbers are represented by $a + bi$, where a and b are real numbers and i represents the imaginary element. When a quadratic equation does not have a real-number solution, the solution can be represented by a complex number. Like real numbers, complex numbers can be added, subtracted, multiplied, and divided.

Vectors and Matrices

A matrix is a set of numbers or elements arranged in rows and columns to form a rectangle. The number of rows is represented by m, and the number of columns is represented by n. To describe the number of rows and columns in a matrix, list the number of rows first using the format $m \times n$. Matrix A is a 3×3 matrix because it has three rows and three columns. To name an element of a matrix, i is used to denote the row, j is used to denote the column, and the element is labeled in the form $a_{i,j}$. In Matrix A below, $a_{3,2}$ is 4.

$$\text{Matrix A} = \begin{pmatrix} 1 & 3 & 5 \\ 0 & 6 & 8 \\ 3 & 4 & 5 \end{pmatrix}$$

A vector is a matrix with only one column or row of elements. A transposed column vector, or a column vector turned on its side, is a row vector. In the example below, row vector b' is the transpose of column vector b.

$$b = \begin{pmatrix} 1 \\ 2 \\ 3 \\ 4 \end{pmatrix}$$

$$b' = \begin{pmatrix} 1 & 2 & 3 & 4 \end{pmatrix}$$

▶ Understand meanings of operations and how they relate to one another

Properties of Addition and Multiplication

Properties are statements that are true for any numbers. For example, $3 + 8$ is the same as $8 + 3$ because each expression equals 11. This illustrates the Commutative Property of Addition. Likewise, $3 \times 8 = 8 \times 3$ illustrates the Commutative Property of Multiplication.

When evaluating expressions, it is often helpful to group or associate the numbers. The Associative

Property says that the way in which numbers are grouped when added or multiplied does not change the sum or product. The following properties are also true:

- **Additive Identity Property:** When 0 is added to any number, the sum is the number.

- **Multiplicative Identity Property:** When any number is multiplied by 1, the product is the number.

- **Multiplicative Property of Zero:** When any number is multiplied by 0, the product is 0.

Rational Numbers

A number that can be written as a fraction is called a rational number. Terminating and repeating decimals are rational numbers because both can be written as fractions. Decimals that are neither terminating nor repeating are called irrational numbers because they cannot be written as fractions.

Terminating decimals can be converted to fractions by placing the number (without the decimal point) in the numerator. Count the number of places to the right of the decimal point, and in the denominator, place a 1 followed by a number of zeros equal to the number of places that you counted. The fraction can then be reduced to its simplest form.

Writing a Fraction as a Decimal

Any fraction $\frac{a}{b}$, where $b \neq 0$, can be written as a decimal by dividing the numerator by the denominator. So $\frac{a}{b} = a \div b$. If the division ends, or terminates, when the remainder is zero, the decimal is a terminating decimal. Not all fractions can be written as terminating decimals. Some have a repeating decimal. A bar indicates that the decimal repeats forever. For example, the fraction $\frac{4}{9}$ can be converted to a repeating decimal, $0.\overline{4}$.

Adding and Subtracting Like Fractions

Fractions with the same denominator are called like fractions. To add like fractions, add the numerators and write the sum over the denominator. To add mixed numbers with like fractions, add the whole numbers and fractions separately, adding the numerators of the fractions, then simplifying if necessary. The rule for subtracting fractions with like denominators is similar to the rule for adding. The numerators can be subtracted and the difference written over the denominator. Mixed numbers are written as improper fractions before subtracting. These same rules apply to adding or subtracting like algebraic fractions. An algebraic fraction is a fraction that contains one or more variables in the numerator or denominator.

Adding and Subtracting Unlike Fractions

Fractions with different denominators are called unlike fractions. The least common multiple of the denominators is used to rename the fractions with a common denominator. After a common denominator is found, the numerators can then be added or subtracted. To add mixed numbers with unlike fractions, rename the mixed numbers as improper fractions. Then find a common denominator, add the numerators, and simplify the answer.

Multiplying Rational Numbers

To multiply fractions, multiply the numerators and multiply the denominators. If the numerators and denominators have common factors, they can be simplified before multiplication. If the fractions have different signs, then the product will be negative. Mixed numbers can be multiplied in the same manner, after first renaming them as improper fractions. Algebraic fractions may be multiplied using the same method described above.

Dividing Rational Numbers

To divide a number by a rational number (a fraction, for example), multiply the first number by the multiplicative inverse of the second. Two numbers whose product is 1 are called multiplicative inverses, or reciprocals. $\frac{7}{4} \times \frac{4}{7} = 1$. When dividing by a mixed number, first rename it as an improper fraction, and then multiply by its multiplicative inverse. This process of multiplying by a number's reciprocal can also be used when dividing algebraic fractions.

Adding and Subtracting Integers

To add integers with the same sign, add their absolute values. The sum takes the same sign as the addends. An addend is a number that is added to another number (the augend). The equation $-5 + (-2) = -7$ is an example of adding two integers with the same sign. To add integers with different signs, subtract their absolute values. The sum takes the same sign as the addend with the greater absolute value. The rules for adding integers are extended to the subtraction of integers. To subtract an integer, add its additive inverse. For example, to find the difference $2 - 5$, add the additive inverse of 5 to 2: $2 + (-5) = -3$. The rule for subtracting integers can be used to solve real-world problems and to evaluate algebraic expressions.

Additive Inverse Property

Two numbers with the same absolute value but different signs are called opposites. For example, –4 and 4 are opposites. An integer and its opposite are also called additive inverses. The Additive Inverse Property says that the sum of any number and its additive inverse is zero. The Commutative, Associative, and Identity Properties also apply to integers. These properties help when adding more than two integers.

Absolute Value

In mathematics, when two integers on a number line are on opposite sides of zero and they are the same distance from zero, they have the same absolute value. The symbol for absolute value is two vertical bars on either side of the number. For example, $|-5| = 5$.

Multiplying Integers

Because multiplication is repeated addition, $3(-7)$ means that –7 is used as an addend three times. By the Commutative Property of Multiplication, $3(-7) = -7(3)$. The product of two integers with different signs is always negative. The product of two integers with the same sign is always positive.

Dividing Integers

The quotient of two integers can be found by dividing the numbers using their absolute values. The quotient of two integers with the same sign is positive, and the quotient of two integers with a different sign is negative: $-12 \div (-4) = 3$ and $12 \div (-4) = -3$. The division of integers is used in statistics to find the average, or mean, of a set of data. When finding the mean of a set of numbers, find the sum of the numbers, and then divide by the number in the set.

Adding and Multiplying Vectors and Matrices

In order to add two matrices together, they must have the same number of rows and columns. In matrix addition, the corresponding elements are added to each other. In other words $(a + b)_{ij} = a_{ij} + b_{ij}$. For example,

$$\begin{pmatrix} 1 & 2 \\ 2 & 1 \end{pmatrix} + \begin{pmatrix} 3 & 6 \\ 0 & 1 \end{pmatrix} = \begin{pmatrix} 1+3 & 2+6 \\ 2+0 & 1+1 \end{pmatrix} = \begin{pmatrix} 4 & 8 \\ 2 & 2 \end{pmatrix}$$

Matrix multiplication requires that the number of elements in each row in the first matrix is equal to the number of elements in each column in the second. The elements of the first row of the first matrix are multiplied by the corresponding elements of the first column of the second matrix and then added together to get the first element of the product matrix. To get the second element, the elements in the first row of the first matrix are multiplied by the corresponding elements in the second column of the second matrix then added, and so on, until every row of the first matrix is multiplied by every column of the second. See the example below.

$$\begin{pmatrix} 1 & 2 \\ 3 & 4 \end{pmatrix} \times \begin{pmatrix} 3 & 6 \\ 0 & 1 \end{pmatrix} = \begin{pmatrix} (1\times3)+(2\times0) & (1\times6)+(2\times1) \\ (3\times3)+(4\times0) & (3\times6)+(4\times1) \end{pmatrix} = \begin{pmatrix} 3 & 8 \\ 9 & 22 \end{pmatrix}$$

Vector addition and multiplication are performed in the same way, but there is only one column and one row.

Permutations and Combinations

Permutations and combinations are used to determine the number of possible outcomes in different situations. An arrangement, listing, or pattern in which order is important is called a permutation. The symbol P(6, 3) represents the number of permutations of 6 things taken 3 at a time. For P(6, 3), there are $6 \times 5 \times 4$, or 120, possible outcomes. An arrangement or listing in which order is not important is called a combination. The symbol C(10, 5) represents the number of combinations of 10 things taken 5 at a time. For C(10, 5), there are $(10 \times 9 \times 8 \times 7 \times 6) \div (5 \times 4 \times 3 \times 2 \times 1)$, or 252, possible outcomes.

Powers and Exponents

An expression such as $3 \times 3 \times 3 \times 3$ can be written as a power. A power has two parts: a base and an exponent. $3 \times 3 \times 3 \times 3 = 3^4$. The base is the number that is multiplied (3). The exponent tells how many times the base is used as a factor (4 times). Numbers and variables can be written using exponents. For example, $8 \times 8 \times 8 \times m \times m \times m \times m \times m$ can be expressed $8^3 m^5$. Exponents also can be used with place value to express numbers in expanded form. Using this method, 1,462 can be written as $(1 \times 10^3) + (4 \times 10^2) + (6 \times 10^1) + (2 \times 10^0)$.

Squares and Square Roots

The square root of a number is one of two equal factors of a number. Every positive number has both a positive and a negative square root. For example, because $8 \times 8 = 64$, 8 is a square root of 64. Because $(-8) \times (-8) = 64$, –8 is also a square root of 64. The notation $\sqrt{\cdot}$ indicates the positive square root, $-\sqrt{\cdot}$ indicates the negative square root, and $\pm\sqrt{\cdot}$ indicates both square roots. For example, $\sqrt{81} = 9$, $-\sqrt{49} = -7$, and $\pm\sqrt{4} = \pm2$. The square root of a negative number is an imaginary number because any two factors of the number must have different signs and are not equivalent.

Logarithm

A logarithm is the inverse of exponentiation. The logarithm of a number x in base b is equal to the number n. Therefore, $b^n = x$ and $\log_b x = n$. For example, $\log_4(64) = 3$ because $4^3 = 64$. The most commonly used bases for logarithms are 10, the common logarithm; 2, the binary logarithm; and the constant e, the natural logarithm (also called $ln(x)$ instead of $\log_e(x)$). Below is a list of some of the rules of logarithms that are important to understand if you are going to use them.

$$\log_b(xy) = \log_b(x) + \log_b(y)$$
$$\log_b\tfrac{x}{y} = \log_b(x) - \log_b(y)$$
$$\log_b\tfrac{1}{x} = -\log_b(x)$$
$$\log_b(x)y = y\log_b(x)$$

▶ Compute fluently and make reasonable estimates

Estimation by Rounding

When rounding numbers, look at the digit to the right of the place to which you are rounding. If the digit is 5 or greater, round up. If it is less than 5, round down. For example, to round 65,137 to the nearest hundred, look at the number in the tens place. Since 3 is less than 5, round down to 65,100. To round the same number to the nearest ten thousandth, look at the number in the thousandths place. Because it is 5, round up to 70,000.

Finding Equivalent Ratios

Equivalent ratios have the same meaning. Just like finding equivalent fractions, to find an equivalent ratio, multiply or divide both sides by the same number. For example, you can multiply 7 by both sides of the ratio 6:8 to get 42:56. Instead, you can also divide both sides of the same ratio by 2 to get 3:4. Find the simplest form of a ratio by dividing to find equivalent ratios until you can't go any further without going into decimals. So 160:240 in simplest form is 2:3. To write a ratio in the form *1:n*, divide both sides by the left-hand number. In other words, to change 8:20 to *1:n*, divide both sides by 8 to get 1:2.5.

Front-End Estimation

Front-end estimation can be used to estimate sums and differences quickly before adding or subtracting. To use this technique, add or subtract

just the digits of the two highest place values, and replace the other place values with zero. This will give you an estimation of the solution of a problem. For example, 93,471 − 22,825 can be changed to 93,000 − 22,000, or 71,000. This estimate can be compared to your final answer to judge its correctness.

Judging Reasonableness

When solving an equation, it is important to check your work by considering how reasonable your answer is. For example, consider the equation $9\tfrac{3}{4} \times 4\tfrac{1}{3}$. Because $9\tfrac{3}{4}$ is between 9 and 10 and $4\tfrac{1}{3}$ is between 4 and 5, only values that are between 9×4, or 36, and 10×5, or 50, will be reasonable. You can also use front-end estimation, or you can round and estimate a reasonable answer. In the equation 73×25, you can round and solve to estimate a reasonable answer to be near 70×30, or 2,100.

Algebra

▶ Understand patterns, relations, and functions

Relation

A relation is a generalization comparing sets of ordered pairs for an equation or inequality such as $x = y + 1$ or $x > y$. The first element in each pair, the x values, forms the domain. The second element in each pair, the y values, forms the range.

Function

A function is a special relation in which each member of the domain is paired with exactly one member in the range. Functions may be represented using ordered pairs, tables, or graphs. One way to determine whether a relation is a function is to use the vertical-line test. Using an object to represent a vertical line, move the object from left to right across the graph. If, for each value of x in the domain, the object passes through no more than one point on the graph, then the graph represents a function.

Linear and Nonlinear Functions

Linear functions have graphs that are straight lines. These graphs represent constant rates of change. In other words, the slope between any two pairs of points on the graph is the same. Nonlinear functions do not have constant rates of change. The slope changes along these graphs. Therefore, the graphs of nonlinear functions are *not* straight lines. Graphs of curves represent nonlinear functions. The equation for a linear function can be written in the form $y = mx + b$, where m represents the constant rate of change, or the slope. Therefore, you can determine whether a function is linear by looking at the equation. For example, the equation $y = \frac{3}{x}$ is nonlinear because x is in the denominator and the equation cannot be written in the form $y = mx + b$. A nonlinear function does not increase or decrease at a constant rate. You can check this by using a table and finding the increase or decrease in y for each regular increase in x. For example, if, for each increase in x by 2, y does not increase or decrease the same amount each time, the function is nonlinear.

Linear Equations in Two Variables

In a linear equation with two variables, such as $y = x - 3$, the variables appear in separate terms and neither variable contains an exponent other than 1. The graphs of all linear equations are straight lines. All points on a line are solutions of the equation that is graphed.

Quadratic and Cubic Functions

A quadratic function is a polynomial equation of the second degree, generally expressed as $ax^2 + bx + c = 0$, where a, b, and c are real numbers and a is not equal to zero. Similarly, a cubic function is a polynomial equation of the third degree, usually expressed as $ax^3 + bx^2 + cx + d = 0$. Quadratic functions can be graphed using an equation or a table of values. For example, to graph $y = 3x^2 + 1$, substitute the values -1, -0.5, 0, 0.5, and 1 for x to yield the point coordinates $(-1, 4)$, $(-0.5, 1.75)$, $(0, 1)$, $(0.5, 1.75)$, and $(1, 4)$. Plot these points on a coordinate grid and connect the points in the form of a parabola. Cubic functions also can be graphed by making a table of values. The points of a cubic function form a curve. There is one point at which the curve changes from opening upward to opening downward, or vice versa, called the point of inflection.

Slope

Slope is the ratio of the rise, or vertical change, to the run, or horizontal change of a line: slope = rise/run. Slope (m) is the same for any two points on a straight line and can be found by using the coordinates of any two points on the line:

$m = \frac{y_2 - y_1}{x_2 - x_1}$, where $x_2 \neq x_1$

Asymptotes

An asymptote is a straight line that a curve approaches but never actually meets or crosses. Theoretically, the asymptote meets the curve at

infinity. For example, in the function $f(x) = \frac{1}{x}$, two asymptotes are being approached: the line $y = 0$ and $x = 0$. See the graph of the function below.

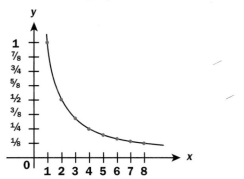

▶ **Represent and analyze mathematical situations and structures using algebraic symbols**

Variables and Expressions

Algebra is a language of symbols. A variable is a placeholder for a changing value. Any letter, such as x, can be used as a variable. Expressions such as $x + 2$ and $4x$ are algebraic expressions because they represent sums and/or products of variables and numbers. Usually, mathematicians avoid the use of i and e for variables because they have other mathematical meanings ($i = \sqrt{-1}$ and e is used with natural logarithms). To evaluate an algebraic expression, replace the variable or variables with known values, and then solve using order of operations. Translate verbal phrases into algebraic expressions by first defining a variable: Choose a variable and a quantity for the variable to represent. In this way, algebraic expressions can be used to represent real-world situations.

Constant and Coefficient

A constant is a fixed value, unlike a variable, which can change. Constants are usually represented by numbers, but they can also be represented by symbols. For example, π is a symbolic representation of the value 3.1415.... A coefficient is a constant by which a variable or other object is multiplied. For example, in the expression $7x^2 + 5x + 9$, the coefficient of x^2 is 7, and the coefficient of x is 5. The number 9 is a constant and not a coefficient.

Monomial and Polynomial

A monomial is a number, a variable, or a product of numbers and/or variables such as 3×4. An algebraic expression that contains one or more monomials is called a polynomial. In a polynomial, there are no terms with variables in the denominator and no terms with variables under a radical sign. Polynomials can be classified by the number of terms contained in the expression. Therefore, a polynomial with two terms is called a binomial ($z^2 - 1$), and a polynomial with three terms is called a trinomial ($2y^3 + 4y^2 - y$). Polynomials also can be classified by their degrees. The degree of a monomial is the sum of the exponents of its variables. The degree of a nonzero constant such as 6 or 10 is 0. The constant 0 has no degree. For example, the monomial $4b^5c^2$ had a degree of 7. The degree of a polynomial is the same as that of the term with the greatest degree. For example, the polynomial $3x^4 - 2y^3 + 4y^2 - y$ has a degree of 4.

Equation

An equation is a mathematical sentence that states that two expressions are equal. The two expressions in an equation are always separated by an equal sign. When solving for a variable in an equation, you must perform the same operations on both sides of the equation in order for the mathematical sentence to remain true.

Solving Equations with Variables

To solve equations with variables on both sides, use the Addition or Subtraction Property of Equality to write an equivalent equation with the variables on the same side. For example, to solve $5x - 8 = 3x$, subtract $3x$ from each side to get $2x - 8 = 0$. Then add 8 to each side to get $2x = 8$. Finally, divide each side by 2 to find that $x = 4$.

Solving Equations with Grouping Symbols

Equations often contain grouping symbols such as parentheses or brackets. The first step in solving these equations is to use the Distributive Property to remove the grouping symbols. For example $5(x + 2) = 25$ can be changed to $5x + 10 = 25$, and then solved to find that $x = 3$.

Some equations have no solution. That is, there is no value of the variable that results in a true sentence. For such an equation, the solution set is called the null or empty set and is represented by the symbol $\varnothing$ or {}. Other equations may have every number as the solution. An equation that is true for every value of the variable is called the identity.

Inequality

A mathematical sentence that contains the symbols < (less than), > (greater than),

≤ (less than or equal to), or ≥ (greater than or equal to) is called an inequality. For example, the statement that it is legal to drive 55 miles per hour or slower on a stretch of the highway can be shown by the sentence $s \leq 55$. Inequalities with variables are called open sentences. When a variable is replaced with a number, the inequality may be true or false.

Solving Inequalities

Solving an inequality means finding values for the variable that make the inequality true. Just as with equations, when you add or subtract the same number from each side of an inequality, the inequality remains true. For example, if you add 5 to each side of the inequality $3x < 6$, the resulting inequality $3x + 5 < 11$ is also true. Adding or subtracting the same number from each side of an inequality does not affect the inequality sign. When multiplying or dividing each side of an inequality by the same positive number, the inequality remains true. In such cases, the inequality symbol does not change. When multiplying or dividing each side of an inequality by a negative number, the inequality symbol must be reversed. For example, when dividing each side of the inequality $-4x \geq -8$ by -2, the inequality sign must be changed to ≤ for the resulting inequality, $2x \leq 4$, to be true. Because the solutions to an inequality include all rational numbers satisfying it, inequalities have an infinite number of solutions.

Representing Inequalities on a Number Line

The solutions of inequalities can be graphed on a number line. For example, if the solution of an inequality is $x < 5$, start an arrow at 5 on the number line, and continue the arrow to the left to show all values less than 5 as the solution. Put an open circle at 5 to show that the point 5 is *not* included in the graph. Use a closed circle when graphing solutions that are greater than or equal to, or less than or equal to, a number.

Order of Operations

Solving a problem may involve using more than one operation. The answer can depend on the order in which you do the operations. To make sure that there is just one answer to a series of computations, mathematicians have agreed upon an order in which to do the operations. First simplify within the parentheses, often called graphing symbols, and then evaluate any exponents. Then multiply and divide from left to right, and finally add and subtract from left to right.

Parametric Equations

Given an equation with more than one unknown, a statistician can draw conclusions about those unknown quantities through the use of parameters, independent variables about which the statistician already knows something. For example, you can find the velocity of an object if you make some assumptions about distance and time parameters.

Recursive Equations

In recursive equations, every value is determined by the previous value. You must first plug an initial value into the equation to get the first value, and then you can use the first value to determine the next one, and so on. For example, in order to determine what the population of pigeons will be in New York City in three years, you can use an equation with the birth, death, immigration, and emigration rates of the birds. Input the current population size into the equation to determine next year's size, then repeat until you have calculated the value for which you are looking.

▷ Use mathematical models to represent and understand quantitative relationships

Solving Systems of Equations

Two or more equations together are called a system of equations. A system of equations can have one solution, no solution, or infinitely many solutions. One method for solving a system of equations is to graph the equations on the same coordinate plane. The coordinates of the point where the graphs intersect is the solution. In other words, the solution of a system is the ordered pair that is a solution of all equations. A more accurate way to solve a system of two equations is by using a method called substitution. Write both equations in terms of y. Replace y in the first equation with the right side of the second equation. Check the solution by graphing. You can solve a system of three equations using matrix algebra.

Graphing Inequalities

To graph an inequality, first graph the related equation, which is the boundary. All points in the shaded region are solutions of the inequality. If an inequality contains the symbol $\leq$ or $\geq$, then use a solid line to indicate that the boundary is included in the graph. If an inequality contains the symbol $<$ or $>$, then use a dashed line to indicate that the boundary is not included in the graph.

▷ Analyze change in various contexts

Rate of Change

A change in one quantity with respect to another quantity is called the rate of change. Rates of change can be described using slope:

$$\text{slope} = \frac{change\ in\ y}{change\ in\ x}$$

You can find rates of change from an equation, a table, or a graph. A special type of linear equation that describes rate of change is called a direct variation. The graph of a direct variation always passes through the origin and represents a proportional situation. In the equation y = kx, k is called the constant of variation. It is the slope, or rate of change. As x increases in value, y increases or decreases at a constant rate k, or y varies directly with x. Another way to say this is that y is directly proportional to x. The direct variation y = kx also can be written as k = y/x. In this form, you can see that the ratio of y to x is the same for any corresponding values of y and x.

Slope-Intercept Form

Equations written as $y = mx + b$, where m is the slope and b is the y-intercept, are linear equations in slope-intercept form. For example, the graph of $y = 5x - 6$ is a line that has a slope of 5 and crosses the y-axis at (0, −6). Sometimes you must first write an equation in slope-intercept form before finding the slope and y-intercept. For example, the equation $2x + 3y = 15$ can be expressed in slope-intercept form by subtracting $2x$ from each side and then dividing by 3: $y = -\frac{2}{3}x + 5$, revealing a slope of $-\frac{2}{3}$ and a y-intercept of 5. You can use the slope-intercept form of an equation to graph a line easily. Graph the y-intercept and use the slope to find another point on the line, then connect the two points with a line.

Geometry

▷ Analyze characteristics and properties of two- and three-dimensional geometric shapes and develop mathematical arguments about geometric relationships

Angles

Two rays that have the same endpoint form an angle. The common endpoint is called the vertex, and the two rays that make up the angle are called the sides of the angle. The most common unit of measure for angles is the degree. Protractors can be used to measure angles or to draw an angle of a given measure. Angles can be classified by their degree measure. Acute angles have measures less than 90° but greater than 0°. Obtuse angles have measures greater than 90° but less than 180°. Right angles have measures of 90°.

Triangles

A triangle is a figure formed by three line segments that intersect only at their endpoints. The sum of the measures of the angles of a triangle is 180°. Triangles can be classified by their angles. An acute triangle contains all acute angles. An obtuse triangle has one obtuse angle. A right triangle has one right angle. Triangles can also be classified by their sides. A scalene triangle has no congruent sides. An isosceles triangle has at least two congruent sides. In an equilateral triangle, all sides are congruent.

Quadrilaterals

A quadrilateral is a closed figure with four sides and four vertices. The segments of a quadrilateral intersect only at their endpoints. Quadrilaterals can be separated into two triangles. Because the sum of the interior angles of all triangles totals 180°, the measures of the interior angles of a quadrilateral equal 360°. Quadrilaterals are classified according to their characteristics and include trapezoids, parallelograms, rectangles, squares, and rhombuses.

Two-Dimensional Figures

A two-dimensional figure exists within a plane and has only the dimensions of length and width. Examples of two-dimensional figures include circles and polygons. Polygons are figures that have three or more angles, including triangles, quadrilaterals, pentagons, hexagons, and many more. The sum of the angles of any polygon totals at least 180° (triangle), and each additional side adds 180° to the measure of the first three angles. The sum of the angles of a quadrilateral, for example, is 360°. The sum of the angles of a pentagon is 540°.

Three-Dimensional Figures

A plane is a two-dimensional flat surface that extends in all directions. Intersecting planes can form the edges and vertices of three-dimensional figures or solids. A polyhedron is a solid with flat surfaces that are polygons. Polyhedrons are composed of faces, edges, and vertices and are differentiated by the shapes of their faces and by their numbers of bases. Skew lines are lines that lie in different planes. They are neither intersecting nor parallel.

Congruence

Figures that have the same size and shape are congruent. The parts of congruent triangles that match are called corresponding parts. Congruence statements are used to identify corresponding parts of congruent triangles. When writing a congruence statement, the letters must be written so that corresponding vertices appear in the same order. Corresponding parts can be used to find the measures of angles and sides in a figure that is congruent to a figure with known measures.

Similarity

If two figures have the same shape but not the same size, they are called similar figures. For example, the triangles below are similar, so angles *A*, *B*, and *C* have the same measurements as angles *D*, *E*, and *F*, respectively. However, segments *AB*, *BC*, and *CA* do not have the same measurements as segments *DE*, *EF*, and *FD*, but the measures of the sides are proportional.

For example, $\dfrac{\overline{AB}}{\overline{DE}} = \dfrac{\overline{BC}}{\overline{EF}} = \dfrac{\overline{CA}}{\overline{FD}}$.

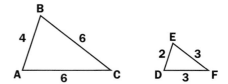

Solid figures are considered to be similar if they have the same shape and if their corresponding linear measures are proportional. As with two-dimensional figures, they can be tested for similarity by comparing corresponding measures. If the compared ratios are proportional, then the figures are similar solids. Missing measures of similar solids can also be determined by using proportions.

The Pythagorean Theorem

The sides that are adjacent to a right angle are called legs. The side opposite the right angle is the hypotenuse.

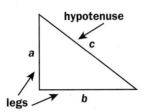

The Pythagorean Theorem describes the relationship between the lengths of the legs a and b and the hypotenuse c. It states that if a triangle is a right triangle, then the square of the length of the hypotenuse is equal to the sum of the squares of the lengths of the legs. In symbols, $c^2 = a^2 + b^2$.

Sine, Cosine, and Tangent Ratios

Trigonometry is the study of the properties of triangles. A trigonometric ratio is a ratio of the lengths of two sides of a right triangle. The most common trigonometric ratios are the sine, cosine, and tangent ratios. These ratios are abbreviated as *sin*, *cos*, and *tan*, respectively.

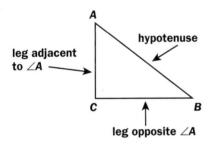

If $\angle A$ is an acute angle of a right triangle, then

$$sin \ \angle A = \frac{\text{measure of leg opposite } \angle A}{\text{measure of hypotenuse}},$$

$$cos \ \angle A = \frac{\text{measure of leg adjacent to } \angle A}{\text{measure of hypotenuse}}, \text{ and}$$

$$tan \ \angle A = \frac{\text{measure of leg opposite } \angle A}{\text{measure of leg adjacent to } \angle A}.$$

▷ Specify locations and describe spatial relationships using coordinate geometry and other representational systems

Polygons

A polygon is a simple, closed figure formed by three or more line segments. The line segments meet only at their endpoints. The points of intersection are called vertices, and the line segments are called sides. Polygons are classified by the number of sides they have. The diagonals of a polygon divide the polygon into triangles. The number of triangles formed is two less than the number of sides. To find the sum of the measures of the interior angles of any polygon, multiply the number of triangles within the polygon by 180. That is, if n equals the number of sides, then $(n - 2)$ 180 gives the sum of the measures of the polygon's interior angles.

Cartesian Coordinates

In the Cartesian coordinate system, the y-axis extends vertically from the origin, and the x-axis extends horizontally from the origin, the point at which the x- and y-axes intersect. Numbers below and to the left of the origin are negative. A point graphed on the coordinate grid is said to have an x-coordinate and a y-coordinate. For example, the point $(1,-2)$ has as its x-coordinate the number 1 and has as its y-coordinate the number -2. This point is graphed by locating the position on the grid that is 1 unit to the right of the origin and 2 units below the origin.

The x-axis and the y-axis separate the coordinate plane into four regions called quadrants. The axes and points located on the axes themselves are not located in any of the quadrants. The quadrants are labeled I to IV, starting in the upper right and proceeding counterclockwise. In quadrant I, both coordinates are positive. In quadrant II, the x-coordinate is negative and the y-coordinate is positive. In quadrant III, both coordinates are negative. In quadrant IV, the x-coordinate is positive and the y-coordinate is negative. A coordinate graph can be used to show algebraic relationships among numbers.

▷ Apply transformations and use symmetry to analyze mathematical situations

Similar Triangles and Indirect Measurement

Triangles that have the same shape but not necessarily the same dimensions are called similar triangles. Similar triangles have corresponding angles and corresponding sides. Arcs are used to show congruent angles. If two triangles are similar, then the corresponding angles have the same measure, and the corresponding sides are proportional. Therefore, to determine the measures of the sides of similar triangles when some measures are known, proportions can be used.

Transformations

A transformation is a movement of a geometric figure. There are several types of transformations. In a translation, also called a slide, a figure is slid from one position to another without turning it. Every point of the original figure is moved the same distance and in the same direction. In a reflection, also called a flip, a figure is flipped over a line to form a mirror image. Every point of the original figure has a corresponding point on the other side of the line of symmetry. In a rotation, also called a turn, a figure is turned around a fixed point. A figure can be rotated 0°–360° clockwise or counterclockwise. A dilation transforms each line to a parallel line whose length is a fixed multiple of the length of the original line to create a similar figure that will be either larger or smaller.

▶ **Use visualizations, spatial reasoning, and geometric modeling to solve problems**

Two-Dimensional Representations of Three-Dimensional Objects

Three-dimensional objects can be represented in a two-dimensional drawing in order to more easily determine properties such as surface area and volume. When you look at the triangular prism, you can see the orientation of its three dimensions, length, width, and height. Using the drawing and the formulas for surface area and volume, you can easily calculate these properties.

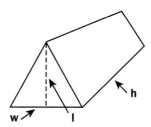

Another way to represent a three-dimensional object in a two-dimensional plane is by using a net, which is the unfolded representation. Imagine cutting the vertices of a box until it is flat then drawing an outline of it. That's a net. Most objects have more than one net, but any object can be measured to determine surface area. At the top of the page is a cube and one of its nets.

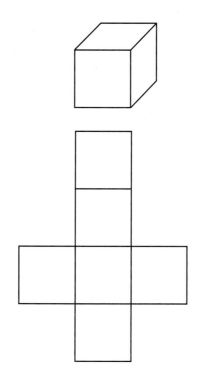

Measurement

▶ **Understand measurable attributes of objects and the units, systems, and processes of measurement**

Customary System

The customary system is the system of weights and measures used in the United States. The main units of weight are ounces, pounds (1 equal to 16 ounces), and tons (1 equal to 2,000 pounds). Length is typically measured in inches, feet (1 equal to 12 inches), yards (1 equal to 3 feet), and miles (1 equal to 5,280 feet), while area is measured in square feet and acres (1 equal to 43,560 square feet). Liquid is measured in cups, pints (1 equal to 2 cups), quarts (1 equal to 2 pints), and gallons (1 equal to 4 quarts). Finally, temperature is measured in degrees Fahrenheit.

Metric System

The metric system is a decimal system of weights and measurements in which the prefixes of the words for the units of measure indicate the relationships between the different measurements. In this system, the main units of weight, or mass, are grams and kilograms. Length is measured in millimeters, centimeters, meters, and kilometers;

and the units of area are square millimeters, centimeters, meters, and kilometers. Liquid is typically measured in milliliters and liters, while temperature is in degrees Celsius.

Selecting Units of Measure

When measuring something, it is important to select the appropriate type and size of unit. For example, in the United States it would be appropriate when describing someone's height to use feet and inches. These units of height or length are good to use because they are in the customary system, and they are of appropriate size. In the customary system, use inches, feet, and miles for lengths and perimeters; square inches, feet, and miles for area and surface area; and cups, pints, quarts, gallons or cubic inches and feet (and less commonly miles) for volume. In the metric system, use millimeters, centimeters, meters, and kilometers for lengths and perimeters; square units millimeters, centimeters, meters, and kilometers for area and surface area; and milliliters and liters for volume. Finally, always use degrees to measure angles.

▶ **Apply appropriate techniques, tools, and formulas to determine measurements**

Precision and Significant Digits

The precision of measurement is the exactness to which a measurement is made. Precision depends on the smallest unit of measure being used, or the precision unit. One way to record a measure is to estimate to the nearest precision unit. A more precise method is to include all the digits that are actually measured, plus one estimated digit. The digits recorded, called significant digits, indicate the precision of the measurement. There are special rules for determining significant digits. If a number contains a decimal point, the number of significant digits is found by counting from left to right, starting with the first nonzero digit. If the number does not contain a decimal point, the number of significant digits is found by counting the digits from left to right, starting with the first digit and ending with the last nonzero digit.

Surface Area

The amount of material needed to cover the surface of a figure is called the surface area. It can be calculated by finding the area of each face and adding them together. To find the surface area of a rectangular prism, for example, the formula $S = 2lw + 2lh + 2wh$ applies. A cylinder, on the other hand, may be unrolled to reveal two circles and a rectangle. Its surface area can be determined by finding the area of the two circles, $2\pi r^2$, and adding it to the area of the rectangle, $2\pi rh$ (the length of the rectangle is the circumference of one of the circles), or $S = 2\pi r^2 + 2\pi rh$. The surface area of a pyramid is measured in a slightly different way because the sides of a pyramid are triangles that intersect at the vertex. These sides are called lateral faces, and the height of each is called the slant height. The sum of their areas is the lateral area of a pyramid. The surface area of a square pyramid is the lateral area $\frac{1}{2}bh$ (area of a lateral face) times 4 (number of lateral faces), plus the area of the base. The surface area of a cone is the area of its circular base (πr^2) plus its lateral area (πrl, where l is the slant height).

Volume

Volume is the measure of space occupied by a solid region. To find the volume of a prism, the area of the base is multiplied by the measure of the height: $V = Bh$. A solid containing several prisms can be broken down into its component prisms. Then the volume of each component can be found and the volumes added. The volume of a cylinder can be determined by finding the area of its circular base, πr^2, and then multiplying by the height of the cylinder. A pyramid has one-third the volume of a prism with the same base and height. To find the volume of a pyramid, multiply the area of the base by the pyramid's height, and then divide by 3. Simply stated, the formula for the volume of a pyramid is $V = \frac{1}{3}bh$. A cone is a three-dimensional figure with one circular base and a curved surface connecting the base and the vertex. The volume of a cone is one-third the volume of a cylinder with the same base area and height. Like a pyramid, the formula for the volume of a cone is $V = \frac{1}{3}bh$. More specifically, the formula is $V = \frac{1}{3}\pi r^2 h$.

Upper and Lower Bounds

Upper and lower bounds have to do with the accuracy of a measurement. When a measurement is given, the degree of accuracy is also stated to tell you what the upper and lower bounds of the measurement are. The upper bound is the largest possible value that a measurement could have had before being rounded down, and the lower bound is the lowest possible value it could have had before being rounded up.

Data Analysis and Probablity

▷ **Formulate questions that can be addressed with data and collect, organize, and display relevant data to answer them**

Histograms

A histogram displays numerical data that have been organized into equal intervals using bars that have the same width and no space between them. While a histogram does not give exact data points, its shape shows the distribution of the data. Histograms also can be used to compare data.

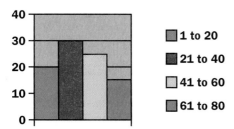

Box-and-Whisker Plot

A box-and-whisker plot displays the measures of central tendency and variation. A box is drawn around the quartile values, and whiskers extend from each quartile to the extreme data points. To make a box plot for a set of data, draw a number line that covers the range of data. Find the median, the extremes, and the upper and lower quartiles. Mark these points on the number line with bullets, then draw a box and the whiskers. The length of a whisker or the box shows whether the values of the data in that part are concentrated or spread out.

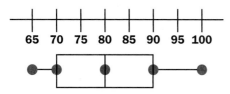

Scatter Plots

A scatter plot is a graph that shows the relationship between two sets of data. In a scatter plot, two sets of data are graphed as ordered pairs on a coordinate system. Two sets of data can have a positive correlation (as *x* increases, *y* increases), a negative correlation (as *x* increases, *y* decreases), or no correlation (no obvious pattern is shown).

Scatter plots can be used to spot trends, to draw conclusions, and to make predictions about data.

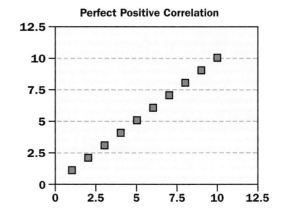

Randomization

The idea of randomization is a very important principle of statistics and the design of experiments. Data must be selected randomly to prevent bias from influencing the results. For example, you want to know the average income of people in your town but you can use only a sample of 100 individuals to make determinations about everyone. If you select 100 individuals who are all doctors, you will have a biased sample. However, if you chose a random sample of 100 people out of the phone book, you are much more likely to accurately represent average income in the town.

Statistics and Parameters

Statistics is a science that involves collecting, analyzing, and presenting data. The data can be collected in various ways, for example, through a census or by making physical measurements. The data can then be analyzed by creating summary statistics, which have to do with the distribution of the data sample, including the mean, range, and standard error. They can also be illustrated in tables and graphs such as box plots, scatter plots, and histograms. The presentation of the data typically involves describing the strength or validity of the data and what they show. For example, an analysis of ancestry of people in a city might tell you something about immigration patterns, unless the data set is very small or biased in some way, in which case it is not likely to be very accurate or useful.

Categorical and Measurement Data

When analyzing data, it is important to understand if the data is qualitative or quantitative. Categorical data is qualitative, and measurement, or numerical, data is quantitative. Categorical data describes a quality of something and can be placed into different categories. For example, if you are analyzing the number of students in different grades in a school, each grade is a category. On the other hand, measurement data is continuous, such as height, weight, or any other measurable variable. Measurement data can be converted into categorical data if you decide to group the data. Using height as an example, you can group the continuous data set into categories such as under 5 feet, 5 feet to 5 feet 5 inches, over 5 feet 5 inches to 6 feet, and so on.

Univariate and Bivariate Data

In data analysis, a researcher can analyze one variable at a time or look at how multiple variables behave together. Univariate data involves only one variable, for example, height in humans. You can measure the height in a population of people then plot the results in a histogram to look at how height is distributed in humans. To summarize univariate data, you can use statistics such as the mean, mode, median, range, and standard deviation, which is a measure of variation. When looking at more than one variable at once, you use multivariate data. Bivariate data involves two variables. For example, you can look at height and age in humans together by gathering information on both variables from individuals in a population. You can then plot both variables in a scatter plot, look at how the variables behave in relation to each other, and create an equation that represents the relationship, also called a regression. These equations could help answer questions such as, for example, does height increase with age in humans?

> **Select and use appropriate statistical methods to analyze data**

Measures of Central Tendency

When you have a list of numerical data, it is often helpful to use one or more numbers to represent the whole set. These numbers are called measures of central tendency. Three measures of central tendency are mean, median, and mode. The mean is the sum of the data divided by the number of items in the data set. The median is the middle number of the ordered data (or the mean of the two middle numbers). The mode is the number or numbers that occur most often. These measures of central tendency allow data to be analyzed and better understood.

Measures of Spread

In statistics, measures of spread or variation are used to describe how data are distributed. The range of a set of data is the difference between the greatest and the least values of the data set. The quartiles are the values that divide the data into four equal parts. The median of data separates the set in half. Similarly, the median of the lower half of a set of data is the lower quartile. The median of the upper half of a set of data is the upper quartile. The interquartile range is the difference between the upper quartile and the lower quartile.

Line of Best Fit

When data are collected, the points graphed usually do not form a straight line, but they may approximate a linear relationship. A line of best fit lies very close to most of the data points. It can be used to predict data. You also can use the equation of the best-fit line to make predictions.

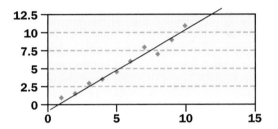

Stem and Leaf Plots

In a stem and leaf plot, numerical data are listed in ascending or descending order. The greatest place value of the data is used for the stems. The next greatest place value forms the leaves. For example, if the least number in a set of data is 8 and the greatest number is 95, draw a vertical line and write the stems from 0 to 9 to the left of the line. Write the leaves to the right of the line, with the corresponding stem. Next, rearrange the leaves so they are ordered from least to greatest. Then include a key or explanation, such as 1|3 = 13. Notice that the stem-and-leaf plot below is like a histogram turned on its side.

```
0|8
1|3 6
2|5 6 9
3|0 2 7 8
4|0 1 4 7 9
5|1 4 5 8
6|1 3 7
7|5 8
8|2 6
9|5                    Key: 1|3 = 13
```

▷ Develop and evaluate inferences and predictions that are based on data

Sampling Distribution

The sampling distribution of a population is the distribution that would result if you could take an infinite number of samples from the population, average each, and then average the averages. The more normal the distribution of the population, that is, how closely the distribution follows a bell curve, the more likely the sampling distribution will also follow a normal distribution. The larger the sample, the more likely it will accurately represent the entire population. You are more likely to gain more representative results from a population of 1,000 with a sample of 100 than with a sample of 2.

Validity

In statistics, validity refers to acquiring results that accurately reflect that which is being measured. In other words, it is important when performing statistical analyses to ensure that the data are valid in that the sample being analyzed represents the population to the best extent possible. Randomization of data and using appropriate sample sizes are two important aspects of making valid inferences about a population.

▷ Understand and apply basic concepts of probability

Complementary, Mutually Exclusive Events

To understand probability theory, it is important to know if two events are mutually exclusive, or complementary: The occurrence of one event automatically implies the nonoccurrence of the other. That is, two complementary events cannot both occur. If you roll a pair of dice, the event of rolling 6 and rolling doubles have an outcome in common (3, 3), so they are not mutually exclusive. If you roll (3, 3), you also roll doubles. However, the events of rolling a 9 and rolling doubles are mutually exclusive because they have no outcomes in common. If you roll a 9, you will not also roll doubles.

Independent and Dependent Events

Determining the probability of a series of events requires that you know whether the events are independent or dependent. An independent event has no influence on the occurrence of subsequent events, whereas a dependent event does influence subsequent events. The chances that a woman's first child will be a girl are $\frac{1}{2}$, and the chances that her second child will be a girl are also $\frac{1}{2}$ because the two events are independent of each other. However, if there are 7 red marbles in a bag of 15 marbles, the chances that the first marble you pick will be red are $\frac{7}{15}$, and if you indeed pick a red marble and remove it, you have reduced the chances of picking another red marble to $\frac{6}{14}$.

Sample Space

The sample space is the group of all possible outcomes for an event. For example, if you are tossing a single six-sided die, the sample space is {1, 2, 3, 4, 5, 6}. Similarly, you can determine the sample space for the possible outcomes of two events. If you are going to toss a coin twice, the sample space is {(heads, heads), (heads, tails), (tails, heads), (tails, tails)}.

Computing the Probability of a Compound Event

If two events are independent, the outcome of one event does not influence the outcome of the second. For example, if a bag contains 2 blue and 3 red marbles, then the probability of selecting a blue marble, replacing it, and then selecting a red marble is $P(A) \times P(B) = \frac{2}{5} \times \frac{3}{5}$, or $\frac{6}{25}$.

If two events are dependent, the outcome of one event affects the outcome of the second. For example, if a bag contains 2 blue and 3 red marbles, then the probability of selecting a blue and then a red marble without replacing the first marble is $P(A) \times P(B$ following $A) = \frac{2}{5} \times \frac{3}{4}$, or $\frac{3}{10}$. Two events that cannot happen at the same time are mutually exclusive. For example, when you roll two number cubes, you cannot roll a sum that is both 5 and even. So, $P(A$ or $B) = \frac{4}{36} + \frac{18}{36}$, or $\frac{11}{18}$.

How to Use This Glossary

- Content vocabulary terms in this glossary are words that relate to this book's content. They are **highlighted yellow** in your text.

- Words in this glossary that have an asterisk (*) are academic vocabulary terms. They help you understand your school subjects and are used on tests. They are boldface blue in your text.

- Some of the vocabulary words in this book include pronunciation symbols to help you sound out the words. Use the pronunciation key to help you pronounce the words.

Pronunciation Key

a .... **a**t	**ô** .... **fo**rk, **a**ll	**ⁿ** ..... indicates preceding sound is pronounced with an open nasal passage
ā .... **a**pe	**oo** .. w**oo**d, p**u**t	
ä .... f**a**ther	**ōō** .. f**oo**l	**th**... **th**in
e .... **e**nd	**oi** ... **oi**l	**th**... **th**is
ē .... m**e**	**ou** .. **ou**t	**zh** .. trea**s**ure
i ..... **i**t	**u** .... **u**p	**ə** .... **a**go, tak**e**n, penc**i**l, lem**o**n, circ**u**s
ī ..... **i**ce	**ū** .... **u**se	**'** ..... indicates primary stress (symbol in front of and *above* letter)
o .... h**o**t	**ü** .... r**u**le	
ō .... h**o**pe	**u** .... p**u**ll	**'** ..... indicates secondary stress (symbol in front of and *below* letter)
o .... s**a**w	**ŋ** .... si**ng**	

abdominal thrust A quick, upward thrust with the heel of the hand into the abdomen that forces air from the lungs out to expel an object caught in the throat. (p. 121)

*abstractly Thinking separately from any specific object or occurrence. (p. 368)

accessible Easily used by those with disabilities. (p. 401)

accommodation (ə-ˌkä-mə-ˈdā-shən) Children changing their thinking about concepts to make new information fit. (p. 329)

accommodations Classroom changes made to allow children with special needs to more fully participate. (p. 389)

accreditation criteria A set of standards that represents high-quality, developmentally appropriate programs. (p. 219)

*acquaint To make familiar with. (p. 490)

active listening Listening to understand the meaning of a speaker's words; a strategy in which

a teacher listens to what a child says and then repeats to show that he or she had heard the child (p. 22)

active play Fun physical activities in which children participate. (p. 510)

*adequate Enough or sufficient. (p. 255)

advisory board A group of people who give directors only recommendations on decisions to be made. (p. 225)

advocacy The process of pleading a cause to influence change for the best interest of others. (p. 69)

advocates People who inform legislators (or policy makers) of their clients' needs. (p. 69)

*alternative Offering a choice between two or more options. (p. 151)

anecdotal record (a-nik-ˈdō-təl) A written description that focuses on a specific incident. (p. 136)

aphasia (ə-ˈfa-zh(ē-)) A language impairment that affects a child's (or adult's) use of speech and understanding of language. (p. 392)

assimilation (ə-ˌsi-mə-ˈlā-shən) Children taking in new information and trying to make it fit with what they already know and understand. (p. 328)

at-risk Environments that interfere with proper development and well-being of children. (p. 94)

attachment behavior A sign of bonding, when an infant shows a strong preference for one person. (p. 302)

attention deficit hyperactivity disorder (ADHD) A disorder of the central nervous system, caused by a lack of certain brain chemicals, whose characteristics include having difficulty paying attention and following instructions and being aggressive, impulsive, and overly active. (p 393)

attention span The time spent on one activity. (p. 327)

auditory discrimination The skill of hearing similarities and differences in sounds and words. (p. 448)

au pair A person from another country who lives with a family and cares for its children to receive exposure to American culture as a part of his or her employment. (p. 7)

autism spectrum disorder A brain disorder that impacts normal development, communication, and social interaction. (p. 393)

authentic assessment Collections of children's work that can be shared during parent-teacher conferences to illustrate children's development; teacher's assessment of children's growth and development in many different areas by observing and participating in natural play situations. (p. 139)

automated external defibrillation (AED) An electrical shock that reestablishes normal heart rhythm. (p. 122)

autonomy (ö-ˈtä-nə-mē) A sense of independence. (p. 330)

B

*bias (bī ˈ-əs) A tendency to favor one person's side over the other's. (p. 132)

bilingual Able to speak more than one language. (p. 54)

biohazardous Materials that have come into contact with bodily fluids and are potentially hazardous. (p. 108)

Bloom's taxonomy (tak-ˈsä-nə-mē) A system of ranking mental abilities from very basic thinking skills to more complex thinking skills. (p. 423)

board (board of directors) A group of individuals who support a program's purpose and are designated to make decisions about the program but are not employed by the program. (p. 224)

body language The way you move your hands and arms, hold your body, and use facial expressions. (p. 23)

C

call-and-response songs Songs in which an adult sings questions and children sing back the answers. (p. 506)

cardiopulmonary resuscitation (CPR) An emergency technique used when a heartbeat or pulse is not detected for 10-12 seconds. (p. 122)

caregiver report form A form used to organize and record the routine care provided each day to children. (p. 311)

centration Children's ability to focus on only one characteristic at a time. (p. 347)

cesarean section A surgical procedure used to deliver some babies. (p. 95)

checklist A list of specific information for which an observer is looking that can be checked off, indicating demonstration of a behavior or skill. (p. 135)

child abuse An intentional injury afflicted on a child. (p. 146)

child care The broad term that describes any situation in which children are provided with supervision, support, and sometimes training by individuals outside the child's immediate family. (p. 6)

Child Development Associate (CDA) A nationally recognized credential program for early childhood professionals. (p. 14)

child neglect The failure to provide a child with basic life necessities, including food, clothing, shelter, and medical care. (p. 148)

choice time A transition technique that lets children decide which activity they would like to participate in next. (p. 243)

chore board A board that features pictures of different cleanup activities, such as washing paintbrushes and putting away tricycles, in various sections of the board and allows children to select a classroom chore to perform. (p. 243)

close-ended materials Items primarily used in one way, with an expected result. (p. 421)

cognitive development How children think, communicate, make decisions, and solve problems. (p. 85)

collage (kə-'läzh) A picture made by gluing many different pieces of materials onto a backing. (p. 502)

collective bargaining The process of workers and employees agreeing to working conditions, contracts, and benefits. (p. 45)

compassion The ability to respond sensitively to others' feelings and experiences. (p. 178)

compensatory time Extra pay or time off for hourly employees who work overtime. (p. 45)

***comply** To follow the rules of. (p. 8)

concept A general idea formed from other information. (p. 328)

concrete operations period The developmental stage between ages 7 and 11 during which children learn to think more rationally and less magically. (p. 368)

conferences Meetings between family members and staff. (p. 59)

confidentiality The practice of always maintaining the privacy of others. (p. 66)

***consensus** Mutual agreement. (p. 282)

consequences Events that occur as the result of a particular behavior—either positive or negative. (p. 190)

conservation The act of considering several variables at one time. (p. 368)

***consistent** Continually the same. (p. 339)

constituents The residents of electoral districts. (p. 71)

continuing education Updating career knowledge and acquiring new job skills. (p. 63)

cool-down moment A short period of time in which the child must sit apart from group activities that he or she is interrupting, yet still be in clear sight of the teachers. (p. 192)

cooperative learning A child's ability to investigate a specific topic of interest with other children. (p. 355)

cooperative play Children playing together and agreeing on play activities and themes. (p. 343)

core learning skills Life skills, which affect learning not just during childhood but also throughout the life span. (p. 415)

creative movement Responding to music or a mental image with physical motion. (p. 508)

crisis nursery A 24-hour service for parents who feel at risk to hurt their child. (p. 151)

curriculum Experiences and activities that support and guide children's learning. (p. 422)

custody rights The rights to care and guardianship of a child. (p. 283)

D

deficiency A lack in one or more nutrients, especially over a long period of time. (p. 161)

dehydrated Ill from loss of water or body fluids. (p. 266)

depth perception The ability to judge distance and to see objects in perspective. (p. 367)

***designated** Set apart for a specific purpose. (p. 252)

developmentally appropriate Items and activities that fit the abilities and ages of children. (p. 250)

developmentally appropriate curriculum Activities teachers offer that are geared to the varying abilities and levels of development of a whole group of children. (p. 422)

discrimination Unfair treatment based on age, gender, race, ethnicity, religion, physical appearance, disability, or other factors. (p. 45)

diversity The individual qualities people have that make them different from one another. (p. 374)

documenting Providing a written record of activities or information related to suspected child abuse or neglect. (p. 150)

dramatic play Realistic or fantasy situations that children act out. (p. 480)

dress codes Rules for professional dressing in the workplace. (p. 63)

dyscalculia (dis-'kal-kyə-'lē-ə) A math-skills disorder in which children may be unable to count objects or to recognize basic shapes. (p. 392)

dyslexia (dis-'lek-sē-ə) A reading disorder in which a child (or adult) may have trouble recognizing letters of the alphabet and difficulty reading. (p. 392)

E

egocentric (ˌē-gō-'sen-trik) Children's way of thinking, during their first year of life, about the world only from their own points of view. (p. 304)

emergent literacy Children's gradual development of literacy skills over time. (p. 440)

empathy ('em-pə-thē) The skill of putting yourself in another's place; the ability to understand another person's feelings. (p. 41)

*encounter To first see or meet. (p. 397)

entrepreneur (äⁿ-trə-p(r)ə-'nər)A person who owns and operates a business. (p. 13)

environment The people, culture, and physical and social surroundings in which a person lives. (p. 90)

ethics ('e-thiks) Internal guidelines for distinguishing right from wrong. (p. 42)

*evaluate To determine the value of a program. (p. 131)

*expand To increase. (p. 506)

*exposure Experience with or access to. (p. 166)

eye-hand coordination The ability to move the hands and fingers precisely in relation to what is seen. (p. 300)

*facilitate To help or bring about learning without controlling it. (p. 420)

*factors Things that contribute to a result. (p. 90)

fall zones Areas designated to keep children from walking into unsafe areas, or safety factors that will prevent injuries. (p. 264)

family relations policy A child care program's policy for how families should be treated and included in the program. (p. 274)

fiber A plant material that helps the body eliminate waste. (p. 161)

field guide A book for identifying natural items such as flowers, insects, trees, and birds. (p. 471)

financial management Balancing income and expenses to meet the costs of the daily operation of a working program. (p. 227)

finger plays Specific hand motions that accompany a song. (p. 448)

flexibility The ability to adapt willingly to change. (p. 25)

food-service sanitation certificate A state-issued document indicating that proper food-service practices are being followed. (p. 120)

for-profit Programs that are designed to bring in more income than they spend on their services. (p. 210)

*foundation A base that you build upon. (p. 22)

frequency count A record of how many times a particular behavior or situation occurs during a specific period of time. (p. 136)

frostbite The freezing of body tissue, usually in feet, hands, face, and ears. (p. 110)

*functions Purposes. (p. 187)

governing board A group of individuals who have the ability to tell directors what actions to take and have final authority for decisions. (p. 225)

growth plateau Growth that is slow and steady in young school-age children. (p. 366)

guidance Involves behavior modeling and corrective actions by adults, which help children learn about appropriate behavior. (p. 181)

heat exhaustion Physical stress on the body caused by overheating and the loss of fluid and salt through profuse sweating. (p. 110)

heredity Qualities and traits passed from parents to children through their genes at conception. (p. 90)

*highlight To bring attention to. (p. 459)

hormones Chemical substances carried in the blood that impact growth and development. (p. 366)

hypothermia (ˌhī-pō-'thər-mē-ə) A health condition that results when body temperature becomes dangerously low. (p. 110)

I-messages A communication method that includes a specific description of behavior, how it affects you, and your feelings about it. (p. 187)

GLOSSARY

immunizations Vaccines that protect people from certain diseases. (p. 106)

inclusion A federal law that states that children with disabilities must be educated whenever possible with children who are not disabled. (p. 396)

*__inanimate__ Nonliving. (p. 480)

*__individual__ Separate and personalized. (p. 238)

Individualized Education Plan (IEP) A written document that outlines how to encourage the development of a child with special needs. (p. 400)

Individualized Family Service Plan (IFSP) A plan that sets goals to meet the overall special needs of a child, including assessment, goals for development, and ways to promote family support and involvement. (p. 400)

industry The desire to perform skills, to succeed at tasks, and to make social contributions. (p. 369)

inferiority A feeling of not having met expected standards. (p. 369)

*__inhibit__ To discourage. (p. 500)

*__initiative__ The ability to take first steps. (p. 9)

intelligence quotient The ratio between mental age and chronological age. (p. 418)

intentional teaching A strategy that teachers use to plan activities that are responsive to individual children's abilities and needs. (p. 422)

*__interact__ To have contact with and communicate with one another. (p. 54)

intervention services Resources and specialized help for children and their parents. (p. 98)

invented spelling Spelling a word the way it sounds. (p. 450)

inventory record A list of equipment and supplies on hand. (p. 255)

*__investigate__ To observe or look into by close examination. (p. 150)

isolation room A separate room for children who become ill. (p. 251)

*__jeopardy__ Danger. (p. 280)

job jar A container filled with pieces of paper that show pictures of activities that students use to select classroom chores. (p. 243)

labor union An organization of workers in a similar field. (p. 45)

language arts Activities that teach children to listen, speak, read, and write. (p. 440)

latchkey children Children who stay home alone before or after school. (p. 374)

learning centers Clearly defined spaces for specific types of play or investigation. (p. 258)

learning disability A disorder that affects the way the brain processes information. (p. 392)

learning specialists Professionals trained to identify learning disorders and to help children overcome them. (p. 393)

lesson plan A detailed, written explanation of an activity, including the purpose, materials needed, step-by-step instructions, evaluation, and possibly follow-up activities. (p. 430)

license exempt Not required to have a license to operate a program. (p. 216)

light table A low, lighted table with a white plastic top on which children can put objects for close inspection. (p. 467)

literacy The ability to read and write language. (p. 356)

locomotion The act of moving from place to place. (p. 509)

lyrics Words to songs. (p. 504)

*__major__ Very important. (p. 242)

mandated Required by law. (p. 15)

manipulatives Toys or materials that children can handle and change with their hands. (p. 414)

mathematical vocabulary Words that express numbers, quantities, shape, size, or volume. (p. 458)

mathematics The study of shapes and numbers and the use of numbers. (p. 458)

maze A deliberately confusing series of pathways. (p. 514)

melody The tune of a song. (p. 504)

minimum wage The lowest hourly amount a worker can earn. (p. 45)

multiple intelligences Gardner's belief that people vary in terms of type of intelligence and learning strengths, just as they differ in learning styles. (p. 418)

MyPlate A tool developed by the U.S. Department of Agriculture to help individuals make healthful food choices and be active every day. (p. 162)

nanny An in-home care provider who may or may not live with the family. (p. 7)

naturalistic observation A record of natural behaviors of children as they occur. (p. 133)

nature education Teachings about the environment and life on Earth. (p. 469)

networking Making use of all your personal and professional contacts to further your career goals. (p. 28)

neurons Nerve cells in the brain. (p. 91)

nonprofit Programs that have no owners or stockholders who receive money from the program's income. (p. 210)

nontoxic Not poisonous. (p. 263)

numerals Written symbols that represent numbers. (p. 461)

nutrients Substances in food that the body uses to function, to grow, to repair tissue, and to produce energy. (p. 160)

nutrition The process through which the body uses the nutrients in food. (p. 160)

objective observation Recorded facts without personal opinion or bias. (p. 132)

objectives Learning outcomes for children to achieve or to experience through participation in a specific curriculum activity. (p. 423)

object permanence The understanding that an object continues to exist even when out of sight. (p. 300)

on demand Conducting routines according to each child's individual needs. (p. 310)

one-to-one correspondence Counting each object once. (p. 348)

open door policy A policy that allows parents or approved family members to visit an early childhood program at any time. (p. 54)

open-ended materials Items that can be used in a variety of ways, with no single correct result. (p. 421)

open-ended questions Questions that require more than a yes or no answer and often begin with how, what, when, where, and why. (p. 433)

organizational chart A document letting staff know to whom they report. (p. 222)

*outcome Result. (p. 421)

parallel play Children playing near each other but not with each other. (p. 331)

parent or guardian report form A document that parents or guardians complete that details an infant's activities and behavior before arrival at the center. (p. 312)

participant observer Someone who interacts with children while observing them. (p. 133)

pathogens Disease-causing organisms. (p. 107)

perceptual motor skills Skills that require the coordination of vision, intellect, and movement. (p. 299)

*period Length of time. (p. 446)

perishable Foods that will become spoiled if not refrigerated or frozen. (p.167)

perspective taking When children learn to consider and respect other children's points of view as well as their own. (p. 87)

philosophy General beliefs, concepts, and attitudes about learning, such as in programs for children. (p. 208)

pitch The highness or lowness of musical sounds. (p. 504)

positive reinforcement A consequence that rewards a particular behavior, making it more likely to be repeated. (p. 190)

prenatal Before birth. (p. 95)

prenatal development Changes that occur to humans during the nine months of pregnancy. (p. 296)

preoperational period The period when children are between 2 and 7 years old in which they start to think symbolically and imaginatively. (p. 327)

*prevention Taking action to keep something from happening. (p. 117)

print-rich environment The use of printed materials throughout the classroom in meaningful ways. (p. 441)

*primary The first in rank or importance. (p. 54)

prioritize To put tasks in order of importance. (p. 39)

probation A period of time in which an employer observes the employee's work and behavior in order to assess whether the employee is fit to remain with the company. (p. 45)

* process A series of changes. (p. 304)

process versus product The principle that what children learn while making art is more important than the product they create. (p. 500)

productive language The ability to use words to express oneself. (p. 335)

professional ethics The standards of right and wrong that apply to your professional behavior. (p. 62)

program goals Identify basic skills, concepts, and attitudes to develop and encourage in children. (p. 208)

program governance The process of a director and a board making decisions about a program's policies and procedures. (p. 224)

program sponsors Specific groups that fund or manage a program, such as an early childhood program. (p. 210)

*prohibits Forbids. (p. 389)

project approach A method of teaching that allows children to explore projects, or in-depth investigations of specific topics, in developmentally appropriate ways. (p. 425)

prop box A container for storing items used for specific dramatic play themes. (p. 483)

proportion The size relationship of parts. (p. 499)

props Items that suggest and support dramatic play themes. (p. 483)

puberty A transition stage when children undergo a series of physical changes and begin to look like adult men and women. (p. 366)

public relations Communicating information about your program to the public. (p. 55)

rating scale A recorded letter or numerical evaluation of listed items by an observer. (p. 137)

rational counting The understanding that the last number counted in a group represents the entire number of objects in the group. (p. 348)

rebus recipe A recipe that shows ingredients and directions with picture symbols. (p. 468)

receptive language The ability to understand spoken words. (p. 335)

redirection Steering a child's disruptive behavior to a different, more acceptable activity that still meets the child's basic needs. (p. 190)

reference checks Contacting people who know the applicant's character, job performance, and employment skills. (p. 223)

referral Sending a family that needs assistance to a support service or resource. (p. 99)

*refine To perfect. (p. 370)

reflexes Instinctive, involuntary bodily reactions to a stimulus such as a noise or touch. (p. 298)

Reggio Emilia Approach A unique approach to teaching, which originated in Reggio Emilia, Italy, in which children are considered competent, capable, and motivated learners and full of potential, and collaborative learning is stressed (p. 426)

registration The written notification to city or state officials by a care provider of pertinent information, including intention to provide services, instead of a formal program license. (p. 216)

*require To need. (p. 448)

resilience Learning to cope with and recovering from difficult situations, such as the hardships of neglect and abuse. (p. 152)

*resort (to) Use. (p. 330)

*resources Sources of information. (p. 472)

*responsibility A required task or duty. (p. 39)

*restrict To avoid or limit. (p. 166)

résumé ('re-zə-ˌmā) A summary of your career objectives, work experience, job qualifications, education, and training. (p. 33)

rhythm instruments Musical instruments with which children experiment to make their own rhythms. (p 505)

risk management plan Written emergency procedures. (p. 116)

rote counting Memorizing and reciting numbers in order without any real understanding of what the numbers represent. (pp. 348, 460)

routine A regular, expected procedure that is followed to accomplish something. (p. 239)

running record A record in which an observer creates a sequential record of anything that happens during a specific time period. (p. 136)

safety policy A policy that states the rules and procedures that protect children and staff at a child care facility. (p. 116)

sanitized Cleaned in a way that will kill organisms that can cause illness. (p. 256)

scaffolding Building the support needed for children's learning of emerging concepts or skills. (p. 422)

schedule A plan for how time will be used. (p. 236)

science A process of collecting knowledge about the physical world and how the world works. (p. 463)

screenings Examinations given to a group of children to look for one specific health problem. (p. 111)

self-directed Learning to cooperate in class activities in an independent fashion with less physical or verbal direction needed from the teacher. (p. 237)

self-discipline The ability to guide your own behavior. (p. 183)

self-help skills Skills that allow children to help take care of their personal needs. (p. 325)

*sensitivity A physical reaction to a common substance. (p. 113)

sensorimotor (sen(t)s-rē-ˈmō-tər) Learning through the senses of sight, touch, taste, hearing, and smell. (p. 85)

sensorimotor period (ˌsen(t)s-rē-ˈmō-tər ˈpir-ē-əd) The time frame during which infants develop their intellect. (p. 300)

sensory Involving or related to the senses. (p. 85)

sensory table A table with a boxlike, hollow top that can hold water, sand, beans, or other substances for children to explore. (p. 467)

separation anxiety A child's fear of separation from familiar people. (p. 336)

*sequence A certain order of things. (p. 299)

seriation Children's ability to organize objects according to increasing or decreasing size; identifying size relationships between objects. (pp. 347, 460)

service learning Community service that is part of your schoolwork. (p. 30)

sexual harassment An act of discrimination; any unwelcome verbal or physical behavior of a sexual nature. (p. 45)

social competence (ˈsō-shəl ˈkäm-pə-tən(t)s) A person's ability to get along with others in acceptable and appropriate ways. (p. 178)

social responsibility The practice of making a positive contribution to a community and obeying community laws. (p. 491)

social studies A curriculum area that teaches about self, families, communities, and the world. (p. 485)

sociocultural theory Vygotsky's theory that children learn their culture's beliefs, customs, and skills through social interactions with skilled peers and adults. (p. 354)

solitary play Children playing alone rather than with other children. (p. 331)

specialized lessons Lessons that are similar to clubs in that they allow children to apply skills, to expand interests, and to form friendships. (p. 378)

special needs Circumstances that cause a child's physical, cognitive, and behavioral development to vary significantly from the norm. (p. 388)

spontaneous dramatic play Dramatic play that children engage in without suggestion or direction from adults. (p. 480)

*stable Firmly established. (p. 353)

staff turnover The rate at which employees leave their jobs, creating the need for hiring new employees. (p. 310)

stranger anxiety An infant's fear of unfamiliar people. (p. 304)

subjective description An observation based on personal judgments. (p. 132)

*subside To lessen in frequency. (p. 349)

*subsidy A governmental financial assistance program. (p. 227)

support groups Groups that meet regularly to discuss common concerns and needs. (p. 278)

symbolic thinking Children's more advanced thought process in which they understand that one thing can stand for something else. (p. 327)

synapses Electrical connections between neurons in the brain. (p. 91)

teachable moments Unplanned opportunities for learning. (p. 421)

temperament A typical way a child responds to people and situations; a person's inborn style of reacting to the environment. (pp. 86, 302)

temper tantrum An episode in which a child shows anger or frustration in an aggressive or destructive way. (p 336)

tempo The rhythm and speed at which a song is sung. (p. 504)

*terminate To fire. (p. 222)

theme One central topic around which the teacher selects activities because he or she thinks the topic will entice children. (p. 427)

*theories ideas and principles about a subject that can be investigated using the scientific method. (p. 88)

three dimensional Shapes and objects that have height, width, and depth. (p. 502)

toddler A child between the ages of 12 and 36 months. (p. 324)

toxic Poisonous. (p. 254)

toxins Harmful substances that can cause disease or illness. (p. 119)

trade publications Magazines and newsletters written for people in an industry by organizations that support the industry. (p. 29)

traffic pattern The pattern of the room and the direction the children take to get from one area to another. (p. 259)

transition A short activity or procedure used to guide children smoothly from one activity, routine, or event to another. (p. 242)

transition techniques Signals or short activities that prompt children to move from one place or routine to another. (p. 242)

trend The overall direction in which a society moves within a given time frame. (p. 6)

universal precautions Infection-control guidelines that protect individuals from infectious disease and limit its spread. (p. 107)

*vary To be different. (p. 184)

visual discrimination The ability to notice similarities and differences in shapes and alphabet letters. (p. 449)

vocalizations Sounds made by infants that imitate adult language. (p. 301)

wellness Overall good health and well-being. (p. 160)

whole language The inclusion of reading and writing in various classroom activities. (p. 441)

work ethic A personal commitment to work hard and to do one's very best. (p. 25)

workers' compensation State laws requiring your employer to provide financial help if you are injured on the job and cannot work. (p. 45)

INDEX